Michael Cooper

Wine Atlas

of New Zealand

Michael Cooper

Wine

Atlas
of New Zealand

Michael Cooper

Photographs by John McDermott

Hodder Moa Beckett

Contents

Preface

Right from the start, it was understood that geography has a crucial bearing on viticulture and wine styles. After making the first recorded planting of grapevines at Kerikeri in the Bay of Islands, in 1819, Samuel Marsden wrote: 'New Zealand promises to be very favourable to the vine as far as I can judge at present of the nature of the soil and climate.' New Zealand, he enthused, 'will be the finest country in the world for wine . . . '

Yet until recently the idea of a *Wine Atlas of New Zealand* would have been premature. Not until the late 1960s did vineyards spread far beyond Auckland and Hawke's Bay, and only since the 1980s have New Zealand wines commonly acknowledged their region of origin on the label. Today's widespread interest in the links between soil, climate, topography, people and wine styles was the trigger for this book.

Successive editions of my previous volume, *The Wines and Vineyards of New Zealand*, between 1984 and 1996, laid the foundations for the *Atlas*. While the basic structure of those books has been retained, especially the detailed commentaries on each significant winery and the colour photographs, here the explorations of soil and climate are much more in-depth, both on a regional and sub-regional basis, and the maps are far more numerous and detailed.

With a string of books, including the last edition of *The Wines and Vineyards of New Zealand*, in recent years John McDermott has emerged as one of New Zealand's finest photographers. For the *Wine Atlas of New Zealand*, John returned to the wine trail, capturing fresh images of the country's wine-growers and the landscapes — so often strikingly beautiful — in which they live and work.

In any atlas, maps hold centre stage. Here, the major goal was to map the wine regions and sub-regions of New Zealand in far greater detail than had previously been attempted. My thanks to cartographer Jan Kelly for her pivotal contribution. For their invaluable help with pinpointing the major areas of vines in the three key regions, I am indebted to James and Annie Millton (Gisborne), Steve Smith MW (Hawke's Bay), and Ivan Sutherland (principally) and Glenn Thomas (Marlborough).

All over the country — from the Karikari Peninsula in Northland to Ettrick, south of Roxburgh in Otago — vineyards are sprouting. To research the *Atlas*, I visited each of the regions to talk to leading viticulturists and winemakers. Their contributions (and enthusiasm for the project) have been invaluable.

Several people agreed to read parts of the *Atlas* in manuscript. I am indebted to Philip Gregan, chief executive officer of New Zealand Winegrowers, for help with the laws and labels section; Steve Smith MW, of Craggy Range, for reading the viticulture chapter; and Neill Culley, of Cable Bay, for checking the chapter on winemaking. Dr Alan Limmer, of the Stonecroft winery, read the introduction to Hawke's Bay; Brian Bicknell, of Seresin Estate, did the same for Marlborough and the Wairau and Awatere Valleys; and Alan Brady, of the Mount Edward winery, helped with the introductions to Central Otago and its sub-regions.

Librarians Brian Marshall and Thelma Braggins kept pointing me in the right direction while I studied in the Geography Department Library at the University of Auckland. Dr Claudia Orange, of the Department for Culture and Heritage, kindly gave me permission to include in the *Atlas* revised versions of my profiles of Bernard Chambers, Assid Abraham Corban, Josip Babich and Tom McDonald, first published in the *Dictionary of New Zealand Biography*. Thanks also to Peter Fredatovich, of Lincoln Vineyards, who generously supplied labels from his collection to illustrate the chapter on the history of wine in New Zealand.

Kevin Chapman, managing director of Hodder Moa Beckett, first suggested the need for a *Wine Atlas of New Zealand*, and publishing manager Linda Cassells steered the project throughout. Editor Brian O'Flaherty and designer Nick Turzynski have also played key roles.

At the head of the support team was my wife, Linda, whose contribution was even greater than she realises.

Michael Cooper

Understanding the Maps

The maps in this Atlas vary in scale and level of detail, depending on the complexity of the areas mapped. There are two styles of map — the regional maps, which show the topography of the main wine-growing areas and the relevant weather stations; and sub-regional maps, which provide details of the locations of wine companies and notable individual vineyards. This information is also included on those regional maps which are not subdivided into sub-regions, such as Northland, Waikato/Bay of Plenty, Gisborne and Hawke's Bay. The glass symbol for a wine company in most cases indicates the presence of an on-site winery (production facility) and tasting and retail outlet, but some companies operate neither, perhaps owning only a vineyard and wine brand. For this reason, the term 'wine company' is shown on the maps, rather than the common but inconsistently used term 'winery'.

The key areas of vineyard plantings are shown for the three principal wine-growing regions, Gisborne, Hawke's Bay and Marlborough, which in 2002 had 80 per cent of the total producing vineyard area. Vine plantings in other regions, which are markedly lighter, have been omitted due to the lack of detailed information available from the local wine industry organisations. The vineyard locations in the three principal regions have been checked with local winemakers, but total accuracy is impossible to achieve as plantings are changing constantly. The areas shown are correct to the best of our knowledge at the time of going to press.

Introduction

In the romantic cellars of Château Cantemerle, a fifth-growth of the southern Médoc in Bordeaux, I once had an unforgettable conversation. The *maître d'chais* (cellarmaster) was refusing to acknowledge that a Hawke's Bay claret-style red could even remotely resemble a red Bordeaux.

'Your climate is different,' he declared.

'Both regions have a maritime climate and a fairly similar amount of heat over the growing season,' I replied, stirring gently.

'Then your soils must be different,' he said.

I mentioned the gravel country in Gimblett Road had some parallels with the stony, free-draining soils of the Médoc.

'Then your grapes must be different,' he protested.

'They grow Cabernet Sauvignon and Merlot in Hawke's Bay, just like you,' I replied.

Then he pounced: 'Well, your *men* must be different!'

That youngish winemaker knew little about wine beyond his own patch (and nothing about vinification techniques in St Émilion, 40 kilometres away), but he understood what gives wine its style and personality. Now New Zealand's wine-growers are also starting to explore the ways in which their wines are influenced by climate, soil, topography — and people.

The much-debated French concept of *terroir* (which embraces not only soil but all the physical, ecological and human factors that influence a particular wine style) has over the past decade captured the imagination of New Zealand's wine-growers. Hampering the understanding of *terroir* influences in New Zealand is the extreme youthfulness of the country's vineyards; plantings have doubled in the past six years. Young vines cannot express the nuances of *terroir* as clearly as mature, 20-year-old vines, their roots anchored deeply in the land.

Yet you can smell and taste clear differences between the wines from New Zealand's regions. Sauvignon Blanc from Hawke's Bay is typically more mouthfilling, riper and rounder than the penetrating, zingy Sauvignon Blancs of Marlborough. Auckland reds have an earthy, spicy warmth that contrasts with the fresh, vibrant fruit characters of southern reds. And within the various regions and sub-regions — even within individual vineyards — there is a growing awareness of the extent to which different soils and climates influence wine styles.

'Site selection' is currently a buzz word in the New Zealand wine industry, but it is hardly a new concept. At the 1896 Conference of Australasian Fruitgrowers held in Wellington, Whangarei grapegrower Lionel Hanlon enthused: '. . . on the gently sloping limestone hills that are so characteristic of the [Hawke's Bay] district . . . may be found hundreds of ideal sites for vineyards. In some places the hills present the peculiar truncated appearance of the vine-clothed hills of the celebrated Côte d'Or district in France . . . ' However, most winemakers ignored Hanlon's advice and planted their vineyards on the fertile, easy-to-cultivate flats.

Given the general competence of New Zealand's winemakers, most are able to produce good wine. For the next step up — to great wine — the key challenge is to understand how to fully exploit the grapes from individual sites, believes Dr Neil McCallum, of the Dry River winery in Martinborough.

Rugby is a traditional cornerstone of New Zealand culture, but wine (represented here by Mission Vineyards at Taradale, Hawke's Bay) adds colour and sophistication to the contemporary scene.

'Winemakers in Burgundy have been fortunate that their forebears have spent many years working out the best ways of making wine to suit their various regional grapes. . . . The information has been passed down in the form of tradition and many aspects have even been codified into law. In my view this represents a real advantage for the new generations of winemakers — nobody has to try to reinvent the wheel and make the same old mistakes in the process.'

Jackie Barthelme, a regular visitor to New Zealand from the prestigious Domaine Albert Mann in Alsace, told *WineNZ* in 2001 that 'there has not yet been enough time in New Zealand to determine the various *terroirs*. You need to observe the vines carefully over a number of years and this is a process which cannot be hurried. The vines, the character of the soils and the climate determine the differences in the grapes and the complexity and structure of the wine. It takes a long time to understand these relationships and even in Alsace, where many of our vines and sites go back over fifty years [some *grand cru* sites have been vineyards for centuries] we are still learning.' Clearly, the unravelling of New Zealand *terroirs* has only just begun.

The *Wine Atlas of New Zealand* opens with a brief history of New Zealand wine, including profiles of several influential winemakers. It is commonly supposed that the story began a few decades ago, but New Zealand wine has a long and intriguing history, with several false starts before the prosperity of the modern era. Other introductory sections focus

Vineyards have transformed the landscape in the Wairarapa and many other New Zealand regions.

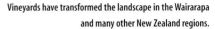

on New Zealand's burgeoning international wine trade; fundamental aspects of the country's climate and soils; the principal grape varieties; winemaking techniques; wine legislation and how to read a New Zealand wine label.

The heart of the book follows: a region-by-region guide to all of the significant wine companies in New Zealand. With hundreds of wineries jostling for space, I have given the most in-depth coverage to the large and middle-sized producers (whose wines you are most likely to drink) and the smaller companies with top-flight wines (for more details on the wines themselves, see my annual *Buyer's Guide To New Zealand Wines*). Scattered through the book are profiles of key individuals and discussions of such topics as sustainable viticulture and Martinborough issues.

In most of the wine regions, where distinct sub-regions exist (such as Marlborough's Wairau and Awatere Valleys) the text is arranged accordingly, discussing each region's and sub-region's viticultural history, climate, soils and wine styles. The overriding goal has been to provide more information about — and greater insight into — the geographic influences on New Zealand wine than ever before.

The GDD (growing degree day) figures in the regional introductions are a measure of the warmth available to the vines over the growing season to ripen their grapes. It should be clearly understood that such statistics — in the past inconsistent from one publication to another and hotly debated by winemakers — only hold true for the meteorological stations (pinpointed on the maps) where they were collected; sites only a short distance away may have quite different readings. The GDD (or heat

The South Island was long believed to be too cold for winemaking on a commercial scale, but Mountford Vineyard, at Waipara in North Canterbury, produces strikingly rich Pinot Noirs and Chardonnays.

summation) figures in the *Atlas* were especially commissioned from the most authoritative source available, the National Institute of Water and Atmospheric Research (NIWA).

'Maps, to me, since first I started on the happily absorbing study of wine, have been the vital, logical ally,' wrote Hugh Johnson in 1974, introducing the first edition of his classic *World Atlas of Wine*. 'Bit by bit, it dawned on me that maps on a large enough scale are more than aids to navigation: they are pictures of the ground and what goes on on it. That it was possible, as it were, to take a reader up into a high mountain and show him all the vineyards of the earth.'

Compared to the world's other fine wine-producing nations, New Zealand has been poorly mapped. The goal in the *Atlas* has been to pinpoint the locations of the wine companies and also, for the three principal regions of Gisborne, Hawke's Bay and Marlborough, the principal vineyard areas (but not every single row, no matter how isolated). The regional maps also show relief, and all the maps include such key natural features as ranges, peaks, rivers and lakes, as well as towns and roads.

With dozens of maps, an extensive collection of colour labels and John McDermott's evocative photographs, this is a richly illustrated book. I hope it does justice to the modern New Zealand wine industry, with its meteoric growth and mounting air of excitement.

A Brief History of Wine

in New Zealand

At first glance the history of wine in New Zealand appears singularly short. Wines from classic *Vitis vinifera* grape varieties have only been widely procurable since the early 1970s; only since the mid-1980s have the new breeds of Sauvignon Blancs and Chardonnays carved out their elevated international reputation. Yet the grapevine was a common sight in the early colonists' gardens, and by the time of the signing of the Treaty of Waitangi in 1840, the first recorded New Zealand wine was already bottled. Wine has in fact had a long, tortuous and fascinating history in this country.

The first recorded planting of grapevines, at Kerikeri in the Bay of Islands, derived from the Anglican missionary Samuel Marsden's belief that Maori should be taught the civilising pursuits of agriculture and handicrafts before being converted to Christianity. In his journal for 25 September 1819 Marsden wrote: 'We had a small plot of land cleared and broken up in which I planted about a hundred grapevines of different kinds brought from Port Jackson [Sydney]. New Zealand promises to be very favourable to the vine as far as I can judge at present of the nature of the soil and climate.'[1]

Twenty years were to pass, however, before the first recorded New Zealand wine flowed. James Busby, a Scot also acknowledged as the father of Australian viticulture, was appointed British Resident at the Bay of Islands in 1832. In 1836 a tiny vineyard sprouted between the house and the flagstaff at Waitangi. Visiting Busby in 1840, the French explorer Dumont d'Urville observed 'a trellis on which several flourishing vines were growing . . . with great pleasure I agreed to taste the product of the vineyard that I had just seen. I was given a light white wine, very sparkling, and delicious to taste, which I enjoyed very much.'[2]

Although Busby's vineyard was ruined in 1845 by troops camped at Waitangi, the flame he had ignited was to be preserved throughout the nineteenth century. Bishop Pompallier, the first Catholic Bishop of the South Pacific, brought French vine cuttings to the Hokianga in 1838; thereafter, wherever French mission stations sprang up, vineyards were planted to supply the Marist priests with table grapes and sacramental and table wines. At Akaroa, French peasants who planted vines in 1840 sold fresh grapes to visiting whalers and also produced a rivulet of wine for their own tables.

The honour of being the first to capitalise on

Samuel Marsden

James Busby

winemaking's commercial potential in New Zealand, however, belongs to an Englishman. Charles Levet, a Cambridge coppersmith and his son, William, in 1863 planted a 7-acre (2.8-hectare) vineyard on an inlet of the Kaipara Harbour. For over four decades the Levets made their living exclusively from producing and selling wine.

Joseph Soler, a Spaniard, was equally successful. Soler made his first wine in Wanganui in 1869 and each year until his death in 1906 despatched about 20,000 bottles of wine to customers throughout the colony.

Winemaking, however, was an extremely precarious pursuit in nineteenth-century New Zealand. Those who laboured with peasant tenacity in isolated vineyards faced crushing odds. Oidium, a powdery mildew that covered the grapes with mould, splitting their skins and exposing their juice to fungi and insects, caused widespread havoc.

Powerful cultural factors also tethered the fledgling industry. The predominantly British-born and descended population lacked any national tradition of viticulture. Wine was also perceived as a 'class' drink, consumed not by working men and women but by the elite — who demanded true port and sherry and largely ignored the antipodean substitutes.

Another increasingly formidable foe was the temperance movement, which in its early years campaigned against public drunkenness and also advocated abstention from spirits — but not wine. A meeting held in Kororareka (Russell) on 11 May 1836, which founded the New Zealand Temperance Society, was chaired by that fervent wine advocate, James Busby. As the temperance movement gathered momentum, however, it increasingly called for the prohibition of all alcoholic beverages. The passage of more and more restrictive

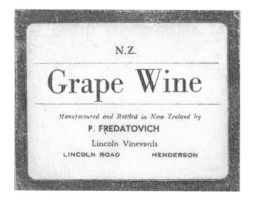

Previous page: Planting is underway in Montana's vineyards in 1973. When most of the vines perished in a drought, the company learned a harsh lesson about the need to irrigate.

[1] Rawson-Elder, J., *Letters and Journals of Samuel Marsden*, Otago University Council, 1932.
[2] Thorpy, F., *Wine in New Zealand*, first edition, 1971, p. 20.

Bernard Chambers

■ **A key pioneer of Hawke's Bay wine, Bernard Chambers was born in 1859, the son of John Chambers, a sheep farmer at Te Mata, on the outskirts of Havelock North. When the property was divided in 1886 between three of Chambers' five sons, Bernard Chambers became a major landowner in his own right.**

His interest in winemaking was kindled by a French guest at Te Mata homestead, who pointed out the viticultural potential of the surrounding slopes. Visits to wineries in France, California and Australia motivated him further. In 1892, cuttings of Pinot Noir were obtained from the Society of Mary's Mission Vineyards at Taradale and the first vines struck root at Te Mata Vineyard.

The business flourished. Chambers converted a brick stable into his cellar and by March 1895 the first wine was flowing. 'My wine is turning out very well,' he wrote in 1898.'I made claret and chablis and have given a lot away. I won't begin selling for another year, until the wine is more matured.'

By 1900, on 5430 acres (2197 hectares) of freehold land, Bernard Chambers had 10,328 sheep and six acres (2.4 hectares) of grapevines. Among the stream of eminent visitors to the vineyard were the premier, Richard Seddon, and the governor, Lord Ranfurly.

By 1906 Te Mata Vineyard had spread to 26 acres (10.5 hectares). Three years later, with a full-time winemaker, J.O. Craike, and manager, Travers Twiss, at the helm, production was the highest in the country, with an annual output of 12,000 gallons (54,552 L) of claret, hock and madeira from the 35 acres (14.2 hectares) of Meunier, Syrah, Cabernet Sauvignon, Riesling and Verdelho vines. Craike won gold medals for Te Mata overseas. In 1914 Sidney Anderson, the government vine and wine instructor, wrote that Te Mata Vineyard 'is now the leading one in the Dominion'.

However, not all was plain sailing. From 1909 onwards, Chambers did not extend his vine plantings. The local market preferred sweet fortified wines to fine table wines, and the prohibition movement peaked in the second decade of the twentieth century, forcing many winemakers out of business. Birds, mildew, frost

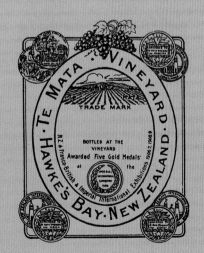

Portrait of Bernard Chambers, painted about the time he gained control of Te Mata in 1885.

and labour posed further problems. Chambers wrote in 1916,'the vines are in a disgraceful state, unhoed under the rows, and generally neglected'.

In 1917, Bernard Chambers, now 58, sold his winery, wine stocks and part of the vineyard to Reginald Collins Limited; Chambers retained a minority shareholding. By 1923, when Reginald Collins sold its interests to TMV Wines, the vineyard had shrunk to 10 acres (4 hectares) and the peak period of Te Mata Vineyard was over. Chambers died at Havelock North in 1931, aged 72.

When André Simon, the famous writer on gastronomy and wine, visited Hawke's Bay in 1964, he tasted the 1912 vintage of Te Mata Claret. 'Remarkable, quite remarkable,' was the verdict.'One wouldn't have thought it would have kept that long. This is really quite good, there is not the slightest trace of acidity or vinegar. No sign of decay at all. A very mellow wine.'

Chambers' winery has since experienced a renaissance. In 1974 Michael Morris and John Buck acquired the run-down company and more than a century after the first vintage flowed in Chambers' vats, Te Mata Estate ranks among the foremost wine producers in Hawke's Bay.

Winemakers of distinction

liquor legislation between 1881 and 1918 severely retarded the wine industry's progress and soon threatened its survival.

Winegrowers succeeded in extracting a few concessions from the government before the power of the prohibition movement peaked in the early twentieth century. These reforms were sparked by the Colonial Industries Commission, which reported in 1880 that 'wine of good quality is produced in various parts of the colony, and that, but for the restrictions placed upon it by the existing licensing laws, this industry is likely to grow to considerable proportions'.[3]

In 1881 special licences were introduced to govern the sale of New Zealand wine. Previously vineyard sales had been banned and hotels had been the sole legal outlet. Vineyard sales were now authorised but restricted to a minimum quantity of two gallons (9.1 L) for consumption off the premises. In 1891, Parliament awarded winemakers the right to operate their own stills to produce spirits for wine fortification, thereby releasing them from the financial burden of having to purchase heavily taxed imported spirits.

Before the prohibition storm-cloud burst, however, several Hawke's Bay landowning families eager to explore new economic ventures plunged into commercial winemaking. They were encouraged by the success of William Beetham, a Wairarapa farmer, who planted his first vines in 1883 and by 1897 was making about 1850 gallons (8410 L) of wine from Pinot Noir, Meunier and Hermitage (Syrah) grapes.

At Henry Tiffen's Greenmeadows Vineyard — praised by a contemporary observer as 'the premier vineyard of New Zealand' — Pinot Noir and Meunier were the principal varieties planted. In 1897, a *New Zealand Farmer* reporter 'came across a bottle of Burgundy in private life and it bore on the bottle the Greenmeadows label. The excellence of the wine had drawn my curious attention to the label, and I was both surprised and pleased to find wine so matured and of such high-class quality produced, so to speak, at one's elbow. For good, sound, light wine we have really no occasion to go outside the colony.'[4] The Burgundy was made from Pinot Noir and Meunier, and Tiffen's 1899 Claret was a blend of Shiraz, Cabernet Sauvignon and Malbec. The 1890s also witnessed the first recorded sales of Mission wines.

Henry Stokes Tiffen

Romeo Bragato

At the Te Mata station, Bernard Chambers planted his first vines as a hobby in 1892 and his first wine flowed in 1895. By 1909 his 35-acre (14.2-hectare) vineyard of Meunier, Syrah, Cabernet Sauvignon, Riesling and Verdelho was the largest in the country, annually producing 12,000 gallons (54,552 L) of wine. The *New Zealand Journal of Agriculture* observed in May 1914: 'Mr. Chambers' wines are principally hocks, claret and sweet, and are commanding a large sale.'

An overseas expert's fervent advocacy of viticulture as an industry 'that will by far eclipse any other that has hitherto been prosecuted here' also stimulated a surge in vineyard plantings in the late 1890s. Romeo Bragato, a Dalmatian-born graduate of the Royal School of Viticulture and Oenology at Corregliano, Italy, arrived in New Zealand on loan from the Victorian Government in 1895 to assess the colony's potential for winemaking.

Bragato's far-sighted *Report on the Prospects of Viticulture in New Zealand* enthused that 'there are few of the places visited by me which are unsuitable to the vine. The land in your colony, if properly worked, should yield a very large quantity of grapes per acre from which wine of the finest quality, both red and white and Champagne could be produced.'[5] Bragato also made an identification of phylloxera, a root-sucking aphid which was then devastating many of the country's vineyards.

At the turn of the century, 'the largest and most successful vine-grower up North' was W. Heathcote Jackman, observed the *Graphic*.[6] When phylloxera inspectors arrived at Whakapirau, on a north-east arm of the Kaipara Harbour, in the summer of 1898–99, they discovered in Jackman's vineyard 'a large quantity of vines cultivated . . . four and a half acres of trained vines, about six thousand'.[7] The vineyard they inspected had been established in classic varieties: Cabernet Sauvignon, Pinots, Chasselas, Riesling and Syrah.

Jackman's wines were dry — he avoided adding sugar except in poor years — and when his customers baulked at their lack of sweetness they were 'educated up to them'. Bragato was much impressed, telling an audience of fruit-growers that he 'had tasted wine, that of Mr Jackman in the Kaipara, equal, and very likely superior, to any wine imported into the country'.[8]

Further impetus was given to the burgeoning industry

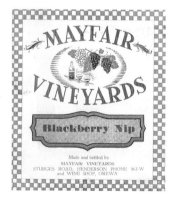

---

[3] *Report of the Colonial Industries Commission*, AJHR, H-22, 1880, p. 3.
[4] *New Zealand Farmer*, April 1896, p. 126.

[5] Bragato, R., *Report on the Prospects of Viticulture in New Zealand*, Department of Agriculture, 1895, pp. 8–10.
[6] Scott, D., *Seven Lives on Salt River*, 1987, p. 65.
[7] Ibid, p. 65.
[8] Ibid, p. 65.

when Dalmatians working in the gumfields of the Far North began producing wine. Dalmatians had first planted vines at Pahi in north Kaipara in 1896. By 1907 some 14 miniscule vineyards at Herekino, south of Kaitaia, had an output of about 2000 gallons (9092 L) of wine per year. *The Auckland Weekly News* in May 1906 was struck by the 'curious fact' that 'although men of British blood were the first to prove that the vine would flourish in New Zealand, and even now have the largest and most up-to-date vineyards, the expansion of vine-growing is due at the present time largely to the efforts of foreigners'.[9]

Those who had endured the struggle to make wine in the generally adverse social climate of nineteenth-century New Zealand enjoyed in the early 1900s a notable rise in fortune. In 1902 Romeo Bragato returned to New Zealand to accept the newly created post of Government Viticulturist and took personal charge of the war on phylloxera. The government viticultural research station at Te Kauwhata was swiftly upgraded; classic *vinifera* vines grafted onto phylloxera-resistant American rootstocks were widely distributed to growers; a programme of experimental winemaking started. The wine industry looked to be on the verge of prosperity: in 1902 a Lebanese stonemason, Assid Abraham Corban, established a 4-acre (1.6-hectare) vineyard at Henderson and Stipan Jelich made the first wine at the Pleasant Valley winery in Henderson. By 1913 some 70 winemakers were producing a total of 81,450 gallons (366,525 L) of wine per year.

The market gave growers no incentive to produce high-quality table wines. 'The natural uneducated British taste, when it calls for wine, craves something that is red and sweet and strong,' observed the *New Zealand Farmer*. 'Good wine of a lighter kind might be better for the average drinker, but the ascent to that better state of affairs seems long and slow.'[10]

Most growers were producing fortified wines, the Department of Agriculture reported in 1912, yet New Zealand's climate was suited to producing 'pure light wines. . . . High in alcohol, very sweet, and wanting in that fruity body which should accompany a sweet wine, [they] are a poor imitation of the wine they are named after — port.'[11]

The steady growth of two decades was largely destroyed when the influence of the prohibitionists peaked in the second decade of the century. When Masterton and Eden — an electorate including part of Henderson — voted 'no-licence' in 1908, many winemakers denied the right to sell their wines locally were forced out of business. Official support began to wither away; the Viticultural Division of the Department of Agriculture was disbanded and in 1909 Bragato left the country, frustrated and disillusioned.

The New Zealand Viticultural Association was formed in 1911 and promptly petitioned the government for aid, but the beleaguered winegrowers soon found themselves embroiled in a bitter controversy over their own winemaking standards. Prime Minister W.F. Massey, altogether untroubled by the fact that he had 'never seen the stuff', in 1914 lambasted the Dalmatians' wine as 'a degrading, demoralising and sometimes maddening

Stipan Jelich (Stephan Yelas), pictured here with his family, planted the first vines at Pleasant Valley, New Zealand's oldest family-owned winery, in the 1890s.

drink'.[12] The government subsequently tightened its control by setting up a new system of winemakers' licences, although accusations of adulteration continued to hound the country's winemakers until the early 1980s.

Prohibition fervour gradually went off the boil in the 1920s and 1930s, bringing an interval of steady although unspectacular growth in the wine industry. On the east coast, Friedrich Wohnsiedler of Waihirere, Tom McDonald of McDonald's and Robert Bird of Glenvale all entered the industry during this period. An influx of Dalmatians at Henderson soon brought to the area, according to the *New Zealand Herald* in July 1935, 'something of the charm of a home industry with simple apparatus and unpretentious sheds'.[13] The number of licensed winemakers soared from 40 in 1925 (barely more than half the 70 operating in 1913) to 100 in 1932.

For much of the first half of the century, Corbans dominated the New Zealand wine scene. Assid Abraham Corban made his first recorded sale in 1909 and swiftly won recognition for the quality of his wines. By the mid-1920s, with his son, Wadier, in charge of winemaking and another son, Khaleel, travelling the country in a Dodge van in search of sales, Corbans winery was the largest in New Zealand, and was to retain its ascendancy until the early 1960s.

The health of the country's vineyards was, however, declining. Most classic *vinifera* vines had been so weakened by blight and viruses that it was popularly believed that *vinifera* varieties could not successfully be cultivated in New Zealand. Growers turned instead to disease-resistant Franco-American hybrid vines or to the extraordinary Albany Surprise, a particularly heavy-bearing clone of the American Isabella variety. The outcome: wines that at best were coarse and at worst undrinkable.

[9] *The Auckland Weekly News*, 31 May 1906, p. 47.

[10] Quoted in Scott, D., *Pioneers of New Zealand Wine*, 2002, p. 50.

[11] Quoted in Thorpy, F., op. cit., p. 129.

[12] New Zealand Parliamentary Debates, 1914, Vol. 168, pp. 829–30.

[13] *New Zealand Herald*, 12 July 1935.

Assid Abraham
Corban

■ The sturdy figure of Assid Abraham Corban, with his magnificent walrus moustache and trademark waistcoat and chains, for many years gazed sternly down from a wall in the entrance to the head office of Corbans Wines, at Henderson. For much of the first half of the twentieth century the winery Corban founded dominated the New Zealand wine scene.

Assid Corban was born in Lebanon in 1864. In his youth, he worked principally as a stonemason but he also worked and ploughed the family vineyard. Three years after his 1888 marriage to Najibie Tanyus Ataia, spurred by tales of the riches amassed by Lebanese emigrants to the New World, he set out alone for Australia. In 1895 he opened a shop in Queen Street, Auckland (advertising himself as an 'Eastern Importer of Fancy Goods, Jewellery, Drapery, etc.'), and in 1897 sent for his wife and two children to join him in New Zealand.

The origin of Corbans Wines lies in Assid Corban's purchase in 1902 of a 10-acre (4-hectare) block of scrub-covered Henderson gumland. The property had a two-roomed cottage, an orchard and vines of the native American variety Isabella. His first 3.5-acre (1.4-hectare) vineyard was planted in a mix of wine grapes that included the classic red varieties Syrah, Meunier and Cabernet Sauvignon, and dual-purpose table grapes such as Black Hamburgh. Romeo Bragato, government viticulturist from 1902 to 1909, was very impressed with Mt Lebanon Vineyards, praising it as 'the model vineyard of New Zealand, and an object lesson to vinegrowers'.

A.A. Corban stands guard against the birds at Henderson.

A three-level wine cellar, started in 1903, was completed in 1907. The first grapes were crushed by hand with a wooden club, and an open hogshead was used as the fermenting vat. By 1908 Corban had a simple crusher and two small presses for his first commercial vintage. His first recorded sale, in September 1909, was to James Cottle of Taupaki, who purchased two gallons (9.1 L) of wine in his own jar at 10 shillings per gallon.

Recognition of the quality of Corban's wines came swiftly. At the 1913–14 Auckland Exhibition, competing against wines from other countries in the British Empire, the company won silver medals for its claret and red wine, and gold medals for its sherry and port.

Both the Corban family (another eight children were born in New Zealand) and its holdings steadily expanded. In 1909 Assid bought a neighbouring 20-acre (8.1-hectare) property, planting the first 5 acres (2 hectares) in vines in 1912. Eight years later he opened a wine depot in Auckland city and in 1923 built a two-storeyed, 17-room family homestead on Great North Road.

In 1925 the Department of Agriculture's vine and wine instructor, Charles Woodfin, wrote that in the previous year 'only 20 acres [8.1 hectare] of vines were [newly] planted and one brave man was responsible for eight of these'. A.A. Corban and Company had become the largest winery in the country.

Although the arrival of a rotary hoe in 1934, and a caterpillar tractor soon after, greatly eased the vineyard toil, by all accounts Assid Corban remained a patriarch in the Old Testament mould and a strong believer in the virtues of hard work. He never retired.

Assid Corban died in 1941; his wife, Najibie, died in 1957. The business became a public company in 1963 and passed out of the family's hands in the 1970s, but remained one of the country's winemaking giants until 2000, when it was finally absorbed by Montana.

Father and son team, Assid (right) and Wadier Corban, at the crusher.

Winemakers of distinction

Walter Nash, prime minister during the 1957–60 Labour government, addresses an early Viticultural Association field day. On his left sits the Hon. H.G.R. Mason. Behind, standing, are Peter Fredatovich of Lincoln Vineyards, Mate Selak and Mate Brajkovich of San Marino (now Kumeu River).

Having languished without political encouragement for three decades, the wine industry benefited greatly from Labour's ascension to power in 1935. A key ally was the Hon. H.G.R. (Rex) Mason, Minister of Justice in the new government, who as Member of Parliament for Auckland Suburbs and then Waitakere strongly promoted his west Auckland winegrower constituents' interests for a period spanning 37 years.

The Te Kauwhata research station was now expanded and upgraded and a new Government Viticulturist, Bruce Lindeman, appointed. Duties on overseas wines were raised and import licences for wine halved. Merchants, required by the Department of Industries and Commerce to buy two gallons of New Zealand wine for every gallon they imported, suddenly found themselves forced to clamour for local brands they had long held in disdain.

Demand for New Zealand wine soared, and then further escalated during the war when American servicemen on leave flooded into the country. As one grower put it: 'I sold some wine to an American serviceman for ten shillings a gallon — he was very happy. Then a fortnight later I heard that wine was being sold at thirty shillings a gallon. So I bought a distillery, put in a cellar, and planted five or six acres in grapes. In 1943 in went another five acres. . . .'[14]

With wine selling easily and at top prices, the financial position of winegrowers rapidly improved. Brick wineries supplanted tin sheds, concrete vats replaced wooden, and many sideline winemaking operations emerged as profitable small businesses.

Unfortunately, quality took a back seat in the wartime rush for easy profits. With demand for wine exceeding the supply, the growers made up the difference less from grapes than from sugar and water. In 1946 the Royal Commission on Licensing was scathing in its criticism of New Zealand wine. 'The Department of Agriculture states that more than 60 per cent of the wine made by the smaller winemakers is infected with bacterial

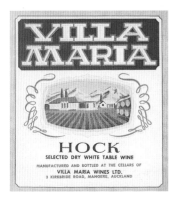

14 *Wine Review*, Vol. 12, No. 4, Summer 1975.

PINOTAGE CABERNET

Produced and Bottled by
BABICH WINES LTD.
Henderson N.Z.

■ **In 1916, in a windowless tin shed on the desolate gumfields of New Zealand's Far North, the young Josip Petrov Babich trod grapes with his feet, fermented wine and opened a wine shop. From that humble beginning has grown Babich Wines, a leading example of the family-owned companies of Croatian origin that have played a crucial role in the emergence of the New Zealand wine industry.**

He was born Josip Babic (later anglicised to Babich) in 1895 in Dalmatia, a part of Austrian-ruled Croatia known for its red wines. To escape economic hardship and military conscription, in 1910 Josip and his brother Stipan journeyed to New Zealand to join their three brothers, who were already toiling in the northern gumfields.

In 1916 the Babich brothers planted Isabella vines and established a pocket-sized vineyard at Kaikino, north of Awanui. Three surviving glass negatives, with 'Kaikino Wineshop 1916' scratched on the plates, show a tin shed near the Babich homestead. Inside are a stack of barrels (the word 'Babich' chalked on their heads), copper jugs, syphon tubing, a funnel, bottles and a worn bottle-cleaning brush. For a £1 sale, Josip would sometimes make an 80-mile (129-km) delivery trip on horseback, a dozen bottles of wine slung over his saddle.

In 1919 Josip Babich and three of his brothers shifted to land they had bought earlier at Henderson in west Auckland. At first the property was farmed jointly, but later it was divided between the brothers. A tall, strongly built man, Josip cleared the land, milked cows, grew vegetables and planted fruit trees — and established another vineyard.

Winemaking resumed in the 1920s, with Babich hawking his port and sherry in bottles, half-gallon jars and clay jeroboams of varying sizes around the streets of Auckland. For decades the family grew a variety of fruit, as well as grapes. The company's name, at first New Era Orchard and Vineyard, later changed to Pinot Vineyards, Northern Vineyards and finally Babich Wines.

By the late 1930s most of Babich's income was derived from winemaking. Along with a 5-acre (2-hectare) orchard, he owned 7 acres (2.8 hectares) of Meunier, Black Hamburgh, Baco, Seibel and Albany Surprise vines. Each year,

about 3000 gallons (13,638 L) of wine were sold directly from the winery or delivered to customers throughout Auckland.

By the 1950s Babich Dry White, Dry Red, Palomino Sherry and other wines enjoyed a small but growing clientele. Although he remained active in the company, during the 1950s Josip (usually called 'Joe') passed responsibility for its day-to-day running to his two sons, Peter and Joe. When the wine boom gathered momentum in the 1960s, the family seized the opportunity, investing in a major expansion of the winery. By the 1970s, the company was a nationally distributed producer of quality, award-winning table wines.

Josip Babich died at Henderson in 1983; his wife, Mara, died in 1994. During a period when New Zealand wines were not highly regarded, he early won a reputation for well-priced, consistently sound wines. After several decades of steady, controlled growth, the company Josip founded is still family-owned and operated, and ranks among New Zealand's leading wine producers.

Pioneer winemaker Josip (Joe) Babich — a man of voracious reading habits and infectious wit — and his wife, Mara.

disorders . . . [and] a considerable quantity of wine made in New Zealand would be classified as unfit for human consumption in other wine-producing countries.'[15]

A first step towards making New Zealand wine more freely available to the public was taken in 1948, when the wine-reseller's licence was created, allowing growers and others to establish retail outlets for New Zealand wine throughout the country. However, the wartime wine boom collapsed in the late 1940s after the easing of import restrictions when a wave of Australian wine entered the local market. The demand for local wine fell and by 1949 prices had fallen appreciably below wartime levels. Yet the modern era of New Zealand wine was about to begin.

Thousands of New Zealand soldiers had their first, fumbling encounters with table wine when stationed in European wine districts during the Second World War. An anonymous 'Kiwi Husband', writing in 1952, recalled that 'most New Zealand soldiers made their first acquaintance with wine only when the supply of beer ran dry. It was a rough and ready meeting, and many of us dealt with wine in the manner to which we had become accustomed. We drank it from the bottle, and by the bottle-full, often with sad results to ourselves . . . We collected our wine in water carts that held some hundreds of gallons and imparted a taint of chlorine and foul lime sediments; we dispensed it in jerrycans designed for petrol and drank it from the mugs we used for hot tea. And we abandoned it for beer whenever we had the chance . . . '[16]

Some, like 'Kiwi Husband', later developed a more appreciative understanding of wine. Migration of Italians, Yugoslavs and Greeks also brought thousands of wine drinkers to New Zealand. The post-war boom in overseas travel also exposed countless New Zealanders to the traditional European enthusiasm for wine.

Yet in the mid-1950s, apart from in hotel dining rooms, it was still exceptionally difficult to enjoy wine with a restaurant meal. The custom was to smuggle in a bottle and hide it under the table. Some restaurants took the wine away and decanted it into soft-drink bottles, to look more innocent in the event of a police raid.

'Today may go down as a gastronomic landmark,' the *New Zealand Herald* observed on 8 February 1954, 'for at 7.30 tonight a little group of food enthusiasts . . . will inaugurate a Wine and Food Society in New Zealand, dedicated to the cause of better eating and drinking.' Dr Tom Childs was interviewed about 'neglected' practices in New Zealand, including 'the habit of drinking wine moderately and intelligently with meals'.[17] Alex Corban, and Dudley Russell of Western Vineyards, were among the society's inaugural officers.

Four years earlier, George Mazuran had been elected president of the Viticultural Association, composed mainly of small-scale growers of Dalmatian origin. Convinced that the future prosperity of the wine industry hinged on relaxation of the country's restrictive licensing laws,

Mazuran carved out a long career for himself as one of the most successful lobbyists that New Zealand has known. He extracted a string of legislative concessions from successive governments that laid the foundation for the industry's phenomenal growth rates of the 1960s and 1970s.

An annual dinner and field-day for parliamentarians and government officials was launched in 1952 and subsequently brought the wine industry to the favourable attention of a host of politicians. A crucial breakthrough came in 1955 when Parliament reduced the minimum quantities of wine that could be sold by winemakers and wine resellers, from two gallons (9 L) to a quart (1.14 L) for table wines and temporarily to a half-gallon for fortified wines.

An even more important contribution was made by the Winemaking Industry Committee, set up in 1956 to investigate all aspects of the manufacture and sale of New Zealand wine. For several years the breweries had succeeded in preventing the spread of wine-resellers' licences, arguing that such outlets were unnecessary where New Zealand wine could already be bought from hotels. The Committee recommended that wine-reseller licences should be more freely granted, and by 1965 the number of New Zealand wine shops had doubled.

The Second Labour Government (1957–60) rendered further assistance to the winegrowers. Imports of wines and spirits dropped in 1958 and 1959 to half their former volume. Another shot in the arm came with the high taxes slapped on beer and spirits in the 'Black Budget' of 1958. The *Weekly News* in September 1958 declared that 'the beer drinker was rocked on his heels by the sharp bump upwards in beer tax that came with the Nordmeyer Budget. Today, New Zealanders who wend their way homeward after 6 p.m. with brown parcels under arm will often have a bottle of wine as well as the traditional nut-brown brew.'[18]

The effects of Labour's moves are well described in the 1959 Annual Report of the Department of Agriculture. The tax and licensing adjustments had 'created an immediate and unprecedented demand for New Zealand wines. The market position for New Zealand wines changed from one of difficult and competitive trading to a buoyant market capable of absorbing all the wine that producers could supply'.[19]

A critical turning point in the industry's fortunes had been reached. Winemakers now entered a 20-year period of unbroken growth and prosperity. Overseas funds began to pour into the industry. McWilliam's of Australia had set the precedent, establishing vineyards and a winery in Hawke's Bay between 1947 and 1950. Penfolds Wines (NZ) was founded at Henderson in 1963, with the Australian parent company holding the majority of the capital. Montana's rapid expansion, which began in the 1960s, acquired greater momentum in 1973 when Seagram of New York acquired a 40 per cent shareholding.

Having failed to block the emergence of an indigenous wine industry, local wine merchants and brewers began to display a more positive attitude

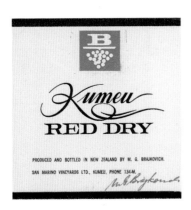

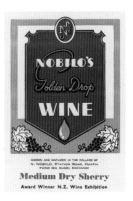

[15] *Report of the Royal Commission on Licensing*, 1946, p. 255.
[16] 'Observations at the Shrine of Bacchus', *Here and Now*, 2, No. 4, January 1952, p. 2.
[17] *Silver Jubilee History of the Wine and Food Society of Auckland*, 1979.
[18] Bolster, T.N., 'Lucky Break for New Zealand Winemakers', *Weekly News*, 24 September 1958.
[19] Annual Report, Department of Agriculture and Fisheries, 1959.

Harold Innes in his favourite role — spreading the gospel of New Zealand wine at an early Connoisseurs Club festival.

towards New Zealand wine. Hotel bottle-stores throughout the country now stocked and promoted the products of the large wine companies (especially McWilliam's and Penfolds) in which the breweries acquired a substantial financial stake. During the 1960s the dominant force of the New Zealand wine industry — with its dry white Cresta Dore, hybrid red Bakano and sparkling Marque Vue virtually household names — McWilliam's (NZ) was wholly Australian-owned until 1962. A branch for the distribution of McWilliam's Australian wines had opened in Auckland in 1928, but the McWilliam's family later decided that their interests would be better served by establishing a winery locally. McWilliam's first vines were planted at Te Awanga in Hawke's Bay, in 1947, and the first wine flowed in 1952.

McWilliam's grew rapidly until 1961, when it merged with McDonald's Wines to become the largest winery in New Zealand. With a string of unprecedentedly fine (although by modern standards light) Cabernet Sauvignons from 1965 onwards, and its multiple gold medal-winning 1974 and 1978 Chardonnays (labelled as Pinot Chardonnays), McWilliam's proved beyond doubt New Zealand's ability to produce high-class table wines. The financial involvement of Lion Breweries and Dominion Breweries guaranteed McWilliam's more freely available wines a prominent position on hotel wine lists and wine merchants' shelves.

An ambitious and high-profile new company burst on the scene in the late 1960s. David Lucas, the founder of Cooks, observed that his Dalmatian friends in Henderson had 'large cars, small vineyards and went for trips back home . . . [Yet] the industry has only a limited number of vines and these in

the main are large bearers, planted by pioneers who knew and cared little about quality wine'. Cooks was planned as 'a model vineyard, devoted only to quality, that will raise the standard of New Zealand wines'.[20]

The company's first vine — a Müller-Thurgau — was planted at Te Kauwhata in May 1969. By the end of the year, a 50-acre (20-hectare) vineyard of Pinot Gris, Chasselas, Müller-Thurgau, Cabernet Sauvignon, Pinotage and Meunier had been established. When Cooks' 1972–73 Cabernet Sauvignon scooped the trophy for champion wine at the 1974 Easter Show Wine Competition, the winery emerged as one of New Zealand's leading table wine producers.

Rising affluence encouraged more and more New Zealanders to seek new experiences in food and drink. No longer, as in winemaker Paul Groshek's day, was wine viewed as 'plonk, to be consumed in shame behind hedges and bullrushes [sic]'. Wine was becoming fashionable. The industry's own marketing efforts, the improving quality of local wine and the emergence of wine competitions, wine clubs and wine columns (notably by J.C. Graham in the *New Zealand Herald* and Michael Brett in the *Auckland Star*, both started around 1970), combined to raise the level of public wine awareness in New Zealand to new heights.

Brewer turned wine promoter Harold Innes launched the Connoisseurs Club in 1965. 'The title was presumptuous then, and perhaps still is now,' he declared in 1970, 'but we have brought the average man into contact with wine and food. And we have developed the idea of bringing New Zealand table wines into the home.'[21]

Two thousand Aucklanders consumed almost 5000 bottles of wine while dancing on the green at Redwood Park, Swanson, in 1966. In 1974 — the first year the event was held at Kumeu — the 4000 festival-goers drained 8000 bottles of New Zealand wine.

The wine industry also benefited from a proliferation of new forms of liquor licences. From the 1960s the trend towards liberalisation of the licensing laws, evident since 1948, grew much more decisive. Restaurants were licensed in 1960 and taverns in 1961. Theatres, airports and cabarets became licensed between 1969 and 1971, all offering new opportunities for wine sales. The creation of a permit system in 1976 gave belated legislative recognition to the BYO wine phenomenon by allowing the consumption of wine in unlicensed restaurants. Another amendment that year introduced vineyard bar licences, allowing the sale of wine for on-premise consumption at wineries.

Vineyard acreages tripled between 1965 and 1970 as contract grapegrowing swept the Gisborne Plains. An average winery grew 96 per cent of its grape requirements in 1960. Today, contract grape-growers produce and sell 60 per cent of the country's grape crop.

The emergence of contract grapegrowing reshaped the structure of the viticultural industry in New Zealand. Traditionally, wineries had grown all their own grapes; viticulture and winemaking formed integral

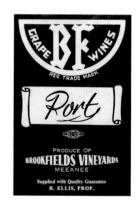

20 Lucas, D., and Ujdur, S., 'New Zealand Wine', unpublished report, 17 May 1967.
21 *Cooks Wine Bulletin*, December 1970, p. 2.

Tom McDonald

■ Tom McDonald, *Cooks Wine Bulletin* declared in April 1971, was 'like a benevolent grizzly bear ... big, bald. [He] lords it over the Bay. He rules by force of personality, his views influencing those outside his domain, his insistence on tradition admired there and mostly copied.'[22] Today, Tom McDonald is honoured as the driving force behind New Zealand's first prestige red.

In 1921, 14-year-old Thomas Bayne McDonald started work at Bartholomew Steinmetz's Taradale Vineyards. 'We made only fortified wines, such as sherries, ports and muscats then ... I was very fortunate that the old fellow was a talented winemaker brought up in the European school, and it was from him I got my basic principles.'[23] In 1926, when Steinmetz, born in Luxembourg, decided to return to Europe for a few years, he leased his business to McDonald and George Hildred. McDonald subsequently took over the business, carrying on trading as Taradale Vineyards.

The 1931 earthquake damaged McDonald's winery but in 1932, and again in 1938, he extended his landholdings. During the Depression, however, wine sales slumped. McDonald supplemented his income by growing fruit and vegetables, and on his 1931 marriage certificate gave his occupation as orchardist. 'Table wines were just a sideline then. The main grapes were Pinot Meunier, Chasselas and Cabernet Sauvignon. White wines were made from Pinot Meunier [a black-skinned variety] fermented off the skins.'[24]

In 1944, McDonald sold out to the Christchurch-based brewers and merchants, Ballins. 'I had two reasons for selling. The first was that I had two daughters and no sons to hand the business on to, and the other was that it brought in the necessary finance to allow for expansion.'[25] McDonald stayed on, however, as manager; new vineyards were planted and a modern winery built. The company's name was finally changed to McDonald's Wines.

There now flowed a rivulet of Cabernet Sauvignon under the McDonald label that pioneered the modern era of red-winemaking in Hawke's Bay. McDonald himself was inspired by the past. Born in Taradale, he was acquainted with Henry Tiffen's daughter and heir, Mrs Amelia Randall, and keenly aware of the table wines from classic varieties produced from the mid-1890s onwards at Tiffen's Greenmeadows Vineyard.

When André Simon, the famous food and wine writer, visited Hawke's Bay in 1964, McDonald served him cheek by jowl the 1949 vintages of his own 'Cabernet' and Château Margaux. To Simon, this was 'a rare and convincing proof that New Zealand can bring forth table wines of a very high standard of quality. ... The Margaux had a sweeter finish and a more welcoming bouquet, greater breed, but it did not shame the New Zealand cousin of the same vintage.'[26]

In 1962 McDonald's Wines merged with the dominant force in the Bay, McWilliam's Wines (NZ). McDonald climbed to the influential post of McWilliam's production director. In 1965 came the first vintage of the great string of white-labelled McWilliam's Cabernet Sauvignons that were so excitingly superior to anything else in the country.

John Buck, now of Te Mata Estate, was highly impressed by the 1965. 'Aptly described as "Tom McDonald's baby", this wine is of darkish, Cabernet colour and has a lovely varietal nose which, although rather strong in new oak, should improve with age. It also has good body (perhaps still fractionally light but a great improvement by New Zealand standards) and a palate well balanced in tannin and acid ... it looks a certain winner.'[27]

With McWilliam's financial resources, McDonald and his winemaker Denis Kasza — who made a vital contribution — were not only able to purchase French oak barriques in which to mature their Cabernet Sauvignon for a year; it was then bottle-aged until it was four years old. Each vintage was snapped up by wine lovers who put their names on allocation lists; few bottles ever reached retail shelves. McDonald also made a series of fine white wines from such varieties as Chardonnay, Gewürztraminer and Riesling.

Awarded the OBE in 1971 — the year of his fiftieth vintage — McDonald retired from McWilliam's in 1976, but stayed on as a consultant and director until 1982, and even chaired the Wine Institute from 1980 to 1982.

A burly man with a powerful intellect and shrewd, sparkling eyes, McDonald died in 1987, aged 79. His memory lives on in the richly atmospheric Tom McDonald Cellar at Montana's Church Road Winery in Hawke's Bay, and in the name of the company's most prestigious wine — Tom.

Winemakers of distinction

22 *Cooks Wine Bulletin*, April 1971, p. 6.
23 *Wine Review*, Summer 1971, p. 39.
24 *Wine Review*, Autumn 1976, p. 22.
25 *Wine Review*, Summer 1971, p. 39.
26 Thorpy, F., op. cit., p. 87.
27 Buck, J., *Take a Little Wine*, 1969, p. 109.

Frank Yukich

■ He took the helm of an obscure, fortified-producing winery and with a cyclonic explosion of energy constructed the largest wine company in the land. In 1973 he led Montana into the almost virgin territory of Marlborough, triggering the emergence of New Zealand's most internationally acclaimed wine region. Ambitious, ruthless and far-sighted, in the 1960s and 1970s Frank Yukich revolutionised the New Zealand wine industry.

'He has ... a tack-sharp mind and a squared-away muscularity which would make you think three times before tangling with him,'[28] declared the *Dominion* in 1972. To call Yukich hard-driving would be an understatement — he reputedly drank two bottles of wine and slept no more than three or four hours daily.

Montana was founded by Ivan Yukich, a Dalmatian immigrant who planted his vineyard in the Waitakere Ranges west of Auckland and marketed his first wine in 1944. Under the direction of Ivan's sons, Frank and Mate, in the 1960s Montana admitted new shareholders to build up its financial clout, and then plunged into a whirlwind of expansion.

'This virile young company has now risen to the top bracket in the industry,' observed *Wine Review* in 1966. 'Through the medium of major distributors and the company's own wine-shops throughout both islands, Montana wines, sherries, ports, cocktails and liqueurs have become some of the best known.'[29] Montana led the way with such novelties as Cold Duck and Montana Pearl, and was the first to put classical labels in quantity on the market. Between 1961 and 1972, the winery's output soared from 13,500 litres to 5.85 million litres. A year later, Frank Yukich bought New Zealand's first mechanical grape-harvester.

Above all else, Yukich is remembered as the driving force behind the foundation of the Marlborough wine industry. Alerted to the region's viticultural potential by a favourable report from Wayne Thomas, then a young DSIR scientist, Yukich, according to *Marlborough Wines and Vines*, 'set out, under the cover of the company Cloudy Bay Developments, to buy 1600 hectares of flat land on the southern side of the Wairau Plain.

'He paid the deposit on the land out of his own pocket, then told the [Montana] board what he had done. His plan was rejected. The board, still convinced that the North Island was the only place to be, argued that Thomas' research was inconclusive. Professor Berg [of California] subsequently studied Thomas' report, agreed with the conclusions, the board then reversed its decision, and gave Yukich the go-ahead to start planting in Marlborough.'[30] The first vine in the modern era of Marlborough wine was planted on 24 August 1973.

Bold in action, Yukich was also an indefatigable planner. His five-year plan was the springboard for Montana's initial flurry of growth; 1966 brought an 800-page, 10-year plan. The *Dominion* was agape at 'such planning and analysis as one would regard as being far beyond the capacity of a young man who reached form two at a country school'.[31]

In 1973 Seagram, the multinational liquor giant, took a 40 per cent shareholding in Montana. The investment was trumpeted as 'basically an export deal ... [to] export three million gallons [13.64 million L] a year within five years'[32] to the United States. Yukich's relationship with Seagram, however, proved stormy. In 1974, with the winery reporting a $178,000 loss, Yukich stepped down from the top post and cut his ties with Montana, although his brother, Mate, stayed on as production director.

In 1977 Frank Yukich rebounded with the purchase of a controlling 64 per cent share in Penfolds (NZ). By buying most of the Australian parent company's stake in Penfolds, the man responsible for heavy overseas investment in Montana turned Penfolds into a New Zealand company. The large Henderson winery, Yukich declared, had been 'just standing still ... nobody has been pushing to expand the company'.[33] Penfolds' traditional emphasis on sherry and port was swiftly shifted to table wines, and by January 1978 Yukich was back in Marlborough looking for new contract growers.

'The stormy, often controversial rise of Penfolds,' wrote the *Auckland Star* in 1984, 'has been accompanied by bloodletting ... the rush to become big brought so many problems.'[34] Short of grapes, in 1981 Penfolds was apprehended importing concentrated grape juice, in an effort to satisfy its burgeoning market for restaurant bulk wines. When its hock and moselle catering kegs were seized by the Health Department, the ensuing controversy damaged the company's reputation. Penfolds' profitability nose-dived. A proposed $2.5 million share-issue had to be withdrawn, and in 1982 Yukich bowed out by selling his shares in Penfolds to Lion Breweries. As a condition of the sale, Yukich agreed to have no involvement with the wine industry for at least five years. His tumultuous career in New Zealand wine was at an end.

In 1993, in recognition of his mammoth contribution to the industry, Frank Yukich was elected a Fellow of the Wine Institute. 'I take my hat off to Frank Yukich,' says David Lucas, the founder of Cooks. 'He always wanted to be the biggest — and for a long time, he succeeded.'[35]

[28] 'Man Who Produces the Food of the Sun', *Dominion*, 3 June 1972.
[29] *Wine Review*, Spring 1966, p. 11.
[30] Brooks, C., *Marlborough Wines and Vines*, C. and B.H. Brooks, Blenheim, 1992.
[31] *Dominion*, 3 June 1972.
[32] *Wine Review*, Summer 1972, p. 5.
[33] *Auckland Star*, 8 August 1978.
[34] Ibid, 31 August 1984.
[35] Lucas, D., personal interview, March 1992.

parts of each winery's activities. This pattern altered in the late 1960s when several large companies, seeking to avoid the heavy capital expenditure required to establish new vineyards, persuaded farmers to plant their surplus acres in grapevines.

Auckland's share of the national vineyard area dropped between 1970 and 2000 from nearly 50 per cent to 3.4 per cent. Shifts occurred within the province as many Henderson wineries developed new vineyards further north, in the more rural Huapai-Kumeu area.

As vineyard expansion slowed in Auckland and the Waikato, further south in Gisborne, Hawke's Bay and Marlborough the pace was hot. Corbans' plantings, for example, spread from Henderson to Kumeu and Taupaki in west Auckland, and then to the East Coast and finally Marlborough. Montana planted at Mangatangi, south of Auckland, before contracting large acreages in Gisborne and pioneering the spread of viticulture to Marlborough.

During the 'Cold Duck' era of the early 1970s, an undiscriminating public snapped up large volumes of cheap sparklings, white wines, sherries and ports. In 1971, wine writer J.C. Graham listed the criticisms still commonly levelled at New Zealand wine: 'Each winemaker attempts to produce every type of wine, instead of specialising; many wines are too thin and watery; unacceptable quantities of sugar and water are added in manufacturing; undue use is made of heavy-yielding hybrid grapes which do not make the best wine.'[36]

At the 1971 Industries and Commerce Competition (forerunner of the Air New Zealand Wine Awards), the gold medal winners were Vidal Extra Dry Special Reserve Sherry, McWilliam's Pinot Chardonnay 1968, McWilliam's Cabernet Sauvignon 1969, Totara Gold Special Selection (a sweet white table wine), Mazuran Rich Port and Mazuran Special Port.

The 1970s brought an overall improvement in wine quality and heavy emphasis on the production of table wines. Wine production soared between 1960 and 1985 from 4.1 million litres to 59.6 million litres. Table wines, which captured 12 per cent of the market in 1962, by 1985 accounted for 91 per cent of production and slightly sweet, fruity white wines dominated the market.

The emergence of these wines reflected sweeping changes in the composition of New Zealand vineyards. Forty years ago, less than one-third of the vines planted in New Zealand were of classical European varieties — the most common varieties were the heavy-cropping but poor wine-producing Baco 22A and Albany Surprise. As a Cooks publication noted in 1979: 'The first is prohibited in most European winemaking districts. The second would be if anyone proposed to plant it.'[37]

By 1983 Müller-Thurgau was by far the most heavily planted variety in the country, and Cabernet Sauvignon was the major variety for red wine. Classic *vinifera* varieties constituted over 95 per cent of all vines in New Zealand.

The radical changes in the wine industry during the 1970s produced a

So beautiful was Dudley Russell's Western Vineyards at Henderson, its terraced vines several times graced the covers of popular magazines.

number of casualties. To switch from the production of fortified wine to more delicate table wines required heavy expenditure on vineyards and equipment. While some companies acquired the necessary technical and marketing abilities, others fell behind in the race to expand and improve.

Western Vineyards — founded by 19-year-old Dudley Russell in the Waitakere Ranges in 1932 — had helped pioneer the modern era of classical table wines and enjoyed formidable competition success in the sixties. At its height of production, the winery put out 35–40,000 gallons (157,500–180,000 L) of wine a year, with its Cabernet Sauvignon, 'Gamay de Beaujolais', Pinot Chardonnay and private bin Flor Sherry all enthusiastically received.

The stunning 40-acre (15-hectare) terraced vineyard in 1964 excited the legendary wine writer, André Simon, to jot in the visitors' book: 'I have never seen a more picturesque vineyard anywhere but in Tuscany.' For many years thereafter, Western Vineyards' advertisements brandished this memorable Simon quote — minus the last three words.

In his later years, Dudley Russell began to lose interest in winemaking; beef farming increasingly absorbed his energies and investments. After his eldest son chose not to enter the family wine business, Russell announced in 1979 that the 1978 vintage had been his last; the vineyard would be uprooted and all wine stocks auctioned off. He died less than a year later, aged 67.

After a labyrinth of many years' negotiations, agreement was reached in 1975 to form a single, united wine organisation to represent all New Zealand winemakers. Previously, the industry's representation was fragmented. The Viticultural Association spoke on behalf of the small-scale, principally Dalmatian-owned wineries and the New Zealand Wine Council and the Hawke's Bay Grape Winegrowers' Association pursued the interests of the larger companies. Their contrasting economic fortunes kept the two camps apart — and often at each other's throats — until, spurred on by the industry's increasingly complex problems,

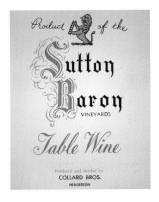

[36] Graham, J.C., *New Zealand Wine Guide*, 1971.
[37] Cooks brochure, 1979.

The historic first meeting of the provisional executive committee of the Wine Institute, held on 1 October 1975. (From left) Terry Dunleavy (acting executive officer) Montana; Peter Fredatovich, Lincoln; Russell Gibbons, Montana; George Mazuran (deputy chairman); Alex Corban (chairman); Mate Selak; Tom McDonald, McWilliam's; Stan Chan, Totara SYC; Mate Brajkovich, San Marino; Peter Babich.

they finally reached agreement to form a united body.

The Wine Institute in 2002 joined forces with the New Zealand Grape Growers Council to form a new, unified body, New Zealand Winegrowers. What does New Zealand Winegrowers do? Since the environment in which the wine industry operates is vitally influenced by government policies and decisions, lobbying occurs on such crucial issues as the licensing laws, taxation and trade liberalisation. A multitude of other tasks are accomplished, from behind-the-scenes subcommittee work on such areas of special concern as viticulture and winemaking regulations to more visible promotional activities, including administration of the Air New Zealand Wine Awards and generic export campaigns.

As part of a government policy of economic restructuring, in 1979 the wine industry was referred for study to the Industries Development Commission (IDC). In its 'Wine Industry Development Plan to 1986', published in December 1980, the IDC concluded that the wine industry deserved special encouragement, but strongly criticised the price of most New Zealand wine as being too high.

In the IDC's view, over-protection of the local industry from imported wine had placed a price burden on the consumer unjustified by the wine industry's 'poor' export performance. Distortion of competition in the wine market also derived from the commercial dominance of a select cluster of wineries, merchants and resellers described by the IDC as 'a highly cartelised group characterised by their oligopolistic influence in the market'.[38]

Several of the IDC's recommendations, designed to contain escalating costs by encouraging stiffer competition, were acted on by the government. Wine was freed from import licensing in 1981, although not from tariff restrictions. To stimulate more competition in the distribution arena, a new class of wine distributor licence was created. Sales tax on wine was altered from a value basis to a volume rate, which made cheap wines more expensive but lowered the price of finer wines.

Despite the progress in quality during the 1970s, in the early 1980s a wine scandal unfolded of major proportions. A group of scientific studies yielded clear evidence that wine-watering, although illegal, was common in New Zealand. For decades the government had turned a blind eye on the grounds that adding water to wine (or more accurately unfermented grape juice) enabled winemakers to reduce the coarse flavours and sharp acidity found in hybrid wines. By the early 1980s, however, most of the water was being added not to ameliorate wine but to 'stretch' it.

'The fact is,' wrote David Lucas of Cooks in 1980, 'the New Zealand wine industry has been following thoroughly fraudulent winemaking practices for many years, and if this news gets into the overseas press, our chances of getting into the world's wine markets will be irreparably damaged.'[39] The issue was finally resolved in 1983 when winegrowers agreed to support new regulations setting a minimum 95 per cent grape-juice level for all table wines; thenceforth water could only be added to wine in small amounts as a processing aid for legal additives. Cask wines were

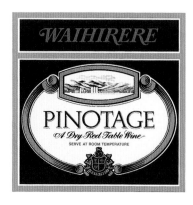

[38] Report of the Industries Development Commission: The Wine Industry Development Plan to 1986, 1980.   [39] Lucas, D., '1980 Vintage: Influence of Wine Quality Requirements', unpublished paper, 1980.

transformed in quality as a result.

Yet by 1982, serious doubts had arisen about the successful achievement of the aims of the Wine Industry Development Plan. The plan had projected an annual per capita consumption of New Zealand wine of 15 litres by 1986, but consumption eased from 12.2 litres in 1981 to 12.1 litres in 1982, then to 12 litres in 1983. The drop in sales, linked to heavier imports and consumer price resistance, proved a serious setback to an industry geared to rapid growth.

Heavy planting of new vineyards in the early 1980s — encouraged by distortionary tax incentives then offered to many land-based products — raised the spectre of a wine glut. From the bumper 1985 vintage, the industry needed 55,000 tonnes of grapes to satisfy demand, but crushed 78,000 tonnes. Production climbed by 43 per cent on 1984, sales rose by 2 per cent, and a surplus resulted of record proportions.

The history of wine in New Zealand can be portrayed as an industry embarked on a century-old rollercoaster ride, soaring and plunging through successive periods of growth and optimism, decline and disillusionment. Between mid-1985 and early 1986, following the sustained prosperity of the 1960s and 1970s, the rollercoaster once again turned groundwards, carrying three privately owned wineries — the Villa Maria/Vidal stable and Delegat's — into receivership and, by their own admission, Nobilo and Glenvale to the brink of it.

Although criticised by two government committees for having divorced themselves from market realities, the winemakers blamed the crisis on the Labour Government's November 1984 Budget, which had lifted the sales tax on sherries and ports by 54 per cent, from $1.05 to $1.62 per bottle, and on table wines from 54 cents to 99 cents per bottle — a searing hike of 83 per cent. In concert with the rapid expansion of vine plantings and the slowdown in consumption growth, this brutal tax hike brought the wine industry to its knees.

The decision by the giant Cooks/McWilliam's company — formed by a merger in September 1984 — to unload its surplus stocks by cutting prices then set alight the ferocious price war of 1985–86. Villa Maria/Vidal, Penfolds, Montana, Delegat's, Corbans and Glenvale all chopped their ex-winery trade prices to as low as one-half the production cost. The cut-throat discounting brought an explosion in the sale of cheap sparkling wines and casks, sliding demand for the wineries which stayed aloof from the price slashing, and a battle for life for the family vineyards lacking corporate financial backing.

In February 1986 the government intervened. Growers were offered $6175 per hectare to eradicate up to 25 per cent of the national vineyard, and 1517 hectares of vines were torn from the soil. The heaviest vine pulls were on the East Coast: Hawke's Bay lost 534 hectares of vineyards and Gisborne 586 hectares. Müller-Thurgau, the grape variety upon which most bulk white wines were based, suffered the severest loss: 507 hectares.

The industry's travails also resulted in a severe loss of investor confidence and sweeping ownership changes at Montana, Penfolds, Villa Maria/Vidal, Cooks/McWilliam's and Delegat's.

Seagram's decision to divest itself of its 43 per cent shareholding in Montana was not difficult to understand — in the half-year to 31 December 1985 the company chalked up a net loss of $4.62 million. In August 1986 Montana succeeded in a takeover of Penfolds Wines (NZ), thereby creating the country's biggest wine company, commanding about 40 per cent of the market for New Zealand wines.

Corbans bought the vineyard and winery assets of Cooks/McWilliam's in early 1987 for $20 million. The enlarged Corbans emerged as the second largest wine company in the country, holding over 30 per cent of the market.

For the second time in 25 years, the wine industry embarked on the traumatic task of restructuring. During the 1960s and 1970s, the replacement of hybrid vines with classic *vinifera* varieties, especially Müller-Thurgau, and heavy investment in modern equipment, enabled the industry to switch from fortified to table wine production. Now, faced at home with a tidal wave of imported wines, the industry at last focused seriously on export, planting extensive new vineyards in Sauvignon Blanc and Chardonnay.

Overseas wines, which in 1987 held 5 per cent of the total New Zealand wine market, by 1991 had grabbed 21 per cent. The government, although funding the vine-uprooting scheme, had also moved in 1985 to speed up the removal of barriers against overseas wines. The heavy duties with which cheap imported wines were previously saddled were slashed. By mid-1990, trans-Tasman tariffs on wine had been abolished, allowing Australian wineries to contest the New Zealand market on an equal footing with local producers. The Australian invasion was spearheaded by its richly flavoured reds, but Australia also dominated the imported still white, sparkling and fortified wine markets.

The galvanising effects of the government's moves have been well summarised by the Wine Institute. 'The New Zealand wine industry originally developed to serve the domestic market within a heavily regulated economy. From 1984 onwards, as tax breaks were phased out and imports were substantially liberalised, the industry underwent a traumatic adjustment which greatly improved its long-term health and viability . . . the new emphasis on competition within a predictable medium-term economic framework increased the industry's confidence in its own future. Grape-growers and wineries responded with a burst of new investment in quality plantings and unprecedented emphasis on international standards of quality. The industry began for the first time to explore the world in search of significant export markets.'[40]

The relentless pressure on the winemakers to find export markets can be seen on the graph on page 27 showing domestic sales, imports and exports for the period 1982–2002. In 1990, New Zealand winemakers sold 39.2 million litres in their domestic market, and 8 million litres of wine were imported.

40 *New Zealand Wine 1993–2000, A Working Paper*, 1992, p. 1.

Ernie Hunter stormed the UK wine scene in the mid-1980s, winning high critical praise and festival awards for his Marlborough Sauvignon Blancs and Chardonnays.

By 2002, the industry's local sales were only 32.2 million litres (estimated), but imports (strongest in the red wine category and at the cheap end of the market, in casks and bottles) had surged to 41.9 million litres. The local industry's growth in volume terms during the 1990s derived entirely from exports, which soared from 4 million litres in 1990 to 23.0 million litres in 2002.

A highlight of recent decades has been the emergence of Wairarapa, Nelson, Central Otago and Canterbury as successful wine regions. Of the major established regions, Marlborough has emerged as by far the most heavily planted in the country, with a projected 6823 hectares of bearing vines in 2004. Hawke's Bay, with an estimated 3813 hectares, is well ahead of Gisborne with 1857 hectares. The far smaller Northland, Auckland, Waikato/Bay of Plenty, Wairarapa, Nelson, Canterbury and Otago regions will account for 18.5 per cent of the total area of bearing vines in 2004 (2940 hectares).

Over the past decade, new wineries have mushroomed, from Kaitaia to Alexandra. In 1984 the Wine Institute had 93 members; in 1992, 166; and in 2002, 398. The wine industry is forever abuzz with the excitement of new companies, new faces and new labels. Attracted by New Zealand's proven ability to produce world-class wines, a wave of overseas producers has swept into the industry. A prestigious Western Australian winery, Cape Mentelle, founded Cloudy Bay (now part of LMVH, the French luxury goods conglomerate), and set the wine world alight with the stunning quality of its debut 1985 Marlborough Sauvignon Blanc. The Australian-funded Craggy Range winery in Hawke's Bay; the Swiss-owned Fromm winery in Marlborough; the Marlborough operation currently being established by a top Sancerre producer, Henri Bourgeois; the American-owned Tasman Bay winery in Nelson; and the German-owned Giesen winery in Canterbury are just a few examples of the extensive international investment in New Zealand wine.

Far more conspicuously, the start of the new millennium has brought dramatic changes to New Zealand's biggest wine companies, reflecting a global trend towards consolidation of ownership. Faced with the growing retail power of giant supermarket groups and the high cost structures of an industry in rapid expansion, large Australian wine producers have been endeavouring to improve their economies of scale and market share through merger and acquisition.

BRL Hardy, the Australian wine giant, gained control of New Zealand's then fourth largest winery, Nobilo, in early 2000. Soon after, the industry giant, Montana, purchased its largest competitor, Corbans. In early 2001 Matua Valley, New Zealand's sixth largest producer, was acquired by Beringer Blass, the wine division of the Australian Foster's Group; in mid-2001 the world's second largest spirits and wine conglomerate, UK-based Allied Domecq, gained control of Montana. Within a single dramatic year, three of the country's six largest wine producers had passed into overseas hands. The full impact of foreign ownership on Montana, Nobilo and Matua Valley remains to be seen, but an immediate benefit was improved access to international distribution channels. Further rationalisation, especially among the ranks of medium-sized producers, has been widely predicted.

The New Zealand wine industry is still at an early stage of its development — barely out of its infancy. Marlborough's winemakers have processed just 27 vintages, leaving much to be learned about the crucial links between topography, soil, climate, variety, vine management and winemaking techniques. Around the country, new districts and sites with viticultural potential are waiting to be identified; overseas, new markets are waiting to be explored.

Samuel Marsden observed over 180 years ago that 'New Zealand promises to be very favourable to the vine'.[41] With its area of bearing vines having doubled between 1996 and 2002, the industry is now reaping the benefit of its recent heavy investment. Although the value of its sales rose markedly over the past decade, volumes remained static as winemakers switched from cheap, everyday-drinking wine to premium-quality wine with export potential. Today, the outlook is for strong sales growth in both volume and value terms.

By 2005, more New Zealand wine is expected to be consumed in the UK, the United States and Australia than in domestic markets (see page 29). A new era in the history of the New Zealand wine industry — as a quality niche player on the international stage — is now unfolding.

[41] Rawson-Elder, J., ibid.

Producing Vine Area in New Zealand
1984–2004 (Hectares)

Year	Hectares
1984	5 500
1985	5 900
1986	4 300
1987	N/A
1988	N/A
1989	4 270
1990	4 880
1991	5 440
1992	5 800
1993	5 980
1994	6 110
1995	6 110
1996	6 610
1997	7 410
1998	7 580
1999	9 000
2000	10 197
2001	11 648
2002	13 173
2003	14 802
2004	15 829

Production of New Zealand Wine
1982–2002 (Millions of litres)

Year	Millions of litres
1982	47.0
1983	57.7
1984	41.7
1985	59.6
1986	42.4
1987	37.7
1988	39.2
1989	45.3
1990	54.4
1991	49.9
1992	41.6
1993	32.5
1994	41.1
1995	56.4
1996	57.3
1997	45.8
1998	60.6
1999	60.2
2000	60.2
2001	53.3
2002	89.0

Number of Wineries
1987–2002

Year	Number
1987	112
1988	112
1989	123
1990	131
1991	150
1992	166
1993	175
1994	190
1995	204
1996	238
1997	262
1998	293
1999	334
2000	358
2001	382
2002	398

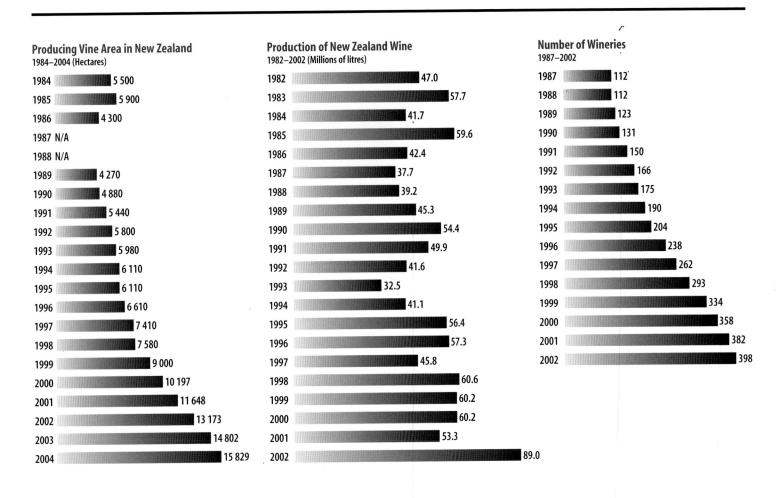

Domestic Sales of New Zealand Wine, Wine Imports into New Zealand and Wine Exports
1982–2002 (Millions of litres)

Year	Domestic sales of NZ wine	Wine imports into NZ	NZ wine exports
1982	38.2	3.4	0.5
1983	38.2	2.5	0.6
1984	41.9	3.2	0.7
1985	42.6	3.9	0.8
1986	50.8	2.8	1.1
1987	46.6	3.7	1.0
1988	45.0	4.4	2.9
1989	39.1	6.8	2.7
1990	39.2	8.0	4.0
1991	41.1	11.4	5.6
1992	43.6	8.4	7.1
1993	37.4	19.7	8.6
1994	28.5	32.7	7.9
1995	30.9	25.5	7.8
1996	35.6	21.3	11.0
1997	38.8	22.4	13.1
1998	38.2	28.2	15.2
1999	38.4	27.9	16.6
2000	40.9	28.6	19.2
2001	37.4	30.4	19.2
2002	32.2	41.9	23.0

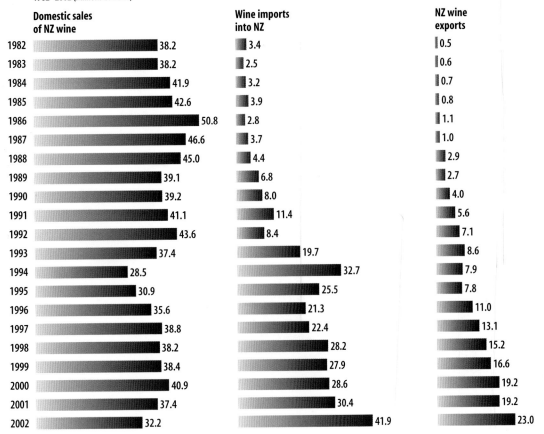

New Zealand Wine in a Global Market

Most wine lovers would be surprised to learn that, on a list of wine-producing countries by output, New Zealand ranks in the low to mid-30s; the same territory occupied by Cyprus, Azerbaijan and the Czech Republic.

New Zealand accounts for just 0.2 per cent of the international wine trade, but since the 1980s its white (especially), red and sparkling wines have carved out a high profile in the United Kingdom and established valuable footholds in the United States and Australia. The recent growth trend in New Zealand wine exports has been steep; the future promises an even sharper ascent.

For more than a century and a half, enthusiasts have predicted a buoyant overseas trade in New Zealand wine. Walter Brodie, for instance, ignoring the almost total absence of wines in the colony, declared in 1845 that 'New Zealand, in a few years, will export much wine'.[1] Brodie was wrong. Andrew Tod, a Scotsman who made wine at Wanganui as early as 1873, later shipped a batch home, and in December 1874 the *Dundee Advertiser* reported: 'We have seen some samples of the New Zealand wine . . . it appears to be of excellent quality, and has improved rather than deteriorated in bouquet by the long voyage.'[2]

This, the first recorded export of New Zealand wine, came to nought. In 1934 the British newspaper the *Daily Mail* enquired whether there were any 'New Zealand or West Indian wines that could be offered in this country?' Observed the paper generously: 'We Englishmen are prepared to try anything once.'[3]

A tiny overseas trade in New Zealand wine was maintained from 1963, when Corbans received a trial order from the British Columbia Liquor Control Board for 25 cases of medium-sweet sherry. Repeat orders followed, both for sherry and the company's Montel Sauternes. By 1972, Corbans was also making small, regular shipments of table wine to Melbourne, California, Chicago and New York.

One early flirtation with export to the United Kingdom was a 480-case shipment in 1971. Organised by Graeme Reid, a leading Auckland wine merchant, the selection included four Corbans labels — Montel Sauternes, Riverlea Riesling, Riverlea White and Medium Sherry — and other wines from Aspen Ridge, Penfolds (NZ), San Marino, McWilliam's (NZ), McDonald's and Western Vineyards.

The result was seen as a disaster. No interest was displayed by New Zealand firms operating in the United Kingdom. Four months after the wines arrived there, 104 cases had been sold, 16 cases had been broken in transit, 133 cases were unsaleable because of inadequate labelling, and the other 227 cases were unsold.

February 1982 brought a turning point, when a small group of merchants and writers assembled in the penthouse of New Zealand House, London, to taste 47 wines. Not only was this the first generic tasting of New Zealand wines in the United Kingdom, it marked the start of the industry's sustained and successful courtship of the British market.

A string of triumphs in London wine competitions boosted the image of New Zealand wine. At the 1986 *Sunday Times* Wine Club Festival, Hunter's topped the popular vote with its Fumé Blanc 1985. A year later, Hunter's Chardonnay 1986 scooped one of only 12 gold medals awarded to 380 wines in the formal judging at the *Sunday Times* festival, and was also voted best wine of the show at two of the three public tasting sessions. These results reflected not only the high quality of the wines, but the limitless energy and irresistible charm of the winery's founder, a dynamic expatriate Irishman, Ernie Hunter.

At the International Wine and Spirit Competition, New Zealand began to monopolise the trophy for champion Sauvignon Blanc, winning in 1990 with Montana Marlborough Sauvignon Blanc 1989; in 1991 with Oyster Bay Sauvignon Blanc 1990; and in 1992 with Hunter's Marlborough Sauvignon Blanc 1991.

The International Wine Challenge 1991, staged by *Wine* magazine, awarded the trophy for best Chardonnay to Kumeu River 1989, and the trophy for best white wine of the show to Te Mata Elston Chardonnay 1989. Such early triumphs helped put New Zealand on the world wine map.

By the late 1980s, New Zealand wines had built up a reputation for good quality, according to the wine buyer at Selfridge's, the London department store. 'Many of our customers now realise that for half or even a third of the cost of white Burgundy, they can buy a decent New Zealand Chardonnay, or your even better known dry white, Sauvignon Blanc.'[4]

It was Marlborough Sauvignon Blanc that 'established New Zealand on British retail shelves,' Tim Atkin, the *Observer*'s wine correspondent, wrote in 1995. 'It has led to a lot of navel-scrutiny in Sancerre and Pouilly-Fumé. . . . For punters previously resigned to one good Sancerre in three, New Zealand Sauvignon Blanc has been a godsend. The market-leading Montana Marlborough Sauvignon Blanc is an admirably consistent wine.'

Today, British consumers pay more for New Zealand wine than that of any other country. In 2000, when the average price of a bottle of table wine in the United Kingdom was £3.52, New Zealand wine sold at an average of £5.20, ahead of Australia (£4.45) and the United States (£4.34). A minor player in volume terms, New Zealand has nevertheless carved out a valuable 8 per cent share of the British premium (over £5 per bottle) wine market.

The value of New Zealand's wine exports to the United Kingdom skyrocketed from $0.4 million in 1985 to $7.8 million in 1990, $27.6 million in 1995 and $118 million in 2002.

For a niche player like New Zealand to penetrate overseas markets, it has been crucial for the industry to adopt a cohesive approach. The wines have been consistently positioned under the slogan 'the riches of a clean green land', and a united strategy in terms of target markets has boosted growth.

[1] Quoted in Scott, D., *Pioneers of New Zealand Wine*, 2002 p. 14.
[2] *Listener*, 8 February 1971, p. 49.
[3] *New Zealand Herald*, 12 July 1935.
[4] *Cuisine*, No. 11, Oct./Nov. 1988, p. 115.

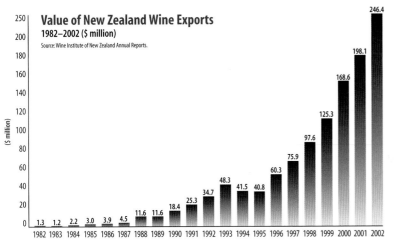

Value of New Zealand Wine Exports
1982–2002 ($ million)
Source: Wine Institute of New Zealand Annual Reports.

New Zealand Wine Exports: Percentage of Total Sales
By volume, 1990–2010
Source: Wine Institute of New Zealand Annual Reports.

Since the initial focus on the British market, to spread the potential risk and rewards a policy of diversification has been pursued since the early 1990s. Core markets have been identified, with the United Kingdom, United States and Australia in the top tier; Canada, Japan and Germany in tier two; and Ireland and the Netherlands in tier three. The top tier markets have recently received about 80 per cent of the industry's generic promotional funds and returned almost 80 per cent of the sales.

The hot new target for New Zealand winemakers is the United States, which leapfrogged Australia in 2000 to become the industry's second largest export market. The value of New Zealand's wine exports to the United States has skyrocketed from $1.05 million in 1995 to $48.2 million in 2002.

As in the United Kingdom, the critical response to New Zealand wines in the United States has generally been enthusiastic. 'Few wine lovers here have tasted anything other than one or two of New Zealand's justly famous Sauvignon Blancs,' Michael Franz noted in the *Washington Post* in 2000. '[But] in terms of sheer quality, the most exciting of all emerging wine-producing countries is New Zealand.'[5]

New Zealand's other most valuable market lies across the Tasman. When the first Cloudy Bay hit the shelves in 1985, many Australians were alerted to the phenomenon of Marlborough Sauvignon Blanc. Progress has been much slower than in the United Kingdom or United States, reflecting the local industry's dominance in its domestic market, and many New Zealand wine companies have put Australia in the 'too hard' basket. However, Montana recently intensified its promotional effort in Australia and between 1996 and 2002 the value of New Zealand's wine shipments rose by over 500 per cent to $38.1 million.

New Zealand winemakers are being helped by a global pattern of significant growth in the wine trade, fuelled by lower tariffs and removal of other trade barriers. New World countries — especially Australia and the United States — have become major players and taken market share from the traditional, still dominant European producers, France, Italy and Spain.

New Zealand's progress on the world stage has also been aided by rising demand for premium wines from better educated, more discerning consumers. Fresh, fruity New World wines with easy-to-understand varietal labels have catered for a growing interest in new taste experiences.

Moreover, in many traditional beer-drinking countries, wine consumption is soaring. In the United Kingdom, for instance, beer drinking fell between 1990 and 2000, while adult wine consumption soared from 15.7 to 24 litres per head.

Despite their international successes, New Zealand winemakers have been warned not to take their future for granted. 'There have been some price hikes lately which the United Kingdom has resisted,' observed British wine writer Oz Clarke in 1998. 'There's been discounting of important quality [New Zealand] producers, some £20 a case off, £30 off some of those wines.'[6] Katherine O'Callaghan, the Wine Institute's United Kingdom marketing manager, reported in 2000 that 'there is a perception [in the United Kingdom trade and press] that some (not all) of New Zealand's reds are overpriced and do not represent value for money'.[7]

Despite that, the outlook is rosy for New Zealand wine exporters. Between 1990 and 2000, exports leapt from less than 10 per cent of the industry's total sales to a third. The country's major wine exporters predict that by 2005 exports will exceed domestic sales and two-thirds of the country's wine could be exported by 2010. Exports, in short, will dominate the industry's future.

New Zealand Wine Exports by Grape Variety and Style
By volume, for the year to June 2002
Source: Wine Institute of New Zealand Annual Reports.

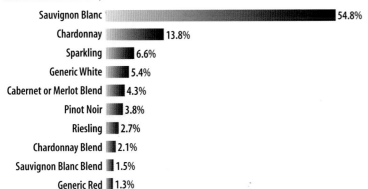

New Zealand Wine Exports by Destination
By volume, for the year to June 2002
Source: Wine Institute of New Zealand Annual Reports.

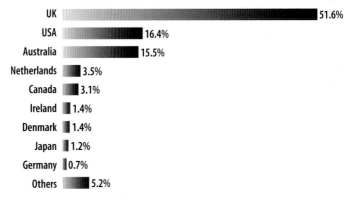

[5] Quoted in *New Zealand Winegrower*, Winter 2000, p. 9.
[6] Quoted in *New Zealand Winegrower*, Summer 1998, p. 16.
[7] Quoted in *New Zealand Winegrower*, Summer 2000, p. 25.

Climate, Soil and Topography

'Man has the first say on what he plants and where; and the last say on how he makes his wine. In between, through soil and climate, nature has much to say.'

— James Wilson, *Terroir*

Through the combination of climate, soil and topography, each of New Zealand's regions and individual vineyard sites has its own unique environment, expressed from year to year in the style and quality of its wines. Such geographic limitations (as opposed to blending from all quarters) can produce distinctive wines with a sense and taste of 'somewhereness'. The Sauvignon Blanc variety is cultivated extensively around the world, but Marlborough Sauvignon Blanc comes only from Marlborough, and Stonyridge Larose Cabernets can only be grown in the Stonyridge vineyard on Waiheke Island.

Climate

Anyone poring over the globe could be forgiven if he or she failed to realise that the South and lower North Islands of New Zealand have cool viticultural climates. Marlborough (at 41.5°S) lies at a comparable latitude to the sweltering Douro Valley in Portugal, home of the great fortified wine, port.

New Zealand's wine regions, however, have markedly lower temperatures during the vine's growth than their latitudinal equivalents in the northern hemisphere. Encircled by the sea, New Zealand has a temperate, maritime climate with cooler summers and milder winters than those experienced in Europe. Isolated from adjoining continents, and thus removed from the influence of continental hot-air masses, New Zealand escapes the summer heat waves that descend on wine regions at similar latitudes in the northern hemisphere.

Three factors have a critical bearing on New Zealand's climate: its latitudinal position, oceanic setting and topography. Spread between latitudes 34°S and 47°S, New Zealand lies south of the subtropics and wholly within the temperate zone. Hot-air masses from Australia and freezing winds from Antarctica are substantially tamed by their long ocean passage, giving New Zealand a lack of temperature extremes. The winds pick up abundant moisture from the ocean, giving the country a generally wet, humid climate.

Topography enters the picture because the chain of high mountains that spans both islands is a formidable obstacle to the prevailing westerly winds. The orographic (mountain-generated) rains fall heavily in western regions, giving the east coast a much drier and sunnier climate.

New Zealand's climate can be classified broadly as temperate oceanic, but its three main islands have a north-south span of 1500 kilometres. From subtropical Northland to the arid inland basins of Central Otago, New Zealand is a land of diverse regional climates. The day-to-day weather pattern is dominated by a progression of eastward-moving anticyclones, at average intervals of six days, separated by low-pressure troughs that bring strong winds and unstable weather.

Garden-fresh and enlivened with crisp, racy acidity, Marlborough's Sauvignon Blancs taste like classic cool-climate whites; so do the Rieslings and Chardonnays of other South Island regions. Yet the wines of the North Island are out of a different mould — weightier, riper and rounder. These clearcut variations in style reflect the significantly different climates in which the wines were grown.

Until a few years ago, New Zealand was promoted as 'the home of cool-climate wines'. This slogan was dropped, however, after winemakers realised that New Zealand's viticultural environment was more complicated than that.

According to Richard Smart and John Gladstones, prominent Australian viticultural scientists, New Zealand's cool-climate areas for grapegrowing are the South Island and the southern North Island. 'The distinguishing characteristic of cool viticultural climates [including the Loire Valley, Champagne, Burgundy, Germany, Tasmania and parts of the Adelaide Hills and Victoria] is that they will regularly ripen only early-maturing varieties such as Gewürztraminer, Chardonnay and Pinot Noir. Only in especially warm mesoclimates [site climates] can varieties such as Riesling, which ripens early to mid-season, be ripened.'[1]

Slow ripening of the grapes in relatively cool autumn temperatures is the key advantage of cool-climate regions for wine quality, according to Professor David Jackson and Danny Schuster, Canterbury-based co-authors of *The Production of Grapes and Wine in Cool Climates*. 'In warm climates ripening of grapes occurs early, when the weather is still warm or even hot. These hot conditions cause rapid development of sugars, rapid loss of acids and high pHs . . . and the grape appears to have insufficient time to accumulate those many chemical compounds which add distinction to the wine. A cool autumn — often with considerable diurnal temperature variation — slows down development; better balances can be achieved and more aroma and flavour constituents are accumulated.'[2]

Where does that leave the rest of New Zealand? According to Smart and Gladstones, Hawke's Bay, Gisborne and the northern regions (which together have 40 per cent of the total vineyard area) have intermediate viticultural climates, 'with growing seasons long and warm enough for regular ripening of mid-season grapes such as Merlot and Syrah, and late to mid-season, such as Cabernet Sauvignon.'[3] This classification places most of the North Island in the same broad viticultural climate camp as Bordeaux, the northern Rhône Valley, Tuscany, the Napa and Sonoma valleys of California, Coonawarra in South Australia and Margaret River in Western Australia.

[1] Robinson, J. (ed.), 'Cool Climate Viticulture' in *The Oxford Companion to Wine*, 1994.
[2] Jackson, D. and Schuster, D., *The Production of Grapes and Wine in Cool Climates*, 1994.
[3] Robinson, J. (ed.), ibid.

Chad Douglas argued in a recent geography thesis that New Zealand can be divided into three distinct climate zones for viticulture.[4] The northern zone — from Northland to Hawke's Bay — is characterised by plenty of heat and sunshine during the growing season and a low frost risk, but also high humidity, with an associated high risk of disease. The central zone — the Wairarapa, Nelson and Marlborough — is cooler, with fewer frost-free days but the highest sunshine hours in the country. In the southern zone — Canterbury and Central Otago — the major challenges facing grape-growers are low heat accumulation during the growing season and increased frost risk.

Based on the climatic indices (and how the wines taste) I would suggest a slight refinement to Douglas' classification. Inclusion of Waipara in the central zone would reflect the fact that, in terms of heat during the ripening season, this North Canterbury region is climatically much more akin to Marlborough, Nelson and the Wairarapa, than it is to the Canterbury Plains.

Temperature is the crucial climatic influence on viticulture, because it determines the timing of the vines' growth stages and grape ripening. Mean day and maximum temperatures are important; so too are diurnal (day/night) variations in temperature. Compared to Europe, during the peak of the growing season most New Zealand wine regions are cooler at night, which slows ripening and is believed to be an important factor in fruit quality. But other elements of climate are important to viticultural success, including rainfall, humidity, sunshine hours, frost and wind.

If moderately cool weather during the vine's growing season is New Zealand's greatest viticultural advantage, unpredictable and frequently heavy rainfall is its greatest liability. Vines need sufficient rain to promote healthy plant growth (unless they are linked to irrigation systems), but excessive rain can lead to luxuriant foliage growth and a wet, humid microclimate within

Sunny days and cold nights give Sauvignon Blanc from the Nautilus vineyard in the Awatere Valley an aromatic intensity and crisp acid spine that is pure Marlborough.

the canopy (leaves and fruit), which retards ripening and encourages disease.

In New Zealand, typically three or four tropical cyclones arrive each year between December and March, bringing gale-force winds and torrential rain. In adverse seasons, heavy rains can descend on all the major regions during summer and the crucial autumn weeks leading into the harvest.

The marked swings in vintage quality reflect the fact that the country's areas with the least consistent annual rainfall — those most prone to long, unusually wet or dry periods — include all of the major winegrowing regions: Gisborne, Hawke's Bay and Marlborough. New Zealand's seasonal rainfall is also least reliable in late summer and autumn, during the final stages of ripening, when drought sometimes develops east of the central ranges.

Overall, growing season (October–April) rainfall decreases southwards in New Zealand, from 562–663 mm in Auckland, to 487–522 mm in Gisborne, 366–387 mm in Hawke's Bay, 357–398 mm in Marlborough, and 243–276 mm in Central Otago. The relative dryness in the east coast regions of both islands sharply lowers the risk of disease. Growers are thus able to hang their grapes longer on the vines in pursuit of optimal ripeness and flavour development, instead of being forced to pick prematurely to avoid such wet-weather diseases as botrytis and downy mildew.

By world standards, all of New Zealand's wine regions have a high level of humidity (slightly lower away from the coast), but this is not necessarily a drawback for wine quality. High humidity raises the risk of fungal diseases, but it also encourages steady photosynthesis, which maximises the production of berry sugars, colours, aromas and flavours.

[4] Douglas, C., 'Latitudinal Limit of Commercial Viticulture in New Zealand', University of Otago, 2000.

The contribution of sunlight to grape ripening is hard to pinpoint, because temperatures and sunlight hours often go hand in hand. New Zealand's sunniest areas are both wine regions — Nelson and Marlborough.

In regions with relatively high temperatures, vines need more sugar for their normal metabolism but do not photosynthesise any faster. To generate the sugar surplus needed to ripen their fruit, they require more sunshine hours. This explains why the warm but cloudy Auckland region generally produces only medium to full-bodied table wines.

Frost — which can kill the vine's shoots and leaves and decimate its crop — poses a significant threat to New Zealand's grape-growers, especially in the deep south, but the major wine regions have a low to moderate incidence of frost. The length of the frost-free period at Napier, in Hawke's Bay (306 days) and Blenheim, in Marlborough (233 days) compares favourably with Geisenheim, in the Rheingau (197 days) and Bordeaux (214 days).[5]

The frost danger, lowest in the north and close to the coast, rises with latitude and altitude, reaching a peak in Central Otago. (Most vineyards in New Zealand are less than 100 metres above sea level, and none is higher than 500 metres.) Frostiness often varies even on a local scale, with warm, north-facing slopes the least affected.

The strong winds common in New Zealand pose another challenge for grape-growers. Some air movement is needed, to reduce the risk of fungal diseases by drying the foliage and bunches, but severe winds can inflict major shoot and leaf damage, delaying flowering and ripening. Young vines, especially Chardonnay and Merlot, are the most vulnerable.

Changes over the past 20 years to New Zealand's climate, coinciding with global warming, have included rising temperatures, fewer frosts and an increase in very hot days in eastern regions. Philip Manson, of New Zealand Winegrowers, believes the projected temperature rises of the future 'could be beneficial, providing warmer conditions for ripening fruit in marginal areas. [However] climate change could spell bad news on the disease front . . . due to warmer, wetter summers.'[6]

Note: the climatic data used in this atlas, supplied by NIWA (the National Institute of Water and Atmospheric Research) and taken from recording stations within the wine regions, is not necessarily indicative of the site climates of individual vineyards. The possible effect of urban warming on the recording station, or such differences as altitude, slope and aspect, must be taken into account. The full understanding of a particular vineyard's mesoclimate requires lengthy, on-the-spot records, which are rarely available.

Soil

Geologically, New Zealand is a young country. Its most ancient rocks, on the west coast of the South Island, are believed to be 600 to 700 million years old (only a fifth the age of the world's oldest rocks), and most of its surface rock is less than 100 million years old.

Bedrock has often been cited as an important influence on wine quality and flavour, but around the world, good wines are grown on virtually any geological base. Rather than the core parent rocks — in New Zealand, principally greywackes, argillites and schists — it is the soils derived from them that play the decisive role in wine quality.

New Zealand's soils are young — most are less than 10,000 years old

A note on *terroir*

A new word recently started appearing on New Zealand wine labels. It's a French term that lacks a precise English equivalent and is used in different ways by different people. The word is 'terroir'.

In France, *terroir* (pronounced tare-wah) has at least two meanings. In its narrowest sense, *terroir* relates to the soil; the tasting term 'goût de terroir', used about wine, means 'earthy'. In its broader sense *terroir* means a defined area of land, including its natural and human characteristics, which takes its meaning close to the English word territory. When New Zealand winemakers mention the *terroir* of a region, sub-region or vineyard, they are generally referring to its soil, topography and climate, which crucially influence wine styles. But so do people.

'The soil exists,' notes Professor Warren Moran, a geographer at Auckland University, 'but the *terroir* arrives when somebody makes an expressive wine from grapes grown in it.' In Burgundy, winemakers deliberately use different techniques to achieve a distinctive village style with the desired quality.

For English wine writer, Hugh Johnson, *terroir* means 'the whole ecology of a vineyard: every aspect of its surroundings from bedrock to late frosts and autumn mists, not excluding the way the vineyard is tended, nor even the soul of the vigneron'.

A decade ago, several vineyards promoted the Martinborough Terraces as a unique wine-growing *terroir*. When some key players started processing grapes from beyond the delineated area, the move faltered.

In 2001, a group of companies launched the Gimblett Gravels Winegrowing District in Hawke's Bay, delineating the area on the basis of its soils and referring constantly to its favourable *terroir*. As other producers unravel and promote the links between their natural environments, wine styles and standards, we'll be hearing more about *terroir*.

[5] Fitzharris, B. and Endlicher, W., 'Climatic Conditions for Wine Grape Growing,' *New Zealand Geographer*, 52 (1), pp. 1–11, 1996.

[6] Manson, P., 'Changes Are Inevitable in Global Climate Within Decades', *New Zealand Winegrower*, Autumn 2000, p. 25.

and some are less than 100. In the South Island, since the end of the last glaciation period 10,000 years ago, large amounts of alluvial material and loess have been deposited on lowland areas. In the North Island, where many soils are of volcanic origin, the oldest, most highly weathered soils are in the far north.

Which soils produce the best wine? Around the world, great wines are grown in gravel, sand, loams, even clay. However, a famous study of Bordeaux by Dr Gerard Seguin found the soils of leading vineyards shared two key characteristics: moderate fertility and excellent drainage, with the ability to store and supply just enough water to meet the vines' needs.

In highly fertile soils, vines grow luxuriantly, producing a tangle of canes and leaves which retard fruit quality by casting the ripening bunches into shade. In poorer soils, by contrast, vines grow smaller canopies, which allow the leaves and ripening grapes greater exposure to direct sunlight. Waterlogged soils restrict root activity and the supply of nutrients to the vine, contribute to poor berry 'set', and produce large grapes with low skin to pulp ratios and diluted colour pigments and flavours. They also prevent the development of a deep, effective root system, leaving the vine vulnerable to drought or excessive water uptake after heavy rain.

Until the 1980s, most New Zealand vineyards were planted in soils of high — or, as English wine writer Jancis Robinson put it, 'almost embarrassing' — fertility. The rich alluvial silts of the Gisborne flats and much of the Heretaunga Plains in Hawke's Bay are poorly drained and often wet. The search for sites that can both reduce vine vigour and advance fruit ripening led growers to establish vineyards in the freer-draining, shingly soils of Marlborough, Canterbury, Wairarapa and parts of Hawke's Bay. Drip irrigation systems have even been widely installed in these regions to alleviate vine stress and maintain yields during very dry years. This trend to locate new vineyards in well-drained soils of low-to-moderate fertility has yielded major advances in wine quality.

Many New Zealand vineyards are established on alluvial soils of silt, sand and gravel, deposited by flowing water across the coastal flood plains. Rich, silty loams, with a high capacity for storing water and plant nutrients, can encourage excessive vine vigour. However, although generally fertile and of inconsistent texture and drainage (often varying within a few metres), the stonier alluvial soils — as in Marlborough — are highly sought after by grape-growers.

Heavy-textured clays warm up slowly in spring and often drain poorly. However, clays can still be suitable for quality wine-growing, provided they contain plenty of organic matter and calcium, which boost drainage by giving the soil a crumbly texture.

Chalk and other limestones are highly rated in France, especially for Pinot Noir and Chardonnay, but most New World viticulturists see no special magic in such soils, other than their free-draining nature and the good water-storage capacity of their sub-soils.

Much stronger is the link between stony soils — such as those of Marlborough and the Gimblett Gravels district of Hawke's Bay — and fine quality wine. A high proportion of stones reduces soil fertility, improves drainage and encourages the growth of extensive root systems. By absorbing and storing heat efficiently on sunny days and warming the above-ground parts of the vine during cloudy periods and at night, stony soils are also believed to enhance ripening in cool-climate regions.

Topography

Topography — like climate and soil — is a key component of a vineyard's natural environment. A standout European example is the cold Mosel-Saar-Ruwer region of Germany, where the land surface features of individual sites can determine whether such late-ripening varieties as Riesling achieve ripeness at all.

At the Matariki vineyard in the Gimblett Road area of Hawke's Bay, individual grape varieties are carefully matched to the varying soil types. Here, Merlot vines are planted in a shallow layer of silt overlying free-draining, shingly soil.

The elevation, slope, aspect and proximity to water masses of sites all have implications for viticulture. Height above sea level strongly influences a site's ripening potential, because for every 100 metres of altitude, temperatures typically fall by 0.6°C.

For ease of cultivation, until recently most New Zealand vineyards were planted on valley floors, but lately winegrowers have started to explore the potential of the hills. Hillside sites typically have shallow soils, which reduces vine vigour, and are less vulnerable to frosts, because cold air is able to drain away at night. North-facing slopes are the warmest, absorbing heat during the day that is radiated to the vines at night, promoting ripening.

Most of New Zealand's vineyard area lies within 20 kilometres of the Pacific Ocean. In the afternoon, sea breezes move in to replace heated air rising over the land. Their proximity to the sea gives these vineyards significantly lower temperatures than would otherwise be the case. By slowing the ripening of such early ripening varieties as Chardonnay, this maritime influence can contribute to wine quality in the warmer regions. However, cooling sea breezes are viewed as less desirable in regions with more marginal viticultural climates, such as the Canterbury Plains.

The Principal Grape Varieties

Several basic factors influence the emergence of all wine styles — climate, soil, vineyard site selection, grape varieties, vine management and the winemaker. The careful matching of climate and soil with suitable grape varieties is of critical importance in New Zealand where, in general, the vineyard site climates (mesoclimates) allow the selected grape varieties to only just ripen.

The 2001 national vineyard survey, conducted by Winegrowers of New Zealand, like its forerunners revealed drastic changes in the varietal composition of our vineyards and projected a dramatic 159 per cent leap in the area of producing vines between 1995 and 2004, from 6110 to 15,829 hectares. The two major white-wine varieties, Sauvignon Blanc and Chardonnay, have increased their dominance since 1995 — up from 38 per cent to 51 per cent of the country's total producing vineyard area in 2004. Pinot Noir (also used in sparkling wine production) and Merlot have pushed Cabernet Sauvignon off its pedestal to become the most widely planted red-wine varieties.

Rarer grapes which are occasionally produced as varietal wines or named on labels are Breidecker, a crossing of Müller-Thurgau with the white hybrid Seibel 7053, which yields mild, unmemorable wine; Pinot Blanc, a white mutation of Pinot Noir which can yield weighty, savoury dry wines; Osteiner, a crossing of Riesling and Sylvaner, thus far not impressive in New Zealand; Viognier, which produces impressively perfumed and robust dry whites in the northern Rhône and is starting to yield finely scented, sturdy and smooth wines in New Zealand; Gamay, the foundation of the seductively soft reds of Beaujolais; Grenache, a red-wine grape traditionally found in the hot, dry vineyards of Spain and southern France; Petite Syrah, which yields dark, sturdy, tannic reds in South America and California; and Sangiovese, Italy's most extensively planted red-wine variety, so far producing generally high-acid reds in New Zealand.

National Total Area of Producing Vines

	2004		1995	
	Hectares	% of Total Plantings	Hectares	% of Total Plantings
Sauvignon Blanc	4488	28.4	936	15.3
Chardonnay	3699	23.4	1385	22.7
Pinot Noir	2743	17.3	415	6.8
Merlot	1276	8.1	282	4.6
Cabernet Sauvignon	816	5.2	526	8.6
Riesling	636	4.0	289	4.7
Pinot Gris	315	2.0	22	0.4
Müller Thurgau	286	1.8	885	14.5
Sémillon	253	1.6	183	3.0
Gewürztraminer	202	1.3	124	2.0
Cabernet Franc	176	1.1	80	1.3
Malbec	158	1.0	11	0.2
Syrah	144	0.9	14	0.2
Chenin Blanc	129	0.8	145	2.4
Muscat varieties	129	0.8	204	3.3
Pinotage	88	0.6	66	1.1
Reichensteiner	56	0.4	98	1.6
Other/unknown	235	1.3	445	7.3

White wine varieties

White-wine grapes predominate in New Zealand's vineyards. Chardonnay and Sauvignon Blanc — the big two — account for over half of the country's total vine plantings, and other classic white-wine varieties — Riesling, Pinot Gris, Sémillon, Chenin Blanc and Gewürztraminer — are well established. Nevertheless, the proportion of the national producing vineyard devoted to white-grape varieties is declining (down from 75.6 per cent in 1995 to 65.4 per cent in 2004) due to the burgeoning plantings of Pinot Noir, Merlot and other red-wine varieties.

Chardonnay

Intensely flavoured and finely textured, Chardonnay is the foundation of many of New Zealand's greatest dry whites. During the 1990s, plantings of this internationally fashionable variety exceeded those of every other grape, but have recently been overtaken by Sauvignon Blanc.

Chardonnay's success here is hardly surprising: it is a versatile variety that thrives in many parts of the world. In its homeland, the Côte d'Or of Burgundy, where its plantings cover only one-sixth of the area devoted to Pinot Noir, it reaches its full glories in the vineyards of Puligny-Montrachet and Meursault. California and Australia, infatuated with Chardonnay, now boast wines capable of challenging the Burgundians at all but the very highest level.

Chardonnay used to be commonly referred to here as Pinot Chardonnay, but it is not a true Pinot. The clones imported into New Zealand in the late 1920s never grew well, being infected with leaf-roll virus, and the vines languished, raising doubts — later proved unfounded — as to whether the variety was the same vine as the classic Chardonnay of Burgundy.

The Mendoza clone of Chardonnay, imported in 1971, is now the most widely planted in New Zealand. Called UCD1 (University of California, Davis, clone no. 1) in California and originally known here as the McCrae clone, it was renamed in the 1980s by government viticulturist Dr Richard Smart, to identify its origins in the Mendoza region of Argentina.

Mendoza vines in New Zealand are infected with a weak strain of leaf-roll virus. Relatively low-yielding because of its characteristically poor grape 'set', which produces the 'hen and chicken' (large and small berries) effect, Mendoza is nevertheless favoured by most Chardonnay producers because its smaller berries give a higher skin to juice ratio and more intense flavour. As a later-ripening clone, with high levels of extract and acidity, Mendoza produces wine that develops relatively slowly.

Also widely planted is Clone 6 (UCD6). Imported by Delegat's from Australia and released in New Zealand in 1982, Clone 6 has a more even berry size than Mendoza, crops more heavily, and is the basis of many of New Zealand's mid-priced Chardonnays. Mature, low-cropped vines have yielded some excellent wines in northern parts of the country.

Other established clones in New Zealand are the big-bunch, heavy-cropping UCD4 and UCD5, which form the basis of the Californian industry and are used in sparkling wine production in New Zealand; UCD15, which crops more heavily than Mendoza but less than Clone 6, and has yielded some high quality wines in New Zealand; MVIG1, the country's first locally selected Chardonnay clone, which crops consistently well in Marlborough with lower than average acid levels; and Bernard 95 and Bernard 96, New Zealand's first Chardonnay clones imported directly from Burgundy. Chardonnay vines are spread throughout all the wine regions, but are most heavily concentrated in Marlborough, Gisborne and Hawke's Bay (which each have between 27 and 30 per cent of the country's total plantings). The variety is as popular in the vineyard as it is in the market, adapting well to a wide range of climates and soil types and yielding an average of 8 tonnes per hectare. Chardonnay's early bud-burst renders it vulnerable to damage from spring frosts in colder regions, but the grapes ripen mid-season in small bunches of yellow-green berries harbouring high sugar levels (hence the sturdy alcohol typical of its wine).

Viticultural expert Steve Smith, of Craggy Range, has summarised the key requirements for making top Chardonnay in New Zealand. 'The fruit needs to be concentrated and very ripe to handle the winemaking techniques used. Yields must be low, below 8 tonnes per hectare. Don't let botrytis play a part. Hand-pick. And for the real result, you'll have to wait for some vine age.'

New Zealand's Chardonnays are full-bodied, with fruit flavours ranging from the crisp, flinty apple and lemon flavours found in cooler regions, through to the lush stone-fruit — peach and apricot — flavours of very ripe grapes. Styles produced range from fresh, 'fruit-driven' wines (with little or no wood influence) through to multi-faceted wines made with varying use of whole-bunch pressing, barrel fermentation, malolactic fermentation, aging on yeast lees, lees-stirring and oak maturation.

The hallmark of New Zealand Chardonnays is their delicious varietal intensity. The leading wines display such concentrated aromas and flavours, supported by crisp, authoritative acidity, that they have rapidly emerged on the world stage.

Leading labels
Ata Rangi Craighall, Babich Irongate, Babich The Patriarch, Church Road Reserve, Clearview Estate Reserve, Cloudy Bay, Coopers Creek Swamp Reserve, Dry River, Esk Valley Reserve, Isabel Marlborough, Kumeu River Kumeu, Kumeu River Mate's Vineyard, Martinborough Vineyard, Millton Clos de Ste Anne, Montana Ormond Estate, Morton Estate Black Label, Neudorf Moutere, Palliser Estate, Pegasus Bay, Sacred Hill Riflemans Reserve, Te Awa Farm Frontier, Te Mata Elston, Trinity Hill Gimblett Road, Vidal Reserve, Villa Maria Reserve Barrique Fermented, Villa Maria Reserve Marlborough, Wither Hills Marlborough

Projected producing area in 2004
3699 hectares

Chardonnay

Chenin Blanc

At their best, New Zealand's Chenin Blancs are full in body, with a fresh, buoyant, pineappley, peachy flavour and mouth-watering acidity. In the past, they were typically over-acidic and lacked charm and drinkability, but the latest releases are much riper and more attractive.

Chenin Blanc is only a workhorse variety in Australia and California — where it wins favour for its abundant yields of fresh, medium-dry wines that usefully retain an invigorating acidity — but in the Loire it achieves greatness. The finest dry Vouvrays are substantial, fruity wines with tongue-curling acidity and an ability to unfold in the bottle for decades.

In New Zealand the wine industry is less enthusiastic than it used to be about this vigorous variety, which is largely concentrated in Hawke's Bay and Gisborne. Although Chenin Blanc ripens early in warm climates, in New Zealand the grapes tend to ripen late and its tight bunches are highly susceptible to wet weather and to botrytis. Many growers have discarded their vines; plantings plummeted from 372 hectares in 1983 to 145 hectares of bearing vines in 1995, and are still gradually declining.

Chenin Blanc reveals its full personality only in cooler growing conditions, and should therefore feel very much at home in New Zealand. It demands careful vineyard site selection and long hours of sunshine, however, to build up its potentially high sugar levels. In New Zealand, as in France, its acid levels can be searingly high.

Ripe fruit is essential if New Zealand is to master Chenin Blanc. The vine's vigour must be controlled, crop levels reduced and the grapes exposed to maximum sunshine. With yields in New Zealand averaging 16 tonnes per hectare, most of the vines are still being managed to produce bulk wine. However, by cultivating Chenin Blanc in stony, devigorating vineyards and reducing crop loads, a few viticulturists have achieved higher grape sugars, lower acid levels and richer, riper flavours.

Chenin Blanc's past role in New Zealand was as a blending variety, adding body and 'spine' to its blends with Müller-Thurgau in casks, and it also had a substantial presence in many low-priced dry whites. However, only Millton, Collards and Esk Valley have consistently mastered Chenin Blanc as a strong, distinctive varietal with seductive, steely, tropical-fruit flavours.

Small-bunched, relatively early-ripening Loire Valley clones of Chenin Blanc have yet to be imported into New Zealand. Interest is slowly building in this classic variety's potential; New Zealand's finest Chenin Blancs are yet to come.

Leading labels
Collards Hawke's Bay, Esk Valley Hawke's Bay, Millton Te Arai Vineyard

Projected producing area in 2004
129 hectares

Gewürztraminer

Gewürztraminer, which is at its ravishingly perfumed and pungently seasoned best in Alsace, in New Zealand's cool climate yields less opulent but still impressive wines with clearcut varietal characters, aromatic and spicy.

Pronounced Ge-vertz-truh-meen-uh, with the stress on the 'meen', the name of the wine is sometimes shortened to Traminer. 'Gewürz' means spicy. In Germany it was customary to call the wine Gewürztraminer if it was spicy, Traminer if it was not. In Alsace the current practice is to label all the wines Gewürztraminer.

In New Zealand, Gewürztraminer had an inauspicious debut: in 1953 the Department of Agriculture imported a strain known as Roter Traminer which, after McWilliam's established a plot at Tukituki, bore poorly and produced disappointing wine. As a result many winemakers became convinced that Gewürztraminer could not be cultivated successfully here.

The heaviest plantings are in Gisborne (with 35 per cent of the country's vines), Marlborough and Hawke's Bay, with smaller pockets in Nelson and Central Otago. However, Gewürztraminer has never risen to the popularity of Chardonnay or Sauvignon Blanc. Between 1983 and 1998, its plantings plummeted from 284 to 85 hectares, but have since started to expand again.

Gewürztraminer is a grower's nightmare. The vine is notoriously temperamental, ripening its grapes easily in New Zealand with plenty of sugar and fragrance, but highly susceptible to adverse weather during flowering — which can dramatically reduce the crop — and also vulnerable to powdery mildew and botrytis. The average Gewürztraminer crop in New Zealand is below 7 tonnes per hectare. To plant a vineyard exclusively in Gewürztraminer is a risk, one that few local viticulturists would contemplate.

Clonal variation is marked. The country's older clones, such as UCD1 and UCD4 (imported from the United States by Bill Irwin of Matawhero in 1976), with small berries and light crops, make the best wine. Other clones (GM11, GM12 and GM14) imported from Germany in the early 1980s, crop more regularly with less concentrated flavour. Gewürztraminer is a wine to broach occasionally, when you're in the mood to delight in its overwhelming aroma and lingering, full-flavoured spiciness.

Leading labels
Dry River, Lawson's Dry Hills Marlborough, Montana Patutahi Estate, Stonecroft, Te Whare Ra Duke of Marlborough

Projected producing area in 2004
202 hectares

gewürztraminer

Müller-Thurgau

New Zealanders once drank oceans of Müller-Thurgau, packaged in casks and bottles. During the gap between the early hybrid era and today's classic wines, a glass of floral, fruity Müller-Thurgau made easy summer sipping. Now, this mediocre German grape is fast vanishing from New Zealand vineyards.

Müller-Thurgau (pronounced Mooler-Ter-gow) was bred at Geisenheim in the 1880s by Professor Hermann Müller, a native of the Swiss canton of Thurgau. Müller wrote of his ambition to combine 'the superb characteristics of the Riesling grape with the reliable early maturing qualities of the Sylvaner', but it has never been proven that the variety named after him is indeed a crossing of Riesling and the more humble Sylvaner; he may have crossed two different Riesling clones.

Müller-Thurgau was originally regarded as a bulk producer of low merit. Later, German growers unable to ripen Riesling grapes on less favoured sites discovered that the new vine could produce large quantities of attractive wine, with less susceptibility to weather conditions. The drawback is that Müller-Thurgau as a wine cannot match the flavour and aroma intensity or longevity of Riesling.

In the 1930s, Government Viticulturist Charles Woodfin imported the vine into New Zealand. The commercial value of Müller-Thurgau became apparent much later, when the demand for white table wines escalated in the 1960s. Then the vine spread rapidly, prized for its early ripening ability and high yields. A rush of plantings in the early 1970s rapidly established Müller-Thurgau as New Zealand's leading grape variety. By 1983, 1873 hectares were planted.

Alex Corban made his first Müller-Thurgau, labelled Corbans Riverlea Riesling, in 1957, and the legendary 1965 vintage won international acclaim. It was Nobilo, in the early 1970s, that was the first to take the plunge and use the variety's correct name, Müller-Thurgau.

However, over a third of all Müller-Thurgau vines were uprooted in the 1986 vinepull scheme. Since then, plantings have nosedived to a projected 286 hectares of bearing vines in 2004, concentrated in Gisborne (which has 47 per cent of the remaining vines), Hawke's Bay and Marlborough.

Müller-Thurgau grows vigorously in New Zealand and on most soils yields heavy crops of about 20 tonnes per hectare. The berries, yellow-green and flecked with small brown spots, ripen early, and Müller-Thurgau is generally the first variety to be picked. The grapes are susceptible to wet weather at vintage and to fungus diseases.

Müller-Thurgau's popularity in New Zealand fell when local tastes swung to fuller-bodied, more flavoursome dry whites, such as Chardonnay and Sauvignon Blanc. In recent years, the big companies have found it cheaper to fill their wine casks with bulk wine imported from Europe, South America and Australia. And when the industry turned seriously to export, Müller-Thurgau's pleasant but unmemorable wine had limited potential.

Most Müller-Thurgau is light-bodied and slightly sweet, with a mild, distinctly fruity flavour that lacks Riesling's intensity and acid spine. Müller-Thurgau is a beverage wine: an easy-drinking, enjoyable, low-priced white wine to consume anywhere, any time.

Leading label
Villa Maria Private Bin

Projected producing area in 2004
286 hectares

Muscat varieties

Muscat varieties form a large, instantly recognisable family of white and red grapes notable for their almost overpowering musky scent and sweet grapey flavour. The vines grow all over the Mediterranean and in the New World wine regions, yielding a diversity of styles ranging from scented dry whites in Alsace through to the full-bloomed sweet Asti sparklings of Italy and the delicious fortified wines of Victoria.

Muscat Dr Hogg, an old English table grape, is by far the most common Muscat variety cultivated in New Zealand. Over 80 per cent of all plantings are in Gisborne, with the rest virtually confined to Hawke's Bay.

The vines are heavily cropped in New Zealand, averaging over 20 tonnes per hectare of large fleshy berries with a typical Muscat aroma and flavour. Bumper yields and New Zealand's relatively cool temperatures inhibit any prospect of greatness; in Gisborne, Muscat Dr Hogg is one of the last white-wine varieties to be harvested. Another, earlier-ripening Muscat variety grown in Gisborne, Early White Muscat, although very susceptible to rot, may have the potential to produce wines with more concentrated varietal character.

Following the German practice, Muscat is often blended with Müller-Thurgau to enhance the wine's bouquet. It also gives a lift — again, often as a minor partner of Müller-Thurgau — to charmingly light and perfumed Asti-type sparklings. However, Muscat has traditionally been viewed as a bulk-wine variety in New Zealand, and since 1983 its plantings have contracted from 331 hectares to a projected 129 hectares of bearing vines in 2004.

Leading label
Matua Valley Eastern Bays Late Harvest Muscat

Projected producing area in 2004
129 hectares

Pinot Gris

An outstanding Chardonnay substitute, weighty and deep-flavoured, Pinot Gris is spreading rapidly in New Zealand vineyards. The variety belongs to the Pinot family of vines and is cultivated in Italy (where it is known as Pinot Grigio), Germany (Rulander) and France. In Alsace, Pinot Gris

pinot gris

produces outstanding wine, robust, peachy, spicy and lush.

Although Bragato praised the variety in 1906 ('in the far north it is an early grape, bears heavily and produces an excellent white wine'), Pinot Gris later fell out of favour with most growers because of its tendency to crop erratically. Now the tide has turned, with the area of bearing vines exploding from 22 hectares in 1995 to 315 hectares in 2004. Nearly 40 per cent of the vines are concentrated in Marlborough, but there are also significant plantings in Central Otago, Hawke's Bay, Canterbury, the Wairarapa and Auckland.

A thin-skinned, tight-bunched variety, Pinot Gris has a tendency to overcrop, which produces green-edged, phenolic wines with hard tannins. It adapts well to most soils but performs best in low-vigour soils, since small crops and open vine canopies are needed to build the concentrated, ripe stone-fruit flavours of quality Pinot Gris. Its blue-grey, or sometimes reddish pink, berries mature fairly early with lowish acidity and high sugars (hence the strong alcohol typical of the wine).

With its ability to produce wines of impressive weight and flavour richness (without the assistance of oak — a major plus-point), Pinot Gris has high potential in New Zealand and has proven its versatility by yielding impressive wines from Auckland to Central Otago. This classic cool-climate variety is now the country's fourth most widely planted white-wine grape, after Sauvignon Blanc, Chardonnay and Riesling.

Leading labels
Bilancia Reserve, Brick Bay, Dry River, Fairhall Downs, Martinborough Vineyard, Seresin

Projected producing area in 2004
315 hectares

Riesling

New Zealand wine lovers were so captivated by Chardonnay and Sauvignon Blanc a decade ago, winemakers could hardly give their Rieslings away. Now hundreds of labels are on the market, ranging in style from bone-dry to honey-sweet, and the grape's ravishing perfume and piercing, racy flavour have captured many admirers. Riesling, at last, is fashionable.

Riesling is the greatest and most famous grape variety of Germany. In the Rheingau and the Mosel its wine is strongly scented, the flavour a harmony of honey-like fruit and steely acid. Riesling also performs well in Alsace, Central Europe, California and Australia.

The proper name of the variety is Riesling, but for many years it was called Rhine Riesling here, to avoid confusion with Riesling-Sylvaner (as Müller-Thurgau was labelled originally in New Zealand). Since the mid-1990s, however, the classic name Riesling has prevailed.

Government Viticulturist Romeo Bragato in 1906 declined to recommend Riesling vines, 'being only fair bearers'. The 1975 vineyard survey revealed the scarcity of Riesling vines in the country; 8 hectares in Hawke's Bay and half a hectare in Auckland. During the 1980s, planting gathered momentum and between 1995 and 2004, the area of bearing Riesling vines is expanding from 289 to 636 hectares. Now New Zealand's third most widely planted white-wine grape, over 55 per cent of the vines are concentrated in Marlborough (and 85 per cent in the South Island), with further significant plantings in Canterbury and smaller pockets in Nelson, Central Otago, Hawke's Bay, the Wairarapa and Gisborne.

Riesling is a moderate bearer, yielding an average of 8 to 10 tonnes per hectare in New Zealand. To achieve flavour intensity, low yields are essential. The grapes ripen late in the season but hang on well, resisting frosts and cold. Riesling's tight bunches are vulnerable to botrytis rot, but the lower humidity in the South Island reduces the disease risk.

This variety needs a long, slow period of ripening to fully develop its most intricate flavours. Thus the finest Rieslings tend to be grown in cooler areas enjoying long dry autumns; in New Zealand, the best results have come from the Wairarapa and the four South Island regions.

Noble rot, a beneficial form of *Botrytis cinerea* that shrivels and dehydrates the grapes, can transform Riesling's quality. Depending on the extent of botrytis infection, the bouquet of the grape variety itself is replaced by an aroma strongly reminiscent of honey. The wine tastes richer, more luscious, smoother and honeyed. The majority of New Zealand's most ravishingly beautiful sweet white wines are late-harvested, botrytised Rieslings.

The overall standard of New Zealand Riesling has soared in the past decade, with achieving full ripeness the key to rich, expressive wines. For drink-young styles, many winemakers hold the unfermented juice in contact with the grape skins, which boosts the young wine's flavour, but the most delicate and refined wines, made without skin contact, develop better over the long haul.

Leading labels
Dry River Craighall, Felton Road, Neudorf Moutere, Palliser Estate, Pegasus Bay, Stoneleigh Vineyards Marlborough, Villa Maria Reserve Marlborough, Villa Maria Reserve Noble Riesling

Projected producing area in 2004
636 hectares

riesling

Sauvignon Blanc

Nowhere else in the world does Sauvignon Blanc yield such pungently aromatic and explosively flavoured wine as it does in Marlborough. The variety enjoys an exceptionally high profile in New Zealand — higher than in all other wine countries — and in 2004 will account for 28.4 per cent of the country's total area of bearing vines.

In Bordeaux, where Sauvignon Blanc (or Sauvignon, as the French call it) is widely planted, traditionally it has been blended with the more neutral Sémillon, to produce dry white Graves and sweet Sauternes. But in the regions of Sancerre and Pouilly in the upper Loire Valley, the Sauvignons are unblended and here the wines are assertive, cutting and flinty, in a style readily recognisable as cool-climate Sauvignon Blanc.

Sauvignon Blanc, a vigorously growing vine, typically yields well, with an average crop in New Zealand of 9 tonnes per hectare. The grapes ripen mid to late season, retaining a high level of acidity, but in wet weather (especially the more humid conditions of Gisborne and Hawke's Bay) are prone to split, causing rot.

Sauvignon Blanc has been grown in New Zealand for over 30 years. Ross Spence, fresh from studying winemaking in California, where he first encountered Sauvignon Blanc, in the late 1960s obtained severely virused, low-yielding cuttings of the variety from the Te Kauwhata Research Station, from which Matua Valley produced its first trial wine in 1974. The same year, Spence found a cleaner, virus-free clone in a Ministry of Agriculture and Fisheries trial block in Corbans' Kumeu vineyard. The improved clone, known as UCD1 (University of California, Davis, no. 1) is the source of most of the current plantings (although five new clones, including three from Bordeaux, were released from quarantine in 1992).

After procuring cuttings from Matua Valley, Montana produced its first Marlborough Sauvignon Blanc in 1979. By the mid-1980s, its penetratingly herbaceous wine and (in smaller volumes) the riper, more subtle Cloudy Bay had alerted the world to the startling quality of New Zealand Sauvignon Blanc. The area of bearing vines is soaring by 375 per cent between 1995 and 2004. Over 80 per cent of the vines are concentrated in Marlborough (where it thrives in clear, sunny days and cool nights and is the number one variety); there are also significant plantings in Hawke's Bay and smaller pockets in Wairarapa, Nelson, Canterbury and Gisborne. In the North Island's warmer climate, Sauvignon Blanc generally yields riper, softer, less assertive wines than the forthright style typical of Marlborough (although the top Wairarapa wines are fully a match for Marlborough's best).

Why are New Zealand's, and especially Marlborough's, Sauvignon Blancs so brimful of varietal character? The secret ingredient is an organic compound that is far easier to drink than it is to pronounce — methoxypyrazine. The green, grassy scent of methoxypyrazine is detectable in miniscule amounts by humans, and New Zealand's Sauvignon Blancs harbour about three times as much as Australia's.

The pungent, grassy bouquet of cool-climate Sauvignon Blanc leaps from the glass with a forcefulness some criticise as unsubtle. Others adore its distinctiveness. The flavour ranges from a sharp, green capsicum character — stemming from a touch of unripeness in the fruit — through to a riper, fruity gooseberry style and, finally, to the tropical-fruit (melons and passionfruit) overtones and lower acidity of very ripe fruit.

The grower can manipulate these Sauvignon Blanc flavours in the vineyard. In Marlborough, where shaded fruit tends to yield wine with nettley aromas and flavours, markedly riper flavours can be achieved by canopy division and leaf-plucking.

'In New Zealand it is not difficult to make herbaceous Sauvignon Blanc,' says Kevin Judd, winemaker at Cloudy Bay. 'This fresh edge and intense varietal aroma are the reason for its international popularity. [But] the better of the wines have these herbaceous characters in balance with the more tropical-fruit characters associated with riper fruit.'

Two distinct styles of Sauvignon Blanc are today produced by Marlborough winemakers. Traditionalists place their accent on the grape's pungent, racy, nettley varietal character. Other winemakers, striving for greater complexity, pursue riper, less herbaceous fruit characters, with subtle use of smoky oak and maturation on yeast lees. The result is a less ebullient wine, but more multi-dimensional.

Leading labels
Cloudy Bay, Goldwater Dog Point Marlborough, Grove Mill Marlborough, Hunter's Marlborough, Hunter's Winemaker's Selection, Isabel Estate Marlborough, Lawson's Dry Hills Marlborough, Matua Valley Matheson, Montana Brancott Estate, Nga Waka, Palliser Estate, Seresin Marlborough, Thornbury Marlborough, Vavasour Single Vineyard, Villa Maria Reserve Clifford Bay, Villa Maria Reserve Wairau Valley, Whitehaven Marlborough, Wither Hills Marlborough

Projected producing area in 2004
4488 hectares

sauvignon blanc

Sémillon

In New Zealand's cool ripening conditions, Sémillon tends to be crisp and green-edged. Overseas, the grape gives rise to a diversity of styles ranging from the fine dry whites of Graves and Australia to the sweet, late-harvested wines of Sauternes and Barsac. Sémillon imparts softness to its blend with Sauvignon Blanc in Graves. In Sauternes, infection of Sémillon grapes with *Botrytis cinerea* brings a distinctive, 'noble rot' character to the best wines. Although in Europe the variety is invariably blended with other grapes, Sémillon reaches its apogee as an unblended varietal in the tight, slowly evolving, honey- and toast-flavoured dry whites of the Hunter Valley in New South Wales.

The commercial plantings of Sémillon in New Zealand initially yielded confusing results. The vines, which grew vigorously, yielded moderately heavy crops (at an average of 11 tonnes per hectare, they are still significantly higher than Sauvignon Blanc) and their tough-skinned, greenish-yellow berries appeared to have good weather resistance.

This last quality was very surprising, especially in New Zealand's often humid growing conditions, because the compact grape cluster typical of Sémillon usually renders it highly vulnerable to bunch rot. The clone at first widely planted in New Zealand — UCD2 — grew much looser bunches. Doubts (now proven unfounded) were expressed as to whether UCD2 is true Sémillon.

Sémillon's past extreme herbaceousness in New Zealand, and its apparent resistance to rot, are now known to have been the result of widespread virus infection, which retarded ripening. Attractive, riper flavours are now being achieved by leaf-plucking and other vineyard practices aimed at exposing the fruit to higher levels of sunshine. A newer Sémillon clone, BVRC-14, imported from the Barossa Valley in Australia and now widely planted in New Zealand, is also yielding wines that are much less pungently herbaceous.

Sémillon is New Zealand's sixth most important white-wine variety. The area of bearing vines is expanding slowly between 1995 and 2004, from 183 to 253 hectares. Sémillon's strongholds are Gisborne and Marlborough (which each have over a third of the total vines), with most of the remaining plantings in Hawke's Bay. Sémillon is often (but usually anonymously) added to Sauvignon Blancs in New Zealand, contributing complexity and aging potential. It is a useful, flavour-packed blending variety in lower-priced wines (often labelled Sémillon/Chardonnay), and has recently yielded some attractive varietal wines with fresh, ripe, melon and lime flavours.

Leading labels
Alpha Domus AD, Sileni Estates

Projected producing area in 2004
253 hectares

sémillon

Viognier

Still rare in New Zealand but yielding promising wines, Viognier is a traditional Rhône variety whose most famous expression is the perfumed, robust white wine of Condrieu. Plantings spread into the south of France, California and Australia during the 1980s, and in 1993 Te Mata Estate imported some of the first Viognier vines into New Zealand.

Viognier is regarded as a light cropper in the Rhône. In New Zealand, where the vines' flowering and fruit-set have been highly variable, the deeply coloured grapes go through bud-burst, flowering and *veraison* (the final stage of ripening) slightly behind Chardonnay, and are harvested about the same time as Pinot Noir.

Fermented in old oak barrels, Viognier produces sturdy, high-alcohol wines in New Zealand with subtle flavours and gentle acidity. Its softly mouthfilling, distinctive wine is an intriguing amalgam of the scentedness of Riesling and the weightiness of Chardonnay.

Leading labels
Collards, Millton, Te Mata

Projected producing area in 2004
Not recorded

Red wine varieties

The range of red-wine grapes cultivated in New Zealand is narrower than that of white-wine varieties; of the country's 17 most widely planted grapes, seven are red. However, Pinot Noir and Merlot, both spreading rapidly, are New Zealand's third and fourth most important varieties, with the more slowly expanding Cabernet Sauvignon in fifth place. The 2001 national vineyard survey also revealed the rapid expansion of such up-and-coming red-wine grapes as Syrah and Malbec. Between 1995 and 2004, the proportion of the national bearing vineyard devoted to red-wine varieties soared from 24.4 to 34.6 per cent.

Cabernet Franc

Cabernet Franc, a happier vine in cooler regions than Cabernet Sauvignon (because it buds, and thus ripens, earlier) is one of New Zealand's most important red-wine varieties. It is much valued in Bordeaux, particularly in St Émilion where, under the name of Bouchet, it is the grape primarily responsible for the esteemed Château Cheval Blanc. Cabernet Franc is also widely planted in the middle Loire and in north-eastern Italy.

The vine was established here early last century and 'succeeded well in the northernmost parts of the colony,' observed the Government Viticulturist, Romeo Bragato, in 1906. 'Unfortunately, it seems to be subject to *coulure* [failure of the vine flowers to develop] in southern districts.' It is a moderate yielder, averaging 7 tonnes per hectare in New Zealand.

Cabernet Franc is expected to yield its finest wines in New Zealand in the warmest sites. The *coulure* problem is greater in cooler vineyards, and when not fully ripe, the variety can taste very green. Planted in warmer vineyards, Cabernet Franc crops more consistently with riper flavours.

The New Zealand wine industry has derived almost all its Cabernet Franc from trial vines imported in the late 1960s from the University of California, Davis. Virtually unknown prior to the 1980s, Cabernet Franc is now our fourth most widely planted red-wine variety (although far behind Pinot Noir, Merlot and Cabernet Sauvignon). The area of producing vines is expanding from 80 hectares in 1995 to 176 hectares in 2004, particularly in Hawke's Bay (which has 60 per cent of the vines) and Auckland.

Cabernet Franc's wine is more genial than that of Cabernet Sauvignon, lower in tannin, acids and extract, with an instantly appealing aroma variously described as raspberries, violets and pencil shavings. Its key role in New Zealand is as part of the *encepagement* (varietal recipe) of claret-style reds, where it contributes a buoyant, fruity character and seductive softness to its blends with Cabernet Sauvignon, Merlot and Malbec.

Leading labels
Clearview Estate Reserve, Harrier Rise,
Mission Reserve

Projected producing area in 2004
176 hectares

Cabernet Sauvignon

Cabernet Sauvignon is to the red-wine world what Chardonnay is to the white: both are of impeccable pedigree and huge international popularity. Yet over the past decade, Cabernet Sauvignon has lost its long-standing primacy in New Zealand to Pinot Noir and Merlot.

Cabernet Sauvignon — often abbreviated to Cabernet — has a long history in New Zealand, arriving with Busby or with the French settlers at Akaroa, and was well known in the nineteenth century. In 1906, Government Viticulturist Romeo Bragato pronounced it to be 'one of the best varieties grown here . . . the wine produced is of an excellent quality'. Nevertheless, interest in Cabernet Sauvignon slumped during the wasted

cabernet franc

cabernet sauvignon

years of cheap 'plonk' manufacture. The current commercial revival dates from the early 1970s, when Cabernet Sauvignon came to be regarded as the ideal grape to upgrade the overall standard of red wines.

The arrival of Montana Cabernet Sauvignon 1973 ushered in a new era: for the first time a decent quality New Zealand red was widely available. By 1983, Cabernet Sauvignon — the aristocratic grape of the Médoc in Bordeaux — was the second most common variety in the country. Since then, however, other varieties have expanded more swiftly and it is now in fifth place.

Producing fine quality Cabernet Sauvignon in New Zealand is a challenge: many regions are simply too cool for the late-ripening variety. Poor site selection in the past compounded the problem. Fertile soils, except in dry years, cause luxuriant foliage growth, which shades the grapes and inhibits ripening. Another inhibiting factor has been widespread leaf-roll virus, which retarded ripening and lowered yields.

Often labelled a shy bearer, Cabernet Sauvignon produces an average of 7 tonnes per hectare in New Zealand of small, blue-black, tough-skinned berries tasting of blackcurrants or blackberries. The grapes are usually picked last, in April and even May, with high levels of tannin.

Cabernet Sauvignon has performed best in the warmer temperatures of the North Island. Over 70 per cent of all plantings are in Hawke's Bay, where in favourable vintages the grape yields fragrant, sturdy wine of a richness and complexity only consistently rivalled by the Cabernet-based reds of Waiheke Island. There are also significant plantings in Auckland (where it is the third most common variety) and Marlborough (where its wine has typically been light and green-edged and plantings have declined steeply).

Most of the early New Zealand Cabernets were thin and marred by unripe, excessively herbaceous flavours. Today this problem lingers, although reduced. Other common faults of New Zealand Cabernet Sauvignon have been lightness of colour, high natural acidity and coarse, green tannins. The most widely planted clones of Cabernet Sauvignon are UCD7 and UCD8, imported from California in 1976.

The sharp rise in the standard of New Zealand's Cabernet-based reds over the past decade can be attributed to: the planting of healthier, less virused vines; the maturing of those vines; the planting of vines on warmer sites with less fertile, stonier soils; lower crop levels per vine; improved canopy management; greater appreciation of the way new oak casks enhance quality; and blending with the classic Bordeaux varieties, Merlot and Cabernet Franc.

Small amounts of high-class, Cabernet Sauvignon-predominant reds are made in New Zealand, but larger-volume claret-style reds are increasingly Merlot-based blends, in which Cabernet Sauvignon adds its firmness, concentration and longevity to the fruitier, softer Merlot.

Leading labels

Babich The Patriarch Cabernet Sauvignon, Brookfields Reserve Vintage Cabernet/Merlot, Goldwater Cabernet Sauvignon & Merlot, Mills Reef Elspeth Cabernet/Merlot, Mills Reef Elspeth Cabernet Sauvignon, Newton/Forrest Cornerstone Cabernet/Merlot/Malbec, Stonyridge Larose Cabernet, Te Mata Awatea Cabernet/Merlot, Te Mata Coleraine Cabernet/Merlot, Trinity Hill Gimblett Road Cabernet/Merlot, Vidal Reserve Cabernet Sauvignon/Merlot

Projected producing area in 2004

816 hectares

malbec

Malbec

Malbec is the fourth traditional red-wine grape of Bordeaux — after Cabernet Sauvignon, Merlot and Cabernet Franc — to stir up interest in New Zealand.

Although of declining importance in Bordeaux (due at least partly to its great vulnerability to *coulure* (poor fruit-set that drastically reduces yields), Malbec is still fairly common in Bourg, Blaye and the Entre-Deux-Mers region. In the nineteenth century, Malbec was the foundation of the famous flavour-crammed, tannic 'black wine' of Cahors, in south-west France (where it is still widely planted). In Argentina, where plantings now far outstrip those in France, it produces dark, muscular wines capable of lengthy aging.

Government Viticulturist Romeo Bragato praised Malbec in 1906 as 'a very fine grape which grows well in the Hawke's Bay district . . . [but] in northern districts it does not set so freely'. Today, Malbec still often 'sets' poorly, although on warmer sites it crops more heavily. Today, the average crop is only 5 tonnes per hectare, but many of the vines are still in their infancy.

Malbec's area of bearing vines is expanding rapidly between 1995 and 2004, from 11 to 158 hectares, making it the country's fifth most widely planted red-wine variety. Over 60 per cent of the vines are in Hawke's Bay, with much smaller plantings in Gisborne, Auckland and Marlborough.

When planted in favourable sites in New Zealand, Malbec achieves sugar-ripeness very early, while retaining good acidity.

This early-ripening ability is a major asset, especially in cooler seasons when Cabernet Sauvignon struggles to ripen. Its large berries harbour strong tannins and rich, plummy, spicy, pruney, non-herbaceous flavours.

Six clones of Malbec have been identified in New Zealand, but only two are planted widely, including the 'old' clone, known for highly unpredictable yields. Clone 595, which originated in Bordeaux, is a much

merlot

where a typical vineyard is planted two-thirds in Merlot, with the rest in Cabernet Franc.

In Bordeaux, Merlot flourishes in clay — precisely where Cabernet Sauvignon vines, which prefer the relative warmth of gravel, struggle to ripen their fruit. Merlot's early — compared to Cabernet Sauvignon — budding and flowering can be a problem in cooler regions prone to spring frosts. The vine grows vigorously, producing in New Zealand an average of 7 tonnes per hectare of blue-black, loose-bunched berries, harbouring less tannin than Cabernet Sauvignon. One of Merlot's crucial assets in New Zealand is that its grapes typically harbour less than half the level of methoxypyrazines (flavour components that give wine a herbaceous character) found in Cabernet Sauvignon.

Merlot's major drawback is its susceptibility to *coulure* (poor fruit-set), which can drastically reduce the size of the crop. Clonal selection can reduce, although not eliminate, the threat. Most of the early Merlot plantings in New Zealand were of the clone TK 05149, imported from California and released in 1970. More popular now is the better-setting clone UCD6, from California, released in 1978. Two Bordeaux clones, released in 1992, have also aroused considerable enthusiasm.

At first, Merlot was principally used as a minority blending partner in New Zealand, adding its lush fruit flavours and velvety mouthfeel to the more angular, often leaner, predominant Cabernet Sauvignon. Now that Merlot's status as a premium red-wine variety in its own right has been recognised by winemakers, since the mid-1990s many unblended Merlots and Merlot-predominant blends have also reached the shelves.

Corbans, Babich and Collards produced unblended Merlots in the late 1970s and early 1980s, but Kumeu River Merlot 1983 was the first stylish red produced from the variety in New Zealand.

For wine lovers, Merlot's early-drinking appeal is a boon. A high quality Cabernet Sauvignon can need three to five years before it becomes a pleasure to drink; Merlot can knock your socks off in two. At first as Cabernet Sauvignon's bridesmaid, and now increasingly as the bride, Merlot has added a lush, sensuous appeal to our reds.

Leading labels
C.J. Pask Reserve, Clearview Estate Reserve, Esk Valley Reserve Merlot/Malbec/Cabernet Sauvignon, Matua Valley Ararimu Merlot/Cabernet Sauvignon, Te Awa Farm Boundary, Unison Selection, Villa Maria Reserve, Villa Maria Reserve Merlot/Cabernet Sauvignon

Projected producing area in 2004
1276 hectares

Pinotage

New Zealand's seventh most important red-wine grape, Pinotage is not one of the classic European red-wine grapes, but it is a direct descendant of one of them. It was bred in South Africa in 1925 by Professor A.I. Perold, whose goal was to combine the superb quality of Pinot Noir, the great grape of Burgundy, with the heavier yields of Cinsaut.

Cinsaut is extensively planted in the south of France, where it is valued for its drought-resistance and ability to add fragrance, fruitiness and softness to a sea of blended reds, including Chateauneuf-du-Pape. Cinsaut was at that time wrongly called Hermitage in South Africa, which explains the third syllable in the name Pinotage.

As a commercially grown wine variety Pinotage is unique to South Africa and New Zealand, where it yields soft, rounded reds that are often underrated.

more consistent bearer, although it has a tendency to overcrop.

With its brilliant colour and ripe, sweet fruit flavours, Malbec yields a dark, soft varietal red in New Zealand, ideal for early consumption. It also adds colour density and rich berry-fruit characters to many of the country's claret-style blends.

Leading label
Esk Valley The Terraces

Projected producing area in 2004
158 hectares

Merlot

A vital ingredient in classic Bordeaux, Merlot has enormous potential in New Zealand. Over the lengthy ripening season in our cool climate, Merlot is able to slowly build and concentrate its flavours. And with its early ripening nature — two to three weeks ahead of Cabernet Sauvignon — it can achieve higher sugar levels, lower acidity and riper fruit flavours before late autumn's coolness descends.

With its producing area soaring by over 350 per cent between 1995 and 2004, Merlot is New Zealand's fourth most common grape and second most widely planted red-wine variety, well ahead of Cabernet Sauvignon. Over 70 per cent of the vines are concentrated in Hawke's Bay, with most of the remaining vines in Marlborough, Auckland and Gisborne.

Merlot produces red wines of alluring richness, plumpness and suppleness. In Bordeaux, Merlot's plantings are almost double those of Cabernet Sauvignon (most wine lovers think the reverse). To the Cabernet Sauvignon-based reds of the Médoc and Graves, Merlot imparts richness and softness. Merlot truly comes into its own in St Émilion and Pomerol,

Pinotage was established in New Zealand in the 1960s (Corbans Pinotage 1964 was the first commercial release) during the rush to replace hybrids with *vinifera* material. The vine grew prolifically, ripening mid-season with good yields (currently averaging 11 tonnes per hectare) of medium-sized, thick-skinned berries. The variety proved especially popular in Auckland, because of its ability to withstand humid conditions, although it succumbs to bunch rot sooner than the more loosely clustered Cabernet Sauvignon.

Pinotage's area of bearing vines is spreading slowly between 1995 and 2004, from 66 to 88 hectares. The vines are largely confined to four regions — Hawke's Bay, Auckland, Marlborough and Gisborne.

Pinotage has had a turbulent career in New Zealand. Once heralded as a premium variety capable of producing 'the great New Zealand red', it was later much criticised as 'coarse'. The criticism derived partly from the fact that many so-called Pinotage wines used to include substantial amounts of hybrids, ostensibly to improve the wine's colour. Even today, many of the vines are virus-infected and planted on excessively vigorous rootstocks in heavy soils.

A well-made Pinotage is an early-maturing, peppery, slightly earthy and gamey wine, with a buoyant, berry-like flavour and smooth finish. Two styles are made. Extensive use of skin contact and maturation in oak yields a heavier, firmer wine, while others are in the Beaujolais mould — fresh, vibrantly fruity and supple.

Leading labels
Babich Winemakers Reserve, Okahu Estate Paula's Reserve, Pleasant Valley Signature Selection, Saints, Soljans, Te Awa Farm Longlands

Projected producing area in 2004
88 hectares

Pinot Noir

With an array of notably perfumed, richly flavoured and supple wines, Pinot Noir has staked its claim to be New Zealand's star red wine of the future. By far our most widely planted red variety (although much of the crop is grown for sparkling wine), Pinot Noir is also New Zealand's third most commonly planted grape overall. Between 1995 and 2004, the area of bearing Pinot Noir vines is soaring from 415 to 2743 hectares.

Single-handedly responsible for the majestic reds of Burgundy, Pinot Noir tastes of strawberries and raspberries in its youth, with fairly high alcohol and often a suggestion of sweetness. Mature Burgundy can be arrestingly complex, with an array of aromas and flavours suggestive of red berry fruits, violets, rotten vegetables, coffee and fruit cake. Pinot Noir is also of pivotal importance in Champagne, where it is prized for its body and longevity; great care is taken to keep the white juice free of tint from the skins. But the vine is notoriously temperamental in its choice of residence and has not readily adapted to regions beyond Europe.

Twenty years ago, most New Zealand Pinot Noirs were pale and thin rosé look-alikes. Yet today, New Zealand is internationally recognised as one of the world's tiny band of successful Pinot Noir producers. Burgundy stands pre-eminent, but elsewhere, only in Oregon, cooler parts of California and Victoria, and in New Zealand, has this minx of a vine yielded truly distinguished reds.

Government Viticulturist Romeo Bragato observed in 1906 that Pinot Noir 'ordinarily bears well and yields a nice wine'. The vine is a challenge to viticulturists, however; as an early budder, it is vulnerable to spring frosts, and its compact bunches are very prone to rot. (Pinot Noir hates autumn humidity more than any other variety.) One advantage is it ripens ahead of Cabernet Sauvignon, typically producing 7 to 8 tonnes per hectare of small berries of varying skin thickness. Compared to other classic red-wine grapes, Pinot Noir has fewer anthocyanins (colouring pigments), tannins and flavouring substances, so is very vulnerable to overcropping.

To produce fine wine from Pinot Noir in New Zealand, older stony soils with good drainage and some clay content are favoured, which reduce the vines' vigour but give a consistent, slow supply of water. Yields must be kept low, with intensive shoot-thinning, bunch-removal and leaf-plucking.

The first New Zealand Pinot Noir of recognised quality was Nobilo Huapai 1976, followed by the first gold medal winners, Babich 1981, from Henderson, and St Helena 1982, grown in Canterbury. The first experimental Martinborough Pinot Noirs flowed in the mid-1980s, followed in the late eighties by a trickle from Central Otago.

There are hundreds of Pinot Noir clones, of widely varying performance. The first two readily available clones in New Zealand were the well-performed AM 10/5, which yields wine with good colour and a soft, fruity palate, and Bachtobel, whose wine lacks colour and weight and is not highly regarded (except as a base for high-volume bottle-fermented sparkling wines). A second wave of planting material involved clones 5, 6 and 13 from the University of California, Davis; UCD5 ('Pommard') was especially sought after for its deep-hued, firm-structured wine. Since the early 1990s, attention has swung to the Dijon clones from Burgundy, bred by Bernard (clones 113, 114, 115, 375, 667 and 777). A range of clones is believed to produce wines of the greatest character and complexity.

pinot noir

Pinot Noir thrives in coolish climates, where the grapes are able to hang on the vines for extended periods, picking up the most subtle scents and flavours. The majority of Pinot Noir vines are found from the Wairarapa south, in regions characterised by cool night temperatures and relatively low autumn rainfall (and thus a reduced risk of bunch rot). In the Wairarapa, Canterbury and Central Otago, Pinot Noir is now the single most important variety. However, over 40 per cent of the vines are clustered in Marlborough, where much of the crop is reserved for bottle-fermented sparkling wine. Hawke's Bay, Gisborne and Nelson also have extensive plantings.

New Zealand's Pinot Noir production is small — in 2001 accounting for just 2.7 per cent by volume of the country's exports — but fast-expanding. Styles produced vary from the sturdy, warm and spicy Pinot Noirs of Martinborough to Central Otago's fresh, vibrant and racy reds.

Leading labels
Ata Rangi, Cloudy Bay, Dry River, Felton Road Block 3, Fromm La Strada Fromm Vineyard, Gibbston Valley Reserve, Greenhough Hope Vineyard, Kaituna Valley, Martinborough Vineyard, Mountford, Neudorf Moutere and Moutere Home Vineyard, Palliser Estate, Pegasus Bay, Pegasus Bay Prima Donna, Seresin, Walnut Ridge, Wither Hills Marlborough

Projected producing area in 2004
2743 hectares

Sangiovese

Still rare in New Zealand, Sangiovese is by far the most widely planted variety of Italy and is the foundation of such great Tuscan reds as Chianti and Brunello di Montalcino. In Tuscany, Sangiovese ripens late in the season, giving substantial, richly flavoured reds in warm years, but more astringent, high-acid wines in cool vintages. Being fairly thin-skinned, it is susceptible to rot, a distinct disadvantage in regions with frequent late-season rains. In New Zealand, Sangiovese is sometimes confused with Montepulciano — also widely planted across central Italy — and the precise identity of some of the wines released so far is being debated by industry experts. Jane Hunter, in Marlborough, and Ken Sanderson, in Hawke's Bay, have found Sangiovese to be a very late ripening variety, needing more heat. However, David Hoskins, of the Heron's Flight winery at Matakana, reports his Sangiovese ripens 'beautifully, with deep colour, very ripe tannins and deep, rich flavours'.

In the past, New Zealand's grape-growers planted the French and German varieties they were familiar with. Now, Italian grape varieties are starting to add an exciting diversity to New Zealand wine labels.

Projected producing area in 2004
not recorded

Syrah (Shiraz)

Syrah is still rare in New Zealand, but has recently started to carve out a presence in North Island vineyards. It was long believed that this country was too cool and wet for Syrah, but the wines that have emerged over the past decade have been unexpectedly classy.

Syrah is the principal black grape of the upper Rhône Valley of France, has spread widely through the south of France and is Australia's most extensively planted red-wine variety. In France it is called Syrah and in Australia, Shiraz. Lauded in France as the foundation of such great reds as Côte Rotie and Hermitage, it is also the basis of such sought-after Australian reds as Penfolds Grange and Henschke's Hill of Grace.

Regardless of the name of the vine or the location of its vineyard, Syrah typically yields robust, richly flavoured reds with a heady perfume. Top versions are almost opaque, with a characteristic spicy, black pepper aroma and flavour.

Syrah has a long history in New Zealand. Government Viticulturist Romeo Bragato declared in 1906 that 'Hermitage', as it was then known, 'bears well here, is free from mould and gives a good wine'. However, in many areas the grapes failed to ripen, lacking sugar and colour, and remaining overly acid. Government Viticulturist S.F. Anderson wrote in 1917 that Syrah was being 'grown in nearly all our vineyards but the trouble with this variety has been an unevenness in ripening its fruit'.

After decades of eclipse, Syrah is now enjoying a resurgence of interest. New clones and virus-indexed vines show an improved ripening performance. Syrah grows very vigorously and normally crops well, although with most of the vines here still in their infancy, the current average yield is only 4 tonnes per hectare. To curb its natural vigour, stony, dry, low-fertility sites are crucial.

Syrah also needs plenty of heat, achieving ripeness in Hawke's Bay late in the season, at about the same time as Cabernet Sauvignon.

The bearing area of Syrah vines is expanding between 1995 and 2004 from 14 to 144 hectares. Over two-thirds of the vines are clustered in Hawke's Bay, with other pockets in Auckland, Wairarapa and Marlborough. Substantial, firm and peppery, the top New Zealand wines are more reminiscent of Rhône reds than the lush, jammy style typical of Australia.

Leading labels
Dry River, Fromm La Strada Reserve, Matariki, Mills Reef Elspeth, Okahu Estate Kaz, Stonecroft, Te Mata Bullnose

Projected producing area in 2004
144 hectares

syrah

Winemaking in New Zealand

Where is wine made — in the vineyard or the winery? Take a bow if you answered 'in both places'. A common saying in the wine industry is that 'you can't make good wine from bad grapes'. Although in New Zealand the media spotlight is invariably focused on winemakers rather than grape-growers, it is in the vineyards that the raw materials of wine are cultivated, and there that each wine's basic potential is set.

Climate and soil (see pages 30–33) are the two crucial factors the viticulturist evaluates before planting a new vineyard. When choosing a site on which to cultivate grapes for a wine of superior quality, viticulturists today look for a combination of adequate, but not excessive, heat; a relatively dry autumn; and well-drained soils.

The annual cycle in the vineyard

Vineyard toil itself is peaceful, with fixed seasonal routines. Winter's cold, damp months are devoted to pruning, the most time-consuming and costly of all vineyard jobs.

By trellising and pruning the vine, the viticulturist is able to control and shape its foliage growth and potential yield, gaining greater ease of cultivation and finer fruit quality. A small percentage of New Zealand vineyards are close-planted, but due to the generally high soil fertility, which encourages vigorous vegetative growth, most vines are planted about 2 metres apart in rows 2 metres wide, and trained along trellises varying between 1 and 1.7 metres in height.

Cane pruning is the most popular system in New Zealand. Between two and four canes are chosen to carry the new season's growth, each having 10 to 20 buds. A few spurs, carrying several buds, are also retained to provide the fruiting canes for the following season. After the canes are cut, the bearing arms are laid along the bottom wire and later the new season's foliage is trained above.

In spring the buds swell and eventually burst, unfolding tender shoots, leaves and flower clusters. Tractor-towed spraying machines are soon swinging into action against fungus diseases and insects, and another battle is fought against weeds. Late in spring the flower clusters shed their caps; by early December the flowers 'set' as small, green, pea-like berries.

Drip irrigation systems are a common sight in vineyards from Hawke's Bay south, where summer droughts can cause the vines to suffer severe water stress. On sites with light, free-draining soils, irrigation is used to assist ripening and maintain yields in dry years — a sort of viticultural insurance policy.

In mid-summer, when the vineyards reach their peak period of growth, the sides and tops of the vines are mechanically trimmed to control the shape of their canopies. The removal of excess vegetative growth enables light to more easily penetrate the canopy, which improves fruit ripeness and reduces disease problems. Plucking (removing) the leaves around the bunches, by hand or machine, produces similar benefits. Many small vineyards have recently adopted the 'Scott Henry' vine-training system (installed on the standard New Zealand vertical trellis by adding a pair of movable foliage wires), which reduces fruit-shading problems by dividing the canopy into two separate curtains, trained both upwards and downwards.

As ripening proceeds, the fruit gradually evolves its mature skin colours — yellow-green for 'white' varieties, blue-black for 'red' varieties — and its juice composition alters markedly: acids decline and sugars soar.

The fungus *Botrytis cinerea* can be the wine-grower's worst enemy or best friend. Late in the season warm, wet weather encourages grapes to swell with moisture and split open. Botrytis, which appears as a grey, fluffy mould on the bunches, causes the grapes to rot on the vines. Fine dry autumn weather can allow botrytis-infected grapes to develop an intense concentration of flavour and sweetness. In New Zealand's frequently wet autumns, however, botrytis can severely damage the grapes. To combat botrytis, growers rely heavily on the precisely timed applications of fungicide sprays.

'Vintage' starts late in February or early March with the gathering-in of the early-ripening varieties: Gewürztraminer and Müller-Thurgau. Mechanical harvesters, which pick grapes at the speed of about 80 vineyard labourers, straddle the trellises and lumber up and down the rows, slapping the berries — but not their stalks — off with fibreglass rods. The traditional hand-pickers now survive only in the most quality-focused, isolated or hilly vineyards.

By mid-May the harvest is over; the vineyards fall silent, and in a flaming shower the vines shed their leaves. The annual cycle in the vineyards is now at an end. The viticulturist's job is done; the pressure is now on the winemaker to ensure that the potential inherent in the fruit is carried through into the finished wine.

Winemaking

Winemakers returning from visits to the classic wine regions of Europe have often claimed that New Zealand leads the French and Germans in the standard of their winery operations. Although most wineries were technically ill-prepared when public demand switched from fortified to white table wines, New Zealand's late development of interest in wine science allowed the industry to adopt only the established best. An outstanding example is refrigeration, a late arrival on the New Zealand wine scene, but now widely used to stabilise wine and control fermentation.

As Corbans' production manager from 1952 to 1976, Alex Corban was

the first New Zealand winemaker to adopt such modern technical wizardry as pressure fermentations, stainless steel, refrigeration and yeast starter cultures. Only the second New Zealander to gain a diploma in oenology from Roseworthy College, Adelaide, Corban was exposed during his Australian studies to winemaking equipment and techniques unknown to an older generation.

In 1949, the entire Corbans range was fermented with cultured yeasts — the first time natural, 'wild' yeasts were not used in New Zealand. Stainless-steel tanks made their New Zealand wine industry debut in 1958 at Corbans. Then the company's Dry White 1962, based on hybrid Baco 22A grapes, was pressure-fermented at controlled temperatures — another first. Refrigeration, centrifuges, freeze concentration, pasteurisation, cold sterile bottling — the range of equipment and techniques Corban introduced to New Zealand is vast.

Nevertheless, when commercial volumes of premium grape varieties like Chardonnay and Sauvignon Blanc first came on stream, few winemakers had any specialist knowledge of how to handle them. 'During the late 1970s and early 1980s, when more Chardonnay grapes became available, the winemaking procedures followed the pattern of white winemaking of that time,' recalls Kerry Hitchcock, formerly Corbans' chief winemaker. 'This involved quick separation of the juice from its skins and stainless-steel fermentation at low temperatures, followed by aging in oak barrels for a short period. Then as the market became more demanding, winemakers looked at Chardonnay-making in the traditional French way, and we saw different styles being produced in New Zealand. These involved: longer skin contact time to extract flavour; fermenting in oak barrels with higher solids in the juice; leaving the wine on its lees for

Barriques of maturing wine in the Tom McDonald Cellar at Montana's Church Road Winery in Hawke's Bay.

flavour development; and a partial or complete malolactic fermentation in the traditional French way.'

New Zealand initially derived most of its winemaking technology and skills from Australia. As Michael Brajkovich, of Kumeu River, has put it: 'It would have made much more sense to study and adapt the practices of a climatically similar region, such as the cooler regions of France.' A busy programme of winemaker exchanges between New Zealand, Australia, the United States, South America and Europe has since exposed the industry to a far greater diversity of oenological influences.

Whites

To produce a fine white wine the winemaker must be meticulous, because the delicate juices of white grapes are vulnerable to oxidation and browning. To protect the quality of the fruit, sulphur dioxide is frequently — although not always — added at the harvester.

The transport of freshly picked grapes from vineyard to winery can itself influence the quality of the eventual wine. Wines made from machine-harvested fruit trucked long distances (Gisborne or Hawke's Bay to Auckland is common) reflect the inevitable 'skin contact'. The greater extraction of polyphenols — flavour compounds including anthocyanins (colouring matter) and tannins — from the skins into the grape juice produces deeper-coloured, more strongly flavoured wines. To eliminate this problem, some Auckland-based wineries have recently established crushing and de-juicing plants close to their vineyards in Hawke's Bay.

Upon their arrival at the winery, therefore, white-wine grapes are swiftly crushed and de-stemmed. Sulphur dioxide may be added to the crushed fruit ('must') or the juice after pressing to guard against oxidation and to inhibit bacteria and indigenous ('wild') yeasts.

To separate the juice from the skins, the must can be pumped into a 'drainer' tank with a slotted screen at its base. The majority of the juice is this way able to be recovered by the winemaker without pressing; 'free-run' juice of superior quality is the result. Only the residue of pulp, pips and skins, which is still juice-saturated, is conveyed to the press to extract the coarser juices, called 'pressings'.

In most wineries, however, tank presses have superseded the combined use of drainer tanks and multi-stage continuous presses. By giving the grapes a much gentler pressing, modern tank presses are able to obtain a greater volume of juice without extracting unwanted, harsh phenolics and compounds.

Although it is usual to make a swift separation of white-wine juice from the skins, this is not a hard-and-fast rule, as the period of contact depends on the style of wine being made. Where the goal is a light, delicate white, the juice is removed immediately. If a more substantial style is sought, the juice may be allowed up to 24 hours' skin contact in an effort to step up the colour and flavour of the finished wine. A precisely opposite approach to 'whole-bunch pressing' (below), the skin-contact method boosts the juice's level of phenols, and is thus believed by many (not all) winemakers to be well-suited to delicately flavoured wines with low natural levels of phenols.

Whole-bunch pressing is a gentle, increasingly in-vogue technique whereby the winemaker bypasses the crusher and places bunches of hand-harvested grapes directly into the press. Whole-bunch pressing yields juices with greater flavour delicacy — due to the lack of skin contact — lighter colours and much lower levels of solids and phenols. Flavoursome grapes with high phenolic levels are especially well suited to whole-bunch pressing; conversely, delicately flavoured juices with low levels of phenols may benefit from a greater degree of skin contact.

Prior to its fermentation, the juice is cold-settled to rid it of suspended particles of skin, pulp and yeast cells. Next its sugar and acid levels are adjusted if necessary. ('Chaptalisation', or supplementing the grapes' natural sugars, to produce a wine with a desired level of alcohol is legal in New Zealand, as in other cool-climate wine countries.) Finally, it is normally inoculated with a selected 'pure' yeast culture (although interest is growing in fermenting with indigenous yeasts, also known as 'natural' or 'wild' yeasts, to enhance the wines' individuality). A faint stirring of bubbles on the juice's surface is the first sign that the fermentation is under way. Fermentation — the conversion of sugar by yeasts into ethyl alcohol, carbon dioxide and energy — is also the happiest of miracles: the transformation of grape juice into scented, delectable, life-enhancing wine.

The vast majority of New Zealand white wines are fermented in enclosed stainless-steel tanks at low temperatures (12–15°C). Compared to traditional, warmer fermentation methods, this long (up to about three weeks), cool fermentation technique retains much more of the juice's fragile aromas and flavours in the finished wine.

After the fermentation has subsided, the new wine is racked off its yeast lees, stabilised, sweetened if necessary (usually by 'back-blending', the addition of unfermented grape juice, or by 'stop-fermentation', whereby the fermentation is arrested by chilling before all the grape sugars have been converted into alcohol), filtered and then generally bottled early.

A crucial aspect of the winemaking process is blending, and not just of grape varieties, such as Sauvignon Blanc and Sémillon. 'In a world where the vineyard now rules in terms of quality, blending is the last bastion for the winemaker to express his craft,' believes Matua Valley's chief winemaker, Mark Robertson. 'For instance, our Judd Estate Gisborne Chardonnay always has four or five components to blend. We have a reductive, fruit-driven component, a full-blown natural-ferment bit, and barrel-aged, lees-stirred, malolactic fermentation components out of an eclectic mixture of oak. It's the proportions that are the trick, and the fun, of making these wines.'

Lusciously sweet white wines are produced by stop-fermenting late-harvested, ultra-ripe, botrytis-infected fruit, or by the 'freeze concentration' method, whereby a proportion of the natural water content in the grape juice is frozen out, leaving a sweet, concentrated juice to be bottled.

The last of the whites to be bottled are those matured in oak casks — the vast majority of Chardonnays as well as wood-aged Sauvignon Blancs, Pinot Gris, Chenin Blancs and Sémillons. The finest wines are not just aged, but also fermented in the barrel. By fermenting a full-bodied dry white wine in the cask (most often a 225-litre French oak barrique, although American oak is also used), and then barrel-maturing it on its yeast lees for six months to a year (with regular lees-stirring another option), yeast-related flavour complexity and a superior integration of wood and wine flavours can both be achieved.

Another technique widely used is to put full-bodied dry white wines, or at least a part of the final blend, through a secondary, bacterial malolactic fermentation. The search here is for a softer-acid style with heightened complexity.

Reds

Red wines are typically more substantial than whites, with more grape 'extract' (stuffing) and flavour richness. Unlike white wines, reds are fermented in contact with their skins, which enables colouring pigments and tannins — key aspects of the wine's flavour, hue and longevity — to gradually dissolve from the skins into the fermenting juice.

During fermentation (mostly in stainless-steel tanks, although large oak cuves are used by several producers), the incessant rise of carbon dioxide bubbles causes the skins to rise to the surface. This dense cap is periodically re-immersed in the juice by drawing off the juice below the cap and pumping it back over the skins until they are broken up, or, less often, by regular hand-plunging. Red-wine fermentations are usually markedly warmer than for whites; 25–32°C is ideal to secure the richest possible extraction of colour and tannin.

For drink-young styles, where fruitiness and a soft tannin structure is desired, after the fermentation the young wine is swiftly removed from the skins. However, if the goal is a more robust, complex and tannic style, following the fermentation the winemaker may continue to macerate the skins in the new wine for up to a month. The current trend among New Zealand's red-wine makers is towards longer periods of skin contact.

Some New Zealand Pinot Noirs also show the fresh, floral fruit characters and suppleness to be derived from partial use of carbonic maceration (also known as whole-berry fermentation), the traditional technique of Beaujolais. Instead of being immediately crushed, whole berries are piled inside a fermenting vessel. The weight of the upper layers crushes the fruit below, which commences a normal fermentation, giving off carbon dioxide that blankets the intact fruit on top. Here, enzyme activity triggers an individual fermentation within each berry, extracting both colour and flavour from the inner skins.

A wide range of winemaking techniques are used for New Zealand Pinot Noir, including pre- and post-ferment maceration, and partial whole-berry or even whole-bunch (stalks and all) fermentation — all adding individuality between labels to the regional differences in wine style.

After their primary alcoholic fermentation, New Zealand red wines all undergo a secondary, softening malolactic fermentation, based on the bacterial conversion of malic acid to lactic acid and carbon dioxide. Since lactic acid is softer than malic acid, and there is also a decline in total acidity, the malolactic fermentation produces a rounder, more palatable wine.

All of New Zealand's top reds spend a year to 18 months in the cask, most commonly 225-litre French oak barriques, although often (more often than stated on the labels) a combination of French and American oak is used. The influence of new oak varies, typically being 25 per cent for Ata Rangi Pinot Noir, 25 to 30 per cent for Dry River Pinot Noir, 65 per cent for Esk Valley Reserve Merlot/Malbec/Cabernet Sauvignon, and 70 per cent for Te Mata Coleraine Cabernet/Merlot.

Several types of French oak are encountered in New Zealand wineries — Nevers, Limousin, Alliers, Tronçais, Vosges and centre of France. A cheaper alternative is American oak, which contributes more of the colour and flavour of oak to wine than does French oak, but less extract and tannin. American oak-aged wines have a lifted perfume and pungent, sweeter, more vanilla-like oak flavour, which experienced tasters can easily pick.

An even cheaper method to secure some of the flavouring effects of wood is to simply suspend oak chips in the wine.

Rosés

Rosés, which range in hue from pink to onion-skin, are made using primarily white-wine production techniques. The accent with rosés, as with whites, is on achieving flavour delicacy and freshness.

The best rosés are produced by giving the juice of black grapes one or two days' skin contact before or during the fermentation; the juice is then promptly separated from the skins and fermented alone. The precise duration of the skin contact determines the rosé's colour.

Merlot (especially), Cabernet Sauvignon and Pinot Noir are the grape varieties most often used in New Zealand to produce rosés.

Sparklings

The searching yet delicate flavours and crisp, appetising acidity of New Zealand's white wines are well suited to the production of top-class sparkling wines. Low-priced, 'carbonated' bubblies are made by simply injecting carbon dioxide into the base wine, and a few other sparklings are made by the 'Charmat' method, which involves a secondary fermentation in a sealed tank. However, New Zealand's greatest sparklings are all produced by the classic technique first perfected in Champagne, previously known as 'méthode champenoise' but now (following protests by the French) usually called 'méthode traditionnelle'.

Pinot Noir and Chardonnay are the two principal grapes grown for premium sparklings, but a small amount of Pinot Meunier is also used; all three are traditional Champagne varieties. Grapes for sparkling wine are typically harvested three to four weeks earlier than those for still wine, at a sugar level of 19–20 brix — after they have lost all herbaceous character, but before they have developed rich, ripe fruit flavours. By leaving plenty of leaves on the vines, the viticulturist can also induce more shading of the fruit, which leads to higher acidity and, for Pinot Noir, less skin colour.

Marlborough is New Zealand's most acclaimed region for sparkling wines, with the cooler South Island climate giving elegant base wines with relatively high levels of natural acidity. Hawke's Bay and Gisborne also produce a significant amount of sparkling wine, typically weightier and richer than the crisper, more vibrant South Island styles.

The méthode traditionnelle involves a secondary, bubble-inducing fermentation that takes place not in a tank, but in the individual bottle. The grapes are generally whole-bunch pressed, with minimal skin contact, giving a delicate, softly textured base wine. (Although a black-skinned variety, Pinot Noir has little or no colour in its juice and when swiftly separated from its skins gives a clear juice.) Following cold settling, racking and the addition of dried 'Champagne' yeast strains, the base wine undergoes its primary, alcoholic fermentation at 10–14°C in stainless-steel tanks or (in the search for greater complexity) oak barrels. It also typically undergoes a malolactic fermentation, to soften the wine's acidity and enhance its flavour complexity.

After sugar and yeasts have been added to the base wine, it is ensconced in heavy-duty bottles and stored in a temperature-controlled cellar for its secondary fermentation. Low temperatures of 10–12°C are essential, as the resulting long, slow fermentation in the bottle helps to give the wine a fine 'bead' (stream of bubbles). After the secondary fermentation, which lasts six weeks to several months, the yeast cells gradually break down, conferring on the wine distinctive, bready, nutty characters. The bottles are then stacked away to mature on their yeast lees for nine months to four years, or even longer for some of the most prestigious labels.

'Riddling' is the next stage, in which the yeast sediment is gradually shaken from the sides of the bottle down to the cork. Small batches are still hand-riddled, but for larger production runs, automatic riddling machines have provided welcome relief from the traditional wrist-wrenching labour.

Next comes the 'disgorging'; the neck of the bottle is frozen, allowing the cork and plug of sediment to be removed without losing much wine. Finally the bottle is topped up, sweetened, corked and wired.

The 'transfer' method (used by Montana for Lindauer) is a modern approach to bottle-fermentation evolved to speed up the final stages. Instead of riddling and then disgorging the wine, after its fermentation in the bottle it is transferred into pressurised tanks where it is cleaned up and sweetened in bulk, before being re-bottled.

Most sparkling wines are sold as non-vintage blends, but a significant number of vintage wines are also produced. Wines labelled Blanc de Blancs are typically based entirely on Chardonnay, but a few wines have also appeared made solely from Pinot Noir.

Laws and Labels

In 2002 a new Wine Act is currently winding its way through Parliament — the first major review of wine legislation in New Zealand for 20 years. The first regulations for the control of winemaking, issued in 1924 under the Food and Drugs Act 1908, would have forced many growers out of business, had they been rigidly enforced. The addition of water, then commonly used to reduce acidity (and stretch supplies) was banned, and growers with fewer than 5 acres (2 hectares) of vines were prohibited from distilling, or even buying, grape spirit to fortify their antipodean 'sherries' and 'ports'.

Yet the production and labelling requirements imposed on winemakers in New Zealand have generally been less rigorous than in the traditional wine-producing countries of Europe. Four major pieces of legislation controlled the production, labelling, ex-winery sale and export of wine during the 1980s and 1990s, but the current review is expected to lead to major reforms.

A new trans-Tasman wine standard, designed to harmonise winemaking rules in Australia and New Zealand, recently replaced the Food Regulations 1984, which previously governed the production of New Zealand wine. To be enforced from December 2002, the new standards define wine and the products that may be used in winemaking, and address health and safety issues.

The standard provides a simple definition of wine: 'Wine means the product of the complete or partial fermentation of fresh grapes, or a mixture of that product and products derived solely from grapes.' During the winemaking process, the new standard allows various food products to be added — grape juice and grape juice products; sugars; brandy or other potable spirit; and water, where necessary to incorporate any permitted food additive or processing aid.

Past limits on alcohol levels, processing aids and additives have been dropped. For instance, the limit on sulphur addition (previously 200 parts per million for dry wines and 400 parts per million for sweet wines) is simply given as 'good manufacturing practice', and there is no longer a maximum limit (previously 5 per cent) on the addition of water to wine.

Other current legislation includes the Wine Makers Levy Act 1976, which gives legislative recognition to the Wine Institute and secures its funding via a mandatory levy on all grape winemakers based on their annual level of sales; and the Sale of Liquor Act 1989, which covers the sale of wine directly to the public from the winery.

Ensuring that wines shipped overseas are of sound quality falls within the jurisdiction of the Wine Makers Act 1981. To be eligible for export, all New Zealand wines must undergo a chemical analysis and pass a blind tasting by a panel of wine industry personnel. As a negative, rather than positive, test of quality, New Zealand's export certification system makes it difficult for faulty wines to be exported, but does not attempt to prevent the shipment of sound but mediocre wines.

Wine-labelling regulations require several key facts to appear on all labels — the producer's name and address, the wine's country of origin, its alcohol strength and contents by volume. Identifying the use of sulphur dioxide has been mandatory since 1995 by use of the additive declaration 'Contains Preservative (220)'. The 'e' marks on the labels of most exported wines are a European Union requirement, whereby the producer guarantees that the 'contents by volume' figure stated is accurate. Under the new trans-Tasman wine standard, New Zealand wines must also carry a declaration of the number of 'standard drinks' (based on their alcohol content) they contain.

Most New Zealand wines boldly feature the name of a specific grape variety or blend of varieties, and the rules governing their use are clearcut. A wine carrying the name of a single grape must contain at least 75 per cent of the stated variety. A Sauvignon Blanc, for instance, must be made from no less than 75 per cent Sauvignon Blanc juice. (This rule is designed to allow blending to improve the final product. A winemaker might decide, for instance, that a Sauvignon Blanc would be enhanced by the addition of up to 25 per cent of another variety — probably Sémillon). A wine carrying the names of two or more varieties — for instance, Cabernet Sauvignon/Merlot — must also comply with the 75 per cent rule and name the principal grapes in descending order of their contribution to the blend.

Sparkling wines have their own nomenclature. Those labelled as 'bottle-fermented' must contain carbon dioxide gas generated by their own natural fermentation in a bottle no larger than 5 litres. Low-priced, carbonated bubblies may only carry the description 'sparkling wine'. Since use of the name 'Champagne' is illegal in New Zealand, and the term *méthode champenoise* cannot be used on wines exported to the European Union, the trend in New Zealand is to identify bottle-fermented sparkling wines with the EU-acceptable term *méthode traditionnelle*.

New Zealand's current wine-labelling regulations nevertheless have major loopholes. The labelling safeguards are often not specific to wine and do not guarantee the integrity of geographic claims made on New Zealand wine labels.

The Geographical Indications Act 1994, which is not specific to wine, established a system for the delineation and naming of geographic areas in New Zealand, with a hierarchy of geographical indicators including New Zealand, the North and South Islands, regional government areas and specific localities. These boundary definitions are potentially of critical importance to the wine industry, because the inclusion or non-inclusion of a vineyard within a delineated area can have an enormous impact on the value of its wine. However, for political reasons — linked to the stalling of negotiations for a wine agreement between New Zealand and the European Union — the Act has not yet come into force.

When the Geographical Indications Act is finally implemented, the use of geographic terms on wine labels will simply indicate the origin of the grapes. Unlike European appellations of origin, the right to use place names on New Zealand labels will not be linked to the cultivation of specific grape varieties, or maximum yields, or other production practices.

Requesting a review of the country's wine laws in 1999, the Wine Institute argued that 'the current legislation is increasingly out of date, revealing gaps and omissions in the industry's regulatory regime'. The Institute also noted that the 'enforcement of existing industry standards has been inadequate. . . . In particular, wine regulation had no priority for government departments such as the Ministry of Health, and little or no funding'.

The new Wine Act is expected to come into force in early to mid-2003. Among the Wine Institute's key objectives for the revised regulatory system are the setting of minimum standards for record-keeping and labelling; the establishment of auditing procedures to ensure compliance with the rules; and the setting up of a new regulatory authority with the ultimate power to remove the licence of any winemaker who breaches industry standards.

The final form of the legislation, however, remains to be seen.

Reading a New Zealand wine label

Stoneleigh
The brand of the wine. The Stoneleigh brand, always reserved for Marlborough wine, was launched in the 1980s by Corbans and is now owned by Montana.

Wine of New Zealand
Country of origin.

Produced and Bottled by Stoneleigh Vineyards, Main Road South, Blenheim
The producer's name and address.

13.5% vol.
Alcohol content by volume.

Marlborough
The region of origin in which the grapes were grown.

Sauvignon Blanc
The principal grape variety.

2002
The vintage.

750ml
Volume of wine.

Contains approximately 8.0 standard drinks
A measure of alcohol content, initially required on Australian wines and from late 2002 on New Zealand labels.

Preservative (220) Added
Sulphur dioxide is the preservative most commonly used by winemakers.

Antioxidant (300) Added
Erythorbic acid is an antioxidant, used to protect a wine's freshness.

The Principal Wine Regions of New Zealand

The New Zealand wine trail rises hesitantly in the Far North, winds busily through west Auckland and Waiheke Island, proceeds in fits and starts through the Waikato and Bay of Plenty, then runs boldly through Gisborne, Hawke's Bay and the Wairarapa. Over Cook Strait, the wine trail snakes across the Waimea Plains and Upper Moutere hills of Nelson, criss-crosses the Wairau and Awatere valleys of Marlborough, and plunges south from Waipara to South Canterbury, before finally ascending to the vineyards burgeoning in the majestic inland hills and basins of Central Otago.

With almost 80 per cent of the country's vines concentrated in only three regions, New Zealand wine is overwhelmingly of Marlborough, Hawke's Bay or Gisborne origin. Over the three-year period 1999 to 2001, 91 per cent of the total national grape crop was harvested in the big three regions, reflecting the high natural fertility of many Gisborne and Hawke's Bay vineyards, the bulk-wine varieties sometimes (but decreasingly) cultivated there, and management of some vineyards to produce bumper crops for low-priced wine. Many other regions, however, also boast significant vineyard plantings. This far-flung spread of viticulture has greatly enhanced the diversity — and hence fascination — of New Zealand wine.

Clearcut regional differences can often be discerned in the wines. Why does a Canterbury Riesling taste different from a Hawke's Bay Riesling? Climate is the key influence: our winegrowing regions in northern latitudes are markedly warmer than those in the south. Sunshine hours, rainfall and soil types also vary markedly from region to region. These factors influence the grape varieties suitable for each region and also the styles of wine they yield. Grapes cultivated in the cooler southern regions tend to produce delicate, mouth-wateringly crisp wines, whereas fruit grown in the warmer northern regions typically produces more mouthfilling, softer styles.

At various stages of our history, grapevines have been planted, with or without success, over most parts of the country. Bragato in 1895 encountered vines growing in Central Otago, Akaroa, Nelson, the Wairarapa, Hawke's Bay, Bay of Plenty, Wanganui, the Waikato, Auckland and Northland. Such a widespread scattering of early grapegrowing and winemaking reflected the isolated, far-flung nature of the first settlements. Although, ideally, considerations of climate and soil should have been uppermost in selecting areas to establish vines, in fact it was the influence of cultural traditions and the availability of cheap land which played leading roles in the early location of the industry in New Zealand.

The early exploitation of the Auckland region was due to the scale of the available market and the presence of Croatians and others eager to make wine, rather than to any major climatic or physical advantages. Hawke's Bay, with ideal natural conditions for grapegrowing, was sufficiently distant from Auckland to compete for markets in the south. Auckland and Hawke's Bay thus remained the two centres of New Zealand wine for more than half a century. Then in the 1960s, when it became obvious that extensive new plantings would be necessary to cater for the soaring demand for table wines, vineyards spread beyond the traditional grapegrowing zones into Taupaki, Kumeu, Mangatangi and, above all, Gisborne.

Corbans, Cooks and Montana encouraged contract growers in Gisborne to establish substantial areas in vines. The answer lay in the fertility of Gisborne's soils, which yield bumper crops. The subsequent move into Marlborough by Montana (attracted by the availability of large blocks of cheap land), Corbans and others paid an unexpectedly rich dividend. Although the vines' yields are typically lighter, the region proved to be brilliantly suited to the production of intensely flavoured cool-climate white wines.

The 1980s and 1990s brought the emergence of the Wairarapa, Nelson, Canterbury and Central Otago as small but important features of the national wine map. By shifting to cooler climate zones in the south, New Zealand winemakers have been paralleling a common trend overseas. The search for riper, more disease-free grapes has for the past 25 years led most newcomers to the industry to avoid the higher rainfall areas of the upper North Island in favour of the long dry belt extending down the east coast of both islands from Hawke's Bay through the Wairarapa and Marlborough to Canterbury.

Numerous regional strengths have emerged, as an analysis of the results of the Air New Zealand Wine Awards in 1999, 2000 and 2001 underlines. Of the 40 gold medals won by red wines made from traditional Bordeaux varieties (Cabernet Sauvignon, Merlot, Cabernet Franc and Malbec), 37 went to Hawke's Bay. Of the 24 golds awarded to Sauvignon Blancs, 18 went to Marlborough and four to the Wairarapa.

Marlborough also dominated the top awards for Riesling (with 11 out of 19 gold medals), Gewürztraminer (four out of five), sweet white wines (six out of 10) and sparkling wine (six out of nine). However, the 38 Chardonnay golds were more widely spread, with 14 going to Marlborough, 10 to Hawke's Bay, five to Nelson and four to Gisborne. Of the 15 gold medals for Pinot Noir, five went to Central Otago, four to the Wairarapa and three to Marlborough.

Each of New Zealand's wine regions has its own distinctive personality. The exploration of the links between the various landscapes, climates, winemaking communities and wine styles is the focal point of this atlas.

The Principal Wine Regions of New Zealand

Northland/Auckland

Climate challenging; plentiful rain (slightly less on east coast) and high humidity lead to serious threat of fungal diseases; mild winters; warmth favours red-wine production.
Soils heavy clays (drain poorly)
Degree Days 1404–1662°C
Oct–April Rainfall 562–842 mm
Producing Area in 2002 427 hectares (3.3% NZ total)
Major Varieties Chardonnay, Merlot, Cabernet Sauvignon, Cabernet Franc, Pinot Noir, Pinotage

Waikato/Bay of Plenty

Climate temperatures and sunshine hours high, but so are rainfall and humidity
Soils heavy loams over clay
Degree Days 1395°C
Oct–April Rainfall 590 mm
Producing Area in 2002 133 hectares (1% NZ total)
Major Varieties Chardonnay, Cabernet Sauvignon, Sauvignon Blanc

Nelson

Climate warm summers with very high sunshine hours; significant autumn rainfall
Soils range from alluvial loams (Waimea Plains) to heavier clays (Upper Moutere)
Degree Days 1129–1175°C
Oct–April Rainfall 535–562 mm
Producing Area in 2002 357 hectares (2.8% NZ total)
Major Varieties Chardonnay, Sauvignon Blanc, Pinot Noir, Riesling

Gisborne

Climate warm temperatures (lead to early grape harvest) but frequent autumn rainfall (causes strong disease risk)
Soils rich alluvial loams of high fertility
Degree Days 1379–1468°C
Oct–April Rainfall 487–522 mm
Producing Area in 2002 1724 hectares (13.4% NZ total)
Major Varieties Chardonnay, Müller-Thurgau, Muscat varieties, Sémillon, Merlot, Pinot Noir

Hawke's Bay

Climate high sunshine hours, warm summer temperatures, dryish autumns
Soils diverse range from fertile, silty loams with high water table to free-draining shingle
Degree Days 1270°C
Oct–April Rainfall 366–387 mm
Producing Area in 2002 3375 hectares (26.3% NZ total)
Major Varieties Chardonnay, Merlot, Cabernet Sauvignon, Sauvignon Blanc, Pinot Noir, Cabernet Franc

Wairarapa

Climate warm summer; cool, dryish autumn; exposure to strong winds reduces yields
Soils preferred sites have free-draining, shallow loams with gravelly sub-soils
Degree Days 1081–1189°C
Oct–April Rainfall 381–447 mm
Producing Area in 2002 458 hectares (3.6% NZ total)
Major Varieties Pinot Noir, Sauvignon Blanc, Chardonnay, Pinot Gris, Riesling, Cabernet Sauvignon

Marlborough

Climate warm with very high sunshine hours but cool nights to preserve acidity; dryish autumn gives a slow, flavour-intensifying ripening period
Soils variable, even within individual vineyards; less fertile, more shingly sites most sought after
Degree Days 1127–1218°C
Oct–April Rainfall 357–398 mm
Producing Area in 2002 5449 hectares (42.4% NZ total)
Major Varieties Sauvignon Blanc, Pinot Noir, Chardonnay, Riesling, Pinot Gris, Merlot

Canterbury

Climate hot summer days (especially in the north at Waipara) with cool nights to preserve acidity; favourably dry autumns; some sites too cool for regular, full ripening
Soils free-draining, silty loams overlying river gravels; chalky loams in the north
Degree Days 973–1117°C
Oct–April Rainfall 339–379 mm
Producing Area in 2002 501 hectares (3.9% NZ total)
Major Varieties Pinot Noir, Chardonnay, Riesling, Sauvignon Blanc, Pinot Gris

Central Otago

Climate NZ's most continental, with hot summers, cold winters and marked diurnal (day/night) temperature range; low heat summation and high frost danger makes site selection critical; extremely dry autumn allows an extended ripening period
Soils variable, but mostly derived from loess or alluvial deposits, often with underlying gravels
Degree Days 910–989°C
Oct–April Rainfall 243–276 mm
Producing Area in 2002 420 hectares (3.3% NZ total)
Major Varieties Pinot Noir, Chardonnay, Pinot Gris, Riesling, Sauvignon Blanc

Sources: **1** Jackson, D. and Schuster, D., *The Production of Grapes and Wine in Cool Climates*, 1994, p. 42. **2** Bank of New Zealand Wine and Grape Industry Statistical Annual 2001. **3** National Institute of Water and Atmospheric Research (report to author) 2001.

Northland

Principal grape varieties

Cabernet Sauvignon

Chardonnay

Merlot

Syrah

Note: no definitive figures have been published for varietal plantings in Northland. The above list of principal grape varieties was compiled with the assistance of Monty Knight, proprietor of Okahu Estate.

Vintage chart
(1994–2002)

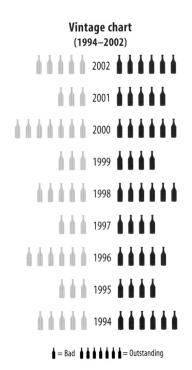

🍾🍾🍾🍾🍾 2002 🍾🍾🍾🍾🍾🍾

🍾🍾🍾 2001 🍾🍾🍾🍾🍾

🍾🍾🍾🍾🍾🍾 2000 🍾🍾🍾🍾🍾🍾

🍾🍾🍾 1999 🍾🍾🍾🍾

🍾🍾🍾🍾🍾 1998 🍾🍾🍾🍾🍾🍾🍾

🍾🍾🍾 1997 🍾🍾🍾🍾

🍾🍾🍾🍾🍾🍾 1996 🍾🍾🍾🍾🍾

🍾🍾🍾 1995 🍾🍾🍾🍾

🍾🍾🍾🍾🍾 1994 🍾🍾🍾🍾🍾🍾

🍾 = Bad 🍾🍾🍾🍾🍾🍾 = Outstanding

Previous page: Syrah has been the biggest success in the Okahu Estate vineyard, near Kaitaia and the southern end of Ninety Mile Beach.

Northland is the minnow of New Zealand's wine regions, producing an average of 7000 cases in the 2000 and 2001 vintages — just 0.1 per cent of the country's wine. Stretched out over 300 kilometres of rolling hill country, its almost subtropical climate — abundant rainfall, high humidity and relatively warm winters — is less well suited to viticulture than the drier regions to the south.

In contrast to the younger, more rugged landforms of the South Island and central North Island, Northland has the less dramatic topography of older landscapes. The land climbs to over 600 metres above sea level in its central ranges, but most of the region lies below 150 metres.

Northland's main industries are forestry, dairy farming and tourism, but the region boasts seven licensed winemakers — mostly on the eastern side of the peninsula — with a cluster of new vineyards on the horizon. Most of the wine is consumed in the region's several vineyard restaurants and can be hard to find outside Northland.

History

Northland was the cradle of New Zealand wine: here Marsden made the first recorded planting of vines in 1819 and here too, in the 1830s, Busby made the first wine. However, after 1840 and the Treaty of Waitangi, the region was exploited mainly for its magnificent kauri forests and later for its gum. Descendants of Croatian gumdiggers and the sons and daughters of more recent Croatian arrivals until recently almost alone preserved the winemaking traditions of Busby.

Mario Vuletich, proprietor of the Longview winery, near Whangarei, recalls that his father 'retired to the site in 1964, after clearing the scrub by hand. He began to make wine for his own consumption, as was the Croatian way, and then began to sell some. Father did a reasonable trade, selling "Mate's Medicinal Tonic" to the locals!'

Between 1976 and 1995, demand for the traditional sherries and ports of Northland declined, and the number of licensed winemakers in the region nose-dived from 19 to four. By the early 1990s, the total area under vines — 18 hectares in 1983 — had contracted to 7 hectares.

Now a revival is underway. Continental Wines propelled itself into a new era by changing its name to Longview Estate in the mid-1990s and has since released some sturdy, richly flavoured Cabernet Sauvignon and Merlot-based reds.

The launch in 1992 of Okahu Estate Ninety Mile Red 1989, grown near Kaitaia, heralded the arrival of a new, quality-orientated winery in the Far North. Since then, other vineyards have emerged at Kerikeri (famous for its citrus and other subtropical fruits), Russell and Tutukaka.

On the Karikari Peninsula, jutting out into the Pacific Ocean north-east of Kaitaia, expatriate American Bob Haig has established a substantial, 17-hectare vineyard, principally in Merlot, Cabernet Sauvignon and Syrah, with smaller plots of Grenache, Malbec, Cabernet Franc, Chardonnay, Viognier, Sémillon and Sauvignon Blanc. The first wines under his Carrington Farm label are due in 2004.

The Matakana/Mahurangi district lies in Auckland, rather than Northland (Ross Road, north of Te Hana, is the southern boundary of the Northland Regional Council). However, the recent flurry of vineyard plantings there and the high reputation of its wine have played a key role in stimulating others to explore the potential of districts further north of Auckland.

Climate

Its northern location and closeness to the sea give Northland a mild climate — warm, sunny and humid.

The mean annual temperature is the highest in New Zealand, especially in eastern and northern parts of the region. In February — the warmest month — Northland's temperatures are no higher than in Auckland, but winter temperatures are higher than elsewhere (hence the popular expression, 'the winterless north'), and day/night temperature variations are relatively minor.

Relative humidity is high throughout the year, due to the close proximity of the sea (nowhere more than 50 kilometres away). The abundant rainfall is heaviest in the ranges, but decreases by almost half in low-lying coastal areas in the east. Tropical cyclones can bring tremendous downpours in summer, but dry spells of

Summary of climate statistics

Meteorological station	Latitude	Height	GDD	MTWM	Rainfall, Oct–Apr	Air frost days (annual)
Kaitaia Observatory	35.08'S	85 m	1662	20°C	618 mm	0
Kerikeri	35.10'S	79 m	1536	19.6°C	842 mm	0

Height — *above sea level* **GDD** — *growing degree days, Oct–Apr, above 10°C* **MTWM** — *mean temperature, warmest month*

two weeks or longer also occur during late summer and early autumn.

The most common winds are from the south-west, especially in winter and spring, but in summer easterlies are equally common, and are typically very moist. Cooling sea breezes are common during summer and autumn.

During an average growing season (October to April), Northland's vineyards receive twice as much rain as Marlborough's and three times as much as Central Otago's. Sloping, well-drained sites, sea breezes and good canopy management can reduce rain-related problems. However, the challenge facing Northland viticulturists is well summed up by Mario Vuletich, of Longview Estate: 'Give me good sprays, a good raincoat, a good sense of humour and thick-skinned grapes, and I can make very good red wines from this property.'

Soils

The geology of Northland is patchy and complex, with a great variety of rocks and landforms. Heavy, greyish brown, clay-rich loam soils are the most common, over a sub-soil of compact clay. 'The forests of the past have left their imprint on the soil,' observes Les Molloy in *Soils of the New Zealand Landscape*. 'In particular, kauri produced deep layers of highly acidic litter . . . that have contributed to the poor physical properties of many of the region's soils.' At Kerikeri, where Marsden Estate and Cottle Hill Winery are based, the principal soils are friable volcanic clays.

In Northland's mild, moist climate, plant growth is almost continuous. For quality winemaking, well-drained soils that give the vines a balanced, rather than excessive, uptake of water are the most sought after.

Wine styles

Northland's small plantings are not recorded separately in the annual national vineyard survey, but are instead added to those for the Auckland region. As a result, there are no authoritative figures available for the total area now in vines or the plantings of individual grape varieties.

In the best (relatively dry) vintages, such as 2000, some excellent white wines flow from Northland — full-bodied, ripely flavoured and soft Chardonnay, Sémillon and Pinot Gris. However, the region is best known for its reds — claret-style and substantial, warm, spicy Rhône Valley look-alikes. Cabernet Sauvignon and Merlot are well established, but the highest hopes are held for Syrah.

Sub-regions

Given the tiny scale of Northland viticulture, it is too early to identify key sub-regions. However, given the scattered, isolated nature of the vineyards (not including Matakana/Mahurangi, in Auckland), it is not surprising they experience significant climate differences (such as Kaitaia's lower rainfall, compared to Kerikeri's) that will inevitably be reflected in the wines.

🍷 wine company

Ⓘ weather station

0   20 km

Longview Estate

■ Longview is playing a vital role in the resurgence of winemaking in the north. For a long time Continental (as it was known until the mid-1990s) seemed content to produce sound *vin ordinaire*, but in the past decade the fruits of a major vineyard replanting programme have come on stream and the standard of the wines has risen sharply. Now winemaker Mario Vuletich's ambition is to 'make a *really* good red, as good as Goldwater or Morton — it can be done here. If we really play hard at it, as good as any Australian.'

The pretty, terraced vineyard alongside the state highway at Otaika, just south of Whangarei, was established by Mate Vuletich who, as his widow, Milica, relates, was born under a grapevine on the family vineyard in Dalmatia. Vuletich planted his first Baco 22A and Niagara vines in 1964 to produce wine for his own medicinal purposes.

Mario Vuletich, the effusive, dark-haired, moustachioed managing director, admits he only 'really got serious about winemaking about 15 years ago — when I got married'. The original hybrid and native American vines were uprooted and the 7-hectare estate vineyard is now planted principally in Chardonnay, Cabernet Sauvignon, Merlot and Syrah, with smaller plots of Gewürztraminer, Malbec, Pinot Noir and Cabernet Franc.

The hill-grown clay vineyard, with its 'long view' over Whangarei Harbour to Mt Mania, is mainly laid out in east-west rows that follow the fall of the land. However, the latest plantings, on flatter terrain, run in the conventional north-south direction to maximise the vines' exposure to the sun. 'We get clean fruit here,' reports Vuletich. 'There's a steady breeze from the harbour, which promotes the circulation of air through the vines' canopies, drying them and reducing disease.' Longview's grapes are currently all estate-grown, although in future Syrah grapes will be bought from a grower at Te Hana, near Wellsford, north of Auckland.

Longview's annual production of about 2500 cases is mostly sold directly to the public at the cream-coloured, Mediterranean-style winery. The key white wines are the attractive Unwooded Chardonnay, which offers tangy, lemony, appley flavours, fresh, crisp and lively; and the more variable Gewürztraminer, at its best rich, ripe and well-spiced.

In favourable vintages, the French and American oak-aged Scarecrow Cabernet Sauvignon and Mario's Merlot are dark and weighty, with concentrated, brambly flavours. In keeping with tradition, Longview also produces a Gumdigger's Port — sweet, smooth and chocolate-rich.

Address Longview Estate,
State Highway One,
Otaika,
Whangarei

Owners The Vuletich family

Key Wines Scarecrow Cabernet
Sauvignon, Mario's Merlot,
Unwooded Chardonnay,
Gewürztraminer,
Gumdigger's Port

Okahu Estate

■ Seductively smooth, warm, rich-flavoured reds oozing ripe, sweet fruit are the most memorable wines at one of New Zealand's most northern vineyards. Okahu Estate lies near Kaitaia, on the road to Ahipara, at the southern end of Ninety Mile Beach.

Monty Knight, the founder, is famous in the Far North, although more for his entrepreneurial career as a home appliance retailer than as a winemaker. He and his wife, Bev, live on the crest of their west-facing, 2-hectare, hillside vineyard. 'We didn't come here to make wine,' he recalls. 'When I planted the first vines in 1984, the idea was just to make wine for our own consumption.' The first experimental wine flowed in 1986. Four years later, the Knights erected an Australian farmhouse-style winery and set out to overturn the common belief that you can't make good wine in the North.

The combination of high humidity and high temperatures in Kaitaia, conducive to extremely vigorous vine growth and the spread of fungal diseases, have encouraged Knight to convert the vineyard from the VSP (vertical shoot position) trellising system to split-canopy systems that create more open vines, less susceptible to disease. 'With reds, the Rhône styles seem to do best at Okahu, so we are planting more and more Syrah,' says Knight. Cabernet Sauvignon (difficult to ripen fully) and Sémillon (difficult to sell) have been discarded. 'Pinotage and Chambourcin [the densely coloured French hybrid] are being grown for us in other Northland vineyards.'

By 2004, Knight predicts Okahu Estate's wines will be based entirely on Northland grapes, grown in the estate vineyard or on contract at Okahu and further afield. Meanwhile, the company still draws much of its fruit from growers at Te Hana, near Wellsford, north of Auckland; other parts of the Auckland region; and Hawke's Bay.

Ben Morris, a winemaking graduate of Lincoln University, joined Okahu Estate in late 2000 after working at the St Helena winery, in Canterbury. A slight rusticity and dullness detracted from some Okahu Estate wines in the past, but Morris has successfully introduced new techniques and is determined 'to retain more fruit characters' in the white wines. Production is growing steadily, from 3000 cases in 1996 to 8000 cases in 2002.

The wines are marketed under a three-tier system. At the top are the 'ultra premium' wines, labelled Kaz after Karen ('Kaz'), Monty and Bev's eldest daughter. The 'premium' Clifton and Ninety Mile labels are named after Monty's brother and the famous west coast beach. Designed for early drinking, the Shipwreck Bay wines are named after a local surfing haunt.

Okahu Estate's notably robust and rich-flavoured Kaz Shiraz 1994 achieved a unique double at the 1996 Liquorland Royal Easter Wine Show — the first gold medal anyone could recall for a Northland wine, and the first gold ever awarded to a New Zealand Syrah. Matured in French and American oak casks, this is typically an

Address Okahu Estate Vineyard
and Winery,
Okahu Road,
Okahu,
Kaitaia

Owners Monty and Bev Knight

Key Wines Kaz Shiraz, Cabernet and
Sémillon; Clifton
Chardonnay and Proprietor's
Reserve Chardonnay; Paula's
Pinotage Reserve; Ninety
Mile Cabernet/Merlot;
Shipwreck Bay PCM and
Lightly Oaked Chardonnay.

'I decided I wouldn't attend a wine awards dinner until I won a gold medal,' Monty Knight told the audience in 1996 while accepting the first gold medal for a Northland wine.

impressive wine with strong, plummy, spicy, nutty flavours. The Kaz range also features a concentrated, cassis and dark plum-flavoured Cabernet.

Both the Clifton Chardonnay and Proprietor's Reserve Clifton Chardonnay have been of variable quality, but the latest vintages are deliciously creamy and complex. Paula's Pinotage Reserve — one of the finest Pinotages in the country, bursting with sweet fruit characters, rich and smooth — is slightly more intense than the Ninety Mile Cabernet/Merlot, which offers satisfying depth of berryish, spicy flavours.

Shipwreck Bay PCM is a good, honest, multi-region blend of Pinotage, Cabernet Franc, Chambourcin and Merlot, made in an easy-drinking style. If you like old fortified wines, don't overlook the sweet, raisiny, seven-year-old Don de Monte Oloroso Sherry, or the amber-green, nutty and mellow Saint Jakob's Tawny, blended from estate-grown and west Auckland stocks with an average age of 15 years.

Other producers

■ Cottle Hill Winery

Escaping from 'the Southern California rat race', Mike and Barbara Webb sailed around the South Pacific for several years before settling in the Bay of Islands. On the corner of Cottle Hill Drive and State Highway 10, just south of Kerikeri, in 1996 they planted a trial block of red-wine grapes — Pinot Noir, Pinotage, Cabernet Sauvignon and Merlot — followed in 1997 by Chardonnay and more Pinot Noir. The sloping, 2.5-hectare estate vineyard, planted in volcanic soils, yielded its first commercial crop in 2000. However, the early 1996 to 1999 vintages (made on-site since 1997) were based entirely on Hawke's Bay grapes and the Webbs continue to draw Chardonnay, Sauvignon Blanc, Sémillon, Merlot and Cabernet Sauvignon from Hawke's Bay. The annual output of about 1500 cases per year includes Bay Breeze, a Sémillon-based quaffer, popular with tourists; a good, sometimes outstanding Reserve Chardonnay; and a complex, savoury, leathery Reserve Merlot.

■ Marsden Estate

To judge from the impressive quality of its 2000 vintage releases, this is a winery to watch. Rod MacIvor, formerly a Wellington builder, and his wife, Cindy, planted their first vines — Chardonnay and Cabernet Sauvignon — in Wiroa Road, Kerikeri, in 1993. Pinot Gris, Pinotage, Merlot, Malbec and Chambourcin have since been added and the vineyard has grown to over 4 hectares, yielding about 3000 cases of wine per year. Made by Rod MacIvor in his lime-washed concrete winery and consumed in Marsden Estate's popular lakeside vineyard restaurant, the range includes a full-bodied, fresh, peachy and spicy Pinot Gris with true varietal character; a barrel-fermented Black Rocks Chardonnay of variable quality; a vibrantly fruity and supple Pinotage; Cavalli, a firm, powerful blend of Cabernet Sauvignon (principally), Malbec and Merlot; and a robust Chambourcin with loads of fresh, plummy flavour.

■ Omata Estate

Over the water from Paihia, in the Bay of Islands, Omata Estate is a luxury lodge with a restaurant (open to the public) and small vineyard. Chardonnay, Syrah and Merlot are cultivated on a sloping site in Aucks Road, a few minutes' drive from Russell. The initial releases were made from Marlborough grapes, but estate-grown wines have recently started to flow. The Syrah is 'especially good — the star in the portfolio', reports Omata Estate. Most of the wine is sold in the estate's restaurant and cellar-door shop.

Auckland

Many of New Zealand's largest wine companies — including Montana, Villa Maria, Nobilo, Babich, Delegat's, Matua Valley and Coopers Creek — have their headquarters in Auckland, processing grapes grown all over the country. A unique feature of the Auckland wine trail is the opportunity to taste wines from several regions, especially Auckland, Gisborne, Hawke's Bay and Marlborough.

Principal grape varieties

	Producing area 2002	% total producing area 2002
Chardonnay	99 ha	23%
Merlot	90 ha	21%
Cabernet Sauvignon	70 ha	16%
Cabernet Franc	31 ha	7%
Pinotage	21 ha	5%
Pinot Noir	20 ha	5%

History

From the early 1900s, with a cluster of Croatian winemakers and others of Lebanese (the Corbans) and English backgrounds, Auckland rivalled Hawke's Bay as one of the two key centres of New Zealand wine.

Today, however, Auckland has just 3 per cent of the country's total vineyard area. Auckland's importance started to decline in the 1960s, with the southward shift of viticulture in pursuit of cheaper land and a drier climate. But the fall in vine plantings, from 455 hectares in 1983 to 241 hectares in 1992, has lately been reversed, with 487 hectares planted in 2001. The successes of Kumeu River, Collards, Goldwater, Stonyridge and others with Auckland-grown wines has recently brought a resurgence of confidence in this historic region.

Climate

With Auckland's high rainfall and humidity throughout the growing season, disease control is the major challenge for the region's grape-growers. Its warm temperatures assist the ripening of late-season grape varieties, but Auckland is also a cloudy region, with sub-optimal sunshine hours for viticulture (especially in the west). The rainfall, highest in the Waitakere Ranges, is significantly lower in eastern districts. Frosts are infrequent and generally light.

Leigh, on the east coast, has a mean daily temperature range of 6°C, compared to 10°C inland at Henderson, showing that Auckland — although sprawled across a narrow isthmus — does experience some continental temperature effects.

Soils

Auckland's bedrock is up to 250 million years old. Many of the young volcanic soils on the narrow isthmus between the Waitemata and Manukau harbours have been formed by volcanic activity over the last 150,000 years. However, layered sandstone and mudstone are the most common rocks in the region, uplifted from the ocean floor many thousands of years ago and since weathered to clay-rich soils. Most Auckland vineyards are planted on heavy clays, often with poor natural drainage.

Wine styles

Auckland's relatively warm temperatures favour Bordeaux-style reds, increasingly based on Merlot rather than Cabernet Sauvignon, which in the heavy clay soils often struggles to achieve full ripeness. Pinot Gris is set to overhaul Sauvignon Blanc as the second most popular white-wine variety, but Chardonnay is far ahead, producing weighty, ripe, tropical fruit-flavoured wines with rounded acidity.

Vintage chart
(1993–2002)

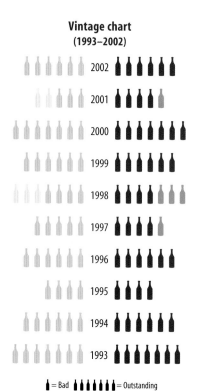

2002

2001

2000

1999

1998

1997

1996

1995

1994

1993

🍾 = Bad 🍾🍾🍾🍾🍾🍾 = Outstanding
🍾🍾 = variation between wine varieties

Sub-regions

Auckland's vineyards are clustered in several distinct sub-regions: Matakana/Mahurangi, Kumeu/Huapai, Henderson, Waiheke Island and South Auckland. In the absence of high mountains and frequent strong winds, Auckland's sub-regions have relatively similar climates. All five districts have the warm temperatures and high rainfall typical of Auckland, although the east coast areas — which have attracted most of the recent vineyard expansion — are slightly drier.

Summary of climate statistics

Meteorological station	Latitude	Height	GDD	MTWM	Rainfall, Oct–Apr	Air frost days (annual)
Leigh	36.16'S	27 m	1601	19.9°C	562 mm	0
Warkworth	36.26'S	72 m	1404	19°C	716 mm	2
Waiheke	36.48'S	30 m	1438	19.8°C	626 mm	1
Henderson	36.51'S	4 m	1617	20°C	663 mm	9

Height — *above sea level* **GDD** — *growing degree days, Oct–Apr, above 10°C* **MTWM** — *mean temperature, warmest month*

Previous page: Looking north from Matakana Estate across the tranquil Matakana Valley.

0   10 km

N

⊕ weather station

Port
Albert
Wellsford
Oruawharo River
Tapora
Tauhoa
River
Hoteo River
HARBOUR
Kaipara
Flats
Atuanui
305m
Ahuroa
Moir Hill
358m
Shelly
Beach
Kakanui
Makarau
Kanohi
Kaukapakapa
Waitoki
Parakai
Helensville
Woodhill
Rewiti
Muriwai
Piha
WAITAKERE
RANGES
Dairy
Flat
Coatesville
Riverhead
Whenuapai
Paremoremo
Albany
Waimauku
Huapai
Kumeu
Laingholm
Titirangi
HENDERSON
AUCKLAND
Waitemata
Harbour
TAKAPUNA
EAST
COAST
BAYS
Ōkura
Redvale
Long Bay
Silverdale
Whangaparaoa
Stanmore
Bay
Orewa
Waiwera
Puhoi
MAHURANGI
Warkworth
Sandspit
Snells Beach
Matakana
Omaha Flats
Omaha
Omaha Bay
Whangateau
Leigh
Cape
Rodney
Kawau Bay
Kawau
Island
Motuora Island
Whangaparaoa
Peninsula
Tiritiri Matangi
HAURAKI
GULF
Rakino Island
Motutapu Island
Rangitoto
Island
Motuihe Island
Waiheke Island
Onetangi
Tamaki
Strait
Ponui
Island
Pakihi
Island
Maraetai
Beachlands
Whitford
HOWICK
Puketutu
Island
MANUKAU
HARBOUR
Auckland
International
Airport
East Tamaki
Papatoetoe
MANUKAU CITY
Manurewa
SOUTH AUCKLAND
Clevedon
PAPAKURA
Red Hill
Hunua
HUNUA
RANGES
Mangatangi
487m
Kingseat
Karaka
Drury
Matakawau
Waiau Pa
Te Hihi
Ararimu
Ramarama
Paerata
Papakura
Papakura
Pollock
Te Toro
Glenbrook
Beach
Patumahoe
Mauku
Waipipi
Pukekohe
Bombay
Mangatangi
Mangatawhiri
Buckland
Waikato River
Papakura
Papakura

Matakana/Mahurangi

Think Matakana, think red wines, especially Cabernet Sauvignon and Merlot-based reds in the Bordeaux mould, pioneered in the mid-1980s by The Antipodean. But recently, the district's Pinot Gris and Chardonnay have looked at least the equal of its reds.

An hour's drive north of Auckland, most of the vineyards are at Matakana, draped across the hills between Warkworth and the coast at Leigh, but others lie slightly to the south, at Mahurangi. This is a small, fast-expanding wine area, with about 80 hectares of vines planted in 2001, less than 1 per cent of the national vineyard.

The winemakers are a diverse community, approaching the business of making a living from wine in very different ways. Some, such as Ascension, sell most of their output through their winery restaurant, while others, including Providence, are not open to visitors and concentrate almost exclusively on export.

This is not an easy place to make fine wines. 'It is wet, humid and often overcast, with clay soils,' says one winemaker. 'In other words, fertile and vigorous, with consistently high disease pressure.'

Not all the soils are heavy and poorly drained. 'The white clays are less suitable for grape-growing,' says James Vuletic of Providence, 'but the reddish, granulated clays often found about a

metre under the topsoil are high in iron and relatively free-draining.' To improve their natural drainage, almost all the vineyards in the area have been planted on slopes.

The frost risk is low, but botrytis bunch rot is a major challenge and at sites near the sea, salt-laden easterly winds can damage the vines. 'You must look seriously at what you grow and how you manage the vines,' says Christine Didsbury of Brick Bay. Various trellis systems are employed in the area to combat vine vigour, and the vines are trimmed, shoot-thinned and leaf-plucked to open their canopies, allowing air to circulate and dry the leaves and bunches.

In favourably dry seasons, the wines from Matakana/Mahurangi shine, with the Chardonnays and Pinot Gris offering ripe stone-fruit characters and the reds reflecting the area's northern warmth in their substantial body and rich, spicy, earthy flavours. With its lovely hills, fields and vineyards, burgeoning wineries and snowballing number of tourists, the Matakana/Mahurangi area is even being promoted by the locals as 'Auckland's answer to Tuscany'.

Ascension

Address   Ascension Vineyard, 480 Matakana Road, Matakana

Owners   The Soljan family

Key Wines   Riesling, Chardonnay, The Ascent Chardonnay, Pinotage, Pinotage Barrique Selection, The Ascent Cabernet/Merlot/Malbec

Ascension's hillside vineyard and striking restaurant are a popular feature of the Matakana wine trail.

◼ Drive over the hill from Warkworth, and right at the entrance to the Matakana Valley lies Ascension's handsome, Spanish mission-style winery restaurant. 'As soon as we opened in late 2000,' recalls Darryl Soljan, 'the place just took off.'

The name Soljan is already known to many wine lovers. Rex Soljan, Darryl's father, was until 1994 a partner in Soljan's Wines in Henderson. Darryl can trace his heritage back over five generations of winemaking Soljans, through Rex to Frank, Bartul and his great-great-grandfather, Frano.

After working in the trucking business as an operations manager (where he 'learned to think outside the square') Darryl Soljan worked at his father and uncle's Henderson winery, then at De Redcliffe, in winemaking and sales roles, from 1995 to 2000. 'After Dad left the Henderson winery, he offered to help my wife, Bridget, and me set up Ascension. We bought the land in 1994 and started planting in 1996.'

Today, the sloping, 4-hectare vineyard is planted in a wide array of grapes — Pinotage, Merlot, Cabernet Sauvignon, Malbec, Chardonnay, Viognier and Pinot Gris. Grapes are also purchased from other regions, including Marlborough and Hawke's Bay. The winery is currently only equipped for red-wine fermentation, but the wines are all matured on-site.

Soljan, who each year produces about 2000 cases, mostly sold in the popular restaurant, wants to make wine 'that's accessible, that people can afford'. His Barrique Selection Pinotage is fresh, vibrant and berryish; the partly barrel-fermented Chardonnay is an easy-drinking, creamy-smooth style.

The top range, labelled The Ascent, features a high-flavoured, toasty Chardonnay, full of character; and a perfumed Cabernet/Merlot/Malbec with good depth of plummy, slightly leafy flavour.

Brick Bay

◼ One of New Zealand's finest Pinot Gris — at its best weighty, rich and soft, in the classic Alsace mould — flows from this small, elevated coastal vineyard. In the bay below, a brickworks operated during the nineteenth century, producing building materials for Sir George Grey's projects on Kawau Island, not far offshore.

Christine Didsbury, a former English teacher, and her husband, Richard, a property investor, bought the 65-hectare Brick Bay Farm in 1986. 'I'd always enjoyed drinking wine and we wanted to do something more intensive than running cattle. So we hired a consultant, who identified part of the property as being "very favourable" for grapes.'

In a warm, sheltered hollow, sloping to the north, the first vines were planted in 1994. Today, the 3-hectare vineyard is devoted principally to Cabernet Sauvignon, Merlot and Pinot Gris, with smaller plots of Cabernet Franc and Malbec. The grapes are all estate-grown.

Christine Didsbury, who has a Certificate in Wine Production from Eastern Institute of Technology in Hawke's Bay, oversees the vineyard, but the wine is made by Anthony Ivicevich at the West Brook winery, in Waimauku. Only about 800 cases flow each year, sold by mail order and in a few restaurants and wine shops.

The first, 1998 vintage Brick Bay Pinot Gris attracted a gold medal; a promise confirmed by later vintages. Didsbury is after 'a weighty, fruit-driven Pinot Gris style, with considerable elegance', and is hitting the target. Powerful, with an oily texture and fresh, rich flavours of peaches and lychees, this is a distinguished wine, worth tracking down.

The debut 1999 Cabernet, blended from Cabernet Sauvignon (principally), Cabernet Franc and Malbec, was less successful — full-flavoured and spicy, but green-edged. Merlot (slow to produce a decent-sized crop) should in future impart riper fruit characters to the blend.

Address   Brick Bay Wines, Kauri Drive, Sandspit

Owners   Christine and Richard Didsbury

Key Wines   Pinot Gris, Cabernets

Address	Heron's Flight Vineyard, 49 Sharp Road, Matakana
Owners	David Hoskins and Mary Evans
Key Wines	Sangiovese, La Cerise Merlot/Sangiovese, Barrique Fermented Chardonnay, La Volee Unoaked Chardonnay

Heron's Flight

■ With a string of good — sometimes excellent — Cabernet Sauvignon/Merlots from 1991 onwards, David Hoskins and Mary Evans confirmed the red-wine potential of the Matakana district first suggested in the 1980s by The Antipodean. Then, in a dramatic change of direction between 1998 and 2001, they replaced all their French red-wine grapes with Italian varieties — Sangiovese (predominantly) and Dolcetto.

Hoskins is a Pennsylvania-born science and philosophy graduate who worked as a teacher and community worker before plunging into full-time winemaking. He and his wife, Mary Evans, a former teacher with an MA in English, planted their first vines on a north-facing clay slope overlooking the Matakana Valley and Sandspit Estuary in 1988.

Named after the herons which nest down by the river (and fly up and perch on the vineyard posts), the 5-hectare vineyard is planted mainly in the great grape of Chianti, Sangiovese (3.5 hectares), supplemented by 1 hectare of Chardonnay and a half-hectare plot of Dolcetto. Why grow Sangiovese, almost unknown in New Zealand?

'After making some very good Cabernet Sauvignon-based wines, in 1995 we found the weather patterns changing,' says David Hoskins. 'It became increasingly difficult to fully ripen the Cabernet. About this time, we were becoming increasingly fascinated by Italian wines. In 1993 we managed to track down two clones of Sangiovese in New Zealand, planted a trial block in 1994, and made our first Sangiovese wine in 1997. So excited were we by its potential, a couple of years ago we made the decision to replant all our French red vines with Sangiovese and Dolcetto [for a lighter style red].'

Much of the wine is consumed in the relaxed, cosy vineyard café. Modelled on a small Tuscan farm, Heron's Flight has large kitchen gardens and produces olive oil and wine vinegar. 'The café is important to us,' says Hoskins, 'because our vision is that wine is not an end in itself, but something to be enjoyed with food, in the company of friends.'

Two white wines are made: a fresh, lively, vibrantly fruity La Volee Unoaked Chardonnay and a peachy, buttery, full-flavoured Barrique Fermented Chardonnay. La Cerise Merlot/Sangiovese is a good luncheon red — ruby-hued, light and cherryish.

Dark, with intense plum/spice flavours strongly seasoned with French oak and a firm underlay of tannin, the strikingly packaged Sangiovese is a powerful wine, designed for cellaring. Bold and youthful, it is much closer in style to the new breed of Tuscan reds, the barrique-aged Supertuscans, than the traditional, more mellow Chianti Classico riservas.

Address	Hyperion Wines, 188 Tongue Farm Road, Matakana
Owners	John and Jill Crone
Key Wines	Phoebe Pinot Gris, Helios Chardonnay, Eos Pinot Noir, Gaia Merlot, Kronos Cabernet/Merlot

Hyperion

■ 'I'd rather lose money in pursuit of a passion than be stuck with something more certain and boring,' says John Crone, a former computer consultant. Crone named his winery after the Greek sun god, Hyperion, whose mythological family also inspired the names given to the individual wines.

John and Jill Crone own two small blocks of vines in Matakana, covering a total of 2.5 hectares. Both the white, wooden Hyperion winery — a converted cowshed and the oldest winery in the district — and the vines adjacent to it, mostly planted in the late 1980s and early 1990s, once formed part of the original Antipodean property, in Tongue Farm Road. A second, slightly larger vineyard, planted in the mid-1990s, lies in Omaha Flats Road, near Providence. Cabernet Sauvignon is the major variety, with smaller plots of Merlot, Chardonnay, Pinot Gris, Pinot Noir and Malbec.

The wines, first produced in 1997, are all estate-grown and made by John Crone. Volumes are small, averaging about 1200 cases per year.

Phoebe Pinot Gris is a slightly sweet style, lemony, peachy and soft. Helios Chardonnay is peachy and toasty, with a strong oak influence.

One of the country's northernmost examples of the variety, Eos Pinot Noir is a light style, solid but not exciting. The Bordeaux-style reds are more convincing, including a berryish, earthy, moderately intense Kronos Cabernet/Merlot. Hyperion's flagship, however, is the supple, raspberry and plum-flavoured Gaia Merlot. The deliciously perfumed and rich 1998 vintage scooped the trophy for champion Merlot at the 2000 New Zealand Wine Society Royal Easter Show.

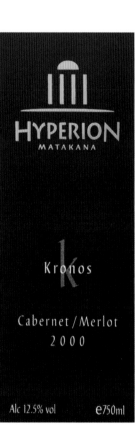

Matakana Estate

■ Not only is Matakana Estate the largest vineyard in the district; for quality across the range, it is one of the best — arguably *the* best.

Draped along north-facing clay slopes alongside the main road through the valley, Matakana Estate is a family affair, owned by Kevin Fitzgerald, his wife, Patricia (Pat) Vegar-Fitzgerald, and Pat's sons, Peter and Paul. The first vines were planted in 1996, and the first wine flowed two years later.

Winemaking is in Pat's blood. Her Croatian grandfather, Luka Lunjevich, made wine at Kaitaia from before the First World War until the mid-1960s, and Pat spent much of her childhood helping at Golden Vineyard. A row of vines at Matakana Estate — no longer producing — is descended from cuttings taken from her grandfather's vineyard.

Merlot, Cabernet Sauvignon and Chardonnay are the major varieties in the 16-hectare vineyard, with smaller plots of Pinot Gris, Cabernet Franc, Malbec, Syrah and Sémillon. A second local vineyard of equal size, Monarch Downs, managed by Matakana Estate on leased land, will yield its first crop in 2003.

Kevin Fitzgerald, a former dairy farmer and Catholic priest, heads the winemaking team, assisted by Ben Dugdale, formerly of Dry River and Coopers Creek. The average annual output is 4000 cases.

Right from the start, Matakana Estate's wines have been immaculate, with impressive concentration, complexity and finesse. The Chardonnay is sophisticated, with fresh, citrusy, mealy, biscuity flavours. Partly barrel-fermented, the Pinot Gris offers strong stone-fruit and spice flavours, fresh, finely balanced and long. The Sémillon, also partly handled in oak, is rounded and persistent, with fresh cut-grass, hay and nut aromas.

A Bordeaux-style red is high on the list of priorities. The Merlot/Cabernet Sauvignon/Franc/Malbec is spicy and cedary, with very good depth and the earthiness typical of Auckland reds. But the debut 1999 Syrah was even better, with smooth, rich flavours of blackcurrant, plum and pepper, hints of dark chocolate and herbs and impressive complexity.

The owners of Matakana Estate also produce a selection of wines under the Goldridge Estate brand. Wines labelled as Matakana Estate are all estate-grown at Matakana, whereas the Goldridge Estate range is based on grapes grown on contract in various regions. The Goldridge Estate range is sold through restaurants and wine shops but is not available for tasting or purchase at Matakana Estate.

Address Matakana Estate,
568 Matakana Road,
Matakana

Owners Kevin Fitzgerald,
Patricia Vegar-Fitzgerald,
Peter and Paul Vegar

Key Wines Sémillon, Pinot Gris,
Chardonnay, Syrah,
Merlot/Cabernet
Sauvignon/Franc/Malbec

Providence

■ Promoted overseas as 'the best Bordeaux-style wine outside France' and sold locally at $185, Providence is New Zealand's most expensive wine. Yet for a New Zealand wine that costs twice as much as any other, this classy Matakana red has an amazingly low profile here.

That doesn't bother Providence's owner, Auckland lawyer James Vuletic. New Zealand wine drinkers simply aren't high on his priority list. Instead, Vuletic makes crazily scheduled trips to Europe, Asia and the United States, where in blind tastings he frequently pits Providence against such brilliant Bordeaux as Château Petrus, the super-prestigious Pomerol, and Château Cheval Blanc, the great St Émilion.

The strategy obviously works, because Providence's profile is far higher in the United Kingdom. After a vertical tasting of the 1993 to 1998 vintages, *Decanter*, the influential British wine magazine, accurately summed up the Providence style as 'not thick, massive, awesome . . . [but] silky, succulent, flowing, graceful.'

After emigrating from Croatia, Vuletic's parents made wine on Auckland's North Shore; James grew up in a world of vines, barrels and corks. He and his brother, Petar, founded The Antipodean vineyard at Matakana in the late 1970s, but the partnership collapsed.

In 1990, James set up another vineyard on a steep, north-facing clay slope, a couple of kilometres from The Antipodean. Cabernet Sauvignon had not ripened easily at the first site, so Vuletic planted 2.5 hectares of Merlot (principally), Cabernet Franc and Malbec vines. The inspiration for The Antipodean had been the Cabernet Sauvignon-based Château Latour. Now, the model was the world's great Merlot wine — Petrus. (There is also a rarer, Cabernet Franc-based blend, called PR — Private Reserve.)

Cultivated without fertilisers and herbicides, the vines are close-planted and short-pruned, yielding only 4 tonnes of grapes per hectare. Fermentation is with natural yeasts and hand-plunging of the skins every four hours, and the wine is matured for up to two years in all-new French oak barriques.

Providence is clearly superior to those vintages of The Antipodean I have tasted. Vuletic wants a wine with 'fatness in the mouth, ripe, soft tannins and a presence that is all pleasure' — and hits the target with ease.

Just how good is Providence? There are no gold medals, because Vuletic doesn't enter it in competitions. 'To the people who'll pay the sort of money I'm asking, a medal would be irrelevant.'

Years ago, I tasted the first 1993 vintage blind with several top Auckland reds, including the Waiheke heavyweights. Fragrant, lush, silky and sustained, Providence held its own, but did not overshadow the field. The 1998 is also a stylish and seductive red that impresses not with sheer power, but perfume, harmony and subtlety. It's a world-class wine.

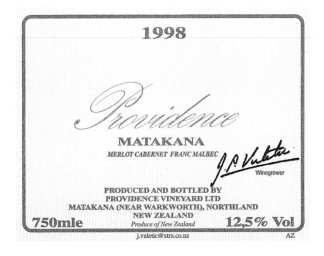

Address Providence Vineyard,
Cnr Omaha Flats Road and
Takatu Road,
Matakana

Owner James Vuletic

Key Wines Providence, PR

Address	Ransom Wines, Valerie Close, Warkworth
Owners	Robin and Marion Ransom
Key Wines	Clos de Valerie Pinot Gris, Gumfield Chardonnay, Barrique Fermented Chardonnay, Mahurangi Cabernet Sauvignon, Dark Summit Cabernet/Merlot

Ransom

■ In a district best known for red wines, Ransom stands out for its whites, with a pair of stylish Chardonnays and a classy Pinot Gris.

On the main highway south of Warkworth, in the Mahurangi district, the property was at first covered in kauri forest, then cleared for an orchard and in the 1920s converted into a dairy farm. The first vines were planted in 1993.

Proprietor Robin Ransom, who has an MA in sociology, was a social worker and alcohol counsellor, then founded and later sold a market research company. 'Had we appreciated back in 1992, when we conceived the improbable notion of growing grapes and making wine, just what was involved, we may have had second thoughts,' admits Ransom. He still works on a part-time basis for ACNielsen.

On north-facing clay slopes, the 6-hectare vineyard is planted principally in Pinot Gris, Cabernet Sauvignon and Chardonnay, supplemented by Cabernet Franc, Malbec and Merlot. The wines are all estate-grown.

The striking winery (winner of a New Zealand Institute of Architects award in 2001), has a gallery built with lots of glass, chunky timber columns and exposed steel beams, opening to a semi-walled, paved courtyard with an expansive view of the valley and vines.

The first vintage flowed in 1996. Once in full production, the vineyards are expected to yield about 3500 cases of wine. From the start, Robin Ransom made the red wines, but did not take over the white-wine reins until 2000.

An unabashed Cabernet Sauvignon fan, who is less enchanted with Merlot, Ransom makes a firm, sturdy Dark Summit Cabernet Sauvignon/Merlot, with strong, spicy, nutty, herbal flavours, and a solid but green-edged Mahurangi Cabernet Sauvignon, designed for earlier consumption.

Named after the road on which the vineyard lies, the Clos de Valerie Pinot Gris displays pure, incisive varietal characters, lemony, spicy and lingering. The gently wooded Gumfield Chardonnay is fresh and full-bodied, with good depth of citrusy, peachy flavours, and the Barrique Chardonnay is typically very rewarding, with rich, well-ripened fig/melon flavours and a deliciously creamy texture.

RANSOM
Clos de Valerie
Pinot Gris
2000

750 ml · 13% alc by vol

Grown and Produced by R & M Ransom
Valerie Close, Mahurangi, Auckland Region, New Zealand
PRODUCT OF NEW ZEALAND

Contains Preservative 220

Other producers

■ **The Antipodean**
This tiny Matakana winery, founded by brothers James and Petar Vuletic, in 1988 launched with tumultuous fanfare an attractive but extraordinarily overpriced ($93 per bottle) Cabernet Sauvignon/Merlot/Malbec 1985. However, after the brothers experienced 'a personal falling out', the company was wound up and in early 1990 all its wine stocks were sold by auction. Petar Vuletic emerged from the break-up with the majority of the vines and the right to the company's striking name. From the 1.8-hectare vineyard in Tongue Farm Road, Michelle Chignell-Vuletic and Petar Vuletic produce high-priced but rarely seen, low-profile wines. After tasting the 1990, 1992, 1994 and 1997 vintages, Nicholas Bryant praised The Antipodean in the *National Business Review* in mid-2001 as 'brilliant, in my opinion the best red wines made in this country'. Of The Antipodean's current annual output of 200 to 300 cases, most is exported, but the wine has recently retailed in Auckland in the $160–195 range.

■ **Mahurangi Estate**
Owned by a syndicate of 120 people, Mahurangi Estate is 'a kind of family and friends venture', says the company manager, Hamish McDonald, whose brother Rod is the winemaker at Vidal. 'Our family ambition was always to grow grapes and make wine. When we bought the land here, we had to extend the family involvement, and when Gimblett Road, Hawke's Bay land came up for sale, we took on even more shareholders.' In the 7-hectare estate vineyard in Hamilton Road, south-east of Warkworth, where planting began in 1997, the key varieties are Merlot, Malbec, Syrah, Cabernet Sauvignon and Chardonnay, with a small amount of Viognier. The Gimblett Road vineyard, first planted in 1999, is devoted to Merlot, Cabernet Sauvignon, Cabernet Franc and Malbec. The initial releases have included wines grown in several regions: Gisborne, Hawke's Bay, Marlborough, Nelson and even Chile. The first estate-grown wine from Mahurangi is expected to be a Bordeaux-style blended red from the 2002 vintage.

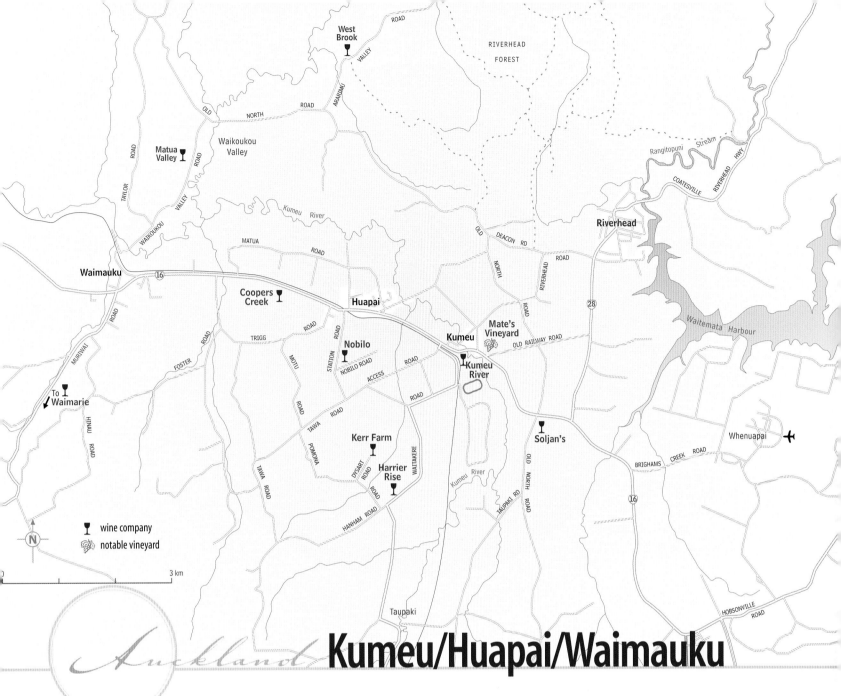

Kumeu/Huapai/Waimauku

Auckland

Scattered across the softly undulating countryside that cradles the west Auckland townships of Kumeu, Huapai and Waimauku are several quality-orientated wineries. The rebirth of interest in Auckland viticulture has been partly based here, with the district's distance from the Waitakere Ranges giving a lower rainfall than at Henderson. The signs of success are everywhere: in the impressive architecture of the wineries and, most importantly, in the wines themselves. Many are ranked among the country's best.

Kumeu-Huapai accounted for 19 per cent of all vine plantings in the Auckland province in 1960, but by 1975 the figure had soared past 50 per cent. Henderson winemakers of the 1960s, wishing to expand to meet increasing demand, faced a serious problem in the lack of inexpensive, reasonably large blocks of land in Henderson. Expansion soon shifted to the much cheaper Kumeu-Huapai area.

Corbans led the charge, buying land at Whenuapai, on the upper reaches of the Waitemata Harbour, in 1959. The heavy, fertile soils of its Riverlea Vineyard soon yielded one of the era's most highly acclaimed wines — Corbans Riverlea Riesling (a Müller-Thurgau, rather than a true Riesling).

Corbans later withdrew from the Kumeu-Huapai district, but Nobilo and Kumeu River have had a presence for well over half a century. Matua Valley and Coopers Creek are more recent arrivals who also chose to base their headquarters there. Several names have disappeared during the past 20 years — Abel & Co, Glenburn, Markovina, Bazzard, Selaks (swallowed by Nobilo) and Limeburners Bay — but new ventures have also sprung up, such as Harrier Rise, Kerr Farm, West Brook (transplanted from Henderson) and Waimarie.

It should be emphasised that the majority of the wines produced here are made from grapes grown in more southern regions, notably Gisborne, Hawke's Bay and Marlborough. However, Kumeu River and Harrier Rise wines are produced exclusively from local fruit.

Rationalisation has been underway in the vineyards as the winemakers single out the grape varieties most adaptable to the region's warm, humid summers and clay loam soils,

which once supported podocarp forest. These are old, leached soils that Harrier Rise reports need the addition of lime and trace elements every three or four years to keep the vines in good heart. In the Kumeu River, Coopers Creek and Matua Valley vineyards, Chardonnay is now by far the most widely planted white-wine variety, and the earlier-ripening Merlot has replaced Cabernet Sauvignon as the principal red. There are also pockets of Pinot Gris, Viognier, Sauvignon Blanc and Pinot Noir.

Winemakers have also been experimenting with new and healthier clones of existing varieties, use of devigorating rootstocks, 'grassing down' to reduce waterlogging of the soil, improved trellising techniques and other methods to upgrade their fruit quality.

While studying winemaking in Australia 20 years ago, Michael Brajkovich of Kumeu River began to worry about the local conditions for grapegrowing. 'I thought that Auckland had a number of problems, including the rain and very fertile soils,' he recalls, 'and that we would have to move or get our grapes from somewhere else. [Instead] we decided to get better varieties and rootstocks, try to eliminate viruses and give the grapes a chance here.' At Kumeu River, adoption of the lyre trellising system proved highly successful. This method enhances ripening and reduces disease problems by dividing the vines' canopies, allowing greater penetration of light and air.

The result of such innovation in the district has been some outstanding wines, with Kumeu River's Kumeu and Mate's Vineyard Chardonnays, and Collards Rothesay Chardonnay the most eye-catching successes.

Address	Coopers Creek Vineyard, 601 State Highway 16, Huapai
Owners	Andrew and Cyndy Hendry
Key Wines	Marlborough Sauvignon Blanc, Reserve Marlborough Sauvignon Blanc, Gisborne Unoaked Chardonnay, Hawke's Bay Chardonnay, Swamp Reserve Chardonnay, Hawke's Bay Riesling, Hawke's Bay Merlot, Hawke's Bay Cabernet Sauvignon/Franc

Coopers Creek

■ This medium-sized winery has lately been on a highly publicised roller-coaster ride. The star of the 1995 Liquorland Royal Easter Wine Show was undoubtedly Coopers Creek, which scored seven gold medals and four trophies, for champion Riesling, Cabernet/Merlot, medium-priced red and high-priced red.

In 1998, however, the company's reputation suffered a severe blow when several wines from the 1996 and earlier vintages were found by an independent auditor to be 'not true to label', containing illegally low percentages of varieties specified on the labels. And since the late 1990s departure of its long-term, high-profile winemaker, Kim Crawford, the flow of awards has been less dramatic.

The pink, Roman basilica-style building housing Coopers Creek's sales, administration and hospitality centre squats alongside the highway just west of Huapai township. Visitors can wander through extensive gardens, with ponds, a pétanque court and open, wood-fired barbecues.

The company was founded by Andrew Hendry, a Wanganui-born accountant with a laid-back manner and ready wit, and Randy Weaver, a highly qualified Oregonian winemaker; these two first worked together at Penfolds in Henderson during the late 1970s. The winery's first vintage was in 1982. The original partnership was dissolved six

From its estate vineyard at Huapai, Coopers Creek produces The Gardener, a Merlot-based red dedicated to the company's viticulturalist, Wayne Morrow.

years later, however, when Weaver returned to the United States, leaving Hendry and his wife, Cyndy, as the principal shareholders in Coopers Creek.

Winemaker Simon Nunns, who joined Coopers Creek in 1997 and was previously an assistant winemaker at Villa Maria, works with fruit drawn from four regions. The 6-hectare estate vineyard is planted in Merlot and Chardonnay (principally), with a small block of Pinot Gris. In Hawke's Bay, the company's 6-hectare Middle Road No. 1 vineyard at Havelock North is planted mainly in Chardonnay; the adjacent, smaller Middle Road No. 2 site, on a steep hillside, is being planted in Syrah. At a fourth, 10-hectare vineyard at Roys Hill, also in Hawke's Bay, Merlot is the most important variety, with some Cabernet Franc and Malbec. Ninety per cent of the winery's grape intake is drawn from growers in Gisborne, Hawke's Bay and Marlborough.

With an annual output of 60,000 cases, Coopers Creek's wines are widely available. The Hawke's Bay Riesling is an intensely aromatic, vibrantly fruity, penetratingly flavoured wine that in most vintages ranks at the forefront of the region's Rieslings. Why is Coopers Creek's so successful?

'It's partly the site,' says Hendry. 'The grapes are grown in Jim Scotland's vineyard at Clive. Good air movement close to the sea reduces the risk of disease, allowing us to hang the fruit out late. The grapes don't get wildly ripe, but they build up intense flavours. And we leave part of the block unsprayed to encourage botrytis.'

In the past labelled as Coopers Dry, the East Coast Sémillon/Chardonnay is a decent quaffer, crisp, lively and slightly grassy. The Marlborough Sauvignon Blanc is consistently good and sharply priced. Made from the pick of the fruit and partly wood-fermented, the Reserve Marlborough Sauvignon Blanc offers rich tropical-fruit flavours, with a subtle seasoning of oak.

The quintet of Chardonnays features a very easy-drinking, slightly buttery Fat Cat Chardonnay; a simple but fresh and vibrant Gisborne Unoaked Chardonnay; a Hawke's Bay Chardonnay that marries sweet, ripe fruit with sweet American oak in a very upfront style, delicious in its youth; a powerful SV (Single Vineyard) Chardonnay, minerally, toasty and complex; and the flagship Swamp Reserve Chardonnay, a French oak-fermented Hawke's Bay wine, beautifully rich, ripe and soft.

The reds include a middleweight, berryish and plummy Hawke's Bay Merlot; a blackcurrant-flavoured, slightly leafy Hawke's Bay Cabernet Sauvignon/Franc; and a spicy, plummy, firm, American oak-aged Huapai Merlot, labelled The Gardener.

Harrier Rise

■ Lawyers are often attracted to the wine industry, usually as ardent imbibers, but also as winery owners. Tim Harris, a lawyer and part-time wine writer turned full-time winemaker, produces some of New Zealand's most Bordeaux-like, yet least-heralded, reds. Harris and several partners bought a 6-hectare block in softly undulating country at Kumeu in 1986, and over the next four years close-planted it in Cabernet Franc, Merlot and Cabernet Sauvignon. The first wine flowed in 1991. After the syndicate disbanded in 1996, Harris emerged as the sole owner.

The main vineyard, which inclines gently to a stream on the northern boundary, is planted in a Pomerol-like mix of Merlot (2.5 hectares), Cabernet Franc (1.8 hectares) and Cabernet Sauvignon (0.4 hectares). A second, leased vineyard nearby is established in 2 hectares of Cabernet Sauvignon. The annual production of wine from these sites averages 3500 cases.

From the start, Harrier Rise Vineyard (until 1997 called Waitakere Road Vineyard) has specialised in red wines. Less overtly fruity, more harmonious, subtle and complex than many New Zealand reds, they are also more downright drinkable.

What is the key to Harris' distinctive, distinctly European red-wine style? 'If you read French winemaking books, it's striking how for generations they've thought about their wine's structure and how best to extract colour and tannins from the skins,' he says. 'The length of time the wine spends on its skins is crucial.'

Harris favours a very long period of skin contact — up to seven weeks. 'The wine starts off with an obvious fruitiness and floral characters, resembling raspberries, then develops hints of coffee. Then it becomes a lot gamier and you get distinctly organic pongs, veering towards silage. But you're looking for structure, and if you keep your nerve you end up with a red with marvellous depth of fine tannins.'

In Harris' eyes, Kumeu is Merlot country: 'It's the first variety to ripen, two weeks before Cabernet Franc and three weeks ahead of Cabernet Sauvignon.' His best known wine, Uppercase Merlot, is always full of character — spicy, earthy and savoury, with moderately firm tannins. Only produced in top vintages, Bigney Coigne Merlot is a generous wine with sweet fruit characters and a greater new-oak influence.

The blackcurrant and spice-flavoured Cabernet Franc shows good depth and complexity. Monza Cabernets is even better — a very stylish, Cabernet Franc-based wine with rich, berryish fruit flavours and firm yet supple tannins.

Address	Harrier Rise Vineyard, 748 Waitakere Road, Kumeu
Owner	Tim Harris
Key Wines	Bigney Coigne Merlot, Cabernet Franc, Monza Cabernets, Uppercase Merlot

Address	Kumeu River Wines,
	550 State Highway 16,
	Kumeu
Owners	The Brajkovich family
Key Wines	Kumeu River Chardonnay,
	Mate's Vineyard Chardonnay,
	Pinot Gris, Pinot Noir, Melba;
	Brajkovich Chardonnay,
	Merlot

Kumeu River

■ Kumeu River's rise to international acclaim in the past 15 years has been founded on its rich, savoury, gloriously full-flavoured Chardonnay. No other white wine grown in the Auckland region enjoys the same status, and few others throughout the country.

The winery lies on the main highway, just south of Kumeu. Early Croatian settlers tended vines on the property for several decades before the Brajkovichs' arrival. When 19-year-old, Dalmatian-born Mate Brajkovich and his parents, Mick and Baba Kate, bought the property in 1944, along with 7 hectares of pasture, they acquired a fermenting vat, barrels and a half-hectare of Isabella and Albany Surprise vines. Under its early name, San Marino, it was one of the first wineries to establish such varieties as Chardonnay and Pinotage, and also enjoyed an early reputation for hybrid quaffing wines, especially its Kumeu Red Dry. The strong impact of San Marino on the Auckland wine scene of the 1950s and 1960s owed much to the Brajkovichs' legendary hospitality.

Winemaking at Kumeu River is still largely a family affair. The charismatic Mate died in 1992 but his widow, Melba, is the financial controller; their eldest son, Michael, controls the winemaking; another son, Milan, oversees the vineyards; and the youngest son, Paul, handles the marketing.

The wines are made exclusively from 39 hectares of Kumeu vineyards, two-thirds company-owned. Nineteen hectares are devoted to Chardonnay, followed by Merlot (9 hectares), Pinot Noir (6 hectares), Pinot Gris (4 hectares) and Malbec (1 hectare). The flagship Mate's Vineyard Chardonnay is produced from the finest grapes harvested from Mate's Vineyard, replanted in Chardonnay in 1990 on the site of the original block. The winery, with its average annual output of 20,000 cases, in reality is much larger than it looks from the front. Should you step through the rear of the vineyard shop, you will be standing in the original concrete-walled winery erected by Mate in the early 1950s.

The range is marketed under two labels: Kumeu River (the premium range), and Brajkovich (for everyday quaffing). New Zealand absorbs much of the winery's output, with the United Kingdom and the United States the two major export markets.

Three Chardonnays are produced. The most famous is Kumeu River Chardonnay, based on fruit grown in several local vineyards, which Michael Brajkovich likens, in Burgundian terms, to 'a village wine'. Grown on the lyre trellising system, which helps to control the vines' vigour and increase bunch exposure to the sun, it is hand-harvested and whole-bunch pressed, fermented with indigenous yeasts and lees-aged in French oak barriques (20–25 per cent new), usually given a full malolactic fermentation, and barrel-matured for a year. One of the great New Zealand Chardonnays, with seamless, persistent flavour and a beguiling creaminess of texture, it typically offers splendid drinking at around three years old.

Mate's Vineyard Chardonnay, likened by Brajkovich to 'a premier cru of the same village', shows a stronger new-oak influence and is more powerful, concentrated and opulent. The lower-tier wine, Brajkovich Chardonnay, usually fermented in a mix of tanks and barrels, is a weighty, moderately complex wine with good depth of sweet, ripe citrus/melon flavours.

Two relative newcomers to the Kumeu River range are a weighty, melon and lychee-flavoured Pinot Gris, not oak-aged; and a firm, cherryish, earthy Pinot Noir, substantial and complex. The other reds include a spicy, berryish Brajkovich Merlot, and Melba, a blend of Merlot (principally) and Malbec, which has the blackcurrant and spice flavours and firm tannin backbone of claret.

From Michael Brajkovich's house, split-canopy vines, netted to guard against feathered vandals, flow down a Kumeu slope.

Michael Brajkovich

■ **More than any other individual, Michael Brajkovich through his outstanding Chardonnays has resurrected west Auckland's reputation as a quality wine region.**

Brajkovich is a quiet, handsome man with a towering physical presence. After training with distinction at Roseworthy College, South Australia, he returned to his family vineyard before spending the 1983 vintage at Château Magdelaine, a leading premier grand cru of St Émilion. Here he developed not only a behind-the-scenes appreciation of Bordeaux winemaking techniques, but also, he says, the conviction that a small-scale New Zealand winery had more to learn from the French about handcrafting wines of individuality and finesse than from the Australians or Californians.

'Despite its obvious climatic differences, New Zealand has derived most of its winemaking technology and skills from the warmer areas of the New World, for no more logical reason than that we speak English,' says Brajkovich. 'On reflection, it probably would have made much more sense to study and adapt the practices of a climatically similar region, such as one of the cooler regions of France.'

In Brajkovich's view, the Chardonnay-based white wines of Burgundy are 'at the summit of white-wine quality in the world.... At Kumeu River, we have taken the best of the techniques that have evolved over time in the production of white Burgundy, and adapted them to our own situation.'

From the start he was convinced that Kumeu could produce grapes of outstanding quality. Brajkovich points to how planting on hill sites improves drainage; to the merits of 'grassing down' between the rows as a way to reduce waterlogging of the soils; to the enhanced fruit ripeness achieved using the lyre trellising system; and to the superior method of fruit selection with hand-harvesting.

The launch of the first Kumeu River Chardonnay caused a major stir. As Brajkovich has written: 'In 1985 Kumeu River produced a Chardonnay that underwent a total malolactic fermentation, to the surprise of many, and certainly to the disgust of the wine judges who relegated it to the no-award level. The style was totally foreign to that of previous New Zealand Chardonnays; it was the style of Burgundy, and unfortunately incorrectly diagnosed as being faulty. Fortunately those people who drink wine for its enjoyment really appreciated the depth, richness and smoothness of this Chardonnay.' The 1987 vintage, which earned accolades in England and the United States, became Kumeu River's first internationally successful wine.

Michael Brajkovich in 1989 became the first New Zealander to succeed in the famously rigorous Master of Wine examination. After winning the right to add the letters M.W. after his name, he recalls: 'I went from being a bit eccentric to being credible.'

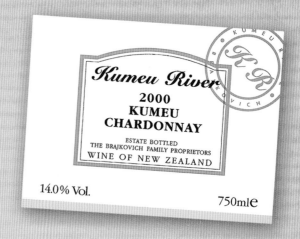

Winemakers of distinction

SHINGLE PEAK

MARLBOROUGH
SAUVIGNON BLANC
2001

PRODUCE OF NEW ZEALAND

Address   Matua Valley Wines,
Waikoukou Valley Road,
Waimauku

Owner   Beringer Blass Wine Estates
(majority)

Key Wines   Matua Valley Ararimu
Chardonnay, Ararimu
Merlot/Cabernet Sauvignon,
Judd Estate Chardonnay,
Eastern Bays Chardonnay,
Matheson Chardonnay,
Hawke's Bay Sauvignon
Blanc, Matheson Sauvignon
Blanc, Hawke's Bay Cabernet
Sauvignon/Merlot, Smith-
Dartmoor Merlot, Matheson
Cabernet/Merlot; Shingle
Peak Riesling, Sauvignon
Blanc, Chardonnay

Matua Valley

■ Matua Valley's handsome, octagonal winery sits on a knoll in the secluded Waikoukou Valley, just a few bends and a climb in the road from Waimauku. One of the modern wine industry's greatest success stories, ranking among the country's six largest producers, it was recently bought by the Australian-based wine giant, Beringer Blass.

Matua, as it is often called (it was named after the original vineyard in Matua Road, Huapai), was established by the Spence brothers, Ross and Bill. They have winemaking in their blood: a grandfather emigrated from Croatia and their father Rod Spence founded Spence's Wines in McLeod Road, Henderson, in the 1940s.

Matua Valley began in a humble, leased tin shed near Henderson, with the Spences holding down full-time jobs elsewhere and producing their wine — including, in 1974, the country's first Sauvignon Blanc — in the evenings and at weekends. The tin shed lasted from 1974 until 1978, when the present vertical-timbered winery at Waimauku was constructed. Right from the start, the wines proved popular. 'People said it's because we produced good wines at a reasonable price,' recalls Ross Spence. 'And Bill and I were accepted as personalities by the trade. People liked to sell "Ross' or Bill's Chardonnay" — that's been very important.'

From the start, members of the Margan family also had a substantial shareholding, and played a key role in decision making at board level. After the Margan family chose to sell their stake, Beringer Blass, the wine arm of Foster's Brewing Group, acquired a 51 per cent shareholding in 2001 for an outlay of $NZ11.2 million. The Spence brothers agreed to stay on until 2004, when Beringer Blass (excited about the potential for exporting Sauvignon Blanc and Pinot Noir to the United States) will complete its takeover. To swiftly boost Matua Valley's exports, in 2002 Beringer Blass purchased two Marlborough producers, Hawkesbridge and Ponder Estate.

In the 17-hectare, undulating estate vineyard, planted on sandy loam soils, Chardonnay and Merlot are the principal varieties. Matua Valley also owns substantial vineyards in Gisborne (32 hectares of mainly Chardonnay, Sémillon and Pinotage); Hawke's Bay (63 hectares of Cabernet Sauvignon, Merlot, Sauvignon Blanc and Chardonnay); and Marlborough (14 hectares of Sauvignon Blanc, Chardonnay and Pinot Gris). Contract grape-growers are also a major source of supply.

About 160,000 cases per year flow from the company's two wineries. The west Auckland winery is the main processing and bottling plant for North Island grapes, while Marlborough wines are produced at the joint venture Rapaura Vintners winery and then freighted to Auckland for bottling.

Mark Robertson, an Otago University science graduate who later spent a year studying at Roseworthy College in South Australia, is in charge of the winemaking. Robertson worked at Nobilo in 1983, in the London wine trade in the mid-1980s, and as an Auckland wine waiter, before joining Matua Valley in 1987. 'Our goal is to produce "food" wines that are fruit-driven and not aggressive in flavour,' says Robertson.

Matua Valley's reputation has spread far beyond its headquarters at Waimauku, encircled by Chardonnay and Merlot vines.

The wines are grouped in five ranges. At the top are the flagship Ararimu wines, followed by experimental Innovator Series wines, single-vineyard wines such as Judd Estate and Matheson, and large volume regional/varietal wines, such as Hawke's Bay Sauvignon Blanc. North Island wines are marketed as Matua Valley, but the Marlborough-grown wines are separately branded as Shingle Peak.

Made only in top years, the Ararimu selection includes a strikingly concentrated, softly textured and beautifully harmonious Chardonnay, based on low-cropping vines in the Judd Estate at Gisborne, and a powerful, brambly, nutty Hawke's Bay Merlot/Cabernet Sauvignon. The single-vineyard wines can offer outstanding value. The popular Judd Estate Chardonnay, fermented in French and American oak barriques, is a softly mouthfilling wine with rich peachy, citrusy flavours and good complexity. The Matheson trio from Hawke's Bay includes a full-bodied, creamy-smooth Chardonnay, a sturdy, flavoursome Cabernet/Merlot, and an often outstanding Sauvignon Blanc, with deep, ripe tropical-fruit flavours and a subtle seasoning of oak.

The moderately priced range of regional/varietal wines features a fresh, fruit-driven Eastern Bays Chardonnay, blended from Gisborne and Hawke's Bay grapes, an easy-drinking, melon/lime-flavoured Hawke's Bay Sauvignon Blanc, and a perfumed, freeze-concentrated Late Harvest Muscat from Gisborne with sweet, orangey flavours.

The Shingle Peak Chardonnay, Sauvignon Blanc and Riesling, grown in Marlborough, have all been winners with their lively, incisive flavours. The newest additions to the range are a crisp, spicy, medium-dry Pinot Gris and a moderately complex but fresh, mouthfilling and supple Pinot Noir.

Nobilo

■ Sixty years after Nikola Nobilo, a Croatian immigrant from the island of Korcula, in Dalmatia, planted his first vines at Huapai, Nobilo ranks among the country's largest wine companies. After many shareholder changes, it is now part of the Australian-based BRL Hardy empire.

During the 1960s, Nobilo's best-known wines were Dry White, Dry Red, Rosé and Sauternes. Thereafter, with the help of several investors — initially Gilbey's of England in 1966, and later Nathans, the PSIS, and the Development Finance Corporation — Nobilo grew rapidly, building a strong reputation based on quality reds (Pinotage, Cabernet Sauvignon and Pinot Noir) and its immensely popular, slightly sweet Müller-Thurgau.

The 1985–86 wine price war caused the company severe financial problems, but soon after the Nobilo family uprooted most of its Huapai vines, sold the land, bought out its partners and regained full control. After almost a decade as New Zealand's largest family-owned winery, in 1995 Nobilo sold a 49 per cent stake to a publicly listed investment company, Direct Capital Limited.

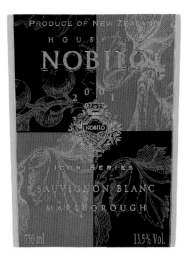

The year 1998 proved pivotal for the company. Firstly, Nobilo bought another long-established Kumeu wine company, Selaks, acquiring not only Selaks' extensive vineyards and gleaming new winery in Marlborough, but also the Selaks brands (better entrenched than Nobilo's in the premium wine market). Soon after, a new company, Nobilo Wines Limited, was formed, incorporating Nobilo Vintners, Selaks Wines and National Liquor Distributors, with BRL Hardy taking a 28.5 per cent shareholding.

BRL Hardy upped its stake in the publicly listed Nobilo Wines Limited in May 2000 to 40 per cent. When a month later the Nobilo family swapped its 29 per cent stake in Nobilo for shares in BRL Hardy, the Australian company gained effective control of Nobilo Wines (since renamed the Nobilo Wine Group). Of the three Nobilo brothers who had run the company for several decades — Nick, firstly as winemaker and later as chief executive, Steve as marketing manager and Mark — only Mark remains, in the role of chief viticulturist.

The 5-hectare estate vineyard at Huapai is planted primarily in Pinotage. Nobilo also has large joint-venture vineyards with Maori trusts on the east coast of the North Island, and is currently planting Merlot, Cabernet Sauvignon, Malbec and Syrah in Hawke's Bay.

In Marlborough, the 16-hectare Drylands Estate is established in Sauvignon Blanc vines (planted in 1980–81) and Chardonnay. Two other vineyards in the Wairau Valley, totalling 124 hectares, have been established in Sauvignon Blanc, Pinot Gris, Gewürztraminer and Pinot Noir. In the Awatere Valley, the 100-hectare Castle Cliffs vineyard was planted in 2002 in Pinot Noir and Sauvignon Blanc. Over half the total fruit intake is supplied by contract growers in Auckland, Gisborne, Hawke's Bay, Nelson and Marlborough.

In its own words, BRL Hardy is providing Nobilo with 'technical assistance, resources and a comprehensive distribution network for international sales'. In a major expansion move, designed to achieve a four-fold increase in production and boost the value of its exports from $20 million to $50 million, between 2001 and 2005 BRL Hardy will pour $30 to $40 million into Nobilo. Around 1000 hectares of bare land and established vineyards are being purchased in Hawke's Bay and Marlborough.

At the two wineries, at Huapai and Marlborough, operations are headed by

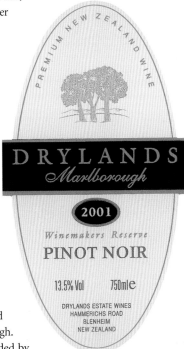

Address	Nobilo Wine Group, 45 Station Road, Huapai
Owner	Nobilo Wine Group
Key Wines	Nobilo Marlborough Sauvignon Blanc, Poverty Bay Chardonnay, Icon Marlborough Sauvignon Blanc, Icon Chardonnay, Fall Harvest Sauvignon Blanc; Selaks Premium Selection Marlborough Sauvignon Blanc, Premium Selection Marlborough Chardonnay, Founders Reserve Oak Aged Sauvignon Blanc, Founders Reserve Chardonnay; Drylands Marlborough Sauvignon Blanc, Drylands Marlborough Chardonnay; White Cloud Medium White, Sparkling, Sauvignon Blanc, Chardonnay

After decades of shareholding changes and acquisitions, Nobilo is now controlled by the Australian-based wine giant, BRL Hardy.

Darryl Woolley, formerly of Selaks, who is now Nobilo Wine Group's general manager of winemaking and viticulture. With the company's output projected to rise from 315,000 cases in 2001 to over one million cases by 2005, Woolley will have his hands full.

At the Drylands winery in Marlborough, the keynote is flexibility, says Woolley. 'We built tank sizes from 5000 to 25,000 litres, rather than concentrate on a small selection of very large tanks. It gives us a lot of flexibility in how we handle the grapes and how we fractionate the juices, searching for the very best wines out of each block.'

Nobilo is not strongly represented at the highest end of the market, but is a fierce competitor in the mid-price and everyday-drinking segments. The internationally popular White Cloud, a light, fresh, slightly sweet blend of Müller-Thurgau (principally), Sauvignon Blanc and Muscat, was inspired by the famous German liebfraumilch, Blue Nun. Numerous other easy-drinking, low-priced white and red wines (not always grown in New Zealand) are sold under the Fall Harvest, Fernleaf and (recently extended) White Cloud brands.

The middle-tier varietal wines under the Nobilo brand include a smooth, ripe, melon/lime-flavoured Marlborough Sauvignon Blanc that offers great drinkability; a lightly oaked Poverty Bay Chardonnay with fresh, strong, citrusy flavours; and a smooth, blackcurrant and green-leaf-flavoured Marlborough Merlot.

The Icon series (based on 'the best possible grapes from the best-performing vineyards') features a lush, richly varietal Marlborough Sauvignon Blanc and a moderately complex, slightly buttery and toasty Chardonnay, over the years blended from various regions. Two single-vineyard wines stand apart — the partly barrel-fermented, typically stylish Tietjen Vineyard Chardonnay, from Gisborne; and the company's top Gisborne wine, Dixon Estate Chardonnay, at its best strikingly fragrant and full-flavoured. The highlights of Selaks' commercial range, labelled Premium Selection, are an aromatic and zingy Marlborough Sauvignon Blanc; a fruit-driven, slightly creamy Marlborough Chardonnay; a floral, crisp Marlborough Riesling; and a freeze-concentrated, light, sweet and lemony Ice Wine. These are moderately priced wines, offering consistently good value.

Selaks Founders Reserve range features a distinctly oaky Marlborough Sauvignon Blanc with rich, ripe tropical-fruit flavours; a peachy, toasty, buttery North Island Chardonnay; and a good, but so far not outstanding, Merlot.

The middle–upper tier Drylands range (originally sold under the Selaks label) has been a deserved success, with an intensely aromatic, penetratingly flavoured Marlborough Sauvignon Blanc and a French and American oak-fermented Chardonnay, rich, vibrant and deliciously smooth.

Soljans

■ After over 60 years in Lincoln Road, Henderson, in mid-2002 Soljans shifted to a new site on the main highway, just south of Kumeu. 'We're looking to the future,' says Tony Soljan, the proprietor. 'To grow, we needed to extend our winery, but Lincoln Road has lost its former image as a wine-producing area. So we thought: Let's move.'

Soljans, traditionally one of the best small Henderson fortified winemakers, has more recently branched out with a sound line-up of white and red varietal table wines. Frank Soljan, Tony's father, bought the original site in 1937 and with his wife, Rona, planted the first vines in 1939. Tony's brother, Rex, maintained the vineyard and its adjacent orchard for many years, but in 1994 withdrew from the company (his son, Darryl, now runs the Ascension winery (see page 65) at Matakana).

At the new property in Kumeu, Soljans is establishing a winery and café, and planting Merlot, Cabernet Franc and Pinotage vines for its future flagship reds. Grapes are bought from growers in several regions: Auckland, Gisborne, Hawke's Bay and Marlborough. The company currently produces about 15,000 cases of wine, of which over half is exported. Matt Ussher, who has worked in Australia, France, Chile and Argentina, took over the winemaking reins in 2001.

In the sheltered barbecue garden at its Henderson winery, a tranquil resting place in the midst of lawns, apple trees and overhead-trellised vines, thousands of visitors each year devoured succulent spit-roasted lamb — washed down, of course, with Soljans' rock-solid wines. At his new property, Tony Soljan plans to keep the tradition alive, catering for functions and staging events to pull in the crowds.

The top wines, grown in Hawke's Bay and labelled Barrique Reserve, include a peachy, mealy, French oak-fermented Chardonnay and a solid but not intense, fresh, plummy Barrique Reserve Merlot.

My favourite is the Auckland Pinotage, for which Soljans has a strong reputation. Savoury, spicy and smooth, it's a gently oaked, characterful wine that drinks well in its youth and is sharply priced.

Soljans makes two bubblies of contrasting styles. Legacy, a fairly complex, bottle-fermented blend of Chardonnay and Pinot Noir, grown in Marlborough and Auckland, is a dryish style with citrusy, slightly toasty flavours and good acid backbone. The seductively sweet Fusion, an Asti Spumante look-alike made from Muscat grown in Hawke's Bay, is charmingly light, grapey and perfumed.

If you are a port lover, try the 10-year-old Founders Tawny — raisiny, sweet and mellow.

Address   Soljans Wines, State Highway 16, Kumeu

Owners   The Soljan family

Key Wines   Barrique Reserve Chardonnay, Merlot; Hawke's Bay Chardonnay, Marlborough Riesling, Lynham Vineyard Sauvignon Blanc, Marlborough Sauvignon Blanc, Gisborne Gewürztraminer, Auckland Pinotage, Hawke's Bay Cabernet/Merlot; Legacy; Founders 10 Year Old Tawny

Address	West Brook Winery, 215 Ararimu Valley Road, Waimauku
Owners	Anthony and Sue Ivicevich
Key Wines	Blue Ridge Marlborough Chardonnay, Blue Ridge Marlborough Sauvignon Blanc, Barrique Fermented Chardonnay, Marlborough Sauvignon Blanc, Marlborough Riesling, Blue Ridge Cabernet Sauvignon

West Brook

■ 'The quiet achievers' is how West Brook once described itself on its winery brochure. A recent arrival in the district, yet with a long winemaking history, it produces good, often outstanding white wines, especially Sauvignon Blanc and Chardonnay.

Tony Ivicevich and his father Mick arrived in New Zealand from their native Croatia in 1934. After only one year, the original property in Awaroa Road, Henderson, had been purchased and planted in trees and grapevines. By 1937 the first port and sherry were on the market, sold for one shilling and sixpence in beer bottles without labels.

After decades of focusing on fortified wines, in the mid-1980s Tony's son, Anthony, and his wife, Sue, took over the reins and switched the emphasis to table wines (their son, Michael, is currently chief winemaker at Delegat's). To symbolise the start of a new era, the winery name was changed from Panorama to West Brook.

Overwhelmed by urban sprawl, in late 1999 the company shifted to the Ararimu Valley in Waimauku, just in time for the first vintage of the new millennium. The 8-hectare estate vineyard, being planted in Merlot, Malbec and Chardonnay, will in future be the source of West Brook's 'ultra-premium' wines. Over 80 per cent of the fruit intake is supplied by growers, especially Charles Wiffen in Marlborough.

In the smart new terracotta winery, producing over 15,000 cases per year, the top-tier wines are labelled Blue Ridge. Of West Brook's wines on sale recently, all those from the 2000 and 2001 vintages had won a silver or gold medal.

The Blue Ridge Marlborough Sauvignon Blanc offers passionfruit and lime characters in a lush, very non-herbaceous style, scented and rich. The 'standard' Sauvignon Blanc is also deliciously ripe, zesty and aromatic.

The Blue Ridge Marlborough Chardonnay and the Barrique Fermented Chardonnay, based on Hawke's Bay grapes, are both finely crafted wines with strong, citrusy, biscuity flavours and a seductively smooth finish.

The range also includes a scented, piercingly flavoured Marlborough Riesling and a decent but not distinguished Blue Ridge Cabernet Sauvignon-based red, grown in Hawke's Bay.

Other producers

■ Kerr Farm Vineyard

After buying an old, 10-hectare Corbans vineyard in Dysart Lane, Kumeu, in 1989, Wendy and Jaison Kerr replaced the hybrid vines with Sauvignon Blanc and Cabernet Sauvignon, and expanded the existing plantings of Pinotage, Sémillon and Chardonnay. Chardonnay grapes have also been purchased from Hawke's Bay. The wines — launched from the 1995 vintage and made on the Kerrs' behalf at a west Auckland winery — have generally been of solid, rather than memorable, quality. Highlights are the plummy, spicy, slightly gamey Pinotage, at its best full of character; and the lightly oaked Sémillon, which displays grass and hay aromas and a touch of nutty complexity.

■ Waimarie Wines

Determined to 'carry on the torch', Nicholas and Stephen Nobilo are third-generation members of the famous winemaking family; their father, Steve, was for decades marketing manager of the Nobilo winery, now owned by BRL Hardy. Founded in 2000, Waimarie ('peaceful waters') is based in Muriwai Valley Road, at Waimauku, on the northern flanks of the Waitakere Ranges. The 3-hectare estate vineyard, on a north-west-facing slope, is planted principally in red Bordeaux varieties — Cabernet Sauvignon, Merlot, Cabernet Franc, Malbec and Petit Verdot — together with Chardonnay, Pinot Gris, Pinot Noir and Tannat. Grapes are also purchased from growers, and the wine is made at the Matariki winery in Hawke's Bay. The first release was a peachy-ripe, toasty, strongly oaked Gimblett Road Chardonnay 2000 and a dark, concentrated, Cabernet Sauvignon-based red from Kumeu, labelled Testament 2000.

Henderson

In the shadow of the Waitakere Ranges at Henderson, 20 kilometres west of Auckland city, are grouped several of the oldest wineries in the country. Strung out along Lincoln Road and Henderson Valley Road, and nestled in the surrounding hills, all (following the closure of the long-dominant Corbans winery) are small or medium-sized. The oldest, Pleasant Valley, produced its first wine in 1902 from vines planted in the nineteenth century.

Here a flourishing Croatian community has imprinted its energetic, wine-loving way of life on the district. Although winemaking in New Zealand is no longer a Croatian preserve, here, numerically at least, they still prevail. Such winery names as Babich, Soljans and Mazuran's have a distinctively Croatian ring. Generally, these vineyards of Croatian background began life as small mixed holdings of fruit trees, vines and vegetables. Croatian settlers who had lived on peasant farms in Dalmatia typically saved funds on the northern gumfields and then looked for self-sufficiency. Cheap parcels of land were available for purchase in the Henderson-Oratia area and the large Auckland market beckoned.

Since 1960 these holdings have shifted towards specialisation in market gardening, orcharding or winemaking. Also there has been a gradual shift of vine plantings away from Henderson itself. Back in 1960, 80 per cent of Auckland's vineyards and orchards were in Henderson and Oratia. Later, the north-western motorway opened west Auckland up to the pressures of urban expansion and reduced the land available for viticulture.

Henderson suffers from serious physical and climatic handicaps for grapegrowing, although no shortage of heat. In a sheltered inland valley alongside the rainy Waitakere Ranges, with relatively high day temperatures and cold, more frost-prone nights, it is a star of the Auckland weather charts. The rainfall — which rises steeply from the city westwards to the Waitakeres —

is far from ideal for viticulture. The plentiful rains, in association with high humidity, create ideal conditions for fungal diseases, especially during the critical February–April ripening period. The heavy clay soils drain poorly and are slow to warm up in spring.

Only Babich, St Jerome and Pleasant Valley now have substantial vineyards at Henderson. Some wineries, often for cosmetic reasons, retain a small plot of vines, and others — surrounded by a sea of houses and factories — have none at all. As Joe Babich says, 'It's so much easier to produce similar quality fruit in Hawke's Bay or Marlborough.'

The past 20 years have been notable for the closure of the large Penfolds and Corbans wineries, the demise of smaller companies such as Bellamour (once called Balic Estate, and before that, Golden Sunset) and Windy Hill, and the lack of visible progress at such wineries as Mayfair, Mazuran's, Mother's Cellar and Fino Valley.

Yet with three sizeable, highly rated wineries — Babich, Delegat's and Collards — retaining their operations here, backed up by many other reliable producers, the Henderson wine trail still has a multitude of vinous delights for the wine lover. Only a few of the finest wines on sale are made from Henderson grapes, but such estate-grown labels as St Jerome Matuka Cabernet Sauvignon/Merlot and Pleasant Valley Signature Selection Pinotage show what can be achieved.

Joe Babich

During the 1970s, while still making the traditional Babich table wines — Dry White, Moselle, Sauternes, Dry Red, Vintara Red and Burgundy — Babich won a strong following for his dry Riesling-Sylvaner and medium-bodied, supple Pinotage/Cabernet, and also released a trickle of widely acclaimed Gewürztraminer and Cabernet Sauvignon. In the first 1976 edition of his *A Guide To New Zealand Wine*, Peter Saunders noted 'the enquiring mind of Joe, who is always willing to talk winemaking and exchange ideas. Joe has a most perceptive palate and is highly respected by other winemakers.'

Finely crafted and harmonious, Babich wines don't scream at you, but offer great drinkability. 'That's what I've always aimed for — wines that offer easy drinking,' says Babich. 'We try not to overdo anything. If a vineyard produces a certain style of wine, we don't force another style on it. We want to produce fruit-driven, subtle wines that are not excessively manipulated by the winemaker.'

The tightly structured, slowly evolving Irongate Chardonnay sums up the Babich style. 'We want ripe fruit characters, a fair measure of alcohol, oak that doesn't dominate and a slightly flinty finish. ' Wines like that, which are restrained in their youth but flourish with cellaring, generally struggle to stand out in competitions. After a judging career of over 35 years, including a 1994–98 spell as chairman of judges at the Air New Zealand Wine Awards, in 1999 Babich withdrew his own company from local wine shows: 'There's often a gap between what critics like and the public likes. We decided to let the market decide.' If that represents a maturing of the Babich policy on competitions, it's also a logical step for a company with an established presence in New Zealand, the United Kingdom, the United States, Australia and other export markets. 'We've done well in competitions over the years,' Babich noted in 1994. 'But we don't make wines specifically to impress the judges — never have.'

After winning the Winemaker of the Year award at the 1994 Liquorland Royal Easter Wine Show, Babich told me candidly: 'It's a good result in a business sense, but in terms of personal excitement, it doesn't mean a great deal.' So what does give this vastly experienced winemaker real satisfaction?

'Above all, acceptance of the wines by consumers,' he says. 'That may seem a small thing, but when people truly like the wines — and that's been ongoing — it's a thrill. In 1969 it was our Riesling-Sylvaner. Now it's the Winemakers Reserve or Irongate wines.'

■ **Is a winemaker's personality reflected in his wines? Extroverted winemakers often produce bold, larger-than-life wines, and there are clear parallels between Joe Babich's controlled, modest personality and the restraint, delicacy and finesse that define his winemaking style.**

For Babich (62), who became general manager of his family's flourishing wine company in the mid-1990s, 'running a wine business is a challenge, all the time. It's more than just being a winemaker. There's the grapes, the money side, the market — they're all a challenge. But I love it.'

From his father, Josip, Joe recalls learning 'sound winemaking principles, in terms of integrity. For instance, stretching the supply of wine with water was once a common practice in New Zealand, but Dad was never one to try to make wine from anything but grapes. He always said: "Never underestimate the customer."' His first vintage in charge of the winemaking was as a 22-year-old, in 1963. 'I'd already worked in the winery for five years, but it came as a surprise, because Peter [his brother], who was still the winemaker, got hepatitis the day the vintage started.' By 1965, Joe had taken over the winemaking duties on a permanent basis.

Babich

■ There's something reassuring about Babich. A long-established, middle-sized company, over the past 30 years it has transformed itself from a predominantly fortified-wine producer (with a loyal following for its dry Palomino Sherry) to an internationally recognised winery with distinguished white and red table wines. Yet through an era characterised by relentless change, the Babich family has remained steadfastly in control, its early reputation for wines of integrity and good quality intact and enhanced.

In 1910, as a boy of 14, Josip (Joe) Babich left Dalmatia to join his brothers toiling in the gumfields of the Far North. His first wine was produced in 1916. At Kaikino, on the last stretch of land leading to Cape Reinga, he grew grapes, trod them with his feet, and opened a wine shop.

The shift to the Henderson Valley came in 1919. On a 24-hectare wilderness property, Joe milked cows, grew vegetables, established a small orchard — and planted classical Meunier vines. During the Second World War, winemaking slowly became the family's major business activity. Josip died in 1983, one of the 'grand old men' of the New Zealand wine industry.

Of Josip and Mara Babich's five children, three are involved in the family winery. For several decades the two brothers, Peter and Joe, neatly divided the company's tasks between them, with Peter as general manager and Joe as winemaker. In the mid-1990s, Joe assumed responsibility for the administration, enabling Peter to ease back, although he is still very actively involved in the company. Their sister, Maureen, works in the office.

David Babich, one of Peter's sons, became the first third-generation family member to take up a permanent position with the company, when in 2001 he was appointed to the role of assistant general manager.

The rolling loam-clay soils of the beautiful 13-hectare estate vineyard, the largest in Henderson, are planted principally in Chardonnay, Pinotage and Pinot Noir. Babich also has full or part ownership of numerous other vineyards in Hawke's Bay and Marlborough.

In a 15-hectare block at Fernhill, in Hawke's Bay, Chardonnay is the major variety, with smaller plantings of other grapes, including Viognier. Another, recently acquired vineyard in Ohiti Road, Fernhill, is currently established in 13 hectares of Merlot and Cabernet Sauvignon, and will be much extended. A 35-hectare block in the gravelly, free-draining soils of Gimblett Road is devoted principally to Cabernet Sauvignon, Merlot, Syrah, Chardonnay and Sauvignon Blanc, with smaller plots of Pinotage, Malbec and Gewürztraminer.

In Marlborough, Babich also owns the 42-hectare Wakefield Downs vineyard in the Awatere Valley, planted predominantly in Sauvignon Blanc. In the recently acquired Cowslip Valley vineyard in the Waihopai Valley, Sauvignon Blanc, Pinot Gris, Riesling and Pinot Noir are being planted. Grapes are also purchased from contract growers in Gisborne and Marlborough.

Its recent land and vineyard investments are vital to Babich's plans to double its output by 2006, in order to satisfy its fast-growing export demand. Its share of the domestic market peaked at 2 per cent between 1970 and 1995, but the current growth is mostly offshore.

Babich
WINEMAKERS RESERVE
2000
SYRAH
GIMBLETT ROAD VINEYARD   HAWKE'S BAY
Produced & bottled by Babich Wines Limited, Babich Road, Henderson, New Zealand
12.5% Vol.   PRODUCE OF NEW ZEALAND   e750ml

Address	Babich Wines, Babich Road, Henderson
Owners	The Babich family
Key Wines	Irongate Chardonnay, Cabernet/Merlot; The Patriarch Chardonnay, Cabernet Sauvignon; Winemakers Reserve Sauvignon Blanc, Chardonnay, Merlot, Syrah; Marlborough Sauvignon Blanc, Marlborough Pinot Gris, Marlborough Riesling, East Coast Chardonnay, Hawke's Bay Cabernet/Merlot, Fumé Vert, Pinotage/Cabernet

Josip Babich planted his first vines at Henderson shortly after the First World War, but today most of the grapes come from Gisborne, Hawke's Bay and Marlborough.

Until recently, Babich wines were as well known for their sharp prices as their consistently sound quality. But the flood of cheap Australian imports in the past decade has forced the company to look overseas for growth opportunities. After rebranding its wines and upping their prices, it is now exporting over half of its annual output (currently well over 100,000 cases) and plans to boost that to 80 per cent.

The winemaker since 2001 has been Adam Hazeldine, who joined Babich in 1996. North Island wines are processed at the Henderson winery, but the Marlborough grapes are fermented within the region at Rapaura Vintners (partly owned by Babich) before finishing and bottling at Henderson.

The two everyday-drinking wines are Fumé Vert ('smoky-green'), a smooth, citrusy, slightly grassy Gisborne blend of Sémillon and Chardonnay (exported as Babich Sémillon/Chardonnay); and the supple, raspberryish Pinotage/Cabernet.

The standard range of varietal wines features a scented, ripely herbaceous Marlborough Sauvignon Blanc, a fruit-driven East Coast Chardonnay, a softly mouthfilling Marlborough Pinot Gris with good concentration, and a medium-dry, richly flavoured Marlborough Riesling.

Highlights of the Winemakers Reserve range — which recently replaced the Mara Estate selection — are a thrillingly intense Marlborough Sauvignon Blanc, grown in the Wakefield Downs vineyard; and a fine value, peppery Syrah, distinctly reminiscent of Rhône reds.

The single-vineyard Irongate wines, grown in Gimblett Road, have been a major success story, especially the Chardonnay. The Cabernet/Merlot displays strong cassis, spice and French oak flavours, braced by taut tannins. Fully barrel-fermented but rarely given a softening malolactic fermentation, the white is one of New Zealand's most refined Chardonnays, with a proven ability in top vintages to mature well for a decade, unfolding intense, citrusy, nutty flavours.

The super-premium wines, labelled The Patriarch (in honour of Josip Babich) include an opulent, arrestingly full-flavoured Hawke's Bay Chardonnay, markedly bolder in its youth than Irongate; and a French oak-aged Hawke's Bay Cabernet Sauvignon, dark and perfumed in a very powerful, concentrated style.

Address Collard Brothers, 303 Lincoln Road, Henderson

Owners The Collard family

Key Wines Rothesay Chardonnay, Rothesay Sauvignon Blanc, Rothesay Cabernet Sauvignon; Queen Charlotte Marlborough Riesling, Queen Charlotte Marlborough Pinot Noir; Hawke's Bay Chardonnay, Hawke's Bay Chenin Blanc, Hawke's Bay Merlot, Marlborough Sauvignon Blanc, Blakes Mill Chardonnay

Collards

■ Collards ranked among New Zealand's most prestigious wineries in the 1970s and 1980s, releasing a stream of beautifully crafted wines from classic grape varieties. Its profile has slipped over the past decade (reflecting its intensifying competition and low-key approach to marketing) but the standard of the wine — especially the whites — has stayed high.

The winery lies just off the north-western motorway in Henderson's traffic-clogged Lincoln Road. Founder John Collard, an English berry-fruit expert, came to New Zealand as an orchard instructor for the Department of Agriculture. He purchased the present Lincoln Road site in 1910, planting it in stone and pip fruits. Although grapes were cultivated at Collard's 'Sutton Baron' property — named after the village in Kent where for generations the Collard family had grown fruit and hops — initially they were for eating, not wine.

John Collard married Dorothy Averill in 1915. Between 1928 and 1963, Dorothy's brothers ran the Averill winery, just along Lincoln Road. At the urging of their uncles — the Averill brothers — in 1946 John Collard's sons, Lionel and Brian, started crushing their own wines. Until 1964, when the present Collards winery was built, Collards wines were always fermented at the Averill cellars.

Today, the indefatigable Lionel (in his early eighties still heavily involved) and his sons, Bruce and Geoffrey, divide the myriad tasks of a modern winery between them. Geoffrey, who once worked for three years in the Mosel, oversees

Lionel Collard, now in his early eighties, still heads his respected family-owned winery.

the grapegrowing; Bruce is the talented, self-effacing winemaker; and Lionel controls the company's financial administration, sales and public relations. Desma Collard, Lionel's wife, is also involved, 'on the clerical side'.

In 2002, Lionel celebrated his fifty-sixth vintage. Steering the winery's transition from a fortified to table wine producer was the greatest challenge of his career. 'In the late 1960s, I could see that we couldn't compete on the world market with golden sherry. So we selected Riesling, Gewürztraminer, Müller-Thurgau, Merlot vines and made some of the first plantings of those varieties in Auckland. My greatest thrill was when we were awarded the first gold medal in New Zealand for a Riesling [Collards 1978]; I planted the vines myself.'

The Collard holding in Lincoln Road, originally 25 hectares, has been decimated by the construction of the surrounding roads; only 2 hectares are still in vines (Merlot and Malbec). The Collards' major company-owned plantings are now in the Waikoukou Valley, near Matua Valley, where the 15-hectare Rothesay Vineyard is established in Chardonnay, Sauvignon Blanc, Cabernet Sauvignon and Viognier. Grapes are also purchased from growers in Hawke's Bay, Te Kauwhata and Marlborough.

At one stage, the Collards planned to shift the winery to Waimauku. After buying land for additional planting, adjacent to the Rothesay vineyard, they were deterred from moving by the threat of a dam being built nearby, which would have raised the water table and affected grapegrowing.

Chardonnay, Sauvignon Blanc and Riesling are the key white-wine varieties, backed up by Chenin Blanc, Sémillon and (most recently) Viognier.

Collards' Chardonnay style emphasises deep, sustained fruit flavours, with subtle wood handling. Rothesay Chardonnay, the flagship, is a powerful wine with rich, well-ripened tropical fruit flavours, fleshed out with quality oak, and the well-rounded finish typical of northern whites. The mid-priced Hawke's Bay Chardonnay is sturdy and full-flavoured, with some barrel-ferment complexity. Blakes Mill Chardonnay, blended from grapes grown in Auckland and elsewhere, is fashioned in a lightly wooded, soft, drink-young style.

The Queen Charlotte Marlborough Riesling is a consistently classy wine, with a beguiling fragrance and notable flavour intensity. Collards Rothesay Sauvignon Blanc, a lush, mouthfilling style with ripe, searching melon and lime-like flavours, is partnered by a verdant, crisp Marlborough Sauvignon Blanc. The Old Vines Sémillon, estate-grown at Henderson, is a distinctive, oak-aged wine with restrained herbal flavours and lees-aging richness in a complex, subtle style.

At its best, the Hawke's Bay Chenin Blanc is rich and vibrantly fruity, with pineappley, faintly honeyed flavours. The first Rothesay Viognier (from the 2000 vintage) offered exceptional value, with very substantial body, lush flavours of peaches and pears and a seductively soft finish.

Collards' reds have long been overshadowed by the whites. At its best, the Rothesay Cabernet Sauvignon is full-flavoured, firm and spicy, but in cooler seasons the wine emerges leafy and austere. The Queen Charlotte Marlborough Pinot Noir is more consistently enjoyable — fragrant and supple, with cherryish, spicy flavours of good but not great depth.

Delegat's

■ Of the country's larger wineries (it currently claims to be the fourth biggest), Delegat's produces one of the tightest ranges. Winemaker Michael Ivicevich focuses exclusively on four grape varieties — Chardonnay, Sauvignon Blanc, Merlot and Cabernet Sauvignon — cultivated in two regions, Hawke's Bay and Marlborough.

Nikola Delegat, the founder, purchased land near the Whau River, an arm of the Waitemata Harbour, in 1947. Delegat first came to New Zealand in 1923 but later returned to Korcula, an island off the Dalmatian coast of Croatia, before he and his wife, Vidosava, finally established a 4-hectare plot of vines at Henderson. If you visit the property, when you step into the concrete-block vineyard shop with its exposed beams you are entering Nikola Delegat's original winery.

At the time of the founder's death in 1973, Delegat's produced fortified and table wines, including five sherries, Glendene Riesling, Rhine Wine, Burgundy, a sparkling called Epernay and a coffee liqueur, Delcafe. With Nikola's son, Jim, and daughter, Rose, now at the helm, followed by the 1979 arrival of a young Australian winemaker, John Hancock, Delegat's changed direction. Almost overnight, Hancock lifted the standard of Delegat's wines: the gold medal won by his 1979 Selected Vintage Riesling-Sylvaner was to be the first of a string of successes. In the early to mid-1980s Delegat's was transformed into a quality-orientated winery with a high reputation for its bold, buttery, richly oaked Chardonnays.

Rocked by the ferocious price war of 1985–86, the family admitted Wilson Neill to a majority shareholding, but in 1991 ownership of the company reverted entirely to Jim and Rose Delegat.

Delegat's is the only sizeable New Zealand winery owned and run by a brother and sister team. As Jim puts it: 'Rose has great empathy and an easy rapport with people which is a huge benefit to our company, whereas my strength lies more in working out where we're going to be in the next few years with our vineyards and winemaking.' Both Brent Marris, winemaker from 1986 to 1998, and his successor, Michael Ivicevich (whose parents own West Brook), have enjoyed formidable competition success.

Delegat's not only specialises in just four classic varieties, the company draws grapes only from regions with a proven strength in each variety and gives each region's wines a separate brand identity. The finest Hawke's Bay

Oyster Bay captures the special character of Marlborough... elegant, assertive wines with glorious fruit flavours

MARLBOROUGH

Sauvignon Blanc

2001

Oyster Bay

NEW ZEALAND

Address	Delegat's Wine Estate, 172 Hepburn Road, Henderson
Owners	Jim and Rose Delegat
Key Wines	Reserve Chardonnay, Cabernet Sauvignon, Merlot; Hawke's Bay Chardonnay, Sauvignon Blanc, Cabernet/Merlot; Oyster Bay Chardonnay, Sauvignon Blanc, Pinot Noir

Jim and Rose Delegat are the only brother and sister team to lead a sizeable New Zealand winery.

wines are reserved for Delegat's Reserve label; a moderately priced range for earlier drinking is labelled Delegat's Hawke's Bay; and three Marlborough wines are marketed under the Oyster Bay label.

Delegat's holdings in Hawke's Bay are extensive: a 25-hectare vineyard in the free-draining shingles of Gimblett Road, supplying Chardonnay, Cabernet Sauvignon and Merlot; a 20-hectare block on State Highway 50, backing onto Gimblett Road, in which the key varieties are Cabernet Sauvignon and Merlot; and 12 hectares of Chardonnay at the silty Vicarage Vineyard in Swamp Road, at the entrance to the Dartmoor Valley. Paving the way for a major production increase, in 2000 Delegat's purchased the 360-hectare Crownthorpe property, on a bend of the Ngaruroro River, 30 kilometres inland from Hastings, being planted in Merlot and Chardonnay.

In Marlborough, Delegat's expansion plans are notably large-scale. In 1999, Delegat's steered the formation of a new public company, Oyster Bay Marlborough Vineyards, which raised $18 million for massive vineyard planting in Marlborough. The Oyster Bay company, itself over 20 per cent owned by Delegat's, is developing 301 hectares of vineyards in the Wairau Valley, focusing on Sauvignon Blanc, Chardonnay and Pinot Noir. Delegat's is also building a $12 million winery near Renwick, predicted to crush 5000 tonnes of grapes (producing over 350,000 cases of wine) by 2004.

Since the last 1996 vintage of its former flagship range, Proprietors Reserve (which featured a notably powerful, peachy-ripe and toasty Chardonnay), Delegat's wines have all been positioned in the sub-$20 category. Research in the mid to late 1990s showed that 'quality wines in this price category [$19], readily available and suitable for early drinking' were increasingly sought after.

The resulting launch from the 1997 vintage of a new Delegat's Reserve range — Chardonnay, Merlot and Cabernet Sauvignon — proved successful, offering Hawke's Bay wines of a consistently high standard, excellent drinkability and outstanding value. The barrel-fermented Reserve Chardonnay is typically weighty, rich and creamy-smooth; the Merlot generous and full-flavoured; the Cabernet Sauvignon dark, fragrant and brambly, with impressive depth. All three rank among the finest sub-$20 New Zealand wines on the market.

For everyday drinking, the tank-fermented, barrel-aged Delegat's Hawke's Bay Chardonnay is fresh, citrusy and smooth; the unwooded Hawke's Bay Sauvignon Blanc offers tropical-fruit flavours, ripe and rounded; and the briefly oak-aged Hawke's Bay Cabernet/Merlot offers blackcurrant and plum, often slightly leafy, flavours of decent depth.

The high-profile Oyster Bay label burst into the limelight when the debut 1990 vintage won the Marquis de Goulaine Trophy for the best Sauvignon Blanc at the 1991 International Wine and Spirit Competition in London. Both the Chardonnay and Sauvignon Blanc are consistently attractive. The Chardonnay, 75 per cent barrel-fermented, showcases Marlborough's pure, penetrating fruit flavours, with a touch of mealiness and a soft finish. The Sauvignon Blanc is typically chock-full of lively, tropical-fruit and cut-grass flavours and the debut 2001 Pinot Noir is beautifully scented, rounded and rich.

Lincoln

■ Lincoln epitomises the west Auckland cluster of old, family-owned wineries of Croatian origin. Founded in 1937, it initially earned a reputation for fortified wines, especially dry sherry. Now the Fredatovich family specialises in table wines, typically sound but not highly distinguished.

Peter Fredatovich, a third-generation member of the family to produce wine in Lincoln Road, took over the reins from his father, Peter, in the late 1980s. Another of Peter Snr's sons, John, was also involved, but he departed the company in 1998.

Peter Snr — awarded the MBE in 1989 for his services to viticulture — had controlled Lincoln since the 1955 retirement of his father, also called Peter. 'For the first few years,' recalls Peter Snr, 'my father worked for the Ministry of Works to earn ready cash so that he could establish our vineyard. He would come home and work on the land, clearing scrub and digging up stumps. It was pretty hard work but he planted one and a half acres (0.6 hectares) of vines on overhead trellises — and got us started.' To accommodate the harvest, he then coopered his own barrels out of totara.

Winemaker Justin Papesch, formerly of Montana, works with grapes purchased from Auckland, Gisborne, Hawke's Bay and Marlborough. The company's Brighams Creek vineyard at Kumeu was uprooted in 1992, and in 1999 the Home Vineyard adjoining the winery was sold to make way for housing, although some vines were retained for decorative purposes. Compared to other wineries of similar background, such as Babich and Delegat's, Lincoln's current lack of high quality, company-owned vineyards is a weakness.

For many years, Lincoln ranked among the industry's medium-sized producers, but in the late 1990s the company embarked on a strategy of slashing its production and lifting quality. After a major labelling revamp, the wines are marketed under a three-tier system, headed by the President's Selection, then the Heritage Collection, and finally the Winemaker's Series range, which consists of low-priced and widely available wines.

The President's Selection Chardonnay, grown in Gisborne and French oak-fermented, has shown varying form, not always proving long-lived, but at its best is rich, ripe and creamy-soft. The President's Selection reds, based on Cabernet Sauvignon and Merlot grown in several regions, have typically been decent but not highly refined.

The middle-tier Heritage Collection range features the names of family members. Patricia Chardonnay, named after the daughter-in-law of the founder, is an upfront style with ripe Gisborne fruit characters and a strong American oak influence. Lukrica Marlborough Sauvignon Blanc, named after the founder's wife, is typically fresh and vibrant, with punchy, strongly herbaceous flavours.

Lincoln has not abandoned fortified wine production, although most of its energies are now poured into table wines. 'There's a market for ports, especially tawny styles,' says Peter Fredatovich. Launched in 2002, after slumbering in oak hogsheads for over 40 years, The Archive Grand Tawny Port is not as mellow as a top Portuguese tawny, but fragrant, smooth, rich and raisiny, with good 'rancio' complexity.

Address	Lincoln Vineyards, 130 Lincoln Road, Henderson
Owners	The Fredatovich family
Key Wines	President's Selection Chardonnay, Merlot, Cabernet/Merlot; Heritage Collection Lakrica Sauvignon Blanc, Patricia Chardonnay, Petar Cabernet/Merlot, Ice Wine; Winemaker's Series Merlot, Chardonnay, Sauvignon Blanc

Peter Fredatovich upholds the family winemaking tradition established by his grandfather in the 1930s.

Address Odyssey Wines,
PO Box 21655,
Henderson

Owner Rebecca Salmond

Key Wines Reserve Iliad Chardonnay,
Merlot; Gisborne
Chardonnay, Kumeu
Cabernet/Merlot,
Blanc de Blancs

Odyssey

■ One of Gisborne's most refined Chardonnays, with intense, ripe fruit wrapped in quality French oak, flows from this small west Auckland-based producer. Rebecca Salmond named her wine venture after Homer's Greek epic, which traces the adventures of Odysseus returning from the siege of Troy.

One of the few women to head a New Zealand wine company, Salmond graduated in biotechnology from Massey University and later gained a postgraduate diploma in wine science from Roseworthy College in South Australia. After working vintages in South Australia, Bordeaux, Chile and Italy, followed by spells as assistant winemaker at Mission Vineyards in Hawke's Bay and winemaker at Pleasant Valley, she now makes most of her wine at Landmark Estate, in Henderson.

Working overseas helped Salmond to develop a clear understanding of the style of wine she wants to make. In her view, too many New Zealand winemakers produce 'overtly fruity and sometimes very oaky wines that are great to taste but difficult to enjoy with food because the wines make such a strong statement'. Wines with harmony and texture, which enhance but don't dominate food, are her goal at Odyssey.

Chardonnay grapes are purchased from Gisborne, and Cabernet Sauvignon and Merlot from Hawke's Bay and Kumeu. In a key step for the future, in 2000 Salmond bought a 22-hectare hill site with a north-easterly aspect and loam clay soils in Marlborough's Brancott Valley, being close-planted in Pinot Noir (principally), Sauvignon Blanc and Pinot Gris.

Since the first 1994 vintage, Odyssey's output (marketed overseas under the Salmond label) has climbed from 200 cases to 5000 cases in 2002.

The lower-tier range features a fruit-driven, slightly honeyed Gisborne Chardonnay, and smooth, flavoursome Cabernet Sauvignon-based reds from Kumeu and Hawke's Bay.

The Reserve Iliad reds, based on Cabernet Sauvignon and Merlot, grown in Hawke's Bay and Kumeu, have been good but not outstanding. Salmond also makes a vintage-dated, Chardonnay-based Blanc de Blancs. A rare example of Gisborne bubbly, it's a moderately complex style with fresh, citrusy flavours overlaid with nutty, yeast autolysis characters.

The pick of the range is the rare Reserve Iliad Chardonnay. Based on a leased 0.4-hectare block in the Kawatiri Vineyard in Gisborne, hand-picked, whole-bunch pressed and French oak-fermented, it is mouthfilling, creamy and complex, with lovely delicacy and intensity. In top vintages, such as 2000, it is a magical wine.

Pacific

■ Will Pacific, like the phoenix on its labels, be a high flier again? Twenty years ago it was a medium-sized producer, focusing on low-priced wine casks and wine coolers. Today its production is heavily reduced, but top vintages of its Gisborne Gewürztraminer are of arresting quality, with several trophies to prove it.

The founder, Mijo (Mick) Erceg, arrived in New Zealand in 1929. After several years' labour on gumfields, roads and the vineyards of other Croatians, he bought a small farm in McLeod Road, Henderson. By 1936, his own vines were in the ground.

Address Pacific Vineyards,
90 McLeod Road,
Henderson

Owners Michael and Millie Erceg

Key Wines Phoenix Gisborne
Gewürztraminer,
Gisborne Chardonnay,
Marlborough Riesling,
Cabernet/Merlot/Franc

After war broke out in 1939, restricting imports of liquor, the demand for New Zealand wine soared. Erceg 'sold some wine to an American serviceman for ten shillings a gallon — he was very happy. Then a fortnight later I heard that wine was being sold for 30 shillings a gallon. So I bought a distillery, put in a cellar and planted five or six acres in grapes. In 1943 in went another five acres. . . .'

Pacific entered into a marketing arrangement with Seppelts of Australia in 1967, and for several years Pacific wines appeared on the shelves under the Seppelt label. Later, the company's wines were sold under the Saint Stefan, Monlouis, Michael's, Willowbrook and other labels.

Today, Pacific is owned by the founder's wife, Millie, who is still actively involved, and her son, Michael, holder of an American doctorate in mathematics, who promotes the wines through his liquor importing, producing and distribution company, Independent Liquor. Steve Tubic, who worked at Corbans between 1979 and 1986, has been the winemaker since the 1987 vintage.

The utilitarian winery, in a suburban street, backs onto a 4-hectare estate vineyard, which is planted in Cabernet Sauvignon (predominantly), Merlot and Cabernet Franc. Another 4-hectare vineyard at Papakura, in South Auckland, has been established in Chardonnay. Gewürztraminer and Chardonnay grapes are purchased from Gisborne growers, and Riesling from Marlborough.

Pacific's output peaked in the 1980s, but now only averages 9000 cases. The wines are all marketed under the Phoenix brand, launched in 1990.

The star attraction is the Gewürztraminer, grown in the Butler (previously Thomas) vineyard in Gisborne. At its best, it is headily perfumed, with slightly sweet, concentrated, pungently spicy flavour. The 1986, 1990, 1995, 1997 and 2001 vintages all collected trophies.

The range also features a creamy-soft, partly barrel-fermented Gisborne Chardonnay, designed for early drinking; a zingy Marlborough Riesling with ample sweetness and fresh apple/lemon flavours; and an estate-grown, American and French oak-aged Cabernet/Merlot/Franc, with solid depth of plummy, spicy, earthy flavour.

Joseph Balic (pictured with his family) founded Golden Sunset in 1912 and built up a healthy trade in 'invalid port'.

The Croatians

■ **Montana, Villa Maria and Nobilo — New Zealand's three largest wine companies — all originated as tiny, family-owned Croatian enterprises. So did Babich, Delegat's, Kumeu River, Lincoln and a host of smaller wineries spread across Auckland, Northland and the Waikato.**

Wine is a pervasive element in Croatian culture; when the early settlers planted vines and made a trickle of wine, they did so principally to satisfy their own thirsts. 'When we came here 50 years ago, I missed my glass of wine with the evening meal,' recalled Zuva Nobilo in 1993. Zuva and her husband, Nikola, planted their first vines on the outskirts of Huapai in 1943.

The Croatians flocked to New Zealand from the terraced vineyards, olive groves and orchards of the central Dalmatian coast. Dalmatia is part of Croatia — itself, until the early 1990s, part of Yugoslavia. Those who emigrated from Makarska and Vrgorac (coastal towns between Split and Dubrovnik), the peninsula of Peljesac and the islands of Hvar and Korcula left behind a backward, peasant society of subsistence agriculture.

Attracted to New Zealand to dig kauri gum, in the 1890s the Croatians also began to make wine north of Auckland. 'At Pahi [north Kaipara], a number of Austrians [Croatia was then a reluctant part of the Austro-Hungarian Empire] are beginning to cultivate the vine on an extensive scale,' stated an Agriculture Department report of 1896. By 1907, 14 Croatian vineyards at Herekino, south of Kaitaia, were producing about 2000 gallons (9092 L) of wine per year. The Frankovich brothers' vineyard at Arkles Bay, on the Whangaparaoa Peninsula, was one of the largest in the country in 1908, covering 16 acres (6.5 hectares).

In west Auckland, by 1904 John Vella, Lovre Marinovich and Stipan Jelich (Stephan Yelas) all had vineyards planted. The *Weekly News* enthused in 1910 that 'the vineyards in the Henderson and Oratia districts . . . stand out as [a] striking example of what may be accomplished in the way of converting the once despised gumlands into highly profitable country'. Government

viticulturist Romeo Bragato was equally impressed by the Croatians' achievements. 'In this way,' he wrote, 'many of these men, who were formerly looked at askance and regarded by some as undesirable immigrants, may now be counted as sober, industrious and thrifty settlers.'

The main influx of Croatians into the west Auckland area came in the late 1920s and 1930s. Josip Babich arrived in 1919; Marino Selak and Mick Ivicevich (West Brook) in 1934; Petar Fredatovich (Lincoln) in 1937; George Mazuran in 1938; George Antunovich (Eastern Vineyards) in 1939; Ivan Yukich (Montana) and Mate Brajkovich (Kumeu River) in 1944; and Nikola Delegat in 1947.

'It was really a cluster effect,' observes Vladimir Vitasovich, of Landmark Estate, in Bruce McLaren Road, Henderson. 'Our relatives tended to settle down where there were others of their own culture around them. It might not have been the perfect place to grow grapes but it worked well enough. Not so much was known then about the relationship between land types and the final wine. In any case there was not really a demand for fine wine as such.'

By the mid-1950s, of the 80-odd vineyards clustered in Henderson-Oratia (mostly smaller than 2 hectares), 90 per cent were owned by Croatians. With New Zealanders beginning to develop a growing appetite for wine, and the second generation of Croatians developing higher economic aspirations, the stage was set for an explosion of winemaking activity by the sons and grandsons of Croatian settlers.

Winemaking history

Address	Pleasant Valley Wines, 322 Henderson Valley Road, Henderson
Owner	Stephan Yelas
Key Wines	Yelas Winemaker's Reserve Chardonnay, Pinotage; Signature Selection Chardonnay, Pinotage, Cabernet/Malbec; Gewürztraminer, Sauvignon Blanc, Amontillado Sherry, Amoroso Sherry, Oloroso Sherry, Founders Port, Anniversary Port

Pleasant Valley

■ Pleasant Valley has the dual distinction of being not only the oldest surviving Croatian vineyard in Henderson, but also the oldest winery in the land under the continuous ownership of the same family.

Stipan Jelich, the founder, arrived in Auckland in 1890, and five years later bought 32 hectares of hill country in the Henderson Valley. Precisely when the first vines were planted is unclear, but Jelich's first crop of grapes, Black Hamburghs, fetched him less on the Auckland markets than the charges of the carrier and auctioneer. By 1902, winemaking had emerged as a better source of income, and from then until Stipan Jelich (Stephan Yelas) retired in 1939, the land was turned over by spade; the vines, tied to manuka stakes, were hand-hoed and sprayed from a knapsack mounted on the back. Not even a horse helped to ease the toil.

Yelas' son Moscow long ago introduced more modern vineyard techniques, replacing manuka stakes with wire trellises and knapsack sprayers with machine sprayers. During the 1960s, the top wines, labelled Château Yelas, won many gold medals, and Moscow continued to make sound, good value wines — including Hock, Pinotage and Fino Dry Sherry — until his death in 1984.

Today, under the guidance of Moscow's son, Stephan, Pleasant Valley no longer has the high profile of 35 years ago, but still produces about 7000 cases per year of rock-solid, often good wines. Made by consultant winemakers, they are mostly sold directly to the public from the winery. The top wines are labelled Yelas Winemaker's Reserve, followed by the middle-tier Signature Selection and a range of Pleasant Valley varietals.

The 12-hectare, hill-grown estate vineyard is established in Pinotage, Cabernet Sauvignon, Merlot and Chardonnay. Most of the grapes, however, are bought from growers in the Auckland, Hawke's Bay and Marlborough regions.

Pleasant Valley's best wines are its estate-grown, multiple silver medal-winning Pinotages, typically deliciously supple and vibrant, with great drink-young charm. Why are they so good?

'It's where the vines are grown — in a bowl on a sunny, north-facing hillside,' says Stephan Yelas. 'It's sheltered from the wind and gets really, really hot.' Both the raspberry, cherry and spice-flavoured Signature Selection Pinotage and the more oak-influenced, gamey Yelas Winemaker's Reserve Pinotage are well worth discovering.

Of Pleasant Valley's traditional range of fortified wines, the barrel-matured Amontillado, Amoroso and Oloroso sherries are all impressively rich, mellow and lingering. The jewels in the crown, however, are the amber-brown, nutty-sweet Founder's Port and the 20-year-old, raisiny, creamy-sweet Anniversary Port.

Pleasant Valley's vineyard café serves lunches on Saturdays and Sundays, all year round. 'It's very casual,' says Ineke Yelas, Stephan's wife. With their three children also involved — Moscow (in the vineyard), Fiona (accounts) and Kristie (in the café) — the Yelas' are this year celebrating a century of family winemaking at Pleasant Valley.

St Jerome

■ 'Red wine is made from skins,' says Davorin Ozich, winemaker at St Jerome. 'That sounds simple but it's far-reaching. All the goodies are in the skins.'

The tiny St Jerome winery lies in the foothills of the Waitakere Ranges, only a kilometre from Babich. Here, Davorin and his viticulturist brother, Miro, produce a muscular, flavour-packed, tautly tannic Cabernet Sauvignon/Merlot, designed to mature well over the long haul.

The sunny, north-facing clay slope behind the winery was originally planted by Mate Ozich, Davorin and Miro's father, in the 1960s. 'Dad made fortified wines for about 25 years under the Nova and Ozich labels,' says Davorin. 'St Jerome is the company Miro and I created in 1981. St Jerome is not an evolution of Nova; it's a whole new beginning.'

The white wines, based on grapes purchased from Gisborne and Hawke's Bay, have typically been of sound, average quality. The Matuka Cabernet Sauvignon/Merlot (named in honour of Mate, who in Croatia was often called 'Matuka'), is clearly the company's flagship. What style of wine are the brothers pursuing?

'We're quite uncompromising in our approach to red winemaking,' says Davorin. 'We aim to get the maximum goodies out of the skins — all the flavours, colour and tannins that give a red wine real character.'

A pivotal step in Davorin's winemaking career came in September and October 1987 when he worked the vintage in Bordeaux, alternating his days between the fabled chateaux, Margaux and Cos d'Estournel. 'I learned that there's no magic formula in red winemaking,' recalls Davorin, 'but I came away confident about how to handle red wine.'

The 8-hectare estate vineyard, planted in Cabernet Sauvignon and Merlot, is harvested by hand. In the winery, the grapes are fermented with indigenous ('natural') yeasts, and the cap of skins is hand-plunged into the fermenting juice four times daily. After the fermentation, the skins are kept submerged in the wine for a further three weeks, boosting its colour, flavour and tannins, and the wine is matured in French oak barriques for up to two years.

The result is a robust wine with blackcurrant and cedarwood flavours, framed by firm tannins. In some years, it can be slightly leafy, but the top vintages are impressively concentrated, with a proven ability to mature well for a decade or longer.

Address	St Jerome Wines, 219 Metcalfe Road, Henderson
Owners	The Ozich family
Key Wines	Matuka Cabernet Sauvignon/Merlot, Chardonnay, Riesling, Sauvignon Blanc

ST JEROME
——
Matuka
CABERNET
SAUVIGNON
MERLOT
1996

Hand Picked & Unfiltered

PRODUCED AND BOTTLED BY ST JEROME WINES
HENDERSON AUCKLAND NEW ZEALAND

75 cl   WINE OF NEW ZEALAND   13.5% vol

Other producers

■ Artisan Wines

Launched from the 2000 vintage, Artisan is a partnership between three grapegrowing couples. Rex (the company head) and Maria Sunde cultivate 2 hectares of Pinot Noir and Syrah at Oratia, near Henderson; Bruce Gaw and Marie Wilmshurst grow 18 hectares of Chardonnay and Gewürztraminer at Tolaga Bay, north of Gisborne; and Robert and Lynne Kennedy have 12 hectares of Sauvignon Blanc, Chardonnay and Pinot Noir in Marlborough. Distinctive, single-vineyard wines are the goal. The initial releases were Sunvale Estate Gewürztraminer 2000, a medium-dry Gisborne wine with decent depth; and Fantail Island Pinot Noir 2000, from Oratia, ruby-hued, raspberryish and rounded.

■ Landmark Estate Wines

Founded in Bruce McLaren Road, Henderson, by the Vitasovich family in 1934 and long known as Public Vineyards, in the past Landmark specialised in bulk wines. From its two 5-hectare vineyards at Henderson and Kumeu, plus grapes grown on contract in other regions, winemakers Zlatomir Vitasovich and Rebecca Salmond (of Odyssey) produce wines under the flagship Earls, middle-tier Landmark and low-priced Albatross Point labels. The Chardonnays can be highly attractive.

■ Mazuran's Vineyard

The Mazuran winery specialised in fortified wines for decades with outstanding success. It was founded in 1939 by George Mazuran, who in the 1950s embarked on a unique lobbying career designed to foster the sales of independent, family-owned wineries such as his own. Ironically, the winegrowing bonanza that owed so much to his efforts passed his own company by. The Mazuran vineyard in Lincoln Road, today run by George Mazuran's son-in-law, Rado Hladilo, and his son, Antony, is small, with 2 hectares of Palomino, Muscat, Cabernet Sauvignon, Merlot and hybrids. The range of products, concentrated on sherries and ports — some matured for over 50 years — has barely changed for decades. The Mazuran port style is unmistakable: these are dark, almost opaque wines with an almost liqueur-like intensity — rich, treacly and creamy-sweet.

■ Seibel Wines

Born and trained in Germany, Norbert Seibel worked in South Africa and later as chief winemaker for Corbans before he launched his own Seibel label in 1987. He and his wife, Silvia, acquired the historic Bellamour winery (once called Balic Estate, and before that, Golden Sunset) in Sturges Road, Henderson, in 1993. The company, which does not own vineyards, buys grapes from growers in several regions. Seibel is a vastly experienced winemaker, and although his wines under the Seibel and One Tree Hill brands do not enjoy a high profile, they can be distinctive and rewarding, especially the tightly structured Rieslings, which age gracefully.

Waiheke Island

Thomas More's *Utopia* told in the sixteenth century of an island of vineyards and wine where 'all things begin little by little to wax pleasant. The air soft, temperate and gentle. The ground covered with green grass. Less wildness in the beasts.' Five hundred years later, his flight of the imagination is a perfect fit for the lovely, sprawling, red wine-producing island of Waiheke in Auckland's Hauraki Gulf.

The Goldwaters at Putiki Bay pioneered the modern era of Waiheke wine, planting their first vines in 1978, but they were not the first vintners the island had attracted. The Gradiska family winery produced both fortified and a trickle of table wines around the 1950s, until a series of personal tragedies overtook the family and winemaking ceased.

When Stephen White planted his first vines at Stonyridge Vineyard in 1982, 'the biggest industries on the island were the dole, sickness benefits, pensions, fishing and marijuana growing'. Today, the island boasts two of the country's top producers of claret-style reds, and there are at least a dozen other brands on the market. Cabernet Sauvignon and Merlot account for about 60 per cent of the plantings, but most vineyards also grow Cabernet Franc and Malbec, and interest in Chardonnay is spreading.

The main viticultural areas lie in the west and central parts of the island, although a few vineyards lie further east, at Stony Batter and Te Matuku Bay. Some growers sell their grapes; others have their wine made at another winery on the island; others have their wine made on the mainland; while still others are fully integrated vineyards and wineries.

The hilly terrain means the vineyards are small, labour intensive and costly to run, and transport costs are heavy. High land prices are a major hurdle for newcomers. Inevitably, the wines are high-priced, although their quality ranges from mediocre to outstanding.

Most of the vineyards are on slopes, so they are typically well-drained, but as one winemaker at Onetangi put it: 'There's a real mix of sites. Some are good, but others are not. Some are very windy. Some slope to the north, but others to the south-east.'

The strongly weathered, yellow-brown clay soils sometimes have a layer of rotten rock beneath, which helps promote drainage. Of generally moderate to low fertility, the soils dry out in early summer but retain enough water for the vines' needs; irrigation is rarely used.

Is Waiheke Island significantly hotter and drier during the growing season than the mainland, as its winegrowers often suggest? The climate figures do not support the claim, but the Awaroa Valley meteorological station lies at the base of the island's highest hill, where 'it is cooler and wetter than at the lower, western end of the island,' says Christopher Lush, of Peninsula Estate. The winemakers themselves report significant heat differences between sites. Lush notes that summer temperatures normally peak in the high 20s at Oneroa, but climb into the mid-30s at Onetangi.

Yields are low at most vineyards, averaging 3.5 to 7 tonnes per hectare. 'Wind is the key problem,' believes viticulturist Dr David Jordan. Sites on the island's north coast are better protected from the prevailing south-westerlies, but strong winds during flowering often reduce the set.

With 113 hectares planted in 2001, principally at Stony Batter, Cable Bay, Goldwater and Obsidian, Waiheke Island had 0.7 per cent of the national vineyard.

At the sparsely populated eastern end of the island, multi-millionaire John Spencer has established Waiheke's largest vineyard, Stony Batter Estate.

Fenton

■ Every month, Auckland businessman Barry Fenton — the owner of Passport United Holidays — drinks two or three bottles of first growth Bordeaux. Fired by his love of great claret, in 1989 he started planting vines alongside his family's holiday retreat at Oneroa, only 400 metres as the crow flies from Peninsula Estate. The first 1993 vintage of Fenton proved exceptional.

The vineyard (called Twin Bays) lies on a headland flanked by two bays. On a gentle north-facing slope, the vines run down to a sheer drop, 40 metres above the sea. The plantings were tripled in 1999 and now cover 3 hectares of traditional Bordeaux varieties: Cabernet Sauvignon, Merlot, Cabernet Franc, Malbec and Petit Verdot.

The early, 1993 and 1994 vintages were made in a highly Bordeaux-like style by Stephen White at Stonyridge. Between 1996 and 1998, the wine was made by Kim Crawford, then at Coopers Creek, in a more early-drinking style with extensive use of American oak. However, since 1999 the grapes have been processed by John Hancock at the Trinity Hill winery in Hawke's Bay, and the goal is once again serious, long-lived reds.

Output is low (550 cases in the 2000 vintage) and just two wines are made. Fenton, the flagship red, is only marketed in top vintages. In lesser years, a lower-priced wine is sold, labelled simply as The Red. Spicy and savoury, The Red is not highly concentrated, but still subtle and satisfying. Fenton has been of varying style, but the magical quality of the 1993 and 1994 vintages (both lovely, supple wines, now showing complex spice, tobacco and leather characters) shows what can be done.

FENTON
WAIHEKE

FENTON

1998
Cabernet Sauvignon
Merlot Franc

Produced and Bottled for
Fenton Vineyards
State Highway 10 Kaeo
from Grapes Grown at Fenton Twin Bays Vineyard
Oneroa, Waiheke Island

750ml℮   PRODUCE OF NEW ZEALAND   13% VOL

Address	Fenton Estate, 56 Korora Road, Oneroa
Owners	Barry and Meg Fenton
Key Wines	Cabernet Sauvignon/Merlot/ Franc, The Red

Goldwater

Address	Goldwater Estate. 18 Causeway Road, Putiki Bay
Owners	Kim and Jeanette Goldwater
Key Wines	Cabernet Sauvignon and Merlot, Esslin Merlot, Zell Chardonnay, Roseland Marlborough Chardonnay, Dog Point Marlborough Sauvignon Blanc

■ Goldwater Estate is being transformed. For long a prestigious producer of Waiheke Island reds, it now makes a far greater volume of Marlborough white wine (including an exceptional Sauvignon Blanc), and also invested recently in a red-wine vineyard in Hawke's Bay.

The modern flush of viticultural enthusiasm on the island was triggered in 1978 when Kim Goldwater — a former civil engineer and fashion photographer — and his wife Jeanette planted their first experimental vines in sandy clay soils on the hillside overlooking Putiki Bay.

The Goldwaters, who were fuelled as students by Babich and San Marino (now Kumeu River) dry reds, recall how they were later 'seduced by the Mediterranean lifestyle and especially the idea of serving wine with food every day'. The Goldwaters are a warm and hospitable couple who take obvious delight in one another's company. Goldwater is a family affair: their daughter, Gretchen, now heads the marketing and her husband, Ken Christie, is the general manager. The 13-hectare estate vineyard is planted principally in Chardonnay, Merlot and Cabernet Sauvignon, with a smaller plot of Cabernet Franc. The production from some of the old vines has fallen to such a low level that they are no longer economic and are gradually being replaced with cuttings from the Goldwaters' best-performing vines.

Further south, an 8-hectare vineyard of red Bordeaux varieties (mainly Merlot and Cabernet Franc) is being developed in the Gimblett Gravels district of Hawke's Bay, in conjunction with Craggy Range. The Goldwaters also have 40 hectares of Sauvignon Blanc and Chardonnay under contract in Marlborough.

On Waiheke Island, a new, colonial-style winery was completed prior to the 2001 vintage. Illustrating the scale of the company's involvement in Marlborough, the Goldwaters also recently acquired a 25 per cent shareholding in the large contract winemaking facility, Rapaura Vintners. With a current annual output of about 28,000 cases, the company is entering the ranks of the industry's medium-sized producers.

Kim's winemaking ambition is 'to win international recognition for making one of the world's great wines'. The Cabernet Sauvignon & Merlot is an aristocratic red with masses of blackcurrant, spice and oak flavour, and the proven ability to flourish in the bottle for many years. How has its style evolved since the first vintage — a straight Cabernet Sauvignon — in 1982?

'To begin with, we were preoccupied with enormity,' recalls Kim. 'Now we aim for elegance. The wine must have balance, finesse and concentration, in that order. Too many winemakers aim at concentration first, and the wine becomes an assault on the senses. Our key criteria are balance and harmony.'

Goldwater says the vinification is 'classic Bordeaux'. The fermenting juice is pumped over the skins, rather than

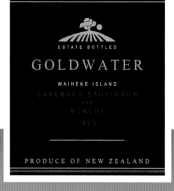

Grown at Putiki Bay, Goldwater Cabernet Sauvignon and Merlot ranks among Waiheke Island's — and the country's — greatest claret-style reds.

hand-plunged; the wine is kept in contact with the skins for 15 to 25 days after the ferment, to soften its tannins, and it is matured for 12 to 21 months in French oak barriques (typically half new). Powerful, brambly and finely structured, with great finesse, the top vintages reward cellaring for at least a decade. Esslin Merlot, also grown at Putiki Bay, offers complex flavours of spice, plum and chocolate, and silky tannins. This is a classy wine, though savoury and supple, but I am not yet convinced it justifies its markedly higher price, compared to its Cabernet Sauvignon & Merlot stablemate.

Although principally celebrated for its reds, Goldwater Estate's white wines can also be of startling quality. The island-grown, barrel-fermented Zell Chardonnay is powerful, lush and soft, with concentrated stone-fruit flavours and impressive complexity. The bold Dog Point Marlborough Sauvignon Blanc is a celebration of splendidly ripe fruit, with lush passionfruit/lime flavours, vibrant and tangy. The Roseland Marlborough Chardonnay is a gently oaked style that places its accent on well-ripened tropical and citrus fruit flavours, fresh and strong.

Mudbrick

■ Constructed solely from mud bricks hewn by hand, the Mudbrick vineyard restaurant has a stunning view across Auckland's Waitemata Harbour to the distant city. The restaurant is better known than the wines, but Mudbrick's reds are consistently impressive, full of warm, spicy flavour.

Nestled into the hillside at Church Bay, Mudbrick is owned by Nick and Robyn Jones. Nick, formerly an accountant, says he and his wife are now 'restaurateurs, with a passion for the island and the nuances of its wines'.

On a north-facing clay slope at Church Bay, the 4-hectare estate vineyard is planted in Cabernet Sauvignon, Merlot, Malbec, Cabernet Franc, Syrah and Chardonnay. Another, 6-hectare vineyard at Onetangi, called Shepherds Point, has been established in the same varieties, except Cabernet Franc. Chardonnay has also been purchased from Hawke's Bay, to produce wine for sale in the restaurant.

Address	Mudbrick Vineyard and Restaurant, Church Bay Road, Oneroa
Owners	Nick and Robyn Jones
Key Wines	Cabernet Sauvignon/Franc, Syrah, Reserve Merlot/ Cabernets/Malbec, Chardonnay

James Rowan, who joined Mudbrick in 2000, is based at the company's winery at the Shepherds Point vineyard, where he makes the wine for several Waiheke brands. Mudbrick's own annual output is only around 1000 cases of wine, but rising as new plantings come on stream.

Launched in 1996, the range includes two Chardonnays: a fully barrel-fermented, generous, sweet-fruited Church Bay Chardonnay, well-balanced and rounded; and a lower-priced Hawke's Bay model, full, peachy and soft.

Mudbrick's most distinctive wines, however, are its reds. The Cabernet Sauvignon/Franc is dark, with concentrated blackcurrant, nut and spice flavours. The Reserve Merlot/Cabernets/Malbec (the proportions of the blend vary, according to the season) is dark and rich, with good complexity and density.

The Syrah is pungently peppery on the nose, with intense plum/spice flavours. These are powerful, ripe, satisfying reds, full of island sunshine.

Obsidian

■ Named after a black volcanic glass traditionally used by Maori settled at Onetangi ('weeping sands'), Obsidian produces a stylish claret-style red, notable especially for its impressive harmony and finesse, rather than sheer power. Obsidian is a partnership of Auckland businessman and Bordeaux enthusiast Lindsay Spilman, Andrew Hendry, proprietor of Coopers Creek, and viticulturist Chester Nicholls. In 1996, the company purchased a vineyard, Gulf Crest, planted three years earlier at Onetangi. Winemaker Kim Crawford, then at Coopers Creek, was also involved at the start, but he withdrew in 1999.

Address	Obsidian Vineyard, Te Makiri Road, Onetangi
Owners	Lindsay Spilman, Andrew Hendry and Chester Nicholls
Key Wines	Obsidian, Weeping Sands

The 7-hectare vineyard is planted principally in Cabernet Sauvignon and Merlot, with smaller blocks of Pinot Noir (unusual for the island), Cabernet Franc and Malbec. About 1500 cases of wine are made annually, based exclusively on grapes from the estate vineyard. The winemaking is all done at the Coopers Creek winery in west Auckland by Simon Nunns, who worked the 2000 vintage in St Émilion.

The first wine flowed in 1997. From the start, Obsidian has been an elegant, smoothly mouthfilling wine with ripe, plummy, spicy flavours and complexity from well-integrated French and American oak. Stonyridge and Goldwater still produce the island's finest reds, but Obsidian is definitely in the second rank and one of Waiheke's rising stars. The second label, Weeping Sands Cabernet/Merlot, also estate-grown, is an American oak-matured blend, deeply coloured, smooth and flavoursome, with plenty of berryish, spicy character.

Address	Passage Rock Wines,
	438 Orapiu Road,
	Te Matuku Bay
Owners	David Evans and Veronika
	Evans-Gander
Key Wines	Forté, Syrah, Unoaked
	Gisborne Chardonnay

Passage Rock

■ One of the highest achievers among the new wave of Waiheke wineries, Passage Rock lies isolated from the rest on the south-east side of the island, overlooking Oakura Bay.

The site, known as Camana Farm Vineyard, is in the Te Matuku Valley, where David and Veronika Evans-Gander planted their first vines in 1994. David — whose sister, Mary, owns Heron's Flight Vineyard at Matakana — has previously made wine in Western Australia and Switzerland; Veronika, from Switzerland, is a former teacher.

On raised, almost flat land, the 3-hectare vineyard is planted mainly in Cabernet Sauvignon, Cabernet Franc and Merlot, supplemented by Malbec, Syrah, Chardonnay and Viognier. Chardonnay grapes are also purchased from Gisborne. In the future, a further 4 hectares of vines will be planted, including Montepulciano.

Made on-site by David Evans, the wines are limited in availability: 1000 cases a year of red wine and 1500 cases of white. But they are worth tracking down. Forté is one of the finest and best-value wines on the island. A blended red with a core of Cabernet Franc, and Merlot and Cabernet Sauvignon in supporting roles, it is dark, fragrant, rich and supple, with excellent concentration and structure.

Passage Rock Oakura Bay Syrah is also classy — weighty and intensely varietal, with deep cassis, plum and pepper flavours, fragrant, firm and long.

Address	Peninsula Estate,
	52A Korora Road,
	Oneroa
Owners	Geoff and Rose Creighton
Key Wines	Peninsula Estate Hauraki
	Cabernet/Merlot/Franc,
	Zeno Syrah, Christopher
	Chardonnay; Oneroa Bay
	Cabernet/Merlot

Peninsula Estate

■ Aiming to produce 'a Bordeaux-style claret of the highest quality', in 1985 Doug and Anne Hamilton planted their first vines on a breathtakingly beautiful, wind-buffeted site overlooking Oneroa Beach. So exposed is the elevated vineyard, their young vines had to be irrigated, an extraordinary requirement in Auckland. However, after '15 years of planting, pruning and picking' — and making some impressive reds — they recently sold the company to their long-term business partners, Geoff and Rose Creighton.

The 4-hectare sloping vineyard of friable clays over broken rock is established mainly in Cabernet Sauvignon and Syrah, with smaller plantings of Merlot and Cabernet Franc, and tiny plots of Chardonnay, Viognier, Malbec and Petit Verdot.

In the winery Doug Hamilton built in 1987, the annual output is currently about 1500 cases of wine. Winemaker Christopher Lush, who joined Peninsula Estate in 1991, is a graduate in horticulture from Massey University. He also holds a postgraduate diploma in viticulture and oenology from Lincoln University, and gathered his initial experience at Montana, Villa Maria, Goldwater Estate and in the Napa Valley of California. The grapes are all hand-harvested and the wine is matured for up to 18 months in French oak barriques, one-third new each year.

'Peninsula Estate is one of the island's cooler vineyard sites,' says Lush. 'It's not a heat trap; we don't get any excessive heat build-up so our harvest is typically two weeks behind most of the others'. So long as we miss bad weather, we see that as an advantage. And it's certainly better for working in!'

Peninsula Estate has never been one of the trendy Waiheke Island wineries. Excited by the challenge of raising the profile, the new owners plan to expand the vineyard and release new label designs, brands and wines.

The flagship Hauraki Cabernet/Merlot/Franc is a big, generous red, savoury, spicy, tannic and full-flavoured, although in cooler seasons, leafy characters have detracted from its quality. At least its equal, the Zeno Syrah (in the past labelled Gilmour Syrah) is sturdy and ripe, with loads of blackcurrant and black pepper flavour.

The second-tier claret-style red, labelled Oneroa Bay Cabernet Sauvignon/Merlot, is typically savoury, spicy and chewy, with lots of character. There is also a rare, estate-grown, French oak-fermented Christopher Chardonnay, at its best weighty and ripe, with peachy, lemony flavours and a rounded finish.

Stonyridge

■ From this small Onetangi producer flows one of the most celebrated and expensive reds in the land. For its arresting power, complexity and richness, and sheer vintage-to-vintage brilliance, Stonyridge Larose must be ranked as New Zealand's greatest claret-style red.

Stonyridge — named after a nearby rocky outcrop — lies a kilometre from the sea. Stephen White planted his first vines here in 1982 on poor, free-draining clay soils saturated with manganese nodules. Today, the 6 hectares of north-facing vines include all five of the traditional red Bordeaux varieties: Cabernet Sauvignon, Merlot, Cabernet Franc, Malbec and Petit Verdot (described by White as 'like a supercharged Cabernet . . . very high in tannin, colour, alcohol and acidity').

Managed organically, with no use of herbicides, insecticides or systemic fungicides, the vines are trained in classic Bordeaux fashion and a lot of time is spent manicuring the vineyard — shoot-positioning, leaf-plucking and crop-thinning. The vines only yield about 5 tonnes of grapes per hectare, well below the New Zealand average.

Closer to Onetangi Beach, a second vineyard, Vina del Mar ('vineyard on the sea') was planted recently in 2 hectares of red Bordeaux varieties, predominantly Malbec. The grapes, first harvested in 2002, are being kept separate from those grown at Stonyridge and will not be blended into Larose.

In his elegant terracotta concrete and timber winery, with its two-tier crush and fermentation areas and underground barrel cellar, White produces a bold, voluptuous red, richly perfumed and awash with lush, splendidly ripe, blackcurrant-like flavours. 'If we put the Larose label on a bottle,' he says, 'it's got to have big, dark, ripe berry fruits — that's what Larose is all about. It's got masses of colour, concentrated fruit and soft tannins, yet it's still a cool-climate style, and avoids going over the top into non-varietal jammy characters.'

Why has Larose been so successful? White points to Waiheke's high sunshine hours, the summer heat at Onetangi (up to 36°C in the shade), and low rainfall compared to the mainland, but those assets are shared with other winemakers. The site's northern aspect is very important, maximising exposure to the sun; clay soils give the wine flesh and richness; the rocks promote drainage; and the adjacent ridge protects the vines from cooling westerly winds.

Matured for a year in French (75 per cent) and American oak barriques (in a top year almost all new or freshly shaved), Larose is a consistently powerful yet stylish red, even in lesser years notably scented and ripe-tasting. It typically improves for seven or eight years, unfolding great complexity, and drinks superbly for at least a decade. Tasted in 2002, the magnificent 1994 vintage is just starting to round out.

The second-string label, Airfield, named after a nearby landing strip, is used 'as a back-up for poorer-performing rows, or for a poor year'. There is also a range of experimental wines — Row 10 Chardonnay, Syrah/Grenache and Malbec — sold in the winery's popular café.

Stonyridge's total annual output has recently ranged between 500 and 1500 cases, of which most is exported or sold to members of the Stonyridge Loyalty Club, who automatically buy an allocation each year. The 1985 vintage of Larose was launched at $17, the 2000 at $85, a clear guide to the stature of this glorious Waiheke red.

Address Stonyridge Vineyard, 87 Onetangi Road, Onetangi

Owner Stephen White

Key Wine Larose Cabernets

The nearby 'stony ridge' shields Stephen White's low-cropping vines at Onetangi from cooling westerly winds.

Stephen White

■ **Anyone reading Stonyridge's unique newsletter could be forgiven for believing Stephen White has devoted his life to hedonism, rather than winemaking.**

Penned under the name Serge Blanco (rumoured to be White himself), the annual letters to Stonyridge's mail-order customers tell of constant parties overseas with the famous and beautiful and an endless flow of fine wine. 'We like to inject a bit of fun into wine,' says White, who believes (or at least Blanco does) that the meaning of life is 'sailing, mountains, geckos, G-strings, islands and red wine'.

Now in his forties, Stephen White graduated with a Diploma of Horticulture from Lincoln University, Canterbury, in 1977. While studying under viticultural expert Dr David Jackson, it dawned on White that 'the whole concept of viticulture and winemaking is different from horticulture, because the fundamental direction of production is towards flavour, not tonnage. It's a fundamental difference in philosophy. You're actually getting into an art form'.

After working in the late 1970s in vineyards in Tuscany and California, and later at Châteaux d'Angludet, Palmer and Prieure-Lichine in Bordeaux, White returned to New Zealand to pursue his high ambition: 'to make one of the best Médoc-style reds in the world.'

Looking for the 'hottest, driest, sunniest climate', he originally intended to buy land in Hawke's Bay. 'But I'm an Aucklander, and I had an uncle with a few farms on the island. He said it was terrible farmland. It was very dry in the summer, he told me, with no fertility in the soil — all the things that were good for grapes. I was going tick, tick, tick on my list of requirements and thought: "This is it."'

In 1982, White bought his 10-hectare block at Onetangi and over the next four years set up Stonyridge while also managing an orchard at Pukekohe, south of Auckland. He was well aware of the shortcomings of almost all New Zealand reds of that era. 'The problem with most New Zealand Cabernet Sauvignons,' White wrote in 1986, 'is that they are too low in grape tannin, have a pH that is too high, have an embarrassingly weak colour and also that unripe

fruit/vegetative character that occurs in wines that have been heavily chaptalised [given sugar additions] and acid-adjusted.'

By contrast, White wanted his own Cabernet-based red to be an expression of fully ripe grapes. 'In terms of Bordeaux, I wanted a wine that had some of the strength of Mouton [Château Mouton-Rothschild] and the elegance of [Château] Margaux.' From the start, he sought to produce a wine in the Bordeaux mould, using low cropping, long skin maceration, a second label to allow 'selection', barrique-aging and selling 'en primeur'. 'Many of these were firsts for New Zealand.'

Nuggety, with a rugged, handsome face, White ran a marathon in his late thirties, finishing in a respectable 3 hours 22 minutes. 'It was a desperate attempt to prove that fine wine consumption and vigorous exercise could halt aging, heighten mental alertness and improve libido,' he wrote in his newsletter.

After 18 vintages and a glowing review from almost every critic who has tasted his wine, what gives Stephen White his greatest satisfaction? 'It's when someone says: "What an amazing place you've got," or "What an amazing wine." I started with no money and a bare field.'

Winemakers of distinction

Te Whau

■ Above a steep (20-degree) slope near the point of Te Whau Peninsula, at Putiki Bay on the south side of the island, soars the striking, Le Corbusier-influenced Te Whau winery and restaurant. Te Whau's red wine, The Point, is one of the island's finest and the restaurant's wine list is one of the greatest in the country, offering over 500 vintages.

Tony Forsyth, formerly head of the personnel consultancy firm Sheffield Consultancy, and his wife, Moira, planted their first vines in 1996. 'This is my second career,' says Forsyth. 'Over the next 25 years, my challenge is primarily to produce great red wine and also develop the wine tourism side. That subsidises the winemaking, as it's very hard to make a living out of such a small vineyard.' Tony's sister, Caroline, a career diplomat, is also involved.

The north-facing clay slope is close-planted in 1 hectare of Cabernet Sauvignon, Merlot (0.6 hectares), Cabernet Franc (0.3 hectares) and Malbec (0.1 hectares). The vines, managed organically, are sheltered from cooling south and south-west winds. For spraying on such steep land, a special tracked tractor (the only one in the country) is used. On another block nearby, 0.3 hectares of Chardonnay have been planted. The three-level winery, which uses gravity rather than pumping to move the grape must and wine, and has an underground cellar and barrel hall, was erected prior to the first vintage in 1999. Swiss winemaker Herb Freidli, a graduate of Roseworthy College in South Australia, worked in Burgundy, Victoria and at Stonyridge before joining Te Whau in 1999.

Te Whau's annual output is tiny — 100 cases of Chardonnay and 500 cases of The Point — but from the start the wines have been classy. French oak-fermented, the Chardonnay is tight and elegant, with sweet, grapefruit-like characters, biscuity oak and a long, poised finish.

The Point is a Bordeaux-style blend, matured in French oak and bottled without filtration. Cabernet Sauvignon-predominant, it is sturdy and warm, with brambly, plummy, savoury, slightly earthy flavours, complex, long and fine. Both the 1999 and 2000 vintages (there is no 2001) are distinguished.

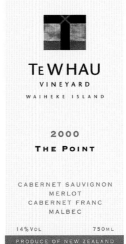

Address	Te Whau Vineyard, 218 Te Whau Drive, Te Whau Peninsula
Owners	Tony and Moira Forsyth, Caroline Forsyth
Key Wines	The Point, Chardonnay

Waiheke Vineyards

■ As executive officer of the Wine Institute from 1976 to 1990, Terry Dunleavy campaigned on behalf of all New Zealand winemakers. Now he crusades on behalf of 'the best red-wine area in New Zealand — Waiheke Island'.

Te Motu — the name of the company's flagship red — is an abbreviation of the original Maori name for Waiheke Island, Te Motu-Arai-Roa (the island-sheltering-long). The driving force in the foundation of Waiheke Vineyards was Paul Dunleavy, one of Terry Dunleavy's sons, a financier who returned to Auckland from Hawke's Bay in 1985 determined to start a vineyard.

Paul's brother, John, was living on Waiheke Island, where the Dunleavys found the summer heat 'reminiscent of Hawke's Bay, where we grew up'. Waiheke Vineyards Limited was formed by the Dunleavy and Buffalora families in 1988. A 12-hectare goat farm separated from Stonyridge Vineyard by a 60-metre-wide airstrip was purchased in 1989, and within months the first vines were in the ground.

The key tasks of running Waiheke Vineyards are divided between the three Dunleavys. 'I oversee everything on the island,' says John Dunleavy, who lives on-site. 'Paul, as managing director, looks after the financial side, and Dad takes charge of distribution and promotion.'

The 6-hectare vineyard, on gently undulating clay land only half a kilometre from the coast, is close-planted principally in Cabernet Sauvignon, with smaller blocks of Merlot and Cabernet Franc. John Dunleavy believes the site is 'very similar to Stonyridge, although a bit more exposed to the wind'. The vines yield a small crop, ranging from 3.5 to 6 tonnes per hectare. The wine was originally crushed, fermented and pressed at the vineyard, then barrel-aged in west Auckland, but has been made on-site by John and Paul Dunleavy since 1999.

Te Motu Cabernet/Merlot is matured in a mix of French (two-thirds) and American oak barriques. The 1994 — especially — and 1996 vintages shone, offering notable concentration and complexity, but to date the wine has been less consistently brilliant than Stonyridge or Goldwater.

Dunleavy Cabernet/Merlot, the second-tier label, is a drink-young style, fresh and lightly oaked, with good depth of plummy, spicy, slightly earthy flavour and gentle tannins.

Address	Waiheke Vineyards, Onetangi Road, Onetangi
Owners	The Dunleavy and Buffalora families
Key Wines	Te Motu Cabernet/Merlot, Dunleavy Cabernet/Merlot

Other producers

■ Cable Bay

Producing its first wines in 2002, Cable Bay is a major new player on the Waiheke wine scene. Its principal shareholders are Neill Culley, formerly chief winemaker at Babich, and his wife, accountant Denise Culley; viticulturist Dr David Jordan and his partner, Morag Fryer, a marketing and business management consultant; and David Irving, formerly chief executive of Heinz Wattie and past owner of the Irongate Vineyard, and his wife, Judy. The vineyards, first planted in 1998, are spread over seven sites at Church Bay, Oneroa and Onetangi. On land leased from local landowners and developed and managed by Cable Bay, 20 hectares have been established in Chardonnay, Merlot, Cabernet Sauvignon, Cabernet Franc and Malbec. The range, made by Culley at a west Auckland winery — until the company's own winery is built at Church Bay — will feature a Merlot-predominant, Bordeaux-style blend and a Chardonnay. Cable Bay's output will eventually top 10,000 cases, making it a real force to be reckoned with.

■ Ferryman

George and Judy Hudson own a vineyard at Church Bay but no winery. Since 1997, they have produced a very solid Cabernet Sauvignon/Merlot with good depth of blackcurrant, green leaf and spice flavour.

■ John Mellars of Great Barrier Island

The viticultural potential of Great Barrier Island, further out in the Hauraki Gulf, is also being explored. John Mellars gave up a 20-year career in computer consultancy to plant Cabernet Sauvignon and Merlot vines on a steep, sheltered clay hillside overlooking Okupu Beach, on the island's west coast. His 1-hectare vineyard, planted in 1990, yielded its first wine in 1993 — 156 bottles of robust, richly flavoured and rounded Great Barrier Cabernet. In favourable years, Mellars' output totals about 1000 bottles, made on-site, but there has been 'a lot of trial and error' along the way. 'At least those wines that are not good enough to sell, you can drink yourself.'

■ Kennedy Point Vineyard

At the western entrance to Putiki Bay, on the south-west side of Waiheke Island, Susan McCarthy and Neal Kunimura own a guesthouse and 1-hectare vineyard, planted in 1996 in Cabernet Sauvignon, Syrah and Merlot. The estate-grown wine — launched from the 1999 vintage, made by Herb Friedli and sold on-site at 44 Donald Bruce Road, Surfdale — is a classy, Cabernet Sauvignon-based blend with satisfyingly rich colour, body and flavour. (The range also includes a decent Marlborough Sauvignon Blanc.)

■ Miro Vineyard

On a steep slope in Browns Road, Onetangi, overlooking Obsidian, Dr Barnett Bond (a GP) and his partner, Catherine ('Cat') Vosper, own a 3-hectare vineyard, established in 1993–94 in Cabernet Sauvignon, Cabernet Franc, Merlot and Malbec. The wines, launched from the 1997 vintage and now made on-site by Bond, include the sturdy, brambly, spicy flagship red, Miro. In lesser years, Archipelago Cabernets, a decent red with blackcurrant, plum and herb flavours, is marketed.

■ Onetangi Road Vineyard

Near Stonyridge, at 82 Onetangi Road, this 3-hectare vineyard of Merlot, Cabernet Sauvignon, Cabernet Franc, Malbec and Chardonnay was established in the mid-1990s by John and Megan Wallace, who released their first wine from the 1998 vintage. It is now owned by George and Debbie Craddock, who also have a micro-brewery on the same site, producing ales under the Baroona brand. George Craddock makes about 1000 cases of wine each year. The early releases have included a smooth, slightly sweet Rosé, blended from Merlot and Cabernet Sauvignon; a flavoursome but only moderately ripe Merlot/Cabernet Sauvignon; and a dark, warm and concentrated Reserve Cabernet Sauvignon/Malbec/Merlot.

■ Putiki Bay Vineyard

Owned by Detlev Dannemann, a German who plans to retire to New Zealand, the 4.5-hectare Putiki Bay Vineyard at Te Whau Point is planted principally in Pinot Noir, with smaller plots of Malbec and Merlot. The wines, first produced in 1997 and made by Jamie Zapp, include a solid, ruby hued, firm and savoury Pinot Noir, a warm, berry and spice-flavoured Malbec and a fresh, buoyantly fruity Merlot.

■ Stony Batter Estate

At Man O'War Farm, at the north-east end of the island, John Spencer has established Waiheke's largest vineyard. A grandson of Berridge Spencer, who founded Caxton Printing Works, Spencer is one of New Zealand's richest men. On an elevated, windy site, the first vines were planted in 1993 and a trickle of wine has flowed since 1996. Planting began 'in earnest' in 1998, and the Stony Batter vineyard now covers 24 hectares of Merlot, Cabernet Sauvignon, Cabernet Franc and Pinot Noir, with small plots of Chardonnay, Sauvignon Blanc and Syrah. Once production gets into full stride (with 70 hectares of vines yielding an estimated 25,000 cases of wine), Stony Batter will be a medium-sized producer by New Zealand standards — and the giant of the Waiheke scene.

Stony Batter's vines at Man O'War Farm lie apart from the main cluster of Waiheke vineyards in the west.

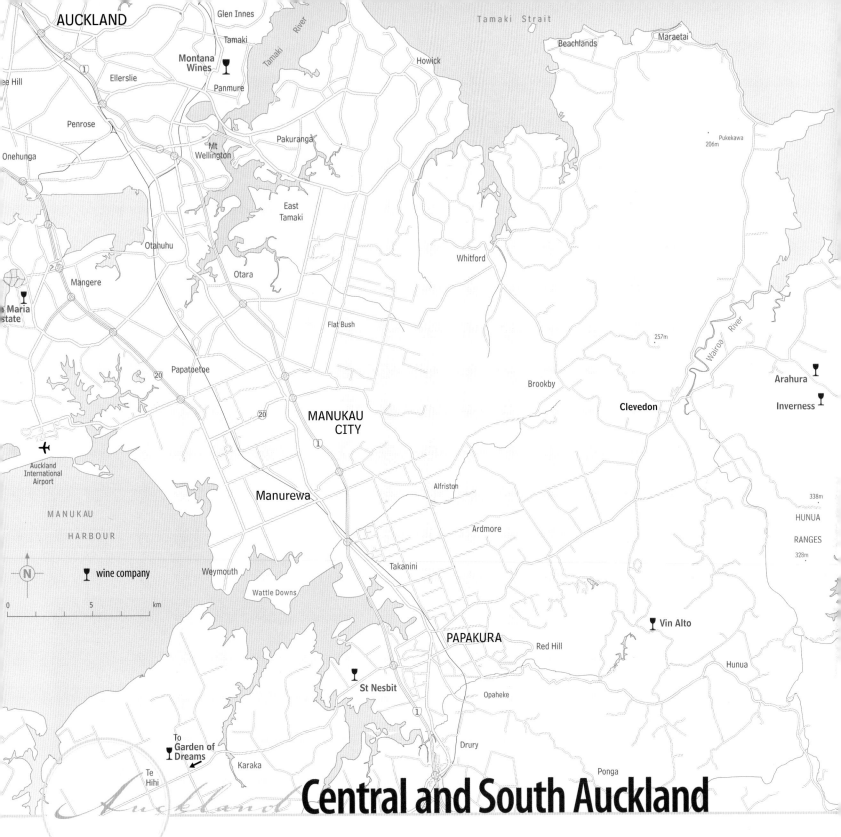

AUCKLAND
Glen Innes
Tamaki
Montana
Wines
Ellerslie
Panmure
Penrose
Mt
Wellington
Pakuranga
Onehunga
Otahuhu
East
Tamaki
Mangere
Otara
Maria
state
Flat Bush
Papatoetoe
MANUKAU
CITY
Auckland
International
Airport
Manurewa
Alfriston
MANUKAU
HARBOUR
N
wine company
Ardmore
0   5   km
Weymouth
Takanini
Wattle Downs
PAPAKURA
Red Hill
St Nesbit
Opaheke
To
Garden of
Dreams
Drury
Te
Hihi
Karaka
Ponga

Tamaki Strait
Beachlands
Maraetai
Howick
Whitford
Pukekawa
206m
Wairoa River
Arahura
Brookby
Clevedon
Inverness
257m
338m
HUNUA
RANGES
328m
Vin Alto
Hunua
Ponga

Central and South Auckland

Two of New Zealand's largest wine companies have their headquarters within Auckland's urban sprawl. Montana is based in a light industrial and state housing area in east Auckland, while Villa Maria is situated in Mangere, on the other side of the Auckland isthmus, near the Manukau Harbour. To the south-east lies the fledgling Clevedon region, starting to build a reputation for Bordeaux-style and (far less predictably) Italian-style red wines.

Clevedon

In the hills and valleys of Clevedon, in south Auckland, grapevines are sprouting. Arahura Vineyard, Vin Alto and Inverness Estate already have wine on the market, and several other producers are on the horizon.

Think Clevedon, and polo, horses and Champagne spring readily to mind. The district looks too lush and green for grapegrowing, but the local grape-growers are swift to point out that Waiheke Island lies over the water, just a few kilometres away. Many of the traditional dairy and dry stock farms have been subdivided in recent years, allowing diversification into export flowers, strawberries, equestrian centres — and vineyards. For several of those planting vines at Clevedon, the area's close proximity to Auckland city is an attraction, for family or business reasons.

The vineyards lie draped across sheltered blocks in the valleys and hilly sites angled to the sun. The first wine to flow from the Clevedon area was Ken and Diane Mason's Arahura Vineyard Merlot 1994. The focus has stayed on red wines, reflecting Auckland's warm climate. Radio personality Leighton Smith is determined to produce a top Syrah from his 2-hectare vineyard. By contrast, expatriate Americans Paul and Judy Fowler are inspired by the great reds of Pomerol, in Bordeaux, and have planted Merlot (mainly), Cabernet Sauvignon and Malbec at their 2-hectare Puriri Hills vineyard.

On the road to Kawakawa Bay, Callum and Jan McCallum have a north-facing 2-hectare vineyard, planted in Cabernet Sauvignon (principally) and Merlot. Callum is a cousin of Neil McCallum, owner of the Dry River winery in Martinborough. Made by Mark Robertson, of Matua Valley, the McCallums' first Clevedon Coast Cabernet Sauvignon flowed from the 1999 vintage.

Address Arahura Vineyard,
146 Ness Valley Road,
Clevedon

Owners Ken and Diane Mason

Key Wines Arahura Franc/Malbec/
Cabernet Sauvignon,
Merlot/Cabernet Sauvignon;
Ness Valley Merlot/Cabernet
Sauvignon, Cabernet
Sauvignon/Merlot

Arahura Vineyard

■ Ken Mason has often been in the public eye, chairing commissions of enquiry into such subjects as the status of mental health in New Zealand. A former judge, raised on the South Island's West Coast, in 1994 he produced the first wine from the Clevedon district.

'When I retired from the bench, I was only 53,' Mason recalls. 'Diane, my wife, and I had always had an interest in wine. After we got married, on Friday nights we'd have chicken chow mein and sparkling Barossa Pearl.' Veuve Clicquot, the great Champagne, later launched the Masons on their love affair with fine wine.

In 1990, the Masons toured France. 'We saw people tending their little plots of vines, and we had the land at Clevedon . . . Diane and I wanted to keep fit. We thought: let's see if we can make wine.'

After seeking advice from Tom van Dam, then at the Rongopai winery in Te Kauwhata, and Tony Molloy QC, of the St Nesbit winery at Te Karaka, in 1991 the Masons planted their first vines on a north-facing clay slope in Ness Valley Road, between Clevedon and Kawakawa Bay. The Masons named their winery after Arahura, just north of Hokitika — the traditional home of the Mason family of Poutini Ngai Tahu.

Two hectares of Merlot (50 per cent), Cabernet Sauvignon, Cabernet Franc and Malbec are now established. In a winery erected for the 1997 vintage, the Masons' son, Tim, an experienced winemaker who has worked for Montana since 1990, each year produces about 1000 cases of characterful, often classy, claret-style reds.

The lower-tier wines, sold under the Ness Valley label, have included a subtle, satisfying Merlot/Cabernet Sauvignon and a plummy, spicy Cabernet Sauvignon/Merlot, savoury and mellow. Both wines are reminiscent of a minor Bordeaux.

The premium range, carrying the Arahura brand, has featured a deliciously rich and supple Merlot/Cabernet Sauvignon and a generous, plump Franc/Malbec/Cabernet Sauvignon with deep blackcurrant and plum flavours and the earthiness typical of Auckland reds. These are consistently rewarding reds, priced right.

Montana

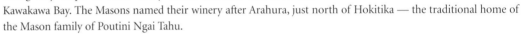

Address Montana Wines
Head Office:
171 Pilkington Road,
Glen Innes,
Auckland

Owner Allied Domecq

■ Montana is the Croatian word for mountain — a strikingly apt name for the colossus of New Zealand wine.

Statistics reveal the extent to which Montana bestrides the New Zealand wine industry. In the wake of its 2000 purchase of its largest competitor, Corbans, Montana produces about 50 per cent of all New Zealand wine and accounts for almost half of the country's wine exports. It owns or has management control over 3000 hectares of vines, operates wineries in Auckland, Gisborne, Hawke's Bay and Marlborough, and has a full-time staff of 1000. Over the past five years, it has poured more than $240 million into the wine industry, and in the year to 30 June 2001 had earnings (before interest and tax) of $55.2 million.

The company markets its wines under a wide array of brands, including Montana, Church Road, Saints, Deutz and Lindauer. The Corbans takeover has added such brands as Corbans, Stoneleigh Vineyards, Longridge and Huntaway to the portfolio. If you add in the New Zealand and imported brands the company distributes throughout the country, Montana claims a whopping 57 per cent share of its domestic market.

With Peter Hubscher in the top job since 1991, Montana has sharpened its wine quality and marketed its wines with increased sophistication. The company has also been highly profitable (posting an after-tax profit of almost $39 million in the 15 months to 30 September 2001). Inevitably, its international success attracted the interest of foreign buyers. In 2001, after a six-month battle with brewing giant Lion Nathan, UK-based Allied Domecq, the world's second-largest wine and spirits company, gained control of Montana.

Philip Bowman is Allied Domecq's chief executive officer. 'We bought Montana because it has some very good assets — dirt and vines, great brands and some very good people,' says Bowman. 'We'll be ramping up capital investment to accelerate the planting of new vines and getting the Montana brand integrated into our distribution network.'

Allied Domecq owns wine businesses in France (including Mumm and Perrier-Jouët Champagne), California, Spain, Portugal and Argentina, but its biggest wine asset is Montana. Between 1973 and 2000, Waihirere Wines at Gisborne, Penfolds Wines (NZ), the old McDonald's winery in Hawke's Bay, and finally Corbans (which itself had earlier swallowed Cooks/McWilliam's), had all fallen into Montana's embrace.

Ivan Yukich, the founder of this giant company, arrived in New Zealand from Croatia as a youth of 15. After returning to his homeland, he came back to New Zealand in 1934, this time with a wife and two sons. After years devoted to market gardening, Yukich planted a one-fifth-hectare vineyard high in the bush-clad folds of the Waitakere Ranges west of Auckland, and is believed to have sold his first wine in 1944.

Under the direction of sons Mate, the viticulturist, and Frank, winemaker and salesman, the vineyard grew to 10 hectares by the end of the 1950s. The company then embarked on a whirlwind period of expansion unprecedented in New Zealand wine history. To build up its financial and distribution clout, Montana joined forces with Campbell and Ehrenfried, the liquor wholesaling giant, and Auckland financier Rolf Porter. A new 120-hectare vineyard was established at Mangatangi in the Waikato and in the late 1960s Gisborne farmers plunged into grapegrowing at the Yukichs' urgings. A gleaming new winery rose on the outskirts of Gisborne in 1972 and a year later Montana absorbed the old family firm of Waihirere.

Although production was booming the company at this stage earned a reputation for placing sales volume goals ahead of product quality. The launch-pad for Montana's spectacular growth was a series of sparkling 'pop' wines — Pearl, Cold Duck and Poulet Poulet — which briefly won a following. For those with a finer appreciation of wine the company somehow managed to produce an array of classic labels.

The real force behind Montana's rise was the indefatigable and far-sighted Frank Yukich. He early perceived the trend away from sherry to white table wine and was the first to adopt aggressive marketing strategies. 1973 was a momentous year. The giant multinational distilling and winemaking company Seagram obtained a 40 per cent share holding in Montana, contributing money, technical resources and marketing expertise. Seagram's investment was originally trumpeted as 'basically an export deal . . . [to] export three million gallons [13.6 million L] a year within five years', but the anticipated river of wine from New Zealand to the United States never flowed.

The same year, Montana made an issue of 2.4 million public shares. Seagram's investments, shareholders' funds and independent loans together provided $8 million over the next three years for development purposes.

Also in 1973 came the pivotal move into Marlborough, as part of a major vineyard planting programme. Wayne Thomas, then a scientist in the Plant Diseases Division of the DSIR has related: 'Although plenty of suitable land was available in both the Poverty Bay and Hawke's Bay regions, my own impression was that it was too highly priced for vineyards.' Thomas suggested the Marlborough region as an alternative, and the area's wine-growing suitability was independently confirmed by the Viticulture Department at the University of California, Davis.

The first vine was planted in Marlborough on 24 August 1973: a silver coin, the traditional token of good fortune, was dropped in the hole and Sir David Beattie, then chairman of the company, with a sprinkling of sparkling wine dedicated the historic vine. The first grapes were harvested on 15 and 16 March 1976; 15 tonnes of Müller-Thurgau were trucked aboard the inter-island ferry at Picton and driven through the night by Mate Yukich to Montana's Gisborne winery. A 'token' picking of Cabernet Sauvignon followed in April.

Montana was moving swiftly to rectify its quality problems. The standard of the 1974 and subsequent vintages soon lifted the company into the ranks of the industry's leaders. Still pursuing the mass market, the company now shifted its emphasis to non-sparkling table wines. Bernkaizler Riesling (later called Benmorven) began to open up a huge market for slightly sweet white wines later developed with Blenheimer (still available in 3-litre casks). Its 1973 to 1977 Cabernet Sauvignons, grown in Gisborne, pioneered the production of quality New Zealand reds in large volume; the memorable, red label 1973 Reserve Bin won the top trophy at the 1975 National Wine Competition.

A year after the pivotal moves of 1973, Frank Yukich, the key visionary behind Montana's rapid rise, was gone — the loser when his relationship with Seagram turned sour. Soon after, the company also severed its link with the old Yukich vineyard at Titirangi. The 20-hectare vineyard site and substantial winery was unsuited to further development and the company chose instead to expand elsewhere. The old winery was dismantled and most of the equipment sent to Blenheim.

By the early 1980s, Montana was producing some of the country's top wines — notably its Marlborough Sauvignon Blanc and Marlborough Rhine Riesling — and had an enviable record in wine competitions. In 1985 Corporate Investments Limited took control of Montana, by adding Seagram's 43.8 per cent stake to its own already substantial shareholding. Seagram pulled out when the industry's fortunes turned sour: in the year to 30 June 1986 the company recorded a loss of almost $1.6 million. The principal shareholder in Corporate Investments was Peter Masfen, a son-in-law of Rolf Porter and a Montana director since the early 1970s. After acquiring Penfolds Wines (NZ) Limited in late 1986 from Lion Corporation Limited, in 1987 Corporate Investments secured a 100 per cent shareholding in Montana and then de-listed the company from the stock exchange.

During the late 1980s, Montana's policy was to supply the market with large volumes of sound, often excellent, wines at affordable prices. However, its top wines were no longer a match for those of some of its smaller rivals. In 1988, the company made a crucial decision: to expand its share of the premium wine market. Previously, geared to crush huge tonnages, it simply wasn't able to handle small, superior batches of grapes. It now reserved two locations for small-scale, premium wine production: a separate flow system at its Marlborough winery for hand-picked, whole-bunch pressed grapes, and the Church Road winery in Hawke's Bay.

By the early 1990s, Montana's top white wines were again capable of matching the boutiques for quality (and outperforming them in the value-for-money stakes), and the stylish Hawke's Bay reds under the Church Road label

Key Wines   Tom; Virtu; **Montana** Ormond Estate Chardonnay, Renwick Estate Chardonnay, Brancott Estate Sauvignon Blanc, Patutahi Estate Gewürztraminer, Fairhall Estate Cabernet Sauvignon; **Montana Reserve** Sauvignon Blanc, Chardonnay, Riesling, Merlot, Pinot Noir; **Church Road** Chardonnay, Reserve Chardonnay, Cabernet Sauvignon/Merlot, Reserve Cabernet Sauvignon/Merlot, Sauvignon Blanc; **Saints** Gisborne Chardonnay, Gisborne Gewürztraminer; **Montana** Marlborough Sauvignon Blanc, Marlborough Riesling, Gisborne Chardonnay, Gisborne Sémillon, Cabernet Sauvignon/Merlot; **Corbans** Cottage Block, Private Bin, varietal and White Label selections; **Stoneleigh** Sauvignon Blanc, Chardonnay, Riesling, Pinot Noir; **Longridge** Chardonnay, Sauvignon Blanc, Gewürztraminer, Cabernet Sauvignon/Merlot; **Huntaway Reserve** Chardonnay; **Lindauer** Brut, Special Reserve, Grandeur; **Deutz** Marlborough Cuvée, Blanc de Blancs; **Verde**

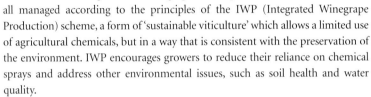

had started to flow. Today, under such brands as Montana Estates, Montana Reserve, Church Road and Deutz, Montana consistently produces some of the country's finest wines, white, red and sparkling.

All Montana's wines are bottled at its Glen Innes, Auckland winery, where chief winemaker Jeff Clarke is based. A graduate of Roseworthy College in South Australia, he worked at Penfolds in the Barossa Valley, and then at the Tisdall winery in Victoria, before joining Montana in 1993.

About half of Montana's grapes are grown in vineyards under its direct control, either company-owned or leased, and at least 75 per cent of the grapes for its premium wines. The vines are all managed according to the principles of the IWP (Integrated Winegrape Production) scheme, a form of 'sustainable viticulture' which allows a limited use of agricultural chemicals, but in a way that is consistent with the preservation of the environment. IWP encourages growers to reduce their reliance on chemical sprays and address other environmental issues, such as soil health and water quality.

In 2002, Montana's vineyard holdings included 350 hectares in Gisborne, 700 hectares in Hawke's Bay and 2500 hectares in Marlborough. In Gisborne, 200 hectares of Chardonnay, Gewürztraminer and Sémillon are established in clay loam soils at Montana's Patutahi and Saints vineyards in the Patutahi district; in the Ormond area, another 110 hectares of Chardonnay are grown in Waihirere clays at the Ormond and Whitmore vineyards.

In Hawke's Bay, between Taradale and Fernhill, 175 hectares of Chardonnay, Gewürztraminer, Sauvignon Blanc, Merlot and Cabernet Sauvignon are planted in silt loam soils at the Fernhill and Korokipo vineyards. At Ngatarawa, 140 hectares of Merlot and Cabernet Sauvignon have been planted in free-draining light silts overlying red metal. East of Havelock North, in clay pans and low-vigour river silts, both overlying gravels, 210 hectares of Merlot, Cabernet Sauvignon, Cabernet Franc, Malbec, Chardonnay and Sauvignon Blanc are grown in the company's Tukituki and Montana Terraces vineyards.

In Marlborough, at its sweeping Brancott vineyard on the south side of the Wairau Valley, Montana has 305 hectares of Sauvignon Blanc, Riesling, Chardonnay, Sémillon and Pinot Noir established in old glacial outwash soils, which although stony have a higher clay content than younger alluvial soils.

In the middle of the Wairau Valley, in soils ranging from silt loams to gravels, 260 hectares of Chardonnay, Sauvignon Blanc, Merlot, Cabernet Sauvignon and Pinot Noir are cultivated at the Fairhall and Renwick vineyards. On the north side of the valley, in silt loams and extremely stony Rapaura soils, the Stoneleigh and Squires vineyards have 265 hectares of Sauvignon Blanc, Riesling, Chardonnay, Gewürztraminer, Sémillon, Pinot Noir, Merlot and Cabernet Sauvignon.

In the upper Wairau Valley, Pinot Noir, Sauvignon Blanc and Chardonnay are planted in sandy loams and gravels at the 260-hectare Kaituna vineyard. Over in the Awatere Valley, at its Awatere Terraces vineyard — the coolest, windiest and driest of all the company's Marlborough sites — 245 hectares of Sauvignon Blanc, Riesling, Pinot Gris and Pinot Noir have been planted in silt loams and stony river terraces.

Making its first planting move into a new region for over a decade, in 2001 Montana established 55 hectares of Riesling and Pinot Noir in Waipara, North Canterbury, to extend a 5-hectare plot of 16-year-old Riesling vines it acquired as part of the Corbans purchase.

Montana's production of Sauvignon Blanc is one of the largest in the world, and it has the same ambition for Pinot Noir. Montana Marlborough Sauvignon Blanc, launched from the 1979 vintage, has introduced more overseas wine lovers to the delights of New Zealand wine than any other. Fermented at cool temperatures in stainless-steel tanks, it is an intensely varietal Sauvignon Blanc with pungent, zesty, capsicum-like aromas and flavours threaded with fresh, appetising acidity.

In 1996, Montana set out to become a force in the international red-wine market. Having decided, in Jeff Clarke's words, that 'the sites with high potential for Merlot or Cabernet Sauvignon are limited in New Zealand', it saw no reason, in terms of climate and soil, why Pinot Noir couldn't succeed on a large scale in Marlborough. Much work has been done to select low-vigour rootstocks, superior clones and soils with some clay content, which are believed to give greater depth of flavour. Between 1996 and 2002, Montana's total output of Marlborough Pinot Noir soared from 600 cases to 100,000 cases.

Montana's lowest-priced wines, packaged in bottles and 3-litre casks, are often blended from bulk wines imported from such countries as Australia and Chile. In the declining cask-wine market — which still accounts for over 40 per cent by volume of supermarket wine sales — its Wohnsiedler, Blenheimer, Country, Red Ridge, Woodhill's Vineyard and Oaklands casks enjoy a huge following. Montana's everyday-drinking bottled wines, marketed under such brands as Wohnsiedler, Jackman Ridge, Timara, Robard & Butler and Corbans White Label, are also frequently based on imported wines.

Peter Hubscher

■ **1973 was a pivotal year at Montana — Seagram bought a stake and the first vines were planted in Marlborough. A young winemaker, Peter Hubscher, also joined the company that year, embarking on his long, highly successful career at Montana.**

When named FCB Marketer of the Year at the TVNZ/Marketing Magazine Awards in 2001, Peter Hubscher was praised by the judges as 'inspirational, insightful and impassioned . . . at Hubscher's Montana everyone has the right to speak their mind. He clearly adores lateral thinking, questions conventional thinking and remains a very humble man'.

Awarded an honorary doctorate from Massey University in 2002 for 'outstanding contributions to winemaking, the wine industry and the wider field of business', in 1998, Hubscher was also made a Member of the Order of New Zealand for services to the wine industry. Chairman of the Wine Institute since 1999, during the past few years this notably experienced and versatile winemaker has been showered with honours.

The son of Czechoslovakian immigrants Otto (a violinist) and Suse Hubscher, who fled Prague and Hitler's anti-Jewish terror just before the Second World War, Peter grew up in Glen Eden in west Auckland, near the vineyards of Henderson and Oratia. 'My parents drank wine; I remember them buying Babich Dry Red and Western Vineyards Dry Sherry.'

His entry to the wine industry came 'by accident'. Planning a career as a cheesemaker, he studied for a degree in food technology at Massey University. In 1964 Tom McDonald, then production manager at McWilliam's, visited the university on a staff recruiting drive. Twenty-one-year-old Peter Hubscher was soon off to Hawke's Bay, the country's first graduate to be employed in a non-family owned wine company.

Hubscher spent eight years with McDonald at McWilliam's, then 'a big factory for making sherry, mainly out of sugar and water'. However, in 1965 McDonald and his Hungarian winemaker, Denis Kasza, started producing the famous series of McWilliam's Cabernet Sauvignons. In Hubscher's eyes, he was learning 'half what to do and half what not to do . . . and about what could be, what I could aim at'.

After joining Montana as winemaker in 1973, Hubscher initially used Müller-Thurgau grapes to produce slightly sweet, German-style wines like Bernkaizler

and Niersteiner. As the Marlborough vineyards started to come on stream, there followed increasingly sophisticated varietal wines from Chardonnay, Sauvignon Blanc, Riesling and Cabernet Sauvignon, and the country's first high-quality, widely available sparklings, Lindauer and Deutz Marlborough Cuvée.

Yet when he stepped into the top job in 1991, Hubscher felt all was not well at Montana. 'It had allowed itself to get too middle of the road. There was not enough focus on excellence, and that irritated me. Because I'd been in the industry a long time, I knew something about making wine and what was achievable. As managing director, I've had the opportunity to put some of my hare-brained ideas into practice.'

One of Hubscher's great strengths has been his willingness to employ overseas wine companies, such as Cordier (from Bordeaux) and Deutz (from Champagne), to show Montana what to do. 'I've always sought to get excellence from outsiders,' he says, 'so we don't end up trying to reinvent every wheel known to man. The problem is that in such a young industry, we didn't know what we didn't know.'

An arts lover who drinks 'a glass-and-a-half' of wine with dinner, Hubscher is quietly spoken, with a low-key manner, but no one in the wine industry doubts his astuteness and drive. 'Since university I've wanted to make something special and unique in New Zealand,' he says. 'Nothing else gives me more opportunity to do that than here. Montana is a collection of individuals creating something special.'

2001

MARLBOROUGH
Vineyard Selection
SAUVIGNON BLANC

PRODUCE OF NEW ZEALAND

75cl   Produced and Bottled by Montana Wines Ltd, RD4 Blenheim, New Zealand.   13.5% Vol

At the pinnacle of the company's wines — at least in terms of price — are Tom and Virtu. Tom, named in honour of the legendary winemaker Tom McDonald, is Montana's top Hawke's Bay red, made with input from the Bordeaux house of Cordier. Blended from Cabernet Sauvignon and Merlot, matured in French oak barriques, it is savoury, leathery and spicy, in a concentrated and complex style that steers away from the typically more fruit-driven reds of the New World and resembles a quality Médoc.

Made from botrytised Hawke's Bay Sémillon grapes and French oak-fermented, Virtu is a distinctly Sauternes-like wine, amber-hued, with superbly deep honey and apricot flavours in a very sweet, mouthfilling and complex style.

The Estate range features some of the company's greatest wines: the weighty, stylish Ormond Estate Chardonnay from Gisborne, which offers great depth of peachy, biscuity flavour, complex and creamy; an intense, nutty, steelier Renwick Estate Chardonnay from Marlborough; a pick-of-the-crop, partly barrel-fermented Brancott Estate Sauvignon Blanc from Marlborough with lush, incisive tropical-fruit flavours fleshed out with subtle oak; a mouthfilling, musky, rich, pungently peppery Patutahi Estate Gewürztraminer from Gisborne; and a fragrant, delicately flavoured Fairhall Estate Cabernet Sauvignon that proves (in favourable vintages) Marlborough's ability to produce top class claret-style reds. Dressed in labels featuring a bold single letter ('O' for Ormond, 'P' for Patutahi, and so on), this is a striking quintet.

The Montana Reserve range offers several Marlborough wines that, although produced in very large volumes at moderate prices, offer excellent quality. Fermented and matured in French and American oak casks, the Reserve Marlborough Chardonnay is fragrant, full-bodied and flavoursome, with fresh, ripe, grapefruit-like characters, biscuity, mealy complexities and a creamy-smooth texture; a string of major awards in New Zealand, Australia and the United Kingdom have highlighted its outstanding value. The Reserve Marlborough Sauvignon Blanc exhibits beautifully fresh passionfruit/lime flavours, vibrant and long. The Reserve Marlborough Pinot Noir is plummy and spicy, with substantial body, French oak complexity and very satisfying depth.

The impressive Chardonnays and Cabernet Sauvignon/Merlots produced under the Church Road label are

Sweeping across the south side of the Wairau Valley to the Wither Hills, Montana's Marlborough vineyards yield some of the world's most sought-after Sauvignon Blancs.

discussed on pages 140–41. The black-label Saints range offers several mid-priced wines of good quality. Saints Chardonnay, usually grown in Gisborne, is a delicious drink-young style, packed with toasty, buttery-soft flavour. Saints Gisborne Gewürztraminer is musky, with rich lychees, pear and spice flavours, a sliver of sweetness and plenty of personality.

In terms of sheer volume, and value-for-money, the company's key varietals are the long-popular wines marketed under the Montana brand: Marlborough Sauvignon Blanc, Marlborough Riesling, Cabernet Sauvignon/Merlot, Gisborne Chardonnay and (the latest addition) Gisborne Sémillon.

Since the first 1979 vintage, Montana's Marlborough Riesling has appealed as a floral, slightly sweet wine with an abundance of lemon/lime flavour and refreshing acidity. The huge-selling Gisborne Chardonnay places its accent on soft, peachy, citrusy fruit flavours, with a very subtle backdrop of oak (about 20 per cent of the final blend is barrel-aged). The Gisborne Sémillon is an easy-drinking style with ripe, tropical-fruit flavours, a subtle twist of oak and a fractionally sweet, smooth finish.

Montana Cabernet Sauvignon/Merlot, matured in French and American oak casks, is vibrantly fruity, with good depth of blackcurrant, plum and green-leaf flavours and gentle tannins. In most recent vintages it has been a blend of Marlborough and Hawke's Bay fruit, but it is not always made entirely from New Zealand grapes.

With its huge-selling Lindauer, Montana dominates New Zealand's sparkling wine output. Launched in 1981 and sold in Brut (dry), Sec (medium), Rosé, Special Reserve and Grandeur (ultra-premium) versions, Lindauer was the country's first readily available bottle-fermented sparkling. The Brut, the best-known label of the quintet, is based on three grapes — Pinot Noir (40 per cent), Chardonnay (40 per cent) and Chenin Blanc (20 per cent) — grown in Marlborough, Hawke's Bay and Gisborne, and disgorged after 15 months' maturation on its yeast lees. Fresh and lively, yeasty and vivacious, it's a four-star wine at a two-star price, and fully deserves its runaway popularity.

Each year, New Zealanders drink more than three million bottles of Lindauer, and more Lindauer goes overseas (especially to the United Kingdom, where it is the top-selling New World sparkling) than any other New Zealand wine. If Lindauer were a company in its own right, it would rank as New Zealand's third-largest winery.

Lindauer Special Reserve — a blend of Pinot Noir (principally) and Chardonnay, grown in Hawke's Bay and Marlborough and matured on its yeast lees for two years — is fuller, richer and creamier than the standard wine, with impressive depth of strawberryish, yeasty flavour and a smooth finish.

Montana's flagship sparkling wine was formerly Deutz Marlborough Cuvée, but in its key export markets Montana is now keen to play down the Deutz brand and build on the strong reputation of Lindauer. The recipe for Lindauer Grandeur, launched in 2000, was Pinot Noir (70 per cent) and Chardonnay, grown in Marlborough (90 per cent) and Hawke's Bay. A blend of several vintages, it spent an average of four years maturing on its yeast lees. A notably Champagne-like wine, Lindauer Grandeur is slightly pink-hued, with an enticingly fragrant and complex bouquet, a powerful, rich and yeasty mid-palate, developed flavours and a seductively smooth finish.

Deutz Marlborough Cuvée has been produced since 1988 under a joint agreement between Montana and the Champagne house of Deutz and Geldermann. André Lallier, the owner, managing director and chairman of Champagne Deutz, set out to tone down the aromatic fruitiness of Marlborough fruit. 'In Champagne, where the grapes don't have strong character, we aim for a wine without fruit aromas, preferring yeast autolysis characters.' Designed as an apéritif style, Deutz Marlborough Cuvée is based on hand-picked Marlborough Pinot Noir and Chardonnay, disgorged after two to three years on its yeast lees. Light, yeasty, delicate and flinty, it's a very refined, non-vintage style. The vintage-dated, Chardonnay-based Deutz Marlborough Cuvée Blanc de Blancs offers piercing, lemony, appley fruit characters with nutty, bready complexities and a crisp, lingering finish.

After absorbing Corbans in 2000, Montana kept most of its labels, including the popular bottle-fermented sparkling, Verde. Now a Chardonnay-predominant style, to provide a clear contrast with the similarly priced Lindauer Special Reserve, Verde is a stylish wine with strong, citrusy, yeasty flavours and good yeast-derived complexity.

Corbans' flagship Cottage Block and second-tier Private Bin ranges have in the past offered some arrestingly lush Gisborne Chardonnays and classy Marlborough Chardonnays, Sauvignon Blancs and Rieslings. These were recently

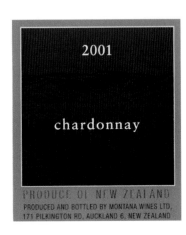

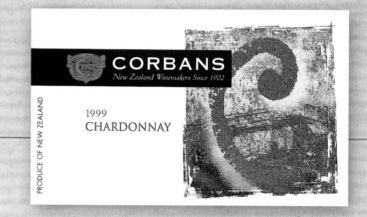

A pivotal event in Montana's recent history was its November 2000 acquisition of its biggest rival, Corbans, for $151 million. By swallowing the country's second-largest wine company, Montana greatly enhanced its grape resources, production capability and brand portfolio, and boosted its production of New Zealand wine by 70 per cent.

Within two months, Montana and Corbans were reportedly functioning 'as one company in every respect. All vineyard, winery, bottling, marketing, sales and distribution operations are fully integrated.'

The total cost of integrating the two wine giants, including some redundancies, was $9.5 million. 'The hardest thing I did shortly after the merger was announced was to wear a Stoneleigh-labelled [Corbans] T-shirt,' recalls Peter Hubscher, Montana's managing director.

Corbans had owned vineyards in the Gisborne, Hawke's Bay (245 hectares) and Marlborough (210 hectares) regions, wineries in all three regions, and a final blending, bottling and warehousing centre in Auckland. Under its key brands — Corbans, Stoneleigh Vineyard, Longridge of Hawke's Bay and Robard & Butler — it marketed a great diversity of labels.

In the first half of the twentieth century, the adroit management of the Corban family had ensured their domination of the New Zealand wine industry. From humble beginnings as a 1.5-hectare vineyard founded by Lebanese immigrant Assid Abraham Corban at Henderson in 1902, the winery flourished through prohibition and depression and early established itself as a household name. By the time of the Montana purchase, however, the company was Corbans only in name, being a wholly owned subsidiary of DB Group Limited, itself owned by Singapore-based Asia Pacific Breweries Limited, controlled by Dutch brewer Heineken NV.

During 1998 and 1999, DB had invested $32 million in expanding Corbans' vineyards and wineries. However, despite an annual turnover of around $120 million and export sales to over 30 countries, the company had been less profitable than its major New Zealand competitors. Viewed by DB as vulnerable on the New Zealand market to giant Australian producers, and at risk internationally because of its lack of shareholding ties to its principal overseas distributors, in mid-2000 the company was put up for sale.

After buying Corbans, most of the bottling equipment at the company's Ti Rakau Drive complex in Auckland was moved to Montana's bottling hall at Glen Innes. In Gisborne, Montana linked the two companies' adjacent wineries through pipelines, forming a single winery with the largest production capacity in New Zealand.

Corbans' winery in Thames Street, Napier, was extended and now processes the majority of Montana's Hawke's Bay grapes. In Marlborough, after transferring some equipment to its Brancott Winery, Montana sold Corbans' Stoneleigh Winery: 'It made sense to integrate all our winemaking in the region at one location,' said Peter Hubscher.

Corbans' key brands — Corbans, Stoneleigh, Longridge, Huntaway and Robard & Butler — all survived the takeover. After absorbing its long-standing and most formidable competitor, it would be difficult to argue with Montana's claim that 'increasingly, the history of Montana is becoming the history of New Zealand wine'.

Alex Corban (pictured in the early 1980s) for decades kept Corbans at the forefront of New Zealand wine quality.

joined by a moderately priced range of Corbans varietal wines, including a smooth, green-edged Corbans Sauvignon Blanc and a crisp, lively, slightly sweet Corbans Marlborough Riesling.

The Huntaway Reserve range, acquired from Corbans, includes a typically upfront, peachy, toasty, high-flavoured Chardonnay, blended from Gisborne (principally) and other grapes, and a soft, ripe and weighty Gisborne Pinot Gris.

The Longridge range, Corbans' Hawke's Bay equivalent of its Stoneleigh Vineyards Marlborough wines, included a solid, gently wooded Chardonnay, a fresh, limey, tangy Sauvignon Blanc, a pungent, peppery Gewürztraminer and a typically slightly leafy Merlot/Cabernet Sauvignon. However, under Montana's direction the Longridge brand has not been restricted exclusively to Hawke's Bay wines.

Of all the Corbans brands Montana recently added to its portfolio, the most internationally famous is Stoneleigh. The Sauvignon Blanc is awash with the pure, fresh and zingy flavours of Marlborough fruit, and has shown outstanding form in recent vintages.

Stoneleigh Riesling is dryish, with excellent depth of lemon/lime flavour and a tight, freshly acidic finish. The Chardonnay is typically crisp, with vibrant lemon/apple flavours and a subtle oak and lees-aging influence. Fragrant, generous, spicy and supple, Stoneleigh Pinot Noir is the country's best Pinot Noir in the sub-$20 category.

The premium Rapaura Series trio under the Stoneleigh brand features a fully barrel-fermented, soft, richly flavoured Chardonnay; a faintly oaked, intense, ripely herbaceous Sauvignon Blanc; and a weighty, complex Pinot Noir with deep cherry and spice flavours.

Villa Maria

■ Villa Maria occupies a unique place in the New Zealand wine industry. The only one of the three major companies still in private hands, it has also been by far the most successful exhibitor in local wine competitions during the last 15 years, winning an avalanche of gold medals and trophies. The Villa Maria empire includes three wineries: Villa Maria itself, and Esk Valley and Vidal in Hawke's Bay.

The origins of Villa Maria lie in a tiny operation called Mountain Vineyards, which was run as a hobby by Croatian immigrant Andrew Fistonich, who arrived in New Zealand just before the Depression. After working on the gumfields, Fistonich became a market gardener, and made a few bottles of wine for himself and friends before he became a licensed winemaker in 1949. When illness slowed him down, his son George abandoned his career plans in carpentry, leased his father's 0.8-hectare vineyard, formed a new company, and bought a press, barrels and pumps from Maungatapu Vineyards at Tauranga. In 1961, Villa Maria Hock nosed out into the market.

The winery initially made its presence felt at the bottom end of the market. The slogan 'Let Villa Maria introduce you to wine' associated with the sale of sherries and quaffing table wines, created an image the company for years struggled to overcome.

The commercial range in 1977 included six sherries, two ports, four sparklings, Moselwein, Hock, Sauternes, Burgundy, Claret and a slightly sweet Seibel Red. More importantly, in terms of the company's future direction, there was also a batch of experimental wines: Pinotage, Melesconera, Riesling, Cabernet Sauvignon, Pinot Chardonnay and Pinot Noir.

Villa Maria expanded rapidly through the 1970s — absorbing Vidal in 1976 — and early 1980s. To throw off its old image, recalls George Fistonich, 'around 1980 we changed the label by introducing the red "V", and decided to focus on quality and gold medals'. John Spencer, of the Caxton group of companies, was then a silent but substantial shareholder.

At the height of the wine industry's price war late in 1985, Villa Maria slid into a much-publicised receivership. With its limited capital reserves, the winery was simply unable to survive in the heavy loss-making trading environment created by its larger rivals. It was rescued by a capital injection from a new part-owner, Grant Adams, then deputy chairman of the investment company Equiticorp. Barely a year later, Villa Maria astounded observers by absorbing the Bird family's ailing Glenvale (now Esk Valley) winery. Villa Maria was on the comeback trail.

In 1991 Grant Adams sold his 50 per cent share in Villa Maria to Mangere grapegrower Ian Montgomerie. When Montgomerie sold his shares to the Fistonich family in 1996, the company returned to full family control.

Villa Maria relies on contract grape-growers for over half of its total fruit intake, but its top wines are usually grown in vineyards either owned or managed by the company. It owns Esk Valley's small estate vineyard, and in 1992 planting began at the gravelly Ngakirikiri vineyard on State Highway 50, near Gimblett Road, inland from Hastings. Twenty-five hectares have been planted in Cabernet Sauvignon and Merlot (principally), with small plots of Malbec, Cabernet Franc and Chardonnay. The vines (1.6 m apart, with 1.8 m between rows) are planted at twice the normal density in New Zealand, which enables the company to reduce cropping levels per vine without sacrificing yield per hectare.

Villa Maria also owns three other vineyards in the Gimblett Gravels area of Hawke's Bay. The 72-hectare Soler vineyard is planted principally in Merlot and Gewürztraminer; the 47-hectare Omahu vineyard in Merlot, Cabernet Sauvignon and Syrah; and the 18-hectare Vidal vineyard in Cabernet Sauvignon and Merlot. As a key alternative source of grapes, George Fistonich has pioneered in New Zealand the development of specialist, publicly owned vineyard companies. In 1993, small investors in Seddon Vineyards funded the establishment of an 80-hectare block of Sauvignon Blanc (principally), Chardonnay, Sémillon, Riesling and Pinot Noir in Marlborough's Awatere Valley. Villa Maria is contracted to manage the vines and buy the grapes.

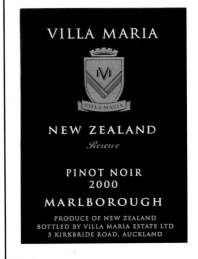

Address   Villa Maria Estate,
5 Kirkbride Road,
Mangere

Owners   The Fistonich family

Key Wines   Reserve Barrique Fermented Chardonnay, Marlborough Chardonnay, Hawke's Bay Chardonnay, Wairau Valley Sauvignon Blanc, Clifford Bay Sauvignon Blanc, Riesling, Gewürztraminer, Noble Riesling, Pinot Noir, Merlot, Merlot/Cabernet Sauvignon; Cellar Selection Chardonnay, Sauvignon Blanc, Riesling, Pinot Noir, Merlot/Cabernet Sauvignon; Private Bin Chardonnay, Sauvignon Blanc, Gewürztraminer, Riesling, Cabernet Sauvignon/Merlot

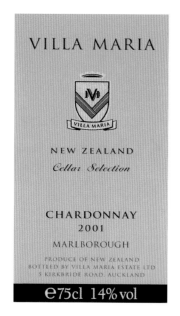

VILLA MARIA

NEW ZEALAND
Cellar Selection

CHARDONNAY
2001
MARLBOROUGH

PRODUCE OF NEW ZEALAND
BOTTLED BY VILLA MARIA ESTATE LTD
5 KIRKBRIDE ROAD, AUCKLAND

e 75cl 14% vol

Watch out! Picking the grapes by hand (rather than giant mechanical harvesters) enhances the quality of wines from Villa Maria's vineyards in Hawke's Bay.

The Terra Vitae share float in 1998 funded more new plantings in Hawke's Bay and Marlborough. The Keltern and Twyford Gravels vineyards, totalling 74 hectares near Roys Hill, in Hawke's Bay, have been planted in Merlot, Cabernet Franc, Cabernet Sauvignon, Syrah, Pinot Noir, Chardonnay, Gewürztraminer and Sémillon. In the Awatere Valley, another 80 hectares of Sauvignon Blanc (principally), Riesling, Chardonnay and Pinot Gris have been planted at Taylors Pass.

Villa Maria's vineyards in Marlborough are managed by Dr Mike Trought, a viticultural scientist formerly based at the Marlborough Research Centre and then Lincoln University. In 2000, the company opened a $7.5 million concrete and cedar winery in Marlborough.

Villa Maria's long-established, pseudo-Spanish winery at Mangere, in south Auckland, does all the bottling and distribution for the company's other wineries further south. However, in 2000 the company bought land in an old volcanic crater at Ihumatao, near Auckland Airport, where a 12-hectare vineyard is being established in Gewürztraminer, Chardonnay and Pinot Noir, and a new winery, bottling hall, distribution complex and visitors' centre is being erected. The Montgomerie Road winery will be able to handle 7000 tonnes of grapes, double the production capacity of the old winery.

Michelle Richardson, who joined Villa Maria in 1992 and became Villa Maria's winemaker in 1994, headed the group's winemaking team from 1998 until her resignation in 2002. Her successor is New Zealander Alistair Maling MW. Directly beneath the chief winemaker in the company's production pyramid are a trio of winemakers based at Villa Maria, Vidal and Esk Valley. The Vidal and Esk Valley winemakers prepare their wines to a 'ready for bottling' state, before they are tankered by road to Villa Maria for their final filtering and bottling.

Villa Maria's top wines, marketed under a Reserve label, have of late enjoyed a phenomenal run of gold-medal and trophy-winning successes. At the 2001 Air New Zealand Wine Awards, for instance, Villa Maria won gold medals for its Reserve Marlborough Chardonnay 2000, Reserve Riesling 1999, Reserve Noble Riesling 1999, Reserve Merlot 1999, and the 2000 and 1998 vintages of its Reserve Merlot/Cabernet Sauvignon. The Reserve Merlot 1999 also scooped the trophies for champion Merlot and Reserve champion (runner-up) wine of the competition.

George Fistonich

■ With his quiet manner and easy drawl, it would be easy to underestimate George Fistonich. He also generally avoids the limelight, happily stepping back in favour of his winemaking team. Yet Fistonich, Villa Maria's managing director, ranks among the wine industry's most powerful figures.

After leaving school at the age of 16, Fistonich served a five-year apprenticeship as a builder and joiner. 'Then I went out building on my own, but my father was suffering from asthma, so I came home to do a bit of work in the winery.' Forty years later, he's still there.

'I initially started off selling at the gate,' recalls Fistonich, 'but then we branched out to supply half a dozen wine shops. In the early days, a lot of retailers took the attitude they had never heard of Villa Maria. I travelled virtually the whole of the North Island, and we made contact with strong and independent people who supported us right from the start. Eventually, as our popularity grew, we put on a full-time sales manager in 1968. We kept concentrating on getting outlets throughout New Zealand, and then we started an advertising campaign in 1970. We were pretty much doubling our sales every year at that stage.'

Today, George Fistonich likes being involved in most aspects of the company. 'Some GMs are accountancy-orientated; I'm not. I find people much more fascinating. I love the element of psychology in business; it surfaces in marketing, negotiating and motivating. I'd be bored as a small-scale winemaker. There's much more scope for what interests me in a large company.'

In the eyes of Kym Milne, his former chief winemaker, Fistonich is 'an entrepreneur, an ideas man, rather than someone who gets bogged down in paperwork. Above all, he's a great "people" person.'

The word 'culture' often pops up in conversation with George Fistonich. He prides himself on creating a strong team culture at Villa Maria, and defines the company culture as 'being at the leading edge of quality across a broad range of wines at price points for all consumers. We have an overriding desire to be the best.'

Fistonich has always been a staunch supporter of local wine competitions. 'I see no other way to encourage our winemaking team to strive for better viticultural and winemaking practices than having the ultimate test of subjecting their wines to open competition.'

And how do you explain the company's brilliant track record in show judgings over the past 15 years? 'It's George,' says his former chief winemaker, Michelle Richardson, unhesitatingly. 'He realised very early that you need top viticulturists, and he got them living in the grapegrowing regions, where they could liaise constantly with the company's growers.'

Apart from his policy of employing top winemakers (there have been one or two failures along the way), Fistonich himself stresses the key role of viticulture in Villa Maria's competition successes. 'It's been our commitment to site selection within the regions best suited to our wine styles; our employment of top viticulturists to advise our growers; and our innovative "price based on quality" payment schedule, which rewards growers for their efforts in producing good-quality grapes.'

When George Fistonich was voted Winemaker of the Year at the 1993 Liquorland Royal Easter Wine Show, Michael Brett wrote in the *Sunday Star*: 'Fistonich has not made wine since the 1960s and cynics would probably say that Villa Maria's success began once he stopped making the wine. Rather, the award honours a man — a survivor, a juggler, an innovator — who has been the catalyst for the country's most consistently successful winner of wine show awards for close on a decade.'

The honours have flowed in recent years. In 2000, Fistonich was given a special award for Wine Industry Service to Hawke's Bay by the chairman of Hawke's Bay Vintners, and in 2001 he was inducted into the Manukau Business Hall of Fame. Fistonich is single-minded in his devotion to Villa Maria. If you ask him about his range of interests, he confesses: 'Wine has been all-absorbing.'

Now in his early sixties, Fistonich has no children involved in the company on a full-time basis, but his daughter, Karen, who is married to Milan Brajkovich, of Kumeu River, sits on the board of directors.

Will Fistonich eventually sell Villa Maria? 'I just passed a medical with flying colours,' he said in early 2002, 'and certainly don't plan to retire in the short term. I'm a bit like a conductor here — I could always hire a general manager and become the chairman.'

Winemakers of distinction

VILLA MARIA

NEW ZEALAND

Private Bin

SAUVIGNON BLANC
2002

MARLBOROUGH

PRODUCE OF NEW ZEALAND
BOTTLED BY VILLA MARIA ESTATE LTD
5 KIRKBRIDE ROAD, AUCKLAND

e 75cl 13% vol

Villa Maria's two top Chardonnay labels over the past decade, the Reserve Barrique Fermented and the Reserve Marlborough, afford an absorbing style contrast. The softly mouthfilling Reserve Barrique Fermented Chardonnay, usually based on Gisborne fruit, is powerful, mealy, creamy and rich. A lush, high-impact style made from super-ripe grapes off low-cropping vines, it has a strong new oak influence (currently averaging 80 per cent) and layers of citrusy, figgy, toasty flavour. Also fully French oak-fermented but with less new wood (60 per cent), the less voluptuous but equally classy Reserve Marlborough Chardonnay offers intense grapefruit, butterscotch and nut flavours, threaded with fresh, authoritative acidity.

The prestigious Reserve range also features two thrillingly intense Sauvignon Blancs: the pungently herbaceous and zingy Reserve Clifford Bay, grown in the Awatere Valley, and the faintly oaked, slightly weightier and rounder, but still explosively flavoured Reserve Wairau Valley. Also grown in Marlborough, the Reserve Riesling is typically mouthfilling, with intense, dry flavours, citrusy and minerally.

The Reserve Noble Riesling is a gloriously perfumed, honey-sweet Marlborough wine, with beautifully ripe fruit characters enriched but not dominated by botrytis. This is New Zealand's most acclaimed sweet white on the show circuit.

Pinot Noir entered the Reserve range with the dark, rich 2000 vintage, a plump, soft wine crammed with sweet, plummy, spicy fruit. Grown in Hawke's Bay and matured in French (principally) and American oak barriques, Villa Maria's Reserve Merlots and Merlot/Cabernet Sauvignons are the equal of any in the land, with dense blackcurrant, plum and spice flavours and notable complexity and harmony.

The second-tier Cellar Selection wines place their accent on intense fruit characters, with less use of new oak than in the Reserve range. The Cellar Selection white wines include two classy Chardonnays, from Hawke's Bay and Marlborough, with rich, vibrant fruit flavours delicately seasoned with wood; a deliciously intense and tangy, melon and green capsicum-flavoured Marlborough Sauvignon Blanc; a fragrant, strong-flavoured and supple Marlborough Pinot Noir; and a dark, sturdy Hawke's Bay Merlot/Cabernet Sauvignon with plum, blackcurrant and spice flavours, smooth and rich.

The quality of Villa Maria's third-tier Private Bin range has improved sharply in recent vintages. The Private Bin Gewürztraminer is an easy-drinking, fruity wine with fresh lychees and spice flavours and a splash of sweetness. In some vintages based on Marlborough fruit, in others blended from Marlborough and North Island grapes, the Private Bin Sauvignon Blanc is typically fresh, vibrant and flavour-packed, delivering outstanding value at its moderate price.

The Private Bin Marlborough Riesling offers crisp, dryish lemon/lime flavours, fresh and punchy. With its straightforward, citrusy flavours and light oak influence, the Private Bin Chardonnay, usually grown in Gisborne, is a no-fuss style designed for early consumption. There is also a solid but rarely exciting Private Bin Cabernet Sauvignon/Merlot, grown in Hawke's Bay and matured in seasoned oak barrels, with blackcurrant, plum and green-leaf flavours.

From the 2000 vintage, Villa Maria released a new collection of single-vineyard wines, including a notably subtle and complex Single Vineyard Waikahu Chardonnay, grown in Hawke's Bay, and a densely coloured Single Vineyard Pinot Noir from Marlborough with a powerful surge of sweet, ripe cherry and plum flavours and plenty of muscle.

Villa Maria's vineyard and winery complex (currently being developed) near Auckland Airport will be a Mecca for wine lovers.

Vin Alto

■ On steep, north-facing slopes of the Clevedon hills, 200 metres above sea level, Enzo and Margaret Bettio have set out on a revolutionary project: 'To use Italian grape varieties to make traditional Italian-style wines in New Zealand.'

Born in Switzerland but of northern Italian descent, Enzo Bettio worked in his father's business, importing and exporting food and wine, then travelled the world. After he 'fell in love' with New Zealand in 1980, Bettio and his English-born wife, Margaret, established one of the country's foremost importers of specialty foods, Delmaine Trading.

In the belief that there are distinct parallels between the climate and soils of Clevedon and those of Verona and Piedmont, in northern Italy, in 1994 the Bettios planted their first vines at Vin Alto ('high wine'). Their 8-hectare vineyard (which also includes varieties of French origin, such as Chardonnay and Merlot), has reputedly the largest collection of Italian grape varieties and clones in the southern hemisphere, including Nebbiolo, Sangiovese, Montepulciano, Rabose, Barbera, Dolcetto, Pinot Grigio (Pinot Gris), Corvina and Arneis.

Since the first 1996 vintage, the wines have been made on-site by Enzo and Margaret Bettio, using grapes grown on the estate and by other local growers, including radio personality Leighton Smith. Margaret Bettio has studied viticulture and winemaking by correspondence from Charles Sturt University in Australia. Enzo, who has worked in wineries in Italy, also benefits from technical assistance from Masi, a leading Veronese producer whose New Zealand agent is Delmaine.

To make Clevedon's equivalent of the traditional *amarones* of Verona, in late autumn the grapes are selectively hand-picked into trays and taken to drying sheds specially designed to enhance air movement. Over the next two months the fruit shrivels, losing up to 40 per cent of its weight and concentrating its flavour and sugar content. The grapes are then lightly crushed, de-stemmed and fermented. Partway through the fermentation, the free-run wine is drawn off and put into barrels to produce Vin Alto's most prized wine, Retico.

Left behind in the fermenting vat is a residue of pulp and skins that still contains some of the flavour and sugar of the original dried grapes. By pouring a young wine onto the remaining skins and continuing the fermentation, the Bettios create Ritorno, a wine in the Veronese *ripasso* tradition.

Leathery and spicy on the nose, Ritorno is a richly alcoholic wine with sweet fruit characters and strong, plummy, spicy flavours, framed by firm tannins. Best served at the end of a meal, 'with cheese, in front of the fire', Retico is a strapping, tawny-hued wine with a touch of sweetness and rich, raisiny, nutty, almost port-like flavours.

These are expensive wines — Ritorno retails at $65 and Retico at $89. 'I could make several bottles of normal wine with the grapes in one bottle of Retico,' says Enzo Bettio. 'If we want great red wines in New Zealand, people have to be prepared to pay for them.'

Vin Alto also produces more conventional wines, including a bone-dry, crisp and lemony Pinot Gris; a moderately complex, buttery-smooth Chardonnay; and a spicy, leathery, savoury, oak-aged blend of French and Italian red-wine grapes, labelled unpretentiously as Ordinario.

Address	Vin Alto, 424 Creightons Road, Clevedon
Owners	Enzo and Margaret Bettio
Key Wines	Retico, Ritorno, Ordinario, Chardonnay

Other producers

■ Garden of Dreams

One of New Zealand's rarest reds flows from the tiny Garden of Dreams vineyard on the Awhitu Peninsula. On a cliff-top site overlooking the Manukau Harbour, Craig Miller (best known for Miller's coffee) has established a 0.4-hectare plot of Merlot (predominantly) and Cabernet Franc. The classy 2000 vintage of Miller's Serious One is a fine debut — fragrant and generous, with excellent depth of ripe blackcurrant, spice and dark chocolate flavours.

■ Inverness Estate

At their 2.8-hectare vineyard in Ness Valley Road, Clevedon, John and Yolande Robinson cultivate Sémillon, Chardonnay and Cabernet Franc. The wines, made on their behalf by Anthony Ivicevich at West Brook, include a toasty, peachy, well-rounded Chardonnay and a spicy, earthy Reserve Cabernet Franc, which displays good depth and complexity.

■ St Francis

Auckland-based Simon Lampen, who in the past worked at Dry River and Delegat's, has since 1997 produced a rivulet of Hawke's Bay and Marlborough wines under the St Francis label. He is also part-owner of a 9-hectare vineyard in Marlborough's Omaka Valley, planted in 1999 in Pinot Noir, Pinot Gris, Sauvignon Blanc, Riesling and Gewürztraminer. Lampen's finest wine to date is the weighty, deliciously full-flavoured and creamy-smooth St Francis Hawke's Bay Chardonnay 2000.

■ St Nesbit

Owned by tax lawyer Dr Tony Molloy QC, St Nesbit is a small winery tucked away on a southern arm of the Manukau Harbour in Hingaia Road, Karaka, a couple of kilometres from Auckland's southern motorway. Molloy planted his first vines in Karaka's fertile, loamy soils in 1981, and from 1984 to 1991 released a stream of stylish, highly acclaimed claret-style reds. Today, the 2.6-hectare vineyard is planted principally in Merlot, with smaller plots of Cabernet Franc (15 per cent), Petit Verdot (15 per cent) and Malbec (4 per cent). During the 1990s, the vineyard was extensively replanted to reflect Molloy's changing ideas about the most suitable grape varieties, rootstocks, row orientations and vine spacing. After the release of the 1991 St Nesbit, red-wine production ceased until the 2001 vintage, which yielded about 500 cases.

Waikato/
Bay of Plenty

Vineyards and wineries are scattered very thinly across the Waikato and Bay of Plenty regions, yet several important wine companies are based there, including Morton Estate, Firstland Vineyards (formerly De Redcliffe) and Mills Reef. The northern and middle Waikato, where most of the vineyards are found, is a region of gently undulating lowlands, with broad valleys and rolling hills. Grass is the main crop and the dairy cow rules. To the east, in the Bay of Plenty, there is a sharp contrast between the inland volcanic landscapes and heavily forested ranges, and the coastal lowlands bordering the Pacific Ocean.

History

The foundation of the government Viticultural Research Station at Te Kauwhata in 1897 gave an early boost to grapegrowing in the Waikato. During the 1960s, Montana planted the country's largest vineyard south of the Bombay Hills, at Mangatangi, and in 1969 Cooks established extensive vineyards and a modern winery at Te Kauwhata. At the 1974 National Wine Competition, the trophy for champion wine was awarded to Cooks Cabernet Sauvignon 1973, grown at Te Kauwhata. By 1982, growers had 336 hectares, or 5.7 per cent of the country's total plantings, under vines.

A decade later, however, the Waikato was languishing as a wine region. Both the Cooks winery and the old research station had closed down, plantings were declining and new winemaking ventures were rare.

With the general industry shift to drier regions in the south, the Waikato's area in vines has plummeted. In 2002, only 133 hectares of producing vines (1 per cent of the national bearing vineyard) were planted in the Waikato/Bay of Plenty. Yet the number of licensed winemakers has not dropped over the past decade: 11 in 1991, 12 in 2001.

Climate

Warm summer temperatures and mild winters are typical of the Waikato, with high humidity levels and an ample, year-round supply of rain. With its high temperatures, humidity and rainfall, the Waikato shares the Auckland region's strengths and weaknesses for viticulture. Te Kauwhata has an almost identical heat summation figure to Warkworth, north of Auckland, but is marginally drier on average during the growing season than most of Auckland's wine districts. The Bay of Plenty is sunny, very warm and mild in coastal areas, with higher rainfall and a greater temperature range inland, where frosts can be severe. Sheltered by the ranges from the prevailing westerly winds, the coastal Bay of Plenty records high sunshine hours, but it is also exposed to rain-bearing winds from the north and north-east.

Soils

The clay loam soils common in the Waikato are generally deep and free-draining. Derived from a type of tephra (volcanic rock) known as Hamilton Ash, these lightly textured clays have a good structure for plant growth, provided organic matter levels are maintained. Volcanic loams are also widespread in the coastal Bay of Plenty, where their high soil temperatures and good water-holding capacity are ideal for citrus and kiwifruit growing.

Wine styles

Mouthfilling and rounded, with substantial body, ripe flavours and moderate acidity, the wines of the Waikato reflect the warm growing conditions of the upper North Island. The Chardonnays and Sauvignon Blancs are soft, with tropical-fruit flavours, and the claret-style reds are typically full-bodied, spicy and earthy. Chardonnay, Cabernet Sauvignon and Sauvignon Blanc (the last two classic Bordeaux varieties) are the most extensively planted grapes, but the latest national vineyard survey also revealed a significant presence of 'other white' and 'other red' varieties. These include Breidecker, Sylvaner, Blauburger, Seibel hybrids and Albany Surprise (cultivated for eating, rather than winemaking, purposes).

Sub-regions

Te Kauwhata, in the north, has been the hub of the Waikato wine industry since the 1890s. More recently, another cluster of vineyards has emerged south of the city of Hamilton — as far south as Te Awamutu — and there are also isolated plots of vines in the Bay of Plenty.

Principal grape varieties

	Producing area 2002	% total producing area 2002
Chardonnay	21 ha	16.1%
Cabernet Sauvignon	19 ha	14.0%
Other White Varieties	16 ha	11.8%
Sauvignon Blanc	16 ha	11.8%
Other Red Varieties	13 ha	10.0%

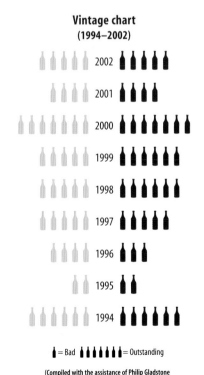

Vintage chart (1994–2002)

🍾 = Bad 🍾🍾🍾🍾🍾🍾 = Outstanding

(Compiled with the assistance of Philip Gladstone of Rongopai Wines, this chart is based on the Te Kauwhata sub-region.)

Previous page: Pinot Noir is the most promising wine from David and Margaret Higham's Pukawa Vineyard, on the southern shores of Lake Taupo.

Summary of climate statistics

Meteorological station	Latitude	Height	GDD	MTWM	Rainfall, Oct–Apr	Air frost days, annual
Te Kauwhata	37.25'S	32 m	1395	19.1°C	590 mm	10

Height — *above sea level* **GDD** — *growing degree days, Oct–Apr, above 10°C* **MTWM** — *mean temperature, warmest month*

Address	Firstland Vineyards, Lyons Road, Mangatawhiri
Owner	Leeward Investments Limited
Key Wines	Firstland Marlborough Sauvignon Blanc, Chardonnay, Reserve Chardonnay, Marlborough Riesling, Pinot Noir, Hawke's Bay Cabernet Sauvignon/Merlot, Reserve Cabernet Sauvignon/Shiraz

Firstland

■ The lovely, hill-ringed Firstland vineyard and winery (until recently known as De Redcliffe) lies north of Te Kauwhata, in the tranquil Mangatawhiri Valley. Here, winemaker Mark Compton, who arrived in 1987, produces good, often excellent wines.

Chris Canning, the founder, planted his first vines in 1976. His entrepreneurial talents were demonstrated in the late 1980s by the rise at De Redcliffe of the $8 million Hotel Du Vin, which boasts a top-class restaurant. De Redcliffe Group, incorporating the vineyard, winery and hotel, was floated on the stock exchange in 1987, with Canning the majority shareholder.

Following early financial difficulties, the Group was purchased by a Japanese-owned company, Otaka Holdings (NZ), whose principal shareholder, Michio Otaka, made his fortune in the construction industry. However, by the mid-1990s De Redcliffe's image was not strong, and in its own words its 'future looked decidedly bleak'. In a major move to lift its production and profile, the company embarked on three vineyard projects on a joint venture basis. 'In essence, we established our own vineyards, without having to own the land,' says Mark Compton.

In Hawke's Bay, working with landowner Bob Newton, the company established Cabernet Sauvignon and Merlot vineyards in the Gimblett Road district. These grapes are transported to Mangatawhiri for processing in Firstland's handsome, riverstone and cedar winery.

At Renwick, in Marlborough, Riesling and Sauvignon Blanc were planted in partnership with John Forrest, at whose winery the grapes are processed. About 10 per cent of Firstland's grapes come from the 7-hectare estate vineyard at Mangatawhiri, on river silts with a gravel base, where Chardonnay is the key variety, with smaller blocks of Pinot Noir and Sémillon.

A new era was launched in 2002 when the winery and hotel were purchased by Ed Aster, previously owner of one of America's largest publishers of trade magazines. Preferring to 'compete on quality rather than price', Aster promptly withdrew Firstland from the New Zealand market and will focus solely on export, especially to the United States.

The new Firstland range features an excellent, richly flavoured Marlborough Sauvignon Blanc; a citrusy, biscuity, mealy, impressively complex Reserve Chardonnay; and a sturdy Reserve Cabernet Sauvignon/Shiraz with plum and black pepper flavours, deep and firm.

Address	Mills Reef Winery, 143 Moffat Road, Bethlehem, Tauranga
Owners	The Preston family
Key Wines	Elspeth Chardonnay, Cabernet/Merlot, Merlot, Cabernet Sauvignon, Pinot Noir; Reserve Chardonnay, Riesling, Sauvignon Blanc, Merlot, Merlot/Cabernet; Mills Reef Chardonnay, Riesling, Sauvignon Blanc, Cabernet/Merlot/Franc, Traditional Method, Traditional Method NV

Mills Reef

■ Mills Reef is making waves. Some of the country's most compelling claret-style reds and an equally arresting Syrah flow from this sumptuous winery at Bethlehem, on the outskirts of Tauranga.

A former builder, 'Paddy' (Warren) Preston came to the Bay of Plenty from Wellington in the late 1970s to make wine — from kiwifruit. 'I'd previously made all sorts of wine at home. Kiwifruit was going well in the Bay, and I thought kiwifruit wines could succeed in Japan.' The Preston family soon dominated the Fruit Winemakers of New Zealand competition.

In 1989, the Prestons plunged into grape winemaking. 'The whole family was keen to make something well that's more widely recognised than fruit wine,' recalls Paddy Preston. The new venture was named Mills Reef in honour of the memory of Charles Mills, Paddy's great-grandfather, a sea captain and miner who 'watched for reefs at sea and mined for reefs of gold'.

Mills Reef's annual output is about 40,000 cases, making it a medium-sized winery by New Zealand standards. Its shingly 16-hectare vineyard in Mere Road, Hawke's Bay, close-planted since 1993 with red Bordeaux varieties and Syrah, is a key source of fruit for its top labels. Mills Reef also buys grapes from other growers in Hawke's Bay, the Coromandel Peninsula and the Kapiti Coast, north of Wellington.

The art deco style winery (reflecting the company's reliance on Hawke's Bay grapes) is a showpiece. Italian ceramic tiles run through the public areas and onto a deck that runs almost right around the building. The deck flows to a paved and grassed area that includes several pétanque courts.

The elegant winery restaurant seats 150. From the spacious wine-tasting room, which has large viewing windows into the bottling and labelling areas, stairs lead down to a cellar with traditional vaulted ceilings and older vintages of Mills Reef wines for sale. Huge wooden doors lead into a spacious cellar for barrel maturation.

The wines are made by Paddy Preston and his son, Tim. Mills Reef produces a three-tier range, with those labelled Elspeth (after Paddy Preston's mother) at the summit, followed by a mid-priced range of Reserve wines and everyday-drinking varietals called simply Mills Reef (these were previously branded as Mere Road and Moffat Road). Chardonnay and sparkling wines were at first the highlights of the Mills Reef range, but of late the red wines have stolen the limelight.

The Elspeth reds are powerful and concentrated, with exceptional depth, complexity and harmony. The Elspeth selection includes several claret-style reds — usually Cabernet Sauvignon or Merlot-predominant blends, but also straight varietal wines — and a superb Syrah. Among the most distinguished wines in the country, with a host of five-star awards, gold medals and trophies to prove it, the Elspeth reds also achieve excellent vintage-to-vintage consistency.

The Chardonnays are skilfully crafted, from the bottom-tier Hawke's Bay Chardonnay, typically easy drinking and creamy-smooth, to the well-structured, grapefruit, peach and butterscotch-flavoured Reserve Chardonnay, and the fully barrel-fermented Elspeth Chardonnay, a richly fragrant wine with sweet, ripe melon/grapefruit flavours and nutty, mealy, toasty characters adding richness.

The Reserve Sauvignon Blanc is a satisfying example of the Hawke's Bay regional style, with good weight, ripe tropical-fruit flavours and a touch of complexity from oak and lees-aging. The Reserve Riesling is a dryish style, fragrant, intense and lively in cool vintages. The Reserve claret-style reds show much of the character and style of their Elspeth stablemates.

For his top sparkling, the vintage-dated Mills Reef Traditional Method, Paddy Preston believes barrel-fermenting the base wine, before it goes into the bottle, is a key factor in the wine's quality. A blend of Hawke's Bay Chardonnay and Pinot Noir, it shows good intensity of nutty, yeasty flavour, crisp, complex and refined.

Not all of the wines are grown in Hawke's Bay. From the Shakespeare Cliff vineyard, overlooking Cooks Beach on the Coromandel Peninsula, comes a fat, ripe and rounded Reserve Cooks Beach Chardonnay, an appley, limey Sauvignon Blanc, and a smooth, strawberryish Reserve Cooks Beach Pinot Noir. There is also a lush, flavour-crammed Elspeth Pinot Noir, with sweet fruit delights and easy tannins, grown at Te Horo, on the Kapiti Coast.

When its Elspeth Syrah triumphed at London's International Wine and Spirit Competition in 2002, Mills Reef won the first international gold medal for a New Zealand Syrah (Shiraz).

Morton Estate

■ With its fast-expanding annual output of over 200,000 cases, Morton Estate ranks among the largest of New Zealand's middle-sized wineries. It markets a diverse array of sharply priced Hawke's Bay and Marlborough wines, with its super-stylish Black Label Hawke's Bay Chardonnay the jewel in the crown.

For several years after its first vintage in 1983, the Bay of Plenty winery sold all its output with impressive ease. The gold medal success of its 1983 White Label Chardonnay spurred interest, the striking Cape Dutch-style winery on the highway near Katikati attracted widespread attention, and South Australian winemaker John Hancock had already built a cult following during four spectacularly successful vintages at Delegat's.

Morton Brown, the entrepreneurial founder of Morton Estate, planted his first vines at Katikati in 1978. According to Hancock, Brown 'wasn't a wine man at all, but he was very progressive, very marketing orientated'. Morton Estate Chardonnays achieved great popularity, but in 1988 Brown sold his shares to Mildara Wines of Australia. Five years later, the company was purchased by Appellation Vineyards Limited, returning Morton Estate to New Zealand ownership.

When the current owner, John Coney, purchased Morton Estate in 1995, it was the final act in the unravelling of the Appellation Vineyards venture, which briefly merged Morton Estate, Cellier Le Brun and Allan Scott but never proceeded with its planned public share float. Coney, a New Zealander, was described by former Morton Estate marketing manager Paul Treacher as 'a property developer and financier with a real enthusiasm for New Zealand wine'.

Hancock departed in 1996, to set up the Trinity Hill winery, and the chief winemaker is now Evan Ward, based in Hawke's Bay, who carved out a strong reputation during his long spell as Corbans' winemaker in the region. The Hawke's Bay grapes are all processed at Morton Estate's Riverview winery at Mangatahi, before the wine is sent to the Bay of Plenty for final bottling. The Katikati-based winemaker is Chris Archer, an Australian who gained much of his early experience at the Tyrrell's and Pepper Tree wineries. Morton Estate is a diverse operation, spread across four regions. Its head office is in central Auckland; it has a winery and warehouse in the Bay of Plenty; most of its vineyards and a crush facility are in Hawke's Bay; and it owns the Stone Creek vineyard in Marlborough.

Central to the company's success has been its lovely Riverview Vineyard, established in 1988 on an elevated, relatively cool inland site on the banks of the Ngaruroro River. The upper terraces, protected by hills from the prevailing westerly winds, are especially warm. Here Morton Estate has planted 57 hectares of vines — half Chardonnay, with smaller blocks of Sauvignon Blanc, Pinot Noir, Cabernet Sauvignon, Merlot, Meunier and Syrah. This late-ripening site has yielded brilliant Chardonnay, with good acid spine and great flavour richness.

The nearby, slightly more elevated and wind-exposed Colefield vineyard is the coolest of Morton Estate's sites. Here, 25 hectares have been planted in Sauvignon Blanc, Chardonnay, Pinot Noir and Merlot. On the opposite bank from Riverview lies the company's largest vineyard, Kinross, where 158 hectares of Chardonnay and Pinot Noir (principally), Pinot Gris and Sauvignon Blanc have been planted.

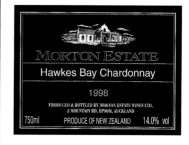

Address Morton Estate,
State Highway 2,
Katikati

Owner John Coney

Key Wines Coniglio; Black Label Chardonnay, Merlot/Cabernet, Merlot, Pinot Noir, Méthode Traditionnelle; White Label Chardonnay, Sauvignon Blanc, Riesling, Pinot Gris, Syrah, Pinot Noir, The Mercure; Stone Creek Sauvignon Blanc, Pinot Noir; Colefield Sauvignon Blanc, Riverview Chardonnay, Premium Brut

One of New Zealand's largest wineries, Morton Estate is especially acclaimed for its stylish, intense, Hawke's Bay Chardonnays.

Down on the plains, in the 'Ngatarawa Triangle', the relatively warm, 42-hectare Tantallon vineyard is devoted mainly to Chardonnay, but has also yielded some top Merlot. With sheltering hills to the south, the adjacent, even warmer Campbell's Brook vineyard has 36 hectares of Merlot, Cabernet Franc and Cabernet Sauvignon.

Morton Estate also owns the 41-hectare Stone Creek vineyard in Rapaura Road, Marlborough, planted in Sauvignon Blanc (principally), Chardonnay and Riesling. In a rare approach for a company of its size, Morton Estate does not buy grapes from contract growers, relying exclusively on its own vineyards.

The most prestigious wines carry a Black Label, with White Label wines positioned in the middle, and a selection of everyday-drinking wines, labelled Mill Road, at the bottom. The company also produces single-vineyard wines from Riverview, Colefield and Stone Creek, some impressive sparklings and a new super-premium Chardonnay, Coniglio.

Forty-five dollars was the highest price for a New Zealand Chardonnay until 2001, when Coniglio Hawke's Bay Chardonnay 1998 was launched at $80. A sort of Reserve version of the Black Label, it's a notably classy wine with layers of grapefruit and hazelnut flavours and a rich, resounding finish. Although expensive by New Zealand standards, the 1998 Coniglio is a match for many more expensive overseas Chardonnays.

The classic Black Label Chardonnay, grown at Riverview, is fully fermented in French oak barriques, typically 80 per cent new. A refined, tightly structured wine, in its youth intense, vibrant and citrusy, it flourishes with cellaring, building up complex, minerally, toasty characters.

The Black Label range also includes a smooth, biscuity, buttery Méthode Traditionnelle; a mellow, savoury and spicy Pinot Noir; and a Merlot/Cabernet Sauvignon that in warmer than average vintages (such as 1995 and 1998) is very classy and complex — savoury, leathery, nutty and brambly.

The middle-tier White Label selection includes two Chardonnays: the long-popular Hawke's Bay version, which offers plenty of peachy, citrusy flavour and a delicate seasoning of French oak; and a fruity, moderately complex, smooth Marlborough wine. Of the two White Label Sauvignon Blancs, the Hawke's Bay version is appley and limey, with a fractionally sweet finish, and the Marlborough model is fresh and punchy, with plenty of melon/lime flavour.

Grown in Hawke's Bay, the White Label Pinot Noir and White Label Syrah are both sharply priced wines, not intense, but offering good varietal character and some complexity. The Mercure, based on Merlot and Cabernet Sauvignon, is sometimes green-edged, but has plenty of savoury, leafy, spicy flavour.

The Individual Vineyard range features an elegant Riverview Chardonnay with lively melon/citrus flavours showing good complexity and depth; and a partly oak-fermented and lees-aged Colefield Sauvignon Blanc, tropical fruit-flavoured, soft and full.

Of Morton Estate's sparkling, the most popular is the Premium Brut, a Pinot Noir/Chardonnay blend with delicate, yeasty flavours and a seductively smooth finish.

Rongopai

■ The Rongopai — meaning 'good taste' or 'good feeling' — winery was founded by Dr Rainer Eschenbruch and Tom van Dam, who worked together at the Te Kauwhata Viticultural Research Station. The company originally earned a high profile for its rampantly botrytised, honey-sweet white wines, but now also produces dry whites and reds.

Rongopai produced its first wines in 1985, but in 1993 Eschenbruch withdrew from the company. Van Dam stayed on, but he also retired from the company in 2001. The company is now owned by a Scottish businessman, Derek Reid, who began investing in Rongopai in 1994. Reid — who made his fortune in the food industry, is a director of several Scottish companies and lectures in tourism — appointed viticulturist Phil Gladstone to the key post of Rongopai's operations manager. The original winery, in Waerenga Road, was built between the First and Second World Wars by Lou Gordon, who also operated under the name Rongopai. In 1995, however, Rongopai purchased the historic Viticultural Research Station's winery in Te Kauwhata Road. The rambling (1600 sq m), white-walled winery, with ancient casks and a three-storey high copper pot-still, works on a three-level, gravity-feed system, with the crusher at the top and the barrels at the bottom.

On loam-clay soils sloping gently to the north in Waerenga Road, Rongopai has a 1.4-hectare vineyard of close-planted Riesling and Chardonnay. Rongopai also owns another 2-hectare vineyard in Swan Road, planted in Chardonnay, Würzer, Pinot Noir, Merlot and Malbec. However, 80 per cent of the company's grapes are purchased from growers in Te Kauwhata, Gisborne and Marlborough. In a swing away from its traditional, heavily botrytised sweet wines, Rongopai is now aiming for a late harvest style, using grapes with about 20 per cent botrytis infection. The wines, totalling 15,000 cases in an average year, are made under the supervision of consultant winemaker Steve Bird, of Thornbury. The Rongopai range — currently in a state of flux — will in future include a Reserve selection, based on varietal wines from the major grapegrowing regions; a Heritage selection of single-vineyard wines, including late harvest styles from Te Kauwhata; and in an especially favourable season, sweet whites under the Romeo brand (in memory of the pioneer government viticulturist, Romeo Bragato).

Recent releases, which have been of variable quality, have included a smooth, ripe, barrel-fermented Vintage Reserve Chardonnay, with considerable complexity; a citrusy, limey, grassy Te Kauwhata Sauvignon Blanc; and an American oak-perfumed, weighty, full-flavoured and smooth Vintage Reserve Cabernet Sauvignon/Merlot.

Address	Rongopai Wines, 55 Te Kauwhata Road, Te Kauwhata
Owner	Derek Reid
Key Wines	Vintage Reserve Chardonnay, Riesling, Pinot Gris, Riesling Selection, Pinot Noir, Cabernet Sauvignon/Merlot

Other producers

■ Covell Estate

The remote Covell Estate lies at Galatea, near Murupara in the inland, eastern Bay of Plenty. Bob Covell planted his first vines 10 years before his first 'commercial' wine flowed in 1991. In the 7-hectare, frost-prone vineyard, 200 metres above sea level, Pinot Noir and Chardonnay are the key varieties. The wines, made on-site, have included a light, mellow Pinot Noir, a Chardonnay of variable quality and a lemony, freshly acidic Riesling.

■ Judge Valley

On the back roads of Te Awamutu, in 1997 Kevin Geraghty and Sheena Harrison planted Cabernet Franc on a north-facing slope in front of their farmhouse. In heavy, ash-based soils, with a high clay content, they plan to establish a 6-hectare vineyard of Merlot, Cabernet Sauvignon, Malbec and Cabernet Franc. Released in late 2000, the first vintage of 50 cases 'got the thumbs up from friends and neighbours'.

■ Kanuka Forest

This tiny winery sits right on the coast at Thornton, 15 kilometres west of Whakatane. Tony Hassall and his wife, Julia, planted the first vines in 1988 and in 1993 bottled their first commercial wines, but in 1997 they sold Kanuka Forest to Gerrit and Wil Kruithoed. The sandy, 3-hectare vineyard, run organically, is planted primarily in Cabernet Sauvignon, Merlot, Sauvignon Blanc and Chardonnay. The Cabernet Sauvignon/Merlot has been a solid red with moderately ripe blackcurrant and red berry flavours.

■ Ohinemuri Estate

In the bush-tangled slopes of the Karangahake Gorge, between Paeroa and Waihi, Horst and Wendy Hillerich have established a charming chalet-style winery. Horst Hillerich, born and trained in Germany, made the first Ohinemuri Estate wines in 1989. The grapes are bought from Gisborne and Hawke's Bay. The wines, made on-site and sold directly to the public over the counter or in the popular winery café, include a tangy, incisively flavoured Riesling and a perfumed, slightly sweet Gewürztraminer.

■ Pukawa Vineyard

One of the highest altitude vineyards in the country, Pukawa Vineyard lies on Lake Taupo's southern shores, near Turangi. David and Margaret Higham planted their first vines in 1996 and now have 2.5 hectares of Pinot Noir (primarily), Riesling, Chardonnay and Pinotage. The wines, launched from the 1999 vintage and made on the Highams' behalf at a Hawke's Bay winery, include a green-edged, high acid Riesling and a good, full-coloured Pinot Noir with strong plum/raspberry flavours.

■ Quarry Road

Now owned by Toby Cooper and Jenny Gander, this Te Kauwhata winery began life in 1963 as Aspen Ridge. The 5-hectare vineyard is planted in Sauvignon Blanc, Chardonnay, Riesling, Cabernet Sauvignon and Merlot. The Sauvignon Blanc is typically fresh, with crisp, grassy, limey flavours and good varietal definition; the Chardonnay is peachy and buttery-smooth; and the Merlot/Cabernet Sauvignon is medium-bodied, berryish and slightly leafy.

■ Totara

Out on a limb near Thames, Totara is New Zealand's only predominantly Chinese-owned winery. Founded by Stanley Chan in 1950, the company once had a strong following for its slightly sweet, blended Fu Gai and kiwifruit and coffee-based liqueurs, but the wines are no longer widely seen.

■ Vilagrad

The oldest wine company in the Waikato is Vilagrad, founded in 1922 by Ivan Milicich near Ngahinapouri, south of Hamilton. Pieter and Nelda Nooyen, the third generation of the family (their three sons are also involved) have a 5-hectare vineyard planted in Chardonnay, Gewürztraminer, Pinot Noir, Merlot, Malbec and Cabernet Sauvignon. The range includes a citrusy, spicy, medium Chardonnay/Traminer, a Reserve Chardonnay that can be highly impressive (especially in its youth), a plummy, green-edged Reserve Pinot Noir and a soft, slightly raisiny Reserve Cabernet/Merlot/Malbec.

Gisborne

Principal grape varieties

	Producing area 2002	% total producing area 2002
Chardonnay	966 ha	56.0%
Müller-Thurgau	157 ha	8.6%
Muscat varieties	102 ha	5.9%
Sémillon	91 ha	5.3%
Merlot	74 ha	4.3%
Pinot Noir	69 ha	4.0%
Gewürztraminer	55 ha	3.2%
Reichensteiner	51 ha	3.0%
Sauvignon Blanc	38 ha	2.2%
Chenin Blanc	22 ha	1.3%

Vintage chart
(1993–2002)

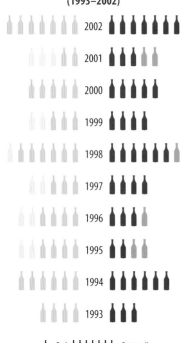

🍾 = Bad 🍾🍾🍾🍾🍾🍾 = Outstanding
🍾🍾 = variation between wine varieties

Previous page: From the Gisborne Plains flows a river of deliciously soft, rich, tropical fruit-flavoured Chardonnay, hard to resist at only six months old.

Over a quarter of New Zealand's wine flows from Gisborne in most vintages, yet the area does not have the powerful profile of the country's two other major wine regions, Marlborough and Hawke's Bay. Chardonnay accounts for over half of all plantings and has enjoyed glowing competition success, but much of Gisborne's grape crop is grown for low and moderately-priced wines, and with fewer than 10 wineries open to the public, the region's wine trail is remarkably short.

The hilly East Cape of the North Island is dominated by the Raukumara Range, leaving limited lowland areas suitable for viticulture. Grapegrowing is largely confined to the Poverty Bay flats near Gisborne city, which at just over 20,000 hectares form the largest of the coastal alluvial plains, and a much smaller one further north at Tolaga Bay.

The richness of its soils, warm summers and mild winters make Gisborne an ideal place for growing maize, grapes, kiwifruit, citrus and subtropical fruits. In the hill country, sheep, cattle, deer and goats are farmed and huge forests have been planted in *Pinus radiata*.

This is one of the most unstable landscapes in New Zealand. The soft, easily eroded mudstones and clays of the back country are drained by the narrow, silty Waipaoa River, which meanders across the western side of the plains to the coast at Poverty Bay. In the past, the river frequently flooded, inundating the plains with clay and silt sediment up to 7.5 centimetres thick. A flood control scheme was introduced in 1953, and since then the plains have rarely been flooded.

At the lower end of the Waipaoa Valley, the Gisborne Plains are shaped roughly like an isosceles triangle, with its apex near Te Karaka, 20 kilometres from the coast, and its base running 13 kilometres along the coast from Young Nick's Head to the mouth of the Turanganui River. On the north-east side of the valley — where the first vineyards were planted — five kilometres inland steep, strongly sculptured hills rise to 370 metres. On the western side of the valley, within 10 kilometres of the city, the hills climb to 450 metres.

At least half of the vines are clustered at Patutahi, north-west of the city, where Montana expanded its plantings so markedly in the late 1990s that the locals recently dubbed the area 'Montanaland'. Warm — being inland — with relatively low rainfall and heavy clay soils that drain well because the land is gently sloping, Patutahi has considerable advantages for viticulture, but a less obvious factor in Montana's recent surge of investment is simply that the largest land-holdings available for purchase were at Patutahi.

The second major grapegrowing district lies north of the city, in the Ormond, Waihirere and Hexton areas, where Gisborne's first commercial vineyards were planted. Here, on the eastern edge of the plains, at the foot of a long, irregular escarpment, lies the 'Slope of Gold', a gentle, clay-based slope with 20–30 centimetres of sandy topsoils which has given rise to many of Gisborne's top Chardonnays.

The 'Slope of Gold' faces south-west, rather than the preferred northerly aspect, but its soils are more free-draining and drier than those on the flats. There is also a crucial human factor in the medal-winning success of wines from the 'Slope of Gold' — some of Gisborne's most dedicated grape-growers, such as Geordie Witters and Paul Tietjen, are based there.

Closer to the coast, there are also substantial vine plantings in fertile, sandy soils at Matawhero, where afternoon sea breezes keep temperatures relatively cool.

The hunt for new, more favourable sites up off the valley floor is gathering pace, although the ruggedness of the hill country makes it difficult to find north-facing slopes large enough for vineyards. At its new McDiarmid Hill Vineyard on leased land at Patutahi, Villa Maria has close-planted 6 hectares of Chardonnay in low-vigour pumice soils. This elevated, sloping site is expected to yield 'exceptional' fruit for the company's top Barrique Fermented Chardonnay label. Villa Maria has also planted 11 hectares of Chardonnay and Gewürztraminer at the gently sloping Katoa Vineyard in a warm, sheltered bowl at Manutuke, surrounded by low hills.

At Naboth's Vineyard, James and Annie Millton have 2 hectares of Chardonnay and Pinot Noir on a steep, north-east-facing hillside at Manutuke, and grape-grower Chris Parker also has a hillside vineyard at Patutahi.

Reservations about Gisborne's viticultural potential have centred principally on the fact that although the vines get ample amounts of sunshine and heat, the typically highly fertile nature of the soils and plentiful autumn rains can easily combine to produce excessive vine-foliage growth and bumper crops.

Summary of climate statistics

Meteorological station	Latitude	Height	GDD	MTWM	Rainfall, Oct–Apr	Air frost days (annual)
Gisborne Airport	38.41'S	5 m	1468	19.2°C	522 mm	5
Manutuke	38.41'S	9 m	1379	18.8°C	487 mm	10

Height — *above sea level* **GDD** — *growing degree days, Oct–Apr, above 10°C* **MTWM** — *mean temperature, warmest month*

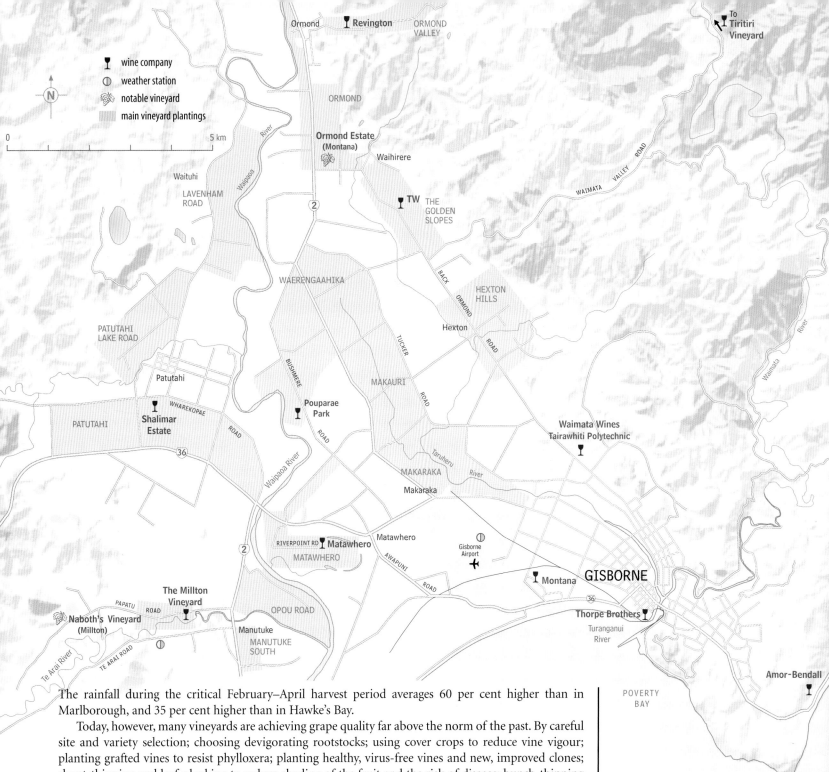

The rainfall during the critical February–April harvest period averages 60 per cent higher than in Marlborough, and 35 per cent higher than in Hawke's Bay.

Today, however, many vineyards are achieving grape quality far above the norm of the past. By careful site and variety selection; choosing devigorating rootstocks; using cover crops to reduce vine vigour; planting grafted vines to resist phylloxera; planting healthy, virus-free vines and new, improved clones; shoot-thinning and leaf-plucking to reduce shading of the fruit and the risk of disease; bunch-thinning to increase ripeness and flavour depth; harvesting later to advance fruit ripeness; and a range of other approaches, many Gisborne viticulturists are starting to explore their region's fine wine potential. Such consistently impressive wines as Millton Clos de Ste Anne Naboth's Vineyard Chardonnay and Montana Patutahi Estate Gewürztraminer show what can be done.

History

Friedrich Wohnsiedler pioneered winemaking in Gisborne after a false start by Marist missionaries, who landed by mistake at Turanganui (Gisborne) in 1850 and planted vines before departing for their original destination, Hawke's Bay. Wohnsiedler, born on a tributary of the Rhine, arrived in New Zealand around the turn of the twentieth century. When patriots laid waste his Gisborne smallgoods business during the First World War, in 1917 Wohnsiedler moved out and onto the land, planting vines at Waihirere. His first vintage, a sweet red, was labelled simply as 'Wine', with his own name beneath.

When Wohnsiedler died in 1958, his Waihirere vineyard covered only 4 hectares. (His name lives on, of course, on the labels of Montana's Wohnsiedler range.) In 1961, a rapid expansion programme began which, after a series of financial restructurings, saw the Wohnsiedler family eventually lose control. By 1973 Montana had completely absorbed Waihirere.

From a paltry acreage of vines supplying the old Waihirere winery, since 1965 viticulture has established a strong presence on the Gisborne Plains. It was a decline in the profitability of small-holding pastoral farming in the 1960s that aroused farmers' interest in grapegrowing. When Corbans and Montana offered lucrative contracts, vineyards spread rapidly. Corbans opened a gleaming new winery in

Gisborne in 1971, followed by Montana and Penfolds. By 1982, vine plantings reached a total of 1922 hectares, more than in any other region.

During the 1970s and early to mid-1980s, Gisborne was the wine industry's bread basket, the prime source of grapes for its hungry bulk-wine production lines. The tag 'carafe country' was easy to apply.

However, after New Zealand's fierce 1985–86 wine price war, as part of the government-funded vine extraction scheme, nearly 600 hectares of Gisborne's vines were uprooted and many growers left the industry. Since then, plantings have gradually returned to the extent of the early 1980s, with Chardonnay replacing Müller-Thurgau as the region's mainstay variety. In 2002, Gisborne is New Zealand's third most heavily planted wine region. Its 1724 hectares of producing vines (up from 1447 hectares in 1999) constituted 13.1 per cent of the country's total producing area — a steep drop from 25.8 per cent in 1990, reflecting the recent flurry of vineyard expansion in less fertile, drier regions to the south.

Some of the middle-sized wine companies have abandoned Gisborne in recent years and now draw their grapes from further south, on the grounds that their export markets prefer Hawke's Bay and Marlborough wine. For Gisborne, however, all is not lost. After massive plantings by Montana, the region's area of bearing Chardonnay vines soared from 590 hectares in 1999 to 966 hectares in 2002, enabling the company to expand overseas sales of its big volume Montana Gisborne Chardonnay, middle-tier Saints Gisborne Chardonnay and flagship Ormond Estate Chardonnay.

But with only 15 producers in 2001, the Gisborne wine community is tiny compared to Hawke's Bay (which had 51 producers) and Marlborough (with 64). If Gisborne wines are ever to enjoy a similar profile, many more producers and labels will be needed.

Climate

One of the sunniest regions in New Zealand, Gisborne has also recorded some of the highest temperatures, with 38°C at Gisborne city. Such early-ripening grapes as Müller-Thurgau and Reichensteiner are typically among the first in the country to be harvested, and Chardonnay ripens in Gisborne up to six weeks ahead of southern regions.

That Gisborne is warm enough to mature its grapes early is of critical importance — especially in wet seasons — because its rainfall figures are relatively high. High hills at the coast collect moisture from easterly and south-easterly winds, making the region markedly wetter than Hawke's Bay. The western side of the Gisborne Plains, however, is drier than the east. During the 1996 to 2000 grapegrowing seasons, 30 per cent less rain fell on Montana's vineyards at Patutahi than at Ormond.

Gisborne's climate is strongly influenced by the surrounding mountains, with the North Island high country and nearby hills providing much shelter from westerly and northerly weather systems. The prevailing north-westerly winds are usually warm and dry and southerlies, although cold and wet, are generally of short duration. However, Gisborne is highly exposed to easterly winds and the coastal hills intensify the precipitation, bringing lengthy spells of wet weather. Sea breezes are common in summer, especially in the afternoons, cooling the vineyards in the Matawhero area but having less effect on the more extensive plantings further inland. In Gisborne's relatively wet climate, the challenge facing viticulturists is to ripen their grapes fully in clean, rot-free condition. Bunch rot, especially botrytis, is the chief disease threat and a much greater problem than in the drier regions to the south.

A major plus-point for Gisborne, however, is its ability, at least in drier years, to fully ripen grapes on vines carrying 'commercial' (that is, heavy) crop loads. In the cooler regions to the south, smaller crops are necessary to achieve ripe fruit flavours. Gisborne's ability in favourable years to fully ripen relatively heavy crops is a bonus for companies seeking to produce moderately priced wine of sound, average quality.

Soils

The young alluvial soils of the Gisborne Plains, derived from the soft, sedimentary rocks of the back country, rank among the most naturally fertile soils in New Zealand.

James Millton, the region's leading small winemaker, sees two key soil types in the lower Waipaoa Valley for grapegrowing. 'The fine silt loams closest to the river produce aromatic wines, whereas the heavier clay soils on the edge of the plains give a fleshier character.' At Patutahi, the widespread Kaiti soils are principally clay loams with near-white sub-soils and black topsoils that dry out and crack in summer.

Soils of the Waipaoa type, found close to the Waipaoa River, include silt loams near the river banks and clay loams further afield. These are the newest soils on the plains, deposited by floods during the twentieth century after heavy erosion of the river's catchment area. Waipaoa soils are the least popular with viticulturists; they are the most flood-prone and in Montana's view produce less richly flavoured grapes and wines. Matawhero and Waihirere soils lie on the rarely flooded, higher parts of the plain. Deep, friable and well-drained, with an ample supply of nutrients, they are regarded as the finest all-purpose soils and are widely used for viticulture. Matawhero soils have distinctly organic topsoils, with some areas possessing a layer of humus-enriched sediment up to 100 cm thick; Waihirere soils are chemically similar and are again highly fertile.

Wine styles

Gisborne's greatest asset is the enormous drink-young appeal of its Chardonnays. Fragrant and soft, with lush, ripe citrus and tropical fruit flavours, they can knock your socks off barely six months after they were a bunch of grapes. Gisborne Chardonnay can also mature gracefully. Revington Vineyard Chardonnay 1989, the champion Chardonnay of the 1990 Air New Zealand Wine Awards, was in magical condition in 1999 and could easily have been taken for five, rather than 10, years old. The exceptionally stylish and multi-faceted 1994 and 1995 vintages of Corbans Cottage Block Gisborne Chardonnay also matured superbly.

Gisborne is largely white-wine country. In the 2000 vintage (more representative than 2001, an exceptionally low-cropping year) the region produced 85 per cent of New Zealand's Muscat; 49 per cent of the Müller-Thurgau; 48 per cent of the Sémillon; 39 per cent of the Gewürztraminer; 38 per cent of the Chardonnay; and 24 per cent of the Chenin Blanc. Plantings are expanding of Chardonnay, Sauvignon Blanc, Malbec, Pinot Noir, Chenin Blanc, Sémillon and Gewürztraminer. However, Müller-Thurgau, Muscat and Reichensteiner (all grown for low-priced white or sparkling wines) are declining. Sauvignon Blanc, which has proved vulnerable to botrytis and ripens too swiftly to retain herbaceous varietal characters, is nevertheless expanding slowly. Sémillon, with its greater disease-resistance, has a brighter future and has yielded some attractive, well-ripened, tropical fruit-flavoured wines.

Gisborne has produced some of New Zealand's most striking Gewürztraminers, at first under the Matawhero and more recently Montana Patutahi Estate labels. However, the variety's tight bunches are vulnerable to botrytis and the quality of Gisborne Gewürztraminer is highly variable, reflecting the dryness or wetness of the season. Montana reports that thin-skinned, tight-bunched Pinot Gris has not performed well in Gisborne's relatively wet autumn weather.

Few Gisborne reds stand out. The region has sufficient heat to grow later-ripening red-wine grapes, but rain is the bugbear, swelling the berries at the cost of flavour and colour intensity. With the occasional exception, Cabernet Sauvignon has not performed well and plantings are rare.

Some promising Merlots have been made in drier seasons, but most growers accept that the variety performs better in Hawke's Bay. Thin-skinned Pinot Noir is too susceptible to Gisborne's autumn rain to make quality reds, but may have a future when harvested early for sparkling wine. Malbec's early-ripening ability has recently aroused strong interest and plantings are expanding swiftly.

Sub-regions

The most heavily planted district is Patutahi, a relatively warm and dry, slightly inland area north-west of Gisborne city, where Montana has recently established extensive Chardonnay vineyards. The older-established Ormond area, more affected by rain-bearing easterlies, lies on the other side of the plains. Afternoon sea breezes cool vineyards in the Matawhero district, closer to the coast.

Gisborne's fertile alluvial soils typically yield heavy crops of grapes for everyday-drinking wines, but some lower-vigour sites are producing exceptionally powerful, intense Chardonnays.

Address Matawhero Wines,
Riverpoint Road,
Matawhero

Owner Denis Irwin

Key Wines Reserve Gewürztraminer,
Chardonnay; Estate
Gewürztraminer,
Chardonnay; Bridge Estate

Matawhero

■ 'In a "Woman's Weekly" world, I'm doing Hemingway,' claims Denis Irwin, the proprietor of Matawhero and one of the great individualists of the New Zealand wine scene.

Twenty years ago, Matawhero enjoyed a reputation second to none for its handling of Gewürztraminer. Bill Irwin (Denis' father) planted his first vines as a contract grower in 1968. The first 1976 vintage of Matawhero Gewürztraminer, made in a converted chicken shed, scored a silver medal at that year's National Wine Competition; the 1978 later won gold. Today, the winery's star has dimmed, but the wines flowing from the end of Riverpoint Road can still be absorbing.

Matawhero's 31-hectare vineyard surrounding the winery is planted predominantly in Chardonnay and Gewürztraminer. The nearby 2.5-hectare Bridge Estate vineyard, established in 1985, is planted in red Bordeaux varieties: Merlot, Cabernet Sauvignon, Cabernet Franc and Malbec.

A restless spirit, Irwin spent the majority of the 1980s across the Tasman, unsuccessfully attempting to establish a second winery in Victoria. Unlike the intensely varietal wines on which the company's fame was built, Matawhero now set out to produce wines with more restrained varietal characters, using indigenous rather than cultured yeasts, malolactic fermentation and lengthy wood handling. But the standard of the wines — even judged as 'style' rather than 'varietal' wines — was uneven.

Today, the Gewürztraminer is musky, substantial, honeyish and soft. 'There are a lot of more pungent, obvious Gewürztraminers on the market than mine,' says Irwin. 'But there's no challenge for me in that. I want structure, subtlety, complexity. Varietal character is the last point I'm interested in, although it does come as the wines age.'

In 1999, Matawhero noted that its Gewürztraminer is 'served at the Queen's table and is reputed to be one of her favourite wines'. Of the two models recently on the market, the Estate Gewürztraminer is soft, gingery and well-spiced, but lacks the intensity of the Reserve label.

The Reserve Chardonnay is robust, rich-flavoured and complex at its best, but has sometimes simply looked tired. Bridge Estate, the sturdy, single-vineyard blend of Merlot, Malbec, Cabernet Sauvignon and Cabernet Franc, can be highly impressive, with concentrated, blackcurrant and plum flavours, spicy, leathery, savoury complexities and a proven ability to mature well for at least a decade.

Address The Millton Vineyard,
119 Papatu Road,
Manutuke

Owners James and Annie Millton

Key Wines Gisborne Vineyards
Chardonnay, Riesling Opou
Vineyard, Chenin Blanc Te
Arai Vineyard, Chardonnay
Opou Vineyard,
Merlot/Cabernet Te Arai
Vineyard; The Growers Series
Viognier, Gewürztraminer;
Clos de Ste Anne Naboth's
Vineyard Chardonnay, Clos
de Ste Anne Naboth's
Vineyard Pinot Noir

The Millton Vineyard

■ It is a startling fact that only one wholly Gisborne-based winery has built a national — indeed international — reputation for wines of consistent excellence. The Millton Vineyard lies west of the city at Manutuke, on the banks of the Te Arai River.

Once expelled from a South Island private school for making blackberry wine in the prefects' study, James Millton spent two years with Montana before leaving to pursue his wine career overseas. After working on a small estate in the Rheinhessen, he returned to a vintage with Corbans and then went to work for John Clark — his wife, Annie's, father — who first planted vines at Manutuke in the late 1960s. The Milltons' first vintage flowed in 1984; by 1985 they had their first gold medal.

Now the Milltons' four vineyards have spread out over 20 hectares in the Manutuke and Matawhero districts. In the original Opou Vineyard in Papatu Road, Manutuke, 8 hectares of Chardonnay and Riesling are cultivated in Waihirere heavy silt loams and Kaiti clay loams. Bounded on three sides by the Te Arai River, the silty, 3-hectare Te Arai Vineyard is planted in Chenin Blanc, Viognier, Malbec and Merlot. In the Matawhero silt loams of the 7-hectare Riverpoint Vineyard — along the road from Denis Irwin in Riverpoint Road, Matawhero — the Milltons have planted Chardonnay and Viognier.

The top of the range Clos de Ste Anne wines are grown at Manutuke, on a steep north-east-facing slope with a commanding view over Poverty Bay. Here, in volcanic loess overlying pumice and calcareous base rock, the 2-hectare Naboths Vineyard is planted in Chardonnay and Pinot Noir.

In the conviction that 'we are what we eat', the Milltons have set themselves the difficult task of making organically grown wines in commercial volumes. In 1986, their vineyards were the first in the country to be certified organic. The 'Bio-Gro' status given by the New Zealand Biological Producers' Council affirms that the Milltons do not use herbicides, insecticides, systemic chemicals or artificial fertilisers.

James Millton readily agrees that Gisborne's warm, moist climate is not well suited to organic viticulture: 'But we can do it. Far from being a convenient way of marketing our wine, it is the protection of our own health and the environment in which we work that motivates us to pursue this direction.' (For further details, see pages 128–29.)

Not all of the Milltons' wines are grown organically. The Growers Series, launched from the 2001 vintage, is based on grapes purchased from Gisborne growers whose vineyards are managed according to IWP standards (see pages 128–29).

After many years making wine in Gisborne, James Millton has decided to focus on Chardonnay, Riesling, Chenin Blanc and Viognier for white wines and Merlot and Malbec for reds. Pinot Noir, rarely successful this far north, is also part of the range, 'for adventure'. Production has doubled since the early 1990s but with its average annual output of 15,000 cases Millton is still a smallish producer.

The Chenin Blanc Te Arai Vineyard is the best in the land. 'I want honey and acidity and almond flavours,' says Millton — and he gets them. The grapes are hand-harvested at three different stages of ripening, culminating in

On a steep, north-east-facing slope overlooking Poverty Bay, James Millton grows his memorable Clos de Ste Anne Naboth's Vineyard Chardonnay, dedicated to his wife, Annie.

the final picking of botrytis-affected fruit. Fermented in a mix of stainless-steel tanks and seasoned French oak casks, but fully barrel-aged, this is a delectable, fractionally off-dry wine. In dry years it is fresh and vibrant, with intense fruit flavours, pure and tight; in wetter seasons, with a stronger botrytis influence, the wine is more forward and honeyed.

With its rich, citrusy, limey, often honeyed flavours and lively acidity, the medium-sweet Riesling Opou Vineyard is New Zealand's northernmost fine-quality Riesling. The Chardonnay Opou Vineyard (in the past labelled Barrel Fermented) has shown strong form in recent vintages, with good mouthfeel and depth and a deliciously soft texture. There is also a moderately priced, gently oaked Gisborne Vineyards Chardonnay with smooth, ripe, citrus/melon flavours and a slightly buttery finish.

The outstanding Clos de Ste Anne Naboths Vineyard Chardonnay, produced only in top vintages, is not put through malolactic fermentation, in order to achieve a 'pure, crisp, mineral flavour'. Savoury, nutty and firm, it's a powerful, concentrated, multi-faceted wine, full of extract and flavour. The less memorable but still rewarding Clos de Ste Anne Naboths Vineyard Pinot Noir is fragrant, cherryish and spicy, with earthy, savoury characters and strong personality.

Fermented with indigenous yeasts in old barrels, at its best the Growers Series Viognier is strikingly scented, powerful and rich, with deep, pear-like, slightly nutty flavours and a softly seductive finish.

Thorpe Brothers

◼ Winemaker John Thorpe's career has taken several twists and turns since his first vintage in 1989. After helping to set up his family's horticulture blocks and producing fruit wines and mead, with Ross Revington, a Gisborne lawyer, Thorpe set up a partnership originally called White Cliffs and later, Landfall. After Revington (who has his own Revington Vineyard label) withdrew from the business in 1993, Thorpe formed a new partnership with his brother, Bill, to produce wine under the Landfall (now discontinued) and Longbush labels.

For several years the winery was based at Manutuke, alongside the original vineyard established by the Thorpe family in the 1970s. After selling that property, the company is now based at The Works, a former freezing works overlooking the port of Gisborne.

Today, Thorpe Brothers does not own vineyards; the company's annual output of about 5000 cases is based entirely on Gisborne grapes grown on a contract basis. Chardonnay, Gewürztraminer and Merlot are the mainstays of the range, marketed under the flagship Longbush Woodlands Reserve, Longbush (middle-tier) and Nicks Head (everyday-drinking) labels.

The wines have been of variable quality over the years, but the latest releases are solid. Longbush Chardonnay, fermented in French and American oak barriques, is full-bodied, with a core of ripe, peachy fruit overlaid with buttery, toasty characters. The Woodlands Reserve Chardonnay (French oak-fermented) offers rich, smooth tropical and citrus flavours and toasty oak in a classic regional style.

Longbush Gewürztraminer is softly mouthfilling and gently spicy. Longbush Merlot is typically of moderate depth, but the American oak-aged Woodlands Reserve Merlot/Cabernet Franc is a full-coloured wine with good depth of blackcurrant and plum flavours and some earthy, leathery complexity.

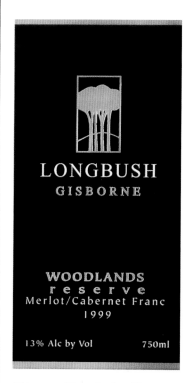

LONGBUSH
GISBORNE

WOODLANDS
r e s e r v e
Merlot/Cabernet Franc
1999

13% Alc by Vol   750ml

Address	Thorpe Brothers Wines, 265 Lytton Road, Gisborne
Owners	Bill and John Thorpe
Key Wines	Longbush Woodlands Reserve Chardonnay, Gewürztraminer, Merlot/Cabernet Franc; Longbush Chardonnay, Gewürztraminer, Merlot

Other producers

■ Amor-Bendall

Meticulous white wines flow from this boutique winery at Wainui Beach, run by food technologist Noel Amor and his partner, Alison Bendall. First produced in 1999 and made from grapes purchased from Gisborne growers, the range includes an unoaked but highly attractive Gisborne Chardonnay, a classy, concentrated and complex Reserve Chardonnay, a Gewürztraminer with considerable richness, and a less exciting, green-edged Merlot/Pinotage.

■ Pouparae Park

Keen to diversify beyond kiwifruit, in 1994 Alec Cameron purchased grapes and had his first 1994 vintage processed by a local winery. The workmanlike wines — sold at Cameron's Bushmere Road property, set in a country garden — include Chardonnay, Riesling, Solstice Blanc (blended from Müller-Thurgau and Muscat Dr Hogg), Merlot and a Cabernet Sauvignon/Merlot Dessert Wine.

■ Revington Vineyard

From a small, hill-flanked vineyard tucked away in Gisborne's Ormond Valley, north of the city, sometimes flow one of New Zealand's finest Gewürztraminers and a top-class Chardonnay. Lawyer Ross Revington and his wife, Mary Jane, in 1987 purchased a 4.5-hectare vineyard of Chardonnay and Gewürztraminer, planted in flat, sandy loams over clay. The wines, produced at various times at wineries in Gisborne and Marlborough, and not made every year, are unusually rich and full of character — the Gewürztraminer powerful and intensely spicy, the Chardonnay stylish, complex and (at least from dry seasons) long-lived.

The greening of New Zealand's vineyards

■ 'New Zealand wine: the riches of a clean, green land', has been the wine industry's positioning statement for several years. Yet until recently, admits Tony Hoksbergen, national vineyards manager for Montana, 'if anyone had chosen to scratch the surface, they would have found little substance to the claim in the context of viticultural production'.

Today, half of the country's vineyard area is managed according to the principles of the IWP (Integrated Winegrape Production) scheme, which Hoksbergen describes as 'a pragmatic balance between environmental concerns and productivity. We could go down the organic route, but that raises issues in terms of productivity, viability and international competitiveness'.

Around the world, there is confusion as to the exact nature of organic viticulture, but the primary focus is on the soil. Organic grape-growers concentrate on increasing microbial activity in the soil, while avoiding adding to the soil substances which are not derived directly from nature. For instance, compost and manure are used as fertilisers, in preference to chemicals.

An extreme form of organic farming is bio-dynamics, based on the teachings of Rudolf Steiner. In the belief that plants respond not only to nutrition but to various forces of nature, bio-dynamic viticulturists plan their activities according to the positions of the moon and stars. Adherents include Domaine LeRoy, in Burgundy, Chapoutier in the northern Rhône and The Millton Vineyard in Gisborne.

The Millton Vineyard's Bio-Gro status affirms that in their own vineyards (they sometimes buy grapes from other growers) the Milltons do not use herbicides, insecticides, systemic fungicides or soluble fertilisers.

For fungus control (botrytis is a major disease risk in Gisborne's warm, moist climate), a limited amount of copper and sulphur is sprayed on the vines, supplemented by waterglass, seaweed extract and vegetable oils. 'Most importantly, we use bio-dynamic herbal preparations applied to the soil,

compost and liquid manures,' says James Millton.

Parasites and predators are used to biologically control insect pests. Weed control is by mechanical means, rather than sprays. Sulphur dioxide is added to Millton wine as a preservative, in controlled amounts.

Of the almost 400 wine producers in New Zealand, only six are certified as organic: Millton; Kingsley Estate in Hawke's Bay; Covell Estate in the inland Bay of Plenty; Sunset Valley Vineyard and Richmond Plains in Nelson; and Kawarau Estate in Central Otago. Most of these producers are tiny.

Bio-Gro wine in New Zealand must not only be made from organically grown grapes, the fruit must be processed with a minimum of chemicals in the winery. Traditionally in New Zealand, dry wines have been able to contain up to 200 parts per million (ppm) of the age-old preservative, sulphur dioxide. For wine to carry the Bio-Gro stamp of approval, the maximum permitted level of sulphur dioxide is 110 ppm.

Do organic wines taste different? 'Customers tell us that our wines have clearer varietal characteristics than others,' says Annie Millton. However, in 'blind' tastings where the country's best organically grown wines (from Millton, Kingsley Estate and Kawarau Estate) have been included, I have not found significant flavour differences.

Will you feel better after drinking organic wine? 'People who are allergic to sulphur dioxide in wine often say they can drink ours,' says Annie Millton. But before you rush out to buy organic wine, note that most winemakers use only 110 to 120 ppm of sulphur dioxide for dry white wines, and around 50 ppm for dry reds.

So why are most Kiwi winemakers not going down the organic road? The viability of organic wine production is related to each region's climate. In areas with a favourably warm, dry climate (such as the south of France, the home of organic wines), it is much easier to adopt a chemical-free grapegrowing

Shalimar Estate

Shalimar's terraced vineyard is at Patutahi, on the western edge of the plains. Alec Stuart, who grew grapes for Montana from 1969 until 1986, planted the first vines in his new vineyard in 1992; Shalimar's first vintage, based on bought-in grapes, followed in 1994. The 8-hectare vineyard is planted in numerous varieties: Cabernet Sauvignon, Merlot, Pinotage, Sauvignon Blanc, Chardonnay, Pinot Gris, Sémillon and Riesling. The early wines were mediocre, but subsequent releases have been sound and clearly varietal.

Tiritiri Vineyards

Duncan and Judy Smith's tiny, 0.27-hectare vineyard is at 'Pooh Corner', in Waimata Valley Road, 25 kilometres north-west of the city. After planting their first vines in 1994, the Smiths released their first wine from the 1998 vintage, made on their behalf by John Thorpe. The wines, grown organically, include an easy-drinking Estate Chardonnay and a more stylish and complex Chardonnay Reserve.

TW

'TW' stands for Tietjen Witters. Long-term grape-growers Paul Tietjen and Geordie Witters own vineyards on Gisborne's 'Golden Slope', north-west of the city (their company name is Golden Slope Limited). Using fruit selected from their own vineyards and the services of a contract winemaker, they market a consistently excellent Chardonnay with soft grapefruit, fig and melon characters, an oaky, mealy richness and a seductively creamy texture.

Waimata

Students involved in the one-year wine industry certificate course at Gisborne's Tairawhiti Polytechnic each year produce and sell about 1000 cases of wine under the Waimata Vineyard label (previously Tai-Ara-Rau). The grapes are grown in the polytechnic's 2.5-hectare vineyard in the Waimata Valley, planted in Chardonnay, Pinot Gris and Merlot. I have tasted an easy-drinking Merlot and a barrel-fermented, deliciously fragrant, fat and ripe Reserve Chardonnay.

Wild flowers in Montana's vineyards attract beneficial insects which aid natural pest control.

programme, simply because the risk of disease is far lower.

Instead of organics, most modern viticulturists advocate 'sustainable viticulture', which permits a limited use of agricultural chemicals, but in a way that is held to be consistent with the preservation of the environment. The local version of sustainable viticulture is IWP.

Launched in the mid-1990s, IWP is a scheme that combines education, financial incentives (lower spray costs and bonuses from wine companies to growers who have joined the scheme) and monitoring to encourage grape-growers to reduce their reliance on chemical sprays and address other environmental issues, such as soil health and water quality. The scheme was born out of growing concern within the industry that its vastly increased reliance on chemicals since the Second World War was not environmentally sustainable in the long term.

The wine industry's desire to close the gap between its clean, green image

and the reality of what happens in the vineyards also reflects the growing concern of its overseas customers about the environment and food safety issues. Local winemakers also worry that foreign governments could use the issue of spray residues in wine as a non-tariff trade barrier, enabling them to block the entry of New Zealand wines.

The large and medium-sized wineries — those most heavily involved in export — have been the most enthusiastic adopters of IWP. Many smaller wineries, selling mainly to a local clientele, have been less interested, simply because they are under less pressure to do so. And in the humid climate of west Auckland, growers are naturally more cautious about reducing anti-fungal sprays than in the much drier climate of Central Otago, where growers are closer to organic production.

Montana, the industry giant, is strongly committed to IWP. 'Disease and pest control are the areas where growers can readily make dramatic improvements,' says Hoksbergen. 'Rather than calendar spraying (applying agrochemicals every 14–21 days regardless of disease or pest pressure), vineyard blocks should be formally monitored weekly for pest and disease incidence.' Only when a pest or disease reaches a certain threshold or infection period is the area sprayed.

On Montana's vineyards, chemical spraying has dropped markedly since the adoption of IWP. For instance, the number of spray applications on Sauvignon Blanc at Brancott Estate in Marlborough has fallen by 45 per cent, giving an annual saving of $300 per hectare.

IWP also encourages some form of cover crop or permanent sward between the vines. Chicory, fescues and rye grasses are used in Montana's vineyards to reduce the vines' vigour (associated with higher quality wine); oats, mustard, lupins and red clover are sown for organic matter and nitrogen; and to attract beneficial insects, buck wheat, alyssum and wildflowers are grown.

Despite Montana's dominant position, Hoksbergen believes the IWP scheme needs the support of all growers if the industry's clean, green image is to be protected. 'Every grower who chooses not to belong should seriously consider the message they are sending to their communities and customers.'

Hawke's
Bay

Eskdale

Linden E

5

Poraiti

Sacred Hill

Woodthorpe
(Te Mata)

Riverside

DARTMOOR ROAD

Tutaekuri River

DARTMOOR
VALLEY

Puketapu

PUKETAPU ROAD

Moteo

OMARUNUI ROAD

SWAMP ROAD

Mission

Church
Road

TARADA

Riverview
(Morton Estate)

Ngaruroro River

MANGATAHI

Kemblefield

KERERU ROAD

OHITI ROAD

TAHAPE ROAD

ROAD

Omahu

Stonecroft

Mere Road
(Mills Reef)

MERE RD

Fernhill

Cross
Roads

50

Ngaruroro River

50

Twyford

OMAHU ROAD

Unison

Newton Forrest
Irongate
(Babich)

Matariki

C. J. Pask

ORMOND ROAD

Bilancia

Trinity Hill

Roys Hill

Te Awa
Farm

GIMBLETT ROAD

Kingsley

FLAXMERE

PLAINS

HASTINGS

NGATARAWA

Ngatarawa

Bullnose
(Te Mata)

Matheson
(Matua Valley)

MARAEKAKAHO

Alpha
Domus

Huthlee

NGATARAWA ROAD

MONTANA ROAD

VALENTINE ROAD

Vidal
Estat

ST AUBYN E

HAVELOC

Maraekakaho

Sileni

Redmetal

ROAD

Bridge
Pa

Bridge Pa
Aerodrome

HERETAUNGA

Lucknow

Longlands

wine company

weather station

notable vineyard

main vineyard plantings

Gimblett Gravels
Winegrowing District

N

0   5   10 km

50

Pukahu

Pakipaki

2

Hawke's Bay is the aristocrat of New Zealand's wine regions. In the 1890s a source of pioneering white and red table wines made from classic *vinifera* varieties, it has preserved its traditional importance and with such prestigious grapes as Chardonnay, Cabernet Sauvignon and Merlot, its regional reputation is the highest in the country.

In 2002, with 3375 hectares of bearing vines, Hawke's Bay ranked second to Marlborough in the extent of its vineyards. In the decade from 1992 to 2002, the region's area of bearing vines expanded by 114 per cent, increasing its share of the national vineyard from 22 to 28 per cent. After a lull in the mid-1980s, when few new wineries emerged, the Hawke's Bay wine scene has of late been abuzz with the emergence of new sub-regions, new varieties and new labels.

Apart from the relatively flat Heretaunga Plains, which surround the twin cities of Napier and Hastings, most of Hawke's Bay is rolling hill country, ascending inland to over 1600 metres in the rugged Ruahine and Kaweka Ranges, which form the backbone of the North Island. Fast rivers — notably the Tutaekuri, Ngaruroro and Tukituki — run west-east, from the mountains to the sea. In this sheltered environment, protected from the prevailing westerly winds, agriculture thrives: pastoralism, process cropping, orcharding, market gardening and viticulture.

To the north and south of the plains, the steep hill country and wild coast are sparsely populated. There are isolated vineyards in the north of the region — at Nuhaka, near the Mahia Peninsula, Wairoa and Raupunga, on the Mohaka River — and to the south, at Takapau in upland, central Hawke's Bay. But the vast majority of the vines are on the Heretaunga Plains.

Once an inlet of the Pacific Ocean, the lowlands cover 35,000 hectares, all within 20 kilometres of Napier and Hastings. At first, grain-growing flourished on the plains, followed by intensive pastoralism, but after the Second World War the Heretaunga Plains became the most specialised cash cropping and horticultural district in the country. As orchards and market gardens (and eventually vineyards) spread, Hawke's Bay acquired the tag 'the fruit bowl of New Zealand'. However, poor export prices have recently hit hard at the horticultural industry, encouraging growers to look to alternatives, such as organics and olives. The early Hawke's Bay winemakers battled prohibition, the phylloxera aphid, imported wines and public apathy. Today, the greatest challenge facing Hawke's Bay's flourishing wine-growers is far more benign yet highly complex — the extreme diversity of the region's climate and soils. Across the Heretaunga Plains, Chardonnay harvest dates vary by more than a month and Te Mata Estate's best and worst Cabernet Sauvignon sites lie less than a kilometre apart at Havelock North. 'The defining characteristic of Hawke's Bay is the extreme variation within the region,' says Dr Alan Limmer of Stonecroft. 'But that's what makes it possible to produce styles ranging from cool-climate bottle-fermented sparklings to Bordeaux-style reds.'

Previous page: Looking north from the summit of Roys Hill to the spreading Gimblett Gravels vineyards and the crumpled Hawke's Bay hill country.

Principal grape varieties

	Producing area 2002	% total producing area 2002
Chardonnay	910 ha	27.0%
Merlot	715 ha	21.2%
Cabernet Sauvignon	537 ha	15.9%
Sauvignon Blanc	303 ha	9.0%
Pinot Noir	231 ha	6.8%
Müller-Thurgau	130 ha	3.9%
Cabernet Franc	95 ha	2.8%
Chenin Blanc	90 ha	2.7%
Malbec	71 ha	2.1%
Syrah	62 ha	1.8%

From the Heretaunga Plains flow powerful, citrusy Chardonnays and most of New Zealand's top Merlot and Cabernet Sauvignon-based reds.

History

Marist missionaries from the Society of Mary planted the first vines in Hawke's Bay at Pakowhai (south of Napier) in 1851. In the 1890s, the Mission made its first recorded sales and several wealthy landowners produced and sold table wines from classic *vinifera* grape varieties.

A conference of Australasian Fruitgrowers, held in Wellington in 1896, heard that 'more pioneer work in viticulture has been done at the Greenmeadows Vineyard, Taradale, than elsewhere. Here we find the premier vineyard of New Zealand.' Henry Tiffen had about 8 hectares of vines planted in 1894, mostly Pinot Noir and Meunier. In 1897 his Greenmeadows Burgundy attracted high praise from a *New Zealand Farmer* reporter: 'I was both surprised and pleased to find wine so matured and of such high-class quality produced, so to speak, at one's elbow. For good, sound, light wine we have really no occasion to go outside the colony.'

In 1909, Bernard Chambers' 14-hectare Te Mata vineyard at Havelock North — planted in Meunier, Syrah, Cabernet Sauvignon, Riesling and Verdelho — was the largest in the country, annually producing 12,000 gallons (54,552 L) of wine (see pages 13 and 158).

Chambers, Tiffen and J.N. Williams of Frimley Orchards, Hastings, were essentially hobbyists, determined to prove the possibilities of commercial winemaking. In 1903, a state vineyard, the Arataki Experimental Station, opened at Havelock North on land purchased from Bernard Chambers, and soon after the region's first commercial winemaker arrived. Spanish-born Anthony Vidal in 1905 purchased a half-hectare Hastings property, planted grapevines and converted the existing stables into a winery.

Prohibitionist sentiment, two world wars and the Depression hampered the industry's development, but by the 1930s Tom McDonald at Taradale, Robert Bird of the Glenvale winery at Bay View, and Richard Ellis of Brookfields Vineyards, at Meeanee, were all producing fortified wines for an undiscerning local clientele.

For decades, the dominant force in the Bay was McWilliam's, established in 1947, with its brewery-distributed sherries and ports and popular Marque Vue (sparkling), Cresta Doré (dry white) and Bakano (dry red).

Yet only in the past 35 years has viticulture reached significant proportions in Hawke's Bay. In the late 1930s, for instance, only 25 hectares of vines were grown in the province. Then in 1967 contract growing extended to Hawke's Bay. Such varieties as Müller-Thurgau, Chardonnay and Cabernet Sauvignon were identified as having potential in the region, but it was not until the mid-1970s that some winemakers began to realise the critical importance of soil and site selection if superior wines were to be produced.

During the past decade, the Hawke's Bay wine industry has flourished. Between 1990 and 2002, the area of producing vines expanded from 1328 hectares to 3375 hectares (an increase of 154 per cent). In the same period, the number of licensed winemakers soared from 14 to 51.

Today, this historic, thriving wine region boasts the oldest winemaking concern in New Zealand still

Summary of climate statistics

Meteorological station	Latitude	Height	GDD	MTWM	Rainfall, Oct–Apr	Air frost days (annual)
Hastings	39.37'S	5 m	1273	18.3°C	366 mm	21
Havelock North	39.39'S	9 m	1270	18.6°C	387 mm	36

Height — *above sea level* GDD — *growing degree days, Oct–Apr, above 10°C* MTWM — *mean temperature, warmest month*

under the same management — Mission Vineyards, established by the Catholic Society of Mary in 1851 — and at Te Mata Estate can be seen the oldest winery still operating, erected in stages from the 1870s.

Climate

Hawke's Bay is one of the sunniest areas of the country, with vineyards on the Heretaunga Plains basking in an annual average of over 2200 hours of sunshine.

The heat summation figures for Hastings and Havelock North suggest that those parts of Hawke's Bay, at least, are warmer than Burgundy but cooler than Bordeaux. This theory is supported by Hawke's Bay's major success with Chardonnay but its struggle to consistently ripen Cabernet Sauvignon, except on the warmest sites.

In the past, Hawke's Bay was often described as a sort of antipodean Bordeaux, but viticulturist Steve Smith, of Craggy Range, believes that 'in general Hawke's Bay is slightly cool for making red wines from the Bordeaux red varieties and Syrah. The lack of real heat during berry development is the limiting factor. The cause of this lack of really hot summer days is the sea, less than 15 kilometres from most vineyards, which generates a cool sea breeze from about lunch-time on most summer days.'

Yet most Hawke's Bay sites are too warm for Pinot Noir. Compared to regions further south, Hawke's Bay cools down slowly at night. Pinot Noir grapes therefore ripen swiftly and miss out on the extended ripening period necessary to retain skin colour and sweet, varietal fruit characters.

On the Heretaunga Plains during summer, afternoon temperatures typically climb to 23–25°C. Along the coast, maximum temperatures are lower and minimum temperatures are higher, due to the moderating influence of the sea.

Further inland, away from the ocean breezes, sites are typically hotter. In 1998, the Mission recorded mean temperatures for January (usually but not always the warmest month) at several of its vineyards. At Meeanee, nearest the sea, the mean temperature was 19.1°C, rising to 19.7°C at Taradale, 20.5°C at Gimblett Road and 21.0°C at Moteo, in the lower Dartmoor Valley. Further inland again, for each 100-metre rise above sea level, air temperatures typically fall by 0.6°C, gradually limiting the potential for viticulture.

On clear nights in the lowland areas, frosts are a risk. Low-lying, frost-prone areas, such as the Heretaunga Plains near Havelock North, each year have an average of almost 100 ground frosts. One grower with vineyards at Gimblett Road and Ngatarawa was hard hit by spring frosts in 1995, 1997 and 2000. Most growers, however, do not view the risk as high enough to invest in permanent frost-fighting equipment, and instead rely on helicopters.

Sheltered by the high country, Hawke's Bay is less windy than many other coastal regions of the country, with a high frequency of light winds. During spring and summer, when westerly winds prevail, hot, dry nor'westers can cause droughts, inhibiting the vines' canopy growth.

Spells of cold, wet, southerly weather are frequent during the growing season; more than half Hawke's Bay's rain comes from the south or south-east. Gales from the east and north-east bring warm, humid weather, conducive to botrytis bunch rot, and Hawke's Bay is also vulnerable to periodic tropical cyclones. Disease control can be a challenge to the region's grape-growers after consistent wet spells, but vines with open canopies and small crops are least at risk.

The pattern of rainfall across the region is closely linked to its orography. In both westerly and easterly winds, rain increases towards the high country. Over most of the Heretaunga Plains, the mean annual rainfall is 800–1200 mm, less than half the 2400 mm in the ranges.

The quality of each vintage is largely determined by the rain, which is highly variable in Hawke's Bay. The driest period of the year is usually spring and early summer, when the warm, dry nor'westers hold sway. Dry spells (less than 1 mm of rain daily for at least 15 days) occur on average three times per year, and at least one drought (with no measurable rain for at least 15 days) can also be expected.

For the quality of the vintage, the timing of the rains is critical. March and April are the key period. Autumn rains can cut short the ripening period, especially for late-season varieties, but in favourable years an Indian summer allows the grapes to reach full maturity.

Soils

A distinguishing feature of Hawke's Bay is its extreme diversity of soils. The Heretaunga Plains consist mainly of fertile alluvial soils over gravelly sub-soils, deposited by the rivers and creeks that drain the uplands. As the rivers have meandered across the plains, they have laid down a patchwork of soils. Of the dozens of categories of soil on the Heretaunga Plains, ranging from stones to hard pans to heavy silts, each has a profound influence on the wine.

The mosaic of soils varies widely in texture, depth and water-storage capacity. Loamy, clayey Hastings soils, deep and fertile, with a very high capacity for storing plant-available water, are ideal for orchards but not for vineyards. Havelock soils, consisting of sandy loams over a clay pan, are moderately fertile and dry out rapidly.

Twyford soils (including the famously arid and free-draining soils of the Gimblett Gravels Winegrowing District, see pages 136 and 162), range from stony gravels that dry out swiftly to more

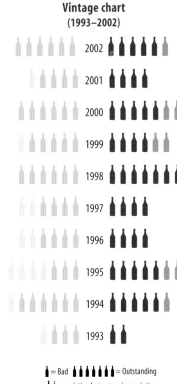

Vintage chart
(1993–2002)

2002

2001

2000

1999

1998

1997

1996

1995

1994

1993

🍷 = Bad 🍷🍷🍷🍷🍷🍷 = Outstanding
🍷🍷 = variation between wine varieties

fertile, silty and sandy loams. Takapau soils, with a layer of fine alluvium overlying greywacke gravels, are similarly free-draining and dry.

In the past, Hawke's Bay's vineyards were often established on very fertile soils with a high water table, such as those between Hastings and the sea. 'A guy would diversify by ripping out peaches and putting in vines on a site originally chosen as ideal for orchards,' says Dr Alan Limmer of Stonecroft. 'Those sites were only good for servicing the bulk-wine industry.'

A comprehensive regional study published in 1985 by the Hawke's Bay Vintners stated frankly that 'many soils on the Heretaunga Plains are quite wet and vines grow too vigorously, giving large yields of grapes with poor balance and insufficient ripeness [notably the areas of fertile silty loams having a high water table]. . . '

Most of the expansion in the past decade has been on lower fertility sites, inland from Hastings, where the vines grow less vigorously, yielding lighter crops with riper, more concentrated flavours. Wines grown in these districts, including Gimblett Gravels and the Ngatarawa Triangle, vary much less in quality from one vintage to the next than those from lesser areas.

To complicate matters, soils often vary markedly within a single vineyard (in one 8-hectare Hawke's Bay vineyard, 17 different soil types were identified). 'We go through our vineyards and break each block down by its soil types,' says John Hancock of Trinity Hill. 'Then we manage the vines on those soils differently, with more or less irrigation or shoot removal.'

How much impact do the different soils have on wine quality? In 2001, growers and winemakers at a workshop on 'making red wine in the vineyard' tasted a quartet of 2001 Hawke's Bay Merlots, from vines grown in gravel and silt soils. The consensus was that, although the grapes had all been harvested with similar sugar levels, the gravels produced the most substantial, tannic and ripely flavoured wines.

A recent doctoral thesis by Dejan Tesic showed that the 'soil factor' (defined as the interaction between soil temperature, soil moisture, soil texture and rooting depth) has a significant effect on vine performance and wine quality. According to Steve Smith of Craggy Range, 'the sites with the highest soil factor score were the Gimblett Gravels and, in the driest years, those with shallow pan soils around Havelock North and on the gentle slopes adjacent to the Tukituki River'.

Few Hawke's Bay vineyards are in the high country, where limestone and clay are found, often clothed in volcanic ash from the Taupo eruptions. Winemakers are divided on the potential of the hills. Some are put off by their steepness and relatively high rainfall (as well as the need for hands-on viticulture and the problem of hard pans); others argue that the drainage and heat benefits from planting on hillsides are simply not needed in Hawke's Bay.

Others are excited by the hills. Esk Valley's steep, 1-hectare Terraces vineyard at Bay View has produced some stunningly concentrated blended reds and on its new, 0.6-hectare hill site at Havelock North, Te Mata has predicted it will grow its finest Cabernet Sauvignon. Several other vineyards have been planted on hillsides, but rather than large developments, the prospect is for a trickle of premium quality, high-priced wines.

Wine styles

Hawke's Bay's two most important wine styles are Chardonnay and Merlot-based reds, which dominate the region's production. The Chardonnays are powerful, while retaining elegance and varietal intensity, and the top wines mature gracefully for several years.

In New Zealand, only Hawke's Bay produces large volumes of high quality, claret-style reds. Cabernet Sauvignon has only ripened consistently on the warmest sites in the Bay and its plantings now lag behind Merlot, but both varieties (and their blends) are producing distinguished reds.

Hawke's Bay's mouthfilling, tropical fruit-flavoured, oak-aged Sauvignon Blanc is arguably New Zealand's most underrated wine style. Some good Gewürztraminers, Rieslings, Pinot Gris, Sémillons, Chenin Blancs, Viogniers, Pinot Noirs, sweet white wines and bottle-fermented sparklings have appeared. A possible star of the future is Syrah, which ripens ahead of Cabernet Sauvignon and is yielding notably dark, weighty and flavour-crammed wines.

Sub-regions

From the Esk Valley in the north to central Hawke's Bay in the south, Mangatahi inland to Te Awanga on the coast, the wines of Hawke's Bay are strongly influenced by soil types, proximity to the sea and elevation. Vineyards near the coast are cooled by afternoon sea breezes, but 10 to 20 kilometres inland, the more sheltered sites are significantly warmer. Further inland again, on more elevated land, the daily temperature range increases, the nights are cooler and the climate is more continental. These climatic differences, coupled with the extreme soil variation characteristic of Hawke's Bay, produce a notably diverse array of wines, from crisp, delicate bottle-fermented sparklings to robust, richly flavoured, claret-style reds.

Of the dozen or so, typically ill-defined sub-regions (each wine-grower suggests a different group), the most publicised in recent years has been Gimblett Gravels, at the base of Roys Hill, on the outskirts of Hastings. Here, in exceptionally free-draining soils and high summer temperatures, the vines' vigour is

reduced and their typically light crops harbour ripe, concentrated flavours (see page 163). Gordon Russell, of Esk Valley Estate, views the area as 'the ultimate spot in the Bay for Cabernet Sauvignon. It's hot during the day, the shingles radiate the heat at night and it's very free-draining.'

On the south side of the plains, within a roughly triangular area formed by Maraekakaho Road, State Highway 50 and Ngatarawa Road, lies the 'Ngatarawa Triangle', also known as the 'Redmetal Triangle'. The soils, slightly more fertile than around Gimblett Road, have a 30–50 centimetre layer of sandy silt overlying red metal gravels. 'Infertile, dries off', is the succinct description of these 'Ngatarawa sandy loam gravels' on a Hawke's Bay soil map from the 1930s. So well-drained are the soils that the vines are all irrigated, otherwise they would be unlikely to survive.

In the 'Ngatarawa Triangle', where the grapes typically ripen four to seven days later than at Gimblett Road, according to Grant Edmonds of Sileni Estate and Redmetal Vineyards, Merlot has been the big success so far. 'In a hot, dry season, we may perform better than Gimblett Gravels,' says Edmonds, 'but in a cooler year, they'll have the advantage.' Jenny Dobson of Te Awa Farm, who worked for a decade in Bordeaux, believes vineyards in the 'Ngatarawa Triangle' yield 'softer, rounder wines, plummy and less tannic than those from Gimblett Road'.

Te Mata Estate — Hawke's Bay's top-rated producer of Cabernet Sauvignon-based reds since the early 1980s — believes that the hills of Havelock North are the region's finest Cabernet Sauvignon country. 'They're our hottest sites,' says proprietor John Buck. 'They're angled to the sun, they don't get frost and they're sheltered from the south, where the coldest winds come from. We can get Cabernet Sauvignon fully ripe there eight years in 10 — as often as they do in Bordeaux.'

The Esk Valley, which runs inland from Bay View, on the coast north of Napier, is a relatively cool area. Buck refers to it as 'Carneros-like' (a reference to the foggy, coastal California wine region renowned for its Chardonnay and Pinot Noir). With its cooling sea breezes and relatively fertile soils, Gordon Russell sees the Esk Valley as 'white-wine country, although there are more red grapes planted there'.

In the Dartmoor Valley, behind Taradale, vineyards are draped alongside the Tutaekuri River for many kilometres. The sandy, silty soils have yielded some very fine Chardonnay, but 'it's generally too wet in autumn for top reds,' according to Steve Smith of Craggy Range. At Moteo, near the village of Puketapu, the local marae owns large contract vineyards and Montana has planted its McDonald Estate in Chardonnay, Merlot and Cabernet Sauvignon. Te Mata has planted mainly Chardonnay and Sauvignon Blanc in its Woodthorpe Terraces vineyard, with Merlot the principal red variety.

Along State Highway 50, from Fernhill to Taradale, where Montana has its extensive Korokipo Estate and Fernhill Estate plantings, the silt loam soils suit white-wine grapes, according to viticulturist Jim Hamilton. Closer to the sea, the heavy, high-fertility soils at Meeanee are not well suited to quality viticulture. At Te Awanga, right on the coast, the cooling influence of the sea favours earlier-ripening varieties, such as Chardonnay, Pinot Noir and Merlot.

In the inland, elevated Mangatahi sub-region, about 100 metres above sea level, where Morton Estate has its famous Riverview vineyard, temperatures at night are markedly lower and the grapes are usually harvested 10 days later than at Maraekakaho. A relatively frost-prone area with stony river terraces, Mangatahi has produced brilliant Chardonnay and high hopes are held for Pinot Noir.

An hour's drive south of the plains, small plots of vines have been established at Waipukurau and Takapau, in central Hawke's Bay. These inland, high altitude (300 metres above sea level) vineyards are yielding a trickle of racy, high-acid white wines and fresh, appley, lively bottle-fermented sparklings. Pinot Noir is a possibility.

Address	Alpha Domus, 1829 Maraekakaho Road, Bridge Pa
Owner	The Ham family
Key Wines	The Aviator, The Navigator, Merlot/Cabernet, Merlot, AD Chardonnay, Chardonnay, Sauvignon Blanc, Sémillon, AD Sémillon

Alpha Domus

■ The soaring Tiger Moth on Alpha Domus' label reflects the winery's location near Bridge Pa airfield, where many of New Zealand's pioneer pilots earned their wings. Today, the area is better known for its high-flying producers of some of Hawke's Bay's finest Merlot-based reds.

Alpha Domus is owned by the Ham family: Anthonius (Ton) and Lea Ham, who emigrated from Holland to New Zealand in the 1960s, and their three sons, Paul, Henry and Anthony. The name Alpha is derived from the first letter of each of their names; Domus is Latin for 'house' or 'family'. Ton and Lea are now retired and the wine company is run by the youngest of their three sons, Anthony, a graduate in information technology.

The first vines were planted in 1991 but for a few years their crop was sold to other wineries. Alpha Domus' first wine flowed in 1996. Today the company's 30 hectares of vineyards in the Ngatarawa Triangle are planted principally in Merlot, Cabernet Sauvignon and Chardonnay, with smaller plots of Sauvignon Blanc, Pinot Noir, Cabernet Franc, Malbec, Sémillon and Viognier. In most years the wines are entirely estate-grown.

Dutch-born Evert Nijzink joined Alpha Domus as winemaker in 1997, after training in Hawke's Bay and working several vintages in Bordeaux, Burgundy and the south of France. The company's output reached 17,000 cases in 2002 and the wines, made on-site, are consistently rewarding.

The top Chardonnay, branded AD (for Alpha Domus), is a powerful wine, fully French oak-fermented, with rich, citrusy, mealy, toasty flavours. The standard Chardonnay is a lightly wooded style with a touch of biscuity oak seasoning its fresh, strong, well-ripened fruit flavours. The white-wine range also features a crisp, lively Sémillon with tropical fruit and fresh-cut grass aromas and a weighty, rich, more strongly oak-influenced AD Sémillon.

Designed for early drinking, the French and American oak-aged Merlot/Cabernet is typically dark, warm and deeply flavoured, with a rounded finish. The Navigator, the top Merlot-based blend, is savoury, earthy and leathery in a distinctly Bordeaux-like style. The Aviator, a French oak-aged, Cabernet Sauvignon-dominant blend with smaller portions of Merlot, Cabernet Franc and Malbec, is at its best densely coloured, with beautifully rich blackcurrant, plum and spice flavours.

Askerne

Address	Askerne Vineyard, 267 Te Mata-Mangateretere Road, Havelock North
Owners	John and Kathryn Loughlin
Key Wines	Sauvignon Blanc, Chardonnay, Gewürztraminer, Sémillon

■ A single-estate producer of mostly white wine, Askerne is owned by John Loughlin — until recently chief executive of Richmond, New Zealand's largest meat processor and exporter — and his wife, Kathryn, who from the outset has run the wine company near Havelock North. Askerne is named after a Yorkshire spa town that was Kathryn's birthplace.

On the western side of the Tukituki River, only 3 kilometres from the sea, the Askerne vineyard sits on a relatively cool site, which the Loughlins feel is ideal for aromatic white wines. The 8-hectare vineyard, first planted in 1993, has a wide range of soils — gravels, silt, sand and clay. The most important grape varieties are Sauvignon Blanc, Chardonnay and Gewürztraminer, with smaller plots of Bordeaux red grapes, Sémillon, Optima and Pinot Noir.

The wines, first produced in 1996, are made on-site by Kathryn Loughlin, assisted since 2002 by Craig Thomas, who formerly worked at Te Awa Farm. At about 3000 cases per year, Askerne's annual output is small, but growing.

The wines are typically fresh, crisp and mouthfilling, with good varietal character. The Sauvignon Blanc, of which a minor portion is barrel-fermented, is full-bodied and rounded, with fresh, vibrant melon/lime flavours and a subtle twist of oak. Two Sémillon-based white wines have been produced: a nutty, leesy Barrel Fermented Sémillon and a lightly wooded, crisp, lemony and grassy Sémillon/Sauvignon Blanc.

In peak form, the Gewürztraminer is perfumed and weighty, with excellent depth of lychees and spice flavours. The Chardonnay, French oak-aged, is smooth, mouthfilling and complex, with strong, peachy, nutty flavours.

Bilancia

■ One of Hawke's Bay rarest wine labels, well worth tracking down, Bilancia (pronounced 'be-larn-cha', Italian for 'balance' or 'harmony') is the source of very good Chardonnay and distinguished, trophy-winning Merlot and Pinot Gris. In the wings are Syrah and Viognier.

First produced in 1997, the wines are made by two Roseworthy College graduates: Lorraine Leheny, previously assistant winemaker at Delegat's, and her partner, Warren Gibson, who is the full-time winemaker at Trinity Hill (where the Bilancia wines are processed).

Leheny and Gibson were totally reliant on growers for their early vintages, drawing grapes from Hawke's Bay (principally) and Marlborough. In 1998, however, they planted the first Syrah vines at their terraced vineyard, Collina (Italian for 'hill') on a north-west slope on Roys Hill, overlooking the Gimblett Gravels district. Viognier followed in 2000.

Fully fermented in French oak barriques, the Chardonnay is typically weighty and finely balanced, with a smooth spread of lemon and stone-fruit flavours. The Reserve Pinot Grigio (the Italian name for Pinot Gris) shows lovely freshness and intensity, with vibrant, peachy, spicy flavours and a subtle wood influence from its fermentation and brief maturation in old oak casks. Both a straight Merlot and a blended Merlot/Cabernet Sauvignon have been marketed, showing impressive concentration of cassis/plum flavours, oak complexity and a firm finish.

Address	Bilancia, State Highway 50, Hastings
Owners	Lorraine Leheny and Warren Gibson
Key Wines	Chardonnay, Reserve Pinot Grigio, Merlot/Cabernet Sauvignon

Brookfields

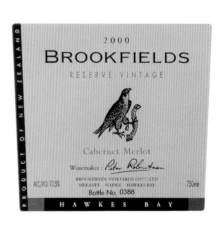

■ Peter Robertson, the quiet owner of the Brookfields winery, a couple of kilometres from the sea at Meeanee, is rarely in the publicity spotlight. 'I just putt along, concentrating on making the wines,' he says. 'The wines can talk for themselves' — which they manage to do most eloquently.

Brookfields' flagship, the 'gold label' Reserve Vintage Cabernet/Merlot, is one of the darkest, most powerful and richly flavoured reds found in Hawke's Bay. The robust, savoury Marshall Bank Chardonnay can also reach great heights. These are strapping, generously flavoured wines; richness of body and flavour are hallmarks of the Brookfields style.

Robertson, raised in Otago, had his interest in wine sparked as a student in the early 1970s, when he took a holiday job at Barker's fruit winery at Geraldine. After graduating with a BSc in biochemistry, he joined McWilliam's in Hawke's Bay, working under the legendary winemaker Tom McDonald, initially as a cellarhand, then as a laboratory chemist. 'After a couple of years I had itchy feet,' he recalls. 'I was working in a winery, but couldn't prune a vine. When I left, the first thing I did was go pruning.'

In 1977 Peter Robertson purchased the old Brookfields winery, traditionally a sherry specialist. 'Dick Ellis, the founder, had died and his son, Jack, wasn't interested in carrying on.'

Today, Brookfields still has a fairly small output of 8000 cases of wine per year. Cooled by sea breezes, the

Address	Brookfields Vineyards, 376 Brookfields Road, Meeanee
Owner	Peter Robertson
Key Wines	Marshall Bank Chardonnay, Bergman Estate Chardonnay, Sauvignon Blanc, Pinot Gris, Gewürztraminer, Riesling Dry, Ohiti Estate Cabernet Sauvignon, Reserve Vintage Cabernet/Merlot, Hillside Syrah

Peter Robertson aims to make 'fruit-driven wines that go well with food', including the fine cuisine served at Brookfields' own winery restaurant, which opens for lunch daily.

company's 3-hectare Brookfields and 2-hectare Marshall Bank blocks at Meeanee are planted in Chardonnay. Pinot Gris, Gewürztraminer, Riesling and Sauvignon Blanc are grown in a warmer, shingly vineyard in Ohiti Road, behind Roys Hill, partly owned by Robertson. Syrah, first produced in 2000, is drawn from a north-facing slope at Bridge Pa. Growers supply about 25 per cent of Brookfields' grape intake. The winery is a delight to visit. To enhance the atmosphere of the original building, erected in 1937 from concrete blocks hand-made on the property, Robertson has added a brick entranceway, a new gable and colonial windows. In the cellar, full of rustic, heavy, black wooden tables and benches, the original concrete barrel racks are still nursing casks. Brookfields' winery restaurant opens for lunch daily. 'My wines are made to be drunk with food,' says Robertson. 'They're mouthfilling, with firm alcohol. Food wines also need a bit of acidity. And because of the wines' balance, they live and develop.'

Brookfields' lower-priced range includes a powerful, almost dry Gewürztraminer with soft, rich peach, lychee and spice flavours; a dry but not austere Riesling with strong, citrusy, limey, slightly minerally characters; and a sturdy Pinot Gris with an oily texture, stone-fruit and spice flavours and a smooth, off-dry finish. Two Chardonnays are produced. The French and American oak-aged Bergman Estate Chardonnay is an upfront style with generous grapefruit and peach flavours and soft, buttery, 'malo' characters giving an easy-drinking appeal. The flagship Marshall Bank Chardonnay, fermented in all-new French oak barriques, is robust and complex, with citrusy, biscuity, strongly wooded flavours and a rich, creamy texture. French oak-matured for a year, the mid-priced Ohiti Estate Cabernet Sauvignon is deeply coloured, with fresh, strong blackcurrant and plum flavours. However, the jewel in Brookfields' crown is the 'gold label' Reserve Vintage Cabernet/Merlot.

'It's the one I really go for in the winery,' says Robertson. Grown in the Ohiti Estate vineyard and matured for up to 18 months in new French oak barriques, it is a full-on style, dark, perfumed and muscular, with lush blackcurrant, plum and spice flavours and the power, concentration and tannin backbone to flourish for a decade.

Central Hawke's Bay Wine Company

■ Distinctly cool-climate wines, enlivened by racy acidity, flow from the hill country of central Hawke's Bay, where five pioneering grape-growers have come together under the Three Sisters brand.

South of the Heretaunga Plains and inland from the market towns of Waipawa and Waipukurau, the Ruataniwha-Takapau Plains form one of the driest parts of the North Island, with free-draining sandy silts and gravelly terraces. Fired by a belief in the potential of this elevated sub-region, in 1983 Malcolm Johansen planted the first vines at Takapau. Johansen has since sold Riesling grapes to top Hawke's Bay producers.

Sir Richard Harrison, a former speaker of the House of Representatives, planted his 0.5-hectare vineyard at Takapau in 1987, and after many years of trials has reached the conclusion that 'we should concentrate on the grape varieties of Champagne [Pinot Noir, Chardonnay and Meunier] and Alsace [Riesling, Pinot Gris and Gewürztraminer]'. Other growers include Neil Mathers at Tamamu, and John Ashworth and Shirley Stubbs at Takapau.

The Central Hawke's Bay Wine Company does not operate a winery; the grapes, grown at up to 300 metres above sea level, are transported to Hastings and processed by Rod McDonald at the Vidal winery. Named after hills behind Takapau called the Three Sisters and sold in local supermarkets, the wines are still rare, with the total current output of about 150 cases.

The wines to date have included a lean, steely Riesling; a French oak-fermented Chardonnay, citrusy, minerally and freshly acidic; a crisp, appley, moderately complex bottle-fermented sparkling, Three Sisters Brut; and a light but clearly varietal Pinot Noir.

Church Road

■ The Church Road winery at the foot of the Taradale hills is a Mecca for wine tourists, with the country's first major wine museum, a popular luncheon restaurant and some outstanding Hawke's Bay wines.

With much fanfare, in 1988 and 1989 Montana thrust into Hawke's Bay, snapping up $6 million worth of existing vineyards and the old McDonald winery. Its goal: to elevate the standard of the giant company's previously unspectacular red wines and — to a lesser extent — Chardonnays.

Although deeply rooted in the Gisborne and Marlborough regions, New Zealand's largest wine company had previously been absent in Hawke's Bay. Montana's purchase of Penfold's (New Zealand) in late 1986 first triggered its involvement in Hawke's Bay, by linking it with Penfold's contract growers. By also purchasing 238 hectares of vines, Montana swiftly staked out a significant share of the region's vineyards. Its acquisition of the McDonald winery — which it swiftly rejuvenated and named The McDonald Winery, but later renamed Church Road — also gave it a small-scale production facility ideal for making limited volumes of top-flight wines.

Winemaker Tony Prichard, a Massey University food technology graduate, joined Montana in 1983. To boost its red-wine quality, Montana turned to Cordier, one of Bordeaux's major shippers and chateaux owners, with

Address   Central Hawke's Bay Wine Company,
c/- John Ashworth,
RD2, Takapau

Owners   John Ashworth, Sir Richard Harrison, Malcolm Johansen, Neil Mathers, Shirley Stubbs

Key Wines   Chardonnay, Riesling, Sauvignon Blanc, Method Traditional

Address   Church Road Winery,
200 Church Road,
Taradale

Owner   Montana Wines

Key Wines   Church Road Chardonnay,
Reserve Chardonnay,
Cuve Series Chardonnay,
Sauvignon Blanc,
Reserve Noble Sémillon,
Cabernet Sauvignon/Merlot,
Reserve Cabernet Sauvignon/Merlot; Tom

extensive cru classé holdings. Cordier gave Montana clear guidelines. 'Prior to their involvement, we were trying lots of techniques, but didn't have a clear direction,' says Prichard. 'Cordier focused us on a narrower range of concerns: the quality and amount of tannins, barrel handling [no American oak], blending and — the key thing — eliminating herbaceousness.'

The extended roots of the Church Road winery run back to the closing years of the nineteenth century. In 1896 Bartholomew Steinmetz, a native of Luxembourg, resigned his position as a lay brother at the Society of Mary's Marist Mission to settle in Taradale and marry. Steinmetz purchased 5 acres (2 hectares) from the estate of pioneer winemaker Henry Tiffen, planted vine cuttings supplied by the adjoining Mission, and by 1901 the first vintage of Taradale Vineyards' wines was in the barrel.

For the next 25 years Steinmetz made his living selling table grapes and wine. In 1926, Steinmetz leased his winery to 19-year-old Tom McDonald, whose later exploits with the Cabernet Sauvignon variety were to indivisibly link the name McDonald with fine quality reds (see page 21).

The vineyards Montana purchased in Hawke's Bay in the late 1980s were rationalised, with the removal of low-grade varieties and a new planting emphasis on Cabernet Sauvignon, Merlot and Chardonnay. Montana now owns or has management control over about 800 hectares of vineyards in Hawke's Bay. The steep, half-hectare Park Terrace vineyard behind the winery yielded its first crop of Merlot in 2001.

The popular Church Road Chardonnay places its accent on rich, ripe, citrusy fruit flavours, with barrel-fermentation and lees-aging adding toasty, biscuity characters and partial malolactic fermentation giving a touch of butteriness. This is a deliciously full, flavour-packed and skilfully balanced wine. The Reserve model, fermented in two-thirds new French oak barriques, is more powerful, with intense, grapefruit-like fruit flavours and a savoury, mealy, oaky complexity. There is also a rare, very elegant, subtle and harmonious Cuve Series Chardonnay, made in a Burgundian style, and a ripely herbaceous, gently oaked Sauvignon Blanc, blended from Hawke's Bay and Marlborough fruit.

Church Road Cabernet Sauvignon/Merlot stands out, not as a blockbuster, but for its elegance and finesse, with considerable complexity and fine-grained tannins. The Reserve Cabernet Sauvignon/Merlot offers excellent depth of brambly, spicy, cedary flavour, although the wines from cooler seasons still show a distinct herbaceousness.

Tom, Montana's super-premium red, launched from the 1995 vintage, is a rich, complex and savoury Hawke's Bay Cabernet Sauvignon/Merlot. A Bordeaux fan, Tom McDonald would have loved it.

Housing hundreds of barrels of maturing wine, the Tom McDonald Cellar was used for the first time at the launch of Tom, Montana's flagship red, and hosts many cultural events and winemakers' dinners.

Address   C.J. Pask Winery,
1133 Omahu Road,
Hastings

Owners   Chris Pask, Kate Radburnd
and John Benton

Key Wines   Gimblett Road Chardonnay,
Merlot, Cabernet/Merlot,
Pinot Noir; Reserve
Chardonnay, Merlot,
Declaration; Roys Hill
Chardonnay, Sauvignon
Blanc, Cabernet/Merlot/
Malbec

C.J. Pask

■ From 20-year-old vines in Gimblett Road, among the oldest in Hawke's Bay, the C.J. Pask winery at Hastings fashions some of the region's greatest reds, arrestingly powerful, complex and concentrated.

The winery is owned in equal shares by Chris ('C.J.') Pask, winemaker Kate Radburnd and (since 2000) Wellington financier John Benton. Pask, a former top-dressing pilot, was also from 1969 onwards a contract grape-grower at Fernhill. Having each year turned out a couple of barrels of wine for his friends and relatives and, he says, being 'interested in adding value', in 1985 he elected to move into commercial wine production under his own label.

The original winery — a converted tractor shed — and vineyard in Korokipo Road, Fernhill, were in 1989 sold to Montana. A new Mediterranean-style winery, featuring river stones, stained glass and prominent columns, soon afterwards rose in a built-up area on the north side of Hastings.

The 1985 to 1990 vintages were made by Chris Pask himself, but his white wines lacked the consistently high quality of the reds. 'The company had grown enormously and needed a professional winemaker,' says Kate Radburnd, who joined C.J. Pask in 1990. Born in Adelaide, Radburnd is a Roseworthy College graduate who worked as an assistant winemaker at Vidal and Villa Maria during the mid-1980s and then built a glowing reputation during her 1987–90 spell as winemaker at Vidal.

'It was time for a change,' says Radburnd. 'I wanted to see how a smaller winery works, especially one where you grow your own grapes. I'd already worked with and knew the quality of Chris' Gimblett Road fruit. From his point of view, the reputation I'd built at Vidal was a tremendous bonus.'

When Pask planted the first vines in Gimblett Road in 1981, the area was best known for its rubbish dump, drag strip and shingle quarry. Today, the company's 84 hectares of vineyards in Gimblett Road are an invaluable asset, planted principally in Merlot, Chardonnay, Cabernet Sauvignon, Cabernet Franc, Malbec, Syrah and Sauvignon Blanc. A further 60 hectares are available for planting, and contract growers around the Bay also provide grapes for the winery's bottom-tier Roys Hill range.

Until the late 1990s, Pask reds were often leafy-green, showing a lack of truly ripe fruit characters, but lately the Merlot-based wines have been consistently outstanding, establishing a brilliant track record in local and overseas competitions. In explanation, Radburnd points to the advancing maturity of the vines and the viticulturists' efforts to reduce crops and increase fruit ripeness by opening the vines' canopies to sunlight. C.J. Pask's output of about 45,000 cases (making it a middle-size producer) is based on a three-tier range, with Reserve wines at the top, a Gimblett Road selection in the middle and Roys Hill wines for everyday drinking.

The Roys Hill range features a fruit-driven Chardonnay, fresh and vibrant; a smooth, tropical fruit-flavoured Sauvignon Blanc; and a berryish, plummy, very lightly wooded Cabernet/Merlot/Malbec.

The partly oak-aged Gimblett Road Chardonnay has strong drink-young appeal, with citrusy fruit characters to the fore and restrained use of wood. Matured in French and American oak casks, the Gimblett Road Merlot is highly impressive for a non-Reserve wine, with excellent ripeness and depth and great drinkability. The Reserve Chardonnay shows a strong, new French oak influence, in a tightly structured style with fresh, citrusy, mealy flavours. The star Reserve Merlot is strikingly rich, with a complex array of blackcurrant, plum, spice and coffee flavours, warm, dense and lasting.

There is also a notably dark and perfumed Cabernet Sauvignon and Malbec-based Reserve Declaration, concentrated, spicy and nutty, with a firm tannin grip.

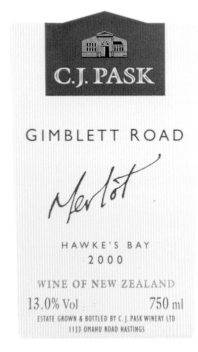

From 20-year-old vines, Kate Radburnd and winemaker Bill Nancarrow fashion one of New Zealand's most internationally acclaimed reds, the arrestingly deep C.J.Pask Reserve Merlot.

Clearview Estate

■ 'Subtle is boring!' declares Tim Turvey, co-owner of the small but spectacularly successful Clearview Estate winery. 'I aim to make vibrant and explosive Chardonnay and red wines that will blow your socks off.'

Turvey made his first wines while still a schoolboy. After graduating with a BA from Massey University, he 'always worked on the land, from contract grapegrowing to growing pineapples in Australia'. His Te Awanga land, right on the coast with a glorious view of Cape Kidnappers, was bought in 1985. The first vines were planted in 1988 and a year later the first wine flowed, based on bought-in grapes.

Helma van den Berg, Turvey's partner, is a viticulturist who also runs Clearview's popular vineyard restaurant. 'We've put enormous work into it,' she says. 'Tim and I have rammed every post, grafted every vine, planted every vine.'

The shingly estate vineyard, an old Vidal block first planted in 1916, today covers 5 hectares of Chardonnay, Cabernet Sauvignon, Merlot and Cabernet Franc vines, pruned for low yields and not irrigated. 'It's a frost-free, amazingly well-drained site,' says Turvey. Turvey and van den Berg also manage another 6 hectares of vines at Te Awanga.

Clearview's winery started life as a commercial garage in Hastings, since dismantled, shifted, reassembled, converted and extended. The original plan was to produce fewer than 1000 cases of wine per year, but production has now risen to around 5000 cases.

Clearview's most celebrated wine is its hefty, explosively flavoured Reserve Chardonnay. Ultra-ripe fruit is the key to the wine's style. 'The grapes are golden, honeyish, with an amazingly luscious fruit character,' says Turvey. 'We never harvest them below 25 brix [sugar], which gives around 14 per cent alcohol.' Fermented in all-new French oak barriques, it is a hedonist's delight — a bold, succulent wine that overflows with peachy, oaky, mealy flavour and has a proven ability to mature gracefully for several years.

Clearview's top reds are powerful, exuberantly fruity wines, crammed with flavour. My favourite is the dark, mouthfilling Reserve Merlot, with its seductive intensity of spicy, vibrant, almost sweet-tasting fruit flavour. The Reserve Cabernet Franc is a serious yet sensuous red, chock-full of colour, body and flavour.

The Reserve Old Olive Block is a Cabernet Sauvignon-based blend, bold and full-flavoured, but less consistently outstanding than the Reserve Merlot. However, The Basket Press, a rarer and far higher priced Cabernet Sauvignon-based red, is a stunning wine, savoury, spicy and nutty, with lovely softness, complexity and richness.

Craggy Range

■ Craggy Range promotes itself as 'New Zealand's specialist producer of single-vineyard wines'. Combining the financial muscle of Australia-based, heavy industry businessman Terry Peabody with the expertise and drive of Steve Smith, a prominent viticulturist and Master of Wine, Craggy Range is one of the most exciting recent arrivals in Hawke's Bay.

Named after rugged hills at Havelock North which form a spectacular backdrop to the winery, Craggy Range is planned to grow to an annual output of over 100,000 cases, making it a medium-large winery by New Zealand standards. Between 1999 and 2004, Peabody is pouring $30 million into the company, establishing vineyards in Hawke's Bay and Martinborough and two specialist wineries in the Bay. Smith, Craggy Range's general manager and wine and viticulture director, was formerly chief viticulturist for the Villa Maria group.

The impressive early wines, first produced in 1999, have been based on grapes bought from specialist growers

Address   Clearview Estate Winery,
Clifton Road,
Te Awanga

Owners   Tim Turvey, Helma van den Berg, David and Betty Ward

Key Wines   The Basket Press; Reserve Chardonnay, Te Awanga Sauvignon Blanc, Cabernet Franc, Merlot, Old Olive Block; Beach-Head Chardonnay, Unwooded Chardonnay, Te Awanga Sauvignon Blanc, Black Reef Riesling, Blush, Cape Kidnappers Cabernet

Address   Craggy Range Vineyards, 252 Waimarama Road, Havelock North

Owners   The Peabody and Smith families

Key Wines   Seven Poplars Vineyard Chardonnay, Avery Vineyard Marlborough Sauvignon Blanc, Old Renwick Vineyard Sauvignon Blanc, Seven Poplars Vineyard Merlot

Named after the prominent bony ridges of Te Mata Peak, at Havelock North, Craggy Range produces a top-flight array of Hawke's Bay, Wairarapa and Marlborough wines.

in Hawke's Bay and Marlborough. In 1999, however, planting began in Craggy Range's own extensive vineyards. In the Gimblett Gravels district (of which Smith is a passionate advocate), 100 hectares have been planted in Merlot (especially), Cabernet Franc, Malbec, Cabernet Sauvignon, Syrah and Chardonnay. The vines are trellised low to the ground and densely planted.

In a bid to make fine Pinot Noir and Sauvignon Blanc, Craggy Range has planted a further 120 hectares in the Wairarapa, on old river terraces in Te Muna Road, a few kilometres south-east of the village of Martinborough. The stony higher terrace, an extension of the famous Martinborough Terrace, has been planted in 32 hectares of Pinot Noir. On the lower terrace, strewn with greywacke stones — similar to the Wairau Valley — and some limestone, are 41 hectares of Sauvignon Blanc. The balance of the plantings are Chardonnay and Riesling.

Two specialist wineries are being erected in Hawke's Bay: one to focus on Chardonnay and Bordeaux-style reds, the other on Sauvignon Blanc, Pinot Noir and Syrah. Winemaker Doug Wisor, from upstate New York, who has worked in California and Burgundy, is in charge of Craggy Range's Pinot Noir and Syrah programmes, while Steve Smith specialises in the Bordeaux-style reds and Chardonnay. The two share responsibility for Sauvignon Blanc.

By 'careful harvesting of fully mature fruit and very gentle processing and handling of the juice', Smith has set out to produce wines that are 'more reserved [than the New Zealand norm] and classically structured'. Craggy Range's focus on single-vineyard wines reflects his conviction that the world's most expressive wines are produced from unique plots of land. 'For me, this is the ultimate winemaking challenge: to work intensively in a vineyard, understand it, and then produce a wine with character that is entirely related to that special piece of land.'

Grown in the Todd family's vineyard on the banks of the Tutaekuri River, in the lower Dartmoor Valley, the Seven Poplars Vineyard Chardonnay has concentrated grapefruit, peach and butterscotch flavours, mouthfilling body and a well-rounded finish. Based on very low-cropping vines in Marlborough, the Old Renwick Vineyard Sauvignon Blanc offers ripe melon, gooseberry and passionfruit characters, pure, intense and cut with fresh acidity. There is also an Avery Vineyard Marlborough Sauvignon Blanc, weighty, dry and penetrating.

Seven Poplars Vineyard Merlot is mouthfilling, complex, soft and warm, with a voluptuous fragrance, spice, dark chocolate and vanilla oak flavours and velvety tannins. These early releases have been of auspicious quality, showing excellent intensity, balance and structure.

Cross Roads

■ A new era began at this smallish Fernhill winery in late 1990, when Ager Sectus, a Wellington-based private company controlled by Peter Cutfield, bought out Cross Roads' founding partners, Malcolm Reeves and Lester O'Brien. 'The heart of our plan,' declared Cutfield, 'is to produce premium red wine to rival the best New Zealand has made.'

The terracotta, Cape Dutch-style winery had won gold medals for a range of varieties, but was 'too big to be small and too small to be big,' says Reeves. In particular, it was too small to export seriously. Cutfield intends to substantially boost Cross Roads' annual production, from 10,000 cases to 70,000 cases.

Malcolm Reeves, a former senior lecturer in food technology, set up the winery in partnership with Lester O'Brien, a Victoria University chemistry graduate. O'Brien later established a computing company in Belgium. The company was called Cross Roads because Reeves suggested forming it to O'Brien when the two met in Paris, long after their paths had first crossed in the early 1970s at university.

Cross Roads' 1990 to 1993 vintages were produced at a variety of premises. The existing winery on State Highway 50 (where a new laboratory and temperature-controlled barrel room were recently installed) arose in time for the 1993 vintage. A second winery is also to be erected near Maraekakaho village, where Cutfield is planting a 60-hectare vineyard. In the 5-hectare estate vineyard at Fernhill, which has blocks of shingly and sandy loams, the red-wine varieties have long been kept a secret. However, Hawke's Bay growers have supplied most of the grapes.

After the 2000 sale, O'Brien, the general manager, left the company, but Reeves stayed on as winemaker. However, he also departed in 2002 and was replaced by Matthew Mitchell, who formerly worked at Montana's Church Road Winery. Cutfield plans to narrow the range and concentrate on Merlot, Cabernet/Merlot blends, Syrah and Chardonnay.

The wines have been solid and often good, but rarely outstanding, perhaps reflecting Cross Roads' heavy reliance on bought-in grapes. The 'commercial' range, labelled Classic, has included a flavoursome, rounded, partly barrel-fermented Chardonnay; a crisp, lemony, slightly sweet Riesling; a perfumed, medium-dry Gewürztraminer with plenty of varietal character; and a fresh, raspberryish, moderately complex Pinot Noir.

The Reserve Chardonnay has at best been complex, rich and harmonious, but of slightly variable quality. Matured in French and American oak, the Reserve Cabernet/Merlot has been an ongoing strength, with impressive depth of blackcurrant and plum flavours. The first Reserve Pinot Noir, from the 2000 vintage, was highly successful, with sweet fruit characters of cherries and spice and a lasting finish.

Talisman, the top red, is an estate-grown blend of six grape varieties whose identities Cross Roads has delighted in keeping a secret (Malbec could be a key contributor, but that's just my guess). Matured in French and American oak barriques, with a high percentage of new wood, Talisman is full of personality: dark, perfumed and awash with plum, red berry and spice flavours, seductively smooth and rich.

TALISMAN

1999

CROSSROADS
HAWKES BAY

WINE OF NEW ZEALAND

e1.5l | PRODUCED & BOTTLED BY CROSSROADS WINERY, AGER SECTUS COMPANY LTD HAWKES BAY | 13.0% vol

Address	Cross Roads Wine Company, Korokipo Road, Fernhill
Owner	Ager Sectus
Key Wines	Talisman; Reserve Chardonnay, Pinot Noir, Cabernet/Merlot; Classic Syrah, Merlot/Cabernet, Chardonnay, Riesling, Gewürztraminer, Sauvignon Blanc

Esk Valley Estate

■ Voluptuous, silky, Merlot-based reds are the principal glory of this historic Bay View winery, since 1987 a key part of the Villa Maria group. The wines — including a superb Reserve Chardonnay — are among the best in the Bay.

Villa Maria acquired the old Glenvale winery from Robbie and Don Bird, grandsons of the founder, Englishman Robert Bird. In 1933 Bird bought 5 hectares of land on the coast north of Napier, planning to establish a market garden and orchard. But during the Depression the return for grapes of under twopence per pound soon encouraged Bird to enter the wine industry. In the original cellar, a tunnel scooped out of the hillside, early Glenvale wines were vinted using the humble Albany Surprise variety.

By the time of his death in 1961, Robert Bird owned a 28-hectare vineyard and a large modern winery. His son — the second Robert — extended the vineyards to over 100 hectares of principally hybrid varieties. He retired in 1979, opening the way to the top for Robbie and Don while they were still in their mid-twenties.

Under three generations of Bird family management, Glenvale grew steadily into one of New Zealand's largest family-run wineries. Its production traditionally emphasised fortified wines, but by the mid-1980s the table wines were reliable and competitively priced. The Bird brothers' undoing, however, was to over-expand in the highly price-sensitive cask-wine market. The ferocious wine price war of 1985–86 brought the company to its knees, leading to Villa Maria's takeover a year later.

Villa Maria immediately set about repositioning Glenvale — swiftly renamed Esk Valley — as a top-end-of-the-market, 'boutique' producer.

On terraces carved several decades ago out of the north-facing slope alongside the winery, Merlot, Malbec and Cabernet Franc vines are grown for the premium estate red, The Terraces. The founder, Robert Bird, originally planted these terraces with Albany Surprise; the vines flourished and produced very early-ripening grapes, but owing to high labour costs, in the late 1950s they were replaced by pines.

Today, the 1-hectare hillside vineyard, densely planted and irrigated to ensure adequate vine growth on this hot, drought-prone site, yields only about 250 cases of wine each year. 'I'm the custodian of what is potentially one of New Zealand's greatest vineyards,' says winemaker Gordon Russell. 'What a responsibility and what an honour.' A further 0.3 hectares of Chardonnay is grown at the winery. The rest of Esk Valley's grapes are drawn from Villa Maria's company-owned vineyards and contract growers throughout Hawke's Bay.

Esk Valley sits on one of the most stunning vineyard sites in the country, with magnificent views of the Hawke's Bay coastline and the Pacific Ocean. George Fistonich of Villa Maria, who from the start saw the potential, preserved the heart of the old winery — a strong concrete structure — but the entire complex was modernised. Upgrading included the enclosure of outside tanks, installation of a new press, a huge increase in refrigeration capacity, the addition of a half-underground, temperature-controlled barrel fermentation room, and the purchase of hundreds of casks.

Winemaker Gordon Russell arrived at Esk Valley in 1990. After 'falling in love with wine' and working in the liquor trade in the UK, he came back to New Zealand, worked at the Bellamour winery in west Auckland, then in 1988 joined Villa Maria. After rising to chief cellarhand, Russell was appointed assistant winemaker at Esk Valley, and in 1993 stepped into the top job. 'I'm given a lot of resources,' he says, 'and the freedom to make a lot of choices.'

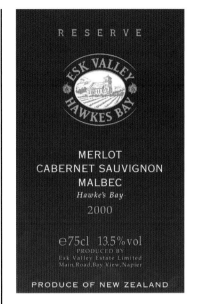

RESERVE

ESK VALLEY
HAWKES BAY

MERLOT
CABERNET SAUVIGNON
MALBEC
Hawke's Bay
2000

e75cl 13.5%vol
PRODUCED BY
Esk Valley Estate Limited
Main Road,Bay View,Napier

PRODUCE OF NEW ZEALAND

Address	Esk Valley Estate, 745 Main Road North, Bay View
Owner	Villa Maria Estate
Key Wines	The Terraces; Reserve Chardonnay, Merlot-predominant blend; Hawke's Bay Chardonnay, Sauvignon Blanc, Riesling, Chenin Blanc, Merlot Rosé, Merlot, Merlot/Cabernet Sauvignon

In Esk Valley's historic cellars, fermentation locks with a one-way valve keep the air out while letting fermentation gases escape.

Gordon Russell crafts majestic, power-packed Reserve reds, but his lower-tier bottlings can also be hard to resist.

I see myself being here a long time.'

Esk Valley is 'Merlot country', according to the winery newsletter. 'Merlot prospers more consistently in Hawke's Bay than other red-wine varieties,' says Russell. In their pursuit of a 'mouth-watering, not mouth-puckering' style of Merlot, Esk Valley's winemakers ferment the wine in open vats, every few hours hand-plunging the grapes' skins into the juice, and mature the Reserve wine for 15 months in French and American oak barriques (typically two-thirds new).

Esk Valley's straight varietal Merlot is a hard-to-resist wine with rich colour, excellent depth of blackcurrant, plum and spice flavours and a seductively smooth finish. The Reserve Merlot-based red (the exact blend varies slightly from vintage to vintage) is a dark, enticingly fragrant, vibrantly fruity wine with an exceptional concentration of ripe, almost sweet-tasting flavour. This is one of New Zealand's most distinguished reds, with great

vintage-to-vintage consistency and a formidable record in show judgings. Esk Valley also produces a dry Merlot Rosé with fresh, crisp, rasberryish flavours, full of drink-young charm.

The Terraces — the estate-grown red — is one of New Zealand's most powerful wines. Merlot and Malbec (up to 45 per cent) are typically the major ingredients, supplemented by Cabernet Franc, and the wine is matured for up to 18 months in all-new French oak barriques. Strikingly dark and bold, it is complex and chewy, with bottomless depth of brambly, spicy, meaty, nutty flavour and firm tannins. Top vintages are staggeringly good.

The Hawke's Bay Sauvignon Blanc, a mouthfilling style with ripely herbal, melon and capsicum-like flavours in warmer vintages, in cooler years is brisker and more green-edged. The Hawke's Bay Chenin Blanc, partly barrel-fermented, is a consistently characterful wine, crisp, peachy and slightly nutty, with good aging potential.

Esk Valley Hawke's Bay Chardonnay, fully fermented and matured in French and American oak barriques, is a generous, mouthfilling, full-flavoured wine with considerable complexity. The Reserve Chardonnay is highly refined, with a core of rich, citrus and stone-fruit flavours and complex, creamy characters from French oak (60 per cent new), lees-aging and lees-stirring and malolactic fermentation. A classic Hawke's Bay style, it matures well for at least five years.

Huthlee Estate

■ When Devon and Estelle Lee were looking for a name for their winery, they weighed up local place-names. 'We live in Montana Road, so that was out!' recalls Devon. 'In the end we chose Huthlee, a combination of Estelle's maiden name, Huthnance, and our married name, Lee.'

This low-profile vineyard lies at Bridge Pa, only a couple of kilometres as the crow flies from the Ngatarawa winery. Devon Lee came to Hawke's Bay from the Waikato as a builder, then worked as a building inspector for the Hastings City Council until 1990.

In 1984, Devon and Estelle bought their 'lifestyle block', planted in peaches and 2 hectares of Merlot and Cabernet Franc vines. 'The vineyard was my hobby,' says Estelle. 'We phased out the peaches and sold the grapes.

Address	Huthlee Estate Vineyard, Montana Road, Bridge Pa
Owners	Devon and Estelle Lee
Key Wines	Sauvignon Blanc, Pinot Gris, Rosé, Kaweka Red, Cabernet Franc, Cabernet Sauvignon/ Merlot, Merlot

We got a half-tonne in 1984 and a year later 25 tonnes.' Why did the Lees plunge into winemaking? 'We toured France in 1990 with Dr David Jackson [a pioneer of Canterbury viticulture] and developed an extreme interest in wine. And we had premium, sought-after grapes.' Huthlee Estate's first vintage flowed in 1991. Show success followed swiftly; the 1992 Cabernet Franc, 1992 Merlot and 1993 Cabernet Sauvignon all won silver medals.

The 6.5-hectare vineyard of Cabernet Franc, Merlot, Cabernet Sauvignon, Pinot Gris and Sauvignon Blanc is planted in free-draining sandy loams overlying river shingles. 'It's only good for grazing sheep or growing grapes,' says Devon. Huthlee Estate's annual production has stayed small, averaging about 2000 cases.

The wines, made on-site since 1994, include a crisp, peachy, spicy Pinot Gris; a punchy, freshly aromatic Sauvignon Blanc; and a raspberryish, zingy Rosé. The bottom-tier Kaweka Red, blended from Cabernet Sauvignon and Merlot, is a decent, flavoursome, oak-aged quaffer.

The trio of top reds — Merlot, Cabernet Franc and Cabernet Sauvignon/Merlot — have been of variable quality, but from favourable seasons show excellent ripeness and depth.

Kemblefield

■ Visiting New Zealand in 1992, California winemaker John Kemble 'picked a couple of dozen wines off the shelves and found vegetative [unripe] qualities in some of the South Island reds. But I was impressed with Morton Estate's Riverview vineyard at Mangatahi and very impressed with the Black Label reds from that vineyard. Then I heard there was a 200-hectare property three kilometres down the road that was potentially available for purchase . . . '

Since then, Kemble and his partner, California tax attorney Kaar Field (the 'field' in Kemblefield) have poured several million dollars into developing a large vineyard and winery at Mangatahi. The stocky, curly-haired Kemble graduated in viticulture from the University of California, Davis in 1983 and for the next nine years was assistant winemaker at Ravenswood, a smallish Sonoma winery renowned for its muscular Zinfandels.

Kemblefield's first wines flowed in 1993. The early releases were generally unspectacular, no doubt reflecting a reliance on bought-in grapes and the time needed to adapt to the local climate. 'In California they just don't get rain,' laughs Kemble. 'The cool climate and general vineyard health issues are more challenging here.' As the company's own grapes have come on stream, the standard of the wine has risen.

Today, on gravelly, free-draining terraces of the Ngaruroro River, over 100 metres above sea level, Kemblefield has 77 hectares of vines, predominantly Chardonnay and Merlot, with significant amounts of Sauvignon Blanc and Cabernet Sauvignon, and small plots of Zinfandel, Cabernet Franc, Sémillon, Gewürztraminer, Malbec and Pinot Gris. The only variety not entirely estate-grown is Gewürztraminer.

With its annual output of about 15,000 cases, Kemblefield is a medium-small producer, labelling its top wines 'The Reserve', middle-tier wines as 'The Distinction' and everyday-drinking wines as 'Winemakers Signature'. Highlights of the Reserve range are the powerful, complex, soft and creamy Chardonnay and the rare, brambly, well-rounded Zinfandel.

The Distinction Chardonnay offers mouthfilling body and deep peach, grapefruit and butterscotch flavours. The Distinction Gewürztraminer — weighty, dryish and rich — and The Distinction Sauvignon Blanc, which offers fresh, crisp, tropical fruit and herbaceous flavours, with toasty oak adding complexity, are also consistently appealing.

Address	Kembiefield Estate Winery, Aorangi Road, Mangatahi
Owners	John Kemble and Kaar Field
Key Wines	The Reserve Chardonnay, Cabernet Sauvignon, Zinfandel; The Distinction Chardonnay, Sauvignon Blanc, Gewürztraminer, Merlot; Winemakers Signature Chardonnay, Cabernet Sauvignon/Merlot

Kim Crawford

■ Formed in 1999 yet already ranked among the country's middle-sized producers, this fast-growing company marries the substantial grape resources of Te Awanga Vineyards and the winemaking talents of Kim Crawford.

Crawford first leapt to prominence at Coopers Creek during the late 1980s and 1990s, where as winemaker he enjoyed glowing competition success. The Te Awanga partnership, in which grape-growers Jim Scotland and Michael Hewitt are the key figures, owns vineyards in Lawn Road, on the Tukituki River, and on the coast at Te Awanga. Kim Crawford Wines, half owned by Crawford and his wife Erica, and half by Te Awanga Vineyards, produces exclusively North Island wines. The Crawfords also market a range of Marlborough wines through their own separate company, which has shareholdings in vineyards in the Awatere and Waihopai valleys and in a winery in Marlborough. 'You need Marlborough Sauvignon Blanc to succeed in export,' says Crawford, 'and you need Pinot Noir, which we're sourcing from Marlborough and Hawke's Bay.'

After graduating with a BSc from Massey University, Crawford gained a post-graduate diploma in oenology from Roseworthy College in South Australia, then worked in wineries in Australia, California, South Africa and France. 'Kim's pretty competitive,' observes Andrew Hendry of Coopers Creek. 'He's certainly motivated to make a good name for himself.'

The cellar door operation is based at Te Awanga, but the wines are made elsewhere in Hawke's Bay. The unusually extensive range is headed by four proprietary blends, including Pia (named after the Crawfords' daughter), a powerful, lush Chardonnay made in a very upfront style with lashings of toasty oak, loads of peachy, buttery flavour and a creamy-rich finish; and the American oak-matured Tane, a blend of Hawke's Bay Merlot and Cabernet Franc, perfumed, densely coloured, notably concentrated and smooth.

The Marlborough Sauvignon Blanc is typically punchy, with very good intensity, and the Marlborough Dry Riesling carries the dry style well, with good body and strong, ripe, lemon, apple and passionfruit flavours. The Tietjen Chardonnay, American oak-fermented, is a classic Gisborne style: richly fragrant, plump and soft.

Address	Kim Crawford Wines, Clifton Road, Te Awanga
Owners	Kim and Erica Crawford and Te Awanga Vineyards Limited
Key Wines	Rory, Pia, Tane, Reka, Te Awanga Merlot, Wicken Vineyard Hawke's Bay Cabernet Franc, Te Awanga Chardonnay, Tietjen Gisborne Chardonnay, Unoaked Marlborough Chardonnay, Marlborough Dry Riesling, Marlborough Sauvignon Blanc

2000

Cabernet Sauvignon Merlot

GIMBLETT GRAVELS, HAWKES BAY, NEW ZEALAND

Address	Kingsley Estate, Gimblett Road, Hastings
Owners	Kingsley Tobin and partners
Key Wines	Gimblett Road Cabernet Sauvignon, Gimblett Road Merlot

Address	Linden Estate, State Highway 5, Eskdale
Owners	Brenda Cha and Peter Wardle
Key Wines	Hawke's Bay Chardonnay, Whole Bunch Pressed Chardonnay, Esk Valley Gewürztraminer, Hawke's Bay Sauvignon Blanc, Dam Block Cabernet/Merlot, Hawke's Bay Merlot, Merlot/Cabernet

Kingsley Estate

■ This small Gimblett Road producer stands out, partly as the first vineyard in Hawke's Bay to have Bio-Gro (certified organic) status, but also because of the consistent excellence of its claret-style reds.

Kingsley Tobin was raised in Hawke's Bay, then spent over a decade in California, where his eight-year spell as a restaurant manager included responsibility for wine purchasing. After returning to the Bay in 1990, he studied viticulture and winemaking, then in 1991 planted his first vines in stony, arid soils at the far end of Gimblett Road.

Today, Kingsley Estate has three vineyards totalling 28 hectares, in Gimblett Road, on the corner of Gimblett Road and State Highway 50, and Mere Road (all are in the Gimblett Gravels Winegrowing District). Cabernet Sauvignon, Merlot and Malbec are the key varieties, with a smaller plot of Syrah added in 2002. The wines are based entirely on estate-grown fruit.

To fund his rapid expansion, Tobin now shares the ownership of the vineyards with an overseas investor, and former television personality John Hawkesby and his wife, Joyce, have invested in the wines' production.

Tobin wants people to judge his wine for its quality, 'not buy it just because it's organic'. Mustard and oats are grown between the rows to increase the soil's organic matter and create an ideal environment for desired insect predators, and sodium silicate, liquid seaweed and a fungal deterrent made from plant oils are used to strengthen the grapes' skins against botrytis bunch rot.

The wines, launched from the 1995 vintage and made at a local winery with Tobin's involvement, have looked impressive from the start, with notable ripeness, intensity and structure. A serious wine with strong personality, the Cabernet Sauvignon is dark, fragrant and warm, with deep, complex flavours of blackcurrants, spice and nuts, and the Merlot is densely coloured, arrestingly rich and supple. These are clearly New Zealand's best organic reds — and splendid wines in their own right.

Linden Estate

■ In the heart of the Esk Valley, near the historic church at Eskdale, lies Linden Estate. For its first decade run by the founders, the van der Linden family, in 2001 Linden Estate was acquired by Canadian architects Brenda Cha and her partner, Peter Wardle.

The first Linden Estate wine flowed in 1991, 20 years after Dutch immigrant Wim van der Linden planted his first vines as a grower for McWilliam's. The early wines were made at a nearby winery, but an on-site winery was operational for the 1993 vintage and in 1995 Nick Chan, formerly of Lincoln Vineyards, was appointed winemaker.

Twenty-two hectares of Sauvignon Blanc, Chardonnay, Cabernet Sauvignon, Merlot and Malbec are cultivated in two major soil types. The majority of the vineyard is planted on the sandy, silty floor of the Esk Valley. The 3-hectare Dam Block, carved out of the hills to create a sheltered, north-facing site with hard limestone soils, is the source of Linden Estate's flagship reds. Grapes are also purchased from other Hawke's Bay growers.

The new owners, still based in Vancouver, have been visiting New Zealand regularly since the early 1970s and previously owned a beef and cattle operation in Northland. Wardle says their interest in wine 'isn't that much greater than anyone else who enjoys fine wine [but] we wanted a land-based operation that also provided some added value, and the wine industry fitted the bill'.

The wines are marketed in a three-tier range, ascending from the Gallery Series, a selection of everyday-drinking Hawke's Bay wines, to the Origin Series, estate-grown in the Esk Valley, and flagship, limited volume wines in the Sovereign Series.

The Hawke's Bay Chardonnay is typically attractive: soft and flavoursome, with citrusy, gently toasty characters and a slightly creamy texture. Fermented with indigenous yeasts in French oak and given a full malolactic fermentation, the Whole Bunch Pressed Chardonnay is tight and minerally, in a crisp, elegant style that matures gracefully. The Esk Valley Gewürztraminer is slightly sweet, with plenty of character, and the Hawke's Bay Sauvignon Blanc is typically solid, although rarely exciting.

The Merlots and Merlot/Cabernets have been of variable quality, sometimes lacking real warmth and depth, but the weighty, generously flavoured and firm 1998 Dam Block Cabernet/Merlot is highly impressive and built to last.

Lombardi

■ This small Havelock North winery has been revolutionised in the past few years. Until the mid-1990s, Lombardi was the oddity of the Hawke's Bay wine trail, preserving the fortified-wine traditions of a largely vanished era. Now the focus is on a tight range of table wines — Chardonnay, Sauvignon Blanc and Merlot-based reds.

In 1948 English-born W.H. Green, who had worked for the Vidal brothers in the 1930s, and his wife, Tina, planted a 1.2-hectare vineyard in Te Mata Road. After Mrs Green, born in the Bay of Naples, turned to her grandparents in Italy for additional winemaking advice, 1959 brought the first Lombardi vintage.

The founders' son, Tony, made the wines for many years, focusing on Italian-style liqueurs and vermouths, supplemented by a range of sherries, ports and quaffing table wines. However, in 1994 the Greens sold the business to their neighbour, Andy Coltart, a property developer and farmer, and his partner, advertising agent Kim Thorp.

Today, there's a lot happening at Lombardi. Concerts are held in a grassed amphitheatre with views across the Bay to Napier and the coast; up-market accommodation is offered at the estate's Rush Cottage and Black Barn; and on Saturdays crowds flock to the rustic Village Growers' Market to buy fresh local produce, including strawberries and asparagus.

Merlot is the principal variety in the replanted, 8-hectare vineyard, which spreads over north-facing clay slopes. Cabernet Sauvignon, Cabernet Franc, Sauvignon Blanc and Chardonnay are also important, with smaller plots of Malbec and (keeping the Italian heritage alive) Sangiovese.

Lombardi's output is low — about 2500 cases per year, entirely estate-grown. The white wines are made at another local winery, but the reds are made and matured on-site by winemaker Dave McKee, who joined Lombardi in 2001 after a decade at the Church Road winery.

The Barrel Fermented Chardonnay is mouthfilling, with melon, lemon and nutty oak flavours, and the Barrel Fermented Sauvignon Blanc is full-bodied, with crisp melon/apple flavours and a touch of oak/lees complexity. The Merlot/Cabernet is plummy and firm, with decent depth, but the star of the range is the markedly more powerful and richly flavoured Reserve Merlot/Cabernet.

There is also a dark, Cabernet Sauvignon-based, French oak-aged Special Reserve Port with intense blackcurrant flavours, sweet and firm.

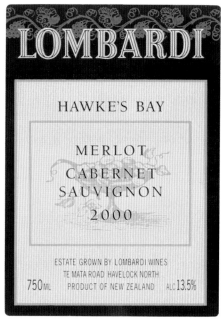

Address	Lombardi Wines, Te Mata Road, Havelock North
Owners	Andy Coltart and Kim Thorp
Key Wines	Barrel Fermented Sauvignon Blanc, Barrel Fermented Chardonnay, Merlot/Cabernet, Reserve Merlot/Cabernet

Matariki

■ 'Matariki,' says John O'Connor, who owns a large area of valuable vineyards in Gimblett Road, 'is the Maori name for the mother of a small cluster of stars. Making her arrival in the sky around the shortest day, Matariki brings light to the barren land and bare vines. If she and her daughters were easily seen, it was believed a bountiful season would follow.'

Since its first vintage in 1997, Matariki, on the outskirts of Hastings, has earned a reputation for impressively rich and concentrated wines. O'Connor, a former drainage contractor ('That's where I developed my interest in vines, soil and wine'), and his wife, Rosemary, planted their first vines in Gimblett Road in 1981. They later sold that vineyard, but in 1992 bought another 170 hectares in Gimblett Road, of which 110 hectares have subsequently been sold to finance the establishment of the Matariki vineyards and winery.

In the 40-hectare vineyard, planted mainly in Sauvignon Blanc, Chardonnay, Cabernet Sauvignon, Merlot, Syrah, Malbec and Pinot Noir, O'Connor has taken great care to match the variable soil types to suitable varieties. Chardonnay and Pinot Noir are planted in the cooler, more silty soils and Bordeaux red varieties and Syrah in the warmer, stonier blocks. A separate, 4-hectare vineyard at Havelock North, on a limestone terrace below Te Mata Peak, has been planted in Chardonnay and Pinot Noir.

The on-site concrete winery has the capacity to produce up to 35,000 cases per year. Greg Foster, an Australian-born and trained winemaker, joined Matariki in 1999 after eight years at the Nobilo winery in west Auckland.

The bottom-tier wines, sold under the Stony Bay brand, include a fruit-driven, crisp and lively Chardonnay and a ripely flavoured, smooth Sauvignon Blanc. The very lightly oaked Matariki Sauvignon Blanc and half barrel-fermented Matariki Reserve Sauvignon Blanc are both weighty, with rich tropical-fruit flavours, dry and long. Both the Reserve and non-Reserve Matariki Chardonnays are highly fragrant, with deep citrus and stone-fruit flavours and well-integrated oak.

The Gimblett Road reds are typically powerful, ripe and generously flavoured. Quintology — blended from Merlot, Cabernet Sauvignon, Cabernet Franc, Syrah and Malbec — is dark and rich, with plum, berry and spice flavours, good complexity and a smooth, peppery finish. The supple, vibrantly fruity Pinot Noirs, which show good varietal definition, and rich, well-spiced Syrahs are among the finest in the Bay.

Address	Matariki Wines, 52 Kirkwood Road, Hastings
Owners	John and Rosemary O'Connor
Key Wines	Matariki Chardonnay, Reserve Chardonnay, Sauvignon Blanc, Reserve Sauvignon Blanc, Quintology, Merlot, Syrah, Reserve Syrah, Pinot Noir, Reserve Pinot Noir, Stony Bay Sauvignon Blanc, Chardonnay

Address	Mission Vineyards, 198 Church Road, Taradale
Owner	Marist Holdings (Greenmeadows) Limited
Key Wines	Reserve Chardonnay, Cabernet Franc, Cabernet/Merlot, Cabernet Sauvignon; Hawke's Bay Chardonnay, Sauvignon Blanc, Gewürztraminer, Pinot Gris, Riesling, Cabernet/Merlot, Cabernet Sauvignon, Merlot, Ice Wine

Mission

■ The old Mission winery at Greenmeadows, nestled against the flanks of the Taradale hills, produces a large volume of sharply priced wines, and its Reserve Chardonnays and claret-style reds are consistently impressive. More than 150 years after planting the first grapevines in Hawke's Bay, the Mission is the country's only nineteenth-century wine producer still under the same management — the Catholic Society of Mary.

The present site is the last of several occupied by the Marist mission during its long history in Hawke's Bay. Father Lampila and two lay brothers, Florentin and Basil, after mistaking the Poverty Bay coast for their real destination, Hawke's Bay, planted vines near Gisborne in 1850. A year later they moved south and planted more vines at Pakowhai, near Napier. The story goes that in 1852, on a return visit to Poverty Bay, Father Lampila found the abandoned vineyard bearing a small crop of grapes, made a barrel of sacramental wine and shipped it to Napier. But the seamen broached the cargo, drank the wine — and the cask completed its journey full of sea water.

A Maori chief, Puhara, took the French missionaries under his protection at Pakowhai. The brothers taught and nursed the local Maori, and gardens and vineyards were laid out. After Puhara was killed, however, in an inter-tribal clash in 1857, the brothers were forced to move again, this time to Meeanee.

For several decades wine production at Meeanee was very limited, sufficient only to supply the brothers' needs for sacramental and table wines. A son of a French peasant winemaker, Brother Cyprian, arrived in 1871 to take charge of winemaking, but not until around 1895 were the first recorded sales made, mainly of red wine.

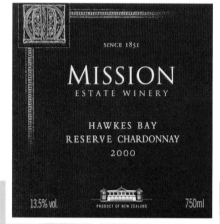

Two years later, local rivers burst their banks, flooding the Meeanee Plains and inundating the Mission cellars. After deciding to shift to higher ground, the Society of Mary bought 240 hectares of Henry Tiffen's estate at Greenmeadows — including 0.2 hectares of Pinot Noir — and established a 4-hectare vineyard there. But not until 1910, after further disastrous floods, was the seminary moved to Greenmeadows; the wooden building was cut into sections and hauled there by steam engine. Fire almost destroyed the wine vaults in 1929, and thousands of gallons of wine were lost in the Napier earthquake of 1931, but of late nature appears to have made its peace with the Mission.

Under the guidance of Brother John, the winemaker from the 1960s until 1982, the

Profits from the sale of Mission wines fund the Society of Mary's seminary and missionary work throughout the South Pacific.

Mission acquired a reputation for sound wines. By the end of the 1970s, however, Mission wines were often mediocre, reflecting a lack both of finance and of advanced winemaking equipment. The church authorities faced a basic decision: to be left further behind the rest of the industry, or to compete. The result was an upgrading of the vineyards and winery equipment, designed to lift both the standards and production level of Mission table wines.

A visit to the Mission is one of the highlights of the Hawke's Bay wine trail. 'For decades, the vineyard and winery were an integral part of the seminary,' recalls winemaker Paul Mooney, who joined the Mission in 1979. 'A lot of the brothers worked in the winery, and the students used to pick grapes by hand.' In 1990, the Society of Mary's seminary shifted to Auckland, but the winery still finances missionary work and the education of young men for the priesthood throughout New Zealand and the South Pacific. The beautiful old seminary building, on the hillside above the winery, was recently restored, and now houses the cellar door operation. An underground cellar contains hundreds of casks, thousands of bottles and a wine library.

About half of the Mission's grapes are drawn from its own vineyards. The relatively low-vigour soils of the 18-hectare vineyard in Church Road are planted mainly in Sauvignon Blanc, Chardonnay and Pinot Gris. At Meeanee, where the Mission has in recent years reduced its vineyard holdings, it has retained a 4-hectare block of Chardonnay. A newer, 14-hectare vineyard, in stony soils in the Gimblett Gravels district, is devoted to Cabernet Sauvignon, Sauvignon Blanc, Merlot, Syrah and Cabernet Franc.

Another crucial factor in the rising quality of Mission wines over the past decade has been the coming on stream of fruit from two vineyards in Ohiti Road, near Roys Hill. 'They're sheltered from the sea breezes and so a little bit warmer,' says Mooney, 'and the shingle in the soil aids ripening. The Cabernet Sauvignon grapes possess very pure, blackcurrant-like flavours and the Cabernet Franc is wonderful — plummy, with fine tannins.'

A medium-sized winery, in the past 15 years the Mission has doubled its annual output from 30,000 to 60,000 cases and penetrated several overseas markets, but 85 per cent of the wine is still sold in New Zealand.

The top wines are labelled Jewelstone, followed by a Reserve range and a selection of moderately priced varietal wines. The Jewelstone label, however, has been rarely seen in recent years, and most of the Mission's finest wines have appeared as part of its Reserve range.

The everyday-drinking wines include a citrusy, ultra-smooth Chardonnay, given a full, softening malolactic fermentation; a slightly sweet, often highly characterful Gewürztraminer; a peachy, spicy, nutty, dry Pinot Gris; a medium-dry Riesling with strong lemon/lime flavours and well-defined varietal characteristics; a solid but not exciting Sauvignon Blanc; and Cabernet Sauvignon, Merlot and Cabernet Franc-based reds which closely mirror the season — light and green-edged in lesser years, but warm and full-flavoured in favourable vintages.

Often distinguished, the Reserve range features an elegant, barrel-fermented Reserve Chardonnay with sweet, ripe fruit characters and a creamy-soft finish; an outstanding Reserve Riesling and Reserve Sémillon (only made occasionally); and a Reserve Cabernet Sauvignon and Reserve Cabernet/Merlot, which both offer firm, concentrated blackcurrant/spice flavours seasoned with quality French oak.

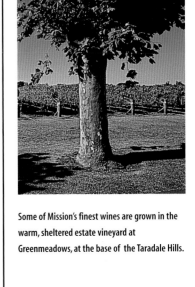

Some of Mission's finest wines are grown in the warm, sheltered estate vineyard at Greenmeadows, at the base of the Taradale Hills.

Ngatarawa

■ The key pioneer of grapegrowing and winemaking in the Ngatarawa Triangle, Ngatarawa is a growing, medium-sized producer, acclaimed for its Chardonnays, Merlot-based reds and richly botrytised, honey-sweet Rieslings.

Ngatarawa (meaning 'between the ridges') began in 1981 as a partnership between Alwyn Corban and the Glazebrook family, of the Washpool sheep station, who had owned the site of the present vineyard for over half a century. The company's first vintage, 1982, was based on Te Kauwhata fruit; the first Hawke's Bay wines flowed in 1983.

Alwyn Corban, a popular and gentle personality, is the son of Alex Corban, the Wine Institute's first chairman. After capping his impressive academic record with a master's degree in oenology and viticulture at the University of California, Davis, Corban spent a year at the Stanley Wine Company in South Australia, followed by four years at McWilliam's in Napier, before founding Ngatarawa with Garry Glazebrook.

In 1999, the Glazebrook family sold their shares in Ngatarawa and the company is now owned equally by Alwyn Corban and his first cousin once removed, Brian Corban. A grandson of 'A.A.' Corban (the founder of Corbans Wines) and a son of Najib Corban, who worked at Corbans for nearly 70 years, Brian Corban is an Auckland businessman and professional company director and chairman, with a long-standing involvement with Ngatarawa.

The winery is based on a converted stables built of heart rimu and totara in the 1890s. The building's soft exterior lines were preserved (creating 'a winery that doesn't look like a winery', says Alwyn Corban approvingly), but the internal walls were gutted to free up space for wine storage. Barely visible at the rear of the old stables winery, a newer building accommodates most of the winemaking equipment.

Ngatarawa's 22 hectares of vineyards are in the 'Hastings dry belt', a recognised low-rainfall district. The irrigated estate vineyards, which have 30 to 60 centimetres of fine

Address	Ngatarawa Wines, Ngatarawa Road, Bridge Pa, Hastings
Owners	Alwyn Corban and Brian Corban
Key Wines	Alwyn Reserve Merlot/Cabernet, Chardonnay, Noble Harvest; Glazebrook Chardonnay, Sauvignon Blanc, Noble Harvest Riesling, Merlot/Cabernet; Stables Chardonnay, Sauvignon Blanc, Late Harvest, Cabernet/Merlot

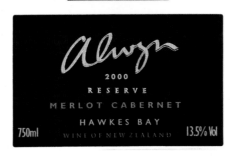

The gravelly estate vineyard at Ngatarawa yields substantial dry wines and (about one year in two) rampantly botrytised, honey-sweet Rieslings.

topsoil over deep gravels — which dry out swiftly in summer — are planted mainly in Chardonnay, Merlot and Cabernet Sauvignon, with smaller plots of Riesling, Sauvignon Blanc, Pinot Noir and Syrah. About 60 per cent of each year's fruit intake is purchased from other Hawke's Bay growers.

Ngatarawa's current annual output of about 37,500 cases is divided between the mid-priced Stables range, premium wines under the Glazebrook label and an ultra-premium selection, called Alwyn Reserve. The wines are made by Alwyn Corban and Peter Gough, who has a postgraduate diploma in oenology from Roseworthy College in South Australia, and for many years ran a vineyard at Moteo, before he joined Ngatarawa in 1993.

Alwyn Corban's devotion to Riesling has few parallels in the region. To encourage the onslaught of 'noble rot' on his Riesling grapes, Corban doesn't use anti-botrytis sprays and hangs the ripening bunches late on the vines. Stables Late Harvest has a pure, delicate, floral bouquet and a medium-sweet, lemony, faintly honeyed palate. Corban sees it as his 'fruit style', meaning it doesn't have the qualities of a heavily botrytised wine.

The honey-sweet Glazebrook Noble Harvest Riesling is made from a high percentage of shrivelled, nobly rotten grapes, for which the hand-pickers make several separate sweeps through the vineyard. Only about one year in two are the humid conditions necessary for the initial botrytis infection followed by the dryness conducive to the development of 'noble rot'. This amber-hued, oily, apricot and honey-flavoured wine is partnered by an even bolder, lusher and more complex Alwyn Noble Harvest, fermented and matured for 18 months in oak casks.

The Stables range features a peachy, citrusy Chardonnay, gently oaked and smooth; a fresh, tropical fruit-flavoured Sauvignon Blanc; and a sturdy Cabernet/Merlot with soft blackcurrant and plum flavours and plenty of drink-young appeal.

The middle-tier Glazebrook Chardonnay (less wood-influenced than in the past, when it was the top label) is a moderately rich, creamy-soft style. Glazebrook Merlot/Cabernet, oak-aged for a year, offers excellent depth of cassis, plum and herb flavours, with a rounded finish.

At the summit of the range are Alwyn Reserve Merlot/Cabernet, a dark, powerful red with notable body and depth of blackcurrant, plum and spice flavours, and Alwyn Reserve Chardonnay, designed for cellaring with its intense, citrusy, slightly minerally, toasty flavours and tight finish.

Redmetal Vineyards

■ Grant Edmonds, who believes New Zealand winemakers often try to do too many things, has a clear focus at Redmetal Vineyards. 'My objective is to make fine red wine — Merlot-based.'

Edmonds first came to prominence in the early 1990s as the Esk Valley winemaker, and from 1993 to 1995 was chief winemaker for the Villa Maria group. He now heads the winemaking team at Sileni, just over the fence from the Redmetal vineyard at Bridge Pa. Named after the soil type in the vineyard — a thin cap of silt loam overlying gravels with a distinct reddish hue — the venture is owned by three couples: Edmonds and his wife, Sue; Auckland lawyer Gary Simpson and his wife, Diane; and Graeme and Gaby Avery, who own Sileni.

The Redmetal vineyard, first planted in 1992, now covers 6.5 hectares of Merlot (principally), Cabernet Franc and Cabernet Sauvignon. Grapes are also purchased from the nearby Prospect Vineyard, planted in Merlot and Cabernet Franc.

Launched from the 1996 vintage and made at the Sileni winery, the wines are produced in fairly small volumes; the 2002 vintage yielded about 3000 cases. The barrel-fermented Rosé is one of the best in the country: dry and substantial, with crisp, strong, berryish, slightly nutty flavours.

The Merlot-based reds are vibrant and overflowing with sweet fruit characters. The lower-priced Merlot/Franc/Cabernet is plump, rich and smooth, with finely integrated oak and gentle tannins. Matured in French and American oak, with a high percentage of new barrels, the Basket Press Merlot/Franc is a highly sophisticated wine with deliciously rich blackcurrant and plum flavours, a silky texture and long, rounded finish. At $90, The Merlot is one of New Zealand's most expensive reds and a real conversation piece. Densely coloured, weighty and supple, with a strong new-oak influence, it's built to last, with great all-round power.

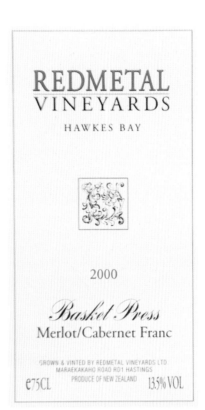

Address	Redmetal Vineyards, Maraekakaho Road, Bridge Pa
Owners	The Edmonds, Simpson and Avery families
Key Wines	The Merlot, Basket Press Merlot/Franc, Rosé, Merlot/Franc/Cabernet

Riverside

■ The rainbow trout that dominate Riverside's labels abound in the Tutaekuri River. The winery sits on a slightly elevated plateau in a peaceful pastoral setting, with sweeping views across the original vineyard and the flat green paddocks of the Dartmoor Valley to the river.

Ian and Rachel Cadwallader planted the first vines at Rosemount, the family farm, in 1981, but sold all the grapes to established wineries until their own first vintage in 1989. Ian Cadwallader, whose great-great-grandparents settled in the Dartmoor Valley in 1851, runs a sheep and cattle farm as well as the 28-hectare vineyard.

The farm, which consists of river flats, old river terraces and rolling hills, has a mix of soil types, with red metals and clay overlying gravels on the terraces. The grape varieties, matched to the soils, include Cabernet Sauvignon (principally), Chardonnay and Merlot, with pockets of Sauvignon Blanc, Sémillon and Pinotage.

The wines are entirely estate-grown (except for the Sauvignon Blanc), and have been made on-site since 1991, originally in a tiny converted boatshed, but since 1993 in a purpose-built winery. Winemaker Russell Wiggins, a Roseworthy College graduate who has worked in Australia, Oregon and France, joined Riverside in 1998. The premium range, labelled Stirling, features a French oak-fermented Chardonnay that in top vintages is beautifully fragrant, intense and refined. Stirling Merlot/Cabernet is spicy, cedary and smooth, with very good depth.

The lower-priced wines, labelled Dartmoor, include a berryish, slightly herbal Merlot with moderate depth; a light, green-edged Cabernet/Merlot; a fresh, smooth Rosé; a melon/lime-flavoured Sauvignon Blanc with reasonable depth; and a straightforward, citrusy Chardonnay.

Rachel Cadwallader has no regrets about plunging into the wine industry. 'You can battle away as a farmer, but who knows about it? As a winemaker, you can make a mark and help bring more tourists to the Bay.'

Address	Riverside Wines, 434 Dartmoor Road, Puketapu
Owners	Ian and Rachel Cadwallader
Key Wines	Stirling Chardonnay, Merlot/Cabernet; Dartmoor Chardonnay, Sauvignon Blanc, Rosé, Merlot, Cabernet/Merlot

Address	Sacred Hill Winery, 1033 Dartmoor Road, Puketapu
Owners	The Mason family
Key Wines	Whitecliff Vineyards Chardonnay, Sauvignon Blanc, Merlot; Barrel Fermented Sauvignon Blanc, Barrel Fermented Chardonnay, Basket Press Merlot/Cabernet, Sauvage, Riflemans Chardonnay, Brokenstone Merlot

Sacred Hill

■ One of the most dynamic wineries in Hawke's Bay over the past decade, Sacred Hill has transformed itself from a small producer of solid but unexciting wines into a medium-large company with good, well-priced, often distinguished Chardonnay, Sauvignon Blanc and Merlot.

Based in the back-country hills of the Dartmoor Valley, Sacred Hill produced its first wine in 1986 — an instantly successful Fumé Blanc, 'which got the boys [David and Mark Mason] very excited'. Their father, John, planted the family's first vines near Puketapu ('sacred hill') in 1982. For many years the company was run by the two brothers, but Mark is no longer involved on a daily basis, leaving David as managing director.

The early years proved a financial struggle, but Sacred Hill now ranks among the country's 20 largest wineries, with an annual output of around 65,000 cases. To strengthen its export portfolio, in 2001 Sacred Hill acquired the vineyards, winery and stock of Cairnbrae Wines, in Marlborough.

The silty, 13-hectare Dartmoor vineyard, just down the road from the Dartmoor Valley winery, is established in Sauvignon Blanc and Chardonnay. A couple of kilometres further up the valley, on a spectacular site overlooking white papa rock cliffs carved by the Tutaekuri River, the 27-hectare Riflemans Terrace vineyard is planted wholly in Chardonnay. Here the soils — a mixture of volcanic ash and red metals overlying limestone — are of very low fertility and the light crops produce rich, concentrated berries, earmarked for the company's top labels.

In the Gimblett Gravels district, a third, 27-hectare vineyard has been planted principally in Merlot, followed by Cabernet Sauvignon, Cabernet Franc, Malbec, Syrah and Chardonnay. Grapes are also drawn from long-term leased vineyards and contract growers. Surrounded by trees alongside the main road through the Dartmoor Valley, the rustic Sacred Hill winery was originally a farm building, extended in 1991 by excavating into the hillside and adding a gravity-fed pressing area and refrigerated cellar for barrel maturation. In 1995, a new, more efficient production facility, Rockwood, was built in Omahu Road, Hastings.

Winemaker Tony Bish has played a key role in Sacred Hill's rising fortunes. Bish, who was first employed at Sacred Hill in the mid-1980s as a vineyard manager, later worked at several other wineries, including Rippon and French Farm, before returning to Sacred Hill as winemaker in 1994. Bish describes himself as 'very much a "vineyard" winemaker, putting into practice the old adage that the best wines are made in the vineyard'.

Designed for early drinking, the Whitecliff Vineyards range includes a minimally oaked but fresh, lively, citrusy and slightly creamy Chardonnay; a frisky, limey, clearly varietal Sauvignon Blanc; and a fragrant, soft and flavourful Merlot. The middle-tier range features a typically delicious Barrel Fermented Chardonnay, marrying rich, ripe, citrus and stone-fruit flavours with toasty oak; a substantial, tropical fruit-flavoured Barrel Fermented Sauvignon Blanc which in favourable years shows good complexity and richness; and a dark, concentrated and seductively smooth Basket Press Merlot/Cabernet.

The bold Brokenstone Merlot, matured in new French oak barriques, has a commanding presence in the mouth, with great intensity and complexity. Riflemans Chardonnay, fermented in new and one-year-old French oak barriques, is a Hawke's Bay classic — powerful and creamy, with beautifully ripe flavours, lush and long.

2000 Hawkes Bay **RIFLEMANS** *Chardonnay* **Sacred Hill** Product of New Zealand

Chardonnay and Sauvignon Blanc dominate Sacred Hill's plantings in the Dartmoor Valley, inland from Taradale, where the Mason brothers made their first wine in 1986.

Sileni

■ Known for his dynamic management and huge entrepreneurial success in the publishing and athletics worlds, Graeme Avery is the driving force behind one of the most exciting recent arrivals on the Hawke's Bay wine scene. Sileni, based at Bridge Pa, is named after the sileni of Roman mythology, demigods of Bacchus, the god of wine.

Avery made his fortune as the founder of medical publishing house Adis International. After selling Adis in 1996, he and his wife, Gabrielle ('Gaby'), set up Vinotica, an award-winning gourmet supply business in Auckland. The Averys' partners in Sileni Estate are Sydney-based chartered accountant Chris Cowper (ex Adis) and his wife, Sally, and Sileni's chief winemaker, Grant Edmonds, and his wife, Sue.

The spectacular winery boasts two restaurants, a cellar door retail area offering wine and gourmet foods, wine education centre, culinary school, and function and conference facilities. Sileni's output is expected to expand from 25,000 cases in 2002 to 60,000 cases by 2005.

The company's vineyards, first planted in 1997, are in two separate, climatically distinct areas. In the relatively warm Ngatarawa Triangle, 44 hectares have been planted, with Merlot (principally), Cabernet Franc, Cabernet Sauvignon and Syrah on the stoniest sites, and Sémillon on the deeper silts. Further inland, between Maraekakaho and Mangatahi, at 110–120 metres above sea level, the markedly cooler Plateau Vineyards have been established with 50 hectares of Pinot Noir and Chardonnay. Grapes are also drawn from contract growers in Hawke's Bay.

Edmonds was previously winemaker at Esk Valley and chief winemaker for the Villa Maria group, and is also involved with the Averys in Redmetal Vineyards. The winemaking team also includes Nigel Davies, who focuses on Bordeaux varieties — Merlot, Cabernet Franc and Sémillon — and Eleanor Dodd, who specialises in Chardonnay and Pinot Noir (for which Sileni has big plans in Hawke's Bay).

The wines, first produced in 1998, are marketed under a three-tier system, headed by rare EV ('exceptional vintage') wines, followed by the larger volume but still excellent quality Estate Selection and an entry-level Cellar Selection.

Partly barrel-fermented, the Cellar Selection Chardonnay is fresh and full, with crisp citrusy, appley flavours and a hint of butterscotch. The Estate Selection Chardonnay, which gets the full treatment in the winery, including a high percentage of new oak, is a powerful, multi-faceted wine, with sweet, grapefruit-like characters, mealy, biscuity complexities and impressive harmony. There is also a subtle, tightly structured, partly oak-aged Estate Selection Sémillon, ripely herbaceous, slightly nutty, crisp and dry.

Like a minor Bordeaux, the Cellar Selection Merlot/Cabernet Franc is supple, with a gentle oak influence but plenty of berryish, spicy flavour. Markedly richer, the French and American oak-aged Estate Selection Merlot/Cabernets shows good density, with strong blackcurrant, plum and spice flavours and complex, savoury, leathery touches.

EV Merlot, one of New Zealand's most expensive reds, is a warm, sweet-fruited wine with a complex array of blackcurrant, spice, coffee and leather characters, cedary French oak and a rich, enveloping bouquet. The future holds an EV Chardonnay and EV Pinot Noir.

Address	Sileni Estates, 2016 Maraekakaho Road, Bridge Pa
Owners	The Avery, Cowper and Edmonds families
Key Wines	EV Merlot; Estate Selection Chardonnay, Sémillon, Merlot/Cabernets; Cellar Selection Chardonnay, Merlot/Cabernet Franc

Graeme Avery has switched his unflagging energy and proven entrepreneurial talents from the publishing world to Hawke's Bay wine.

Address	Stonecroft Wines,
	121 Mere Road,
	Hastings
Owner	Alan and Glennice Limmer
Key Wines	Chardonnay,
	Gewürztraminer,
	Gewürztraminer Late
	Harvest, Syrah, Ruhanui,
	Crofters

Stonecroft

■ If you ask Alan Limmer, of the small Stonecroft winery, to name his favourite wines, he doesn't hesitate: 'Rhône reds. Syrah is very seductive wine.' Acclaimed for his own Syrah, Limmer also produces an increasingly stylish Chardonnay and one of New Zealand's richest and most characterful Gewürztraminers.

Stonecroft (the name means 'stony small farm') lies in Mere Road, in the Gimblett Gravels district, west of Hastings. Limmer studied earth sciences and chemistry at Waikato University, where he earned his doctorate, and then in 1981 moved to Hawke's Bay to manage a private analytical laboratory servicing agricultural needs. After 'drinking plenty and reading a good wine text', he planted the first vines in his silty, sandy, extremely free-draining gravels in 1983. The first Stonecroft wines flowed in 1987.

The 4-hectare estate vineyard, planted in Chardonnay, Gewürztraminer, Cabernet Sauvignon, Merlot and Syrah, is low-yielding and the grapes are left on the vines as long as possible, ripening to very high sugar levels and sometimes shrivelling. A second vineyard, Tokarahi ('many stones') has also been planted in a warm, sheltered, north-facing bowl at the foot of Roys Hill. In this exclusively red-wine vineyard, 3 hectares of Syrah and Merlot have been established, with experimental plots of Zinfandel, Cinsaut and Mourvèdre.

A new, 'clinically efficient' winery rose in 2000, prompted by a lack of space in the original, rustic, stained glass-windowed winery, which Limmer built himself. He currently produces about 3000 cases of wine each year, entirely estate-grown. For many months of the year, the wines are sold out. With his arresting series of dense-coloured, robust, rich-flavoured reds, Limmer was New Zealand's first winemaker to consistently produce a satisfying Syrah. Syrah demands a warm climate and, in the past, growers in New Zealand struggled to ripen its fruit. So what spurred Limmer to plant an experimental row of Syrah vines down Mere Road in 1984?

'Two things. Of the world's top reds, to me Hermitage is the best. The reds of the northern Rhône have everything — fragrance, structure, aging ability. And last century, Syrah looked promising here. So everything pointed to the fact we'd overlooked a good red-wine variety.'

Stonecroft's experimental 1987 and 1988 Syrahs looked promising, so in 1989 Limmer made a whole barrel. 'That wine and the 1990 were successful, so we decided to run with it.'

Limmer is not a great fan of Australia's Shiraz-based reds. 'The Australian wines are big, upfront, with jammy fruit and American oak, but they tend to be one-dimensional. Rhône reds have better structure and length. Our wines are heading in that direction; they're New Zealand wines, but more in the mould of the French.'

Matured for 18 months in French oak barriques (50 per cent new), Stonecroft Syrah is a muscular red with flashing purple-black hues and a powerful surge of red berry, plum and black pepper flavours. So impressed was Michel Chapoutier, head of the great northern Rhône firm, that Chapoutier now distributes Stonecroft wines in France.

Ruhanui, a blend of Cabernet Sauvignon, Syrah and Merlot, has aromas of spice and dark berry fruits, leading into a mouthfilling palate with strong cassis and black pepper flavours in which the Syrah makes its presence well felt. Crofters, numbered rather than vintage-dated, is a sturdy, flavoursome, lower-priced red, based on young vines and wine which, at blending, is not selected for the Ruhanui label.

Sauvignon Blanc was recently dropped from the Stonecroft range, but the 2000 vintage yielded New Zealand's first commercial release of Zinfandel — fresh and moderately ripe, with red berry flavours and a crisp finish. The Chardonnay has grown steadily in stature and is now consistently classy, with sweet, grapefruit-like fruit characters and a savoury, biscuity richness. The Gewürztraminer is pungent and perfumed, weighty and oily, with loads of ripe lychees and spice flavour.

HAWKES BAY
Gewürztraminer
2000
Grown, produced and bottled by
Stonecroft Wines Ltd, R.D.5, Mere Road, Hastings
Produce of New Zealand
CONTAINS PRESERVATIVE (220)
ALC 13.5% Vol.   LG001   750ml.

Zinfandel, Cinsaut and Mourvèdre are among the rarities lurking in Alan Limmer's Tokarahi ('many stones') vineyard, snuggled against the base of Roys Hill.

Te Awa Farm

■ Red wines of notable subtlety, complexity and harmony flow from Te Awa Farm. That's not entirely surprising. Gus Lawson, the proprietor, was determined to produce fine reds from the start and Jenny Dobson, the winemaker, spent 16 years living and working in Bordeaux and Burgundy, including a decade as *maître d'chais* at Château Senejac, a well-respected *cru bourgeois* in the Haut-Médoc.

The Lawson family, contract grape-growers since 1980, searched for five years for a new site to grow top red wines and Chardonnay before purchasing Te Awa Farm, in the Gimblett Gravels district near Hastings, in 1992. Subdivided in 1906 from the original Longlands Station, the name of the 173-hectare property is an abbreviation of Te Awa-O-Te-Atua, which means 'river of God', a reference to the subterranean streams that flow through the district.

Gus Lawson, the head of Te Awa Farm's wine venture, grew up in Hawke's Bay and formerly worked as a viticultural consultant. In the 44-hectare vineyard, where pockets of shingle are interspersed with patches of sand and silt, the various sections are all picked and vinified separately. 'They give us small variations in flavour and texture,' says Lawson, 'and give us more options when it comes to blending.' Sites within the vineyard — sometimes even within rows — where the vines are naturally lower-yielding and produce more intense-flavoured grapes, are the origin of Te Awa Farm's top wines.

Merlot is the most heavily planted variety in the vineyard, followed by Chardonnay, Cabernet Sauvignon, Sauvignon Blanc, Cabernet Franc, Malbec, Syrah and Pinotage.

Te Awa Farm's first vintage flowed in 1994. Entirely estate-grown, the wines are made in a traditional Hawke's Bay farm-style building, with rough-sawn macrocarpa milled from the property adding a rustic charm. With its average annual output of 25,000 cases, Te Awa Farm is a small to medium-sized winery. (The family also grows organic vegetables, served in the winery's popular restaurant and marketed elsewhere under the brand Lawson's True Earth.)

The top selection includes two white wines under the Frontier label. French oak-fermented, Frontier Chardonnay is a powerful wine, mouthfilling, mealy and nutty, with a rich, creamy mouthfeel. Frontier Sauvignon Blanc is a weighty wine with rich, ripe, non-herbaceous fruit characters, strongly seasoned with French oak.

Boundary, the top red, is a Merlot-based blend, French oak-matured for 18 months. Brambly and nutty, savoury, spicy and leathery, in top vintages it is a notably rich and multi-faceted wine.

The more widely available wines, labelled Longlands, are matured in both French and American oak casks (except for the tangy, melon/lime-flavoured Longlands Sauvignon Blanc, which is not barrel-aged). Longlands Chardonnay is attractively fresh, vibrant and crisp, with peachy, citrusy, nutty flavours and a slightly buttery finish.

Longlands Cabernet Sauvignon/Merlot and Merlot are typically stylish reds with excellent ripeness and flavour depth, oak complexity and supple tannins. Less widely seen are the fresh, peppery, strongly varietal Longlands Syrah and the generous Longlands Pinotage, crammed with flavour, plummy, spicy and gamey.

Address Te Awa Farm Winery, 2375 State Highway 50, Hastings

Owner The Lawson family

Key Wines Boundary; Frontier Chardonnay, Sauvignon Blanc; Longlands Chardonnay, Sauvignon Blanc, Cabernet Sauvignon/Merlot, Merlot, Pinotage, Syrah

Te Awa Farm won the 'best commercial garden' award for 2001 from the Hastings District Council. The Frontier Chardonnay and top red, Boundary, are also lovely.

Address   Te Mata Estate Winery,
              349 Te Mata Road,
              Havelock North

Owner   Te Mata Estate Winery
              Limited

Key Wines Coleraine Cabernet/Merlot,
              Awatea Cabernet/Merlot,
              Cabernet/Merlot, Bullnose
              Syrah, Elston Chardonnay,
              Cape Crest Sauvignon Blanc,
              Castle Hill Sauvignon Blanc,
              Woodthorpe Chardonnay,
              Woodthorpe Viognie

Te Mata

■ Two of New Zealand's most sought-after wines — Coleraine Cabernet/Merlot and Elston Chardonnay — flow from this illustrious Hawke's Bay winery. Te Mata Estate is one of New Zealand's top wineries, with consistently outstanding wines and a unique winemaking heritage that stretches back into the nineteenth century.

'The fine vineyard of 35 acres [14.2 hectares] situated at Te Mata, Havelock North, owned by Mr Bernard Chambers, is now the leading one in the Dominion,' wrote S.F. Anderson, the Government vine and wine instructor, in the *New Zealand Journal of Agriculture* in May 1914. 'Mr Chambers' wines are principally hocks, claret and sweet, and are commanding a large sale.'

Chambers, a wealthy grazier and prominent local body politician, had his interest in winemaking kindled by a French guest at the Te Mata homestead, who pointed out the viticultural potential of the surrounding slopes. In 1892, the first vines — cuttings of Pinot Noir obtained from the Society of Mary's Mission Vineyards at Taradale — struck root at Te Mata Vineyard.

The vineyard flourished. Chambers converted a brick stable erected in 1872 into his cellar (still used today for cask storage), and by March 1895 the first wine was flowing. 'My wine is turning out very well,' he wrote in 1898. 'I made claret and chablis and have given a lot away. I won't begin selling for another year, until the wine is more matured.'

With Australian winemaker J.O. Craike (who won gold medals for Te Mata at the Franco-British and Japanese-British Exhibitions) at the production helm, by 1909 Chambers' vineyard was the largest in the country, with an annual output of 12,000 gallons (54,551 L) of 'claret', 'hock' and 'madeira' from the 35 acres (14.2 hectares) of Meunier, Syrah, Cabernet Sauvignon, Riesling and Verdelho vines. Among the stream of eminent visitors to Te Mata Vineyard were Prime Minister Richard Seddon and the Governor, Lord Ranfurly.

But from this early peak, production declined as the influence of the prohibition movement intensified and Chambers ran into problems with birds, mildew, frost and labour. In 1917, Chambers sold his winery, wine stocks and part of the vineyard to Reginald Collins Limited and by 1923, when Reginald Collins sold its interests to a new company, T.M.V. Wines, the vineyard had contracted to 10 acres (4 hectares). A series of new owners failed to restore the vineyard's fortunes.

The revival of Te Mata's reputation began in 1974, when Michael Morris and John Buck, both then active as wine judges, acquired the run-down company. Morris, a Wellington businessman, is a non-working partner; Buck is the managing director and the driving force at Te Mata (see facing page).

After an eight-year search for the right site, during which Buck and Morris looked at 150 properties, they purchased the old Te Mata winery; the cellars, built of brick and native timbers, were restored to their original condition and equipped with stainless-steel tanks and new oak casks.

The new owners' first vintage, 1979, was an unusually wet one, but 1980 brought a rapid change of fortune. 'We were fortunate to acquire the Awatea vineyard and it had a small block of old Cabernet on it,' recalls Buck. 'I guess we picked three or four tonnes off it and the moment we crushed those grapes we knew that our assertion as to the right variety to grow on these hills was correct.' Te Mata 1980 Cabernet Sauvignon then carried off the trophy for the best red at the 1981 National Wine Competition — a feat repeated by the 1981 vintage in 1982 — and Te Mata was on its way.

Coleraine — where John and Wendy Buck live amidst Cabernet Sauvignon, Merlot and Cabernet Franc vines — is by far the country's most-photographed winemaker's residence.

The winery until 1989 marketed all its top wines with a vineyard site designation. Coleraine Cabernet/Merlot, for instance, was sourced from John and Wendy Buck's own 2-hectare vineyard called Coleraine, planted with Cabernet Sauvignon, Merlot and Cabernet Franc. Since the 1989 vintage, however, Te Mata's red wines have been produced in a tiered group, with Coleraine at the top, closely followed by Awatea, and then a third wine called

John Buck

■ In retrospect, it is not surprising that John Buck's career path led finally and triumphantly to the hills of Havelock North. In 1969, while earning a living as a wine merchant, consultant and critic, he wrote in his book *Take a Little Wine*: 'Hawke's Bay wines already possess those essential marks of quality, back palate and finesse. Here, too, soil, climate and topography meet all the requirements for a quality wine area. Thus my choice would be Hawke's Bay, if I wanted land for a New Zealand vineyard.'

Buck, who dropped out of Victoria University after three years' accountancy study, shifted to Auckland, joined a company that imported and sold wine, and 'blundered into my vocation'. He made his first alcoholic drink in 1962. 'We picked up 200 dozen eggs,' he recalls, 'and went out to the Golden Orb vineyard in Sturges Road, Henderson, owned by Hughes and Cossar, to make Finsbury Advocaat.'

After a two-year career in the United Kingdom wine trade and a year's study-visit to Europe, Buck returned to New Zealand in 1966. 'I drove up to Hawke's Bay, spent some time with Tom McDonald, was given a couple of Tom's Cabernets which were served up blind at a luncheon with a Château Haut-Brion, and I also got a thing called McWilliam's Tukituki Rhine Riesling … I saw these wines and I thought, ye gods! There's actually some colossal potential here.' After his first vintage at Te Mata, 1979, proved unusually wet, Buck 'discovered how many friends I had. I'd been a merchant, judge and critic, but many people were dismissive of the whole idea of me going into production.'

He came to Hawke's Bay because he wanted to produce Cabernet Sauvignon-based reds and the 'richer' style of Chardonnay. Buck has long been intrigued by Cabernet-based reds. 'I don't accept the argument that Pinot Noir is the hardest to make. The French concepts of "élevage" [raising the wine, as one would children] and "assemblage" [final selection and blending] really come into play when you are using a multitude of varieties from different soils. Cabernet-based reds therefore have a lot of human input to put the best wines together and often the better the people the better the wine.'

It was the great châteaux of Bordeaux that had most inspired Buck. An admirer of their scientific approach and integrity, he set out to produce reds in the Bordeaux tradition and match as closely as possible their quality. 'Our ideas were based on claret. Not necessarily big wines, but aromatic and complex, with the ability to age.'

Since the early 1980s, Te Mata has ranked among New Zealand's most prestigious wineries. In Hawke's Bay, its reputation is second to none.

Sharp-witted and extroverted, Buck is a forceful personality. Terry Dunleavy, former executive officer of the Wine Institute, described him in 1997 as 'sometimes volatile, but always brilliantly creative and forward-thinking. As chairman [from 1991 to 1996] he brought the Institute to new heights of professionalism, and he is a champion of the value of wine to New Zealand society.'

In recent years, the honours have flowed. Awarded an OBE in 1995, in 1999 John Buck became a Fellow of the Wine Institute. In 2001, he finally got a degree — an honorary Doctor of Commerce from Lincoln University. The citation read in part: 'Known in the wine industry as a great visionary who also has a remarkable ability to get things done, John Buck set out in the late 1970s to make great red wine. He did it — and established the standard for everyone else in the industry.'

Te Mata's Ian Athfield-designed winery produces some of New Zealand's greatest Chardonnay and Cabernet Sauvignon-based reds.

Te Mata Cabernet/Merlot. All three are a blend of wines from Te Mata's spectrum of vineyards. 'This development gives us access to a far greater range of flavours when assembling the wines, providing more flexibility . . . to craft even finer wines,' said Buck.

Te Mata Estate owns no vineyards, although individuals within the company do, and some other vineyards are leased or managed by Te Mata. 'The Havelock North hills — sheltered by Te Mata Peak — provide the hottest vineyard sites in Hawke's Bay,' Buck believes. 'That leads to the principal variety grown being Cabernet Sauvignon, whereas Merlot is our largest red-wine variety at Ngatarawa and Woodthorpe.'

Te Mata's 26 hectares of vineyards at Havelock North are planted principally in Cabernet Sauvignon, Chardonnay and Merlot. In the Ngatarawa district, west of Hastings, where a further 37 hectares have been established, the major variety is Merlot, followed by Syrah, Cabernet Franc and Cabernet Sauvignon, and smaller plots of Sauvignon Blanc, Chardonnay, Pinot Gris and Sémillon.

After a long development period, Te Mata is poised for a huge leap in production from its current level of 35,000 cases. At Woodthorpe Terraces — named after the property's first European owner, O.L.W. (Woodthorpe) Bousefield — an extensive vineyard and fully self-contained winery have been established in a major joint venture between Te Mata Estate and Ghuznee Buildings Limited, a family investment company in which John Buck's wife, Wendy, has holdings. Planting started in 1994 on north-facing terraces above the Tutaekuri River, 14 kilometres inland, on the south side of the Dartmoor Valley. The key soil type is Takapau sandy loam, a free-draining, light volcanic soil with a gravelly base. By 2002, 69 hectares had been established, principally in Chardonnay, Sauvignon Blanc and Merlot, with smaller plots of Cabernet Franc, Cabernet Sauvignon, Viognier, Syrah, Gamay Noir (for a cru Beaujolais-style red) and Petit Verdot. When planting is completed, the 110-hectare vineyard is expected to produce 70,000 cases of wine, all to be processed at the new Woodthorpe Terraces winery.

Te Mata's Ian Athfield-designed, plastered-concrete headquarters, painted throughout in cool pastel shades, houses a boardroom and kitchen on the upper floor, with the offices, sales area and a tasting room at ground level. A landscaped courtyard features a cloistered walkway, sitting steps and fish ponds. The adjacent winery features a temperature-controlled red-wine 'cuverie' (fermentation cellar) with pneumatically operated cap-plungers, and a subterranean barrel hall complete with concrete columns and red-stained barriques.

Winemaker Peter Cowley, a shareholder in the company, is an Auckland University BSc graduate who gained a Roseworthy College diploma and then worked at Delegat's before joining Te Mata. Buck and Cowley's determination to produce long-lived wine styles is a key strand in Te Mata's approach to winemaking. 'To gain true international recognition, an industry has to be capable of making wines that improve with age — that's the ultimate quality factor,' says Buck. '[People need to be able to] put wine into their cellars with confidence and know that when they pull them out they will be a damn sight better than when they put them in.'

A top-vintage Coleraine Cabernet/Merlot matures gracefully for a decade; even longer. With a string of supremely stylish and complex wines since its memorable 1982 debut, Coleraine has carved out a reputation second to none among Hawke's Bay reds. Blended since 1989 from several sites at Havelock North and matured in French oak barriques (typically 70 per cent new), it is typically more wood-influenced and more slowly evolving than its Awatea stablemate.

Cabernet Sauvignon is the cornerstone of the Coleraine blend (varying between 50 and 60 per cent), fleshed out with Merlot (especially) and Cabernet Franc. The standard of the 1989 and subsequent vintages (especially 1991 and 1998) has been markedly superior to the lighter, more herbaceous wines of the 1980s. A top vintage of

Coleraine has the perfume, intensity and complexity that reminds Bordeaux fans of a classed growth Médoc.

Blended from grapes grown at Havelock North, Ngatarawa and Woodthorpe Terraces, Awatea Cabernet/Merlot is voluptuously fragrant, rich and supple, and invariably more approachable in its youth than the Coleraine of the same vintage. Te Mata's third-tier claret-style red, labelled Cabernet/Merlot, is a simpler but highly attractive wine with fresh, vibrant blackcurrant/plum flavours and drink-young appeal.

One of New Zealand's greatest Chardonnays, Elston is grown mostly in the Havelock North hills, fully French oak-fermented, lees-aged and lees-stirred and given a full malolactic fermentation. Powerful, with rich grapefruit and nut flavours in its youth and a creamy-smooth texture, at three to four years old it is complex, richly flavoured and notably 'complete'.

Both tank and barrel-fermented, Woodthorpe Chardonnay is fresh and lively, with grapefruit and melon flavours, subtle oak and a buttery-smooth finish.

Cape Crest and Castle Hill are classic examples of the Hawke's Bay Sauvignon Blanc style — full-bodied and ripely herbal. Castle Hill, grown at Woodthorpe Terraces, is the more clearly varietal of the two, placing its accent on fresh, pure, sweet-fruit characters, crisp and lively. Cape Crest, grown at Woodthorpe Terraces and Havelock North and fully fermented and matured in French oak barrels (mainly second and third-use), shows greater complexity, with a touch of smoky oak and strong, ripe melon/lime flavours enlivened with fresh acidity.

Two relatively recent additions to the range are the densely coloured, powerful Bullnose Syrah, grown at Ngatarawa, which offers densely packed blackcurrant, plum and black pepper flavours, French oak complexity and a long, spicy finish; and Woodthorpe Viognier, floral and softly mouthfilling, with subtle oak, delicate stone-fruit flavours and a crisp, lasting finish. Nicholas Buck, John and Wendy's son, took charge of Te Mata's marketing in 2000. A finance graduate of Massey University, Nicholas worked for eight years in wine production and retailing in New Zealand, the United Kingdom and France, and looks set to play a pivotal role in Te Mata's future.

Trinity Hill

■ The words 'by John Hancock' emblazoned across the label leave you in no doubt that the Trinity Hill range is masterminded by the high-profile winemaker who built his reputation at Delegat's and Morton Estate.

Trinity Hill, at the base of Roys Hill, in the Gimblett Gravels district, was founded in 1993 by three families (hence the winery name): Robert and Robyn Wilson, London developers and restaurateurs; Auckland stockbroker Trevor Janes and his wife, Hanne (early shareholders in Morton Estate); and John and Jennifer Hancock.

Hancock is an affable, irrepressible character, but beneath the popular 'bonhomie' image, there's an ambitious, much more serious side to his personality. Born on a sheep farm near Coonawarra, in South Australia, as a teenager he experimented with fruit winemaking, and in 1973 graduated with a Diploma in Oenology from Roseworthy College. He plunged into the wine industry at the Leo Buring winery in the Barossa Valley and then worked at the giant Berri co-operative winery in the Riverland.

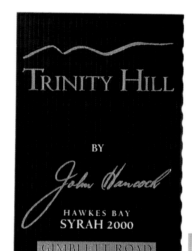

Later, in four spectacularly successful vintages (1979–1982) at Delegat's, and 14 years (1983–1996) at Morton Estate, Hancock built a glowing reputation, above all for Chardonnay.

Trinity Hill's 33 hectares of vineyards in the Gimblett Gravels district, first planted in 1994, are established principally in Merlot, Syrah, Cabernet Sauvignon and Chardonnay, with smaller plots of Viognier, Tempranillo (the great grape of Rioja), Cabernet Franc, Pinot Gris, Petit Verdot and Malbec. The company also buys grapes from Hawke's Bay growers, notably the Shepherds Croft vineyard in the Ngatarawa district. Constructed from tilt-slab concrete, the winery features a modern barrel hall — divided into separate rooms for white and red wines — that gives the winemakers full control of temperature and humidity. 'The idea is to simulate the cellar conditions I saw in Burgundy,' says Hancock, 'and produce finer, more delicate wines with greater aging potential.'

Trinity Hill's first wines flowed in 1996, and with its average output of 35,000 cases, the company is already a medium-sized producer. Warren Gibson — who in the late 1980s worked with Hancock at Morton Estate, has since worked in Australia, California and Europe, and also has his own small label (Bilancia) — is a key member of the production team. The large-volume wines, labelled Shepherds Croft, include a fruit-driven, partly barrel-fermented Chardonnay, citrusy, crisp and refined; a fresh, zippy, limey Sauvignon Blanc; and a berryish, plummy, spicy, moderately flavoursome Merlot/Cabernets/Syrah.

Address	Trinity Hill, 2396 State Highway 50, Roys Hill
Owners	Robyn Wilson, Trevor Janes and John Hancock
Key Wines	Gimblett Road Chardonnay, Cabernet Sauvignon/Merlot, Merlot, Syrah; Shepherds Croft Chardonnay, Sauvignon Blanc, Merlot/Cabernets/Syrah

John Hancock — one of the key pioneers of world-class, increasingly refined New Zealand Chardonnay.

Gimblett G Gravels

So shingly, arid and inhospitable is the land, rabbits rarely venture onto it without taking a cut lunch. Lying at the base of Roys Hill, on the western fringe of Hastings, the stony Gimblett Road area was once the least productive in Hawke's Bay.

Today, 21 years after Chris ('C.J.') Pask planted the first Cabernet Sauvignon vines, the area around Gimblett Road is the source of many of the country's top claret-style reds. To 'define, protect and market' these wines, in 2001 34 companies with over 500 hectares of vines in the area launched the Gimblett Gravels Winegrowing District as a distinct sub-region within Hawke's Bay.

Any wine featuring the Gimblett Gravels brand on its label must be at least 95 per cent from the district. Among the best known examples of the area's reds are those under the C.J. Pask Gimblett Road, Babich Irongate and Patriarch, Mills Reef Elspeth, Unison, Stonecroft, Te Awa Farm, Trinity Hill Gimblett Road, and Vidal and Villa Maria Reserve labels.

Steve Smith of Craggy Range, a driving force behind the Gimblett Gravels concept, believes that Hawke's Bay is slightly cool for making red wines from the traditional Bordeaux red varieties — Cabernet Sauvignon, Merlot, Cabernet Franc and Malbec. However, the Gimblett Gravels district is 'up to 3°C warmer during the day in summer and autumn. This extra heat and the contribution from our soils put the *terroir* [the total natural environment of a vineyard site] of Gimblett Gravels alongside some of the world's famous producers of red wine.' For getting late-ripeners like Cabernet Sauvignon and Syrah to full maturity on the vines, this additional warmth is a crucial advantage.

The boundaries of the Gimblett Gravels district have been defined solely by soil type. The Ngaruroro River, which traverses the Heretaunga Plains between Napier and Hastings, changed its course in 1876. Where the river once flowed, vines now grow in exceptionally free-draining, low-fertility gravel soils (the 'Gimblett gravels'), with bands of sand, silt and clay at various depths. In these warm, stony soils, compared to most other parts of the Bay the vines flower and ripen their grapes relatively early, with higher sugar levels and extract and softer acidity. All of these factors boost the quality of the wine.

Merlot (especially) and Cabernet Sauvignon are the key varieties planted in the Gimblett Gravels, with smaller pockets of Chardonnay, Syrah, Malbec, Cabernet Franc and Sauvignon Blanc. Some outstanding Chardonnays have been grown in the area and the standard of the Syrahs has been high.

Recognition of the Gimblett Gravels district is the result of a careful branding exercise, because the area does not enjoy the official status of wine appellations overseas. An official move in New Zealand to define wine regions, districts and vineyard sites, under the proposed Geographic Indications Act, is proceeding at a snail's pace. The Act also makes no allowance for designating a wine locality solely on the basis of soil, as the Gimblett Gravels group has done.

A vital concern of the group has been to protect the reputation of their wines, by ensuring that vineyards planted nearby but in different soil types cannot use the designation Gimblett Gravels. The group believes a large area of pumice soils directly to the south 'will not offer the same winegrowing benefits ...'

Many of Hawke's Bay's finest reds (from Te Mata, Ngatarawa, Brookfields, Montana, Sileni, Clearview and others) are not grown in the Gimblett Gravels. Winemakers based a few kilometres to the south, producing consistently fine Merlot-based reds in the red-metal soils of the 'Ngatarawa Triangle', are also unlikely to allow Gimblett Gravels to steal all the limelight.

Nevertheless, over the past decade a stream of distinguished Merlot and Cabernet Sauvignon-based reds has flowed from the Gimblett Gravels. The French stress the role of *terroir* in making top wine. Who would criticise the winegrowers of the Gimblett Gravels for doing just that?

Viticulture

For his top, Gimblett Road Chardonnay, Hancock is after finesse. 'We're handling the juice gently, in small batches, to reduce phenolics.' Hand-harvested, whole-bunch pressed and fermented and matured on its yeast lees in French oak barriques (35 per cent new), it's a very stylish, intense and finely structured wine that needs a couple of years to reveal its full class.

In top vintages, the Gimblett Road Cabernet Sauvignon/Merlot is densely packed and tannic, with rich cassis, plum and spice flavours and finely integrated oak. The Gimblett Road Merlot and Gimblett Road Syrah are both firm, concentrated and complex, and well worth cellaring.

Unison

■ Unison is a red wine specialist. Two blends of Merlot, Cabernet Sauvignon and Syrah are produced, both so rich, warm and densely packed that they rank among the most distinctive and consistently rewarding reds in Hawke's Bay.

Anna-Barbara and Bruce Helliwell named their venture Unison because 'we are a husband and wife team who combine Old and New World philosophies and have total control of production, from the vineyard to the finished wine'. Their 6-hectare vineyard was close-planted near Roys Hill, in the Gimblett Gravels district, in 1993. The first wine flowed in 1996.

Anna-Barbara, a German viticulturist and oenologist, and Bruce, a Kiwi winemaker, have worked in Germany, Italy, France, Switzerland, California and New Zealand. Raised in Baden, by the time she was 13 Anna-Barbara had decided to become a viticulturist, and later gained a viticulture degree in Germany and an oenology diploma in Switzerland. While managing a winery in the Chianti Classico zone of Tuscany, in 1992, she met Bruce, from Nelson, who has an MSc in chemistry and was an assistant winemaker at Delegat's from 1987 to 1992.

The Helliwells say their winemaking philosophy is 'based upon low yields per vine and intensive handwork in the vineyard. The wines stand on the concentrated fruit flavours of ripe grapes — not oak.' About 2500 cases of wine are made each year on-site and matured in an underground cellar, 3.5 metres deep.

The Unison varietal recipe of Merlot, Cabernet Sauvignon and Syrah has no classic European model. 'We didn't want a mainstream style,' says Anna-Barbara, 'but the new-wave Tuscan reds are increasingly blended from Merlot and Cabernet Sauvignon. We'd tasted New Zealand Syrah and thought it would "add the dot to the i", so to speak.'

From the start, Unison has stood out for its ripeness, depth and harmony. The top label, Unison Selection, is based on the lowest-cropping vines and is oak-aged longer than the standard label. Matured for a year in French and American oak, then for a further six months in large Italian casks of French and Slovenian oak, it is dark and mouthfilling, with an array of warm, soft, spicy flavours and an almost chocolatey richness.

Designed for earlier consumption, the standard Unison is similarly awash with blackcurrant, plum and spice flavours, smooth and peppery. Both wines are memorable.

Address	Unison Vineyard, 2163 State Highway 50, Hastings
Owners	Anna-Barbara and Bruce Helliwell
Key Wines	Unison Selection, Unison

Vidal Estate

■ The trophies for champion Cabernet Sauvignon/Merlot at the 2000 Air New Zealand Wine Awards and champion Chardonnay at the 2001 New Zealand Wine Society Royal Easter Wine Show both went to Vidal, the historic Hastings winery that is a vital part of the Villa Maria empire.

Anthony Vidal, the founder, came to New Zealand from Spain at the age of 22 in 1888. After 11 years working with his uncle, Wanganui winemaker Joseph Soler, Vidal experimented with viticulture at Palmerston North before shifting to Hawke's Bay. In 1905 he bought a half-hectare property at Hastings, converted the existing stables into a cellar and planted grapevines.

The winery flourished; a new, 3-hectare vineyard was established at Te Awanga in 1916 and, a few years later, another 3 hectares was acquired from Bernard Chambers' Te Mata vineyard. After Anthony Vidal's death, control of the company passed to his three sons: Frank, the winemaker; Cecil, who concentrated on sales; and Leslie, who supervised the vines. For decades the winery enjoyed a solid reputation. John Buck, now of Te Mata Estate, in 1969 stated in his book *Take a Little Wine* that Vidal's Claret and Burgundy were 'the two finest, freely available dry reds on the New Zealand market'. Using Cabernet Sauvignon, Meunier and hybrid grapes, the brothers produced a Burgundy of 'style, good colour, body and balance' and a Claret 'lighter in body and more austere to taste'.

But after 1972, when Seppelt's of Australia acquired a 60 per cent share of Vidal, standard lines were dropped, labels changed and the quality of the wine began to fall away. The slide continued under another owner, Ross MacLennan, from 1974 to 1976.

The restoration of Vidal's reputation began in 1976, after Villa Maria bought the company. In 1979 the first vineyard restaurant in New Zealand opened at Vidal (still open for lunch and dinner, seven days per week).

Address	Vidal Estate, 913 St Aubyn Street East, Hastings
Owner	Villa Maria Estate
Key Wines	Reserve Chardonnay, Cabernet Sauvignon/Merlot, Noble Sémillon; Single Vineyard Pinot Noir; Estate Chardonnay, Sauvignon Blanc, Riesling, Pinot Noir, Cabernet Sauvignon/Merlot

Little remains of the early buildings, but the winery is still on the original Vidal site, some of the large storage casks have survived and the recently re-roofed barrel cellar was once part of the original stables.

Vidal's grapes are drawn from Villa Maria's company-owned vineyards and contract growers based largely but not entirely in the Hawke's Bay region, a reality reflected in the company's 1994 name change from Vidal of Hawke's Bay to Vidal Estate.

Rod McDonald, the winemaker, developed his interest in wine working in restaurants and bars in Christchurch, while studying for a Bachelor of Commerce degree. In 1993, he joined Vidal as a cellarhand, and two years later was promoted to assistant winemaker. After gaining a postgraduate diploma in viticulture and oenology from Lincoln University, in 1998 McDonald was promoted to the top winemaking job at Vidal.

Convinced that 'it is quality, not size that counts,' Vidal produces only half the amount of wine it did a decade ago, but barrel-ages almost five times the volume. In 2001, an exceptionally low-cropping year, its output was 22,000 cases.

Under its commercial Estate range, Vidal markets well-priced, attractive wines, including a crisp, fruit-driven, partly barrel-fermented Chardonnay; a faintly oaked, melon and lime-flavoured Sauvignon Blanc; an easy-drinking, slightly sweet Riesling, which includes varying proportions of Marlborough grapes; a great value Pinot Noir, which couples the weight and firmness typical of Hawke's Bay with the fresh, vibrant fruit characters of Marlborough; and a typically full-flavoured, satisfying, French and American oak-aged Hawke's Bay Cabernet Sauvignon/Merlot. The jewels in the Vidal crown are its Reserve wines, bursting with ripe, concentrated Hawke's Bay fruit flavours. The Reserve Chardonnay, barrel-fermented and lees-aged in French oak barriques (two-thirds new), is robust, peachy and toasty, with layers of flavour.

The Reserve Cabernet Sauvignon/Merlot is matured for up to two years in French and American oak barriques. Dense, ripe and generous, with deep colour and beautifully concentrated cassis, plum and spice flavours, it is only made in favourable vintages, but has an illustrious track record in show judgings. There is also a barrel-fermented, Sauternes-style Reserve Noble Sémillon, golden, powerful, lush and honey-sweet.

A century after Anthony Vidal planted his first vines in Hawke's Bay, the company he founded is still establishing new vineyards in the region.

Other producers

■ Akarangi

This low-profile winery is in River Road, on the banks of the Tukituki, near Havelock North. Morton Osborne, a clinical psychologist, produced his first wine in 1987. The 3-hectare vineyard is planted in Sauvignon Blanc, Chardonnay, Riesling, Cabernet Sauvignon, Merlot, Cabernet Franc and Malbec. Sold on-site in an old church, the range includes a smooth, appley Chardonnay, a restrained Sauvignon Blanc and a light, leafy Cabernet/Merlot.

■ Beach House

Chris and Jill Harrison, both winemaking graduates of Roseworthy College in South Australia, and Chris' family own a 6-hectare vineyard at Te Awanga and another 4-hectare plot in Mere Road, in the Gimblett Gravels district. The wines, first produced in 1996 but still in small volumes, are available at the winery in Clifton Road, Te Awanga. I have tasted a green-edged Cabernet/Merlot and a barrel-fermented Chardonnay with good weight and complexity.

■ Bradshaw Estate

Owned by accountant Wayne Bradshaw and his wife, Judy, the winery, restaurant and 4 hectares of Sauvignon Blanc (principally) and Merlot are in Te Mata Road, Havelock North, on the site of the original Vidal 'No 1' vineyard. Bradshaw's first vintage was 1994. I have tasted a high-flavoured, peachy, toasty Reserve Chardonnay, a medium-bodied, berryish, slightly leafy and nutty Merlot/Cabernet, a perfumed Reserve Merlot/Cabernet Sauvignon with very good depth, and a powerful, plummy, peppery, intensely varietal Legacy Syrah.

■ Chateau Waimarama

John Loughlin, an eye surgeon (whose son, John, owns Askerne Vineyard) produced his first red wine from a sheltered, north-facing slope at the foot of Te Mata Peak in 1991. Overlooking the Tukituki River, the 4-hectare vineyard is planted in Cabernet Sauvignon, Merlot, Cabernet Franc and Malbec. Chateau Waimarama (originally called Waimarama Estate) also draws grapes from a neighbour's 2-hectare vineyard, entirely devoted to Syrah. Loughlin's Cabernet Sauvignon and Merlot-based reds were at best highly impressive, but in 1998 Waimarama was purchased by a Japanese company, So-Con, and today its entire production is exported.

■ Crab Farm

When Hamish Jardine's great-grandfather first acquired land at Petane, near Bay View, it was a mudflat covered with rushes and crawling with crabs. Cooled by sea breezes, the 13.5-hectare vineyard has pockets of shingly and silty soils. The wines, first produced in 1987, are solid and characterful, including a full-flavoured, well-spiced Gewürztraminer, a sturdy, savoury Pinot Noir, and the star Jardine Cabernet Sauvignon, impressively dark, concentrated and firm.

■ Eskdale Winegrowers

Owned by Canadian Kim Salonius and his wife, Trish, Eskdale lies on the highway through the Esk Valley. The first vines were planted in 1973 and the first commercial release of wine followed in 1977. Salonius prefers a low profile, and draws almost all his grapes from the silty, 4-hectare home vineyard, planted in Chardonnay, Gewürztraminer, Cabernet Sauvignon, Cabernet Franc and Malbec. The tiny winery, with wooden trusses, white plastered walls and stained-glass windows, looks every inch like a shrine to Bacchus. Barrel-aged for up to three years, the wines are typically robust and strong-flavoured, including a peachy, nutty, mellow Chardonnay, pungently spicy Gewürztraminer with late harvest richness, and an American oak-aged Cabernet/Merlot with decent depth.

■ Hatton Estate

Viticulturist John Rees and his wife, Ngarita, in partnership with United Kingdom-based Michael and Colleen Daymond-King, own a 14-hectare vineyard in Gimblett Road, planted in Bordeaux red varieties, Syrah and Chardonnay. The wine is rarely seen, but Hatton Estate Cabernet/Merlot/Franc 1999 was praised by wine writer Peter Saunders as a 'lovely soft wine'.

■ Lucknow

Bruce Nimon and Colin Wyllie own a 14-hectare vineyard on Maraekakaho Road, devoted entirely to red-wine varieties: Merlot, Syrah, Malbec and Gamay Noir. Nimon, who previously worked at C.J. Pask and Kemblefield, made the first wine in 1998, based on bought-in grapes. The Lucknow range includes white wines from Marlborough. From Hawke's Bay, I have tasted a fruity, easy-drinking Cabernet Sauvignon/Cabernet Franc and a soft, berryish Dunnegan Road Merlot.

■ Newton Forrest

Australian viticulturist Bob Newton and his partner, Marlborough winemaker John Forrest, produce outstanding reds under the Cornerstone brand. The 30-hectare vineyard, on the corner of Gimblett Road and State Highway 50, is planted mainly in Cabernet Sauvignon and Merlot, with smaller plots of Malbec, Syrah and Cabernet Franc. The wines, launched from the 1994 vintage, include a generous, full-on, fruit-packed Cornerstone Cabernet/Merlot/Malbec and a strapping, densely flavoured straight Cabernet Sauvignon.

■ Park Estate

In Pakowhai Road, Dianne and Owen Park produce both fruit and grape wines. First produced in 1991, the range includes Sauvignon Blanc, Riesling, Chardonnay, Merlot, Cabernet Sauvignon and Cabernet/Merlot. I recently tasted a low-priced, fruity and smooth Bell Tower Cabernet/Merlot, simple but reasonably flavoursome.

■ Sanderson

Ken Sanderson, who has worked in France, Italy and Germany and during the mid to late 1990s at the Cross Roads winery in Hawke's Bay, has since 1999 released a trickle of wine under his own Sanderson label. I have tasted a soft, peachy Chardonnay with good depth; a grassy, honey-and-toast-flavoured, oak-fermented Sémillon; a full-flavoured but green-edged Cabernet Sauvignon; a Pinot Noir with concentrated raspberry, cherry and nut flavours; and a vibrantly fruity, ripe, well-spiced Syrah.

■ Squawking Magpie

Gavin Yortt, one of the original partners in the Irongate vineyard, has 8 hectares of established vines in Gimblett Road and is planting another 20 hectares. Launched from the 1999 vintage and made on Yortt's behalf at local wineries, the Squawking Magpie range includes a stylish, tightly structured Chardonnay and Cabernet/Merlot.

■ Thornbury

Mt Maunganui-based Steve Bird, who worked for many years at Morton Estate, and his wife, Caroline, own this fast-growing company in partnership with Bruce and Sharon McCutcheon. The company's 6.5-hectare vineyard in Gimblett Road is planted in Bordeaux red varieties, and its two vineyards, covering 19 hectares, in Marlborough are planted in Sauvignon Blanc, Chardonnay and Pinot Noir. The Marlborough Sauvignon Blanc is weighty and crammed with zingy tropical-fruit flavours; the Hawke's Bay Chardonnay is powerful and creamy-rich; and top vintages of the Hawke's Bay Merlot are fragrant and concentrated.

Wairarapa

Principal grape varieties

	Producing area 2002	% total producing area 2002
Pinot Noir	192 ha	41.9%
Sauvignon Blanc	86 ha	18.8%
Chardonnay	73 ha	15.9%
Cabernet Sauvignon	25 ha	5.5%
Riesling	23 ha	5.0%
Pinot Gris	20 ha	4.4%
Merlot	17 ha	3.7%

Vintage chart
(1993–2002)

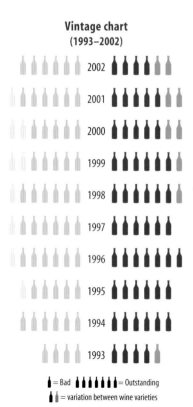

2002	
2001	
2000	
1999	
1998	
1997	
1996	
1995	
1994	
1993	

🍾 = Bad 🍾🍾🍾🍾🍾🍾 = Outstanding

🍾🍾 = variation between wine varieties

Previous page: The flat, stony soils in and around the once-sleepy village of Martinborough yield freshly aromatic, intensely flavoured white wines from several varieties and sturdy, rich Pinot Noir.

The Wairarapa is a small wine region with a big reputation. If you mention the Wairarapa to most wine buffs, the first thing they think about is Martinborough Pinot Noir. Yet there's far more to Martinborough wine than Pinot Noir — and a lot more to the Wairarapa than Martinborough.

Farms run up and over the hills that flank the Wairarapa Plains. To the west lie the rugged, bush-tangled slopes of the Rimutaka and Tararua ranges. Between the plains — where the vineyards are clustered — and the east coast is rolling country, ascending in the south-east to the steep but not high Aorangi Mountains, on the edge of Cook Strait. The major river system is the Ruamahanga, which flows from the Tararuas down the eastern side of the plains, entering the sea south of Martinborough, at Lake Ferry.

The Wairarapa's early vineyards were clustered in and around Martinborough, but of late planting has spread south of the township to Te Muna Road, further north to the Gladstone and East Taratahi areas, near Masterton, and even further north to Opaki. (Not in the Wairarapa at all, but to the west, on the Kapiti Coast, there are also several growers at Te Horo, where since 1990 Te Horo Vineyards has produced a trickle of idiosyncratic, occasionally good wine.)

The Wairarapa is a region of typically tiny vineyards. Only 4 per cent of New Zealand's vines are planted in the region, and from the record 2001 harvest, the Wairarapa's 41 companies produced an average of just 2500 cases of wine.

History
The southern part of the North Island has inherited its own winemaking legacy. In 1883 a wealthy Wairarapa landowner, William Beetham, planted the first vines at his tiny Masterton vineyard (see page 170). Nearly a century passed before publisher Alister Taylor established Martinborough's first vineyard in 1978, followed a year later by Dr Neil McCallum, of Dry River.

Climate
The Wairarapa enjoys long sunshine hours during summer and warm temperatures, reaching over 25°C in sheltered inland areas of the plains. The Rimutaka and Tararua ranges provide some shelter from the strong, warm, north-westerly winds which prevail in spring and summer. East of the ranges, the rainfall declines steeply and droughts and dry spells are common. Southerly or south-easterly winds, forced to rise over the ranges, are the main rain-bearers.

Soils
Shallow silt loams with gravelly sub-soils are a prized asset of the Martinborough Terrace (see page 177), although deep, imperfectly drained soils just south of the terrace are less suitable for viticulture. The fast-expanding vineyards in the East Taratahi/Dakins Road district are planted on river terraces with free-draining, stony silt loams.

Wine styles
The Wairarapa is the driest and coolest of the North Island's wine regions, but slightly warmer than Marlborough. The result: wines that show the flavour intensity and tangy acidity typical of Marlborough, yet also some of the sturdiness and warmth associated with Hawke's Bay.

Pinot Noir has been the great success story in the Wairarapa, yielding sturdy, warm, richly flavoured wines with pronounced varietal character and the ability to mature well. The finest Sauvignon Blancs are strikingly scented, vibrantly fruity and intense, and this versatile region has also produced some top-flight Riesling (dry and sweet), Chardonnay, Pinot Gris and Gewürztraminer.

Sub-regions
Until recently, most of the Wairarapa's vineyards were clustered around the small town of Martinborough, but the latest developments are further afield. In Te Muna Road, 5 kilometres south of the township, substantial vineyards have been planted on gravelly, free-draining soils similar to those in Martinborough itself. Vines are also sprouting 45 minutes' drive up the Wairarapa Valley, to the south and north of Masterton. In a district variously known as East Taratahi or Dakins Road, hundreds of hectares of vines have been planted on terraces above the Ruamahanga River, which meanders down the valley to Martinborough.

Summary of climate statistics

Meteorological station	Latitude	Height	GDD	MTWM	Rainfall, Oct–Apr	Air frost days (annual)
East Taratahi	41.01'S	91 m	1081	17.6°C	447 mm	35
Martinborough	41.07'S	30 m	1189	18.4°C	381 mm	18

Height — *above sea level* **GDD** — *growing degree days, Oct–Apr, above 10°C* **MTWM** — *mean temperature, warmest month*

Otaki

Otaki Forks

TARARUA RANGE

Mt Holdsworth
1470 m

Mt Hector
1529 m

Kiriwhakapapa

2

Kopuaranga

Mikimiki

Rangitumau

Matahiwi

Bideford

Kaituna

Opaki

MASTERTON

Carrington

Te Ore Ore

Waingawa

Tauweru

Homebush

River

Cloustonville

Clareville

Tauweru

Carterton

EAST
TARATAHI

Te Whanga

Wainuioru

Dalefield

Matarawa

Ahikouka

Greytown

Gladstone

Maymorn

Papawai

Ponatahi

Featherston

Morrisons
Bush

Tauherenikau

Battersea

Longbush

53

Pahaoa

River

Te Wharau

RANGE

MUTAKA

Lake
Wairarapa

Flat Point

Martinborough

Tablelands

Kahutara

River

Ruamahanga

Dyerville

Huangarua

River

Tuhitarata

Hinakura

Pirinoa

Ruakokoputuna

Lake
Onoke

Glendhu

Lake
Ferry

Whangaimoana

Palliser

Bay

Tuturumuri

AORANGI

MOUNTAINS

Mt Ross
981 m

weather station

N

Ngawi

Manurewa Point

0   10   20 km

Cape Palliser

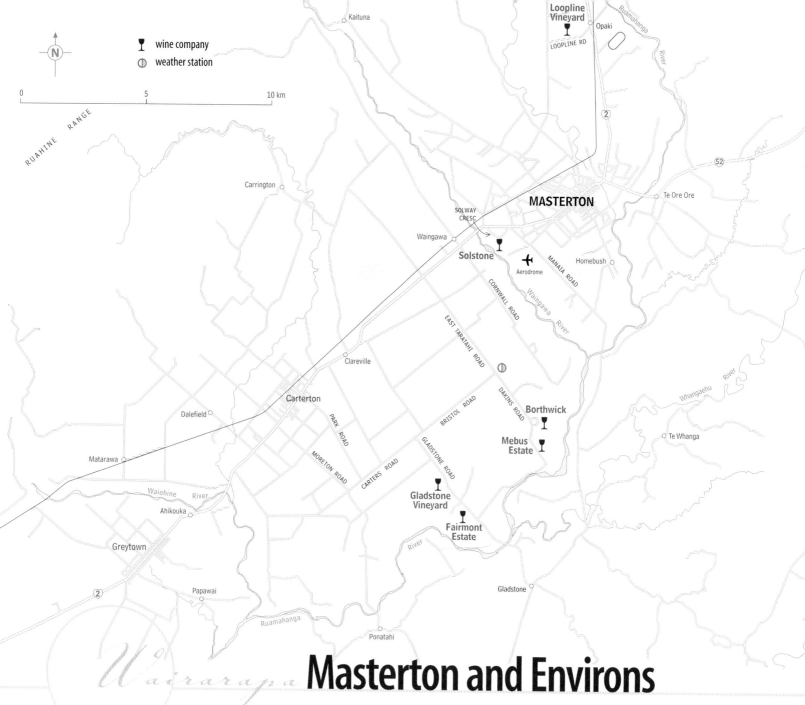

Masterton and Environs

To the north and south of Masterton, the largest urban centre in the Wairarapa, grapevines are mushrooming. By 2004, at least one-third of the region's wine will flow from the Opaki, East Taratahi and Gladstone districts.

From Opaki, 5 kilometres north of the town, the Ruamahanga River skirts Masterton to the east, flowing south to its junction with the Waingawa River. A few kilometres further downstream, Dakins Road, at East Taratahi, runs down to the western banks of the river. From the southern edge of the Dakins Road vineyards, the nearest vines at Gladstone are clearly visible, only a kilometre away (although not by road). At Opaki, three small producers — Loopline Vineyard, Waipipi and Opaki Lodge — have wine on the market and a major, 70-hectare vineyard is being established to supply Sauvignon Blanc and Pinot Noir grapes on contract. At Dakins Road in East Taratahi, where hundreds of hectares of vines are already in the ground, the wine producers are still undecided as to the best name for the district, calling it variously East Taratahi, Dakins Road and Wairarapa Valley.

History

William Beetham planted a tiny vineyard (less than one-tenth of a hectare) at his Masterton town house in 1883. Nine years later, he planted a further 1.2 hectares at Lansdowne vineyard, mostly in Pinot Noir, Meunier and Syrah. Viticulturist Romeo Bragato, who visited Beetham during his 1895 national vineyard tour, reported tasting a Hermitage (Syrah) wine of 'prime quality'. By 1897, Beetham's production had reached 1850 gallons (8410 L) of wine, but following the prohibitionists' no-licence victory in Masterton in 1905, his vineyard was uprooted. In 1985, Beetham's descendants broached a rare bottle of his Lansdowne Claret 1903. Geoff Kelly, then the wine columnist for *National Business Review*, enthused that the 82-year-old wine was 'alive and well . . . with the oak standing firm, yet amazing fruit, body and freshness for the age. The finish is superb, long and lingering.' The new era of Masterton wine began in 1981 when David Bloomfield and his family planted the first vines at Bloomfield Vineyards (now Solstone

Estate). Wellington-based Dennis Roberts, who used to drive through the district thinking 'the eastern hills looked promising', in 1985 planted the first vines in the Gladstone area. Ten years later, attracted by 'the freedom of having no township nearby', Michael Mebus pioneered viticulture in Dakins Road.

Climate

Closer to the Tararua Range, the vineyards near Masterton are viewed by most growers in the Wairarapa as being slightly cooler than those at Martinborough. The rainfall, which comes mainly from the east but also from the south, is also generally slightly higher. Frost is a risk, as elsewhere in the Wairarapa, with cold air descending from Mount Bruce, at the head of the valley, to Masterton.

Soils

At Opaki and Dakins Road, the vineyards are planted in Tauherenikau stony silt loams, typically comprised of 15 to 18 centimetres of topsoil over free-draining gravels. At Gladstone the soils are more variable, changing with increasing distance from the river from light, silty loams with a stony base to heavier, less free-draining soils with a higher clay content.

Wine styles

Most growers prefer Pinot Noir to Cabernet Sauvignon, for its earlier-ripening ability, and the initial releases from Dakins Road have been promising. The Sauvignon Blancs are typically aromatic and lively, coupling cool-climate herbaceousness with riper tropical-fruit characters, and plantings of Chardonnay, Riesling and Merlot are also expanding.

Borthwick

■ Since his first vintage in 1999, Paddy Borthwick has swiftly carved out a reputation for outstanding, gold medal Sauvignon Blancs. For Borthwick, an even greater source of pleasure was 'the look of enjoyment on my father's face, when he drank the first bottle of wine from our vineyard'.

After graduating in oenology from Roseworthy College in South Australia, Paddy Borthwick spent seven years overseas, making wine in France, Switzerland, Australia and the United States, followed by five years at the Allan Scott winery in Marlborough. In 1996, he and his family planted their first vines at East Taratahi, south of Masterton.

Today, the major varieties in the stony, 17-hectare vineyard are Pinot Noir, Sauvignon Blanc and Chardonnay, with smaller plots of Merlot, Riesling and Cabernet Sauvignon. The wines are made next door at the Mebus winery, but Borthwick plans its own winery for the 2003 vintage. All the wines are based entirely on estate-grown grapes, which, says Borthwick, 'enables us to control the primary course for the beginning of great wines'.

From the start, the wines — especially the whites — have shown impressive intensity and finesse. The Sauvignon Blanc is a convincing cool-climate style, with penetrating, ripely herbaceous flavours and good acid spine. The medium-dry Riesling is freshly aromatic, with strong lemon/lime characters. The Chardonnay, fermented in French and American oak barriques, is mouthfilling, peachy, mealy and toasty, with lots of personality.

The Pinot Noir is warm, ripe-tasting and complex, with cherry, plum and smoky oak aromas and flavours. I have also tasted a vibrantly fruity, high-acid Sangiovese and a full-flavoured, finely balanced and minty Cabernet/Merlot/Malbec.

Address	Borthwick Estate, Dakins Road, East Taratahi
Owners	The Borthwick family
Key Wines	Chardonnay, Sauvignon Blanc, Riesling, Pinot Noir

Gladstone Vineyard

■ This beautiful boutique winery was the first in the Gladstone district. Dennis Roberts created a showplace vineyard and winery, won the trophy for champion Sauvignon Blanc at the 1993 Air New Zealand Wine Awards, then in late 1995 sold Gladstone Vineyard to Christine and David Kernohan.

The winery lies 5 kilometres west of the township of Gladstone. Roberts, a veterinarian, and his partner, Richard Stone, planted their first vines at Gladstone in 1985 on old alluvial terraces that once formed the bed of the nearby Ruamahanga River. A handsome, verandahed, two-storey winery, set amid landscaped grounds and thousands of trees, rose in time for the second 1991 vintage. A late nineteenth-century house was also trucked to the site from Masterton.

Today Christine Kernohan, a Scottish MBA with a background in business consultancy and agriculture, runs the company; David lectures at the School of Architecture at Victoria University of Wellington. The Kernohans have increased the company's output from 2000 to 3000 cases and started exporting.

The 3-hectare Gladstone Vineyard home block is planted in Sauvignon Blanc, Riesling, Pinot Gris and Cabernet Sauvignon. The adjacent Carters Block adds another hectare of Riesling, Pinot Gris and Merlot. At Dakins Road, a much larger (10 hectares) vineyard has been planted in Sauvignon Blanc, Riesling, Pinot Gris, Merlot, Cabernet Franc and Pinot Noir. Grapes are also purchased from growers in the northern Wairarapa.

With Dennis Roberts at the helm, Gladstone Vineyard's white wines were classy, with fresh, pure, intense flavours. For a few years after the change of ownership, the wines were less consistently attractive, but the latest vintages have seen a return to form.

At its best, the gently oaked Sauvignon Blanc is full-bodied and impressively rich, with strong, rounded flavours. The lemony, appley, high-acid Riesling has been less enjoyable than the fresh, lively Pinot Gris, which offers strong peachy, lemony, spicy flavours. Top vintages of the Chardonnay possess rich grapefruit and nut flavours, soft and creamy.

In warm seasons, the Cabernet Sauvignon/Merlot is deliciously rich and silky-smooth, although cooler years impart a green, leafy edge. Gladstone Vineyard's top red is the Reserve Merlot, impressively weighty, ripe and concentrated.

Address	Gladstone Vineyard, Gladstone Road, Gladstone
Owners	David and Christine Kernohan
Key Wines	Riesling, Sauvignon Blanc, Pinot Gris, Chardonnay, Cabernet Sauvignon/Merlot, Reserve Merlot, Pinot Noir

Address	Solstone Estate, 119 Solway Crescent, Masterton
Owners	Elizabeth Barrett-Hackel and Lloyd Hackel
Key Wines	Sauvignon Blanc, Chardonnay, Cabernet Franc, Cabernet Sauvignon, Cabernet/Merlot, Merlot, Pinot Noir; Reserve Cabernet Sauvignon, Cabernet Franc, Cabernet/Merlot

Solstone

■ Just off the highway south of Masterton, Solstone was out on a limb for many years as the only Wairarapa winery not based in Martinborough. The vineyard — until 1997 called Bloomfield — was first planted in 1981 by David Bloomfield and his family, who processed their first commercial vintage in 1986.

Bloomfield was born in Masterton, 'and in the late 1970s Dad [an optometrist] and I were looking for something we could do together. We knew there'd been vineyards here previously [planted in the late nineteenth century by William Beetham], looked at the climatic data and chose wine.' However, in 1997 Bloomfield Vineyards was sold to Brendan Meo, who promptly changed its name to Solstone, a reference to the 'warm, sunny Wairarapa climate and the stony river terrace soils'.

The current owners, who took over in 2001, are Elizabeth Barrett-Hackel, a former Wellingtonian who had a long overseas career in banking, and her Canadian husband Lloyd Hackel, who worked in combat and intelligence roles for the Canadian military and says the northern Wairarapa reminds him of 'the mountains, foothills and prairies of Canada'.

The 5-hectare estate vineyard, planted near the Waingawa River in stony river shingles, with large rocks under the vines, contains some of the oldest vines in the Wairarapa. Cabernet Sauvignon is the key variety, with smaller areas of Pinot Noir, Merlot, Cabernet Franc, Sauvignon Blanc and Chardonnay. Grapes are also purchased from two vineyards east of Masterton.

Under David Bloomfield's direction, the vineyard was best known for its flagship Cabernet Sauvignon/Merlot/Cabernet Franc, a full-bodied, dark, spicy red with plenty of flavour and a firm tannin grip. Under the new management, the tradition of richly flavoured, claret-style reds continues, and the standard of the white wines has risen sharply.

The Sauvignon Blanc is weighty and dry, with fresh gooseberry/lime flavours and racy acidity. The Cabernet Sauvignon, Cabernet Franc and Merlot-based reds can be green-edged in cooler years, but in warmer seasons are brambly, spicy and distinctly Bordeaux-like, with good concentration and an earthy, savoury complexity.

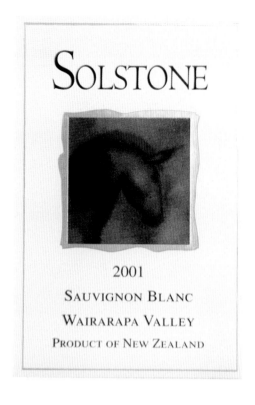

SOLSTONE

2001

SAUVIGNON BLANC

WAIRARAPA VALLEY

PRODUCT OF NEW ZEALAND

Other producers

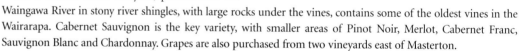

■ Fairmont Estate

The second winery to emerge in the Gladstone district, Fairmont has sizeable plantings of Pinot Noir, Sauvignon Blanc, Chardonnay and Riesling. The wines, made by proprietor Jonathan McNab, have included a crisp, light and appley Riesling, a fresh, green-edged Sauvignon Blanc, and warm, flavoursome Pinot Noirs that sometimes lack refinement.

■ Loopline Vineyard

At Opaki, north of Masterton, Frank and Bernice Parker own a tiny, 1-hectare plot of Riesling. The wines, first produced in 1994, made on-site and sold locally, have included a light, green-edged Cabernet/Merlot, a ruby-hued, moderately complex Reserve Pinot Noir with very good depth of cherry, raspberry and spice flavours and a Sauvignon Blanc of variable but rising quality.

■ Mebus Estate

Dutch immigrants Michael and Hiddle Mebus began planting their extensive, 28-hectare vineyard in Dakins Road, East Taratahi in 1995. Sauvignon Blanc, Pinot Gris, Chardonnay, Pinot Noir and red Bordeaux grapes are the chosen varieties. The wines, made on-site in a gravity-fed winery, have included a green-edged but deeply coloured, vibrant and full-flavoured Cabernet/Merlot/Malbec.

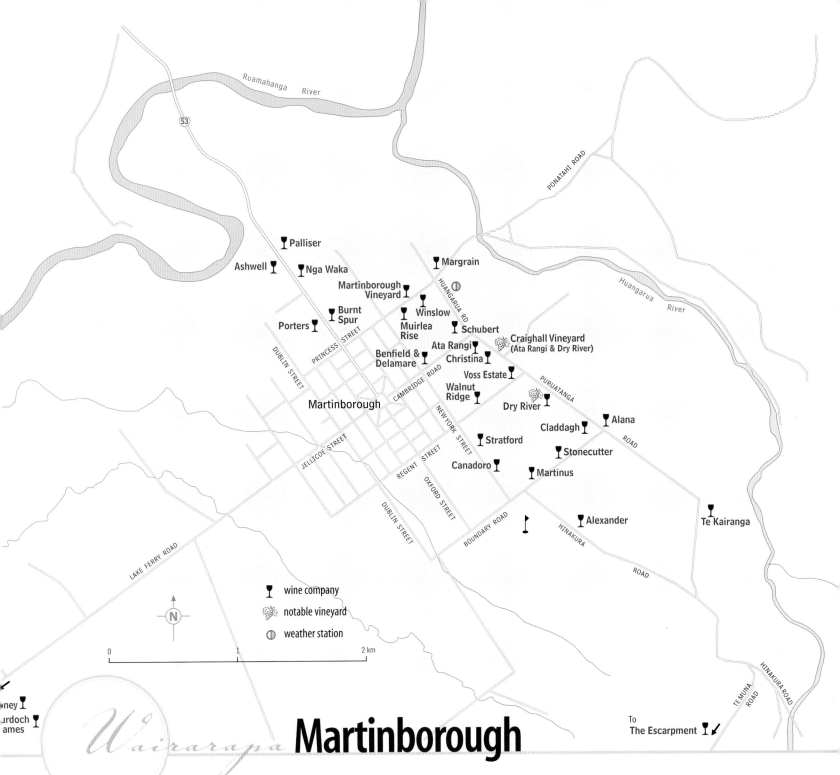

Martinborough

There used to be a joke around Martinborough that 50 per cent of the people who lived there were hiding and the other half were asleep. Today the joke is almost forgotten. The Wairarapa — in particular its most famous wine district, Martinborough — has in the past 15 years emerged as one of New Zealand's most prestigious winegrowing regions.

Martinborough lies just one hour's drive over the Rimutaka Ranges from the capital. As Professor Warren Moran has written: 'Its history is dominated by its proximity to Wellington and its large pool of educated, professional wine drinkers, who have adopted the town as their wine producer — buying its wines, filling its cafés on weekends and supporting its elite winemaking image.'

Martinborough lies in a basin, with the Rimutaka and Tararua ranges looming to the west and low coastal hills to the east, where the sea lies 40 kilometres away (only 30 kilometres to the south). Two rivers loop around the town: the Huangarua, flowing from the south-east; and the Ruamahanga, which just north of the town absorbs the Huangarua on its journey southwards to the coast at Palliser Bay. With land prices in Martinborough soaring and most of the suitable land already planted, vineyard expansion has shifted recently to Te Muna Road, a few kilometres south-east of the town. 'Here I could buy a reasonable area of land at a reasonable price,' says Larry McKenna of The Escarpment Vineyard, 'without the hindrance of the town, yet with all the benefits of Martinborough for wine.'

History

The first Martinborough vineyard was established by the then prominent publisher, Alister Taylor, in 1978. 'It reminded me of Blenheim,' recalls Taylor. He planted Chardonnay, Chenin Blanc and Gewürztraminer, but eventually the vineyard fell prey to the depredations of rabbits, possums and mortgagors. The land was taken over by Tom and Robin Draper, who later founded the Te Kairanga winery.

The major impetus for the resurgence of interest in Wairarapa winemaking came from Dr Derek Milne's 1979 report, pinpointing similarities between Martinborough's climate and soils and those of premium French wine regions. Following a 1977 visit to Germany and Alsace, Milne looked closely at New Zealand's climate regions. 'Climatic comparisons with Europe indicated that there were many areas well suited to *vinifera* [classic] grape production as yet unexploited . . . Martinborough was one of those areas and it was developed because it was closest to Wellington, where the original pioneers [of Martinborough wine] were based.' A 'gang of four' pioneered the planting of commercial vineyards in Martinborough: Dr Neil McCallum of Dry River in 1979, followed in 1980 by Clive Paton of Ata Rangi, Stan Chifney and Derek Milne himself — who put his money where his mouth was as a founding partner in Martinborough Vineyard. The first modern-era Wairarapa wines were bottled in 1984. As Chifney was the only one who could initially afford a winery, the earliest Martinborough wines were all crushed and fermented at his tiny winery.

'Looking back,' said Chifney in 1992, 'I now realise how green everyone was. Neil [McCallum] knew about the theoretical side, being a PhD, and I knew how to use tanks and pumps and pH measuring equipment, because of my laboratory experience, but none of us had technical training in winemaking. We learnt from our mistakes.' A turning-point was the 1986 arrival at Martinborough Vineyard of the area's first experienced winemaker, Larry McKenna. Not long after, recalls Richard Riddiford of Palliser Estate, 'Larry put Martinborough on the map.'

Climate

Despite its location near the bottom of the North Island, Martinborough's viticultural climate resembles Marlborough's more closely than Hawke's Bay's. As in the South Island, cool night temperatures help to preserve the grapes' acidity and fresh, vibrant fruit characters. Small grape crops (widely correlated with high wine quality) are a feature of the area, reflecting Martinborough's weather during spring and early summer, when spells of cold, extremely windy weather often lead to a poor flowering. Spring frosts are a significant threat, especially on the south side of the Martinborough Terrace, where there is less air flow, and these are combated with frost pots, wind machines and helicopters. Martinborough is one of the driest areas in the North Island. Being further south than Gisborne or Hawke's Bay, the district escapes some of the late summer and autumn rains that travel down the east coast. Martinborough's autumns are on average markedly drier than Hawke's Bay's. Droughts are a definite threat in summer. In most years, the vines are in water deficit, and about 80 per cent of the vineyards are irrigated. This relative dryness, however, also encourages the winemakers to hang their grapes late on the vines to achieve full fruit ripeness, without facing any undue risk of disease, although botrytis bunch rot

can be a problem in wetter than average years. In March and April, the vital months leading into the harvest, Martinborough's average daily temperature of 14.7℃ is more akin to Marlborough's 14.3℃ than Hawke's Bay's 15.8℃. The cooler autumns enable the development of intense flavour in the berries without any pronounced loss of acidity. The chief weather drawback here is the wind. Martinborough is pummelled by cold, often rain-bearing southerlies from Cook Strait, and in spring is exposed to gusty, warm and dry north-westerlies which brown the hills, devigorate the vines and sometimes cause severe shoot and leaf damage. Shelter belts are a necessity.

Soils

The most sought-after soils are free-draining, with a thin layer of silt loam over gravels. Sites on the northern side of the Martinborough Terrace (see page 177), closest to the river, generally have the shallowest topsoils, while some of those on the south side have a higher clay content. At Te Muna Road, the vineyards are planted in gravel terraces of the Huangarua River, similar to the Martinborough Terrace. The soil variation in Martinborough contributes to markedly different ripening patterns. Vines on a sheltered site with light, gravelly soils can ripen their crop up to two weeks ahead of a more exposed site with heavier soils. There can also be important variation within individual vineyards: at Dry River, a clay ridge was left unplanted and on a pocket of relatively heavy soil, the owners built their house.

Wine styles

One of the country's northernmost areas for fine quality Pinot Noir, Martinborough produces muscular, well-ripened, richly flavoured Pinot Noirs, less fresh, floral and fruity than those from further south. At their best, the Sauvignon Blancs are of superb quality, scented, vibrant and penetrating. Riesling, Gewürztraminer, Chardonnay and Pinot Gris have all been successful. Cabernet Sauvignon and Merlot are proving tougher nuts to crack, but there are isolated successes.

Alana Estate

■ One of the best of the newer arrivals in the district, since 1998 Alana Estate has produced a stream of impressive whites and reds, full of personality. The vineyard, on a horseshoe-shaped site on the northern edge of the Martinborough Terrace, above the Huangarua River, is owned by Ian Smart and his wife, Alana, who spent 12 years 'travelling the world as a British Airways stewardess, enjoying the cultures of many countries through their food and wine'. After planting their first vines in 1995, the Smarts now have 22 hectares of Pinot Noir (principally), Chardonnay, Sauvignon Blanc and Riesling.

The wines, entirely estate-grown, are made in a multi-level, gravity-flow winery by John Kavanagh, who has worked in Europe and California and for five years was assistant winemaker at Palliser Estate. With an output of 7000 cases in 2002, Alana Estate is a sizeable boutique and the wines are well worth tracking down. The Riesling is very easy to enjoy, with ripe flavours of passionfruit and limes. The Sauvignon Blanc is typically fleshy, ripe and rounded, with excellent depth. Fermented with indigenous yeasts in French oak barriques, the Chardonnay is stylish and complex, lush and mouthfilling, with rich fruit flavours and a slightly toasty, buttery finish. The Pinot Noir is equally fine — sturdy, with excellent depth of raspberry, cherry and spice flavours and gentle tannins in a generous, forward style, full of charm.

Alexander

■ When Kingsley Alexander and his wife, Deborah, came to Martinborough in 1989, rather than joining the trend to plant Pinot Noir, they opted for Bordeaux red varieties. A meteorologist interested in the links between climate and wine styles, Alexander didn't realise 'we were making a political statement by planting Cabernet Sauvignon'.

After producing their first vintage in 1994, the Alexanders built their own winery prior to the 1996 harvest and won a reputation for stylish, middleweight, claret-style reds, rich-flavoured and supple. However, the Alexanders later sold the company and it is now owned by Michael Finucane, an ex-chartered surveyor from the United Kingdom; his wife, Rosalind Walker, a clinical psychologist; and Steve Plowman, the vineyard director.

The vineyard lies on the western side of the town, near a bend in the Ruamahanga River. In a mix of free-draining soils and heavier clays, 4 hectares of high density, low-trellised Cabernet Sauvignon, Cabernet Franc, Merlot and (more recently) Pinot Noir vines have been planted. Alexander Vineyard is a low-volume, red-wine specialist. The wines are produced by consultant winemaker Elise Montgomery, formerly of Vidal Estate.

For their flagship Cabernet/Merlot, the partners aim for 'an elegant, medium-weight' style, which typically shows French oak complexity and excellent depth of fresh blackcurrant/plum flavours, with a slightly minty edge. The Basket Press Cabernet Franc is vibrantly fruity and supple, with fresh, buoyant red berry and plum flavours. Pinot Noir, added to the range in 1997, shows very good depth of plum/spice flavours in a smooth, moderately complex style.

ALANA ESTATE
MARTINBOROUGH

Chardonnay
2000

e750ml   PRODUCE OF NEW ZEALAND   Alc13.5% vol

Address	Alana Estate, Puruatanga Road, Martinborough
Owners	Ian and Alana Smart
Key Wines	Sauvignon Blanc, Chardonnay, Riesling, Pinot Noir

ALEXANDER
MARTINBOROUGH

Pinot Noir
2000

e750ml   WINE OF NEW ZEALAND   13.5% VOL

Address	Alexander Vineyard, Dublin Street Extension, Martinborough
Owners	Michael Finucane, Rosalind Walker and Stephen Plowman
Key Wines	Cabernet/Merlot, Pinot Noir, Basket Press Cabernet Franc

Ata Rangi

■ The 1993, 1994 and 1999 vintages of Ata Rangi Pinot Noir all scooped the Bouchard-Finlayson trophy for champion Pinot Noir at the International Wine and Spirit Competition in London. Most of the world's top Pinot Noir producers do not enter shows, but of those that do, Ata Rangi enjoys spectacular success.

Clive Paton, the founder, is a quietly determined personality who set up his Ata Rangi ('new beginning' or 'dawn sky') winery to specialise in red wines. After taking a diploma in dairying from Massey University, Paton went sharemilking before he planted his first vines in Puruatanga Road in 1980. 'I needed a challenge,' he recalls, 'and striving for a top-performing dairy herd wasn't going to cut it. I loved red wine and figured the Martinborough Terrace had to have wine potential.' In 1983, Clive's sister Alison bought 2 hectares next door, and together they planted five rows of Gewürztraminer, filling the rest of the field with pumpkins and garlic to generate urgently needed cash flow.

The first 1984 vintage was processed at the Chifney winery, but in 1987 Paton built his own small wooden winery. Phyll Pattie, formerly a Montana winemaker at Blenheim, then moved north to join him.

In 1995, Clive Paton and Phyll Pattie formed an equal partnership with Alison Paton and her husband, winemaker Oliver Masters. The restructuring gave this small company (with an average annual output of 8000 cases) the luxury of three winemakers.

Ata Rangi's own vineyards in Martinborough — Ata Rangi, Champ Ali, Boundary Road and Craighall — cover 9 hectares, with Pinot Noir the key variety, followed by Chardonnay, Merlot, Cabernet Sauvignon and Syrah. The company also leases 12 hectares of vineyards and buys grapes from another 12.5 hectares, including the large Petrie vineyard near Masterton. Eighteen kilometres south of Martinborough, Ata Rangi is currently establishing a new vineyard on a north-facing gravel terrace.

The much-acclaimed Pinot Noir combines power and grace. The style goal is a 'complex, sensuous, opulent'

Address	Ata Rangi Vineyard, Puruatanga Road, Martinborough
Owners	Clive Paton, Phyllis Pattie, Alison Paton and Oliver Masters
Key Wines	Pinot Noir, Célèbre, Craighall Chardonnay

Think Ata Rangi, think Pinot Noir. But the Ata Rangi partners also produce a powerful, lush Craighall Chardonnay, one of the country's finest.

Pinot Noir, and Ata Rangi hits the target by marrying highly concentrated, cherryish, sweet-tasting fruit with smoky French oak. Fermented in small batches, with up to 15 per cent whole-bunch fermentation giving 'stalk-derived spiciness and tautness', and matured for a year in French oak barriques, usually 25 per cent new, it typically reveals its full personality at four to eight years old. 'A great site, good clones and low yields [averaging 5 tonnes per hectare]' are the key factors in the wine's quality, according to Paton, who believes the quality of his Pinot Noir can only rise as his vines mature.

Célèbre (pronounced say-lebr) is a Merlot, Cabernet Sauvignon and Syrah blend, sturdy and complex, with impressive depth of blackcurrant, herb, plum and spice flavours. Lightly oaked, the fresh, vibrant, raspberry and spice-flavoured Young Vines Pinot Noir is made for early drinking.

Of Ata Rangi's whites, the flagship is the opulent, strikingly rich Craighall Chardonnay, a weighty wine with a seamless array of grapefruit, peach and toasty oak flavours. There is also a less lush and complex but still impressive Petrie Chardonnay, a rich, well-ripened, partly barrel-fermented Sauvignon Blanc, a strapping, slightly sweet Pinot Gris and a pink, strawberryish, vivacious Summer Rosé.

Address Benfield & Delamare,
35 New York Street,
Martinborough

Owners Bill Benfield and Sue
Delamare

Key Wines Benfield & Delamare
Martinborough, A Song For
Osiris

Benfield & Delamare

■ In a district of small wineries, Benfield & Delamare is microscopic, each year producing 100 to 200 cases of its premium red, Benfield & Delamare Martinborough, and 50 to 150 cases of its second-tier wine, A Song For Osiris. The wines' rarity is not only based on their tiny supply. Encircled by Pinot Noir producers, Benfield & Delamare is passionately committed to Cabernet Sauvignon and Merlot-based reds.

Bill Benfield for many years practised architecture in Wellington. His first contact with wine was as a student at Auckland University, 'going out to Western Vineyards to buy wine for the architects' ball'. After shifting to Martinborough in 1992, Benfield is a full-time winemaker. His partner, English-born Sue Delamare, is a former librarian who also works full-time in the vineyard and winery.

Benfield and Delamare began planting in 1987 and released their first 'commercial' wine (42 cases) from the 1990 vintage. They now own three small vineyards in Martinborough: a 0.8-hectare block in Oxford Street, devoted to Merlot; 0.5 hectares of Cabernet Sauvignon (principally), Cabernet Franc and Merlot in Cambridge Road; and a tiny, 0.2-hectare plot of Cabernet Sauvignon and Cabernet Franc in New York Street (known as 'the house block').

In the Cambridge Road and New York Street blocks, the soils are typically silty loams over old river gravels, while the Oxford Street vineyard has heavier, less free-draining clays. All the vines are trained very low to enhance ripening from ground heat and pruned severely to ensure low yields.

Why the emphasis on Cabernet Sauvignon and Merlot, in a district far better known for its Pinot Noirs? Benfield has written that Martinborough's 'rainfall distribution, length of season, heat summation and frost incidence are all positive pointers towards Cabernet and Merlot grape varieties'. Cabernet Sauvignon and Cabernet Franc have proved to be the most reliable croppers, unlike Merlot, which is highly vulnerable to cool, wet weather during flowering.

In Benfield's small winery, a converted barn, he favours 'simple and traditional' techniques, including high fermentation temperatures, long skin macerations, lots of new French oak (about 50 per cent for the top label), and bottling without filtration.

Although slightly leaner than the foremost claret-style reds of Hawke's Bay, Benfield & Delamare shows excellent colour depth, strong, vibrant, spicy, concentrated flavours, impressive complexity and a firm tannin grip. From warm growing seasons, it can be outstanding. A Song For Osiris, designed for early drinking, is typically buoyantly fruity, with strong, plummy, gently oaked flavours and a smooth finish.

Address Burnt Spur,
40–42 Kitchener Street,
Martinborough

Owner Burnt Spur Martinborough
Limited

Key Wines Fraters Rise Sauvignon
Blanc, Chardonnay, Riesling,
Rosé, Cabernet/Merlot;
Fraters Reserve Pinot Noir,
Vitesse, Cabernet/Merlot

Burnt Spur

■ Chris Lintz always loved 'to do something different', producing a sparkling Riesling, a rosé based on Meunier and a sweet wine made from the rare Optima variety. In the end, he went too far, and was forced to surrender the gold medal and trophy he won at the 1998 Air New Zealand Wine Awards for his 1997 Shiraz, after marked differences were found between bottles of the wine. Burnt Spur, a publicly owned company, has taken over the assets of Lintz Estate. Chris Lintz, of German descent and a zoology graduate from Victoria University, planted his first vines in Martinborough in 1989 and launched his first wine from the 1991 vintage. The company grew rapidly, winning a reputation for burly, flavour-packed reds, and in 1998 made a public share issue, which raised over $4 million and left the Lintz family with a 36 per cent stake in the company.

However, after the medal scandal, sales suffered, vineyard development fell behind schedule, and in the year to 30 June 2000 the company traded at a loss of $388,000. After relations became strained between Chris Lintz and his fellow board members, the company

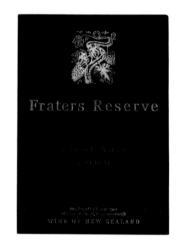

terminated Lintz's management contract in 2001, and the Lintz family is no longer involved financially. The major shareholders now include Wellington businessman Roger Gaskell (formerly a director of Palliser Estate), Dunedin sharebroker Eion Edgar, and investment companies linked to former stock exchange chairman David Wale and Aucklander Geoff Ricketts.

The company owns extensive vineyards, notably the 35-hectare Fraters block, 5 kilometres south of the township, where the major varieties are Pinot Noir, Sauvignon Blanc and Chardonnay. The 8-hectare Moy Hall vineyard (between Dry River and Te Kairanga) is planted mainly in the same varieties; the 3-hectare Kitchener Block is established in Pinot Noir; and the tiny block adjacent to the winery is devoted to Riesling. Grapes are also purchased from growers in Gisborne and Marlborough.

My favourite wines under the Lintz Estate label were the treacly, ultra-sweet Optima Noble Selection and the bold, brambly Vitesse Cabernet Sauvignon. In 1999 a selection of drink-young wines was launched under the Fraters Rise label, but these were not impressive.

In 2001 Sam Weaver, a widely experienced and respected winemaker — who sharpened the quality of the Stoneleigh Vineyards range for Corbans — was appointed contract winemaker. The wines under the Fraters Rise and Fraters Reserve brands are now being phased out and in future will carry a Burnt Spur label.

The Martinborough Terrace Appellation

■ Largely hidden from the public gaze in Martinborough over the past 15 years have been issues that have bitterly divided the wine community. Early claims that the district's climate was similar to Burgundy's — so that Martinborough was logically Pinot Noir country — were challenged by those committed to the Bordeaux varieties, Cabernet Sauvignon and Merlot. Similarly divisive was the Martinborough Terrace Appellation of Origin System.

Launched in 1986, the system was designed to foster and promote wines grown within a designated area of Martinborough, and create an appellation of origin to guarantee the authenticity of the wines. The designated zone had an average annual rainfall of less than 800 millimetres and comprised 'that part of the terrace zone forming the northern part of Martinborough and its environs lying to the north-north-east of a straight line from trigometrical station 2A passing through trigometrical station east base, and bounded in other places by the main terrace scarp... which has for any particular vineyard block 80 per cent or more soils which lack impediments two metres below surface to deep root penetration . . .'

The founding members of the organising committee were Chifney, Martinborough Vineyard, Dry River and Ata Rangi. Wines that met all the rules were eligible to carry a seal on the bottle, confirming they were '100% Martinborough Wine' (the seal was later changed to 'Martinborough Terrace Appellation', to distinguish it from the general Martinborough district). Eight producers eventually qualified to use the seal.

Some newcomers to the district — often those with vineyards outside the appellation's boundaries — argued that the system was less about defining a unique grape-growing area than creating a powerful marketing tool that would enhance its owners' land values and wine prices. One outspoken critic, Bill Benfield, believes the appellation's 'two major flaws are (1) the arbitrary nature of the southern boundary, being a line between two points on a map when the same soils and climate can lie on each side of the line, and (2) the simplistic soil definitions, where a much more complex mosaic exists'.

Winemakers promoting the system insisted that it did not imply other Martinborough wines were of inferior quality, but opposition feeling ran high. The late Willie Brown, of Muirlea Rise (not on the terrace), told MA student Lawrence Mahn in 1994 that the appellation system was 'horseshit, it's a farce, it's a nonsense'.

At a meeting of the Martinborough Winemakers Association in 1990, it was proposed that new appellations — Martinborough Downs or Martinborough Tablelands — be created for vineyards grown on different soil types. No vote was taken. By the early to mid-1990s, support for the original appellation was waning. Its demise was hastened by the small 1992 and 1993 harvests, when Martinborough Vineyard, Ata Rangi and Palliser Estate — advocates of the system — started to purchase grapes from outside the zone's boundaries.

In 1994, when Mahn canvassed 16 Martinborough wine companies for their opinion of the appellation, four were neutral, four were in favour (Ata Rangi, Dry River, Martinborough Vineyard and Palliser Estate), and eight were opposed. Stan Chifney, now neither 'for' nor 'against', admitted the issue had divided the district.

Four years later, the Martinborough Wine 'certified quality mark' was introduced, in an attempt to guarantee the authenticity of the entire district's wines. For a winery to qualify, its annual production had to be at least 85 per cent of Martinborough origin (defined as being within a 10-kilometre radius of the Martinborough Square). The venture proved short-lived.

Yet, even today, the issue has not gone away. Some growers in Te Muna Road argue that, in terms of soil type, they should be part of the Martinborough Terrace; others have suggested they call themselves Martinborough Terrace — Te Muna Extension. The debate goes on . . .

Viticulture

PINOT NOIR
2000

DRY RIVER

Martinborough

No.2198

BOTTLED BY DRY RIVER WINES LTD, PURUATANGA RD, MARTINBOROUGH

e 750ml   PRODUCE OF NEW ZEALAND   13.5% VOL
CONTAINS PRESERVATIVE (220)

Address   Dry River Wines,
Puruatanga Road,
Martinborough

Owners   Dr Neil and Dawn McCallum

Key Wines   Pinot Gris, Gewürztraminer,
Riesling, Chardonnay,
Sauvignon Blanc, Botrytis
Berry and Bunch Selection
sweet whites, Pinot Noir,
Syrah

Dry River

■ Only a trickle flows from Dry River — rare wines with a sky-high reputation. Dr Neil McCallum crafts immaculate, intensely flavoured, slowly evolving white and red wines, tightly structured and full of personality.

The emergence of Neil McCallum as a gifted, individualistic winemaker was greatly assisted by his previous career as a DSIR scientist. Born in Auckland, he capped his high-flying academic record with an Oxford doctorate, awarded for his dissertation on penicillin substitutes. At one memorable Oxford dinner he was 'bowled over' by a Hochheimer Riesling — and launched on his love affair with wine.

McCallum and his wife, Dawn, planted the first vines on their shingly, free-draining block in Puruatanga Road in 1979. Today the 3.6-hectare Dry River estate vineyard is close-planted in Gewürztraminer, Sauvignon Blanc, Viognier, Pinot Gris, Chardonnay and Pinot Noir. Dry River also owns 4.5 hectares of the more sheltered, slightly earlier-ripening Craighall Vineyard, 200 metres down the road, planted in Pinot Noir, Chardonnay, Riesling and Pinot Gris. The vines are not irrigated and cropped at very low levels, and Scott Henry trellising, leaf-plucking and reflective mulch are all used to optimise the bunches' exposure to sunlight and flavour development.

McCallum describes his approach to winemaking as 'low-tech, involving minimum processing and placing an emphasis on cellaring qualities rather than short-term attractiveness for early drinking'. The 'oxidative' approach to winemaking, which involves deliberately exposing grape juice or wine to oxygen in a bid to enhance its early drinking appeal, finds no favour with McCallum. His ability as an organic chemist to precisely control each stage of the winemaking process lies at the heart of the slow-maturing style he has evolved. McCallum wants to produce wines capable of maturing over the long haul and unfolding the subtleties of old age (wines especially recommended for cellaring are designated Amaranth — a name derived from the unfading flower of Greek mythology).

Dry River's annual output is low at 2000 to 3000 cases, and the wines are snapped up within days, principally on a mail-order basis (there are no ex-winery sales). For some wines, you now have to get on a waiting list before you can join the mail-order list.

The wines are extremely stylish, with lots of extract (stuffing). The Gewürztraminer, medium-dry in most vintages, has a weight, richness and softness that reminds experienced tasters of an Alsace *vendange tardive* (late-harvest) style. The Pinot Gris — long regarded as the finest in the country — is substantial, with a subtle bouquet and concentrated stone-fruit, lychee and spice flavours that build in the bottle for several years.

Dry River Sauvignon Blanc is full-bodied and ripely herbaceous, crisp, dry and long. The Chardonnay is tight and savoury, with deep grapefruit and hazelnut flavours in a classically structured style, built to last. The Craighall Riesling, also a classic, shows great purity and intensity of lemon/lime flavours and is a prime candidate for cellaring.

Dessert wines are also a feature of the Dry River range. When the fruit is harvested at 26 to 30 degrees brix (a measure of sugar content) the wine is labelled as a 'Selection'; at 30 to 36 brix it becomes a 'Bunch Selection'; at over 36 brix it is called 'Berry Selection'. The style varies from light, exquisitely fragrant and delicate sweet whites to strapping, excitingly powerful wines, their sweetness unobtrusive amid great richness of flavour and body.

Dry River Pinot Noir has a grandness of scale that places it right in the vanguard of New Zealand's Pinot Noirs. 'The style of our Pinots rests on concentration and structure,' says McCallum. 'The concentration comes from low crop levels (commonly 3.6–4.8 tonnes per hectare).... The structure is generated by ripe fruit tannins, as opposed to oak tannins.' Dark and drenched with super-ripe flavours of plums, cherries and spice, it richly repays cellaring for at least five years. There is also a top-flight Syrah and — currently in the wings — a Viognier.

Hand-picking (rather than machine harvesting) is just one of the many time-consuming and fastidious practices at Dry River that contribute to the eye-catching quality of the wines.

Neil McCallum

■ Apart from the brilliance of his wine, Neil McCallum is also a notably versatile winemaker. Not for him a single-minded focus on one or two varieties — Dry River Rieslings, Pinot Gris, Gewürztraminers, Chardonnays, sweet white wines, Pinot Noirs and Syrahs are all highly distinguished.

'Being labelled a specialist frequently implies that one must surely be producing the best,' says McCallum. He's a great admirer of Olivier Hubrecht, who 'makes literally dozens of Alsace wines each year from six or seven varietals in different styles and from different vineyards. Every wine he makes is sought after as a masterpiece.'

Dry River wines are invariably immaculate, with great delicacy and finesse. His meticulous nature, McCallum admits, can be 'obsessive. I get really tied up with little details, and sometimes it's an effort to let go. But the details can be anything and everything.'

Right from the start, he made a policy decision not to enter wine competitions. 'I strongly suggest that wines viewed individually (at your dinner table) will be seen in a different light than those at a large tasting or show alongside a hundred or so other wines, which all contribute to overworking the palate of the judge who is also required to report on how the wines appear now, when the wines in question may have been nurtured for drinking at their best in four or five years.'

A few winemakers in New Zealand could be great wine writers, if they chose, notably Michael Brajkovich of Kumeu River and Neil McCallum. The tasting notes he pens in *Cellar Notes*, the twice-yearly Dry River newsletter, are technical yet highly evocative. Take this description of Dry River Chardonnay 1999:

'The colour of this wine is clear light gold. It has the aromas of fresh-cut straw, citrus, mineral and even crème brûlée, along with the mealy notes that arose from stirring the yeast lees while the wine was in the barrel (*batonnage*). As would be expected from the warmth of the year, and from the dry autumn and low crop levels (less than one tonne/acre), it has an intense palate with powerful peach/citrus and mineral flavours and added complexity from the *batonnage* and full barrel ferment (27 per cent new oak). The low yields and concentrated palate have delivered a taut structure from fruit-derived phenolics which resemble those of a young Chablis . . . Its complexity and style place it closer to its French than New Zealand counterparts, and consequently the wine offers considerable interest and reward to those who

are prepared to wait and follow its evolution.' After reading that elegantly crafted, gently persuasive prose, who could resist placing an order?

Always the thinker, McCallum is constantly educating his customers. After claims that the hot, dry 1998 vintage was 'the vintage of the century', he pondered: 'What makes a great vintage? One which enforces low cropping levels frequently delivers beyond expectations, as in 1992 and 1993 which were "disastrously" cold but which had uniformly low cropping levels and produced some stunning wines. Other quality factors involve the requirements of individual varieties — sensitivities to wind, different flavour-ripening requirements, different drought tolerances, berry sizes and still more variations imposed by the age of the vines and site peculiarities . . . Our theories tend to be simple, but nature seldom is.'

Somewhere during the 1990s, Neil McCallum's mindset changed from 'pioneer' to 'established'. Having survived financially and gained the recognition he sought from the serious wine-drinking public, with the feeling of security has come 'room for more intellectual involvement and reflection. But the passion remains, and I cannot imagine ever feeling that our goals are attained, or fully understanding how to get there. The more one learns, the more new issues are raised . . .'

Address Margrain Vineyard,
Cnr Ponatahi and
Huangarua Roads,
Martinborough

Owners Daryl and Graham Margrain

Key Wines Chardonnay, Pinot Gris,
Chenin Blanc,
Gewürztraminer, Riesling,
Merlot, Pinot Noir

Address Martinborough Vineyard,
Princess Street,
Martinborough

Owners Derek and Duncan Milne,
Claire Campbell, the Schultz
family, Wharekauhau
Country Lodge

Key Wines Pinot Noir, Chardonnay,
Riesling, Pinot Gris,
Sauvignon Blanc, Late
Harvest Riesling

Pinot Noir is Martinborough Vineyard's
most acclaimed wine, but the Chardonnay,
Riesling, Pinot Gris and Sauvignon Blanc
are also highly impressive.

Margrain

■ Powerful, concentrated wines, full of character, flow from this 'winery, accommodation and conference' complex on the outskirts of Martinborough township.

Daryl and Graham Margrain, who run a construction business in Wellington, planted their first vines in 1992. Adjacent to the 4-hectare estate vineyard — planted in Chardonnay, Pinot Gris, Merlot and Pinot Noir — are a small winery and eight luxury accommodation villas.

The estate vineyard is very low-cropping: 'If we get 4 tonnes per hectare, we're doing well,' says winemaker Strat Canning, who joined Margrain in 1996, two years after the first vintage (and also has his own label, Stratford). To boost its production, in 2000 Margrain purchased land south of the township in Dry River Road, near the Murdoch James winery, where 4 hectares of Pinot Noir and a hectare of Sauvignon Blanc have been planted.

In 2001, Margrain expanded further, acquiring the Chifney vineyard and winery, directly across the road from their own estate vineyard. Stan Chifney's Cabernet Sauvignon vines have been top-grafted to Pinot Noir and his historic little winery has been converted into a café and tasting room, but much of the building's original character has been preserved. The cellar where Stan Chifney fashioned the first Martinborough wines is now known as the Chifney Room.

With its annual output of 3000 cases, Margrain is a small producer, but the wines are worth tracking down. The Chardonnay is powerful, with rich, peachy, mealy flavours. At its best, the Proprietors Selection Riesling shows notable intensity and poise. Since acquiring the Chifney vineyard, Margrain has added to its line-up a robust, beautifully concentrated Gewürztraminer and a fresh, tight Chenin Blanc with excellent depth and varietal definition.

The Merlot is one of the district's top claret-style reds — dark, fragrant and rich, with good complexity. The Pinot Noir is even better, powerful and harmonious, with an array of cherry, plum, spice and nut flavours in a mouthfilling and richly fragrant style.

Martinborough Vineyard

■ Martinborough Vineyard burst into the limelight at the 1989 Air New Zealand Wine Awards, scooping the trophies for top Chardonnay, Riesling, Müller-Thurgau and Pinot Noir, and champion wine of the show. Still a small company, averaging only 7000 cases per year, it produces a tight range of distinguished white and red wines, notably the famous Pinot Noir.

Larry McKenna, the winemaker (and later general manager) from 1986 to 1999, was for many years the public face of Martinborough Vineyard. But the company's success also reflects the talents of its founding partners: Dr Derek Milne, formerly a soil scientist with the DSIR; his brother Duncan, who has a background in agriculture and horticulture, and his wife Claire Campbell; and pharmacist Russell Schultz and his wife Sue.

The company planted its first vines in 1980. After the first 1984 vintage yielded a tiny amount of outstanding Pinot Noir and Sauvignon Blanc, the challenge was to reproduce these standards in larger-volume wines. McKenna arrived in 1986, the first experienced winemaker in the district. The stunning 1986 vintage of Martinborough Vineyard Pinot Noir was the first to transcend the light, simple, shallow style of Pinot Noir that was previously the norm in this country. As one beautifully perfumed, complex and savoury Pinot Noir followed another, McKenna played a pivotal role in putting not only Martinborough Vineyard but the whole district on the wine map.

Claire Mulholland, who took over the winemaking reins in early 2000, was previously assistant winemaker at the Gibbston Valley winery in Central Otago, and has also worked vintages in Victoria, California and Burgundy.

In the company-owned vineyards — all within the Martinborough Terrace — 17 hectares of Pinot Noir have been planted (including nine different clones) and 3.5 hectares of Chardonnay. The original vines are now 22 years old. Grapes are also purchased from growers on the Terrace and further afield. In 1998, the highly rated Wharekauhau Country Lodge acquired a 10 per cent shareholding in Martinborough Vineyard, in exchange for 8 hectares of land.

The acclaimed Pinot Noir in the past impressed more with fragrance and finesse, rather than sheer power, but has become markedly bolder and richer in recent years, perhaps reflecting the decision to discontinue the magisterial Reserve Pinot Noir (last vintage 1998). Based on low-cropped vines of varying ages and clones, it is fermented principally with indigenous yeasts and matured for a year in French oak barriques (typically 30 per cent new). The 1998, 1999 and 2000 vintages are all highly distinguished.

Martinborough Vineyard Chardonnay is almost as widely acclaimed as the Pinot Noir, offering deep grapefruit and peach flavours wrapped in toasty French oak, subtle butterscotch and mealy characters and good acid spine. The Riesling is a distinctly cool-climate style, with a lovely outpouring of citric/lime aromas and strong, slightly sweet, lingering flavours. The Sauvignon Blanc is fresh and zesty, with incisive melon, lime and capsicum flavours. There is also an absorbing Pinot Gris, fermented with indigenous yeasts and matured in seasoned oak barrels. Sturdy and vibrant, with rich peach, pear and spice flavours, a subtle backdrop of oak and a deliciously soft texture, it ranks among the finest Pinot Gris in the country. In some years, a Riesling Late Harvest appears, exquisitely scented, intense and honeyed.

Murdoch James Estate

■ Eight kilometres south-west of the wineries huddled in and around Martinborough township, the Murdoch James winery sits on an elevated, wind-buffeted site commanding lovely views over the southern Wairarapa. Nelson Clark, a sheep and cattle farmer, and his family planted the first vines here in 1986, calling their venture Blue Rock, and produced their first commercial wines in 1991. However, in 1998 the Clarks sold Blue Rock to another small Martinborough producer, Murdoch James.

Murdoch James, named after the father of the founder, Roger Fraser, started life in 1986 when Fraser and his wife, Jill, planted a 2.5-hectare block of Pinot Noir and Syrah in Martinborough. Although the Frasers spent the next decade in Australia — Roger running a large pharmaceutical company — from 1993 onwards a few hundred cases of Murdoch James wines were produced on their behalf at Ata Rangi. Now the Frasers are back, running Murdoch James.

The north-facing Blue Rock vineyard, planted principally in clay soils, after major expansion during 1999 and 2000 covers 19 hectares. Pinot Noir and Syrah are the featured varieties, with smaller plots of Chardonnay, Riesling, Sauvignon Blanc, Cabernet Franc and Cabernet Sauvignon. In the original Fraser Block in Martinborough, 6 hectares of Pinot Noir and Syrah are established.

James Walker, formerly assistant winemaker at Lintz Estate, was appointed winemaker at Murdoch James in 2002, with the assistance of Steve Bird in a consultancy role. Murdoch James' annual output of 4000 cases is still small, but is projected to leap to 12,000 cases by 2004.

The white wines include a typically high alcohol, very fresh and crisp Unoaked Chardonnay; a limey, easy-drinking Riesling, made in a distinctly medium style; and a punchy Sauvignon Blanc with grassy, nettley flavours and racy acidity. Blushing Pinots is a pink/orange, strawberryish, slightly earthy blend of Meunier and Pinot Noir, slightly sweet and smooth.

The Cabernet Sauvignon and Cabernet Franc-based reds are typically slightly crisp and leafy, although full-bodied and flavoursome. The Pinot Noirs, although not outstanding, are generally robust and warm, with a savoury, spicy, nutty complexity. The Shiraz (Syrah) is characterful, with strong peppery aromas in a gutsy style, brambly and spicy.

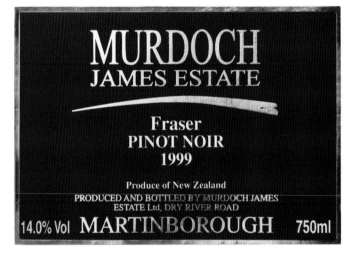

Address	Murdoch James Estate, Dry River Road, Martinborough
Owners	Roger and Jill Fraser
Key Wines	Fraser Pinot Noir, Blue Rock Reserve Pinot Noir, Shiraz, Unoaked Chardonnay

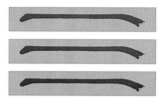

Address Nga Waka Vineyard,
Kitchener Street,
Martinborough

Owners Roger and Carol Parkinson,
Gordon and Margaret
Parkinson

Key Wines Sauvignon Blanc, Riesling,
Chardonnay, Pinot Noir

Nga Waka

■ Nga Waka produces bone-dry, intense, tautly structured wines which in the words of winemaker Roger Parkinson, 'demand and reward cellaring'. At first Nga Waka was a white-wine specialist, but in 1998 Parkinson bowed to the pressure and added Pinot Noir to his range.

The 3.5-hectare vineyard and winery lies between Palliser and Burnt Spur in Kitchener Street. The vineyard was planted in 1988; the first vintage flowed in 1993. The name Nga Waka is derived from the three hills, Nga Waka A Kupe ('The Canoes of Kupe'), which lie like upturned canoes as a backdrop to Martinborough. Nga Waka is family-owned. Parkinson oversees the production and marketing, while his wife, Carol, an accountant, controls the finances. Roger's parents, Gordon and Margaret, are also involved financially. With his father a diplomat, as a child Roger Parkinson lived 'all over the world. When I was 14, Dad was posted to France and got very interested in wine. We drank wine regularly at meals.'

After graduating with a BA in history and French, and working for several years as a training manager, in 1988 Parkinson gained a postgraduate diploma in wine from Roseworthy College in South Australia, and later worked vintages in Victoria, South Australia, Alsace and Bordeaux.

The Winery Vineyard, planted in 'excessively' drained, stony, silty soils, is established in Chardonnay, Riesling and Sauvignon Blanc. Nga Waka is also part-owner of the nearby Old Cemetery Vineyard, where 3 hectares of Pinot Noir are planted.

South-east of the town, near Te Muna Road, Nga Waka leases the Top Block Vineyard, with 2 hectares of Chardonnay, Sauvignon Blanc and Riesling. Compared to its flat blocks on the Martinborough Terrace, this elevated, slightly sloping site is generally warmer at night and less vulnerable to spring frosts. The company also leases another tiny, 0.7-hectare plot of Pinot Noir in Huangarua Road.

In his Colorsteel and concrete block winery, described as a 'designer barn' or 'elegant shed', Parkinson produces about 5000 cases per year of wine, designed to show 'the qualities of the region and our vineyards. The wines need time for those to come out, so I structure them accordingly. That means bone-dry and good acid balance to provide backbone.'

The wines are typically immaculate, with a voluminous fragrance and fresh, deep, lingering flavours. The Sauvignon Blanc is a classic cool-climate style, ripely herbaceous and zingy. With its impressive mouthfeel, searching, bone-dry melon/capsicum flavours and long, steely finish, it is an authoritative wine with a track record of unusual longevity.

The Riesling is also unflinchingly dry, with intense lemon/lime flavours, minerally characters and a tight, freshly acidic finish. The barrel-fermented Chardonnay is tight and restrained in its youth, with citrus/peach flavours threaded with lively acidity, complex, nutty, mealy characters and impressive weight.

The Pinot Noir is not a blockbuster but shows finesse and delicacy, with plum, cherry and spice flavours, well-integrated oak and gentle tannins. These are consistently classy wines.

Robust, intensely flavoured, bone-dry Sauvignon Blanc is a highlight of the tight Nga Waka range.

From one vintage to the next, Palliser Estate produces one of the country's most ravishingly beautiful Sauvignon Blancs.

Palliser Estate

■ Palliser Estate is the largest winery in the Wairarapa, but its size is no bar to quality. Its ravishingly beautiful Sauvignon Blanc has set a benchmark for excellence, and its Riesling and Pinot Noir are also outstanding.

Wyatt Creech, better known as a politician, was 'the driving-force in the early days', according to managing director Richard Riddiford. Creech planted the first vines in his Om Santi vineyard in 1984 and four years later formed an unlisted public company (today with about 150 shareholders) to take over his vineyard and build a winery. The name for the venture, Palliser Estate, was derived from the southernmost tip of the North Island, Cape Palliser.

A scion of a wealthy Wairarapa farming family, Riddiford graduated from Victoria University with a Bachelor of Commerce and Administration degree, spent 10 years at Borthwicks as a marketing manager for such by-products as sheepskins, and was one of the original investors in Palliser Estate. 'I'm not a wine person,' he says. 'My background is in marketing.' Chairman over the years of a host of meat and wine industry organisations, in 1999 Riddiford was made a member of the New Zealand Order of Merit for his contributions to the wine and deer industries.

Palliser's five company-owned vineyards (Om Santi, Palliser, Clouston, East Base and Pinnacles) total 58 hectares, planted principally in Pinot Noir, with significant amounts of Sauvignon Blanc and Chardonnay and much smaller plots of Riesling and Pinot Gris. Grapes are also purchased from contract growers, all in Martinborough.

Allan Johnson, who took over the winemaking reins in late 1990, is a meticulous craftsman whose wines show great harmony and finesse. While growing up in Hawke's Bay, Johnson worked in vineyards during the school holidays, and in 1980 joined McWilliam's as a cellarhand. After graduating from Roseworthy College in 1984, he was winemaker at Capel Vale in Western Australia for the 1985 to 1989 vintages, but says he 'yearned to get back to New Zealand. Our fruit has more concentration of flavour, more power in the middle and end palate.'

With its annual output now exceeding 30,000 cases, Palliser Estate is a medium-sized producer. 'It took 10 years to make a profit,' says Riddiford, but in the year to June 2000 the company posted a net profit of $504,000.

The wines, made in a stylish, twin-gabled, colonial-style winery, are marketed under two brands: Palliser Estate (for the top wines) and Pencarrow (formerly Palliser Bay). The Pencarrow range features a fresh, vibrant, gently oaked Chardonnay; a scented and zesty Sauvignon Blanc; and a sturdy, full-flavoured and smooth Pinot Noir.

The seven wines forming the Palliser Estate range are consistently top-flight. The Chardonnay is stylish, with intense citrusy flavours and a buttery, mealy richness. The Sauvignon Blanc simply overflows with ripely herbaceous aromas and flavours in a mouth-wateringly fresh, vibrant style, proving the district's ability to produce Sauvignon Blancs that are fully a match for Marlborough's finest.

The Riesling is a fractionally off-dry style with great fragrance, searching, lemon/lime fruit flavours and zingy acidity. There is also a Noble Riesling with intense grapefruit/honey flavours and lovely perfume and poise. Recent additions to the range are a substantial Pinot Gris with fresh, strong apple, lychee and spice flavours, and a very refined, lively and yeasty Méthode Champenoise.

The style of Palliser Estate's Pinot Noir reflects Allan Johnson's fondness for 'rich Pinot Noir with the roast coffee aromas of ripe fruit and good structure'. With its lush cherry and plum fruit characters wrapped in subtle French oak, this is an impressively concentrated and supple red. Palliser Estate a few years ago adopted a lower-cropping regime, and since 1996 the Pinot Noir has achieved far greater heights of ripeness and richness, placing it among the district's — and country's — heavyweights.

Address Palliser Estate, Kitchener Street, Martinborough

Owner Palliser Estate Wines of Martinborough Limited

Key Wines Palliser Estate Chardonnay, Sauvignon Blanc, Riesling, Pinot Noir; Pencarrow Sauvignon Blanc, Chardonnay, Pinot Noir

Address Stratford Wines,
115 New York Street,
Martinborough

Owners Stratford Canning and Carla
Burns

Key Wines Chardonnay, Riesling, Noble
Riesling, Pinot Noir

Address Te Kairanga Wines,
Martins Road,
Martinborough

Owner Te Kairanga Wines Limited

Key Wines Reserve Chardonnay, Pinot
Noir; Martinborough
Chardonnay, Martinborough
Pinot Noir, Martinborough
Sauvignon Blanc,
Martinborough Riesling,
Gisborne Chardonnay;
Castlepoint Chardonnay,
Cabernet Sauvignon

Stratford

■ Some of Martinborough's rarest and most characterful wines are made by Stratford ('Strat') Canning, who is also the winemaker at Margrain Vineyard and a half-brother of Chris Canning, founder of De Redcliffe.

Canning and his wife, Carla Burns, planted the first vines on their block near the Dry River winery in 1993. After a decade in marine research, in 1987 Canning joined the wine industry at De Redcliffe and later graduated in winemaking from Charles Sturt University in Australia. After spells as vineyard manager at Palliser Estate and winemaker at Winslow, he is now focused on making wine for Margrain and his own Stratford label.

Pinot Noir is the key variety in the 3-hectare vineyard, with smaller plantings of Riesling and Chardonnay. 'Hands on in the vineyard; hands off in the winery,' is the foundation of Canning's winemaking philosophy. Canning believes 'the production of top quality grapes requires uncompromising manipulation of the vine and its environment, but in the winery, simplicity is the preferred option'.

First produced in 1997, the wines are made in the Margrain winery and only in small volumes, averaging 500 to 600 cases per year. The barrel-fermented Chardonnay is savoury, nutty and complex, with minerally touches and good acid spine.

The slightly sweet Riesling is crisp and tangy, with an outstanding intensity in top vintages. There is also a scented, citrusy and honey-sweet Noble Riesling.

Lush and bursting with sweet, ripe cherry and spice fruit characters, the Pinot Noir is weighty, concentrated and powerful, with a delicious richness through the palate. These are consistently impressive wines.

Te Kairanga

■ Te Kairanga ('the land where the soil is rich and the food plentiful') winery rests on a stunning site above the Huangarua River, against a backdrop of sunlit green hills. The road to success has not been entirely smooth, but Te Kairanga is now the district's second-largest winery, producing consistently impressive Pinot Noirs and Chardonnays. Tom Draper — co-founder of one of Wellington's wine-tasting groups, the Magnum Society — and his wife Robin in 1983 bought the first modern-era Martinborough vineyard, planted in 1978 by Alister Taylor, but then in a run-down state. After the Drapers brought in partners, Te Kairanga's vineyards fanned out on both sides of Martins Road, east of the township.

The original partnership was dissolved in 1991 and Te Kairanga is now a public company with around 180 shareholders, including Tom Draper. As part of a $5 million capital-raising move to fund the development of new vineyards and construction of a new winery, Rangatira, the investment arm of the McKenzie Foundation (set up by the McKenzie family, of the famous department store, to distribute money to charities) purchased a 28 per cent shareholding in 2002. In the year to June 2001, Te Kairanga posted a net after-tax profit of $270,000.

The company's vineyards on the Martinborough Terrace include 28 hectares of Pinot Noir, 10 hectares of Chardonnay, 4 hectares of Sauvignon Blanc and 1 hectare of Riesling. Being at the high point of the terrace and on

Te Kairanga's hundreds of shareholders own the district's second-largest wine company, with particular strengths in Pinot Noir and Chardonnay.

its edge, frosts are not a problem in the Te Kairanga home block or most of the adjacent East Plain vineyard. To boost its grape supply, the company recently planted a 12-hectare vineyard at Springrock, 10 kilometres north-east of the winery, and is also planting a 55-hectare block at Ruakokoputuna, 14 kilometres south of the township. Grapes are also purchased from growers in Gisborne, Hawke's Bay and the Wairarapa.

After the first 1986 vintage, the wines released during the mid to late 1980s proved disappointing. The appointment of Te Kairanga's first full-time winemaker, Chris Buring, in late 1989, was followed by a marked upswing in wine quality. Buring departed in 1998, and the winemakers are now Peter Caldwell, a Tasmanian who previously worked at Nobilo and in Australia, California and Bordeaux, and his French partner, Mayi Caldwell.

With its current annual output of over 20,000 cases, Te Kairanga wines are widely seen. The company markets a three-tier range, with Reserve wines at the top, the key varietal selection in the middle, and Castlepoint wines at the bottom.

Does Te Kairanga have specialities? 'Without question,' says Andrew Shackleton, general manager since 1993. 'Chardonnay and Pinot Noir are the two varieties we're absolutely committed to. They're the best for this area, with the greatest future in terms of quality and demand.'

The oak-aged Martinborough Sauvignon Blanc is verdant and zesty. Fully barrel-fermented, the Martinborough Chardonnay is weighty and crisp, with citrusy, buttery, nutty flavours. The Reserve Chardonnay, based on the ripest fruit, is a powerful, vigorous and complex wine with impressive richness and a firm, slightly flinty finish.

From the 2001 vintage flowed Te Kairanga's first Riesling, a finely scented wine with good intensity of ripe, lemony flavours, balanced sweetness and a rich finish.

The consistently attractive Pinot Noir places its accent on strong, almost sweet-tasting berry/plum fruit flavours, fresh and supple. The Reserve Pinot Noir is more powerful and lush, with typically high alcohol, a stronger French oak influence (30 per cent new) and the ability to flourish in the bottle for several years.

Voss Estate

■ After Gary Voss and his partner, Annette Atkins, bought land next to Ata Rangi in 1987, he tasted Ata Rangi's 1986 Pinot Noir and thought it was 'the best Pinot Noir made in New Zealand or Australia'. Then he tasted Chifney Cabernet Sauvignon and Ata Rangi Célèbre, also Cabernet Sauvignon-based, and liked those too. So in 1988 Voss and Atkins planted both Pinot Noir and Cabernet Sauvignon. Today, with 12 Martinborough vintages behind them, their 'passion' — and the majority of their output — is Pinot Noir.

Voss, who has a BSc in zoology, is a former Fisheries Research diver. He studied oenology for a year in Australia, worked the 1987 and 1988 vintages at De Redcliffe, and the 1989 and 1990 vintages at Ata Rangi, before producing the first Voss Estate wines in 1991. Annette Atkins is a former Fisheries Research kahawai specialist. 'I do more of the work in the vineyard,' she says. 'Gary calls the shots in the winery.'

The 2.7-hectare estate vineyard was originally planted in equal areas of Pinot Noir, Chardonnay, and red Bordeaux varieties: Cabernet Sauvignon, Merlot and Cabernet Franc. After concluding that 'you only get really good red wine from Cabernet Sauvignon here about two years out of five', Voss and Atkins later top-grafted some of their Cabernet Sauvignon vines over to Sauvignon Blanc. The principal varieties are now Pinot Noir and Chardonnay, with smaller plots of Sauvignon Blanc, Cabernet Franc and Cabernet Sauvignon. In 1999, Voss Estate planted the 2.5-hectare Todds Road Block, also on the Martinborough Terrace, devoted exclusively to Pinot Noir. Grapes are also purchased from two other local vineyards managed by Voss Estate.

In their large, unpainted corrugated iron shed ('Any spare money goes into better equipment rather than grandiose architectural statements,' says Gary Voss), the partners produce about 2500 cases per year. With Pinot Noir, the goal is a 'complex, earthy style that has fruit weight but is more than just ripe fruit supported by loads of new oak'. Perfumed, rich-flavoured and supple, with very satisfying weight and depth and silky tannins, this is one of the district's most instantly likeable Pinot Noirs.

Waihenga, blended from Cabernet Franc, Syrah and Cabernet Sauvignon (Merlot was recently deleted) is typically well-coloured, with distinct mint/eucalypt characters amid its blackcurrant, plum and spice flavours.

The Sauvignon Blanc is fleshy and ripely flavoured; the Riesling floral and lively, in a slightly sweet style with excellent depth. Fermented and lees-aged for a year in French oak barriques, the Reserve Chardonnay is powerful, with lush, ripe peach and butterscotch flavours, well-judged oak handling and a slightly creamy texture.

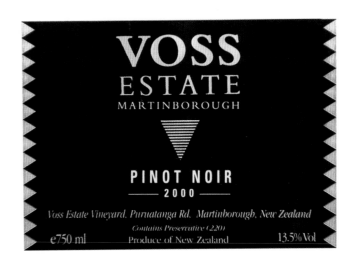

Address	Voss Estate, Puruatanga Road, Martinborough
Owners	Gary Voss and Annette Atkins
Key Wines	Pinot Noir, Waihenga, Reserve Chardonnay, Riesling, Sauvignon Blanc

Address Walnut Ridge,
159 Regent Street,
Martinborough

Owner The Brink family

Key Wines Pinot Noir, Cabernet
Sauvignon, Sauvignon
Blanc, Pinot Gris

Walnut Ridge

■ Iowan Bill Brink (who died in June 2002) came to New Zealand in 1973 after a stint in Samoa with the Peace Corps. After a number of years in the public service, 'doing the *Dominion* crossword', he and his New Zealand wife, Sally, moved to Martinborough in 1986. When Walnut Ridge Pinot Noir 1997 won the trophy for champion Pinot Noir at the 1998 Air New Zealand Wine Awards, it confirmed Brink's status as the producer of one of the district's most muscular, lush and flavour-packed Pinot Noirs.

Walnut Ridge takes its name from a gentle rise that runs the length of the Martinborough Terrace, planted by Brink in walnut trees. He and Sally planted their first vines in Regent Street in 1988. For the first few years, they sold the grapes, producing their first wines in 1994.

Today Pinot Noir is the dominant variety in the 2.5-hectare vineyard, supplemented by Sauvignon Blanc, Pinot Gris and Cabernet Sauvignon. On steep river terraces 10 kilometres from the township, a second vineyard has been planted in Pinot Noir to supply Walnut Ridge.

'I'm a great believer that great wine is made in the vineyard,' said Brink. 'Nothing needs to be done in the winery — it's all been done in the vineyard. Ripe, clean fruit that expresses the *terroir* leads to a wine full of intensity, character and texture.'

Made on-site, Walnut Ridge wines are rare, with a total annual output of only 1000 cases. The Pinot Noir is a hedonist's delight. Perfumed, with substantial body, it simply overflows with ripe cherry, plum and spice flavours, with finely integrated French oak (40 per cent new) adding complexity and a backbone of supple, velvety tannins.

The Cabernet Sauvignon is typically vibrant and full-flavoured, with red berry and green leaf characters. Brink also made a fresh, zesty, passionfruit and lime-flavoured Sauvignon Blanc and a mouthfilling Pinot Gris with pear, apple and spice flavours, crisp and dry.

Winslow

Address Winslow Wines,
Princess Street,
Martinborough

Owners Steve and Jennifer Tarring

Key Wines Petra Cabernet Sauvignon,
Turakirae Reserve Cabernet
Sauvignon/Cabernet Franc,
St Vincent Riesling, White
Rock Chardonnay, Rosetta
Cabernet Rosé, William Ross
Cabernet Liqueur

■ Winslow has a reputation for producing some of the Wairarapa's finest claret-style reds. 'I think we get enough sun and heat in Martinborough to ripen Cabernet Sauvignon,' says proprietor Steve Tarring. 'By New Zealand standards, even in poorer years we make an average Cabernet, and in good vintages we produce a very good wine.' Winslow's red-wine flagship, Turakirae Reserve, blended from Cabernet Sauvignon and Cabernet Franc, has won gold medals in New Zealand and the United Kingdom.

Tarring and his wife, Jennifer, purchased their land in Princess Street, Martinborough, in 1985. A graduate in microbiology and former marine biologist for Fisheries Research, Steve Tarring later spent several years overseas as an executive of a filtration equipment manufacturer. The vineyard was set up by Jennifer's father, Ross Turner, and until recently the wines — first produced in 1991 — were made by Strat Canning.

The 2.5-hectare, shingly estate vineyard is planted in 60 per cent Cabernet Sauvignon, 40 per cent Cabernet Franc. The company also owns a 3-hectare vineyard in Shooting Butts Road, Martinborough, planted in Chardonnay (principally), Riesling and Pinot Noir.

Winslow's output is low. Steve Tarring, who now holds the winemaking reins, currently produces about 1500 cases per year in the on-site winery. Tarring makes white and red wines but, he says, 'in our Cabernets [Petra and Turakirae Reserve] you will find an expression of where our heart truly lies'.

In warm vintages, the reds can be of arresting quality. The Turakirae Reserve Cabernet Sauvignon/Cabernet Franc

(especially) and Petra Cabernet Sauvignon are dark, vibrant, concentrated wines with silky tannins and a delicious burst of blackcurrant, plum and green leaf flavours. Of the pair, the higher-priced Turakirae Reserve is typically the ripest-tasting, most complex and 'complete'.

At its best, the St Vincent Riesling is punchy and tight, with intense lemon/lime flavours. White Rock Chardonnay, briefly aged in American oak, is lemony and appley, with sweet oak aromas. Top vintages of the Rosetta Cabernet Rosé, made from Cabernet Sauvignon and French oak-fermented, are full of charm in their youth, overflowing with red berry flavours, crisp and garden-fresh.

There is also a cinnamon and clove-flavoured, sweet William Ross Cabernet Liqueur, fortified with French brandy to ward off the cold winter nights in the Wairarapa.

Other producers

■ Ashwell Vineyards

Wellington pharmacist John Phipps and his wife, Vivienne, own two small vineyards in Martinborough, totalling 4 hectares of Pinot Noir, Sauvignon Blanc, Chardonnay and Cabernet Sauvignon. The wines, first produced in 1996, are rare (around 300 cases per year) and so far have been of varying quality, but the appointment of Sam Weaver as consultant winemaker should lead to better things. I have recently tasted a weighty and full-flavoured Sauvignon Blanc/Sémillon, with ripe tropical fruit characters, and a dark, fresh, berryish Cabernet Sauvignon/Merlot.

■ Canadoro Wines

Wellingtonians Greg and Lesley Robins planted their 1.2-hectare block of Cabernet Sauvignon and Chardonnay in Martinborough in 1988. The wines, first produced in 1993 and made on the Robins' behalf by a contract winemaker, are a trickle at just 300 cases per year. The Chardonnay is mouthfilling, peachy, toasty and moderately complex; the Cabernet Sauvignon is dark and gutsy, with plenty of brambly, spicy, minty flavour.

■ Christina Estate

In the past called Walker Estate, this 2-hectare vineyard was founded by Brendan and Elizabeth Walker, who in 1988 planted Riesling, Chardonnay and a red-wine variety whose identity has been the focus of much debate in the district, but is still unknown, even after DNA testing. The highlight of the range, launched from the 1993 vintage, was a gutsy, dark, brambly and chewy red, Notre Vigne ('Our Vine'). In late 1999, the company was sold to Christina Egan.

■ Claddagh Vineyard

Russell and Suzann Pearless initially sold most of the crop from their 4-hectare vineyard in Martinborough, retaining only the grapes for their impressively concentrated Cabernet Sauvignon, launched from the 1994 vintage. The vineyard, first planted in 1992, also features Pinot Noir, Sauvignon Blanc and Chardonnay, from which in 2001 an expanded selection of wines was produced on-site.

■ Coney Wines

Tim and Margaret Coney own 4 hectares of Pinot Noir and Riesling vines in Dry River Road, near the Murdoch James winery. The attractive wines, launched from the 1999 vintage, include a charming, vibrantly fruity, cherry and raspberry-flavoured Pinot Noir and a floral, slightly sweet Ragtime Riesling with lush, citrusy flavours. Gate sales will commence by the summer of 2002–03.

■ Martinus Estate

From their 2 hectares of Pinot Noir vines and winery in Todds Road, Martinborough, Robert and Susan van Zanten recently launched a stylish, richly fruity and full-flavoured 2001 Pinot Noir.

■ Muirlea Rise

Willie Brown, wine merchant turned winemaker, and his wife, Lea, planted their first vines in Martinborough in 1988. From 1991 onwards, they made a trickle of mellow, earthy, mushroomy Pinot Noir, a densely coloured, berryish and concentrated Mareth (blended from an unidentified variety they call 'pseudo-Syrah' and Cabernet Sauvignon), and a popular Après Wine Liqueur (a ruby port style). However, the 2.2-hectare vineyard (planted in Pinot Noir, Syrah, Cabernet Sauvignon and 'pseudo-Syrah') was recently leased out, and Willie Brown died in mid-2002.

■ Porters

John and Annabel Porter planted 2 hectares of Pinot Noir (predominantly) and Pinot Gris in Martinborough in 1992, producing their first wines in 1995. At 600 cases per year, the wines are still scarce, but the Pinot Noir is supple, vibrant and substantial, with loads of flavour, and the Pinot Gris has good mouthfeel, with rich stone-fruit and spice flavours.

■ Schubert Wines

Kai Schubert and his partner, Marion Deimling, both graduates of Geisenheim University, say, 'Pinot Noir was the reason for us to come to New Zealand and specifically to the Wairarapa.' Their 1.4-hectare block in Martinborough is planted in five varieties, but far more important is their 12-hectare vineyard in Dakins Road, where Pinot Noir is the most important grape, supplemented by Syrah, Cabernet Sauvignon, Merlot, Pinot Gris, Chardonnay and Sauvignon Blanc. The initial releases featured a trio of strikingly full-flavoured 1999 reds — Cabernet Franc, Cabernet Sauvignon and Syrah — based on grapes contract-grown in Gimblett Road, Hawke's Bay. A winery to watch.

■ Stonecutter Vineyard

Roger Pemberton and Lucy Harper's 4-hectare vineyard in Todds Road, Martinborough, planted in 1995, is devoted principally to Pinot Noir and Pinot Gris, with small plots of Gewürztraminer and Merlot. The wines, launched from the 1999 vintage, include a fresh, mouthfilling Pinot Gris with strong citrus and spice flavours; a fragrant and supple Pinot Noir with sweet-fruit characters; and Topaz, an apéritif style blended from Gewürztraminer and Sauvignon Blanc that offers an array of passionfruit, green capsicum and lychee flavours, sweet and smooth.

■ The Escarpment Vineyard

Larry McKenna — still indivisibly associated with his long and highly successful spell at Martinborough Vineyard, which ended in 1999 — has since been setting up a new venture in Te Muna Road, south-east of Martinborough township, with Australian partners, Robert and Mem Kirby. First planted in 1999, the 24-hectare vineyard is planted in Pinot Noir (70 per cent), Pinot Gris (10 per cent), Chardonnay (10 per cent), Riesling (5 per cent) and Pinot Blanc (5 per cent). The Escarpment Vineyard's debut wines from the 2001 vintage, made from grapes contract-grown in Martinborough, include a notably weighty, concentrated Pinot Gris and a firm, spicy Pinot Noir, built to last. By 2006, production is projected to reach a substantial 15,000 cases.

Nelson

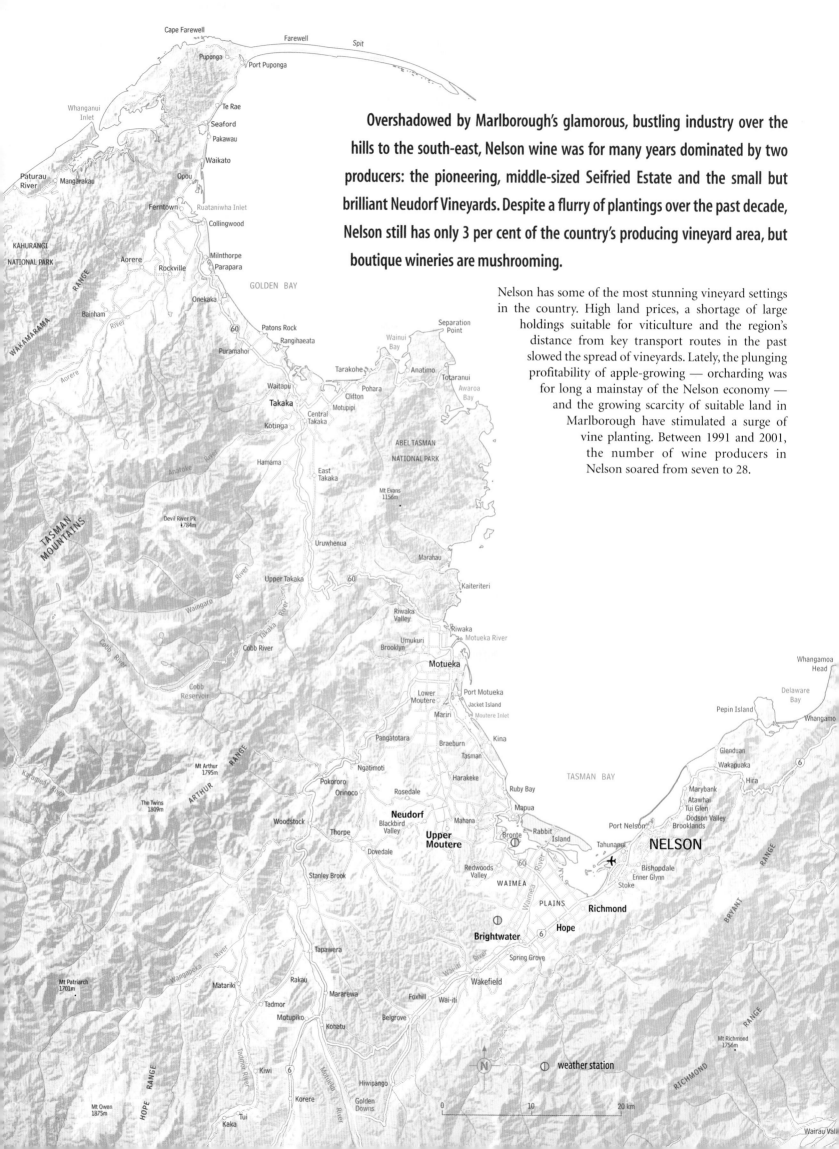

Overshadowed by Marlborough's glamorous, bustling industry over the hills to the south-east, Nelson wine was for many years dominated by two producers: the pioneering, middle-sized Seifried Estate and the small but brilliant Neudorf Vineyards. Despite a flurry of plantings over the past decade, Nelson still has only 3 per cent of the country's producing vineyard area, but boutique wineries are mushrooming.

Nelson has some of the most stunning vineyard settings in the country. High land prices, a shortage of large holdings suitable for viticulture and the region's distance from key transport routes in the past slowed the spread of vineyards. Lately, the plunging profitability of apple-growing — orcharding was for long a mainstay of the Nelson economy — and the growing scarcity of suitable land in Marlborough have stimulated a surge of vine planting. Between 1991 and 2001, the number of wine producers in Nelson soared from seven to 28.

History

Two shiploads of German winemakers who arrived at Nelson in 1843 and 1844 were attracted, according to historian Dick Scott, by 'the glowing prospects for viticulture promised them by the New Zealand Company'. The *Nelson Examiner* enthused: 'No emigrants are more valuable than the Germans and we hail the intended cultivation of the vine by them with unfeigned pleasure.' By 1845, most were already disillusioned and had departed for South Australia.

In the 1890s, F.H.M. Ellis and Sons were 'substantial' winemakers at Motupipi, near Takaka, according to Scott. Established in 1868, making wine from cherries and wild blackberries as well as grapes, the Ellis winery stayed in production for over 70 years, until it was converted into a woolshed in 1939.

Viggo du Fresne, of French Huguenot descent, from 1967 to 1976 made dry red wine at a tiny, half-hectare vineyard planted in deep gravel on the coast at Ruby Bay. The vineyard, dating back to 1918, was originally established with Black Hamburgh table grapes; du Fresne took over in 1948 and waged a long, unsuccessful struggle to establish classical vines. After his Chardonnay, Sémillon and Meunier vines all failed — probably due to viruses — he produced dark and gutsy reds from the hybrid Seibel 5437 and 5455 varieties.

In the late 1960s, Irish-born Rod Neill planted the first vines at Victory, a pocket-sized winery at Stoke. Hermann and Agnes Seifried planted their first vines in the hills at Upper Moutere in 1974. Craig Gass planted the first vines at Korepo Wines (later called Ruby Bay) in 1976, followed in 1978 by Tim and Judy Finn at Neudorf and in 1980 by Trevor Lewis at Ranzau (now Greenhough). Nelson wine was on its way.

Climate

Nelson's topography accounts for its temperate, mild and sunny climate. Mountain ranges to the west, south and east protect it from weather extremes. The Tasman Mountains to the west, climbing to 1775 metres, act as a barrier to the prevailing westerly winds, and ranges to the south and east protect the region from cold weather systems.

Close to the sea, and less windy than most parts of the country, Nelson has a calmer, more temperate climate than most parts of the South Island. On a typical summer's day, temperatures peak at around 25°C, with an overnight low of 14°C. Nelson is often called 'the sunshine capital of New Zealand', a title for which it vies with Blenheim.

Frosts are rare after mid-October, but the region's advantages for viticulture are reduced by the risk of damaging autumn rains as harvest approaches. In this respect, Nelson parallels most of the northern wine regions more closely than other parts of the South Island.

Rainfall during the October–April growing season is much higher than in Marlborough, exceeds Hawke's Bay and even matches Gisborne. Although droughts are occasionally experienced during summer, the likelihood of damaging rain rises during April and May, when susceptible late-ripening varieties such as Riesling can be caught.

Soils

The gravelly silt loams of the Waimea Plains are in many ways similar to Marlborough, although their higher clay content gives greater water-holding capacity. The clay-based soils of the Upper Moutere hill country contrast with the lighter soils found on the flats.

Wine styles

Nelson's wine identity has not been assisted by the fact it does not have a single outstanding wine style, along the lines of Marlborough Sauvignon Blanc or Central Otago Pinot Noir. White wines — Sauvignon Blanc, Riesling, Chardonnay — grown on the Waimea Plains can be distinctly Marlborough-like. Pinot Noir is viewed by most winemakers as the rising star, and has already yielded highly impressive wines at Upper Moutere and on the edge of the plains in heavier, clay-based soils at the base of the hills.

Sub-regions

The majority of Nelson's vines are on the flat, silty Waimea Plains, south-west of the city, but there are also important plantings in the Upper Moutere hills. Wines from less elevated parts of the plains tend to be aromatic, light and fresh, with vivid varietal characters, while those from the hill-country clays are weighty, rich-flavoured and often distinctly minerally. Vines are also sprouting north of Nelson city and in the north-west of the province, at Golden Bay.

Principal grape varieties

	Producing area 2002	% total producing area 2002
Chardonnay	108 ha	30.3%
Sauvignon Blanc	89 ha	24.9%
Pinot Noir	81 ha	22.7%
Riesling	38 ha	10.6%
Cabernet Sauvignon	13 ha	3.6%
Gewürztraminer	11 ha	3.0%
Merlot	9 ha	2.5%

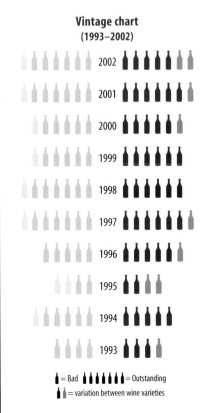

Vintage chart (1993–2002)

2002
2001
2000
1999
1998
1997
1996
1995
1994
1993

= Bad   = Outstanding
= variation between wine varieties

Previous page: Netted to protect their ripening fruit from birds, Tasman Bay's vineyards in the rolling Upper Moutere hill country are planted principally in Chardonnay, Sauvignon Blanc and Pinot Noir.

Summary of climate statistics

Meteorological station	Latitude	Height	GDD	MTWM	Rainfall, Oct–Apr	Air frost days (annual)
Appleby	41.17'S	17 m	1129	17.8°C	535 mm	21
Moutere Hills	41.21'S	110 m	1175	18.1°C	562 mm	15

Height — *above sea level* GDD — *growing degree days, Oct–Apr, above 10°C* MTWM — *mean temperature, warmest month*

Waimea Plains

After descending from the Richmond Range, which divides Nelson from Marlborough, the Waimea River flows north across the plains, absorbing the Wai-iti River, and then pumps into the sea at Rabbit Island. On the sweeping Waimea Plains — in the nineteenth century clothed in bracken, shrubs, native grasses and manuka — apple and pear orchards, olive groves, vegetables, berry fruits, hop gardens, kiwifruit and stone-fruit are cultivated. During the past decade, vineyards have spread like wildfire; the majority of Nelson wine flows from the plains.

History

Rod Neill, who established a 1-hectare vineyard, Victory, at Stoke, just south of the city of Nelson, in the late 1960s, was the first commercial winemaker on the plains. Neill, an orchard manager, planted at various stages Müller-Thurgau, Chasselas, Breidecker, Seibel 5455, 'Gamay Beaujolais' (in fact a clone of Pinot Noir) and Cabernet Sauvignon, and produced his first wines in 1972. Eight years later, another hobbyist, medical technologist Trevor Lewis, planted 2 hectares of Riesling, Müller-Thurgau, Gewürztraminer, 'Gamay Beaujolais' and Cabernet Sauvignon at the Ranzau winery (now known as Greenhough) at Hope, south of Richmond. Despite these pioneering efforts, until a few years ago most of Nelson's wine companies were based at Upper Moutere, and only recently has a significant cluster of wine producers emerged on the plains.

Climate

Vineyards near the coast are moderated by the ocean, with sea breezes during the summer having a cooling effect. Inland districts, such as Brightwater, have marginally higher rainfall and also experience greater day/night fluctuations in temperature.

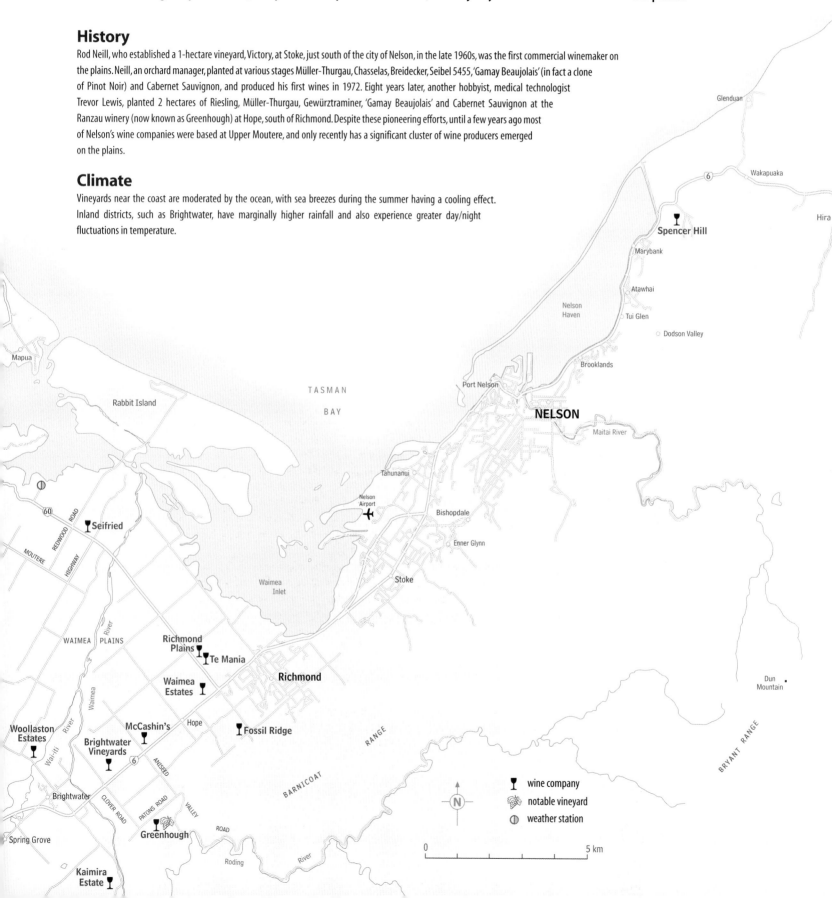

Soils

The friable, free-draining soils of the Waimea Plains feature various types of loams (silty, sandy or stony clay) over a gravel base. Except on the more elevated, inland parts of the plains, the water table is high. Found adjacent to the river, especially on the western part of the plains, 'Waimea silt loams and sandy loams' are friable to a depth of 25 to 30 centimetres, with gravels at a depth of less than a metre and occasionally right on the surface. Most of the vines are planted in 'Ranzau stony clay loams', on the eastern part of the plain, between Stoke and Brightwater. Of low to moderate fertility, with deep underlying gravels and low moisture retention, these soils are found on intermediate river terraces, about 6 metres above the present flood plain of the Waimea River.

Wine styles

White wines grown on the Waimea Plains are scented and vibrantly fruity, with crisp, clear varietal characters. The Sauvignon Blancs are freshly herbaceous and zingy; the Rieslings floral and intense, with good acid spine. Pinot Noir looks especially promising on the margins of the plains, in heavier soils with a higher clay content.

Brightwater Vineyards

■ When surveyor Gary Neale and his wife, Valley, who worked in banking, returned to New Zealand in 1992 after nine years abroad, they were keen to take to the land. 'We thought we'd grow apples,' recalls Valley. 'But an apple-grower said to us: "If you aren't passionate about what you're doing, the bad years are going to be hell." We decided on the drive home we couldn't get passionate about apples — but we were passionate about grapes and wine.'

The Neales' vineyard lies on the edge of Burke's Bank river terrace, overlooking the village of Brightwater. After planting their first vines in 1993, for several years the couple sold all their grapes, until in 1999 they launched their own wine label. The 9-hectare vineyard is planted in Sauvignon Blanc, Chardonnay, Riesling, Merlot and Pinot Noir. The wines, entirely estate-grown and produced by contract winemaker Sam Weaver, were at first not produced on-site, but in 2002 a new winery rose to handle the 2003 harvest.

Brightwater is not content to stay small. Its current output is only 3000 cases, but the Neales plan to eventually produce about 20,000 cases. The style goal is wines with 'regional character, ripe, fruit-driven and food-friendly'.

Partly oak-aged, the Chardonnay is an easy-drinking style with mouthfilling body, ripe citrus/melon characters and a slightly buttery finish. The Sauvignon Blanc — fleshy and rounded from warm seasons, in cooler years more racy — is consistently excellent, with rich melon/lime flavours. The Riesling is lemon-scented and crisp, with strong citrus/lime flavours and a sliver of sweetness. The Merlot is solid — fresh, crisp and buoyantly fruity — but Pinot Noir (now in the pipeline) will surely be the red-wine variety to match Brightwater's stylish, flavour-rich whites.

Address	Brightwater Vineyards, Main Road, Brightwater
Owners	Gary and Valley Neale
Key Wines	Sauvignon Blanc, Chardonnay, Riesling, Merlot

Greenhough

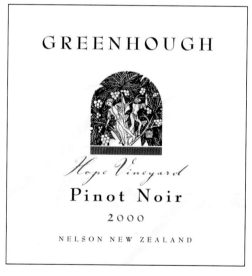

■ A star of the Nelson wine scene, Greenhough is nestled into an elevated south-east corner of the Waimea Plains, on an ancient alluvial plain known as Burke's Bank. Its voluptuous, notably savoury and complex Hope Vineyard Pinot Noir is one of the region's most memorable wines.

Andrew Greenhough and his partner, Jenny Wheeler, bought the property, then called Ranzau, in early 1991. 'We inherited 1.5 hectares of vines and a very rudimentary winery,' recalls Greenhough, who holds an MA in art history and worked at Villa Maria as a cellarhand in 1990. After changing the winery's name to Pelorus, the couple extended the vineyard and converted an adjacent packhouse into the present winery. In 1997, the company name was changed finally to Greenhough.

The 5-hectare estate vineyard is devoted principally to Pinot Noir, with smaller plots of Riesling and Chardonnay. River stones run from surface level to a depth of many metres, and the sub-soil has a high clay content. In a bid to enhance the weight and concentration of the wines, the original Pinot Noir and Riesling vines — now over 20 years old — have been converted from a double to a single fruiting wire, effectively halving their crop; plant density per hectare has risen from 1500 to 4000 vines; and a simple, vertically positioned canopy, open and well ventilated, has been adopted. Sauvignon Blanc grapes, and smaller amounts of Pinot Noir and Chardonnay, will also come on stream in 2003 from a neighbouring vineyard, leased and managed by Greenhough.

The wines are made in small volumes: 3500 cases in the 2001 vintage. Most carry a regional label, but those designated as Hope Vineyard are site-specific and 'have a more distinct stylistic influence,' says Greenhough.

The Nelson Chardonnay, partly barrel-fermented, is a sturdy, upfront style. The Hope Vineyard Chardonnay is powerful and creamy, with intense, ripe grapefruit flavours seasoned with toasty oak. The Sauvignon Blanc is richly scented, weighty, punchy and zingy; the Riesling is dry, tangy and incisively flavoured.

Based on younger vines and made with less new oak, the Nelson Pinot Noir is rich, vibrantly fruity and smooth. The flagship Hope Vineyard Pinot Noir is a strapping, bold red with a seamless array of cherryish, spicy, mushroomy flavours and commanding mouthfeel. This is Pinot Noir on a grand scale, generous, concentrated and opulent.

Address	Greenhough Vineyard and Winery, Patons Road, Hope
Owners	Andrew Greenhough and Jennifer Wheeler
Key Wines	Hope Vineyard Chardonnay, Pinot Noir; Nelson Chardonnay, Riesling, Sauvignon Blanc, Pinot Noir

Address	Kaimira Estate, 121 River Terrace Road, Brightwater
Owners	June Hamilton and Ian Miller
Key Wines	Brightwater Pinot Noir, Estate Chardonnay, Nelson Sauvignon Blanc, Nelson Chardonnay, Golden Bay Gewürztraminer

Kaimira Estate

■ After senior careers in the civil service, June Hamilton and Ian Miller hankered for a change of lifestyle. 'We had an orchard at Brightwater,' says Miller, 'and were planning to plant Gewürztraminer, as a "folly". Then we thought: Let's do wine properly.'

On the banks of the Waimea River, Kaimira (kai = food, mira = mill) takes its name from the old flour mill that is a symbol of Brightwater. The estate vineyard, first planted in stony river soils in 1996, now covers 7 hectares of Riesling, Sauvignon Blanc, Pinot Noir, Chardonnay, Pinot Gris, Gewürztraminer and Viognier. Contract growers in Nelson supply about 30 per cent of the winery's grape intake, and this is projected to rise to 70 per cent.

Kaimira Estate's first wines flowed in 1999, soon after the establishment of a large on-site winery, formerly a kiwifruit packing shed which, strengthened and lined, has the capacity to produce over 20,000 cases of wine. Jane Cooper, who has a graduate diploma in viticulture and oenology from Lincoln University and was winemaker at Seifried Estate in the early to mid-1990s, has made Kaimira Estate's wine from the start.

The Nelson Sauvignon Blanc, blended from grapes grown around the region, is an intensely varietal wine, grassy, full-flavoured and tangy. Lemon-scented, the Brightwater Riesling offers fresh, citrusy, limey flavours, with a crisp, slightly sweet finish.

Grown in the Petros Vineyard at Takaka, the Golden Bay Gewürztraminer has a perfumed bouquet of orange peel and spices and good body and flavour depth. There is also a tense, minerally, rather Chablis-like Golden Bay Chardonnay.

The Estate Chardonnay, fully barrel-fermented, is savoury, complex, smooth and rich. Top vintages of the Brightwater Pinot Noir are generous and ripe, with impressive depth of raspberry, plum, spice and smoky oak flavours.

Kaimira
E S T A T E

Brightwater Pinot Noir

2 0 0 0

Wine of New Zealand

Produced and Bottled by
Hamilton Miller Partnership
River Terrace Rd Brightwater
Nelson New Zealand

75 cl 12.5% VOL

Address	McCashin's Wines, 664 Main Road, Stoke
Owner	The McCashin family
Key Wines	Nelson Sauvignon Blanc, Waipara Riesling, Nelson Chardonnay, Nelson Merlot, Marlborough/Nelson Pinot Noir

McCashin's

■ Beer, not wine, springs to most drinkers' minds when they hear the name McCashin, but in the same year — 1999 — that Terry McCashin sold his beer brand, Mac's, he launched his first wines. 'When I started making beer in 1981,' he recalls, 'my mates were beer drinkers and they still are. But now, like me, a lot of them like wine too.'

Although based in Nelson, McCashin's is a diverse winemaking operation. The early releases, first produced from the 1998 vintage, have been based on grapes grown in Hawke's Bay, Marlborough, Nelson and Canterbury, and the wines are made at a co-operative winery in Marlborough. Craig Gass, who in the past made wine under his own Korepo (Nelson) and Conders Bend (Marlborough) labels, was appointed winemaker in 1999.

Eventually, McCashin's plans to 'bring it all back to Nelson,' says Gass. 'We think Nelson is the next emerging wine region and we aim to be a significant part of it.' As a first step, the company bought an existing 40-hectare vineyard at Hope, planted predominantly in Sauvignon Blanc, Chardonnay and Pinot Noir, with a smaller plot of Merlot. A warm, north-facing block in the hills behind Stoke will also be planted: 'It has huge potential for Pinot Noir,' believes Gass. About 10 per cent of McCashin's fruit intake is still purchased from growers.

With its output of 12,000 cases from the 2001 vintage, McCashin's has quickly shifted into a commercial gear. The Nelson Sauvignon Blanc is freshly herbaceous, with aging on yeast lees adding a touch of complexity and good mouthfeel. The Waipara Riesling is a slightly sweet style with lemon/lime flavours, strong and racy.

The Marlborough/Nelson Pinot Noir is berryish and smooth, with some spicy complexity and solid depth. Reflecting its increasing commitment to the region, the 2001 and 2002 vintages have yielded McCashin's first Nelson-grown Chardonnay and Merlot.

MᶜCASHIN'S

2000
Merlot
Hawkes Bay

Produce of New Zealand

Richmond Plains

■ The first vineyard in the South Island to produce certified organic wines, Richmond Plains is based at The Grape Escape, a vineyard café and tasting venue shared with Te Mania Estate in a 130-year-old cottage near Richmond.

David Holmes used to manage a packaging factory in Yorkshire. After arriving in Nelson with no fixed plans, he saw 'what Seifried, Neudorf and others were doing, and it all looked very viable'. His 5-hectare vineyard in McShanes Road, first planted in 1991 in free-draining, silty clay loams overlying river gravels, is devoted principally to Sauvignon Blanc, Chardonnay and Pinot Noir and has full Bio-Gro certification.

Why did Holmes take the difficult organic route? 'It never occurred to me not to,' he recalls. 'We had an organic garden in England. Other grape-growers see my vineyard and want to tear out the weeds, but the weeds are a psychological problem, not a viticultural problem.'

First produced in 1995, the wines are made by Jane Cooper at a local winery. Richmond Plains' output is small, with 3000 cases from the 2001 vintage.

Sold under the Richmond Plains and Holmes brands, the wines include a consistently attractive Richmond Plains Sauvignon Blanc that is weighty, full-flavoured, ripely herbaceous and zingy. Richmond Plains Reserve Pinot Noir is full of charm, with fresh, smooth cherry/plum flavours and some complexity. Other wines have been less distinguished.

Recent additions to the range, based on bought-in grapes, are an organically grown Holmes Marlborough Sauvignon Blanc and a non-organic, dark, impressively fragrant and concentrated Holmes Nelson Shiraz.

Address	Richmond Plains, 108 McShanes Road, Richmond
Owners	David and Heather Holmes
Key Wines	Richmond Plains Sauvignon Blanc, Chardonnay, Reserve Chardonnay, Escapade White, Pinot Noir, Reserve Pinot Noir, Escapade Red; Holmes Marlborough Sauvignon Blanc, Nelson Shiraz

Seifried

■ One of the great pioneers of South Island wine, Hermann Seifried is big, strong and doesn't waste words. He dominates the Nelson wine scene. The first to grow grapes and make wine commercially at Upper Moutere, he now owns by far the largest winery in the region.

The Seifried label early won respect when, from the first vintage, the Sylvaner 1976 won a silver medal. Austrian-born, Seifried graduated with an oenology degree from Weinsberg in Germany and made wine in Europe and South Africa before arriving in New Zealand in 1971 as winemaker for an ill-fated venture by the Apple and Pear Board into apple-wine production. He planted his first vines in 1974 and a year later his wife, Agnes, a Southlander, resigned her teaching job to join him in the wine venture. Today she oversees the company's administration, exports and public relations.

The original winery in the hills, for many years called Weingut Seifried, is now owned by Kahurangi Estate. In 1993 the Seifrieds opened a vineyard restaurant at Appleby, closer to the city, and in 1996 a handsome winery rose alongside.

Seifried's extensive vineyards are spread around Nelson. On a north-facing clay site at the foot of the Moutere hills, the 32-hectare Redwood Valley vineyard, planted in the early to mid-1980s, is devoted mainly to Gewürztraminer, Sauvignon Blanc and Riesling.

At Rabbit Island, near the winery, 55 hectares were established during the 1990s, mostly in Sauvignon Blanc and Chardonnay. Another 50-hectare vineyard is currently being planted in stony, infertile soils at Brightwater, using irrigation water from a huge dam built by Seifried. Here, the emphasis is on red-wine varieties, including Merlot, Malbec, Cabernet Sauvignon, Cabernet Franc and Syrah.

The winemaking at Seifried is handled by a team, with Hermann overseeing blending and bottling operations. The Seifrieds' son, Christopher, who trained and worked for several years as a winemaker in Australia, oversees the day-to-day running of the cellar.

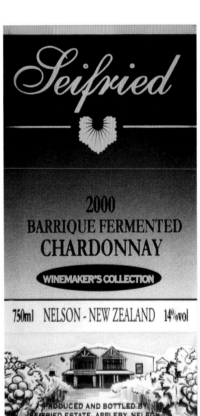

Address	Seifried Estate, Redwood Road, Appleby
Owners	Agnes and Hermann Seifried
Key Wines	Winemaker's Collection Barrel Fermented Chardonnay, Riesling, Sauvignon Blanc, Gewürztraminer Dry, Cabernet/Merlot, Pinot Noir; Nelson Chardonnay, Sauvignon Blanc, Riesling, Gewürztraminer, Cabernet/Merlot, Pinot Noir; Old Coach Road Sauvignon Blanc, Chardonnay, Unoaked Chardonnay

Seifried Estate's extensive vineyards on the Waimea Plains, near the Richmond Hills, yield fresh, crisp, citrusy Chardonnays and vibrant, briskly herbaceous Sauvignon Blancs.

Seifried built its early reputation on a selection of Rieslings and Gewürztraminers in varying styles, but lately Sauvignon Blanc and Chardonnay have also come to the fore. Does the winery specialise in any particular grapes? It has long championed Riesling. 'And we stuck with Gewürztraminer when everyone else was pulling it out,' recalls Hermann. 'Now every year we sell thousands of cases.'

The wines are typically of good quality, especially the whites, and attractively priced. The Seifried label offers the popular range of Nelson varietal wines and an up-market Winemaker's Collection. A selection of cheaper wines is sold as Old Coach Road.

The full-bodied, slightly sweet and tangy Nelson Riesling is partnered by a weighty Winemaker's Collection Riesling, which offers ripe passionfruit and lime flavours, crisp and deliciously rich. The perfumed, well-spiced Nelson Gewürztraminer is markedly sweeter than the Winemaker's Collection Gewürztraminer Dry, a powerful wine with citrus fruit, lychee and spice flavours and a lingering, rounded finish.

The briskly herbaceous Nelson Sauvignon Blanc affords a distinct style contrast with the weightier, more minerally, more tropical fruit-flavoured Winemaker's Collection Sauvignon Blanc, grown at Redwood Valley. Mouthfilling, lemony and crisp, the Nelson Chardonnay is a less complex style than the Winemaker's Collection Barrique Fermented Chardonnay, a bold style with layers of peachy, citrusy, nutty flavour and a creamy-rich finish.

Seifried's reds have rarely been exciting, tending to lack real ripeness and stuffing, but its commitment to major red-wine plantings at Brightwater suggests the best is yet to come.

Te Mania

■ When Jon Harrey came to Nelson from Wellington as a property valuer, he was gripped by the wine industry. 'I could see it was growing and it looked far more complex and rewarding than valuation. My family came from France centuries ago, so maybe there's wine in my blood.'

Harrey and his wife, Cheryl, planted their first vines at Te Mania ('the plain') in 1990. After establishing the 4-hectare Home Block in Riesling, Chardonnay and Sauvignon Blanc, in 1994 they planted the 4-hectare Bartlett Block in white and red varieties, including Pinot Noir, Merlot, Malbec and Cabernet Franc. Another 10-hectare block was purchased in 2001, to be developed as a vineyard, and some grapes are bought from growers as part of Te Mania's plan to double its output from its current level of 5000 cases. 'We need critical mass,' says Harrey. 'Jumping on planes and exhibiting overseas to build your brand is expensive. To justify the outlay, you need the volumes.'

First produced in 1995, the wines are made by Jane Cooper at a local winery. Some barrel-aging takes place at The Grape Escape, a vineyard café and cellar door facility Te Mania shares with Richmond Plains.

The wines are consistently good and the Reserve wines, made in favourable seasons, can be outstanding. Hand-picked and French oak-

Address Te Mania Estate, McShanes Road, Richmond

Owners Jon and Cheryl Harrey

Key Wines Chardonnay, Sauvignon Blanc, Pinot Noir, Three Brothers; Reserve Chardonnay, Late Harvest Botrytis Riesling

Te Mania
2001

NELSON
RIESLING

12% VOL   750ML
PRODUCE OF NEW ZEALAND

fermented, the Reserve Chardonnay is powerful and peachy-ripe, with a strong seasoning of oak, heaps of flavour and a long, silky-smooth finish. The Sauvignon Blanc is a full-bodied style with pleasing depth of melon, passionfruit and lime flavours. The Reserve Late Harvest Riesling is scented and lush, with a lovely surge of apricot, pear and honey flavours. The Pinot Noir shows strong, ripe fruit characters in a smooth, moderately complex style. Three Brothers is a dark, full-flavoured blend of Merlot, Malbec and Cabernet Franc, smooth, spicy and gamey.

Waimea Estates

■ Waimea Estates is on the move. The second largest winery in Nelson, in 2002 it produced 30,000 cases — ranking it among the country's medium-sized producers — and plans to soon reach 50,000 cases.

Trevor and Robyn Bolitho have been pip-fruit orchardists for 20 years and grape-growers since 1993. In their four vineyards at Hope, covering 48 hectares, the key varieties are Sauvignon Blanc, Pinot Noir, Riesling and Chardonnay, with smaller plots of Cabernet Sauvignon, Cabernet Franc and Merlot.

On a spectacular site high above the plains, the 1-hectare, north-facing Hill vineyard is planted exclusively in Cabernet Sauvignon. Contract growers supply about half of the fruit intake.

Pinot Noir is the big hope for the future. 'We will soon be one of the biggest, privately owned producers of Pinot Noir in the country,' says winemaker Michael Brown. 'We plan to be crushing 200 tonnes of Pinot Noir alone [equivalent to about 15,000 cases of wine].' Appointed winemaker in 2000, Brown has worked in Chile, Argentina, Spain, Gascony, California and the Hunter Valley, and in the past in New Zealand at Matua Valley, Vavasour and Corbans.

Waimea Estate launched its first wines from 1997. The wines are made on-site, in a winery adjacent to the Mediterranean-inspired cellar door and café.

The Sauvignon Blanc has a strong reputation, offering lots of fresh, crisp, grassy flavour. Both the medium-dry Nelson Riesling and sweeter Classic Riesling are floral and flavoursome, with good freshness and vivacity. The Noble Riesling, American oak-fermented, is golden, weighty, complex and oily, overflowing with apricot and honey flavours.

The Bolitho Reserve Chardonnay, fermented in French and American oak barriques (80 per cent new), is deliciously mouthfilling, lush, complex and creamy. There is also a standard Chardonnay made in a fruit-driven style with fresh, vibrant fruit characters and a subtle oak. However, the reds — Pinot Noir and Cabernet/Merlot — have yet to stand out, tending to lack warmth and depth.

Address	Waimea Estates, 22 Appleby Highway, Hope
Owners	Trevor and Robyn Bolitho
Key Wines	Bolitho Reserve Chardonnay, Chardonnay, Riesling, Classic Riesling, Sauvignon Blanc, Late Harvest Riesling, Noble Riesling, Cabernet/Merlot, Pinot Noir

Other producers

■ Alexia Wines

Jane Cooper, who acts as winemaker for several small Nelson producers, buys grapes to produce a trickle of wine under her own label, Alexia. The Sauvignon Blanc is fresh and intense, with melon and green capsicum flavours; the Riesling is finely scented, lively and long. Partly barrel-fermented, the Chardonnay is attractively balanced, with subtle oak and strong, ripe grapefruit and apple flavours.

■ Fossil Ridge

Darryl and Tranja Fry have a 3-hectare vineyard of Pinot Noir, Chardonnay and Riesling in the Richmond foothills, first planted in 1998. The wines, not made on-site and launched from the 2000 vintage, include a tight, racy Riesling with very good flavour intensity and a deliciously fresh, full-flavoured and harmonious Chardonnay.

■ Spencer Hill Estate

On coastal ridge-tops at Todds Valley, a few minutes' drive north of Nelson city, Phil Jones, proprietor of Tasman Bay Vineyards, has set out to produce 'some great wines'. In the 4.4-hectare vineyard, first planted in 1995, Pinot Noir is the major variety, with smaller areas of Chardonnay and Viognier. Jones reports the grapes ripen 'earlier than anywhere in Nelson and probably the South Island'. The first 2001 vintage yielded a trickle of Chardonnay and Pinot Noir. A winery and tasting room is planned for 2003, but Spencer Hill's production will be kept small, at around 2500 cases.

■ Woollaston Estates

Philip and Chan Woollaston produced their first wines at Wai-iti River Vineyard, near Brightwater, in 1996. In partnership with American businessman Glenn Schaeffer, the Woollastons recently planted 47 hectares of vines (principally Pinot Noir) at Upper Moutere and another 17 hectares (mostly Sauvignon Blanc) on the plains. A winery will be built at Mahana, in Upper Moutere, with an estimated output by 2008 of 30,000 cases.

Upper Moutere

From the Waimea Plains, the highway to the west climbs into the Moutere hills, past pine plantations and orchards to the tranquil village of Upper Moutere. This is fruit-growing country, but several vineyards and wineries are sprinkled across these lovely blue-green hills.

History

Hermann and Agnes Seifried planted the first vines at Weingut Seifried (now Kahurangi Estate) in 1974. Viggo du Fresne was already producing dark, gutsy hybrid reds down on the coast, at Ruby Bay, but the Seifrieds pioneered commercial winemaking in Upper Moutere. 'The experts told us you couldn't grow grapes in Nelson,' recalls Agnes. 'We were discouraged by the Department of Agriculture and Fisheries, so instead of borrowing money at 2.5 per cent to 5 per cent from the Rural Bank, we had to go elsewhere and pay 14 per cent.' Craig Gass planted his first vines at Korepo (later Ruby Bay) in 1976, followed by the Finns at Neudorf Vineyards in 1978 and Dr David Glover in 1984.

Climate

The climate for grapegrowing is similar to on the plains, but the NIWA figures suggest Upper Moutere is slightly warmer and slightly wetter.

Soils

The common 'Mapua sandy loams' have sandy topsoils, with deep clay sub-soils over strongly weathered gravels. These are low-fertility soils with good water-holding capacity; irrigation is only needed during the vines' establishment period. The top vineyards are on well-drained, north-facing slopes.

Wine styles

Neudorf Vineyards long ago proved the ability of the Upper Moutere hills to yield powerful, richly flavoured Chardonnay. In the past five years, their Pinot Noir has also been impressive — substantial and savoury. The wines grown on the hills are weightier and more 'masculine', with a firmer structure, than most of those from the plains, with impressive mouthfeel and flavour depth.

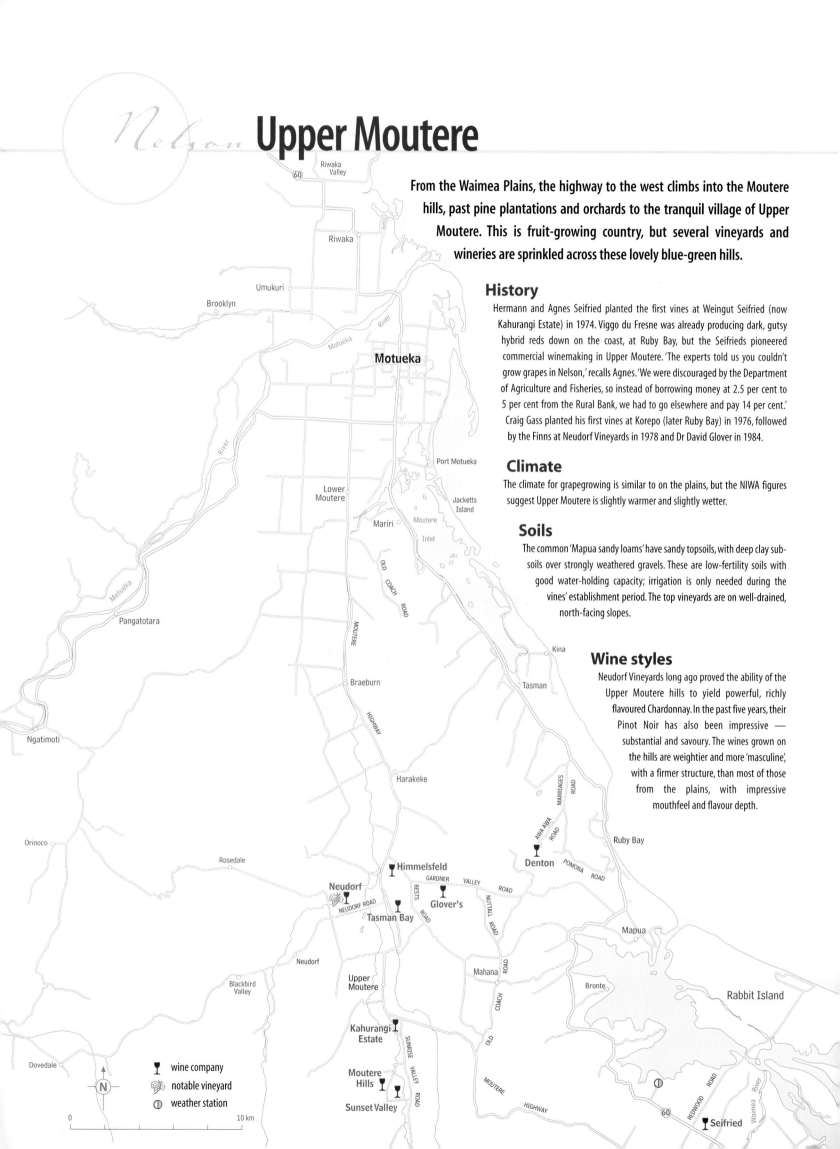

wine company

notable vineyard

weather station

0   10 km

Long renowned for its super-stylish Moutere Chardonnay, Neudorf in recent years has also coaxed exceptionally weighty and intense Pinot Noirs from the clay soils of the Upper Moutere.

Denton

■ On the seaward side of the rolling Moutere hills, Richard and Alexandra ('Alex') Denton planted their first vines in 1995. So popular is their tranquil vineyard and winery, which offers tastings in an old villa, lunch on the terrace overlooking a lake and extensive gardens and walkways, in 2001 they won a supreme tourism award for Nelson.

After taking a degree in psychology in the United Kingdom, Richard Denton ran an electronics manufacturing company; Alex studied art and designed TV props and costumes. After coming to New Zealand on holiday, they 'liked it so much we moved here'. Denton is a self-taught winemaker. 'It's a difficult way of doing things,' he admits, 'but the fastest way to learn winemaking is to get on with the job. After eight vintages, I'm beginning to get the hang of it!'

Planted on gentle, north-sloping Moutere clays, the 6-hectare vineyard is established in Chardonnay, Riesling, Sauvignon Blanc and Pinot Noir. Grapes are also purchased from growers, mostly in Nelson. The wines, first produced in 1997, are made in an old apple-packing shed, built around 1914 and now converted into a winery. Production is low, at 2000 to 3000 cases.

The flagship Reserve Pinot Noir, barrel-aged for a year, is mouthfilling and firm, gamey, earthy and savoury. The Merlot is fresh, crisp and simple, but the Syrah shows more character, with strong plum/spice flavours. Denton Folly, a blend of Merlot and Cabernet Sauvignon, is richly coloured, with very good depth of plum, spice and blackcurrant flavours.

Denton especially enjoys making red wines, but his Riesling can be impressive, with minerally, honeyed characters. The Reserve Chardonnay, fully barrel-fermented, is smooth and mouthfilling, with grapefruit-like flavours and toasty, buttery complexities.

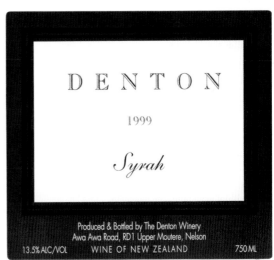

DENTON

1999

Syrah

Produced & Bottled by The Denton Winery
Awa Awa Road, RD1 Upper Moutere, Nelson
13.5% ALC/VOL   WINE OF NEW ZEALAND   750 ML

Address	Denton Winery, Awa Awa Road, Upper Moutere
Owners	Richard and Alexandra Denton
Key Wines	Reserve Chardonnay, Pinot Noir; Chardonnay, Riesling, Folly, Merlot, Syrah

Address	Glover's Vineyard, Gardner Valley Road, Upper Moutere
Owners	Dr David and Penny Glover
Key Wines	Front Block Pinot Noir, Back Block Pinot Noir, Moutere Cabernet Sauvignon, Crusader, Spring Grove Shiraz, Sauvignon Blanc, Richmond Dry Riesling, Richmond Late Harvest Riesling

Glover's

■ TANNIN reads the number-plate on Dave Glover's car. 'I could have got a number-plate reading ELEGANCE,' he says, 'but it has too many letters and in view of our pink capsules might give the wrong impression.' Glover's red wines are sturdy, full of character and renowned for their powerful tannins, which make no concessions to drink-young appeal.

Glover's Vineyard lies in pretty, undulating countryside at Upper Moutere. Glover and his wife, Penny, planted their first vines in Gardner Valley Road in 1984.

A former Wellingtonian, Dr David Glover spent 16 years in Australia, where he gained a PhD in algebra and worked in the Defence Department. After years of making his own wine at home in Canberra, he did an external course in viticulture at Charles Sturt University.

The Glovers came to Nelson for two key reasons. 'I'd always thought the Upper Moutere climate was ideal for winemaking, and after tasting Tim Finn's '82 Neudorf Cabernet Sauvignon, I knew the potential was there,' recalls Glover. 'And Nelson's a hell of a good place to live.'

On a gentle, north-facing slope, in low-fertility clays threaded with decomposing rock, the Glovers planted Pinot Noir, Cabernet Sauvignon and Sauvignon Blanc. 'It's an amazingly low-vigour site,' says Glover. 'We often don't trim the vines at all; just do some leaf-plucking.' Grapes are also bought from growers in Nelson.

Since the first 1989 vintage, the bold, tannic Pinot Noirs have attracted the most attention. 'It's not tannin I'm promoting — it's longevity,' he says. 'The tannins are there as a preservative. Their presence allows one the luxury of "oxidative" methods of winemaking, from which a great wine, in time, may evolve.' Grapes from the hotter slope behind the winery yield a bold, strong-flavoured Back Block Pinot Noir, designed for cellaring. The Front Block Pinot Noir is a slightly more floral and supple style.

The unblended Moutere Cabernet Sauvignon ('Merlot can dissipate Cabernet's structure') is a dark-hued, muscular red with concentrated, brambly flavours and a tightness of structure that *demands* time. Grown at Brightwater, Spring Grove Shiraz is a distinctly cool-climate style, fresh, crisp and pungently peppery. Glover's Moutere Sauvignon Blanc is an austere style, nettley and flinty. The Richmond Dry Riesling is fresh and zingy, with plenty of character, and the medium-sweet Richmond Late Harvest Riesling is scented, light-bodied and lemony in a rather Germanic style.

Address	Kahurangi Estate, Sunrise Road, Upper Moutere
Owners	Greg and Amanda Day
Key Wines	Chardonnay, Gewürztraminer, Riesling, Sauvignon Blanc, Pinot Noir

Kahurangi Estate

■ Kahurangi Estate is a fairly new name, but it owns the oldest Riesling vines in the South Island. They were planted in 1974 by Hermann and Agnes Seifried, who in 1998 sold their original vineyard and winery to Greg and Amanda Day.

Named after Kahurangi National Park, which overlooks the vineyard on the outskirts of Upper Moutere, Kahurangi Estate is expanding quickly. Greg Day, a former liquor industry executive, and his wife, Amanda, an interior designer, both worked at Seifried Estate before the takeover, learning the ropes of viticulture and winemaking.

Riesling is the key variety in the 10-hectare estate vineyard, planted in Moutere clays, with significant areas of Chardonnay, Pinot Noir and Sauvignon Blanc, and small plots of Gewürztraminer and Pinot Blanc. On the northern side of the village, the new, 10-hectare, Five Oaks vineyard is planted in Sauvignon Blanc, Pinot Noir, Pinot Gris, Chardonnay and Gewürztraminer. Grapes are also purchased from Nelson growers.

The 1998 to 2000 vintages were made elsewhere, but since 2001 wine is once again made on the property in the fully re-equipped winery. A New Zealander of Swiss descent, Daniel Schwarzenbach, who has worked in Alsace and Switzerland, and for three years recently at Seifried Estate, was appointed winemaker in 2001. Kahurangi Estate's current output of 6000 cases is projected to reach 15,000 cases by 2005, marketed under the Kahurangi Estate and (mainly for export) Trout Valley labels. The American oak-fermented Chardonnay is peachy and toasty, with plenty of flavour. The medium-dry Riesling also shows good intensity and the Sauvignon Blanc is freshly herbaceous, crisp and dry.

The star of the range so far is the perfumed Gewürztraminer, a medium style crammed with ripe citrus fruit, spice and ginger flavours. The early vintages of Pinot Noir have been less striking, but solid.

Moutere Hills

■ Moutere Hills doesn't make a lot of wine, and is keen to stay that way. 'We'll grow as big as we have to,' says Simon Thomas, 'but stay as small as we can.'

Ex-teachers, Simon and Alison Thomas came to New Zealand from the United Kingdom in 1992. After 'falling in love' with Nelson, in 1993 they planted their first vines in the Sunrise Valley, south of the village of Upper Moutere. The 3-hectare vineyard, established on 'good old-fashioned Moutere clay', is planted in Chardonnay, Sauvignon Blanc, Pinot Noir, Cabernet Sauvignon and Merlot. Grapes are also bought from Nelson growers. Self-taught (but with a useful background in teaching science), Simon Thomas works in a converted shearing shed, which enhances the property's rustic charm. Much of the wine is consumed in the tranquil vineyard café, which serves platters of breads, cheeses, pickles and smoked fish.

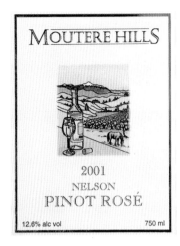

Address	Moutere Hills Vineyard, Eggers Road, Sunrise Valley, Upper Moutere
Owners	Simon and Alison Thomas
Key Wines	Chardonnay, Riesling, Sauvignon Blanc, Pinot Noir, Cabernet/Merlot

Moutere Hills' first wines flowed in 1995. 'Our main successes, at least in terms of medals, have been with Riesling and Pinot Noir,' says Thomas, 'but it has been our Sauvignon that has captured most hearts in our wine bar and local restaurants.'

The Sauvignon Blanc is an easy-drinking style, with a touch of oak seasoning its fresh, ripely herbaceous flavours and a smooth, off-dry finish. Matured in French and American oak casks, the Chardonnay is full-bodied and crisp, with some mealy complexity. The Cabernet/Merlot is a crisp, berryish middleweight, and the Pinot Noir is spicy, supple and mellow. My favourite is the Riesling. A medium style, it is fresh and lively, with firm acidity and slightly honeyed flavours of very good depth.

Neudorf

■ Neudorf is a model vineyard and winery that inspires its visitors to rush off and plant grapes. The setting is idyllic, the powerful, opulent Moutere Chardonnay has long been one of New Zealand's greatest white wines, and in recent years the Moutere Pinot Noirs have also been enthralling.

Neudorf derives its name (pronounced Noy-dorf) from the surrounding district, settled by Germans in the mid-nineteenth century. Tim Finn, the founder, who was raised in Wellington, is an MSc graduate and a former dairying advisory officer with the Ministry of Agriculture and Fisheries. His wife, Judy, a former rural reporter for radio, is deeply involved in the company's sales and administration.

For their second vintage in 1982, Tim Finn built a handsome macrocarpa winery, pitching its roof high to accommodate his fermentation and storage tanks inside. 'In the beginning, people thought we weren't so serious, planting in Nelson rather than Marlborough,' recalls Finn. 'We got 18 tonnes of grapes in our first year; the third year we got 12 tonnes. Our budget didn't go that way at all. We had to buy in grapes and borrow off Judy's mum.'

Address	Neudorf Vineyards, Neudorf Road, Upper Moutere
Owners	Tim and Judy Finn
Key Wines	Moutere Chardonnay, Riesling, Pinot Gris, Pinot Noir, Pinot Noir Home Vineyard; Nelson Sauvignon Blanc, Chardonnay, Pinot Noir

Today, Neudorf ranks among New Zealand's leading small wineries. If you ask Finn for the key reasons behind the consistently outstanding quality of his wines, the soil is the first thing he points to. 'I like heavier soils. Light soils give lightness and clays give depth of flavour; I don't know why it is. I base that observation on Chardonnay — mine has more depth than Marlborough's, yet the two regions' climates are pretty similar.'

The non-irrigated estate vineyard is planted on Moutere clays, threaded with layers of gravel. Having experimented with numerous varieties, the Finns are now concentrating on Pinot Noir and Chardonnay (especially), with smaller plots of Riesling and Pinot Gris. The company now owns or has long-term leases on 13 hectares of vines at Upper Moutere, and a further 7 hectares at Brightwater on the plains (a major source of its Sauvignon Blanc production). Grapes are also bought from Nelson growers, including Sauvignon Blanc from further north, at Motueka.

Long thought of as a 'boutique' winery, Neudorf is now expanding fast. In 2001, it produced 8500 cases, but within a few years it expects to reach 15,000 cases.

The famous Moutere Chardonnay is a magnificently rich and multi-faceted wine with tight, savoury, searching flavours, needing about four years to unveil its full glory. 'Fruit ripeness is the key ingredient,' says Tim Finn. 'To build up fruit intensity and get fullness of flavour through the mid and back-palate, you must be willing to walk a knife-edge towards the end of harvest, even if there's a bit of botrytis around. The length of flavour is also enhanced by a lower crop level.' Once the grapes are in the winery, it's a matter of style. 'I like to layer the fruit with sophisticated oak and lees characters, but they don't swamp the wine,' says Finn. It is fermented with indigenous yeasts and lees-aged for a year in French oak barriques, typically half new.

The Moutere Riesling — partly fermented in old oak barriques 'to enhance texture and mouthfeel' and varying

With its often brilliant wines, white and red, Neudorf has built a reputation second-to-none among the Nelson wineries.

in style from dry to medium-sweet — is also strikingly intense, with pure, limey, minerally flavours. The Nelson Sauvignon Blanc is fresh and zippy, with concentrated tropical/lime flavours, and the Moutere Pinot Gris is fleshy, with rich citrus and stone-fruit flavours and a smooth, slightly sweet finish.

Neudorf's Moutere Pinot Noirs were long overshadowed by the Chardonnay, but in 1997, when new clones came on stream, their quality rose sharply. 'We start off with low-producing, ripe, concentrated fruit,' says Finn. 'Then it's an extraction process. We're looking for more than cherry-like, sweet fruit characters — we want density of fruit and a fine tannin structure running through the wine.' Both the Moutere and Moutere Home Vineyard Pinot Noirs are substantial, softly textured wines, savoury, mushroomy and spicy, with strong personality and great harmony.

Looking back over 22 vintages, Tim Finn is 'happy with progress. I've got a feeling for the site and what it does and how to handle its fruit — it's taken 20 years. I'm more in charge of the viticulture and winemaking, although nature can still hit me for a six!'

Tasman Bay

■ When American Phil Jones came to New Zealand to make wine, he hit the ground running. His first 1994 Chardonnays under the Tasman Bay label instantly attracted attention and gold medal success followed swiftly.

Jones came to the Upper Moutere hills to make great wine. 'The Moutere is a difficult place to grow grapes, especially on the hillsides,' he says. 'The clay is tough and so are the hills. The slowness of the vines' growth is tough. But all over the world, many of the greatest vineyards are on the hills.'

Tasman Bay Vineyards lies in Best Road, off Gardner Valley Road, between Neudorf and Glover's. Jones and his wife, Sheryl, planted their first vines there in 1990, originally calling the winery Spencer Hill, after their first son, Spencer. However, the name (and brand) Spencer Hill were recently transferred to the Jones' new vineyard on the coast north of Nelson city (see page 197).

Address	Tasman Bay Vineyards, Best Road, Upper Moutere
Owners	Philip and Sheryl Jones
Key Wines	Nelson Sauvignon Blanc, Pinot Gris, Pinot Noir; Marlborough Chardonnay, Pinot Gris

Phil Jones studied winemaking at university but then got 'sidetracked' for 18 years before he fulfilled his dream of establishing a winery. Born in London and raised in California, he took degrees in viticulture and pest management 'and did all the winemaking courses at Fresno State University'. The sidetrack came after he started a research station and analytical laboratory that grew to employ 90 people. 'I started coming to New Zealand in 1985 to get away,' he recalls, 'and really liked it. So I decided I'd come to live in New Zealand and plant a vineyard.'

The company's two vineyards at Upper Moutere are planted mainly in Chardonnay, Sauvignon Blanc and Pinot Noir, with smaller plots of Pinot Gris and Viognier. Peter Rose's vineyard in Marlborough is also a key source of grapes.

About 18,000 cases of wine are made in the completely self-sufficient winery, where Jones shares the winemaker's role with Mathew Rutherford, who arrived at Tasman Bay in 1990. Sheryl Jones is involved in the company's marketing.

For several years, the wines were marketed under two brands, with Tasman Bay employed for the most commercial wines, and Spencer Hill reserved for a more vineyard-designated, more oak-influenced range for longer aging. Following the transfer of the Spencer Hill name and brand to the new venture at Todds Valley, the wines are all labelled as Tasman Bay.

The multiple medal-winning Marlborough Chardonnay is deliciously rich and creamy-smooth. It is fermented 'on' rather than 'in' oak — instead of handling his wine in barrels, Jones ferments it in stainless-steel tanks, with French and American oak staves immersed in the wine. The result is a moderately priced wine that typically peaks within two or three years, and can be irresistible at 12 to 18 months.

The Nelson Sauvignon Blanc, partly oak-aged, is a fruit-driven style, fresh and punchy, with a touch of oak and lees-aging complexity. The Nelson Pinot Gris is strongly varietal, with an oily texture and very good depth of lemon, apple and spice flavours. There is also a charming, strawberry and plum-flavoured Nelson Pinot Noir, not concentrated or complex but vibrantly fruity and supple.

Other producers

■ Himmelsfeld

'My dream was to have a small vineyard,' says Elizabeth ('Beth') Eggers, a descendant of German immigrants who arrived in Nelson in 1859. First planted in 1991 on a north-west facing clay hill-top in Gardner Valley Road, Upper Moutere, her Himmelsfeld ('heaven's field') vineyard has 2 hectares of Sauvignon Blanc, Chardonnay and Cabernet Sauvignon. The wines, made by Daniel Schwarzenbach at Kahurangi Estate, include a peachy, creamy-smooth Chardonnay, a fresh, punchy, crisply herbaceous Sauvignon Blanc, and a firm, well-concentrated Cabernet Sauvignon.

■ Sunset Valley Vineyard

Organic wines accorded full Bio-Gro status flow from this vineyard and winery in Eggers Road, Upper Moutere. Ian Newton, who has a postgraduate diploma in viticulture and oenology from Lincoln University, and his partner, Ros Squire, produced their first wine in 1998. Their vineyard, first planted in 1994, has 3 hectares of Pinot Noir, Cabernet Sauvignon, Sauvignon Blanc and Chardonnay. The Sauvignon Blanc is crisp and lively, with solid depth; the Cabernet Sauvignon sturdy, with good depth of blackcurrant and green leaf flavours; and the Pinot Noir vibrantly fruity and supple.

■ Waiwera Estate

Not at Upper Moutere but north-west, at Takaka, Dave Heraud has a tiny vineyard on limestone outcrops overlooking Golden Bay. First produced in 1991, his Pinot Noir is ruby-hued and floral, with sweet, ripe cherry/plum flavours in a moderately complex style, fresh, smooth and mouthfilling.

Marlborough

Greville Harbour
Ragged Point
D'URVILLE ISLAND
Trio Island

D'Urville Peninsula

Paddock Rocks
French Pass (Anaru)
Chetwode Island

Sauvage Point
Bulwer
MARLBOROUGH SOUNDS
MARITIME PARK

Admiralty Bay
Forsyth Island
Forsythe Bay
Alligator Head
Cape Lambert
Cape Jackson

Cape Soucis
Maud Is Tawhitinui
Reach
Guards Bay
Titirangi Bay
Port Gore

Croisilles Harbour
Elaine Bay
Beatrix Bay
Anakoha Bay
Endeavour Inlet
Motuara Island
Cape Koamaru

Whangamoa Head
Okiwi Bay
MARLBOROUGH SOUNDS
Crail Bay
Manaroa
Kenepuru Head
Ship Cove
Long Island

Pepin Island
Delaware Bay
Tennyson Inlet
Pelorus
Sound
Crail Bay
Waitaria Bay
Blumine Island

Hira
Whangamoa
Nopera
Saint Omer
Sound
Portage
Queen Charlotte Sound
Arapawa Island
Perano Head

Rai Valley
Carluke
Kenepuru
Te Mahia
Tory Channel
Cook Strait Ferry

BRYANT RANGE
Rai River
Anakiwa
Curious Cove
Port Underwood
Rununder Point

Moenui
The Grove
Waikawa

Havelock
Linkwater
Picton
Robertson Point

RICHMOND RANGE
Pelorus River
Canvastown
Pelorus Bridge
Wakamarina River
Kaituna River
1
Mount Pleasant
Koromiko

Mt Richmond •1756m
Okaramio
Para

Onamalutu
6
Kaituna
Rarangi
CLOUDY BAY

Te Rou
Rapaura
Spring Creek
Tuamarina
Marshlands
Wairau Pa

WAIRAU VALLEY
Renwick
Woodbourne
Grovetown
Wairau Bar
Wairau River

63
BLENHEIM
Riverlands
Fairhall
Big Lagoon
White Bluffs

Wairau Valley
1
Awatere River

Hillersden
Tyntesfield
Omaka Downs
WITHER HILLS

Craiglochart
Dashwood
CLIFFORD BAY

Summerlands
Avondale
Rossmore
AWATERE VALLEY
Seddon
Blind River

Netherwood
Lake Grassmere
Lake Grassmere
Cape Campbell

Marathon Downs
Hauwai

Malvern Hills
Richmond Brook
Altimarloch

Spray River
Jordan
Welds Hill
Ward

Awapiri
Medway River
Flaxbourne River

Camden
INLAND KAIKOURA RANGE
Mirza

Gladstone
Awatere River
Te Rapa

N
weather station
main vineyard plantings

0   10   20 km

Sheer youthfulness is the striking feature of the Marlborough wine scene. In geological terms, the Wairau Plains is a very young landform — most of the soils were laid down within the last 14,000 years — and since Montana harvested its first grapes in 1976, just 27 vintages have passed. Yet with Sauvignon Blanc, one of the world's few classic grape varieties, Marlborough has wrested the crown from French hands.

With 5488 hectares of bearing vines in 2002 and a further 1374 hectares yet to yield their first crop, Marlborough is by far the country's most extensively planted wine region. Its wine trail features some of the great names of New Zealand wine — Montana, Cloudy Bay, Hunter's — and Marlborough enjoys a far higher international profile than any other New Zealand wine region. Hugh Johnson, the great British wine writer, has summed up Marlborough's key claim to fame: 'No region on earth can match the pungency of its best Sauvignon Blanc.'

Marlborough, the north-eastern edge of the South Island, contains the inland Kaikoura Ranges, which reach an elevation approaching 3000 metres. Rugged mountains and snow-fed rivers make up the great expanse of Marlborough, with farms and pine forests extending far up the valleys, deep into the high country. The Wairau River, draining the ranges of silt and gravel, descends from the back country to the Wairau Plains, where Montana and a host of others have planted the majority of their vines. The original grape plantings were on the southern fringes of the Wairau Plains, but vines have since spread across the river flats of the Rapaura district, west to the Waihopai and upper Wairau valleys, east to the lower Wairau and further south into the Awatere Valley.

Prior to human settlement, the Wairau Plains were a vast swampland, periodically inundated by floodwaters from the Wairau River and its tributaries and covered in flax, raupo, toetoe and cabbage trees. Maori were attracted by the eels and birds of the lagoons; by the plentiful sunshine for cultivating kumara; and by the area's closeness to the fisheries and forests of the Marlborough Sounds.

During the nineteenth century, to create dry land for settlement the swamps were drained and the rivers were stopbanked, channelled and diverted. In 1848 E.D. Sweet was the first European to settle with his family in the Wairau Valley, and by 1855 the town of Blenheim (then known as 'the Beaver', because it was originally built on stilts), was starting to take shape. Sheep early inhabited the Wairau Plains and later mixed farming also gained a stronghold. A host of other crops, including apples, olives and cherries, have more recently flourished. And marching across the pebbly, pancake-flat plains are endless rows of vines. A 1997 study of the economic impact of the Marlborough wine industry found that each year 260,000 people visited the wineries and that the industry generated direct sales of $130 million.

A major problem surfaced in 1984, when phylloxera was discovered in Marlborough. The root-sucking aphid ravaged many of the region's vineyards during the mid to late 1980s, slashing their yields, because the majority of the vines were not grafted onto phylloxera-resistant rootstock. Today, 96 per cent of Marlborough's vines are grafted (above the national average of 87 per cent).

In the past, much of the grape crop was trucked out of the region for processing in the North Island, but three of New Zealand's biggest companies — Villa Maria, Nobilo and Delegat's — have recently built or acquired wineries within Marlborough. Four other, mostly middle-sized, producers — Babich, Shingle Peak (Matua Valley), Nautilus Estate and Goldwater Estate — own Rapaura Vintners, which not only processes their own Marlborough grapes but provides contract winemaking services to several clients. In 2002, Rapaura Vintners expanded significantly by buying the former Corbans winery in Marlborough.

History

The first vine in the modern era of Marlborough wine was planted by Montana on 24 August 1973. Watched by a sceptical group of industry leaders flown south for the occasion, Frank Yukich, the driving force behind Montana's relentless rise, and company chairman Sir David Beattie dropped a silver coin — the traditional token of good fortune — into the hole, and with a sprinkling of sparkling wine dedicated the historic vine. Three years later, the first crops of Marlborough Müller-Thurgau and Cabernet Sauvignon were shipped across Cook Strait and trucked through the night by Mate Yukich, Frank's brother, to Montana's winery at Gisborne.

Montana triggered the modern era of Marlborough viticulture. The region's first wines, however, had

Principal grape varieties

	Producing area 2002	% total producing area 2002
Sauvignon Blanc	2790 ha	51.2%
Chardonnay	1035 ha	19.0%
Pinot Noir	840 ha	15.4%
Riesling	297 ha	5.5%
Merlot	109 ha	2.0%
Sémillon	92 ha	1.7%
Cabernet Sauvignon	76 ha	1.4%
Pinot Gris	73 ha	1.3%

Vintage chart (1993–2002)

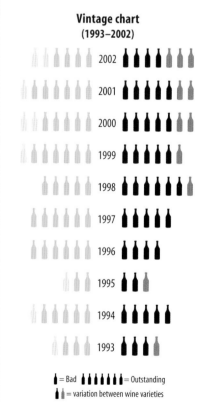

Summary of climate statistics

Meteorological station	Latitude	Height	GDD	MTWM	Rainfall, Oct–Apr	Air frost days (annual)
Blenheim Airport	41.31'S	31 m	1127	17.8°C	398 mm	38
Wither Hills	41.33'S	32 m	1218	18.2°C	357 mm	23

Height — above sea level **GDD** — growing degree days, Oct–Apr, above 10°C **MTWM** — mean temperature, warmest month

Previous page: Bordered by the Wither Hills, Montana's endless rows of Sauvignon Blanc vines on the south side of the Wairau Valley create one of the most memorable images of New Zealand wine.

Mechanical harvesters collect the majority of the Marlborough grape crop, but hand-pickers survive in the most quality-oriented vineyards.

flowed almost a century earlier. David Herd's Auntsfield vineyard, in the hills to the south of Fairhall and Brancott, produced its first commercial harvest around 1875. Auntsfield's sweet red wine was made from red Muscatel grapes. Only about 800 litres were produced each vintage, but the trickle of Auntsfield wine survived Herd's death in 1905; his son-in-law Bill Paynter carried on the family tradition until 1931.

At Mount Pleasant Wine Vaults, just south of Picton, in 1880 George Freeth started making wine from a wide array of fruits, including grapes. No surge of vine plantings in Marlborough followed the 1895 publication of Romeo Bragato's 'Report on the Prospects of Viticulture in New Zealand' — he was more impressed with Nelson's potential and made no mention of Marlborough — but in the first half of this century, in the heart of Blenheim, Harry Patchett and Mansoor Peters grew grapes and sold a trickle of wine. Patchett lived until 1974, just long enough to witness the Montana-led revival of Marlborough wine.

From the start, Montana established a commanding presence (although many of its first vines died, due to a mistaken belief that irrigation was not needed), and its pioneering move into Marlborough is discussed under the Montana entry, pages 100–7. 'Nothing more vividly recalls the sudden realisation of what wine could do for Marlborough,' Terry Dunleavy, Montana's sales manager in the early 1970s, has written, 'than the stunned reaction of Lucas Bros. when faced with a [Montana] order for 26 tractors.'

Despite initial opposition to the spread of viticulture by farmers worried about restrictions on their use of hormone weed sprays, in 1979 the Marlborough County Council relaxed its planning laws, making grapegrowing a 'predominant' rather than 'conditional' land use south of the Wairau River.

Having decided that Montana's bold move into Marlborough had been successful, others in the industry started to follow. The first contract growers' vineyards to supply Penfolds (NZ) were planted in 1979, and Corbans began its vineyard development in the region in 1980. Unlike Montana, which had established its vineyards on the southern margins of the plains, where the less gravelly soil was thought likely to be kinder to machinery, Corbans planted its vineyards in the stony Rapaura district.

On a much smaller scale, in 1979 Allen and Joyce Hogan established the region's first boutique vineyard and winery, Te Whare Ra, at Renwick. Ernie Hunter also planted a contract grower's vineyard in 1979, and three years later startled observers by winning six medals at the National Wine Competition with his first six wines. Determined to make fine-quality sparkling wine, Daniel Le Brun (promptly dubbed 'the mad Frenchman' by locals) and his wife, Adele, planted their first vines near Renwick in 1980.

Marlborough emerged relatively unscathed from the glut-induced vinepull scheme of 1985–86, losing only about 10 per cent of its vines. And since 1985, when Australian capital financed the erection of Cloudy Bay's handsome concrete winery in the heart of the Wairau Valley, overseas investment has streamed into the Marlborough wine scene. French, German and Swiss-owned vineyards and wineries (such as Domaine Georges Michel, Johanneshof Cellars and the Fromm Winery) are scattered across the region and the major overseas companies BRL Hardy (owner of the Nobilo Wine Group), Veuve Clicquot Ponsardin (owner of Cloudy Bay), and S. Smith & Son (owner of the Yalumba winery in the Barossa Valley and Nautilus Estate) are also present. One of the top Sancerre producers, Henri Bourgeois is currently establishing a vineyard and winery in Marlborough. Allied Domecq (via Montana) and Beringer Blass (the division of Foster's which is buying Matua Valley and its Shingle Peak interests in Marlborough) are also deeply involved.

As Peter Perry and Brendon Norrie have pointed out, Marlborough's wine success cannot be explained solely in economic or environmental terms. 'There were elements of good luck — no one could know how well Sauvignon Blanc would perform — [and] there were mundane elements such as land prices . . .'

Climate and soil, foresight and daring, investment and innovation, land prices and luck — all have contributed to the emergence of Marlborough as one of the world's most distinctive and exciting new wine regions.

Climate

At the end of a typically hot and sun-baked day a few years ago, I dined at a friend's house in the Awatere Valley. It was the last day of January. Around midnight, I stepped out into the darkness — and an important lesson on Marlborough's grapegrowing climate. On this perfect mid-summer night, it was freezing.

Isolated by high mountain ranges, Marlborough has one of New Zealand's sunniest and driest climates. The Marlborough Sounds provide some protection from north-westerly gales, the Kaikoura Ranges block cold southerlies and the North Island shelters the region from north-easterly storms. The cities of Blenheim and Nelson are long-term rivals for the title of New Zealand's sunshine capital.

Marlborough's sunny but not excessively hot climate gives the grapes a long, slow period of ripening. The average daily maximum temperature during summer is nearly 24°C, but clear, cold nights keep acid levels high in the grapes, even when their sugars are rising swiftly. The region's marked diurnal variations of temperature (at least 10°C, on most days) are a crucial climatic influence, retaining the grapes' fresh, vibrant fruit characters, promoting the retention of crisp, herbaceous characters in Sauvignon Blanc and enhancing colour development in the skins of Pinot Noir.

During summer, easterly sea breezes frequently cool the vineyards from mid-morning until early evening. The prevailing north-westerly winds bring much of the region's rain, but Marlborough is also regularly swept by hot, dry nor'westers, which by putting extreme transpiration demands on the vines force them to shut down, stopping their photosynthesis and fruit-ripening. So much water is lost by the region's land and plants under extreme north-westerly conditions, most vineyard owners install a trickle irrigation system.

Due to Marlborough's location east of the Main Divide, the vines are cultivated in a significant rain shadow area. Summer droughts are common and in autumn the pre-harvest weather is more reliably dry than in most North Island regions. Humidity levels, slightly lower at Blenheim than at Auckland or Christchurch, are highest near the coast. Botrytis bunch rot poses a challenge in rainy seasons, but is generally less of a threat than in the wetter regions of the north.

Frosts are a danger, having been recorded at Blenheim as early as 28 March and as late as 1 November. In November 2000, some vineyards in low-lying areas of the Fairhall and Waihopai valleys lost all their crop. A heavy frost in the autumn of 1990 turned the Wairau Valley black overnight, cutting the ripening season short by three weeks. The frost risk is highest away from the river, on the south side of the Wairau Valley.

Soils

During the past two million years, glaciers in the high country eroded masses of rock debris, later carried down to the coast by melt-water rivers. As the Wairau River snaked from north to south across the Wairau Valley and its developing plain, the finer particles were separated from the deposits, leaving strips of gravel in the old river channels.

Along Rapaura Road, shallow, stony 'Rapaura Series' soils of low to moderate fertility exist side by side with deep, sandy loams ('Wairau Series') possessing far greater water-holding capacity. In the middle of the Wairau Valley are substantial areas of shallow, stony 'Awatere Series' soils, and the south side has extensive areas of deep 'Wairau Series, Mottled Phase' soils, including sandy loams and silt loams over very stony layers. In the Awatere Valley, the most common soils are 'Dashwood gravelly silt loams' and deep, free-draining 'Seddon silt loams'.

Not all the soil types suit viticulture. Large areas of deep silt loams are very fertile, with a high water-storage capacity. The preferred sites are of lower fertility, with a noticeably stony, sandy loam topsoil overlying deep layers of free-draining shingle with sand infilling. These shallow, stony soils reduce the vines' vigour by improving drainage and reducing the soil's fertility.

Wine styles

Marlborough's keynote wine is its famous Sauvignon Blanc, which simply explodes with ripely herbaceous aromas and flavours, garden-fresh and zingy. For sheer leap-out-of-the-glass intensity, very few wines, from anywhere, can match it.

That Sauvignon Blanc thrives in Marlborough's coolness was demonstrated 20 years ago by Montana. Riesling has been another long-term success — scented, crisp and lively, with clearcut varietal characters. The Chardonnays are slightly leaner than the finest North Island wines, but show good freshness, vigour and acid spine.

James Healy, a senior oenologist at Cloudy Bay, believes that Marlborough is ideal for 'any variety where fruit intensity is a key part of its makeup, such as Sauvignon Blanc, Gewürztraminer and Pinot Noir. However, it is less suitable for grapes such as Chardonnay, Pinot Gris, Cabernet Sauvignon and Merlot, where texture or tannin ripeness are really important.'

Most of New Zealand's top bottle-fermented sparkling wines and botrytised sweet Rieslings flow from the region. The climate is too cool to consistently ripen Cabernet Sauvignon and the Merlots are often green-edged, but there is much excitement about Pinot Noir. The early signs are that Pinot Noir grown on shingly sites is concentrated and tannic, contrasting with a more floral and supple style from soils with a higher clay content.

Sub-regions

Most of Marlborough's wine flows from the Wairau Valley, where Montana began planting in 1973. Thirteen years later, viticulture spread south-east into the smaller, slightly cooler Awatere Valley. Recently, as the supply of available land has dried up between Blenheim and Renwick, there has been significant expansion in the upper reaches of the Wairau Valley and its southern side valleys: Fairhall, Hawkesbury and Waihopai.

The Marlborough scene was for many years dominated by white-wine production, but there is now rising excitement about Pinot Noir.

Wairau Valley

During her childhood, Catherine Scott, co-founder of the Allan Scott winery, would ride across the Wairau Valley with her friends on horses. 'But we never rode around the Rapaura area,' she recalls. 'It was too stony. The horses would be lame.'

The lower Wairau Valley, where most of Marlborough's vines are concentrated, is not a large winegrowing district, but its soils and climate are far from uniform. From the towering Richmond Range on its northern flanks to the Wither Hills in the south is only 10 kilometres, but as winemaker John Forrest puts it: 'The Wairau is not just one homogeneous vineyard. It's a diverse river valley with changes in altitude, temperature gradients, differing rainfalls and a myriad of soil types.' From its headwaters in the Spencer Mountains, the Wairau River flows north then east on its 170-kilometre journey to the sea at Cloudy Bay. The steep, greywacke hills of the back country subside along the valley to more rounded foothills, formed from easily eroded conglomerates with a mantle of loess.

To the south of the plains lie the southern valleys: the Fairhall, Hawkesbury and Waihopai. Compared to the north side of the valley, grapes ripen later in the drier, cooler Fairhall Valley (which winemakers often refer to as the Brancott Valley). The smaller Hawkesbury Valley (sometimes called the Omaka Valley) is similar, but more frost-prone. In the Waihopai Valley, the lower reaches have attracted a flurry of vine planting recently, despite the higher risk of frost than on the plains and — due to the lack of an aquifer — a chronic shortage of water. Vineyards have recently extended into the Kaituna area, on the northern banks of the Wairau River, and there is significant expansion in the very free-draining, 'pea-gravel' soils of Rarangi and Marshlands, near the coast.

History

When Montana planted its first vines in the Wairau Valley on 24 August 1973, it launched the modern era of Marlborough wine, although the first wine was made in the Wairau Valley as early as the 1870s. Marlborough wine stayed of exclusively Wairau Valley origin until 1989, when Vavasour launched its first wine from the Awatere Valley, and today the Wairau Valley still dominates plantings.

Climate

Meso (local) climates commonly identified in the Wairau Valley include a seaward climate with lower peak temperatures in summer; a relatively warm, early-ripening zone around Rapaura; and a cooler inland climate, more subject to frosts. The viticultural climate on the north side of the valley is moderated by the Wairau River, but cold air descends from the mountains into the southern valleys, giving a cooler, later-ripening climate. There is also a rainfall gradient across the plains: during the period January 1999 to April 2000, rainfall near the Wairau River was more than 45 per cent higher than in the Fairhall Valley to the south.

Soils

The Wairau Plains, from Blenheim to Renwick, were formed by greywacke-derived deposits from the last glaciation and post-glacial periods, laid down by the Wairau River and its tributaries. Young soils, they are a mixture of deep, fine alluvium and gravels, overlying an extensive aquifer from which irrigation water is drawn. The soils on the north side of the Wairau Valley are generally the most gravelly. The soils of the southern valleys and inland from Renwick — less extensively reworked by the river system — have higher levels of clay and silt. However, extensive braiding of the soils in an east-west direction (at right angles to the north-south orientation of the vine rows) can cause marked variation in vine vigour and grape ripening patterns within individual vineyards and even single rows.

Wine styles

Marlborough winemakers are exploiting the variations of soil and climate within the valley to produce different wine styles. For instance, to make a strongly herbaceous style of Sauvignon Blanc, you choose a site with medium-high fertility and relatively heavy, more water-retentive soils. For a lusher, riper Sauvignon Blanc, you choose a dry, stony site that matures its fruit earlier. Stonier soils often produce the most aromatic wines, but those cultivated in soils with a higher clay content can show better weight and texture.

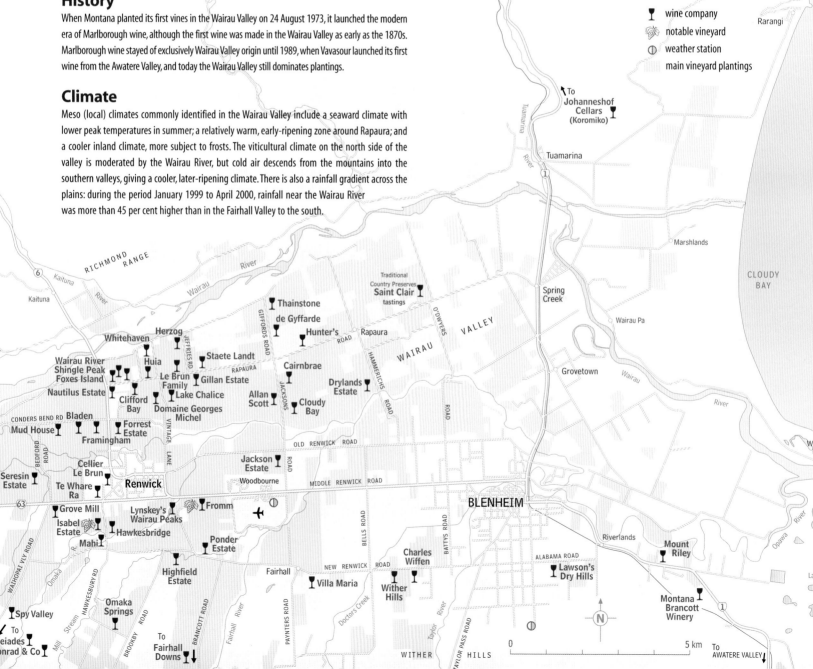

Allan Scott

■ For Allan and Catherine Scott, establishing their vineyards and winery has been 'a fun achievement. But to have our children share that passion has been the highlight.'

Allan Scott, formerly Corbans' national vineyards manager, launched his own label in 1990. After years of growing grapes for Montana and Corbans, and 'wheeling and dealing in land and having faith in the district's wine future', the Scotts now own extensive vineyards in the famously stony Jacksons Road area. Their atmospheric rammed-earth winery was built in early 1992, near Cloudy Bay, with full on-site processing since 1996. Chardonnay, Riesling and — inevitably — Sauvignon Blanc are the mainstays of the Scotts' range.

Allan Scott was a key figure in the development of Marlborough's vineyards. He was born on a North Canterbury farm; Catherine is from Blenheim. When Montana arrived in Marlborough in 1973, Scott got a job as a vineyard labourer, tearing down fences and planting vines. Within a month he was appointed vineyard foreman, and later supervisor of Montana's Fairhall vineyard. Scott switched horses in 1980, joining Corbans to oversee the establishment of their Marlborough vineyards — notably Stoneleigh. After resigning from Corbans in 1989 he set up as a viticultural consultant, but was soon absorbed in developing the Allan Scott range of wines.

In mid-1993, the Scotts sold their vineyards, cellar and restaurant to Appellation Vineyards, in return for a share of Appellation. However, a year later they withdrew from Appellation and regained direct control of the business they founded.

The Scotts' 63 hectares of vineyards encircle the winery on both sides of Jacksons Road and also extend to the south side of the valley. Sauvignon Blanc is the key variety, with substantial plantings of Riesling, Chardonnay and Pinot Noir, and smaller plots of Merlot, Sémillon, Pinot Gris and Gewürztraminer. Contract growers in the region provide about half the winery's grape intake.

Winemaker Graeme Bradshaw, who arrived in 2001, has a postgraduate diploma in viticulture and oenology from Lincoln University and previously worked vintages in New Zealand, Italy and France. Allan and Catherine's son, Joshua, is the junior winemaker, while their daughter, Victoria (and her husband, Daniel) run the winery's popular restaurant, Twelve Trees.

With its annual output of 50,000 cases, Allan Scott is a medium-sized winery. The Sauvignon Blanc offers fresh melon and capsicum-like flavours, in top vintages punchy and zingy. The Chardonnay, French oak-fermented, has lately been classy and harmonious, with subtle wood handling and strong citrus and melon fruit flavours shining through. The star of the range, the strapping Prestige Chardonnay is peachy, figgy and nutty, with outstanding depth, complexity and power.

The Riesling is fresh, with lemon/lime flavours and a crisp, slightly sweet finish. The late-harvested Autumn Riesling is perfumed, citrusy and honeyed, with abundant sweetness cut with fresh acidity.

The non-vintage Méthode Traditionnelle is a crisp, lively and biscuity Blanc de Blancs, based wholly on Chardonnay. The Pinot Noir is floral, berryish and smooth, although not highly complex. The 2001 and 2002 vintages have also yielded a Pinot Gris, Gewürztraminer and Merlot.

Address   Allan Scott Wines and Estates, Jacksons Road, Blenheim

Owners   Allan and Catherine Scott

Key Wines   Marlborough Sauvignon Blanc, Riesling, Chardonnay, Autumn Riesling, Pinot Noir, Méthode Traditionnelle; Prestige Chardonnay

With its lavender garden and adjacent working winery encircled by vines, the restaurant at Allan Scott is one of the region's busiest, serving creamy Marlborough seafood chowder and manuka-roasted cold smoked salmon.

Address Cairnbrae Wines,
Jacksons Road,
Blenheim

Owner Sacred Hill Wines

Key Wines The Stones Sauvignon
Blanc, Old River Riesling,
Clansman Chardonnay,
Pinot Gris, Noble Riesling,
Pinot Noir

Cairnbrae

■ In a rare investment by a Hawke's Bay-based wine company in the region, in 2001 Sacred Hill purchased Cairnbrae's vineyards, cellar door operation, restaurant, stocks and brand. The wines, principally white, are pure Marlborough — fresh, mouth-wateringly crisp and awash with flavour.

Founders Murray and Daphne Brown produced the first Cairnbrae wines in 1992, 12 years after they began planting vines in Jacksons Road. 'After farming in Southland, we came to Marlborough in 1979, looking for a stock property,' recalled Daphne. 'After working for a friend who was developing a vineyard, we decided grapes were a better idea. When Corbans came to Marlborough in 1980, we were the first growers to sign up.' Cairnbrae (meaning 'pile of stones on a hillside') was chosen as the winery name because of the stony ridges that run through the vineyard, traditionally one of the earliest-ripening in the region. Today the 18-hectare vineyard surrounding the winery (with Cloudy Bay just over the fence) is planted mainly in Sauvignon Blanc, with smaller plantings of Riesling, Pinot Gris and Pinot Noir. About 7000 cases of wine have been made each year at a joint-venture winery, Marlborough Valley Cellars, partly owned by the Browns.

Sacred Hill, a much larger Hawke's Bay winery, was attracted to the Cairnbrae acquisition as 'a strategic move to enhance the company's portfolio and ensure a supply of quality Marlborough wines for export growth', especially Sauvignon Blanc and Pinot Noir. The Browns are focusing on the same varieties under their new Cape Campbell label, primarily for export.

Now made by Tony Bish, of Sacred Hill, Cairnbrae wines are based on estate-grown grapes and fruit purchased from local growers. The Stones Marlborough Sauvignon Blanc is fresh, ripe and strongly flavoured, with passionfruit/lime characters and a touch of complexity derived from a splash of Sémillon, malolactic fermentation and lees-aging. The American oak-aged, strongly 'malo'-influenced Clansman Chardonnay is generous, citrusy and creamy-smooth, offering lots of drink-young pleasure.

The Old River Riesling is freshly scented, with vibrant, slightly sweet lemon/lime flavours. Pinot Gris, added to the range in 1999, is a smooth, mouthfilling style with peachy, spicy flavours of very good depth.

The Noble Riesling has typically been a floral, late harvest style with a gentle botrytis influence and pure, sweet, lemony, slightly honeyed flavours. The Pinot Noir, launched from the 2000 vintage, offered sweet, ripe cherry/plum characters in a smooth, moderately complex style.

Diners in the 'Gibbs at Cairnbrae' vineyard restaurant enjoy fresh Marlborough produce seated indoors, outdoors in a sheltered courtyard, or on an upstairs balcony that offers a panoramic view of vineyards carpeting the plains as far as the eye can see.

A significant slice of Cairnbrae's output is consumed on-site in the popular vineyard restaurant.

Cellier Le Brun

■ Founded by Daniel and Adele Le Brun in 1980, Cellier Le Brun swiftly built a reputation for characterful, high-impact sparkling wines that filled your mouth with rich, yeasty, toasty flavour. In 1996, however, the Le Bruns' involvement in the company ended, and today the company that still bears their name is owned by the Wellington-based Nightingale family.

Daniel Le Brun is a Champenois, the scion of a family of French Champagne makers stretching back over 12 generations to 1648. In search of new horizons, Le Brun came to New Zealand and at Renwick, near Blenheim, he discovered the combination of soil and climate he wanted. His ambition: to fashion a bottle-fermented sparkling wine in the antipodes able to challenge the quality of Champagne itself.

Labelled 'the mad Frenchman' by the locals after they got wind of his unorthodox winery plans, in 1980 Le Brun set out to duplicate the cool subterranean storage conditions of Champagne by burrowing 12 metres into his Renwick hillside, to form steel-lined caves under four metres of earth. In these cool caves, varying only a couple of degrees in temperature between summer and winter, the Le Brun bottle-fermented sparklings still age after bottling.

Le Brun was intent on 'carrying on the old techniques — everything is handled according to Champagne tradition'. To make his beloved Brut NV, he blended the base wine from the three traditional varieties — Pinot Noir, Chardonnay and Meunier — and across vintages. After adding yeasts and sugar for the second fermentation, the wine was then bottled and rested on its lees for at least two years.

Regal Salmon Limited gained a controlling interest in Cellier Le Brun in 1987, but Daniel Le Brun stayed on as the winemaker and a director, Adele Le Brun continued to oversee sales, and the Le Bruns and other original investors retained a minority shareholding. The owners of Cellier Le Brun then agreed in mid-1993 to sell their shares to Appellation Vineyards Limited (a holding company for the Morton Estate, Allan Scott and Cellier Le Brun wineries) for shares in Appellation, in which Regal Salmon was the largest shareholder. After Appellation's plans for a public share float collapsed, Resene Paints Limited purchased a majority shareholding in Cellier Le Brun in late 1994, with the Le Bruns retaining (and expanding) their substantial minority stake. However, in 1996 the couple's involvement in the company was abruptly ended.

The Nightingale family is best known as the owner of Resene Paints, a paint manufacturing, distributing and retailing company with an annual turnover of about $120 million. After the departure of the Le Bruns (who soon after founded Le Brun Family Estate), the company's first moves included lowering some prices and the appointment of winemaker Allan McWilliams. 'We want to retain the traditional Le Brun style but improve the quality control,' said McWilliams, a Roseworthy College graduate who was earlier heavily involved in the production of Nautilus Cuvée Marlborough. 'The wines will still be bold and richly flavoured, but less broad, less oxidative.'

The classic varieties of Champagne are naturally featured in Cellier Le Brun's 52 hectares of vineyards, including 18 hectares of Pinot Noir, 11 hectares of Chardonnay and 2 hectares of Meunier. The company also grows Sauvignon Blanc (15 hectares), Pinot Gris (3 hectares) and Riesling (3 hectares), and other grapes are purchased from local growers, especially Sauvignon Blanc. In 2001, Cellier Le Brun produced 13,000 cases of bottle-fermented sparkling wine and 8000 cases of still wine under its Terrace Road brand.

The Daniel Le Brun Brut NV, which constitutes a large slice of the winery's output, is slightly fresher and more delicate than during Le Brun's time, but still a high-flavoured style. Based on Pinot Noir (70 per cent), Chardonnay (20 per cent) and Meunier (10 per cent), and disgorged after three years on its yeast lees, it is crisp and lively, with rich, biscuity flavours and good complexity and length.

The vintage-dated, purely Chardonnay-based Blanc de Blancs is disgorged after three and a half years 'en tirage' (on its yeast lees). The latest releases are scented, citrusy and appley, with well-integrated yeastiness and an appealing freshness and vivacity.

The Brut Taché is a strawberryish, yeasty, non-vintage sparkling, *taché* (stained) with the colour of red grapes. The richly flavoured, toasty and nutty Vintage Brut is a 50/50 blend of Pinot Noir and Chardonnay, matured on its yeast lees for up to five years before it is disgorged. This is traditionally Cellier Le Brun's most distinguished bubbly, at its best strikingly rich and powerful.

The Sauvignon Blanc, Chardonnay and Pinot Noir under the Terrace Road brand have generally been of sound but unexciting quality, but the Terrace Road Classic Brut is typically fine value, offering smooth, delicate, yeasty flavours, fresh and lively.

THE FINEST GRAPES FROM MARLBOROUGH, NEW ZEALAND, COMBINED WITH THE CLASSIC CHAMPAGNE TRADITIONS OF FRANCE

DANIEL LE BRUN

METHODE TRADITIONNELLE

Brut NV

75 CL. PRODUCED BY CELLIER LE BRUN LTD. RENWICK, MARLBOROUGH, NEW ZEALAND ALC 12.0% VOL

Address	Cellier Le Brun, Terrace Road, Renwick
Owner	Resene Paints Limited
Key Wines	Daniel Le Brun Brut NV, Vintage Brut, Blanc de Blancs, Brut Taché; Terrace Road Marlborough Sauvignon Blanc, Chardonnay, Pinot Noir, Classic Brut

Allan McWilliams has successfully taken over the winemaking reins from the founder, Daniel Le Brun.

Address	Charles Wiffen Wines, New Renwick Road, Blenheim.
Owners	Charles and Sandi Wiffen
Key Wines	Sauvignon Blanc, Chardonnay, Riesling, Reserve Merlot

Charles Wiffen

■ Charles and Sandi Wiffen must like travel. Their 31-hectare vineyard lies in New Renwick Road, Marlborough, but the couple live at Cheviot, in North Canterbury — where they farm sheep and cattle at their property, Inverness — and their wines are produced at the West Brook winery in west Auckland.

The Wiffen family have farmed their Marlborough property, Saint Clair, since 1907. After planting their first vines in the Wairau Valley in 1980, for years the Wiffens sold all their grapes to other companies, and they still supply Anthony Ivecivich of West Brook with grapes for his own range of Marlborough wines.

Sauvignon Blanc, Chardonnay, Riesling and Merlot are today the key varieties in the Charles Wiffen vineyard, supplemented in 2001 by new plantings of Pinot Noir. The Wiffens were originally partners in Saint Clair Estate, but subsequently withdrew from that venture and since 1997 have marketed wine under their own brand, Charles Wiffen.

With an output of 4500 cases from the 2001 vintage, the wines are in small but growing supply and their quality is consistently high. The briefly oak-aged, slightly creamy Chardonnay shows good body and flavour depth. The Riesling is a punchy, medium-dry style, and there is also a refined, sweet but not rampantly sweet Dessert Riesling with rich grapefruit, pear and honey characters.

The Sauvignon Blanc is fresh and punchy, with lovely freshness, fragrance and vibrancy. Richly coloured and crammed with blackcurrant/plum fruit flavours seasoned with quality oak, in warm vintages the Reserve Merlot is an excellent claret-style red.

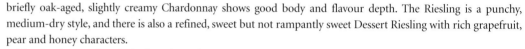

Address	Cloudy Bay Vineyards, Jacksons Road, Blenheim
Owner	Veuve Clicquot Ponsardin
Key Wines	Sauvignon Blanc, Chardonnay, Pinot Noir, Pelorus, Pelorus NV, Te Koko, Late Harvest Riesling

Cloudy Bay

■ No other New Zealand wine has generated as much fervour around the world as Cloudy Bay Sauvignon Blanc. It's been lauded as 'New Zealand's finest export since Sir Richard Hadlee' (David Thomas, *Punch*); as 'the best example of this varietal I have ever tasted from New Zealand' (Robert Parker, *The Wine Advocate*); and as 'like hearing Glenn Gould playing the Goldberg variations, or seeing Niki Lauda at full tilt' (Mark Shields, *Sun Herald*, Melbourne).

When Kevin Judd (see opposite page) arrived in Marlborough in 1985 to take up his new job as Cloudy Bay's winemaker, no fanfare greeted him. 'We had no vineyards, no winery, no equipment, nothing,' recalls Judd. 'Things could only get better.' Explosively flavoured and stunningly packaged, Cloudy Bay's 1985 Sauvignon Blanc swiftly sent a ripple through the international wine world. In the conviction that the quality of New Zealand-grown Sauvignon Blancs could not be equalled in Australia, David Hohnen, part-owner of Cape Mentelle, a prestige Western Australian winery, had crossed the Tasman to set up a second winery, in Marlborough. Cape Mentelle's reputation was based on having captured the Jimmy Watson Trophy — awarded to the top one-year-old Australian red — in successive years, with its 1982 and 1983 Cabernet Sauvignons.

Hohnen had first tasted New Zealand wine when a party of four Kiwi winemakers visited his winery in 1983. 'I had my '82 Sémillon/Sauvignon Blanc in barrels and said: "Get a load of this." They said: "If you think that's herbaceous, see what we've got in the car." Penfolds 1983 Sauvignon Blanc from Marlborough just blew me away. It was a bit sweet, but it had fruit characters that we would never get in Australia.'

When Hohnen plotted to establish a new winery in Marlborough, his accountants advised him to stay out of the New Zealand wine industry, then on the verge of the cut-throat price war of 1985–86. 'It was a terrific gamble. I just had this gut feeling that told me it was the right thing to do. New Zealand Sauvignon Blanc simply hadn't been discovered and seemed to me to have a great future.' Construction of the handsome, concrete-slab winery in Jacksons Road, Rapaura, began in August 1985.

Cloudy Bay, the name of the nearby bay whose waters, when the Wairau River fills them with silt, turn cloudy, was finally chosen as the name of the new venture, but not before the name of a prominent local cape had been entertained but swiftly rejected — Farewell Spit.

Cloudy Bay is now popular in Australia, but the problem in 1985 was persuading Australians to even taste a New Zealand wine. So Hohnen sent key wine retailers a pack containing a bottle, a glass and a jar of New Zealand mussels, carrying the message: 'Before you open this box, get a corkscrew and some fresh crusty bread.' Bottles were broached and almost overnight Cloudy Bay was a smash hit.

Why was the first 1985 Sauvigon Blanc (based on grapes bought from Corbans and made by Judd at Corbans' Gisborne winery) such a roaring worldwide success? 'It all come together,' says Judd. 'We had a simple name, attractive label and a distribution system in place in Australia. The flavour of Marlborough Sauvignon Blanc obviously had wide appeal. When I was working at Selaks in the early 1980s I used to say: "I shouldn't be here making this. I should be in Australia selling it — they'll freak when they see it."'

In 1990 Veuve Clicquot Ponsardin, the illustrious Champagne house, purchased a majority interest in Cape

■ A lean, greying 43-year-old, Kevin Judd (or 'Juddy', as everyone knows him in Marlborough), is not given to idle chatter — far from it — but his work speaks volumes for itself. Ever since Cloudy Bay was just a crazy dream of David Hohnen's, Judd has been there, organising, organising . . . and then swiftly making those early Sauvignon Blancs that made the whole world (or so it seemed) pay attention. Passion and precision are the hallmarks of Kevin Judd's winemaking style, as they are of his stunning wine photography.

Born in England but raised in Australia from the age of nine, in 1979 Judd graduated in wine science from Roseworthy College. 'I thought I had a pretty extensive grounding in all the disciplines required of a winemaker,' he says, 'from soil science to tractor maintenance; from yeast selection to label design and moderation (although I may have slept in that day). Certainly, I felt equipped to handle most vinous challenges.' After working at Château Reynella in South Australia as an assistant winemaker, he came to New Zealand in 1983, attracted by Selaks and the chance to make wine in a cool climate. David Hohnen, the founder of Cloudy Bay, was first introduced to Judd at a tasting following the 1984 National Wine Competition: 'He wasn't making a social event of it, but seriously working his way through the medal-winning wines.'

Hohnen had the vision and the funds — Judd's job was to make the wine. An accomplished red winemaker himself, Hohnen hired Judd for his proven (at Selaks) ability to make white wine, especially fresh, explosively flavoured Sauvignon Blanc. 'I was able to sign up for three years' supply of grapes,' recalls Hohnen. 'With Kevin, all I had to do was give him good tools with which to make wine.'

Judd is a product of the modern winemaking school, where science and technology reign supreme. For him, 'cleanliness is second only to the six o'clock Steinlager'. When James Healy, the company's newly arrived oenologist, suggested in 1991 that it would be a good idea to ferment some Chardonnay with indigenous yeasts, according to the Cloudy Bay newsletter, Judd 'spluttered into his tea leaves. Yeasts should be cultured and well-trained . . .' However, after pondering the suggestion for a few days, Judd gave the go-ahead for a few trial barrels to be set aside, and indigenous yeasts now play a key role in the fermentation of several Cloudy Bay wines.

From the start, Kevin Judd has had responsibility for the day-to-day running of Cloudy Bay. Today, his title is managing director and James Healy is effectively the winemaker, but Judd still heads the winemaking team and has plenty of input into the winemaking style and direction of the company. Hohnen sees Judd as having 'an appreciation of quality, a very acute palate — and a competitive edge'.

Since the late 1980s, Judd has itched to make a great Pinot Noir. After working a vintage in Burgundy, in 1989 he crushed a small amount of first-crop Pinot Noir, fermented it in recycled milk vats and then matured it for 18 months in French oak barrels. Launching the wine in 1992, Judd denied that Pinot Noir was the Morris Minor of Marlborough wines, compared to the Ferrari, Sauvignon Blanc. 'It's a Jensen on blocks. When someone finds the wheels, it'll be up there with the best.'

Judd drinks Cloudy Bay Sauvignon Blanc as an apéritif or with salads or seafood. 'I like it when it's brand new — around Christmas when it opens up with all its exuberance and fruitiness. You get it at the maximum at that age. But at about six years old, when the lifted fruit has gone, it's easier to match with food.'

Kevin Judd, wine photographer, swings into action early in the morning or at sunset: 'The light's better then and it doesn't interfere with the office hours.' His first exhibition, 'Terroir', mounted in Blenheim in 1996, was followed three years later by the publication of his first, internationally acclaimed book, *The Colour of Wine*, featuring photographs of Marlborough vineyards. As both winemaker and photographer, Judd is immersed in the Marlborough wine scene, and one of its quietest but most persuasive champions.

Kevin Judd

On the south side of the Wairau Valley Cloudy Bay has planted mostly Sauvignon Blanc, Chardonnay and Pinot Noir, but also (less predictably) Gewürztraminer, Pinot Blanc and Pinot Gris.

Mentelle — and thus Cloudy Bay. David Hohnen initially retained a 20 per cent shareholding, but in 2001 sold his remaining stake to Veuve Clicquot. In Kevin Judd's eyes, the link with Veuve Clicquot has brought two key benefits: 'Financial stability and greater access to overseas markets.' The total annual output is currently around 100,000 cases.

On flat, stony, well-drained land surrounding the winery, the 39-hectare estate vineyard in Matthews Lane, first planted in 1986, is established in Sauvignon Blanc (principally), with smaller plots of Chardonnay, Gewürztraminer, Sémillon, Pinot Blanc and Malbec. The 50-hectare Mustang Vineyard in the Fairhall Valley is devoted mainly to Chardonnay, Sauvignon Blanc and Pinot Noir, with small plantings of Gewürztraminer, Pinot Gris and Pinot Blanc. At the 44-hectare Widow's Vineyard, near Renwick, Sauvignon Blanc (predominantly) and Pinot Noir are the chosen varieties.

Five growers in the Wairau and Fairhall valleys on 15-year contracts, supported by Cloudy Bay's viticulturist, Ivan Sutherland — himself a grower — supply about two-thirds of the winery's grape intake, but this will drop to about half once the company's own vineyards are in full production. 'We prefer very free-draining, stony soils, like at Rapaura, for Sauvignon Blanc,' says Judd, 'but we prefer to grow Pinot Noir on the even, slightly heavier and more clay-based soils of the southern valleys. Chardonnay seems to perform well on both soil types.' The famous Sauvignon Blanc is a striking wine overflowing with fresh, ripely herbaceous aromas and zingy, downright delicious flavour; one you can devour six months after it was a bunch of grapes on the vine. Judd and his highly respected oenologist, James Healy, seek to produce Sauvignon Blanc having 'a lively gooseberries and lychees — rather than green peas — fruit character and a touch of oak complexity'. Little has changed over the years in the way the grapes are handled in the winery. As David Hohnen puts it: 'Our Sauvignon Blanc winemaking is modern babysitting. It's very different to making a Chardonnay, where you're *inducing* things like malolactic fermentation and yeast autolysis. By contrast, Sauvignon Blanc is early release; it's very straightforward, do-it-by-numbers winemaking to retain fruit characters.'

About 5 per cent barrel-fermentation gives the wine 'a subliminal dimension, something extra, but it's hard to taste oak in the wine,' says Judd. The irresistibly aromatic and zesty style of Cloudy Bay Sauvignon Blanc and its rapier-like flavours stem, Judd is convinced, from 'the fruit characters that are in the grapes when they arrive at the winery. It's our viticulture, rather than our vinification, that's evolved over the years. Scott Henry trellising, leaf-plucking and irrigation management are now giving us much riper flavours in the cooler years.'

With bottle-age, Cloudy Bay Sauvignon Blanc doesn't go from strength to strength, but nor does it run out of steam. It lives for at least 10 years, softening, but staying lively and a pleasure to drink.

Chardonnay, Pinot Noir and the Pelorus bottle-fermented sparklings are the other key wines in the Cloudy Bay line-up. A strapping, citrusy, savoury, tautly structured wine, the Chardonnay is typically 80 per cent barrel-fermented and fully oak-aged on lees, with about 50 per cent malolactic fermentation. A powerful style with impressive concentration and complexity, it ranks among the region's finest Chardonnays, with a proven ability to cellar well for up to a decade.

Pinot Noir, first released on a commercial basis from the 1994 vintage, has emerged as the latest star: fragrant and fleshy, weighty and complex, with rich cherryish, spicy flavours seasoned with toasty oak. The Pelorus sparklings are made in two models: the powerful, lush, creamy-rich, vintage-dated Pelorus, disgorged after at least three years on its yeast lees; and a more Chardonnay-influenced, less complex but refined and refreshing Pelorus NV.

The Cloudy Bay range also includes a trickle of ravishingly perfumed and nectareous Late Harvest Riesling and a strapping, beautifully soft and intense Gewürztraminer. Launched from the 1996 vintage, Te Koko is a substantial, rich, tropical fruit-flavoured, notably complex Sauvignon Blanc, fermented with indigenous yeasts, lees-aged for 18 months in French oak barriques and given a full malolactic fermentation. Compared to the large-volume Cloudy Bay Sauvignon Blanc, in style it's a world apart. 'I knew we were on the right track when I found myself taking it home for dinner,' says Judd.

Cloudy Bay only occasionally enters its wines in competitions and with its illustrious reputation, why should it? Rather than chasing gold medals, it recommends wine drinkers adopt a hedonist's or sensualist's approach to wine. The result? 'Less measure and more pleasure.'

Domaine Georges Michel

■ Owner of Château de Grandmont, a small vineyard and winery in Beaujolais, Georges Michel came to live in New Zealand because 'for a French winemaker, Marlborough is a dream — there's so much freedom. And I wanted to go hunting and fishing, and slow down my life.'

Groupe Georges Michel is a company with diverse interests — stevedoring, car rentals, real estate, wine production and distribution — based on Réunion, near Madagascar. After visiting New Zealand on holiday in 1991, Michel 'fell in love with the country. Meeting Daniel Le Brun in 1997 had a big impact on me. I said to him: "Let me know if anything up-and-running comes on the market."' When the Merlen vineyard and winery, established in the Rapaura district in 1988, came up for sale in 1997, Michel snapped it up.

The vineyard has since been expanded from 7 to 20 hectares and the winery upgraded. Since the first 1998 vintage, the wines have been made by Guy Brac de la Perrière, who each vintage comes to Marlborough from his property, Château Des Pethieres, in Beaujolais. Domaine Georges Michel's current annual output is 8500 cases.

Sauvignon Blanc and Chardonnay are the key varieties planted, with a smaller plot of Pinot Noir. The site is stony, free-draining, flat, frost-free and early-ripening. Growers supply about 30 per cent of the winery's grape intake.

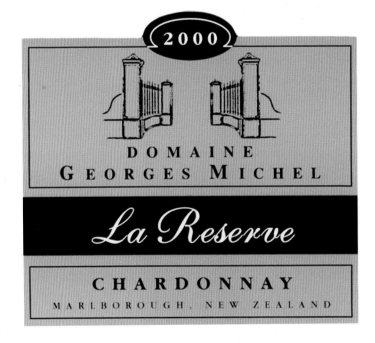

Domaine Georges Michel Sauvignon Blanc is typically a rounder, less assertive wine than the regional norm, but at its best is still full of personality, with great drinkability. 'In France, we try to avoid the very characteristics people here look for in Sauvignon Blanc,' says Michel. 'We're French, so we want a Sancerre style, but we also want the wine to be appreciated locally, so we go for a blend of the two styles. Our wine is more fruity than Sancerre — that's the Marlborough element coming through.'

The La Reserve Chardonnay is typically fleshy, rich, nutty and smooth, with a creamy texture and good complexity and harmony. The Petit Pinot is a no-fuss, light luncheon red. I have also tasted a crisp, grassy and nettley Sauvignon Blanc under the company's Vintage Lane brand.

Address	Domaine Georges Michel, Vintage Lane, Rapaura
Owner	Groupe Georges Michel
Key Wines	Marlborough Sauvignon Blanc, Chardonnay La Reserve, Petit Pinot Noir

Address	Fairhall Downs Estate, 70 Wrekin Road, Brancott Valley
Owners	Ken and Jill Small, Stuart and Julie Smith
Key Wines	Sauvignon Blanc, Chardonnay, Pinot Gris

Fairhall Downs

■ Bold, richly flavoured Pinot Gris and a consistently classy Sauvignon Blanc flow from the Small family's elevated, north-facing site at the head of the Brancott Valley.

Ken and Jill Small, who come from a farming background, planted their first vines in 1982, but for over a decade sold their grapes to established wine companies. After forming a partnership in 1994 with their daughter and son-in-law, Julie and Stuart Smith, two years later they retained a small part of their crop and launched the Fairhall Downs label.

Planted in light-to-medium, free-draining soils with a clay pan over gravels, the 32-hectare vineyard is devoted mainly to Sauvignon Blanc, Chardonnay and Pinot Noir, with smaller plots of Sémillon and Pinot Gris. The wines, fully estate-grown, are made on the partners' behalf at a local winery, where Fairhall Downs has its own tanks and barrels, but a new on-site tasting room, storage and administration building opened in 2002. The company's output of 9000 cases from the 2001 vintage is expected to more than double by 2004.

The Sauvignon Blanc, a regular gold medal winner at the Sydney Top 100 Competition, is typically brimful of character, with substantial body and excellent depth of fresh, crisp, melon/lime flavours. The moderately priced Chardonnay is a gently wooded style — about 25 per cent is handled in American oak casks, the rest in tanks. Fresh, vibrant lemon/apple characters are to the fore, with mouthfilling body, subtle oak and a slightly creamy finish.

The Pinot Gris has typically been robust, with rich stone-fruit, pear and spice flavours and a crisp, dry finish. However, in the search for an easier-drinking wine, Fairhall Downs plans to move to a slightly lower alcohol style with a touch of residual sweetness.

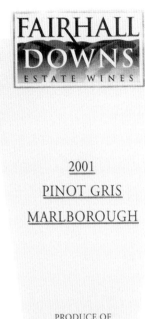

Address	Forrest Estate, Blicks Road, Renwick
Owners	John and Brigid Forrest
Key Wines	Vineyard Selection Sauvignon Blanc, Riesling, Merlot; Marlborough Sauvignon Blanc, Chardonnay, Gewürztraminer, Riesling, Dry Riesling, Rosé, Botrytised Riesling, Indian Summer Late Harvest, Pinot Noir, Gibsons Creek Merlot

Forrest Estate

■ Dr John Forrest makes highly scented, lush, pure and penetrating Marlborough white wines with racy acidity. 'Ripe fruit and big acid defines my style,' says Forrest. 'They're full-on wines — reflecting my personality.'

The Forrest family has deep roots in Marlborough; John Forrest's great-great-grandfather arrived during the first wave of European settlement in the 1840s. Born in Marlborough, Forrest gained his doctorate in biomedical sciences from Otago University. After working as a research scientist in Australia, California and New Zealand, he gained his initial winemaking experience by working as a cellarhand at Corbans Marlborough Winery in 1989 and Grove Mill in 1990. His first wine, a 1990 vintage Cabernet Rosé, enjoyed instant success when it won the trophy for the champion rosé at that year's Air New Zealand Wine Awards.

Forrest is revelling in his second career. 'Winemaking suits my personality because it combines science and art. My scientific training tempers me a bit, but I can express my affable, arty side much better now than when I was a scientist.'

From the Forrest winery, visitors enjoy a stunning view over vine-swept plains to the Richmond Range on the valley's northern flanks. After planting his first vines in 1989, Forrest now owns three vineyards: the 28-hectare estate vineyard at Renwick; a 26-hectare block north of the Wairau River; and another 9 hectares in the Brancott Valley. About 40 per cent of his annual fruit intake is purchased from four growers spread around the Wairau Valley. In a rare reversal of the usual trend of northern investment in the south, John Forrest is also part-owner of Newton Forrest in Hawke's Bay which produces classy claret-style reds under the Cornerstone brand (see page 165).

Forrest Estate's early vintages were made elsewhere, while the Forrests expanded the original garage on their property into a house, wine store and little wine bar with armchairs 'where people sit for hours and become friends'. The company's own winery was erected prior to the 1996 vintage, and Forrest also places a strong emphasis on wine education, offering vineyard and winery tours and tutored tastings. About 25,000 cases of Marlborough wines are produced each year by Forrest and his winemaker, Dave Knappstein.

The popular Sauvignon Blanc is an easy-drinking, fractionally off-dry style with strong melon and cut-grass flavours cut with fresh acidity. The Vineyard Selection Sauvignon Blanc is a drier style with concentrated,

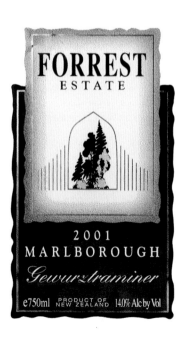

ripely herbaceous flavours and good weight.

Riesling, John Forrest believes, is 'the region's premium grape variety'. His own Marlborough Riesling is typically crisp and lively, with plenty of limey, slightly sweet flavour, and the Dry Riesling is even finer — dry but not austere, with limey, slatey, minerally flavours, intense and long.

The generous, attractively smooth Chardonnay places its focus on rich, vibrant fruit characters enriched by lees-aging and subtle French and American oak. The Gewürztraminer at its best is impressively weighty and lush, with an oily texture and deep, delicate flavours of lychees, spice and ginger.

Of Forrest's several dessert wines, the pick are the perfumed, rich, honey-sweet Botrytised Riesling and the barrel-fermented Botrytised Sémillon/Sauvignon Blanc, which offers lush flavours of dried fruits, honey and nuts.

Fresh, weighty, berryish and smooth, Forrest Rosé is a delicious summertime thirst-quencher. The Pinot Noirs, launched from the 1999 vintage, have not been highly complex, but the Gibson's Creek Merlot is typically vibrantly fruity and supple, with drink-young charm, and the dark Vineyard Selection Merlot offers layers of brambly, minty flavour, complex and firm.

Foxes Island

■ When a century ago the swollen Wairau and Opawa rivers flooded across the Wairau Plains, a small, flat, stony area protruded above the waters, offering a dry haven to travellers and herdsmen. John Belsham's wines are named after the site where his wines are made — Foxes Island.

After working five vintages at Château St Saturnin, a *cru bourgeois* Médoc, in Bordeaux, Belsham built a strong reputation as the winemaker at Matua Valley and later Hunter's. For 10 years he was the winemaker and general manager of Rapaura Vintners, a large contract winemaking facility in Marlborough, of which he was also a foundation shareholder and director. However, in 2000 Belsham resigned from his full-time position at Rapaura Vintners to work as a winemaking consultant and focus on his own label, Foxes Island.

Belsham and his wife, Anne Graham, planted their first vines in the Rapaura district in 1988. Today, they have 5 hectares of close-planted Chardonnay and Pinot Noir vines in their Giffords Road vineyard at Rapaura, established in sandy silt loams over gravelly sub-soils. Paving the way for substantial expansion, in 2000 the couple bought a larger, 20-hectare block in the Awatere Valley, where the Old Ford Road Vineyard is being close-planted in Pinot Noir. Chardonnay grapes are also purchased from growers in the Wairau and Awatere valleys.

The first Foxes Island wines flowed in 1992. Made at the new Wairau River winery at Rapaura (where Belsham is the consultant manager), the wines are still in small supply (2500 cases in 2001), but by 2007 production is planned to rise to about 7500 cases of Pinot Noir and Chardonnay.

As a vastly experienced winemaker who is also chairman of judges at the Air New Zealand Wine Awards, you'd expect Belsham to make meticulous wines — and he does. The Pinot Noir is scented, supple and savoury, and from the 2000 vintage took a big leap in intensity. The Chardonnay, fully French oak-fermented, is a consistently stylish wine with rich, ripe citrus/melon flavours, nutty oak and a creamy-smooth finish.

FOXES ISLAND

MARLBOROUGH
CHARDONNAY
2000

WINE OF NEW ZEALAND
e750ml 14.0%Vol
Produced & Bottled by Foxes Island Wines Ltd RD3 Blenheim New Zealand

Address Foxes Island Wines,
Cnr Rapaura Road and State Highway 6,
Raupara

Owners John Belsham and Anne Graham

Key Wines Chardonnay, Pinot Noir

Address	Framingham
	Wine Company,
	Conders Bend Road,
	Renwick
Owners	Rex and Paula Brooke-
	Taylor, Peter Stubbing, Andy
	Rahs, Gordon Abernethy
Key Wines	Dry Riesling, Classic Riesling,
	Pinot Gris, Gewürztraminer,
	Sauvignon Blanc,
	Chardonnay

Framingham

■ Unlike most Marlborough white-wine producers, which hang their hats on Sauvignon Blanc, Framingham promotes itself — at least within New Zealand — as a specialist in 'aromatic wines. Riesling is our flagship, backed up by Pinot Gris and Gewürztraminer. Sauvignon Blanc is our main export wine.'

Named after a village in Norfolk that is the ancestral home of the founder, Rex Brooke-Taylor, Framingham is a delightful winery to visit, with an atmospheric subterranean cellar and lovely walled gardens. Brooke-Taylor and his wife, Paula, planted their first vines in 1981 and for many years supplied the grapes for acclaimed Rieslings from Corbans, Dry River and Grove Mill. Although co-founders of the Grove Mill winery, they sold their shares in 1990 and four years later launched the Framingham label. Today the company has five shareholders: the Brooke-Taylors, Australian Peter Stubbing, Swiss investor Andy Rahs, and Marlborough businessman Gordon Abernethy. Rex Brooke-Taylor retired from active management of the company in 2002, but Framingham is expanding rapidly, with 130 hectares of vines planted in the Wairau Valley, supplemented by grapes purchased from local growers. When its heavy plantings of Riesling, Sauvignon Blanc and Pinot Noir on the north side of the Wairau River come on stream, Framingham is anticipating an annual production of over 100,000 cases.

Winemaker Antony ('Ant') Mackenzie, who has a degree in viticulture from Lincoln University, worked at Selaks and in the United States before joining Framingham in 1997, but recently shifted to the Spy Valley winery.

In the 16-hectare estate vineyard at Renwick, the 21-year-old Riesling vines ripen their fruit earlier than in nearby, younger vineyards. The flagship Dry Riesling is intense, limey and minerally, with impressive scentedness, delicacy and length. The sweeter Classic Riesling is also fragrant, richly flavoured and tangy.

The Pinot Gris and Gewürztraminer soared in quality recently after Mackenzie visited vineyards in Alsace, noted their lower cropping levels and heavily reduced the yields in Framingham's vineyards. The 2001 vintage yielded perfumed and weighty wines, beautifully ripe, rich and rounded.

The Framingham range also features a beautifully crafted Sauvignon Blanc, fresh and intense, with good acid drive; a vibrantly fruity, gently oaked, moderately complex Chardonnay; a generous, firm and concentrated Pinot Noir; and a richly coloured, deeply flavoured Merlot.

Address	Fromm Winery,
	Godfrey Road,
	Blenheim
Owners	Georg and Ruth Fromm
Key Wines	La Strada Pinot Noir,
	Fromm Vineyard Pinot Noir,
	Clayvin Vineyard Pinot Noir,
	Chardonnay, Reserve
	Chardonnay, Dry Riesling,
	Riesling Auslese,
	Merlot/Malbec, Reserve
	Malbec, Reserve Merlot,
	Reserve Syrah

In its sloping Clayvin Vineyard in the Brancott Valley, Fromm grows a firm, complex Pinot Noir, densely packed with plummy, spicy flavour.

Fromm

■ A decade after the first vintage at one of Marlborough's most individual and respected wineries, Hatsch Kalberer considers his finest achievements as winemaker to be his strikingly powerful Pinot Noirs and delicate, low-alcohol sweet Rieslings. 'As for the company itself, it's been getting to where we are today without smart marketing, wine-show results and compromises — such as a cash-cow Sauvignon Blanc.'

The Swiss founders, Georg and Ruth Fromm, didn't come to Marlborough to produce yet another herbaceous, zingy Sauvignon Blanc. 'Our winery is specialising in reds,' Georg declared in the mid-1990s. 'Everybody makes white wines here. We thought: "If Chardonnay and Sauvignon Blanc thrive in Marlborough, so should reds."'

The Fromm winery lies on the corner of Godfrey and Middle Renwick Roads, between Woodbourne and Renwick. The Fromms planted their first vines here in 1992, producing their first wines from bought-in grapes. Hatsch Kalberer, a tall, gentle Swiss winemaker who previously worked nine vintages at Matawhero, has also been deeply involved from the start.

Georg (commonly called 'George' in New Zealand), whose family has made wine in Switzerland for four generations, still owns a winery and vineyard in Switzerland, planted predominantly in Pinot Noir. 'After my grand-uncle emigrated to New Zealand, we visited in 1991, met Hatsch at Matawhero, and joked that we couldn't go back to Switzerland because of the Gulf War. When we went home, we felt homesick for New Zealand.' The Fromms still spend most of the year in Switzerland, but Georg flies to Marlborough during

the growing season to make critical crop management decisions that affect the wine's quality.

The 5.3-hectare estate vineyard, devoted almost exclusively to red-wine varieties, is planted in richer topsoils than at Rapaura, over layers of clay and free-draining shingles. The vines are close-planted and most tasks are performed manually. In 1998 the Fromms, in association with their United Kingdom agents, Lay and Wheeler, purchased the 15-hectare Clayvin Vineyard, in the upper Brancott Valley. Contract growers supply about 25 per cent of the company's fruit intake, with payments based on a per-hectare rather than yield basis.

The intensity and tannin structure typical of Fromm wines (Kalberer aims to make wines that from a good season will provide pleasure over 10 or 15 years), is clearly derived from the vineyards. 'If we think we are in such a God-given place that we can have 7.5 tonnes of grapes per hectare and still make world class Pinot Noir, we're kidding ourselves,' says Kalberer. Fromm typically harvests only 5 tonnes per hectare, reducing its yields by rootstock and clone selection, and such vineyard management techniques as close-planting, shoot-thinning and bunch removal.

If you pick up a bottle of Fromm wine, the dominant words on the label are 'La Strada'. For Georg Fromm, La Strada ('the road') stands for 'the new impulse of opening up, having the courage to go to the other side of the world and take up the challenge of starting something new — which has enriched our lives enormously'.

Of Fromm's annual output of about 8000 cases, over half is Pinot Noir. 'We want long-lived wine, with tannin structure and generosity,' says Kalberer. 'We can't make Burgundy, but we want the same pedigree as Burgundy, expressing this piece of land.'

The La Strada Pinot Noir, matured in mostly seasoned French oak casks, is typically a robust wine with impressive depth of warm, spicy, complex flavour. The top wine, labelled Fromm Vineyard and exposed to much more new French oak (around 45 per cent), is muscular, spicy, savoury and nutty, with a firm foundation of tannin and notable depth and power. Built to last, it needs five years to show its best.

Syrah is a marginal ripener in Marlborough's cool climate, but Fromm La Strada Reserve Syrah is dark, bold and crammed with firm cassis, plum and black pepper flavours. Both the La Strada Merlot/Malbec and Reserve Merlot are serious, power-packed reds with deep, firm, brambly flavours and hints of herbs and dark chocolate.

Fermented with indigenous yeasts and given a full malolactic fermentation, the La Strada Chardonnay and Reserve Chardonnay are not fresh and vibrantly fruity in the typical Marlborough style, but weighty and creamy, with good mouthfeel. Both the La Strada Dry Riesling and Riesling Auslese are slender, pure and intense, needing years to fully unfold.

Grove Mill

■ For many years, despite glowing overseas successes, a Sauvignon Blanc was never awarded the ultimate prize at a wine competition staged in New Zealand. Finally, at the Liquorland Royal Easter Wine Show 1997, the trophy for champion wine of the show went to Grove Mill Marlborough Sauvignon Blanc 1996.

Founded in 1988, Grove Mill's first decade wasn't easy, with key shareholders coming and going, a winery transplant and constant expansion. A crucial force from the start, however, has been winemaker David Pearce, crafting consistently stylish Sauvignon Blancs, Rieslings and Chardonnays.

As a child, Pearce helped his father make cider for home consumption, and by the time he left school he had decided to be a winemaker. Corbans hired him in 1978 at Henderson as a cellarhand and laboratory technician; then he did a food technology degree at Massey University. After graduating, he returned to the Corbans fold, working his way up at the company's Gisborne winery from trainee to assistant winemaker to the top post — winemaker. In 1988, excited by the potential of Marlborough and the opportunity to 'build everything from scratch', he came south to join the fledgling Grove Mill.

Grove Mill was originally funded by 23 shareholders. By early 2002 the company had 207 shareholders, of whom the largest, Alton Jamieson, also a director, had an 11.6 per cent stake. Announcing its goal of doubling production within five years, in 1999 the company allowed its shares to be publicly traded on the New Zealand secondary exchange. By 2001, its assets totalled $13.8 million. In early 2002 the company was reported to be engaged in acquisition and merger talks with wineries in other regions, and readying itself for transition to the main board of the New Zealand stock exchange.

The winery was at first sited in Blenheim in a brick-walled remnant of the 138-year-old, former Wairau Brewery. Rising output forced a shift in 1994 to a larger winery west of Renwick. A new winery is currently being erected for white-wine production, while the existing winery will focus on reds. Grove Mill's output is rising swiftly, from 63,000 cases in 2001 to a projected 90,000 cases by 2003.

The 17-hectare Home Vineyard, planted in wind-blown loess and stones deposited by the Waihopai River, is established in Chardonnay, Sauvignon Blanc, Riesling, Gewürztraminer and Pinot Gris. Grove Mill also owns the 6-hectare Avenelle Vineyard, in Jacksons Road; the 12-hectare Lansdowne Vineyard in Old Renwick Road; and the sheltered, warm, 24-hectare Seventeen Valley Vineyard in Redwood Pass Road. It also leases the 8-hectare Dowling Vineyard in Hammerichs Road. Contract growers spread across the Wairau and Waihopai valleys supply 70 per cent of the total grape intake.

Address	Grove Mill Wine Company, Waihopai Valley Road, Renwick
Owners	The New Zealand Wine Company
Key Wines	Grove Mill Sauvignon Blanc, Chardonnay, Riesling, Pinot Gris, Merlot, Pinot Noir; Sanctuary Sauvignon Blanc, Riesling, Chardonnay, Pinotage/Pinot Noir

A fast-growing winery with many shareholders, Grove Mill is especially acclaimed for its lush, richly flavoured, hugely drinkable Sauvignon Blanc.

Sauvignon Blanc, Riesling and Chardonnay have been the three principal strings to Grove Mill's bow. The wines are marketed under two brands: Grove Mill for the top-tier wines (including an occasional Winemaker's Selection), and Sanctuary for a range of lower-priced, easy-drinking wines.

The much-awarded Grove Mill Marlborough Sauvignon Blanc is typically mouthfilling, lush and concentrated, with great drinkability. For Pearce, the style of the wine is fixed by its varietal and regional characters. 'On top of that comes the way I like wine, with a degree of opulence, in terms of ripe fruit and weight.' With its lovely mouthfeel and powerful surge of passionfruit/lime flavours, this is one of New Zealand's finest Sauvignon Blancs.

Grove Mill Marlborough Riesling is richly scented, with piercing lemon/lime flavours, abundant sweetness and appetising acidity. The Chardonnay, partly French oak-fermented, partly handled in tanks, places its accent on rich tropical/citrus fruit flavours, with toast and butterscotch characters adding a touch of complexity. The Grove Mill range also includes a substantial Pinot Gris with abundant sweetness and deep peachy, spicy flavours; a warm, concentrated and complex Merlot; and an increasingly distinguished, generous Pinot Noir with deep plum, spice and nut flavours.

Under the Sanctuary brand, Grove Mill also produces a very affordably priced Sauvignon Blanc, Riesling, Chardonnay and Pinotage/Pinot Noir in an attractively fresh, vibrantly fruity and smooth style.

Hawkesbridge

■ Hawkesbridge is a small producer, but its past is a history of Marlborough wine in microcosm. On land where Montana was the first to grow grapes and three lawyers later planted Müller-Thurgau, Mike and Judy Veal established an export trade in Sauvignon Blanc and Chardonnay, then sold out in 2002 to Beringer Blass, the wine subsidiary of Foster's Group.

After 30 years in marketing, advertising and public relations in Wellington, the Veals 'thought we might look at wine. We saw this land in 1990 and fell in love with it.' The property, on the outskirts of Renwick, had 5 hectares of Müller-Thurgau vines, plus another 11 hectares of bare land.

While Mike Veal commuted to Wellington on business, to generate cash flow 3 hectares of Sauvignon Blanc vines were planted on their own roots. When phylloxera spread, the early plantings were replaced with grafted vines. A couple of early Müller-Thurgaus were sold as Marlborough White, followed in 1995 by the first Hawkesbridge Sauvignon Blanc.

By 2002, when the Veals sold to Beringer Blass, the vineyard development was completed and the wines had a secure foothold in the United Kingdom market. In two different soil types — free-draining silts over gravel, and heavier clays — 16 hectares are now planted, principally in Sauvignon Blanc, with smaller plots of Chardonnay, Pinot Gris and Pinot Noir.

Hawkesbridge's output has been running at about 4500 cases per year, made elsewhere on a contract basis, but when the vineyard comes into full bearing, its production is expected to leap to about 9000 cases.

The very easy-drinking Sauvignon Blanc is a slightly off-dry style with passionfruit, melon and lime flavours, fresh, vibrant and strong. The Chardonnay, a lightly oaked style, offers lush, pure, ripe fruit flavours. I have also tasted a vintage-dated Marlborough Brut with a gentle yeastiness and fruity, slightly buttery flavours.

Address	Hawkesbridge Wines and Estates, 83 Hawkesbury Road, Renwick
Owner	Beringer Blass Wine Estates
Key Wines	Marlborough Sauvignon Blanc, Sophie's Vineyard Chardonnay, Marlborough Brut

Herzog

■ Hans and Therese Herzog once owned a respected, Pinot Noir-producing vineyard and Michelin star-rated restaurant in Switzerland. 'We wanted a new challenge — to produce Bordeaux-style reds,' says Hans. 'We looked at California, but land prices were too high. Australia is too hot, so we came to Marlborough.'

After graduating from the wine university of Wadenswil, Herzog ran the 5-hectare Weingut zum Taggenberg vineyard and winery, near Zurich. In selecting the Marlborough region for his bid to make top claret-style reds, Herzog was strongly influenced by the Wairau River: 'It reminded me of the Gironde [in Bordeaux] and the stony soils reminded me of the Médoc. The Wairau has a wide, mostly dry river bed and the heat from the stones turns cool air to warm. The grapes in our vineyard often ripen 10 to 14 days ahead of other vineyards in the area.'

First planted in 1996, the riverside vineyard at Rapaura now has 10 hectares of close-planted Merlot, Cabernet Sauvignon, Cabernet Franc, Malbec, Montepulciano, Chardonnay, Viognier and Pinot Gris vines. At under 5 tonnes per hectare, the vines' yields are extremely low. 'I learned that lesson in Switzerland,' says Herzog, 'There, the climate is cold and the season is short, so if you want quality wine you have to crop the vines lightly.'

First produced in 1998, the wines are entirely estate-grown, with an annual output of around 2500 cases. The flagship Spirit of Marlborough Merlot/Cabernet Sauvignon is a super-charged red, densely coloured and chewy, with huge depth of blackcurrant, plum, spice and new French oak flavours. Built to last, it certainly justifies Herzog's confidence and is backed up by a powerful, deeply coloured Pinot Noir and a strapping Montepulciano with a rich array of liquorice, spice and dark chocolate flavours. The Herzogs also make a small volume of white wines, including a robust dry Pinot Gris with excellent depth of peachy, citrusy, spicy flavour.

Adjacent to the vineyard, Therese Herzog runs the region's most sophisticated restaurant, with exquisite food and a selection of over 350 New Zealand and imported wines.

Address	Herzog's Restaurant and Winery, 81 Jeffries Road, Rapaura
Owners	Hans and Therese Herzog
Key Wines	Spirit of Marlborough Merlot/Cabernet Sauvignon, Montepulciano, Pinot Noir

Highfield

■ When the fledgling Highfield winery changed hands in 1991, its new owners wanted to mark 'the birth of a new tradition'. They did it in style. Highfield's dramatic, 14-metre high observation tower, modelled on a sixteenth-century Tuscan tower, offers a stunning view across the Wairau Valley and each year attracts about 50,000 visitors.

The winery sits on a knoll on the south side of the valley. It was founded in 1989 by Bill Walsh — a grape-grower since the mid-1970s — and his sons Philip and Gerald, but the early wines were not impressive and by 1991 Highfield had slipped into receivership.

The two owners of the company are now Shin Yokoi and Tom Tenuwera. Yokoi, the Osaka-based managing director of Yokoi Manufacturing, which makes fire-fighting apparatus, also holds the Japanese agency for Drappier Champagne. Tenuwera, a Sri Lankan, is the UK-based export manager for Radio Detection, a company making underground cable detectors — whose Japanese agent is also Yokoi Manufacturing.

'We bought Highfield sight-unseen,' recalls Tenuwera. 'It was a bit of an indulgence really. We'd both been coming to New Zealand on business visits, we both loved wine and when we heard the Highfield winery was up for sale, we saw an opportunity that couldn't be missed. In fact, what we bought was a warehouse and a simple winery on a superb hillside site.' Highfield's new owners swiftly focused the range of still wines on four varieties: Sauvignon Blanc, Chardonnay, Riesling and Merlot (since replaced by Pinot Noir).

The 5-hectare estate vineyard, on a rolling north-facing slope with gravel and clay soils, is planted entirely in Pinot Noir. Contract growers supply the vast majority of the company's grapes. To encourage an emphasis on fruit quality rather than quantity, Highfield pays its growers by the hectare rather than tonnage.

Winemaker Alister Soper, who joined Highfield in 1999, has a postgraduate diploma in oenology from Lincoln University and was previously assistant winemaker at Grove Mill. When working on the winery's highly rated bottle-fermented sparkling, Elstree, Soper has the benefit of advice from Michel Drappier, the owner/winemaker of Champagne Drappier, who visits Marlborough regularly. Of Highfield's current annual output of over 20,000 cases, more than 85 per cent is exported, to the United Kingdom, the United States and Australia.

Address	Highfield Estate, Brookby Road, Blenheim
Owners	Shin Yokoi and Tom Tenuwera
Key Wines	Highfield Sauvignon Blanc, Riesling, Chardonnay, Pinot Noir; Elstree Cuvée Brut

The observation tower at Highfield's Tuscan-inspired winery can be seen from afar, and offers a commanding view over the Wairau Valley.

The Sauvignon Blanc, which accounts for over half the company's production, exhibits the incisive melon/capsicum flavours typical of Marlborough in a very fresh, aromatic and springy style, with about 5 per cent barrel fermentation adding a touch of complexity. The Riesling is dry and tight, with strong grapefruit and lime flavours and lively acidity. The Chardonnay, fully French oak-fermented, is robust, with excellent depth of citrusy, mealy, nutty flavour.

The Pinot Noir is substantial, full-flavoured and complex, with cherry, spice and nut flavours. Not marketed under the Highfield brand, the vintage-dated Elstree Cuvée Brut is consistently outstanding. Blended from Chardonnay and Pinot Noir and matured for three years on its yeast lees, its tight-knit structure, delicacy and intense yeastiness are distinctly Champagne-like.

Huia

Address Huia Vineyards, 22 Boyces Road, Rapaura

Owners Mike and Claire Allan

Key Wines Riesling, Gewürztraminer, Pinot Gris, Sauvignon Blanc, Chardonnay, Pinot Noir, Marlborough Brut

■ Claire and Mike Allan like to do things differently. 'We initially stepped right out there with Sauvignon Blanc, going for a subtle, bone-dry style. But we had to come back into the fold, because the market wanted more aromatics.'

The Allans planted their first vines at Rapaura in 1994. Claire Allan studied at Roseworthy College in South Australia and later worked at Corbans in Marlborough and Rapaura Vintners, before coming to prominence as the winemaker at Lawson's Dry Hills between 1992 and 1996. Also a Roseworthy graduate, Mike Allan worked for Cloudy Bay for five years, heavily involved with the sparkling wine, Pelorus, and later at Lawson's Dry Hills and Vavasour, before joining Huia on a full-time basis in 2000.

The 8-hectare estate vineyard is planted in Sauvignon Blanc, Chardonnay and Pinot Noir. Growers around the Wairau Valley supply over half the grapes, with different sites selected 'to give us a variety of flavours that we then blend into the wine to gain complexity. For instance, half the Pinot Noir is grown on a relatively cool, clay-based site, and the other half is grown on the valley floor where the soil is stony and temperatures are warmer.'

First produced in 1997, Huia wines are in reasonable supply at around 12,500 cases per year. Weighty and full-flavoured, they are designed to go well with food. Large, 7500-litre oak vats and 450-litre puncheons are used in preference to 225-litre barriques, in the search for 'softer and more mature flavours; the oak is less obvious and the fruit more pronounced'. Huia wines don't generally leap out of the glass, but seduce you with their fullness, depth and roundness.

The Sauvignon Blanc is full-bodied and smooth, with rich gooseberry, lime and passionfruit flavours. The Chardonnay, barrel-fermented with indigenous yeasts, is weighty and creamy, with a hint of butterscotch and well-integrated oak.

Huia's substantial, full-flavoured and soft Gewürztraminer, fresh, dry Pinot Gris and racy, piercingly flavoured Riesling all reward cellaring. There is also a rich, toasty and yeasty, vintage-dated Marlborough Brut and a vibrant, flavoursome, moderately complex Pinot Noir. These are characterful wines, worth discovering.

Marlborough Sauvignon Blanc

■ Of all New Zealand wine styles, ranging from Gisborne Chardonnay to Hawke's Bay Merlot and Central Otago Pinot Noir, only one can claim to be a world leader — Marlborough Sauvignon Blanc.

Not everyone adores it. 'A lot of winemakers in California can't believe people can actually drink the stuff they make in New Zealand,' says Nick Adams, an English wine merchant. But in the United Kingdom, since the early to mid-1980s the response from the press (at first), then the trade and finally the public has been hugely enthusiastic. 'Where other wines conducted themselves with the demeanour of a svelte ballet dancer,' declared *Wine* magazine in March 2000, 'Kiwi Sauvignons shouted from the rooftops with their pure, unadulterated fruit-driven flavours.'

Why is Sauvignon Blanc, a traditional variety of Bordeaux and the Loire Valley, so successful in Marlborough? Close proximity to the sea is a key factor. In regions with high summer and autumn temperatures, Sauvignon Blanc loses much of its distinctive varietal character, but in Marlborough the maritime influence keeps the summer heat in check — daytime temperatures rarely exceed 30°C.

Marlborough's famously clear skies are also crucial, giving the grapes not only long hours of sunshine in which to ripen, but also cold nights to preserve their fresh, intense aromas and flavours and lively acidity. The region's stony soils are also important, because their low water-storage capacity helps to control Sauvignon Blanc's naturally vigorous growth.

The wines of Sancerre and Pouilly-Fumé, in the Loire Valley, are the classic French expressions of pure, unblended Sauvignon Blanc. Compared to Sancerre, which has a relatively continental climate, Marlborough has lower mean temperatures in the warmest month, but more sunshine hours and overall a strikingly similar amount of heat (over 10°C) during the growing season to ripen the grapes.

The herbaceous, fresh-cut grass aromas and flavours so intense in Marlborough Sauvignon Blanc are derived from methoxypyrazines. The threshold at which tasters are able to detect these compounds (one–two parts per trillion) is equivalent to finding one berry in 500,000 tonnes of grapes (about four times the entire New Zealand harvest in 2002). A key reason Marlborough's Sauvignon Blancs are so intensely herbaceous is simply that, compared to grapes at the same level of ripeness from warm regions, those grown in cooler climates have a higher level of nettley, grassy ('cat's pee' is another popular descriptor) methoxypyrazines.

'Sweaty armpits' is another, less common character found in some Marlborough Sauvignon Blancs. A sulphur molecule, 3-Mercaptohex-anol (which belongs to the mercaptan family, is also found in passionfruit and grapefruit juice and develops in Sauvignon Blanc during fermentation) is believed to be responsible for 'sweaty armpits'.

There are two key styles of Marlborough Sauvignon Blanc. The first, tank-fermented, fresh and fruity, has evolved over the past 20 years from pungent, grassy, stemmy fruit characters to a riper style that mingles both herbaceous and tropical-fruit flavours. 'We blend tropical-fruit characters from the north side of the Wairau Valley, greener, gooseberry flavours from the south, and zingy, nettley characters from the Awatere,' says Clive Jones of Nautilus Estate.

The second style utilises a range of components and techniques in search of a more subtle wine. A small proportion of Sémillon can add length and structure, and indigenous yeasts, barrel-fermentation, lees-aging and malolactic fermentation can add complexity, weight and texture. Classic examples are Isabel Estate and Seresin Estate.

Viticulture

Address	Hunter's Wines, Rapaura Road, Blenheim
Owner	Jane Hunter
Key Wines	Sauvignon Blanc, Winemaker's Selection Sauvignon Blanc, Chardonnay, Riesling, Gewürztraminer, Spring Creek Sauvignon Blanc/Chardonnay, Pinot Noir, Merlot, Brut

Hunter's

■ What thoughts does the name Hunter's conjure up in your mind? I think instantly of Jane Hunter, the famous owner — and a Sauvignon Blanc as aromatic, explosively flavoured and zesty as you can get. Ernie Hunter, his spectacular career tragically cut short at the age of only 38, at the time of his 1987 death in a motor accident had started to savour worldwide applause for the Marlborough wines he toiled so tenaciously to promote. An ebullient Ulsterman, Hunter joined the retail liquor trade in Christchurch, started a hotel wine club, then in 1979 bought 25 hectares of land at Blenheim to grow grapes for Penfolds. After meeting Almuth Lorenz — a young German winemaker here on a working holiday — at a New Year's Eve party in 1981, at her suggestion he elected to plunge into commercial winemaking.

With Lorenz as winemaker the first, 1982 vintage of Hunter's wines was made using Canterbury, Nelson and Marlborough-grown grapes under primitive conditions at an old Christchurch cider factory. Observers were soon startled when, after entering six wines in that year's National Wine Competition, the fledgling company emerged with six medals, including three silvers.

When the local council rejected his application to build a winery at Belfast, on the outskirts of Christchurch, in 1983 Hunter erected a winery at Rapaura. After suffering severe financial and marketing problems in 1984, Hunter turned his formidable energy to exporting — and successfully shipped thousands of cases of wine to the United Kingdom, the United States and Australia. In his widow Jane's words: 'Ernie didn't just sell Hunter's wines. When he was in New Zealand he always talked about Marlborough wines and when he was overseas he talked about New Zealand wines.' His most publicised successes came at the 1986 and 1987 *Sunday Times* Wine Club Festivals in London when the public voted his 1985 Fumé Blanc and 1986 Chardonnay as the most popular wines of the shows.

After Ernie Hunter's premature death, Jane stepped in as managing director (see opposite page). Her brother-in-law, Peter Macdonald, is the general manager. The winemaker since 1991 has been Gary Duke, who grew up in rural Victoria and made his first wine at the age of 11. After working as an assistant winemaker at the Tisdall winery in Victoria, Duke gained a BSc in oenology and then sharpened his cool-climate skills as winemaker for Hanging Rock at Macedon in Victoria. Dr Tony Jordan, an eminent Australian oenologist, has been a consultant since the 1986 vintage.

The company's 37 hectares of vineyards are planted principally in Sauvignon Blanc, Chardonnay, Pinot Noir and Riesling, with smaller blocks of Gewürztraminer, Breidecker, Meunier, Cabernet Sauvignon, Merlot and Malbec. About half the annual fruit intake is drawn from contract growers. Production is planned to leap from 44,000 cases in 2001 to 60,000 cases by 2004.

Deep-scented, elegant white wines of sustained flavour are Hunter's strength. The Sauvignon Blanc is a Marlborough classic, scaling the heights in every vintage. Oak plays no part in the recipe. 'We're after lifted fruit characters and a powerful, round, long palate,' says Duke.

Jane Hunter sees blending as a crucial factor in the Sauvignon Blanc's success. 'We blend fruit from vineyards scattered all around the valley. We get a real mix — some of the grapes are grassy, others give ripe tropical-fruit characters. The trick is the final percentage of each.' Weighty and dry, with pure, searching flavours cut with fresh acidity, it ranks among the region's most stylish white wines.

The Winemaker's Selection Sauvignon Blanc, based on the ripest, least herbaceous grapes, offers rich tropical-fruit flavours, gently seasoned with toasty oak. There is also an easy-drinking, full-flavoured Spring Creek Sauvignon Blanc/Chardonnay, moderately herbaceous, crisp and lively.

The Gewürztraminer and Riesling are impressive, with good weight, sharply defined varietal characters and — especially in recent vintages — excellent depth of flavour. The Chardonnay is also classy, with rich citrusy flavours overlaid with subtle, biscuity French oak (only half the blend is barrel-fermented, but all the wine is oak-aged).

Matured on its yeast lees for over three years, Hunter's Brut is typically refined and incisive, with rich, toasty, yeasty characters and lively acidity. Of the reds, the Merlot is less consistently enjoyable than the full-bodied and supple Pinot Noir, which offers good although not outstanding depth of cherry, raspberry and spice flavours.

Overhead vines at the Hunter's winery offer visitors a shady retreat from the heat of the Marlborough sun.

■ **The most famous woman in New Zealand wine, Jane Hunter was awarded an OBE in 1992 for service to the wine industry, followed in 1997 by an honorary Doctorate in Science from Massey University for her 'outstanding contribution to the wine industry'. Yet when she came to New Zealand (as Jane Arnold) in 1981, she wanted to 'get away from the wine industry' and admits that if the managing director's position at Hunter's 'had been offered to me as a job, I'd never have taken it on'.**

Jane Hunter was brought up in the South Australian wine industry — her father still grows grapes in the Riverland, north of the Barossa Valley. After a short period studying animal husbandry, she switched to viticulture, graduating with a degree in agricultural science from the University of Adelaide.

After a two-year stint running a restaurant at Waikanae, north of Wellington, she came to Marlborough in 1983 to take up a new post as Montana's chief viticulturist, and a year later married Ernie Hunter. Following her husband's death in 1987, Jane thought about leaving the region. 'But then I thought, what's the point? We worked so hard to build it up. It would have been a waste if I'd walked away.'

The charismatic Ernie Hunter had established Hunter's as a 'person' winery, a tradition Jane at first had to work hard to uphold. 'I used to find it difficult, being so much quieter than Ernie,' she recalls, 'but travelling overseas has helped a lot. If we're involved in a dinner or a talk to a wine club, it has to be done by me, or [winemaker] Gary Duke and me. We've built Hunter's around the name — and I'm the only one with the name.'

'Very organised,' is how Duke describes his boss. 'She gets hold of an idea and really goes for it hard, paying very good attention to detail, from A to Z. And she works hard to keep a quality image.'

If you ask Jane Hunter about her strengths and weaknesses, she answers frankly: 'I can be fairly short-tempered and dogmatic. I enjoy management and I'm good at delegating, which lets me get on with planning. Should we source more grapes? Where would we get them from? I always plan five years ahead.'

In 2001, 15 years after Ernie Hunter scooped the white wine of the show award, Jane returned to the *Sunday Times* Wine Festival in London. Once again, the company scooped the award, this time with Hunter's Marlborough Sauvignon Blanc 2000.

Looking back over two decades at Hunter's, what gives Jane the greatest satisfaction? 'I don't know that I'm easily satisfied. I guess it's that we're still here, with basically the same setup we've always had. And I enjoy going overseas and seeing our wine around, and meeting lots of wine lovers who really want to talk to you.'

Address Isabel Estate,
72 Hawkesbury Road,
Renwick

Owners Michael and Robyn Tiller

Key Wines Sauvignon Blanc,
Chardonnay, Riesling, Noble
Sauvage, Pinot Noir

Isabel

■ In the eyes of many wine lovers in the United Kingdom, Isabel Estate must surely be the pre-eminent Marlborough Sauvignon Blanc. When the 2001 vintage was awarded the highest score in a 2002 tasting of New Zealand Sauvignon Blancs by the United Kingdom's *Wine* magazine, it followed the 1998's trophy for Best Sauvignon Blanc at the International Wine Challenge in London, and the 2000's first-equal placing in a tasting of New Zealand Sauvignon Blancs by *Decanter* magazine.

Mike Tiller, a former Air New Zealand pilot, and his wife, Robyn, planted their first vines near Renwick in 1982. The Tillers are 'hard people to catch standing still', according to a member of their staff. 'You almost have to corner them to slow them down.' For many years their grapes were sold to established wine companies, notably Cloudy Bay. In 1994, the couple 'threw a bit of Pinot Noir grape juice into a barrel to see what would happen' — and won a gold medal for the first Isabel Estate Pinot Noir.

Following the departure of Jeff Sinnott, who made a string of outstanding wines between 1998 and 2001, Greg Trought was appointed to the position of winemaker/general manager. A BSc graduate of Canterbury University, Trought studied winemaking at Roseworthy College in South Australia, and later worked at Rothbury Estate and as general manager/winemaker at the St Hubert's winery in Victoria's Yarra Valley.

Isabel Estate wines show outstanding depth, complexity and personality. The keys to their character lie in the soil and the Tillers' uncompromising approach to quality control in the vineyard.

The property's deep, fast-draining gravels combine with a narrow layer of calcium-rich clay in the sub-soil, which prevents excessive water loss and reduces the need for irrigation. Close planting of the vines (at 4400 per hectare, more than double the Marlborough average) allows for lower yields per vine, which contributes to the weight and flavour concentration that is so compelling in the wines.

The extensive, 60-hectare estate vineyard is planted in Sauvignon Blanc (25 hectares), Pinot Noir (15 hectares), Chardonnay (10 hectares), Pinot Gris (5 hectares) and Riesling (5 hectares). So squat are the low-trellised plants, Michael Tiller calls them 'bonsai vines'. The Isabel Sauvignon Blanc, Chardonnay and Pinot Noir are wholly estate-grown, but some Riesling grapes are purchased from 'across the road, where the soil type is the same'.

At 30,000 cases, Isabel Estate is a sizeable producer. The on-site winery, erected in 1997, was significantly extended and upgraded in 2001. In terms of wine style, the Isabel philosophy is 'to allow the vineyard characters to develop complexity and concentration in the wines, rather than modify flavours by winemaking intervention'.

The much-acclaimed Sauvignon Blanc is mostly tank-fermented and lees-aged, but a small portion of the blend is fermented with indigenous yeasts in French oak barriques. Weighty and incisive, it offers lovely depth of passionfruit, gooseberry and lime flavours, tight and long. With its impressive mouthfeel, touch of complexity and strong personality, this is clearly one of the region's greatest white wines.

The Riesling is a cellaring style, dry and tight, with fullness of body and appley, slightly minerally characters. Fermented with indigenous and cultured yeasts in a mix of tanks and French oak barriques, the Chardonnay is weighty and rounded, with rich peach, grapefruit and nut flavours and — in riper years — an almost honeyed richness.

Noble Sauvage is a Sauternes-like wine, golden, substantial, complex and honeyed. The Pinot Noir has not been uniformly exceptional since the debut 1994, but the latest vintages are clearly the best. The powerful, firm and flavour-packed 2000 vintage is one of the most multi-faceted New Zealand Pinot Noirs I have tasted.

Exceptionally concentrated wines, full of personality, flow from Isabel Estate.

Jackson Estate

■ Jackson Estate is well known for its fleshy, rounded Sauvignon Blanc, a lush, ripely flavoured style with great drinkability. 'We don't want a lot of bells and whistles,' says proprietor John Stichbury. 'Using ripe, clean fruit has made us successful.'

Jackson Estate's first vines were planted at the family property in Jacksons Road in 1988. Stichbury's great-grandfather, Adam Jackson (after whom Jacksons Road was named) settled in the heart of the Wairau Valley in the 1840s. The gum tree featured on the Jackson Estate label, planted by Adam Jackson last century, still stands alongside the old, two-storey family homestead.

At first, John Stichbury and his brother, Warwick, planned to grow grapes and sell them rather than make wine: 'That way, we thought we'd have more time to sit in the sun with the kids at Blenheim,' recalled Warwick in 1995. 'Later, we realised that if there was a grape glut we had no security, so we decided to go the whole way.' In 1991, they launched the Jackson Estate label. John, who has farmed the family land since 1977, ran the vineyard while Warwick, an importer and manufacturer, handled the paperwork from his office in Wellington.

In 1997, the venture was restructured when Warwick sold his shareholding. John, who now became managing director, promptly cut his hair, removed his beard and started wearing a tie. 'For image reasons,' he laughs. 'The only change was the box number.' New shareholders were brought into the company, including Dave Williams, a tourism and marketing expert who took over the financial and day-to-day running of Jackson Estate.

The 42-hectare estate vineyard is planted in Sauvignon Blanc, Chardonnay, Riesling and Pinot Noir. The soils are relatively heavy, with good moisture retention, so the vines are not irrigated. 'The only surface stones,' says Stichbury, 'are ones I've carried in my pockets over the years and thrown to the dogs.' Two other vineyards, totalling 15 hectares, were planted in Sauvignon Blanc and Pinot Noir in 2000 and 2001. Further grapes come from growers at Rapaura and in the Waihopai Valley.

Jackson Estate does not own a winery. Martin Shaw, one of the first Australian 'flying winemakers', now part-owner of the Shaw & Smith winery in South Australia, has made the wine since 1992 at a local contract winery. The current annual output is about 40,000 cases, but to cater for unsatisfied export demand, Jackson Estate's production is growing rapidly.

Jackson Estate Sauvignon Blanc is consistently fresh, fragrant and full, with a lovely surge of ripe, melon and capsicum-like flavour and a sustained, rounded finish. The Chardonnay, fully French oak-fermented, is an elegant, mouthfilling wine with citrusy, slightly nutty flavours and fresh underlying acidity. The Reserve Chardonnay, based on older vines and fermented in a higher percentage of new French oak barriques, is tightly structured, with a firm acid spine and strong, grapefruit-like flavours overlaid with savoury, mealy complexities.

The Dry Riesling is a full-bodied style with excellent depth of well-ripened, passionfruit and lemon flavours and good weight. Jackson Vintage, a Pinot Noir-predominant, bottle-fermented sparkling disgorged after up to five years on its yeast lees, is rich and smooth, with good complexity and richness. In favourable vintages, a beautifully scented, honey-sweet Botrytis Riesling emerges, and there is also a moderately concentrated, but vibrantly fruity and supple Pinot Noir.

JACKSON ESTATE

2001
SAUVIGNON BLANC
MARLBOROUGH, NEW ZEALAND

Address	Jackson Estate, Jacksons Road, Blenheim
Owners	John Stichbury and partners
Key Wines	Sauvignon Blanc, Chardonnay, Reserve Chardonnay, Marlborough Dry, Vintage, Pinot Noir

Lush, ripely flavoured and rounded, Jackson Estate Sauvignon Blanc usually scores 10 out of 10 on the drinkability scale.

Address Johanneshof Cellars,
State Highway 1,
Koromiko

Owners Warwick Foley and
Edel Everling

Key Wines Sauvignon Blanc,
Chardonnay, Riesling, Noble
Late Harvest, Emmi,
Pinot Noir

Johanneshof

■ A candle-lit tunnel hewn 50 metres into a Koromiko hillside, full of riddling racks stacked with sparkling wine and barrels of maturing brandy, makes tiny Johanneshof Cellars a memorable place to visit. 'We want to give people a taste of Europe,' say Warwick Foley and his business partner, Edel Everling, who was born at Rudesheim, on the Rhine.

Johanneshof is just south of Koromiko, two-thirds of the way along the road from Blenheim to Picton. The name Johanneshof ('John's courtyard') honours Edel's father, who owned a vineyard in the Rheingau.

Warwick Foley grew up in Marlborough, worked vintages at several wineries and then spent five years in the Rheingau and Baden, which included study at the famous Geisenheim Institute. Returning to Marlborough in 1990, he worked at Corbans and then Te Whare Ra, but is now full-time at Johanneshof. Edel, who has a Geisenheim degree in viticulture and oenology, managed the winery from the start, and now shares the winemaking and marketing with Foley.

When was Johanneshof founded? 'It's a bit confusing,' says Foley. 'Our winery was built in 1993, but we made our first wine in 1991. The first vines were planted back in 1977, after I saw a photo of a steep German vineyard in one of André Simon's books and said to Dad: "Hey, why can't we do something like that?"'

After much trial and replanting, the sloping estate vineyard is planted in 2 hectares of Pinot Noir. 'We harvest about 10 days after the vineyards on the plains,' says Foley, 'and get a bit more rain, but the high iron content in the sandstone soils should give our wine better alcohol and fragrance.' Grapes are also bought from Marlborough growers.

The stone and concrete winery, with fig trees at the entrance, is intended to be 'typical of the Rheingau'. About 3000 cases are produced each year. The wines are typically characterful, with firm acidity, and often unfold well with bottle age. The Chardonnay is a tense, cool-climate style, lemony and slightly nutty.

Johanneshof's most striking wine to date is the Noble Late Harvest. A blend of Chardonnay (95 per cent) and Sauvignon Blanc, harvested in 1995 at a soaring sugar level of 68 brix, it emerged after a three-year-long fermentation as a super-sweet wine with lush tea, apricot, orange and honey flavours. Emmi, the bottle-fermented sparkling wine, is a partly oak-aged blend of Chardonnay and Pinot Noir. Toasty and nutty, it is of solid quality.

Address Lake Chalice Wines,
Vintage Lane,
Rapaura

Owners Phil Binnie, Chris Gambitsis,
Ron Wichman and
Matt Thomson

Key Wines Platinum Chardonnay,
Merlot, Cabernet Sauvignon;
Marlborough Sauvignon
Blanc, Chardonnay, Riesling,
Botrytised Riesling

Lake Chalice

■ Lake Chalice's estate vineyard, at the end of Vintage Lane, off Rapaura Road, is as bony as the next-door quarry. 'You could run the irrigation system here 24 hours a day and it wouldn't flood the vines,' says part-owner Phil Binnie.

The founding partners, Chris Gambitsis and Ron Wichman, have a background in the restaurant trade. Poring over maps in search of a name, they didn't hesitate when they spied Lake Chalice, 40 kilometres away in the Richmond Range — a chalice is a goblet, or wine cup.

Today Lake Chalice is owned and run by Binnie, a former policeman, who is the viticulturist and managing director; Gambitsis, the assistant winemaker and sales manager; Wichman, the cellar manager; and winemaker Matt Thomson. A science graduate, Thomson joined the company in 1997 and each year goes to Italy for the northern hemisphere vintage.

After the vineyard was purchased in 1989 — already planted but badly run-down, having been abandoned several years earlier — the vines were uprooted and replaced with grafted plants. The 11.5-hectare home block, known as the Falcon Vineyard, is established in Sauvignon Blanc, Riesling, Chardonnay, Merlot, Cabernet Sauvignon and Pinot Noir. 'It's so gravelly, we had problems getting the posts in,' says Binnie. 'But we don't have any vigour problems.'

In 2001, the 4.5-hectare Falcon Quarry Block in Vintage Lane was planted in Sauvignon Blanc and Pinot Noir. Another, 12-hectare vineyard of Pinot Noir (principally), Sauvignon Blanc and Riesling is currently being established in Cowslip Valley, in the lower Waihopai Valley. Grapes are also purchased from growers in the Wairau and Awatere valleys.

Since the first 1992 vintage, which yielded just 60 cases, Lake Chalice's output has climbed to 20,000 cases in 2002, made under contract at a local winemaking facility. The top wines, labelled Platinum, include a full-blown, very weighty, lush and creamy-smooth Chardonnay; a full-flavoured, slightly leafy Cabernet Sauvignon; and a Merlot that in favourable vintages shows impressive warmth and concentration.

The Sauvignon Blanc is punchy and crisp, with fresh gooseberry/lime flavours. At its best, the Riesling is finely scented, with vibrant citrus/apple flavours showing good delicacy and depth.

The Chardonnay, fermented and lees-aged in French and American oak barriques, is bold, full-flavoured and softly textured, with excellent drink-young appeal. Another emerging strength are the sweet, citrusy Late Harvest Rieslings and strikingly rich, oak-aged Botrytised Rieslings.

Lawson's Dry Hills

■ High country musterer, champion shearer (300 sheep a day), trade union organiser, possum hunter, swimming pool builder, contract grape-grower … Ross Lawson has been around. Since 1992, he and his wife, Barbara, have produced some of Marlborough's most distinguished white wines.

Lawson's Dry Hills — named after the adjacent Wither Hills, whose low brown folds flank the Wairau Valley to the south — lies on the outskirts of Blenheim. The Lawsons planted their first vines in 1981. 'We had a few acres of land, which we planted for Penfolds,' recalls Ross. 'Before the vines hit the wire, Frank [Yukich, then owner of Penfolds] was in financial difficulties. So we supplied grapes to several wineries.'

Most of the early wines were made by Claire Allan, who now owns Huia Vineyards. The winemaker is Mike Just, a New Zealander of German descent who trained and worked in Germany for several years, and then at the Merlen (now Domaine Georges Michel) winery in Marlborough, before he joined Lawson's Dry Hills in 1997. 'I use a very hands-on approach to winemaking,' says Just, 'and like to be involved at every stage of the process.'

The 4-hectare estate vineyard, planted in moderately fertile, clay-based soils, is devoted exclusively to Gewürztraminer. In partnership with a Singapore-based friend, the Lawsons have also developed a 16-hectare vineyard near the coast at Marshlands, planting Chardonnay, Sauvignon Blanc and Pinot Noir. In the Waihopai Valley, another 25 hectares is being established in Sauvignon Blanc, Pinot Noir, Sémillon, Pinot Gris, Riesling and Gewürztraminer. Grapes are also purchased from local growers.

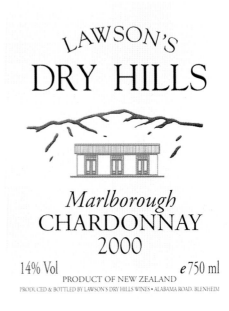

Over 30,000 cases of wine are produced each year in Lawson's Dry Hills' winery, erected prior to the 1995 vintage. The wines, bottled with screwcaps since 2001, are consistently rewarding, with good weight and rich, concentrated flavours.

The bold, intensely varietal Gewürztraminer is one of the country's finest, with substantial body and rich, rounded flavours, ripe, citrusy and strongly spicy. The Riesling is typically full bodied and dryish, with firm acidity and tight, lemony flavours.

The Sauvignon Blanc is a star — freshly scented, vibrant and finely structured, with a powerful surge of gooseberry, melon and lime flavours. Blending of grapes from different sites and subtle use of indigenous yeasts, barrel-fermentation and malolactic fermentation all add richness and complexity, without subduing the wine's strong fruit characters.

The Chardonnay, fermented in a mix of French oak barriques (mostly) and tanks, is typically robust, with grapefruit, peach and biscuity oak flavours woven with fresh acidity. The Pinot Gris is richly alcoholic, with stone-fruit, pear and spice flavours and a faint suggestion of oak.

Launched from the 1997 vintage, the Pinot Noir has been less memorable than the whites, but is steadily gaining in flavour richness and complexity.

Address	Lawson's Dry Hills, Alabama Road, Blenheim
Owners	Ross and Barbara Lawson
Key Wines	Sauvignon Blanc, Gewürztraminer, Riesling, Chardonnay, Pinot Gris, Pinot Noir

From its estate vineyard at the base of the Wither Hills, Lawson's Dry Hills produces a powerful Gewürztraminer, overflowing with citrusy, spicy flavour.

Address	Le Brun Family Estate, 169 Rapaura Road, Rapaura
Owners	Adele and Daniel Le Brun
Key Wines	Méthode Traditionnelle Brut NV, No. 1 Blanc de Blancs NV, Cuvée Virginie

Le Brun Family Estate

■ Daniel Le Brun speaks with a heavy French accent. Born near the legendary town of Épernay, in Champagne, his family winemaking heritage stretches back over many generations. 'The only thing for me to do was to carry on the family tradition,' he recalls.

However, after graduating from the School of Viticulture and Oenology at Avize, Le Brun grew more and more frustrated by the very tight restrictions placed on the size of individual landholdings in Champagne. After visiting New Zealand in 1975, he emigrated here, and three years later met his future wife, Adele. By 1980 they had purchased land near Renwick and begun planting their vineyard.

Following the Le Bruns' departure from Cellier Le Brun in 1996 (see page 213), 'we could easily have retired,' says Daniel. 'But we felt there was the opportunity to come back in a totally independent way, with a smaller level of production focusing solely on sparkling wine. With no other shareholders, life is easier now.' Daniel makes the wine, while Adele controls the marketing.

The 4-hectare estate vineyard in Rapaura Road, with silt loams over gravels, was established in 1997 in Pinot Noir, Chardonnay and Meunier. In a joint venture with Domaine Georges Michel, another, 25-hectare vineyard is being established on the north side of the Wairau River.

In his cream-coloured, concrete block winery, Le Brun does specialist riddling, disgorging, bottling and labelling work for other sparkling wine producers in the region. The Le Bruns' own output of about 3000 cases will rise significantly when the new vineyard plantings come on stream.

The lowest-priced wine, Le Brun Family Estate Méthode Traditionnelle Brut, is a non-vintage blend of Pinot Noir (70 per cent) and Chardonnay, disgorged after three years on its yeast lees. Fragrant, with rich, yeasty flavours and loads of character, it's a great buy.

Cuvée Virginie — dedicated to the Le Bruns' daughter, Virginie — is a vintage-dated, 50/50 blend of Pinot Noir and Chardonnay with tight, citrusy, nutty, yeasty flavours in a very refined style. No. 1 Blanc de Blancs NV is a very elegant, entirely Chardonnay-based style, lemony and crisp, yeasty, lively and long.

Address	Lynskeys Wairau Peaks, 36 Godfrey Road, Blenheim
Owners	Kathy and Ray Lynskey
Key Wines	Chardonnay, Gewürztraminer, Sauvignon Blanc, Pinot Noir

Lynskeys Wairau Peaks

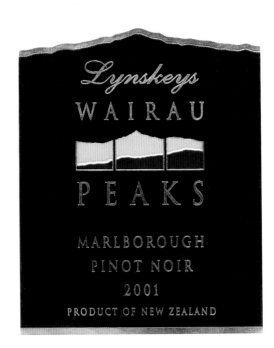

■ 'Unique, but not too boutique' is Kathy and Ray Lynskey's vision for their Lynskeys Wairau Peaks label.

Raised on a Marlborough sheep farm, in 1989 Kathy purchased a newly planted vineyard near the Cloudy Bay coastline. Ray, a commercial pilot and winner of the world gliding championships in 1995, bought a block of bare land in 1993 and also planted vines. The grapes from both vineyards were sold to established Marlborough wineries.

In 1998, after deciding to produce their own wine, the couple bought a new site near the Fromm vineyard, between Renwick and the airport. Once part of the Omaka River bed, the 9-hectare vineyard was planted in Pinot Noir, Sauvignon Blanc, Chardonnay, Gewürztraminer and Merlot.

The early wines, launched from the 1998 vintage, were based on contract-grown fruit, and to supplement their estate-grown grapes the Lynskeys still purchase Sauvignon Blanc and Pinot Noir. The wines — only amounting to 2000 cases per year but steadily increasing in volume — are made on a contract basis by Graeme Paul at the Marlborough Vintners facility in Rapaura Road.

Right from the start, the wines have shown plenty of character. French oak-fermented, the Chardonnay is fragrant, generous and soft, with strong grapefruit and peach flavours, savoury, biscuity characters adding complexity and impressive richness. The Gewürztraminer, fermented in tanks and seasoned oak barrels, is perfumed and slightly sweet, with lychees and spice flavours and a rounded finish.

The Sauvignon Blanc is vibrant and crisp, with good depth of ripely herbaceous flavour and a smooth finish. The Pinot Noir in favourable years is sturdy, spicy and concentrated, with sweet-fruit characters and some savoury complexity.

Mount Riley

■ Named after the predominant peak in the craggy Richmond Range, on the north side of the Wairau Valley, Mount Riley has enjoyed conspicuous competition success since its debut 1996 Sauvignon Blanc won a gold medal at the 1997 Liquorland Royal Easter Wine Show. Part-owner Steve Hotchin noted in early 2002 that 'every vintage [1998, 1999 and 2000] of our Seventeen Valley Chardonnay has won a gold medal in *every* show it has been entered'. A rare performance indeed.

A settled, fast-growing brand in recent years, Mount Riley went through a series of changes in the early to mid-1990s. The existing company was formed in 1994 by John Buchanan and Steve Hotchin, both accountants, in partnership with winemaker Allan Scott. In 1998, Buchanan and Hotchin purchased Scott's stake and hired Bill ('Digger') Hennessy, an Australian graduate of Roseworthy College with winemaking experience in New Zealand (Matua Valley), Australia, Oregon and California.

Mount Riley has established a strong vineyard base in Marlborough. Spread around the Wairau Valley are the 20-hectare Mount Riley Vineyard, the 8-hectare Greystone Vineyard and the 32-hectare Marathon Downs vineyard. Away from the main valley, south of Blenheim, the extremely stony and low-fertility, 14-hectare Seventeen Valley Vineyard is established in Pinot Noir, Merlot, Malbec and Chardonnay. The newest addition is the Blink Bonnie Vineyard, just south of Blenheim, where 17 hectares of Sauvignon Blanc and Chardonnay are being planted. Growers supply only about 20 per cent of Mount Riley's total fruit intake.

With its current annual output of 28,000 cases, Mount Riley ranks among the industry's medium-sized producers. The early vintages were processed at a local contract winery, but a new concrete, glass and steel winery and cellar door is being built at the Blink Bonnie Vineyard in time for the 2003 harvest.

The standard wines are attractive and well-priced. The Chardonnay, 25 per cent barrel-fermented, is a fruit-driven style, fresh, lively and smooth. The Riesling is slightly sweet, with crisp, lemony, appley flavours; the Sauvignon Blanc full-bodied and freshly herbaceous. The Cabernet/Merlot, grown in various regions, is typically berryish and smooth; the Pinot Noir is a drink-young style with moderately complex, raspberryish, plummy flavours.

Savée is unique — a bottle-fermented bubbly made from Sauvignon Blanc. Fresh, grassy and tangy, it's a fun wine for summer sipping.

The two peaks of the Mount Riley range are the Seventeen Valley Chardonnay and Pinot Noir. A blend of grapes from several vineyards, the Seventeen Valley Chardonnay is an opulent, softly mouthfilling wine with grapefruit, toast and butterscotch flavours, rich, rounded and long. The Seventeen Valley Pinot Noir, a single-vineyard wine, is also distinguished: sturdy and deeply coloured, warm, spicy and savoury.

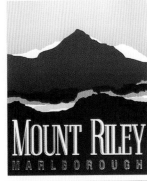

Address	Mount Riley, 10 Malthouse Road, Blenheim
Owners	John Buchanan, Steve Hotchin, Bill Hennessy, Gerard Friedlander
Key Wines	Seventeen Valley Chardonnay, Pinot Noir; Sauvignon Blanc, Chardonnay, Riesling, Pinot Noir, Cabernet/Merlot, Savée

Mud House

■ John and Jennifer Joslin produce a substantial volume of Marlborough whites and reds under two brands, Mud House (the main label in New Zealand) and Le Grys (used principally for export). A mud-brick cottage offering luxury accommodation in their Renwick vineyard was the inspiration for the Mud House brand; Le Grys is Jennifer's maiden name.

The 8-hectare vineyard, planted in 1991 in Sauvignon Blanc, Chardonnay and Pinot Noir, has a *terroir* described by the Joslins as 'typical Marlborough — high sunshine hours, cool nights and the free-draining gravels of an old river bed'. Contract growers make a vital contribution to the wines, and each is named on the company's back labels.

First produced in 1996, the wines are made by Matt Thomson at Marlborough Vintners, a winery owned by Mud House and other producers. With a 2002 output of around 35,000 cases, Mud House ranks among New Zealand's middle-sized wine companies.

The wines under the Mud House and Le Grys labels show subtle differences. For instance, the Mud House Sauvignon Blanc is a typical regional style with forthright, ripely herbaceous flavours, while the Le Grys Sauvignon Blanc is a slightly more restrained but complex style, with about 10 per cent of the blend fermented in new French oak barriques and given a softening malolactic fermentation.

Partly barrel-fermented, Mud House Chardonnay is a slightly creamy wine with a hint of butterscotch and vibrant apple/lemon flavours. The Mud House selection also features a medium-weight, fragrant, blackcurrant and plum-flavoured Black Swan Merlot and a Black Swan Reserve Pinot Noir with good depth of raspberry/spice flavours.

The Le Grys Chardonnay, partly oak-fermented, is full-bodied, lemony, appley and smooth, and the Le Grys Merlot is a medium-weight style, lightly seasoned with oak, vibrantly fruity and rounded.

Address	Mud House Wine Company, Conders Bend Road, Renwick
Owners	John and Jennifer Joslin
Key Wines	Mud House Sauvignon Blanc, Chardonnay, Black Swan Merlot, Black Swan Reserve Pinot Noir; Le Grys Sauvignon Blanc, Chardonnay, Merlot

Address Nautilus Estate,
12 Rapaura Road,
Rapaura

Owner Negociants New Zealand

Key Wines Nautilus Marlborough
Sauvignon Blanc,
Chardonnay, Pinot Gris,
Pinot Noir, Cabernet
Sauvignon/Merlot, Cuvée
Marlborough; Twin Islands
Marlborough Sauvignon
Blanc, Chardonnay,
Merlot/Cabernet
Sauvignon/Cabernet Franc,
Pinot Noir, Brut NV

Nautilus

■ A quality-focused, middle-sized producer exporting to 25 countries, Nautilus Estate produces a consistently impressive Marlborough Sauvignon Blanc and one of New Zealand's greatest bottle-fermented sparklings — Nautilus Cuvée Marlborough.

Nautilus Estate is owned by Negociants New Zealand, one of the country's foremost wine distributors. Negociants itself is Australian-owned, being a subsidiary of S. Smith & Son, whose head office is in the Barossa Valley at Yalumba, Australia's oldest family-owned winery.

'We're in every part of the New Zealand wine industry except retailing,' says Clive Weston, Negociants' managing director. Apart from distribution of the company's range of New Zealand and imported wines, Negociants are also importers and exporters of wine, vineyard owners and winemakers.

The Nautilus brand was launched in the mid-1980s. While in Australia several years ago, Weston stumbled across a surviving bottle of Nautilus Hawke's Bay Sauvignon Blanc 1985, a wine he hadn't realised existed. 'It was probably only ever sold in Australia.'

The first Chardonnay and Hawke's Bay Sauvignon Blanc sold in New Zealand were produced in 1989, and the first Cabernet Sauvignon/Merlot in 1990. The first sparkling wine base was laid down in 1991, and 1992 brought the first Marlborough Sauvignon Blanc (the 1994 vintage had dramatic show success, winning gold medals in Canberra, Hobart, Sydney and New Zealand — and two in London).

Nautilus' company-owned and contract growers' vineyards are located in all of Marlborough's major sub-regions. Seventy per cent of the total fruit intake comes from growers. The company's own plantings include the 12-hectare Opawa Vineyard, adjacent to the winery in Rapaura Road, devoted exclusively to Sauvignon Blanc; the 10-hectare Awatere River Vineyard, established in Sauvignon Blanc, Pinot Gris and Pinot Noir; and the 7-hectare Renwick Vineyard, where Chardonnay, Sauvignon Blanc and Pinot Noir are grown.

Senior winemaker Clive Jones, who has degrees in chemistry and wine science, worked as an analytical chemist and then for six years at Selaks in west Auckland, before he joined Nautilus Estate in 1998. The white wines are made at Rapaura Vintners, in which Nautilus Estate has a 25 per cent stake, but the company also has a 'Kentucky barn'-style winery in Rapaura Road, specifically set up for handling Pinot Noir.

At around 60,000 cases, Nautilus Estate is a substantial producer. Its premium wines are marketed under the Nautilus brand, with a range of 'fruit-driven, value-for-money' wines labelled as Twin Islands. Highlights of the Twin Islands selection are the floral, charming Pinot Noir and the stylish Brut NV, a bottle-fermented blend of Pinot Noir and Chardonnay, citrusy, yeasty and smooth.

Nautilus Marlborough Sauvignon Blanc is typically richly fragrant and weighty, with fresh acidity woven through its ripe passionfruit and lime-like flavours. The Chardonnay, partly wood-fermented and fully barrel-aged, offers fresh, strong citrus and stone-fruit characters, with subtle oak and a slightly creamy texture. Launched from the 2000 vintage, the Pinot Gris is a fractionally off-dry style with citrusy, appley, spicy flavours and good weight.

Refined and intense, the highly acclaimed Nautilus Cuvée Marlborough is a Pinot Noir-dominant style, with Reserve wines from previous vintages, held in old oak casks, included in the blend. Disgorged after 30 months on its yeast lees, it is one of New Zealand's most Champagne-like sparklings — finely scented, crisp and vivacious, with rich yeast autolysis characters and notable complexity and harmony.

Helping to keep the flag flying for claret-style reds in Marlborough, Nautilus Cabernet Sauvignon/Merlot is typically concentrated and firmly structured. The Pinot Noir, matured in new and seasoned French oak barriques, is fragrant, with fine-grained tannins and very good depth of berryish, spicy flavour.

Nautilus Estate draws grapes from several Marlborough sites, including its own vineyard on terraces above the Awatere River.

Omaka Springs

■ Geoffrey Jensen spent 33 years as a pilot, flying jet fighters off aircraft carriers for the Royal Navy and training other pilots as a senior captain for British Airways. After retiring from flying in 1993 to make wine, his first commercial release, Omaka Springs Sauvignon Blanc 1994, won a gold medal.

The Omaka Springs winery is in Kennedys Road in the Omaka Valley, south of Renwick. When Jensen, who was raised in Nelson, and his wife, Robina, purchased the property in 1992, they named it after its three spring-fed ponds.

Today the Jensens own 46 hectares of vineyards in the heavy clay pans of Kennedys Road ('It's like porridge in winter and concrete in summer,' says Jensen) and a kilometre away in lighter, gravelly, free-draining soils in Falveys Road. Sauvignon Blanc accounts for half the plantings, with significant amounts of Chardonnay and Pinot Noir, and smaller plots of Sémillon, Merlot, Pinot Gris, Riesling and Gamay. A windmill towers over the vines, guarding against frost.

Winemaker Ian Marchant, who was born in the United Kingdom and came to New Zealand as a nine-year-old, entered the wine industry in 1978 at Te Mata, in Hawke's Bay. A Roseworthy College graduate, Marchant worked for 13 years in Australian wineries and then for three years at Rapaura Vintners in Marlborough, before joining Omaka Springs in 1998.

Entirely estate-grown, at over 20,000 cases per year the wines are in good supply, and the most recent vintages are markedly more concentrated than those of five years ago. The biggest success of late has been the deliciously aromatic, vibrant, flavour-packed and zingy Sauvignon Blanc. The Riesling is floral and slightly sweet, with fresh lemon and green apple flavours and lively acidity.

French oak-fermented, the Reserve Chardonnay is weighty and creamy, with rich flavours of citrus fruits, apples and butterscotch. The standard Chardonnay, mostly handled in tanks, is mouthfilling and buttery-soft, with strong drink-young appeal. The Merlot is a crisp, berryish middleweight, but the Reserve Pinot Noir offers sweet fruit characters and very good depth of raspberry and plum flavours, with some savoury complexity.

Address	Omaka Springs Estates, Kennedys Road, Omaka Valley
Owner	Geoffrey Jensen
Key Wines	Sauvignon Blanc, Riesling, Chardonnay, Pinot Gris, Merlot; Reserve Chardonnay, Pinot Noir

Ponder

■ Until recently, there was a lot going on at Ponder Estate. Michael Ponder's striking oils and watercolours, exhibited internationally, were on sale in the Shed Gallery. From the olive grove, one of the largest in New Zealand, came olives and Ponder Estate Extra Virgin Olive Oil, and the extensive vineyard supplied grapes for Ponder Estate's often impressive wines. However, in mid-2002 Ponder Estate was purchased by Beringer Blass Wine Estates, the wine division of Foster's Brewing Group, which also owns a controlling stake in Matua Valley.

Michael Ponder's forebears settled in Pelorus Sound in the 1850s. Born in Wellington, he bought and sold property during his twenties, but at the age of 30 elected to become a full-time painter. In 1987, Ponder and his wife, Diane, purchased a block of bare land at the mouth of the Fairhall Valley. Six years after planting the first vines in their silty, gravelly soils, in 1994 the Ponders produced their first wine.

After the sale to Beringer Blass, the Estate's olive trees were swiftly uprooted and replaced with vines. 'We'll reserve the Ponder Estate brand for selling wine through mail-order wine clubs,' says Ross Spence of Matua Valley. 'However, a lot of grapes will be used to boost our exports of Marlborough wine under the Shingle Peak (and in the United States, Matua Valley) labels.'

The 26-hectare vineyard is planted in Sauvignon Blanc (which covers half the total area), Chardonnay, Pinot Noir and Riesling. Stands of native and exotic trees have been planted throughout the vineyard. The company's wine output has grown swiftly, from 1000 cases in 1994 to 25,000 cases in 2001. Contract growers supplied about one-third of Ponder Estate's total grape intake, including all of the Merlot.

Made by consultant winemaker Alan McCorkindale at Marlborough Vintners, a facility partly owned by the Ponders, the range has included a freshly scented, crisp and lively Sauvignon Blanc with melon/lime flavours; a distinctly medium Classic Riesling, at its best perfumed and rich; and a fruit-driven, lightly oaked Chardonnay with fresh, crisp, vibrant lemon and passionfruit characters.

The top selection, labelled Artist's Reserve, features a stylish, impressively full-flavoured, subtly wooded Artist's Reserve Chardonnay, tank-fermented and then French oak-matured; a perfumed, dark and concentrated, French and American oak-aged Artist's Reserve Merlot; and a charming, moderately complex Artist's Reserve Pinot Noir with strong, buoyantly fruity, raspberry/plum flavours.

PONDER
ESTATE

2001
MARLBOROUGH
SAUVIGNON BLANC

Address	Ponder Estate, New Renwick Road, Blenheim
Owners	Beringer Blass Wine Estates
Key Wines	Sauvignon Blanc, Classic Riesling, Chardonnay; Artist's Reserve Chardonnay; Merlot, Pinot Noir

Saint Clair

■ Neal Ibbotson, a former viticultural consultant, has been growing grapes in Marlborough since 1978. Experience counts, because his top wines under the Saint Clair label have enjoyed notable competition success.

The Saint Clair property on the outskirts of Blenheim is named after its original settler, James Sinclair, the founder of the town. Over time, the property's name has evolved from Sinclair to St Clair to Saint Clair.

Ibbotson, born in Dunedin, came to Marlborough as a farm adviser with a Lincoln University diploma. After becoming a private consultant and farm valuer, he began to specialise in viticulture, and for many years grew grapes for other wine companies. Saint Clair's first wines flowed in 1994.

The Ibbotsons' extensive vineyard resources include the 18-hectare Doctors Creek vineyard in New Renwick Road, where Sauvignon Blanc is the key variety; the 15-hectare Awatere Valley vineyard, also devoted principally to Sauvignon Blanc; the 10-hectare Rapaura Road vineyard, planted predominantly in Merlot; and the 7-hectare Omaka Valley vineyard, established in Pinot Noir and Chardonnay. Contract growers supply about 30 per cent of the total grape intake.

Saint Clair's output has soared from 4000 cases in 1994 to 46,000 cases in 2001. The wines are made at a local winemaking facility by two consultant winemakers, Kim Crawford and Matt Thomson.

The trio of Sauvignon Blancs include the scented, full, ripely herbaceous Marlborough Sauvignon Blanc; the deliciously lush, soft and intense, single-vineyard Wairau Reserve Sauvignon Blanc; and the flavour-packed, partly American oak-fermented Awatere Reserve Sauvignon Blanc.

The Marlborough Chardonnay is a fruit-driven style, partly oak-fermented, with ripe, citrusy, appley flavours and a creamy-smooth finish. Weighty and creamy, the Omaka Reserve Chardonnay offers rich grapefruit and stone-fruit characters wrapped in toasty American oak.

The briefly wood-matured Marlborough Merlot is fresh and vibrantly fruity, although green-edged in cooler years. The Rapaura Road Reserve Merlot is much more distinguished, with deep colour, oak complexity and very satisfying depth of red berry and plum flavours.

Address	Saint Clair Estate Wines, 156 New Renwick Road, Blenheim (Cellar door: Cnr Rapaura and Selmes Rds, Rapaura)
Owners	Neal and Judy Ibbotson
Key Wines	Marlborough Sauvignon Blanc, Chardonnay, Riesling, Merlot, Doctor's Creek Noble Botrytis; Reserve Omaka Chardonnay, Fairhall Riesling, Awatere Sauvignon Blanc, Wairau Sauvignon Blanc, Rapaura Road Merlot

Seresin

■ The sentinel stone at the entrance to Seresin Estate bears a subtle handprint. 'The image of the hand is a symbol of strength and the tiller of the soil, a gateway to the heart and the mark of the artisan,' says the company. 'It embodies the philosophy of Seresin Estate.'

Founded in 1992 by Michael Seresin, a New Zealand-born film-maker based in London, Seresin Estate produces

Address	Seresin Estate, Bedford Road, Renwick
Owner	Michael Seresin
Key Wines	Sauvignon Blanc, Chardonnay, Chardonnay Reserve, Pinot Gris, Riesling, Pinot Noir

From its organically managed vineyards, Seresin produces some of the region's most absorbing wines — weighty, subtle and satisfying.

some of Marlborough's greatest wines. Seresin's interest in wine was aroused while holidaying in Tuscany and he originally planned to buy a vineyard in Chianti, before finally deciding in favour of Marlborough.

In the 62-hectare estate vineyard, west of Renwick, Sauvignon Blanc accounts for half the plantings, followed by Chardonnay, Pinot Noir, Pinot Gris, Riesling, Sémillon and Meunier. Two terraces provide distinct mesoclimates and soil types, with Pinot Noir thriving on the upper-level clay soils and white varieties performing best on the silt loams over gravels of the lower terrace. The grapes are grown organically (the vineyard has transitional Bio-Gro status), hand-tended and fermented principally with indigenous yeasts; in 2001, Seresin Estate won the top prize in Marlborough's Rural Environment Awards.

At the head of the Omaka Valley, Pinot Noir has been established on a north-facing clay slope in the 42-hectare Raupo Creek vineyard, with smaller plantings of Sauvignon Blanc, Chardonnay, Riesling and Pinot Gris. At the stony, relatively cool, 15-hectare Tatou Block, inland from Seresin Estate, Sauvignon Blanc is the major variety. No grapes are purchased from growers.

Seresin aims for wines that 'exhibit complexity and palate texture, rather than straight fruit characters.' Chief winemaker Brian Bicknell, who has a BSc in botany and a postgraduate diploma in oenology from Roseworthy College in Adelaide, previously worked in New Zealand, Bordeaux and Hungary, and for three years was chief winemaker at Vina Errazuriz in Chile. First produced in 1996, the wines are made in a partly underground, concrete winery that uses gravity where possible to move the grapes or wine. The 2002 output of 20,000 cases is expected to climb swiftly to 50,000 cases as the new vineyards mature.

The Chardonnay, mostly but not entirely fermented in French oak barriques, has good mouthfeel, with subtle toasty oak enriching its ripe melon/citrus characters. The Chardonnay Reserve is noticeably more powerful, with a lovely array of peachy, mealy, complex flavours and a well-rounded finish.

The Sauvignon Blanc is a very classy wine, subtle and satisfying, with rich, ripe fruit flavours and leesy, nutty characters from a small percentage of barrel-fermentation adding depth and complexity. Built to last, the Riesling is a classic dry style with searching, citrusy, minerally flavours; the Pinot Gris is weighty and oily, with deep peach, lychee and spice flavours, dry and well-rounded.

Moana is a crisp, toasty, limey bottle-fermented sparkling with good yeast-derived complexity and vigour. The Pinot Noir, one of the finest in the region, is fragrant and deeply coloured, with substantial body, beautifully rich cherry, spice and French oak flavours and velvety tannins.

Staete Landt

■ Ruud Maasdam and Dorien Vermaas came from Holland 'with a dream to return to the land and make wine'. Staete Landt is the original name given to New Zealand in 1642 by the Dutch explorer, Abel Tasman.

Maasdam and Vermaas make highly characterful, single-vineyard wines, overflowing with flavour. After 17 years with an American computer company, rising to European managing director, Maasdam itched to get into the wine industry. 'My ancestors were farmers. And there's nothing less tangible than the software industry; nothing more tangible than growing grapes and making wine.'

Visiting New Zealand in 1990 and 1996, the couple noted that 'the winemakers are mostly first generation. In France we wouldn't be accepted, because we're not thirty-second generation.' After exploring all New Zealand's wine regions, they came to Marlborough and thought: 'We should live here.'

First planted in 1998, the 21-hectare vineyard in Rapaura Road is established in Sauvignon Blanc, Pinot Noir and Chardonnay, with a small plot of Pinot Gris. Responding to the two different soil types within the block — stony on the north side, heavier on the south — the vineyard was divided into 18 parcels of different varieties, clones, rootstocks and soil types, all requiring different management techniques. In 1999, Staete Landt won the Marlborough Environmental Award for its intricate irrigation scheme, which took into account the region's limited water resources.

The wines, entirely estate-grown, were launched from the 2000 vintage. Maasdam makes the wines at a local winery, with input from consultant winemaker Sam Weaver. Staete Landt's 2001 production of 5000 cases is projected to grow eventually to 15,000 cases.

The early wines are full of promise. The Sauvignon Blanc, 10 per cent oak-aged, is freshly scented and crisp, with lovely depth of melon and passionfruit characters. The Pinot Gris, fermented in old French oak casks, is muscular, concentrated, peachy and smooth. The Chardonnay, French oak-fermented and given a full malolactic fermentation, is mealy and toasty, with stone-fruit flavours and a creamy-soft texture.

Address	Staete Landt Vineyards, 275 Rapaura Road, Rapaura
Owners	Ruud Maasdam and Dorien Vermaas
Key Wines	Chardonnay, Sauvignon Blanc, Pinot Gris, Pinot Noir

Address	Te Whare Ra Wines, Anglesea Street, Renwick
Owner	Christine Smith
Key Wines	Duke of Marlborough Gewürztraminer, Riesling, Chardonnay, Sémillon; Sarah Jennings Cabernet Sauvignon/Cabernet Franc/Merlot/Malbec

Te Whare Ra

■ Te Whare Ra was the first 'boutique' producer in Marlborough and it has remained small. 'During summer we are open for tasting and wine sales daily, whether or not our "open" sign has been put out at the gate,' says the winery brochure. 'If the tasting room is not staffed, please ring the bell at the top of the steps and wait a couple of minutes for someone to come.'

Allan Hogan, the founder, was one of the fierce individualists of the Marlborough wine scene. He and his wife, Joyce, planted their first vines at Renwick in 1979. Describing himself as a 'self-made, bootstraps winemaker', Hogan fashioned some of New Zealand's most rampantly botrytised sweet white wines, and his strapping, richly alcoholic dry wines were also full of character.

Roger Smith — who worked for the Treasury for many years — and his wife, Christine, purchased Te Whare Ra in 1997, pledging to 'do our best to continue these distinctive styles', but Roger died in 1999. The wine quality faltered in the late 1990s, but the latest releases have been rock-solid. The 2001 output was 2700 cases.

The original 7-hectare vineyard is planted in Gewürztraminer, Chardonnay, Riesling, Sémillon, Cabernet Sauvignon, Merlot, Malbec and Cabernet Franc. An adjacent, 2-hectare vineyard has recently been established in Gewürztraminer, Pinot Noir, Merlot and Malbec. In most years, the wines are entirely estate-grown. Winemaker John McGinlay, an Australian who has also worked in France and the United States, joined Te Whare Ra in 2002.

Most of the white wines are marketed under the Duke of Marlborough label (in memory of the crushing defeat inflicted by John Churchill, Duke of Marlborough, on the French in 1704 at the battle of Blenheim). The jewel in the crown is the exotically perfumed, powerful and rich Duke of Marlborough Gewürztraminer. Based on some of the company's oldest vines, it is a strikingly lush, slightly sweet wine that has won numerous gold medals and trophies.

Te Whare Ra's other white wines include a mouthfilling, strongly oaked, ripe and peachy Duke of Marlborough Chardonnay; a crisp, lemony, medium Duke of Marlborough Riesling; and a Duke of Marlborough Sémillon, citrusy, grassy and tangy. Botrytised sweet whites are no longer a key part of the range ('It's a matter of economics,' says Christine), but the Noble Sémillon is full-bodied, with ripe, gently honeyed grapefruit and lime flavours.

Allan Hogan long crusaded on behalf of Marlborough's Cabernet-Sauvignon based reds, and at the end of his 18-year spell at Te Whare Ra his Sarah Jennings blend (named after the Duke of Marlborough's wife) was 'the wine I am most proud of'. The latest releases have offered plenty of berry and spice flavour, but lack real ripeness and warmth. A Pinot Noir is in the pipeline.

Address	Wairau River Wines, Corner Rapaura Road and State Highway 6, Rapaura
Owners	Phil and Chris Rose
Key Wines	Marlborough Sauvignon Blanc, Chardonnay, Riesling; Reserve Sauvignon Blanc, Chardonnay, Botrytised Riesling

Wairau River

■ A powerful Sauvignon Blanc with excellent depth of lush, nettley flavours and bracing acidity is the finest achievement of Wairau River, whose graceful, low-slung headquarters lies on the corner of Rapaura Road and the main Blenheim–Nelson highway. Phil and Chris Rose, proprietors of Wairau River, pioneered grapegrowing on the north side of the Wairau Valley. Brought up on a dairying and cropping farm near Spring Creek, Phil initially planted his Giffords Road property in vines as a grower for Montana.

The Roses had to fight to establish their vineyard on land that ran 'a quarter of a sheep and one rabbit per acre'. Their 1978 application to the Marlborough County Council for the right to plant a vineyard — the first in the Rapaura area — drew 56 objections, mostly from neighbouring farmers concerned that drift of their hormone sprays would damage the vines. However, a few months later, after intense lobbying, the council amended the district scheme to allow viticulture as a 'predominant', rather than 'conditional', land use on the north side of the valley. 'Many of those who objected now grow grapes, or have sold their land to wine companies,' says Phil Rose.

Today, covering 122 hectares, the Roses' privately owned vineyards are among the most extensive in the valley. In variable silty and stony soils in Giffords Road, right by the river (hence the company name), 72 hectares have been planted, with another 50 hectares in bonier soils in Rapaura Road. Sauvignon Blanc accounts for three-quarters of the plantings, followed by Pinot Noir, Chardonnay, Pinot Gris, Riesling and Gewürztraminer. The wines, entirely estate-grown, are made by John Belsham (of Foxes Island) in Wairau River's new winery in Rapaura Road, which boasts a specialist Pinot Noir cellar and temperature and humidity-controlled barrel hall. The company's headquarters further along Rapaura Road houses a warm, cosy café, serving 'simple, fresh Marlborough food'.

From the start, Wairau River has been strongly export-orientated. 'When we took our first 1991 vintage to the UK, we sold two containers,' recalls Chris. 'That left only 50 cases for New Zealand. Then it won a gold medal and the top Sauvignon Blanc trophy at that year's Air New Zealand Wine Awards.' With an output of 50,000 cases in 2002, the Roses still export a lot more wine than they sell in New Zealand.

The Sauvignon Blanc is full-bodied, with a tantalising interplay of rich, tropical-fruit flavours and more pungent, zingy, herbaceous characters. The Reserve Sauvignon Blanc, fermented and matured in seasoned French oak casks, is mouthfilling and tightly structured, with fresh, concentrated tropical-fruit characters seasoned with toasty oak and a rich, rounded finish.

The Chardonnay, briefly oak-aged, is also a tautly structured style with crisp, ripe fruit characters and a dry, slightly biscuity finish. The Reserve Chardonnay, French oak-matured for a year, is tight and deep-flavoured, in a fresh, elegant style that matures gracefully. There is also an outstanding Reserve Botrytis Riesling, with good acid spine and intense apricot-like, honey-sweet flavours.

Whitehaven

■ The Whitehaven brand is better known overseas than in New Zealand, reflecting the company's strong export orientation. From the start, Whitehaven has shown the ability to make fine wine.

The company was for long based in the original Grove Mill winery — once part of the Wairau Brewery — in the heart of Blenheim. The wines can still be tasted there, but in 2002 a new winery was built in Pauls Road, on the north side of the Wairau Valley, where tank and barrel cellars have been added to the existing apple packhouses. The partners in the venture are Greg and Sue White (the majority shareholders) and winemaker Simon Waghorn.

Greg White is a former merchant banker; Sue White was previously involved in marketing at the Bank of New Zealand. 'After several years cruising around the islands, they developed an interest in entering the wine industry and heard the old Grove Mill winery was available,' recalls Waghorn. 'David Pearce [winemaker at Grove Mill] recommended me to the Whites as a winemaker. He was able to offer them the complete package of a winery, equipment and winemaker.'

Waghorn grew up in rural Canterbury. While studying for a BSc in botany at Canterbury University, he worked in a bottle-store, developing a 'consumer interest' in wine. After working as a cellarhand in New Zealand and Australia, and gaining a Roseworthy College postgraduate diploma in viticulture and oenology, from 1988 to early 1995 he held the top job at Corbans' Gisborne winery. 'I left because I wanted to be a shareholder,' says Waghorn, 'and because instead of overseeing the winemaking process, I wanted to get my hands back on the barrels and pumps.'

Waghorn believes making fine wines in Marlborough requires a different approach than in Gisborne. 'Gisborne grapes are very forgiving, especially Chardonnay. Very ripe fruit can take 100 per cent malolactic fermentation, lots of new charred oak and lees aging, and still produce a harmonious wine. In Blenheim the challenge is not to overshadow the finer fruit characters. I prefer delicate wines; I'm keeping a light touch.'

Whitehaven's annual output has risen from 5000 cases in 1996 (the third vintage) to 23,000 cases in 2001. Contract growers in the past supplied all the grapes, but over the next four years this will reduce to 50 per cent as Whitehaven's own recent plantings come on stream. On three sites around the Wairau Valley, 30 hectares of Sauvignon Blanc and Pinot Noir have been established.

Both the Sauvignon Blanc and Single Vineyard Reserve Sauvignon Blanc are consistently classy, with notable purity and delicacy coupled with satisfying weight and concentrated passionfruit/lime flavours.

The Chardonnay, partly oak-aged, places its accent on fresh, lively, well-ripened fruit flavours. The Reserve Chardonnay, fermented in French and American oak barriques, is a more complex style, crisp, peachy and toasty.

The Single Vineyard Reserve Pinot Gris is weighty, dryish and smooth, with apple and pear characters. I prefer its Gewürztraminer stablemate — weighty, generous and soft, with a richly spiced flavour and fragrance. The Pinot Noir is highly attractive, with subtle oak and plenty of ripe, smooth cherry and plum flavour.

Address	Whitehaven Wine Company, 1 Dodson Street, Blenheim
Owners	Greg and Sue White, Simon Waghorn
Key Wines	Marlborough Sauvignon Blanc, Chardonnay, Riesling, Pinot Noir; Single Vineyard Reserve Sauvignon Blanc, Gewürztraminer, Pinot Gris, Noble Riesling; Reserve Chardonnay

Address	Wither Hills Vineyards,
	211 New Renwick Road,
	Blenheim
Owners	Lion Nathan
Key Wines	Sauvignon Blanc,
	Chardonnay, Pinot Noir

Wither Hills

■ Wither Hills makes just three wines: Sauvignon Blanc, Chardonnay and Pinot Noir. Each has a brilliant record on the show judging circuit, making Wither Hills one of Marlborough's — and New Zealand's — most successful and high profile wineries.

Brent Marris, the driving force behind Wither Hills (see opposite page) made the first vintage in 1992. But in September 2002 the Marris family announced the sale of Wither Hills to the Australasian brewing and wine giant, Lion Nathan.

Brent's father, John, a stock agent with real estate qualifications, was deeply involved in buying land and developing vineyards for Montana between 1973 and 1983, and also one of the region's earliest contract grape-growers. The merger with his son's Wither Hills brand in 1999 added invaluable land holdings and viticultural experience to the company.

The major vineyard, hard against the Wither Hills on the south side of the Wairau Valley, is Taylor River, where 50 hectares of Sauvignon Blanc, 30 hectares of Pinot Noir and 15 hectares of Chardonnay are planted. Here the varying soil pattern includes shingles, silts and clay, and high day temperatures, cold nights and a susceptibility to frost are key aspects of the site's *terroir*. Wither Hills also owns the 14-hectare Benmorven Estate and the St Leonards and Winery vineyards, each covering 8 hectares. At Rarangi, only a kilometre from the coast, another 40 hectares were planted in 2002, with the potential for future expansion. Contract growers supply only about 5 per cent of the annual fruit intake: 'With company vineyards you have more control over your own destiny,' says Brent Marris. With an output of 70,000 cases in 2002, Wither Hills has grown swiftly from the 250 cases produced in 1992. First used for the 2001 vintage, the winery in New Renwick Road started life as an apple packhouse. 'It has been built to be low impact,' says Marris. 'We have top-quality gear [but] basically we are not doing anything extra special with the winemaking. . . . The work has been carried out in the vineyard.' A cellar capable of housing 1600 barrels was built in 2002, with cellar-door sales starting in 2003.

For his much-awarded Wither Hills Sauvignon Blanc, Marris aims for 'a fleshy, ripe, weighty style with charm and elegance'. Lush and lovely, it is a celebration of Marlborough's smashing fruit flavours, with a beguiling richness and roundness. About 5 per cent of the final blend is barrel-fermented, but lees-aging and regular lees-stirring in tanks play a more significant role in the wine's style, 'adding to the layers of complexity, without interfering with the fruit'.

The Chardonnay is powerful and again deliciously intense and rounded, with fermentation and lees-aging in French oak barriques (typically 60 per cent new) giving a distinctly toasty character, balanced by strong, vibrant grapefruit and peach fruit flavours. 'A big wine with a long, soft palate' is the style goal — and Marris hits the target with ease.

Wither Hills Pinot Noir is typically weighty and warm, with deep colour and rich cherry, plum and spice flavours. Matured in French oak barriques (about two-thirds new), it is impressively concentrated and complex, with a backbone of fine, firm tannins and obvious cellaring potential.

For wines in very significant volumes, this is an outstanding trio.

MARLBOROUGH

Wither Hills

2000
CHARDONNAY

Brent Marris
WINEMAKER

750ML   WITHER HILLS VINEYARDS MARLBOROUGH LIMITED   Alc. 14% by Vol.

WINE OF NEW ZEALAND

Brent Marris

■ Brent Marris seems too young to have large overseas companies knocking on his door, offering to buy him out. He's barely turned 40, but the conspicuous success of Wither Hills has indeed been attracting interest — serious interest. 'It got to the point where I woke up one day and thought: "I don't want to work for someone else. We are not after more money. Dad and I are having a fantastic time growing the company together."'*

Raised in Marlborough, Marris graduated from Roseworthy Agricultural College, Adelaide in 1983 with a Bachelor of Applied Science in oenology. During a long spell (1986–1997) as chief winemaker for Delegat's, he won a host of show medals, especially for the Hawke's Bay-grown, powerful, stone-fruit and toast-flavoured Delegat's Proprietor's Reserve Chardonnay.

When the first Wither Hills wines, a 1992 Chardonnay and 1994 Sauvignon Blanc, hit the market together in 1994, Marris showed his talents go well beyond growing grapes and making wine. Two prestigious Auckland restaurants, Iguaçu and The French Café, were offered six months' exclusive supply. A mailing list was set up, with the visitor's book at his daughter's christening supplying the first hundred names.

As one show triumph followed another, the Wither Hills brand swiftly grew in stature. The 1998 Wither Hills Marlborough Pinot Noir won the trophy for champion wine of the 1999 Air New Zealand Wine Awards. Then the 2000 Wither Hills Marlborough Sauvignon Blanc scooped nine gold medals and 10 trophies, making it, according to Marris, 'the most awarded wine in New Zealand history'.

What is the key to the undoubted quality of his wines? 'Created in the vineyard' is the company catch-phrase. 'I identify the different blocks of land — the stonier areas and the siltier areas — and manage the vines' balance and health accordingly, to get clean, botrytis-free grapes with very concentrated flavours. And by keeping each parcel of fruit separate, right through to the stage of completed wine, I get plenty of scope for blending.'

The focus on producing wines for restaurants means they must be smooth and harmonious. 'I try to achieve a long, soft palate,' says Marris. 'A fruit-driven style, with the freshness of Marlborough.' An expert taster himself, he is a regular member of *Winestate* magazine's New Zealand panel and a senior judge in New Zealand, Australian and Californian competitions.

Marris will not be diverted by making wine from other varieties; nor is he interested in private bin or reserve bottlings. 'I can't see the point. We can all make 200 to 300 cases of a reserve,' he told *Grapegrower* magazine in 2002. 'It can be absolutely stunning, but what we have done is taken the heart out of the non-reserve. I would rather just keep focusing on a high quality wine, and build the volume and build the market.'

'Building the market' is one of Marris' great strengths. An outgoing personality, he is as effective at marketing the wine as growing and making it. After Montana took over the distribution of his wine in New Zealand, Wither Hills was listed in 180 cafés and restaurants.

In the United Kingdom, instead of taking the usual route of selecting a national distributor, Marris appointed Oddbins as the exclusive high-street retailer, Waitrose as a supermarket retailer, and the Wine Society to reach mail-order wine drinkers. By shipping the wine straight to the retailers, 'I can achieve the same, or higher, prices to the winery than most of my competition,' says Marris, 'but still be a pound less expensive on the shelf.' In the United Kingdom, Wither Hills Sauvignon Blanc retails at £8, the Chardonnay at £9, and the Pinot Noir at £14. From his Auckland home, Marris is forever flying to Marlborough. Auckland is his key local market, but for Brent Marris, there can be no doubt where his heart lies.

* In early September 2002, the Marris family announced the sale of Wither Hills to Lion Nathan, the Australasian brewing and wine giant, for NZ$52 million.

Other producers

■ Bladen Vineyard

Dave Macdonald and Christine Lowes have an 8-hectare vineyard in Conders Bend Road, Renwick, first planted in 1989. The wines, launched from the 1997 vintage and made by Simon Waghorn, include a full-bodied, well-spiced, slightly sweet Gewürztraminer; a partly oak-fermented Pinot Gris; a floral, distinctly medium Riesling, crisp and vibrantly fruity; and a solid, freshly herbaceous Sauvignon Blanc.

■ Clos Henri

Henri Bourgeois, a tenth-generation producer in Sancerre, in early 2001 purchased 90 hectares of land near Renwick. The family-owned company plans to produce over 35,000 cases at its Marlborough winery, focusing on Pinot Noir and (naturally) Sauvignon Blanc.

■ De Gyffarde Wines

Rod and Di Lofthouse until recently owned a 7-hectare vineyard in Giffords Road, Rapaura, from which they produced a consistently attractive Sauvignon Blanc. Launched in 1995, the wine has been sold in the United Kingdom under the De Gyffarde brand and in New Zealand as Lofthouse. In 2001 the couple sold both the vineyard and Lofthouse label, but will continue to market wine under the De Gyffarde brand.

■ Gillan Estate

Toni and Terry Gillan's first wine scooped the trophy for champion Sauvignon Blanc at the 1994 Air New Zealand Wine Awards. The white Mediterranean-style cellar in Rapaura Road boasts a restaurant, art gallery, function centre and wine education school. Originally a cherry orchard, the land was replanted with 4 hectares of Chardonnay and Pinot Noir for Gillan Estate's bottle-fermented sparkling. At the time of writing, Gillan Estate was on the market and its production of Sauvignon Blanc, Chardonnay, Merlot and Pinot Noir had ceased. However, the flagship, vintage-dated Brut Reserve — matured for up to four years on its yeast lees — is still being distributed. Biscuity and yeasty, it typically shows good vigour, complexity and richness.

■ Goldschmidt Vineyards

Kiwi winemaker Nick Goldschmidt markets a weighty, ripely flavoured and rounded Marlborough Sauvignon Blanc under the Forefathers brand. Most of the wine is sold in the United States, where Goldschmidt is based.

■ Jules Taylor

Raised in Marlborough, winemaker Jules Taylor launched her own label from the 2001 vintage with a very refined Riesling with dry, persistent flavours. The Jules Taylor selection also includes a Pinot Gris and Pinot Noir.

■ Kaikoura Wine Company

Marlborough's southernmost vineyard sits high on a limestone bluff, just south of the town of Kaikoura. A café, winery tours and tastings — and dolphins frolicking in the Pacific below — all add to the tourist appeal. Made by Mike Just, of Lawson's Dry Hills, the range includes a lush, strongly spicy Gewürztraminer; a full-flavoured, distinctly medium Riesling; an excellent Sauvignon Blanc, vibrantly fruity, ripe and rounded; and a smooth Méthode Champenoise with good yeast-derived complexity.

■ Konrad & Co.

Konrad and Sigrun Hengstler, from Germany, own two 20-hectare vineyards at Rapaura and in the Waihopai Valley, planted in Sauvignon Blanc, Pinot Noir and Riesling. Launched from the 1999 vintage and mostly exported, their wines include a dry Riesling, Sigrun Noble Riesling, and a mouthfilling, ripely aromatic Sauvignon Blanc with finely balanced, citrusy and herbaceous flavours.

■ Mahi

Mahi ('your trade, your craft') is the personal label of Brian Bicknell, chief winemaker at Seresin Estate. Made with no concessions to the mass market, the debut Sauvignon Blanc 2001 is a bone-dry wine with tense, strong, melon/lime flavours.

■ Mount Nelson

Designed principally for sale in Italy, the Mount Nelson label is owned by the famous Tuscan producer, Antinori. Waipara-based winemaker Danny Schuster has since 1998 blended batches of wine purchased from South Island companies to fashion an unusually subtle and complex Sauvignon Blanc with deep passionfruit, lemon and lime flavours and excellent mouthfeel.

■ Pleiades Vineyard

Maia, a dark, warm and concentrated, intensely spicy blend of Malbec (principally) and Merlot, is the notable achievement to date of Winston Oliver and Maggie Dewar, who own a 5-hectare vineyard in the Waihopai Valley. The Pleiades range, launched from the 1998 vintage, has been extended in 2002 with a Pinot Gris, and a Pinot Noir will flow in 2003.

■ Spy Valley Wines

Bryan and Jan Johnson's sweeping 120-hectare vineyard in the lower Waihopai Valley was first planted in 1993. At first they sold their grapes, but in 2000 Alan McCorkindale made the first Spy Valley wines, now made by Ant Mackenzie. Named after a local communications monitoring station, the range includes a perfumed and mouthfilling, softly flavoursome Gewürztraminer and a nettley, freshly aromatic Sauvignon Blanc.

■ Thainstone Estate

From their 6-hectare vineyard in Giffords Road, Rapaura, first planted in 1990, Jim and Vivienne Murray have produced a fresh, clearly herbaceous Sauvignon Blanc and impressively mouthfilling and mealy, toasty and creamy Chardonnay under the Cirrus label. However, in 2001 the Murrays announced the Cirrus label was being transferred to a Pinot Noir and Riesling grown in Martinborough. The Thainstone brand is reserved for export.

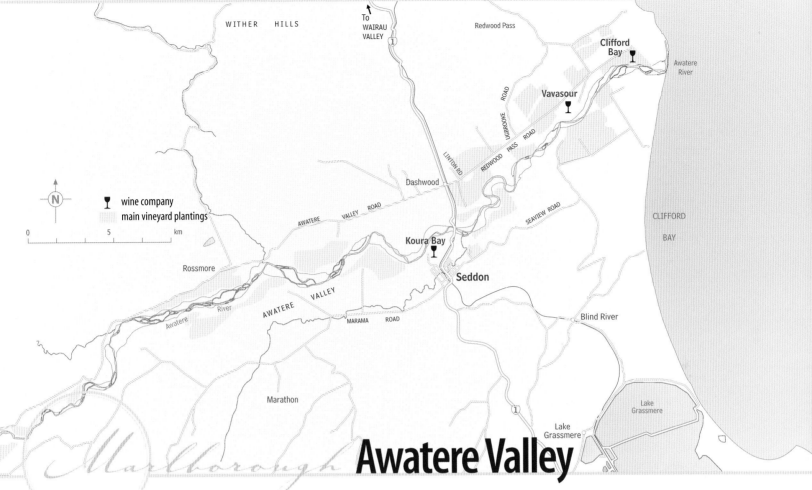

Awatere Valley

South-east of the Wairau Valley, beyond the dry brown Wither Hills, lies the smaller but no less lovely Awatere Valley (pronounced 'Awatree' by the locals). Here the land is more rolling, the horizon closer. From the small town of Seddon, the centre of the valley, the vineyards stretch inland and seaward, up and down the Awatere ('fast flowing river').

The first vineyards were established in the Lower Dashwood, between the highway and the sea. Plantings later spread inland into the Upper Dashwood, more sheltered from cold southerly winds but also more frost-prone. There are also substantial vineyards at Seaview, across the river from Vavasour; at Marama Road, inland from Seddon; and up the valley, above Taylors Pass Road, at Medway.

History

Peter Vavasour, a local landowner and farmer, was the first to sense the Awatere Valley's winegrowing potential. After his hunch was confirmed by viticultural expert Richard Bowling, the two formed a partnership and in 1986 — at a time of glut, when the industry was contracting — the first vines in the Awatere were planted at Vavasour Wines.

Vavasour's first wines flowed in 1989, but it took soaring land prices in the Wairau Valley to trigger further development. In 1993 Villa Maria launched a publicly owned company, Seddon Vineyards, to establish extensive vineyards in the Awatere Valley. In 1996, other Awatere Valley wines finally emerged to join Vavasour, notably Villa Maria Reserve Clifford Bay Sauvignon Blanc and Saint Clair Awatere Reserve Sauvignon Blanc. Koura Bay and Clifford Bay Estate followed in 1997.

Climate

Buds burst and grapes ripen a week later in the Awatere, compared to most of the Wairau Valley. The prevailing wind is the typically warm, dry nor'wester, but the Awatere is cooled by easterly breezes and is more exposed than the Wairau to cold blasts from the south. In the upper reaches of the Awatere Valley, it is cooler again, with greater variation between day and night temperatures.

The vineyards close to the coast or river are protected from frost, but on colder inland sites the risk is higher. The local winegrowers see the Awatere Valley as cooler, drier, windier and typically less fertile than the Wairau, which explains the Awatere's relatively low yields and the higher acid levels of its grapes.

Soils

North of the Awatere River, most of the soils are free-draining 'Dashwood gravelly silt loams', based on alluvium derived from a mix of greywacke, mudstones, sandstones and volcanic rocks. A typical profile is 15 centimetres of gravelly silt loam with a fine granular structure, overlying firm gravelly silt loams at 15 to 35 centimetres, with a gravel base. However, inland from the highway there are also extensive areas of 'Sedgemere silt loams', with compact clay sub-soils that do not drain well.

On the south side of the river the key soil type is 'Seddon silt loam', a deep, free-draining soil derived from loess-like sandstone and dust blown from the adjacent river bed. A typical profile is 25 to 30 centimetres of friable silt loams, over moderately compact silt and clay sub-soils, with a base of sandstone and gravels.

Along both banks of the river, inland from the highway, there are also substantial areas of 'Omaka and Upper Wairau sandy loams' and 'Wairau and Upper Wairau gravelly sands'. Both are free-draining. A water-supply problem has slowed the expansion of vineyards in the Awatere. Irrigation is essential for the vines, but there are no major aquifers — only the seasonal, snow-fed river, which slows to a trickle in a drought year. Some vineyard owners without A-class water rights — whose water supply can be severed during periods of drought — have protected their water supply by building dams.

Wine styles

Awatere Valley Sauvignon Blancs are typically racier and more herbaceous than those from the Wairau Valley, with less tropical-fruit influence and more acid spine. The finest wines are explosively flavoured, with flinty, minerally characters adding individuality. Sauvignon Blancs from the upper reaches of the valley are typically the most aromatic, green-edged and freshly acidic.

Riesling has produced some intense dry wines, although noble rot for dessert wine styles is relatively rare. Vavasour has produced a stream of taut, richly flavoured Chardonnays, but others are less enthusiastic about the prospects for Chardonnay. High hopes are held for Pinot Noir.

Address	Clifford Bay Estate, Lower Dashwood, Awatere Valley (cellar door Rapaura Road, Rapaura)
Owners	Eric and Beverley Bowers, Graham and Thelma Cains, Chris Wilson
Key Wines	Sauvignon Blanc, Chardonnay, Riesling

Clifford Bay Estate

■ Eric and Beverley Bowers' vineyard in the Lower Dashwood lies on a terrace above the Awatere River, just a few bends in the river from the coast at Clifford Bay. Their white wines are freshly scented, with pure, incisive varietal flavours and racy acidity — pure Awatere.

Eric, a former oil company executive, and Beverley bought the property in the early 1990s. With three partners — Marlborough hoteliers Graham and Thelma Cains, and Christchurch businessman Chris Wilson — in 1994 and 1995 they planted 20 hectares of Sauvignon Blanc (principally), Chardonnay and Riesling. The site is silty, dry and low-yielding, with cool sea breezes giving a later harvest than in the Wairau Valley.

First produced in 1997, the wines are made on a contract basis by Glenn Thomas at the nearby Vavasour winery. Over 11,000 cases were produced in 2001. A Tuscan-style 'cellar door' and restaurant in Rapaura Road, in the Wairau Valley, built in 1999 in a joint venture with Woodbourne Estate, is now wholly owned by Clifford Bay (see page 210).

The first 1997 Clifford Bay Sauvignon Blanc won a gold medal at that year's Air New Zealand Wine Awards and the wine is consistently impressive — highly scented, with fresh, zippy melon and lime flavours, intense and long.

Fermented and briefly matured in French oak barriques, the Chardonnay offers strong, vibrant, citrusy, appley flavours and a sustained, slightly creamy texture. Restrained and tight in its youth, the slightly sweet Riesling responds well to cellaring, unfolding strong lemon/lime flavours, underpinned by lively acidity.

Vavasour

■ Vavasour is worth noting for three reasons: its pioneering of winemaking in the Awatere Valley; the outstanding quality of its wines; and finally its glorious site on terraces bordering the Awatere River.

Peter Vavasour is a local farmer whose family settled in the Awatere Valley in the 1850s. (An ancestor served as a cup-bearer for William the Conqueror, thus early setting the family on its wine-tasting path.) Until the mid-1980s, the family property was devoted exclusively to sheep and beef.

The second prime mover in getting Vavasour off the ground was Richard Bowling, a viticultural expert who confirmed Peter Vavasour's hunch about the area's viticultural potential. To fund the $1.3 million venture, Peter Vavasour formed a special partnership in 1986 with carefully chosen shareholders — wine merchants, advertising executives, merchant bankers and accountants. A handsome concrete and cedar winery rose in 1988.

Address	Vavasour Wines, Redwood Pass Road, Lower Dashwood
Owner	Vavasour Wines Limited and Company
Key Wines	Vavasour Awatere Valley Sauvignon Blanc, Single Vineyard Sauvignon Blanc, Riesling, Chardonnay, Pinot Noir; Dashwood Sauvignon Blanc, Pinot Gris, Chardonnay, Pinot Noir

The estate vineyard is planted on the terraced banks of the Awatere River. Mt Tapuaenuku's 2900-metre peak rears to the south; to the north, 4 kilometres away (and reducing the risk of frost) lies the sea. The river's banks reveal an ideal soil structure for vines: a 1-metre-deep surface layer of alluvial silt, over 2 metres of gravelly, silty substrata, down to a base strata of mudstone (papa), rich in calcium and iron. 'It's a low-vigour site,' says winemaker Glenn Thomas, 'with good drainage and hard, bony soils.'

Born in England, Thomas graduated from Roseworthy College in 1979, and then worked in Australian wineries before arriving in New Zealand in 1985. As winemaker at Corbans' Gisborne winery from 1986 to 1988, he was involved in handling Marlborough fruit by making the early Stoneleigh Vineyard wines. Thomas joined Vavasour 'for the challenge of setting up a small winery in a new area'.

The idea of a small winery was abandoned in 1990, when it became clear the company was under-capitalised. Deciding an annual production of 7000 cases was not viable for a non-family-owned winery, Vavasour embarked on a major expansion programme, with the key objective of giving continuity of supply to its popular Dashwood Sauvignon Blanc.

New vineyards were planted and the winery extended. Today, Vavasour owns 28.5 hectares of vines in the Awatere Valley, planted mostly in Sauvignon Blanc, with smaller plots of Pinot Noir, Chardonnay, Riesling and Pinot Gris. Contract growers, some based in the Wairau Valley, are also an important source of grapes. Vavasour's annual output has now climbed to over 30,000 cases.

Vavasour's finest achievement has been its white wines, above all the Sauvignon Blancs and Chardonnays. Yet Vavasour is also committed to producing premium reds. After initially pinning its hopes on Cabernet Sauvignon, its red-wine efforts are now focused on the earlier-ripening Pinot Noir.

The premium Vavasour label is reserved largely — but not exclusively — for grapes grown in the Awatere Valley, whereas those carrying the lower-priced Dashwood label often have a high percentage of Wairau Valley fruit. In Thomas' eyes Dashwood is 'not a second label, just a different style of wine, with greater complexity in the Vavasour wines, and the Dashwood wines more for early drinking'.

The wines are immaculate. The Sauvignon Blancs are awash with vibrant, mouth-wateringly crisp flavour: the Dashwood a fresh, direct style; the Vavasour intensely aromatic, with a powerful surge of passionfruit and green capsicum flavours and the zingy, flinty acidity that is a hallmark of the Awatere. A breathtakingly intense, partly barrel-fermented Single Vineyard Sauvignon Blanc is also made occasionally, with superbly rich melon, gooseberry

and lime flavours, to which a delicate seasoning of oak adds complexity and richness.

Dashwood Chardonnay, partly oak-aged, is a drink-young style with crisp, vibrant, citrusy, appley flavours. French oak-fermented and matured; the Vavasour Chardonnay is a powerful, slightly creamy wine with good acid spine and a lovely harmony of grapefruit, apple and butterscotch flavours.

Vavasour Riesling is pure, incisive and flinty, with intense lemon/lime aromas and flavours that unfold well with cellaring. Dashwood Pinot Gris is weighty and well-rounded, with strong citrus and pear flavours and nutty, leesy characters adding interest.

Designed for early consumption, Dashwood Pinot Noir is mouthfilling and supple, with a touch of smoky oak amid its cherry, plum and raspberry flavours. The Vavasour Pinot Noir is graceful, with strong, firm, cherry/plum flavours and well-integrated French oak.

From its estate vineyard in the lower Awatere Valley and other Marlborough sites, Vavasour produces garden-fresh Sauvignon Blancs, bursting with crisply herbaceous flavour. (The buckwheat in the foreground is grown to attract desired insect predators.)

Other producers

■ Koura Bay Wines

On terraces of the Awatere River at Seddon, since 1993 Geoff and Diane Smith have planted 20 hectares of Sauvignon Blanc (mainly), Pinot Noir, Riesling and Pinot Gris. The wines, launched from the 1997 vintage and made by Simon Waghorn, include a zingy, gooseberry and capsicum-flavoured Whalesback Sauvignon Blanc with good intensity; Mount Fyffe Chardonnay, made in a delicious drink-young style; a fragrant, full-flavoured, slightly sweet Riesling; and a vibrantly fruity and supple, moderately complex Blue Duck Pinot Noir.

■ The Crossings

Set up to take advantage of the strong overseas demand for New Zealand wines, especially Sauvignon Blanc and Pinot Noir, The Crossings grew out of the merger of two public companies, Medway and Brackenfield, which established vineyards in the Awatere Valley in 1996 and 1997. With hundreds of shareholders, total plantings of 140 hectares and its own winery, The Crossings expects to reach full production by 2005.

■ Tohu Wines

A partnership between three Maori business enterprises — Wakatu Incorporation, Ngati Rarua Atiawa Iwi Trust and Wi Pere Trust — Tohu owns a 121-hectare vineyard in the Awatere Valley and another 40-hectare vineyard in the Waihopai Valley, both planted in Sauvignon Blanc and Pinot Noir. The range, first produced in 1998 and primarily for export, includes a fruit-driven Gisborne Chardonnay; a French oak-fermented Gisborne Reserve Chardonnay with some mealy, leesy complexity; a fresh, lively Marlborough Sauvignon Blanc with plenty of gooseberry/capsicum flavour; and a warm, supple Marlborough Pinot Noir with good depth of cherry, plum, raspberry and spice flavours.

Canterbury

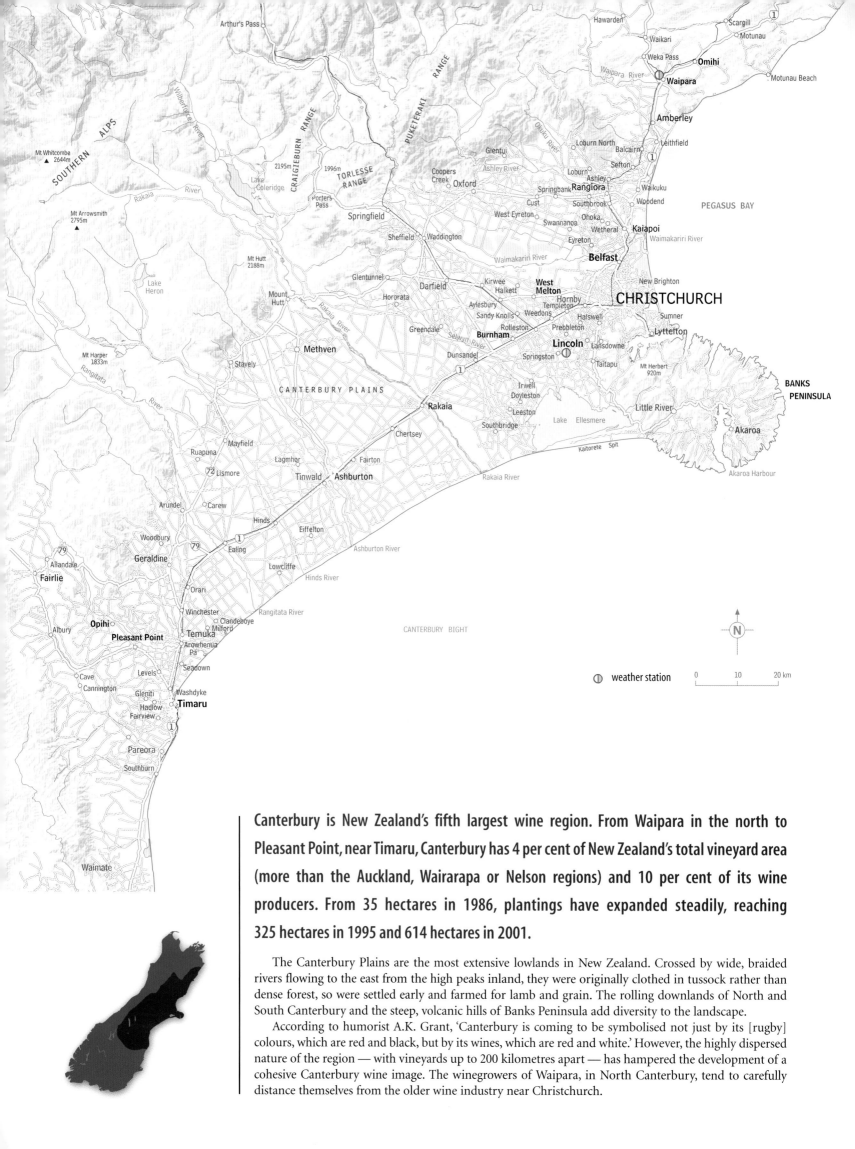

Canterbury is New Zealand's fifth largest wine region. From Waipara in the north to Pleasant Point, near Timaru, Canterbury has 4 per cent of New Zealand's total vineyard area (more than the Auckland, Wairarapa or Nelson regions) and 10 per cent of its wine producers. From 35 hectares in 1986, plantings have expanded steadily, reaching 325 hectares in 1995 and 614 hectares in 2001.

The Canterbury Plains are the most extensive lowlands in New Zealand. Crossed by wide, braided rivers flowing to the east from the high peaks inland, they were originally clothed in tussock rather than dense forest, so were settled early and farmed for lamb and grain. The rolling downlands of North and South Canterbury and the steep, volcanic hills of Banks Peninsula add diversity to the landscape.

According to humorist A.K. Grant, 'Canterbury is coming to be symbolised not just by its [rugby] colours, which are red and black, but by its wines, which are red and white.' However, the highly dispersed nature of the region — with vineyards up to 200 kilometres apart — has hampered the development of a cohesive Canterbury wine image. The winegrowers of Waipara, in North Canterbury, tend to carefully distance themselves from the older wine industry near Christchurch.

History

The modern era of Canterbury wine stems from research conducted at Lincoln University under the direction of Dr David Jackson. When the first trials commenced in 1973, research focused on identifying the most suitable varieties for Canterbury's cool climate. According to the university, the trials demonstrated that Canterbury produces grapes of high acidity and high sugar levels. Jackson saw Canterbury as 'borderline' for such mid-to-late season ripeners as Sauvignon Blanc and such late-season ripeners as Cabernet Sauvignon, but Pinot Noir and Chardonnay were 'particularly promising'.

St Helena was Canterbury's first commercial winery. Robin and Norman Mundy planted their first vines at Belfast, just north of Christchurch, in 1978. St Helena soon electrified the fledgling Canterbury wine community by scoring a gold medal for its 1982 Pinot Noir — a feat repeated by the 1984 vintage.

Climate

'Low rainfall, drying winds and droughty soils' is how R. Mayhill and H. Bawden, co-authors of *New Zealand Geography*, summed up Canterbury's climate and soils. With an average of 2000 hours of sunshine per year, Christchurch has a moderately sunny climate. During summer, temperatures often exceed 25°C, but fronts moving up the east coast also bring cold, subantarctic air.

Commercial viticulture on the Canterbury Plains is more challenging than in regions further north, because in cool seasons there may be insufficient heat to bring the grapes to full ripeness. However, in terms of temperatures over the growing season, the vineyards at Waipara are more comparable to those in Marlborough. (North Canterbury winegrowers like to describe the difference in temperatures between Waipara and the Canterbury Plains on any particular day as: 'There's a jersey in it.')

Cooling sea breezes penetrate large areas of the plains from the east. After losing most of their moisture in the Southern Alps, hot north-westerly winds blast Canterbury, drying out the soils. Droughts are common and in many vineyards irrigation is essential. Canterbury, however, enjoys one crucial advantage over most North Island wine-growing regions — low rainfall. During Canterbury's long dry autumns, the warm days and cool nights enable the fruit to ripen slowly, with high levels of acidity and extract.

Soils

The key distinction in Waipara is between the gravelly deposits close to the Waipara River, and the heavier, limestone-derived clays on the hills on the east side of the valley. Across the Canterbury Plains, most of the soils are shallow, stony and very free-draining, with varying depths of fine alluvial material over gravels.

Wine styles

Pinot Noir, Chardonnay and Riesling are heavily planted in Waipara and on the Canterbury Plains. Sauvignon Blanc is common at Waipara, rivalling Riesling in terms of vineyard area, but is not widely planted on the plains. The biggest plantings of Pinot Gris, a relatively early ripening variety, are on the Canterbury Plains. Riesling and Pinot Noir are Canterbury's most distinguished wines. During the mid-to-late 1980s, the rich, spicy and honeyed Robard & Butler Amberley Riesling (grown at Waipara and from 1993 sold under the Corbans Private Bin label) proved the region's ability to produce top-flight Riesling. Canterbury Rieslings are typically scented and light-bodied, with strong lemon/lime flavours and racy acidity. Many of the region's early Pinot Noirs lacked real ripeness and depth, but the arrival of new, improved clones and reduced crop levels have brought a new breed of far richer and rounder Canterbury Pinot Noirs that rank among the greatest in the country.

Sub-regions

Canterbury's vineyards and wineries are clustered in two main zones: the pancake-flat plains surrounding Christchurch, and an hour's drive north, in undulating terrain at Waipara. Hot, dry nor'westers buffet vineyards in both areas, but the North Canterbury vineyards are protected from the province's cooling coastal breezes by the Teviotdale Hills to the east. You can taste the difference in ripening conditions: the wines from the south are typically leaner and more racy; those from Waipara are more robust and rounder.

Principal grape varieties

	Producing area 2002	% total producing area 2002
Pinot Noir	152.3 ha	30.4%
Chardonnay	120.4 ha	24.0%
Riesling	94.3 ha	18.8%
Sauvignon Blanc	48.7 ha	9.7%
Pinot Gris	26.1 ha	5.2%
Merlot	11.6 ha	2.3%

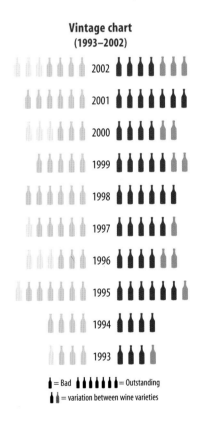

Vintage chart (1993–2002)

2002, 2001, 2000, 1999, 1998, 1997, 1996, 1995, 1994, 1993

🍾 = Bad 🍾🍾🍾🍾🍾🍾 = Outstanding
🍾🍾 = variation between wine varieties

Previous page: Mountford's meticulous sloping vineyard at Waipara yields a robust, rich Chardonnay and a Pinot Noir of outstanding complexity and depth.

Summary of climate statistics

Meteorological station	Latitude	Height	GDD	MTWM	Rainfall, Oct–Apr	Air frost days (annual)
Waipara	43.04'S	64 m	1117	17.8°C	379 mm	35
Lincoln	43.37'S	12 m	973	16.8°C	339 mm	36

Height — *above sea level* GDD — *growing degree days, Oct–Apr, above 10°C* MTWM — *mean temperature, warmest month*

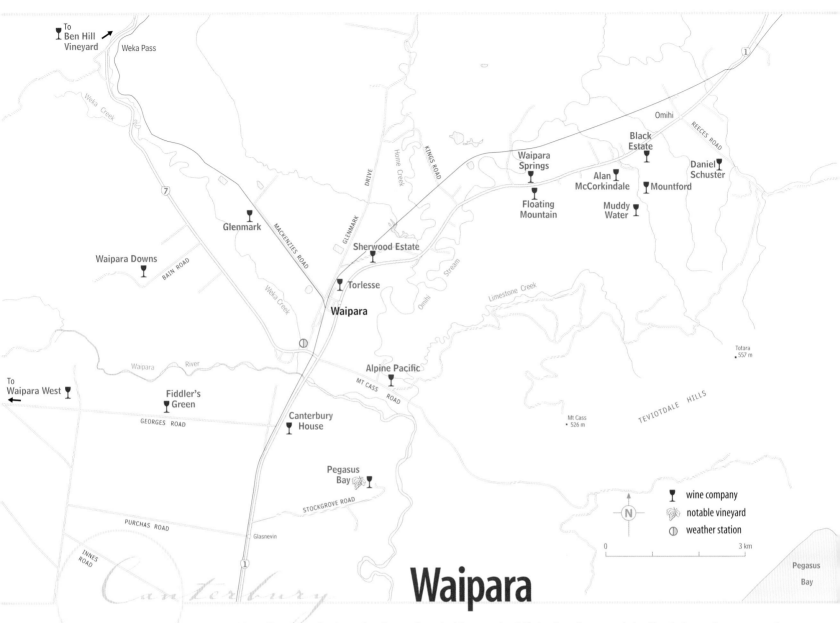

Waipara

Canterbury's most prominent and heavily planted sub-region lies an hour's drive north of Christchurch, around the North Canterbury town of Waipara. Straddling the Christchurch–Picton highway, the vineyards lie draped over flat to sloping — in a few places, steeply sloping — terrain. One of Waipara's greatest assets is that it *looks* like classic wine country.

South of the township, the Waipara River has carved its way through the landscape, leaving stony terraces high above the water. The valley runs in a north-east/south-west direction, flanked by hills long important for their meat and wool production. The entire wine-growing district is promoted by the winemakers as Waipara Valley, but in fact the vineyards east of the Omihi Stream, which runs through the middle of the valley, lie in Omihi; those west of the stream are in Waipara.

History

According to John McCaskey, of the Glenmark winery, Waipara was viewed in the past as 'a drought-prone block of light land of less grazing worth per acre than any around it'. McCaskey experimented with hybrid vines at Waipara in 1965, but poor site selection and a flood arrested progress. After the Glenmark irrigation scheme got underway, McCaskey resumed planting in 1981. Further south, but also in North Canterbury, Jeremy and Lee Prater planted the first vines at Amberley Estate, near the town of Amberley, in 1979. As irrigation water became available at Waipara in the early 1980s, it triggered a flurry of vine planting. In 1982 Derek Quigley, a prominent politician, and his family established the vineyard now owned by Mark and Michelle Rattray, of Floating Mountain; Bruce Moore (now of Waipara Springs) planted a 4-hectare block of Chardonnay to supply Corbans; John Corbett planted Riesling, also to supply Corbans; and Helen and Tony Willy (later of Chancellor Estates) and their partners established their first vines. By 1986, Danny Schuster had started planting the Omihi Hills vineyard and the Donaldson family had established their first vines at Pegasus Bay.

Climate

In terms of heat and rainfall during the October to April growing season, the statistics for Waipara and Blenheim Airport, in Marlborough, are almost identical. According to local winemaker Alan McCorkindale, the major temperature difference is that the vineyards at Waipara experience greater diurnal (day/night) temperature variation.

Nine kilometres from the coast, Waipara's vineyards are protected from cold sea breezes by the Teviotdale hills to the east, which climb at Mt Cass to over 500 metres above sea level. The shelter provided by the coastal hills is a key aspect of Waipara's grapegrowing environment. 'Given the same grape variety and vineyard management, the harvest date in Waipara is typically 10 days to two weeks earlier than on the Canterbury Plains,' says Gwyn Williams of Muddy Water.

Hot, dry nor'westers also dictate Waipara's weather. 'The trees, even the power poles, lean with the winds,' says John McCaskey. These powerful winds can cause severe soil moisture deficits, devigorate the vines, rip off bird nets and even damage posts and trellises.

The cold, southerly winds which bring much of Waipara's rain pose less of a disease threat than would relatively warm easterly winds. Frost is a risk on specific sites, especially on the flats.

Waipara is a small area, yet there is a diversity of mesoclimates. The vineyards on the hills are warm, fast-draining and frost-free, provided they are angled to the north or north-west. However, those with vineyards on the flats (where the frost risk is greatest) claim longer sunshine hours, earlier bud-burst in spring and a longer growing season.

Soils

The two major soil types are gravels in the centre and west of the valley, and richer, clay-based soils on the eastern hills, which also extend onto the flats in the north. The dry, gravelly Glasnevin soils lie south of the Waipara River and in a band on its northern banks. These greywacke-based glacial deposits especially suit Sauvignon Blanc. The 'Rendzina and Related' clay soils on the hills and northern valley floor are richer and more fertile, with limestone improving the drainage on some but not all sites. An analysis of the 10-hectare Muddy Water vineyard, on the hills, found three different soil types varying in texture, sub-soil compactness and limestone content. Irrigation is essential on the gravels, but some vineyards on the heavier soils are not irrigated.

Wine styles

Pinot Noir, Riesling, Chardonnay and Sauvignon Blanc dominate plantings at Waipara. Pinot Noir is the major red-wine success, yielding fragrant, weighty, generous wines that rank among the country's finest. Bordeaux red varieties are not expanding. The top Rieslings are scented, intense and zingy, and the gravelly sites are yielding racy, richly flavoured Sauvignon Blancs. The Chardonnays are of varying quality, but the finest — such as Pegasus Bay and Mountford Vineyard — are deliciously powerful and concentrated.

Alan McCorkindale

■ A big-company man turned small-winery owner, Alan McCorkindale entered the industry as a cellarhand at McWilliam's, in Hawke's Bay. After graduating in 1983 as dux of Roseworthy College in South Australia, he climbed through the ranks and by 1988 had the high profile position of chief winemaker at Corbans Marlborough Winery. Why did he leave?

'Since leaving school, I'd always wanted my own vineyard and winery,' says McCorkindale. 'I felt like a new challenge, and it's a lot easier to make small amounts of quality wines than large volumes.'

First planted in 1996, the 3-hectare McCorkindale vineyard at Waipara is close-planted in Pinot Noir, Chardonnay and Meunier for his bottle-fermented sparkling Brut. The vines are cultivated on a north-west-facing slope in limestone-rich clay loams. For his still white and red table wines, McCorkindale buys grapes from growers in Marlborough and Waipara.

Launched from the 1998 vintage, the wines are made in fairly small volumes (about 8000 cases per year) using contract winery facilities in North Canterbury and Marlborough. McCorkindale is also employed to make the wine for other producers in both regions. The non-vintage Brut holds centre stage in the McCorkindale range. Pinot Noir-dominant, barrel-fermented and disgorged after a minimum of three years on its yeast lees, it offers strong, strawberryish, yeasty aromas and flavours in a complex yet deliciously easy-drinking style.

The Waipara Valley Dry Riesling is floral and appley, with a sliver of sweetness and appetising acidity. The Marlborough wines include a buttery, mealy, well-rounded and concentrated Chardonnay; a fresh, lively and full-flavoured Sauvignon Blanc with a small barrel-ferment component; and a moderately complex, mouthfilling and supple Pinot Noir.

Alan McCorkindale
NEW ZEALAND WINE

Address	Alan McCorkindale, Omihi Road, Waipara
Owners	The McCorkindale family
Key Wines	Brut, Waipara Valley Dry Riesling, Marlborough Sauvignon Blanc, Marlborough Gewürztraminer, Marlborough Chardonnay, Marlborough Pinot Noir

Alpine Pacific

■ Alpine Pacific is the latest name of a company formerly called Chancellor Estates, and before that, Waipara Estates.

Tony and Helen Willy, who planted some of the first vines at Waipara in 1982, later founded Waipara Estates with Marlborough winemakers Allan and Catherine Scott. The partners launched their first wine under the Chancellor label in 1995. After the Willys and the Scotts withdrew, the venture was controlled by Chris Parker, Kevin Dunn and Brian Souter. However, after a share offer in 2000, designed to raise funds for vineyard expansion and a new winery, was under-subscribed, Parker — formerly a shareholder in a chicken marketing company, Santa Rosa — and his wife, Carol, emerged as sole owners. Alpine Pacific owns two vineyards: the 12-hectare Mt Cass Block, originally planted by the Willys, and the 5-hectare Omihi Block, 1.5 kilometres further north. Chardonnay and Sauvignon Blanc are the key varieties, followed by Cabernet Sauvignon, Pinot Noir and Riesling. Grapes are also purchased from the Waipara region.

With an output of 10,000 cases in 2002, Alpine Pacific is a sizeable producer, releasing its wines under the Chancellor and (lower tier) Hanmer Junction brands. The wines are made by Dayne Sherwood at his Waipara winery, but Alpine Pacific hopes to build its own winery on the junction of State Highway 1 and the road to Hanmer Springs. The Mt Cass Road Waipara Sauvignon Blanc is one of the highlights of the range, with punchy melon/capsicum flavours, fresh and zingy. The Riesling is firm and crisp, with substantial body and strong, citrusy aromas and flavours. The Chardonnay is full-bodied, with peach/melon characters and a slightly buttery finish.

The Pinot Noir is robust and rounded, with plenty of ripe cherry/plum flavours and some spicy, savoury complexity. The Cabernet Sauvignon is typically leafy-green, but can show impressive concentration.

Address	Alpine Pacific Wine Company, 133 Mt Cass Road, Waipara
Owners	Chris and Carol Parker
Key Wines	Chancellor Mt Cass Road Waipara Chardonnay, Riesling, Sauvignon Blanc, Pinot Noir, Cabernet Sauvignon

Address	Canterbury House Vineyards, 780 Glasnevin Road, Waipara
Owner	Dr Michael Reid
Key Wines	Waipara Sauvignon Blanc, Chardonnay, Pinot Gris, Riesling, Pinot Noir, Merlot

Canterbury House

■ After touring New Zealand on vacation, 'falling in love with the country and its people', Californian Dr Michael Reid felt it was 'time for a third career, a last fling'. The result: a sweeping 86-hectare vineyard and handsome winery, tasting and restaurant complex that rises dramatically alongside the highway, just south of the Waipara River.

Reid, a professor of radiology at the University of California, Davis, is an expert in the adaptation of engineering to medicine. One reason he chose North Canterbury for his latest venture is that 'winery planning, development and construction is at least twice as expensive in California'.

First planted in 1994 in well-drained, sandy loams overlying gravels, the vineyard is devoted principally to Pinot Noir, Chardonnay, Sauvignon Blanc, Pinot Gris, Riesling and Merlot. Mark Rattray made the debut 1997 to 2001 vintages, but in early 2002 Alan McCorkindale (who also has his own Alan McCorkindale label) took over the winemaking reins.

Canterbury House produced over 48,000 cases from the 2002 vintage (a huge output by the district's standards) and has declared its intention to grow to 130,000 cases. The company vineyard will expand gradually to about 115 hectares, and grapes are also drawn from an adjoining, 30-hectare vineyard, owned by another American.

The wines, mostly sold in New Zealand, have typically been of average quality, with the notable exception of the Sauvignon Blanc, which bursts with fresh, crisply herbaceous aromas and flavours. The Chardonnay is weighty, with smooth lemon/apple flavours and a restrained oak influence; the Pinot Noir is moderately concentrated. At the 2001 Air New Zealand Wine Awards, Canterbury House scooped the trophy for champion wine of the show with an exquisite, thrillingly scented, pure and intense Noble Riesling 2000.

Address	Daniel Schuster Wines, 192 Reeces Road, Omihi
Owners	The Schuster, Petrie and McCauley families
Key Wines	Petrie Vineyard Selection Chardonnay, Twin Vineyards Pinot Noir, Omihi Hills Vineyard Selection Pinot Noir

Daniel Schuster

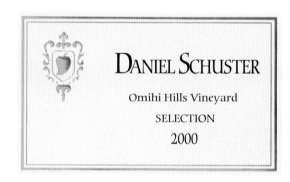

■ Danny Schuster has long been a guru of the Canterbury wine scene. As maker of the second New Zealand Pinot Noir to win a gold medal (the St Helena 1982) and co-author of a textbook on cool-climate viticulture and winemaking, he inevitably aroused high expectations when he planted his own vineyard in rolling hill country at Omihi, north-east of Waipara.

German-born, Schuster gathered his early winemaking experience in Europe, South Africa and Australia. Arriving in New Zealand in the late 1970s, he helped set up the grape trials and microvinification cellar at Lincoln University. Between 1980 and 1985, Schuster carved out a high profile as the winemaker at St Helena, and today he acts as a consultant to such prestigious wineries as Stag's Leap in California and Tenuta del Ornellaia in Tuscany.

The elevated, sloping, 6-hectare Omihi Hills vineyard, first planted in 1986, is well protected from easterly and southerly winds. The close-planted, non-irrigated Pinot Noir vines are planted in heavy clay loams, rich in limestone.

Schuster and his wife, Mari, are in partnership with Don Petrie, who 100 kilometres further south has an 18-hectare vineyard at Rakaia in mid-Canterbury, planted in 1991 in silt loams over gravels. Pinot Noir (principally) and Chardonnay are the chosen varieties. Brian and Shelley McCauley also have a shareholding.

Launched from the 1988 vintage and made on-site, the wines were initially of variable quality, but the latest releases show much greater ripeness and stuffing. Production in the 2001 vintage reached 5000 cases.

The Petrie Vineyard Selection Chardonnay is lemony, appley and nutty, with fresh, strong acidity giving it a Chablis-like steeliness. The Twin Vineyards Pinot Noir, grown in the Petrie and Omihi Hills vineyards, is fresh, supple and vibrantly fruity, with drink-young charm.

Schuster's key claim to fame is his Omihi Hills Vineyard Selection Pinot Noir. There have been few outstanding vintages to date, but at its best — as in 1998 and (to judge from barrel samples) 2001 — it is powerful, rich and firm, with notable complexity and length.

Fiddler's Green

■ Consistently immaculate and concentrated wines flow from this vineyard planted on a terrace south of the Waipara River. Fiddler's Green, the name given to the property by Lieutenant-Commander Sydney Hales, who in 1968 retired from the Royal Navy to Waipara, refers to '. . . the happy land imagined by sailors where there is perpetual mirth, a fiddle that never stops playing for dancers who never tire . . .'

Barry Johns, a former Christchurch lawyer, and his wife, Jennie, planted the first vines at Fiddler's Green in 1994. Their son, Ben, is also actively involved. Barry Johns was previously involved on a hobby basis in the Mountain View vineyard at Halswell, on the outskirts of Christchurch.

On a north-facing site with light, free-draining soils, the Fiddler's Green 14.5-hectare vineyard is planted in Pinot Noir, Riesling, Sauvignon Blanc and Chardonnay vines, irrigated with water from their 22 million-litre reservoir. Over the next three years, another 10 hectares of Pinot Noir will be established.

Entirely estate-grown, the wines were launched from the 1997 vintage and are made on a contract basis by Petter Evans at a local winery. Fiddler's Green's output is low (only 2500 cases from the 2001 vintage), but the wines are well worth tracking down.

The Riesling is a classic cool-climate style with mouth-watering acidity, a sliver of sweetness and intense varietal flavours. The Sauvignon Blanc is punchy and zesty, mingling tropical fruit and green capsicum flavours.

The debut 2001 Chardonnay is stylish, rich, finely balanced and long. The Pinot Noir also shows excellent weight and depth of cherry/plum flavours. These are sophisticated, highly satisfying wines.

Address Fiddler's Green Wines, Georges Road, Waipara

Owners Barry and Jennie Johns

Key Wines Riesling, Pinot Noir, Sauvignon Blanc, Chardonnay

Floating Mountain

■ Mark Rattray, a Pinot Noir and Chardonnay specialist, named his venture after a nearby mountain whose summit often pierces cloud and mists. The Maori name for Mt Grey is Maukatere — 'Floating Mountain'.

The Floating Mountain vineyard and winery are across the highway from the Waipara Springs winery, of which Rattray and his wife, Michelle, were among the founding partners. Born in Christchurch, Rattray studied at the Geisenheim Institute for two years in the early 1970s and worked at the fabled Schloss Johannisberg in the Rheingau. A long-drained bottle of Lorchhausen Rosenberg Riesling Kabinett 1971, with Rattray's name on the label, is a vivid reminder of the 0.2-hectare vineyard he once owned where the Mittelrhein runs into the Rheingau.

After five years with Montana and six years with Penfolds in Auckland, in 1985 Rattray came south to join St Helena, where he was the winemaker until 1990. After producing the first vintages at Waipara Springs, in early 1993 Rattray withdrew from the company. Since then he has acted as a consultant to several other Canterbury producers, and from 1997 to early 2002 was the winemaker at Canterbury House.

After buying former Cabinet Minister Derek Quigley's vineyard, Rattray uprooted the established Gewürztraminer in 1986 and replanted with Pinot Noir, Chardonnay and Sauvignon Blanc. Scheurebe is also grown for a late-harvest style. Seashells are buried in the chalk-based silty loams, revealing that the vineyard, which now totals 5 hectares, once formed part of the sea bed.

Additional grapes to fuel Floating Mountain's expansion will, from 2003, come from Hans Barkell-Schmitz's 8-hectare vineyard near Waipara West winery, planted in Pinot Noir (predominantly), Chardonnay and Gewürztraminer.

The barrel-fermented Waipara Chardonnay is powerful and tightly structured, with strong citrusy flavours, firm acid spine and buttery, nutty complexities. The Waipara Pinot Noir is a muscular style with deep colour, firm, chewy tannins and rich, spicy flavours. Both are bold wines, full of personality.

Address Floating Mountain Winery, 418 Omihi Road, Waipara

Owners Mark and Michelle Rattray

Key Wines Waipara Chardonnay, Waipara Pinot Noir

Address	Glenmark Wines, McKenzies Road, Waipara
Owner	John McCaskey
Key Wines	Riesling Dry, Riesling Medium, Gewürztraminer, Waipara Red

Glenmark

■ With his weathered face, gravelly voice and laconic manner, John McCaskey is one of the great characters of the Canterbury wine scene. A key pioneer of Waipara wine, he produces light, delicate Rieslings that can be quite Germanic in their scentedness and fragility.

McCaskey has spent his life farming his family's property at Weka Pass, which originally formed part of George Henry Moore's 60,000-hectare Glenmark sheep station, 'where peacocks roamed free and swans drifted on the man-made lake'. McCaskey experimented with viticulture at Waipara in the mid-1960s, but it was not until the Glenmark irrigation scheme was under way that diversification began. His first vineyard was planted in 1981 and the first Glenmark wines flowed in 1986.

McCaskey's original 4-hectare vineyard, planted in light silt loams over a base of clay and gravels, features Riesling as the principal variety with smaller plantings of Müller-Thurgau, Gewürztraminer, Chardonnay, Pinot Noir and Cabernet Sauvignon. McCaskey no longer owns but still leases this vineyard, and also plans to plant Merlot, Malbec, Cabernet Franc and Zinfandel on a rocky site further up the Weka Creek.

In 1992 McCaskey sold a share in his winery building, a converted haybarn on the main highway at Waipara, to Torlesse Wines; Glenmark and Torlesse now share the production facility. They also share a winemaker: Kym Rayner, an Australian who formerly worked for Penfolds at Gisborne and Montana at Blenheim, before becoming a shareholder in Torlesse.

Glenmark's annual output is small — about 1500 cases, entirely estate-grown. The Rieslings (both a Riesling Dry and Riesling Medium are produced) are at their best light, floral and vibrantly fruity, with touches of honey and spine-tingling acidity. McCaskey sees Riesling as a Glenmark speciality. The wines can take a year or two to open up, but then age gracefully for five years or longer. Top vintages of the Gewürztraminer are weighty and ripe, with lots of gingery, peppery flavour.

Waipara Red, based predominantly on Cabernet Sauvignon, with some Merlot, Malbec, Cabernet Franc and Seibel, is one of Glenmark's best-known labels. 'We try to give it a soft finish by blending,' says McCaskey, 'and avoid giving it extended maceration on skins or new oak.' Typically an easy-drinking, green-edged red with fresh, strong, red berry-fruit and mint flavours and a well-rounded finish, the 1991 vintage won the trophy for champion red wine at the 1992 Air New Zealand Wine Awards — the first time the trophy had crossed Cook Strait.

Address	Mountford Vineyard, 434 Omihi Road, Waipara
Owners	Buffy and Michael Eaton
Key Wines	Chardonnay, Pinot Noir

Mountford

■ Two of Waipara's most robust, fleshy and richly flavoured wines flow from the lovely hillside vineyard surrounding Mountford Lodge, a luxurious country homestead with just two bedrooms. The property takes its name from the ford in its long driveway and Mt Cass, which looms behind Mountford.

Michael and Buffy Eaton planted their first vines in 1991. Buffy, who grew up in the Hunter Valley, north of Sydney, has studied viticulture and oenology; Michael is a professional painter and a former senior lecturer in art education. Their original 4-hectare vineyard was close-planted entirely in Pinot Noir and Chardonnay, and recently new clones of Pinot Noir have spread up a steep (17 degrees) limestone-rich clay slope at the rear of the lodge.

Danny Schuster made the first 1996 vintage, but since 1997 the winemaker has been Chung Pin ('CP') Lin. Born in Taiwan, Lin, who is blind, has a postgraduate diploma in oenology from Lincoln University. 'The art of winemaking is to distil the essence of a place and bottle it,' believes Lin. 'A great bottle of wine should make you appreciate the minerals in the vineyard's soil, smell the air or the mushrooms that grow there, hear cow bells, think about the literature and poetry of the place.'

Mountford's wines, entirely estate-grown and made on-site, are rare, with an average annual output of 1000 cases. Whole-bunch pressed and fermented and lees-aged in French oak barriques, the Chardonnay is typically a bold, lush wine with rich, peachy, biscuity flavours and commanding mouthfeel. The Pinot Noir is also strapping, with deep colour, a beguiling fragrance and — in top vintages — an arresting concentration of raspberry, plum and spice flavours.

Muddy Water

■ Muddy Water is a literal translation of Waipara ('wai' meaning water and 'para' sediment or mud). One of the district's most consistently impressive small wineries, Muddy Water's flagship Mojo Pinot Noir is outstanding.

Jane East, who has a postgraduate diploma in viticulture and oenology, and her husband, Michael, a Christchurch obstetrician and gynaecologist with 'a passion for wine and hard work', planted their first vines in 1993. Cultivated in limestone-rich soils, the 10-hectare vineyard is managed by expert viticulturist Glyn Williams. Pinot Noir, Chardonnay and Riesling are the key varieties, with smaller plots of Sauvignon Blanc, Pinotage and Syrah.

Entirely estate-grown, the early 1996 to 1999 vintages were made by three winemakers (Mark Rattray, Belinda Gould and Kym Rayner) at two local wineries (Floating Mountain and Waipara Springs). From 2000 onwards, the wines have all been made by Belinda Gould in Muddy Water's own mud-coloured winery, built from straw bales plastered with cement, with vents and fans to take advantage of Waipara's cool night air. The company's output in 2001 totalled 3500 cases. A viticulturist turned winemaker, Belinda Gould graduated with a diploma in horticulture from Lincoln University in 1979, then spent two years studying viticulture at the famous Geisenheim Institute in the Rheingau. After working as a research technician with viticulturist Dr Richard Smart, she joined Waipara Springs as assistant winemaker to Kym Rayner in 1993, and has since held senior winemaking positions in California, at the Calera and Sonoma-Cutrer wineries.

Muddy Water's wines are skilfully crafted and full of character. The Dry Riesling is a flinty, minerally wine with good intensity; the James Hardwick Riesling is a medium style, beautifully scented, poised and rich. At its best, the oak-aged Sauvignon Blanc shows excellent weight and depth of ripe gooseberry and passionfruit characters, gently seasoned with toasty oak. Fermented with indigenous yeasts, the Chardonnay is bold and concentrated, with fresh acidity woven through its peachy, mealy, toasty flavours.

Both the Pinotage and Syrah are promising. The Pinot Noir is generous and well-rounded, with sweet, ripe plum/cherry flavours and lots of drink-young charm. Fermented with indigenous yeasts and bottled without filtration, Mojo Pinot Noir (launched from the 2000 vintage) is savoury, earthy, spicy and gamey in a multi-faceted, rich, firmly structured style that should flourish with cellaring.

Pegasus Bay

■ Pegasus Bay is Canterbury's top winery. It sprang to prominence in the mid-1990s as the first in the region to fashion a range of locally grown wines that could challenge — even match — the best from elsewhere. Today, its Chardonnays, Rieslings, Sauvignon/Sémillons, claret-style reds and Pinot Noirs are consistently top-flight.

Named after the large bay that stretches north up the coast from Christchurch, Pegasus Bay is a family affair. 'There are three things in life I'm passionate about — my family, neurology and wine,' says Associate Professor Ivan Donaldson. A consultant neurologist at Christchurch School of Medicine, Donaldson oversees the vineyard, is a senior wine judge, and for many years contributed a wine column to *The Press*. Chris Donaldson, Ivan's wife, is Pegasus Bay's business manager. Their son, Matthew, a graduate of Roseworthy College, holds the winemaking reins with his partner, Lynnette Hudson, who has a postgraduate diploma in viticulture and oenology from Lincoln University. Another son, Edward, who trained as a chef, oversees the winery restaurant and doubles as the company's marketing manager. The Donaldsons planted their first vines at Waipara in 1986. Today the vineyard

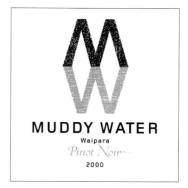

Address Muddy Water,
434 Omihi Road,
Waipara

Owners Jane and Michael East

Key Wines Chardonnay, James
Hardwick Riesling, Dry
Riesling, Sauvignon Blanc,
Pinot Noir, Mojo Pinot Noir

Address Pegasus Bay Winery,
Stockgrove Road,
Waipara

Owners The Donaldson family

Key Wines Pegasus Bay Chardonnay,
Sauvignon/Sémillon,
Riesling, Aria Late Picked
Riesling, Cabernet/Merlot,
Maestro, Pinot Noir, Prima
Donna Pinot Noir; Main
Divide Chardonnay,
Sauvignon Blanc, Riesling,
Pinot Noir

Matthew Donaldson and his partner, Lynette
Hudson, head the winemaking team at
Canterbury's most successful winery.

covers 30 hectares of Pinot Noir, Riesling, Chardonnay, Sauvignon Blanc, Sémillon, Cabernet Sauvignon, Merlot, Malbec and Cabernet Franc, with a tiny plot of Syrah. 'It's lean country,' says Matthew Donaldson. 'The topsoil is loess, never deeper than a foot [0.3 m], and below that it's gravel for 100 metres or so.' The vineyard is planted on north-facing terraces which slope down to the Waipara River, which forms its northern boundary.

Ivan Donaldson is clear about the style of wine he's after. 'New Zealand wines typically have no weakness in flavour, but often lack weight, texture, length and longevity. The style we are emphasising depends on more than just upfront fruit; it has weight in the mouth and plenty of length. In addition, we are after a special mid-palate texture, a type of creaminess.'

Launched from the 1991 vintage, the wines are made in a handsome, terracotta-coloured winery with specially constructed viewing areas for visitors and a large restaurant. Two ranges are produced. The Pegasus Bay selection is made exclusively from estate-grown grapes, while those branded as Main Divide (typically excellent value) are based on grapes purchased from growers in Canterbury and other South Island regions.

The Chardonnay, fully French oak-fermented, is very classy, with substantial body, a delicious surge of citrusy, savoury, slightly buttery flavour and good acid spine. The Sauvignon/Sémillon offers a basket of exotic fruit flavours, with subtle oak and lees characters adding complexity. The scented and zingy, off-dry Riesling is shot through with citrusy, limey, slightly honeyed flavour. The Aria Late Picked Riesling is a sweet (but not super-sweet) style with intense, botrytis-enriched flavours.

The Cabernet/Merlot is sturdy and full-flavoured, but is overshadowed by its stablemate, Maestro, which is based on older vines and matured in a higher percentage of new oak. Dark and robust, generous, brambly and concentrated, Maestro is Canterbury's finest claret-style red. The Pinot Noir is supple and harmonious, with layers of cherry, plum and smoky oak flavours and a lingering, velvety finish. The flagship Pinot Noir, Prima Donna, is highly fragrant, spicy, savoury and complex, with a firm foundation of tannin and a long, rich finish.

Sherwood Estate

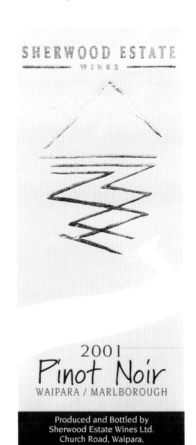

■ Sherwood Estate is a new arrival on the Waipara block, but no stranger to the Canterbury wine scene. Dayne and Jill Sherwood planted their first vines at West Melton, near Christchurch, in 1986.

With export demand skyrocketing, especially from the United States for Sauvignon Blanc and Pinot Noir, Sherwood Estate completely outgrew its original winery at West Melton. 'There's been such pressure on space that most of the tanks and our bottling facility spread outside the winery building,' says Jill Sherwood. 'We simply ran out of room for more extensions.' The new, much larger winery in Church Road, Waipara, is also far closer to the company's major vineyards.

Dayne Sherwood is a Cantabrian who, after graduating with a BA in business administration and history, initially worked for an accountancy company and a bank. After spells at Torlesse and Hunter's, and gaining a postgraduate diploma in viticulture and oenology from Lincoln University, in 1990 Sherwood plunged into full-time winemaking. 'It all started from drinking the stuff,' he recalls, 'and then wanting to know more about it. Now it's a lifestyle and a business.'

In the original, 4-hectare vineyard in Weedons Ross Road, West Melton, Pinot Noir and Chardonnay are planted in free-draining silt loams over a gravel river bed base (Sherwood Estate has retained its administrative office at this site). At Waipara, the company has established another 22 hectares, principally in Pinot Noir and Chardonnay. Sherwood Estate also shares the ownership of 48 hectares of Marlborough vineyards (mostly planted in Sauvignon Blanc) with four other Canterbury-based producers. Grapes are also purchased from growers in Hawke's Bay (Merlot), Marlborough and Canterbury.

At first the Sherwoods planned to produce about 1500 cases of wine per year, but the output has climbed steadily to 7000 cases in 1997 and 17,000 cases in 2001. After many years of trial, the Sherwoods now focus mainly on three varieties: Sauvignon Blanc, Chardonnay and Pinot Noir.

The Chardonnay, grown in Marlborough, is a partly oak-aged style with crisp, citrusy, slightly buttery flavours. The Reserve Chardonnay, grown at West Melton, barrel-fermented and lees-aged, is impressively savoury, mealy and complex, with slightly flinty acidity and good cellaring potential.

Packed with fresh, vibrant, tropical-fruit and herbaceous flavours, the Marlborough Sauvignon Blanc is consistently attractive. Some of the early Pinot Noirs were not impressive, but the latest vintages are the best. The standard Pinot Noir is berryish, spicy and smooth, with satisfying depth, and its Reserve stablemate offers strong, subtly oaked raspberry/spice flavours, fresh and firm.

Address Sherwood Estate, Church Road, Waipara

Owners Dayne and Jill Sherwood

Key Wines Chardonnay, Marlborough Sauvignon Blanc, Pinot Noir; Reserve Pinot Noir, Chardonnay

Torlesse

■ Torlesse produces a selection of solid, often good Canterbury wines, typically bargain-priced.

Named after Mount Torlesse and the Torlesse Range, inland from Christchurch, the company's early history proved turbulent. Founded at West Melton by 20 shareholders, half of whom were grower-suppliers, Torlesse processed its first vintage in 1987. Three years later, however, the winery slid into receivership. 'It was basically a production rather than market-led company,' says Kym Rayner, the winemaker.

The phoenix-like rise of Torlesse came when a new company was formed in 1990 by two of the original shareholders: Andrew Tomlin, an accountant, and Dr David Jackson, who is no longer involved. Rayner, who made the 1990 vintage, soon after also became a shareholder. Today, the shares are spread evenly between Andrew Tomlin (who handles the company's finances); Rayner; Michael and Hazel Blowers, of Christchurch; and Canadian investors Dick and Vivian Pharis and Gary and Ann Fabris.

Kym Rayner is a lanky Australian whose parents were grape-growers in McLaren Vale. After graduating from Roseworthy College in 1975, Rayner worked in Australia until he came to New Zealand in 1983 to run Penfolds' new winery in Gisborne. Following Montana's 1986 takeover of Penfolds, Rayner spent the next three years at Montana's Blenheim winery, then came south to join Torlesse. In 1992, Torlesse purchased a share in the original, red corrugated-iron Glenmark winery building at Waipara, where Torlesse also now offers tastings and wine sales.

Apart from a token 0.8-hectare plot adjacent to the winery, Torlesse does not own vineyards, but its shareholders do (including a site adjacent to Mountford Vineyard, selected recently for its potential for premium Pinot Noir). 'We've aligned our varietal plantings to three distinctive soil types around Waipara,' says Rayner, 'and are starting to reap the benefits.' Torlesse draws grapes from Waipara, other parts of Canterbury and Marlborough.

With its annual output of around 12,000 cases, Torlesse is one of the region's largest producers. The Waipara Riesling is a distinctly cool-climate style, tight and crisp, with appley, limey flavours. Weighty, with fresh, strong passionfruit/lime flavours and a touch of complexity from a small percentage of barrel-fermentation, the Waipara Sauvignon Blanc is full of character. The Waipara Selection Chardonnay is toasty and citrusy, with taut acidity. The Pinot Noir, a Canterbury regional blend, is firm, with ripe plum/cherry flavours and some spicy, smoky complexity. The Waipara Pinot Noir is savoury and nutty, with strawberry and spicy aromas, sweet fruit characters and good flavour depth.

Address Torlesse Wines,
Loffhagen Drive,
Waipara

Owners The Tomlin, Rayner, Blowers,
Pharis and Fabris families

Key Wines Waipara Riesling, Waipara
Sauvignon Blanc, Waipara
Selection Chardonnay,
Waipara Pinot Noir, Lightly
Oaked Chardonnay,
Pinot Noir

Waipara Springs

■ Behind a row of gum trees on the state highway at Waipara nestles a collection of rustic grey farm buildings. Waipara Springs, named after a spring which rises in the nearby hills, boasts one of the region's most popular restaurants and also produces some of its finest wines.

The Moore and Grant families processed their first vintage in 1989. Bruce and Jill Moore, who originally owned the property, planted 4 hectares of Chardonnay in 1982 as contract growers for Corbans. After the Moores formed a partnership in 1987 with Andrew Grant and his mother, Beverley (owners of a local transport company), the vineyard was expanded, and in 1990 a winery was built.

Today, Bruce Moore and his son, Andrew, manage the vineyards; Jill runs the wine bar. Andrew Grant, who has a degree in business management, is the managing director and reports he is 'also a good shoveller at harvest'.

Mark Rattray made the early vintages, followed by Belinda Gould. Stephanie Henderson-Grant, who joined Waipara Springs in 1996 in a

Bruce Moore (right), now in partnership with Andrew Grant and his family, is one of the pioneers of Waipara wine, having planted his first vines in 1982.

marketing role, became assistant winemaker in 1998 and has been the sole winemaker since 2000. Now married to Andrew Grant, she has vintage experience in Oregon and California, and holds an honours degree in agricultural science from Lincoln University.

The 17.5-hectare vineyard behind the winery is planted in Chardonnay (the principal variety), Riesling, Sauvignon Blanc and Pinot Noir. A separate, 3.5-hectare block of Cabernet Sauvignon, Merlot and Pinot Noir is owned by Andrew Grant and Stephanie Henderson-Grant. The loam-clay soils are relatively heavy, with an underlying pan over a limestone and shingle base. A small amount of Pinot Noir and Chardonnay is purchased from an adjacent vineyard, but the wines are predominantly estate-grown.

Waipara Springs' current annual output is about 9000 cases of wine. The Lightly Oaked Chardonnay, 20 per cent

Address Waipara Springs Wines,
409 Omihi Road,
Waipara

Owners The Moore and
Grant families

Key Wines Barrique Chardonnay,
Lightly Oaked Chardonnay,
Riesling, Sauvignon Blanc,
Pinot Noir, Reserve Pinot
Noir

barrel-fermented, is a crisp, lively, drink-young style, at its best full of citrusy, slightly nutty flavour. The Barrique Chardonnay, fully French oak-fermented, is mouthfilling, with strong, peachy, citrusy, toasty flavours.

Aromatic and zingy, the Riesling is a medium-dry style with plenty of lemony, limey flavour. The Sauvignon Blanc is punchy and grassy, with lovely freshness and zing in its youth.

The Cabernet Sauvignon is vibrantly fruity and satisfyingly full-flavoured in warm vintages, but in cooler years light, berryish and crisp. The Reserve Pinot Noir is more consistently impressive, with strawberryish, nutty, spicy flavours of very satisfying depth.

Waipara West

Address Waipara West,
376 Ram Paddock Road,
Waipara

Owners Paul Tutton, Olga Sienko, Vic
Tutton and Lindsay Hill

Key Wines Riesling, Chardonnay,
Sauvignon Blanc, Pinot Noir,
Ram Paddock Red

■ Waipara West's intense, tautly structured wines are better known in London than Christchurch or Wellington. Part-owner Paul Tutton, an expatriate New Zealander, sells most of the wine through his London-based importing and distribution business, Waterloo Wine Company.

Waipara West was founded in 1989 by four partners: Tutton and his wife, artist Olga Sienko, his sister, Vic Tutton, and her husband, Lindsay Hill, who manages the vineyard. The venture is named after a weather station on the property, 6 kilometres inland from the main north–south highway, near the Waipara Gorge. When the partners purchased the property in 1989, it was discovered that the family had owned the land 90 years earlier. The 20-hectare vineyard, on terraces partly surrounded by steep cliffs, is planted in Riesling, Chardonnay, Sauvignon Blanc, Pinot Noir, Merlot, Cabernet Sauvignon and Cabernet Franc. The soil types vary from river stones with limestone to alluvial loams over gravels.

Entirely estate-grown, the wines are made on-site by Petter Evans, winemaker at St Helena from 1991 to 1997. A Cantabrian, Evans is a Roseworthy College oenology graduate who has worked in Auckland, Marlborough, Victoria and Germany. Waipara West's first commercial vintage flowed in 1996. The average annual production is around 3000 cases.

Fermented to full dryness, the Riesling is vibrantly fruity, with intense lemon, lime and spice flavours, fresh, poised and steely. The Sauvignon Blanc is similarly dry, punchy and racy, with piercing melon/lime flavours. Whole-bunch pressed and French oak-fermented, the Chardonnay is fresh and elegant, with a mealy, toasty, minerally richness.

Ram Paddock Red is a smooth, berryish, sometimes green-edged blend of Cabernet Sauvignon, Merlot and Cabernet Franc, with sweet American and French oak characters and good flavour depth. The flagship red is the Pinot Noir — fragrant, full and fresh, with rich, well-ripened cherry/plum flavours seasoned with spicy oak and rounded tannins. These are classy wines.

2000
WAIPARA WEST

Chardonnay
WAIPARA
750ml PRODUCE OF NEW ZEALAND 13.5%vol

Other producers

■ Bell Hill Vineyard
North-west of Waipara and further inland, at 250 metres above sea level, Marcel Giesen and his wife, Sherwyn Veldhuizen, have since 1997 planted a 1-hectare vineyard of Pinot Noir (mainly) and Chardonnay on a north-facing, limestone-rich slope in Old Weka Pass Road. The wines, first produced in 1999, are being marketed under the Old Weka Pass Road brand until the vines reach some maturity.

■ Black Estate
Russell and Kumiko Black own 8 hectares of unirrigated Pinot Noir and Chardonnay vines in Omihi Road, Waipara, first planted in 1993. The range, launched from the 1999 vintage and made by Mark Rattray, features a fragrant, refined and rich Chardonnay and a distinguished, powerful Pinot Noir, warm, complex, firm and persistent.

■ Waipara Downs
'A farm with a vineyard' is how Keith and Ruth Berry promote their 319-hectare property with its 4 hectares of vines planted in friable, free-draining clays. Waipara Downs lies in Bains Road, off the inland highway from North Canterbury to Nelson. Made on-site, the wines include a crisp, strawberryish Pinot Noir and a solid, often highly enjoyable Chardonnay.

■ Waipara Hills Wine Estate
The proceeds from a public share float in 2001 that raised over $2.5 million were used to purchase the assets of Langdale Wine Estate, at West Melton. Waipara Hills will also buy contract-grown grapes from Waipara, other parts of Canterbury and Marlborough, and plans an output exceeding 30,000 cases by 2005. In the four months to the end of 2001, the company reported a start-up loss of $766,000. The wines, initially to be made at the St Helena winery, are all now marketed under the Waipara Hills brand.

Canterbury Plains

In contrast to the tightly confined area of Waipara, the Canterbury Plains is a vast, sprawling sub-region. From Amberley in the north to near Timaru in the south, the plains stretch for 180 kilometres. On the wine trail, you spend a long time behind the wheel.

In sharp contrast to the unrelenting flatness of the plains, south-east of Christchurch looms the hilly, volcanic landscape of Banks Peninsula. Parts of the peninsula are too wet for viticulture — especially the areas exposed to rain-bearing south-easterly winds — but a few sheltered, warm sites are ideal. At the Kaituna Valley vineyard, Pinot Noir is normally harvested several weeks earlier than on the plains. For the numerous wineries at West Melton, Burnham and north of the city, close proximity to Christchurch gives access to a large, supportive market.

History

French peasants who landed in 1840 at Akaroa on Banks Peninsula carried vine cuttings, from which wine soon flowed for their domestic consumption. However, heavy forest cover, oidium (powdery mildew) and the spread of British influence on Banks Peninsula combined to defeat hopes for a flourishing wine industry. A century later, W.H. Meyers built a small winery, Villa Nova, in the Heathcote Valley (near the Ferrymead area, on the way to Sumner Beach). By 1945 he had a tiny vineyard of about 0.8 hectares planted in Verdelho, Pinot Gris, Muscat and other grapes. Although wine was made, Meyers' vines were uprooted around 1949 after they failed to flourish. Mountain View, an experimental, 0.5-hectare vineyard with nine different grape varieties, was established in 1976 at Halswell, on the outskirts of Christchurch. Associate Professor Ivan Donaldson (who now owns Pegasus Bay) made the wines, which were not released publicly. St Helena, the first commercial winery, was established by Robin and Norman Mundy at Belfast, on the northern edge of Christchurch, in 1978. When St Helena Pinot Noir 1982 won the second gold medal ever awarded to a New Zealand Pinot Noir, interest in Canterbury wine snowballed. Today, viticulture on the plains is expanding more slowly than at Waipara (in 2001, there were 336 hectares of vines at Waipara, but only 278 hectares throughout the rest of Canterbury). Sherwood Estate, established at West Melton in 1986, recently shifted its wine production facility to Waipara. 'Land is cheaper at Waipara,' says Dayne Sherwood. 'There are no subdivision pressures. And in marketing terms, Waipara has the higher profile.'

Climate

The vineyards near Christchurch are markedly cooler than those at Waipara, according to the heat summation figures for Lincoln (973) and Waipara (1117). After studying the climate data, the distinguished Australian viticultural scientist, Dr John Gladstones, concluded that 'only a few outstandingly warm sites … [in the Christchurch area] could be expected to ripen any high-quality grape varieties regularly'. Vineyards on the plains are exposed to cooling east-north-easterlies (the predominant wind affecting Christchurch in summer), hot, dry north-westerly blasts, and rain-bearing southerly winds. Shelter belts help, but also increase the frost risk. However, the Canterbury Plains are drier than the North Island wine-growing regions, and the rainfall at Lincoln during the October–April growing season is 10 per cent below that at Waipara. Marcel Giesen views the typically long, dry autumn of the Burnham district, south-west of Christchurch, as its key viticultural asset: 'We never pick our Pinot Noir before 20 April, and sometimes in early May.'

Frosts are a danger, reduced by cultivating the soil between the rows to keep it warmer, rather than 'grassing down', helicopters and overhead sprinklers. On the plus side, low humidity reduces the disease pressure: 'We spend a lot less on sprays at West Melton than at Marlborough,' says Dayne Sherwood. Due to the flat terrain, there is little variation in mesoclimate between close vineyard sites.

Soils

A series of giant, gently sloping fans built up by four major rivers — the Rangitata, Ashburton, Rakaia and Waimakariri — the Canterbury Plains were formed by colossal amounts of greywacke debris, washed down from the back country and deposited on the plains. Soils with less than 45 centimetres of fine material over the outwash gravels are described as 'stony terrace soils'; those with more than 45 centimetres are termed 'deep'.

Across the plains, the majority of the soils are shallow and stony. However, at West Melton, where 50 centimetre-deep Templeton silt loams overlie 'Waimak' river shingles, Dayne Sherwood describes the soils as 'more fertile than at Waipara'.

So fast-draining are most of the soils, irrigation is essential, but there is an abundant supply of water from rivers and aquifers.

Wine styles

Winemaker Marcel Giesen views Riesling and Pinot Noir as the key successes at Giesen's estate vineyard at Burnham, south-west of Christchurch, where Gewürztraminer, Sauvignon Blanc, Merlot and Cabernet Sauvignon have all been phased out. At the Sandihurst vineyard in West Melton, even the birds avoided Cabernet Sauvignon. Dayne Sherwood, who grows grapes at West Melton and in North Canterbury, reports 'higher brixes [sugar levels] in most varieties at West Melton than at Waipara, but the flavours aren't necessarily riper'. The consistently impressive Giesen Reserve Barrel Selection Pinot Noir, grown at Burnham on a fruiting wire close to the warm, stony ground, shows what can be done.

Address	Giesen Wine Estate, Burnham School Road, Burnham
Owners	Theo, Alex and Marcel Giesen
Key Wines	Canterbury Riesling, Marlborough Sauvignon Blanc, Marlborough School Road Chardonnay, Voyage, Pinot Noir, Noble School Road Late Harvest; Reserve Barrel Selection Canterbury Chardonnay, Marlborough Chardonnay, Canterbury Pinot Noir

Giesen

■ From the start, Theo, Alex and Marcel Giesen thought big — the boutique scale typical of Canterbury wineries was never their style. In the 1980s, they upset sections of the fledgling local industry by buying Marlborough grapes. Relentless marketers, they swiftly emerged as the region's largest producer, built a national following, plunged into export, and now run one of New Zealand's 10 largest wine companies.

Giesen's headquarters is at Burnham, south-west of Christchurch. The three brothers were raised at Neustadt, in the wine-growing Rheinpfalz region. Granite quarrying, construction and masonry were the family's chief occupation, but the Giesens, like countless other German families, also owned a small plot of grapevines and made wine for their private consumption.

Why did they uproot themselves to start a new life in New Zealand? 'For opportunity, space, clean air and freedom,' says Marcel Giesen. Winemaking was not part of the brothers' initial plans in the new country, but Marcel recalls being 'confused by the number of Müller-Thurgaus labelled as "Riesling" and astonished by the lack of dry Rieslings. We thought: "Why not make some wine in the style we had produced at home?"'

GIESEN

MARLBOROUGH
SAUVIGNON
BLANC
2001

750ml PRODUCE OF NEW ZEALAND 13%alc/vol
PRODUCED AND BOTTLED BY GIESEN WINE ESTATE CANTERBURY NEW ZEALAND

Raised in the Rheinpfalz, Alex (left) and Marcel Giesen, together with their brother Theo, have built Giesen into Canterbury's largest wine company.

The Giesens bought land at Burnham and planted their first vines in 1981 because they 'particularly wanted to grow Riesling, which flourishes in a cool climate, so in the end it was obvious we should go south.' The brothers' parents, Kurt and Gudrun, helped to fund the new winery, which processed its first harvest in 1984.

Today, the Giesens own 30 hectares of vines in Canterbury and 123 hectares (spread over 11 sites) in Marlborough, where in 2000 the company erected a major new winery. Sauvignon Blanc, Chardonnay, Riesling and Pinot Noir are the key varieties planted. Contract growers currently supply about 25 per cent of the company's total grape intake.

To keep the fast-growing company (125,000 cases in 2001) on the rails, the Giesen brothers have divided between them the myriad tasks of a modern winery. Theo and Alexander are immersed in administration and marketing. Marcel controls production in the utilitarian, corrugated-iron and timber winery, with the assistance of Andrew Blake, a former 'flying winemaker' who joined Giesen in 1997.

Marcel Giesen delights in Riesling's mouth-wateringly crisp acidity: 'You need steely acidity for structure, elegance and longevity. With the low yields we get in Canterbury, our grapes have high extract [stuffing] and the wines can carry more acidity. Riesling like this ages longer than Chardonnay or Sauvignon Blanc.'

Giesen's glorious Botrytised Riesling — in the past one of the country's finest sweet whites — is no longer made (for economic reasons) but at its best the Noble School Road Late Harvest, blended from Riesling and Müller-Thurgau, is a deliciously concentrated and honeyish wine, priced sharply. The medium-dry Canterbury Riesling is also fine value, offering strong lemon/lime flavours and a touch of honey.

The line-up of Chardonnays includes a citrusy Marlborough School Road Chardonnay with biscuity, buttery notes adding complexity; a toasty, minerally and concentrated Reserve Barrel Selection Marlborough Chardonnay that matures well; and an elegant, richly flavoured Reserve Barrel Selection Canterbury Chardonnay.

The large-volume Marlborough Sauvignon Blanc is consistently good, with gooseberry/lime flavours, crisp and punchy. Voyage, a non-vintage, bottle-fermented sparkling, is a Pinot Noir-dominant style, citrusy, yeasty and lively.

Red wine in the past was not an important part of the range, but Pinot Noir is now a key feature. The standard Pinot Noir is a medium-bodied style, floral, berryish and smooth. Showing markedly greater concentration and complexity, the estate-grown Reserve Barrel Selection Canterbury Pinot Noir is savoury, toasty and rich.

Kaituna Valley

■ With a glittering haul of six gold medals and two major trophies at national wine competitions in 2000 and 2001 for their Pinot Noirs, Grant and Helen Whelan are riding high. The Whelans produce exceptional single-vineyard wines from The Kaituna Vineyard on Banks Peninsula and The Awatere Vineyard in Marlborough.

The success of Kaituna Valley reflects not only the Whelans' passion for Pinot Noir, but also their impressive academic backgrounds and lengthy winemaking experience. Helen has a PhD in plant pathology. Grant, who gained his Bachelor of Agricultural Science degree with first class honours and has a postgraduate diploma in viticulture and oenology from Lincoln University, has since 1993 been the winemaker for Rossendale Wines. Helen's parents, Brian and Norma Cameron, also have a financial stake in the venture.

The Kaituna Valley Vineyard lies in a warm, sheltered valley just off the main road to Akaroa, where 2 hectares of Pinot Noir and Chardonnay are planted on a north-facing slope with clay soils. The original block of Pinot Noir vines, planted by Graeme Stean in 1977, is the oldest in Canterbury, according to Grant Whelan.

On terraces of the Awatere River in Marlborough, near Clifford Bay and Vavasour, since 1996 the Whelans have close-planted 7.5 hectares of Sauvignon Blanc, Chardonnay, Pinot Noir and Pinot Gris in shallow, sandy, stony soils with a mudstone base. Another, 3-hectare vineyard of Pinot Noir and Pinot Gris is currently being developed on a warm and windy, north-facing slope near Tai Tapu, also on Banks Peninsula, where a winery is planned for the 2003 vintage.

In all the vineyards, low-yielding vines and intensive canopy management techniques — shoot and cluster thinning, lateral removal, extensive leaf-plucking — are used to maximise grape quality.

Kaituna Valley swiftly made an impact when its debut 1993 Pinot Noir won a gold medal and trophy at the 1995 Liquorland Royal Easter Wine Show — the first New Zealand gold awarded to a Canterbury Pinot Noir since the St Helena 1994. Entirely estate-grown, the wines are still rare: only 1700 cases were produced in 2001, expected to climb to 3000 cases by 2004. The two Chardonnays offer a clear style contrast. The Kaituna Valley Vineyard Chardonnay is tightly structured, with rich grapefruit and nut flavours; the Awatere Vineyard Chardonnay is more open in its youth, with deep grapefruit and peach flavours and a rounded finish. The Awatere Valley Vineyard Sauvignon Blanc is a gently oaked style, full-flavoured, freshly herbaceous and flinty.

The Kaituna Valley Vineyard Pinot Noir, based on the old vines and younger plantings of new clones, is sturdy, plummy, spicy and firm, with impressive intensity, complexity and structure. Its stablemate, the Awatere Valley Vineyard Pinot Noir, is a very elegant style with finely integrated French oak, gentle tannins and notable depth of cherry, raspberry and plum flavours, beautifully rounded and long.

2 0 0 0

KAITUNA
VALLEY

Pinot Noir
Canterbury

The Kaituna Vineyard

13.7% Alc by vol 750ml
Wine of New Zealand

Address Kaituna Valley,
230 Kaituna Valley Road,
Banks Peninsula

Owners Grant and Helen Whelan,
Brian and Norma Cameron

Key Wines The Kaituna Vineyard
Canterbury Pinot Noir,
Canterbury Chardonnay; The
Awatere Vineyard
Marlborough Pinot Noir,
Marlborough Chardonnay,
Marlborough Sauvignon Blanc

Address   Langdale (Waipara Hills),
            Langdales Road,
            West Melton

Owner   Waipara Hills Wine Estate

Key Wines Barrel Fermented Chardonnay,
            Riesling, Marlborough
            Sauvignon Blanc, Pinot Gris,
            Breidecker, Canterbury Pinot
            Noir, Winemaker's Selection
            Pinot Noir

Langdale (Waipara Hills)

■ Down a West Melton driveway lined with English lavendar and vines and across a footbridge lies the two-storey, forest green Langdale vineyard restaurant. The menu features 'creative country cuisine', washed down, of course, with Langdale's attractive — sometimes excellent — Canterbury and Marlborough wines, now labelled as Waipara Hills.

Langdale's first vines were planted in 1989, followed by the first experimental wines in 1992 and 1993 and the first commercial vintage in 1994. Langdale was founded by a large group of shareholders, including manager Lew Stribling (who is still at the helm), but in 2001 the company was purchased by Waipara Hills Wine Estate.

Stribling, a former arts student at Canterbury University, worked in horticulture in Whangarei before he came back to Christchurch in 1989 to plant grapevines on the West Melton property he had purchased two years earlier. 'I developed an interest in wine going around the west Auckland vineyards,' he recalls. 'I was intrigued by the way the winemakers there were able to follow through the full creative process.'

The 4.5-hectare estate vineyard, close to the Waimakariri River, is planted principally in Pinot Noir, Riesling and Chardonnay. Grapes are also purchased from Canterbury and Marlborough growers.

For several years, Langdale's small output of wine was made elsewhere on a contract basis and sold mainly at the cellar door, in the restaurant or by mail order. By 1998, says Stribling, it was clear that 'if we wanted to expand the business, it had to be on the wine production and sales side, rather than the "hospitality" aspect.' A small winery was built and a qualified winemaker, Carol Bunn, was employed.

Now, under the ownership of Waipara Hills, the wines are no longer made on-site, but the company plans eventually to build a joint-venture winery at Waipara. Waipara Hills was launched in 2001, when a public share float raised $2.86 million. Waipara Hills does not intend to own extensive vineyards, but will instead purchase most of its grapes from growers in Waipara, other parts of Canterbury and Marlborough.

The early wines were generally light in body and flavour, but of late have shown markedly greater depth. The Breidecker is a good summertime quaffer, tangy, slightly sweet and appley. The Riesling is scented, with very good depth of lemony, limey flavours, slightly sweet and crisp.

The Marlborough Sauvignon Blanc is full of varietal character — grassy and zingy. The Chardonnay is fresh and lemony, with biscuity, buttery characters and good acid spine. Partly oak-fermented, the Pinot Gris offers plenty of peachy, spicy, nutty flavour.

The Pinot Noir is a medium-bodied, buoyantly fruity style. The Winemaker's Selection Pinot Noir is more substantial and complex, with excellent depth of berryish, spicy, nutty flavour.

Address   Melness Wines,
            1816 Main Road,
            Cust Village,
            North Canterbury

Owners   Norma and Colin Marshall

Key Wines Chardonnay, Riesling,
            Sauvignon Blanc,
            Gewürztraminer, Pinot Noir

Melness

■ When Norma and Colin Marshall established their vineyard in inland North Canterbury in 1990, they planted 11 different grape varieties, not knowing which would flourish in the area's icy winters and hot summers. Seven years later, they had their answer. Melness Pinot Noir 1995 headed off 258 Australian and New Zealand Pinot Noirs to win *Winestate* magazine's trophy for the Pinot Noir of the Year.

Melness lies on the Rangiora to Oxford road, just west of the township of Cust. The Marshalls, both former high-school teachers, named their venture after a coastal village in the far north of Scotland where Norma's great-grandfather was born.

The 0.6-hectare vineyard, on a sheltered, north-facing slope, is now planted in three varieties: Gewürztraminer, Chardonnay and Pinot Noir. 'It's common for temperatures in the vineyard to climb past 40°C,' says Norma. Grapes are also drawn from growers in Canterbury and Marlborough.

The first vintage, 1993, yielded only 160 bottles, which the Marshalls drank themselves. Today, the annual production has reached 1500 cases, made by Matthew Donaldson and Lynnette Hudson at the Pegasus Bay winery.

The Pinot Noir is typically of good quality, although the outstanding richness of the 1995 has yet to be repeated. The Chardonnay is mouthfilling, peachy and smooth, in a very easy-drinking style.

The Riesling offers strong citrusy flavours with plentiful sweetness. The Sauvignon Blanc, of varying regional origin, has also ranged in style, but is typically fresh and full-flavoured.

Opihi

■ When Colin and Brenda Lyon scooped a gold medal for their 1998 Pinot Gris at the 1999 Liquorland Royal Easter Wine Show, they swung the spotlight on the Canterbury region's southernmost vineyard. Opihi, north-west of Timaru, lies 25 kilometres from the coast, near Pleasant Point, and 140 kilometres south of Christchurch.

Opihi ('place of growth') is owned by farmers Colin and Brenda Lyon, who planted their first vines — 1.8 hectares of Müller-Thurgau, Riesling, Chardonnay and Pinot Noir — in 1991. A year later, they added 1.8 hectares of Pinot Gris, and in 2000 a further 1.8 hectares of Pinot Noir.

Planted on a north-facing slope with clay sub-soils, the vineyard is far enough inland to escape some of the cooling coastal winds, and sufficiently steep and frost-free to let the Lyons 'sleep easy'.

Launched from the 1996 vintage and entirely estate-grown, the wines have been made at wineries in the Christchurch area, most recently at Sherwood Estate by Andrew Meggitt. Opihi's output is low — 1000 cases in an average year.

The wines, sold in a restored 1882 limestone cottage, include an enjoyable, floral Müller-Thurgau with fresh, lemony, appley flavours, slight sweetness and enough acidity to keep things lively. Of the few Müller-Thurgaus made in New Zealand today, Opihi is one of the finest. The Riesling is a distinctly cool-climate style with crunchy, green apple flavours.

The Pinot Gris shows clearcut varietal character, with a splash of sweetness, appetising acidity and strong, peachy, lemony, spicy flavours. French oak-matured, the Pinot Noir is a light-bodied style, fresh, crisp and berryish.

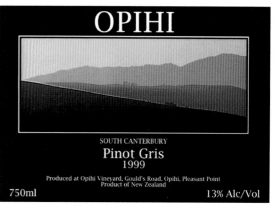

Address	Opihi Vineyard, Gay's Pass Road, Opihi, Pleasant Point, South Canterbury
Owners	Colin and Brenda Lyon
Key Wines	Pinot Noir, Riesling, Pinot Gris, Müller-Thurgau

Rossendale

■ Beefsteak and burgundy are a magical match at dinner tables around the world. Rossendale, a family-owned farm, vineyard, winery and restaurant on the southern outskirts of Christchurch, was the first firm in New Zealand to export wine and beef grown on the same property and marketed under the same brand.

'Farmers have a world of opportunities open to them if they are prepared to diversify,' believes Brent Rawstron, a former member of the New Zealand Meat Board. After diversifying into grapes and opening a restaurant with a 'beef and burgundy' theme, Rawstron boosted the profitability of the family farm fourfold.

Rossendale lies close to the Port Hills, on the edge of Halswell. Brent Rawstron runs the property (named after the area in Lancashire that his paternal grandparents came from) on behalf of the owners, himself and his brothers Haydn and Grant. After cultivating crops during the late 1970s and early 1980s, the Rawstrons diversified into beef and in 1987 the first vines sank root in their silty, sandy soils. Rawstron and his wife, Shirley, a general practitioner, both have postgraduate diplomas in viticulture and oenology from Lincoln University.

Pinot Noir, Chardonnay and Gewürztraminer are planted in the 4.5-hectare estate vineyard, which is sheltered by Banks Peninsula from cooling easterly winds. 'Our grapes typically ripen before those at West Melton but after North Canterbury's,' says Rawstron. Rossendale also owns a 5-hectare Sauvignon Blanc vineyard in Marlborough.

Since the first 1993 vintage, the wines have been made on-site by Grant Whelan, who also has his own label (see Kaituna Valley, page 261). Much of Rossendale's annual output of 6000 cases is consumed in its 127-year-old restaurant, originally a gardener's lodge at the entrance to the Lansdowne homestead of Edward Stafford, Premier of New Zealand for over eight years between 1856–61 and 1866–69.

These are consistently stylish wines. The Canterbury Riesling is scented and light, with excellent depth of crisp, gently sweet, lemon/lime flavour. The Marlborough Chardonnay, partly barrel-fermented, is full, harmonious and well-rounded, with strong, peachy, buttery flavours.

The gently oaked Marlborough Sauvignon Blanc is fresh and ripely herbaceous, with some complexity and good depth. The Canterbury Pinot Noir is a real charmer — fragrant, full and fresh, with ripe, plummy, spicy fruit characters to the fore in a delicious drink-young style.

Address	Rossendale Wines, 150 Old Tai Tapu Road, Halswell, Christchurch
Owners	The Rawstron family
Key Wines	Canterbury Riesling, Canterbury Pinot Noir, Marlborough Chardonnay, Marlborough Sauvignon Blanc

Address	Sandihurst Wines, Main West Coast Road, West Melton
Owners	John and Joan Brough
Key Wines	Gewürztraminer, Pinot Gris, Chardonnay, Pinot Noir, Premier Pinot Noir

Sandihurst

■ 'We're specialising in Pinot Noir,' says John Brough, proprietor of this low profile West Melton winery. Named after the sandy knolls (hursts) that are a feature of the district, Sandihurst lies 25 kilometres from Christchurch, on the inland Christchurch to Arthur's Pass highway. Brough and his wife, Joan, planted their first vines on these wind-swept plains in 1988.

After 33 years in the Christchurch fishing industry, owning a boatyard, fishing boats and a fish-processing factory, John Brough looked around for new fish to fry. In 1987, he recalls, 'There was a fair bit of hype in the papers about the success of Canterbury vineyards.'

Today, the Broughs' 7-hectare vineyard is planted in Pinot Noir, Gewürztraminer and Pinot Gris. Merlot, Cabernet Sauvignon, Sauvignon Blanc and Breidecker have been flagged away over the years, but the Broughs are expanding their Pinot Noir plantings and their son, Andrew, is developing another vineyard at West Melton to supply Sandihurst.

Wind is a key force in the vineyard; shelter belts are essential. Warm, dry nor'westers reduce disease problems but the cool nor'easters slow the grapes' ripening. 'Lincoln University reported that the heat summation here is ideal for Alsace and Burgundy varieties,' says Brough.

In an implement shed converted into a winery, Sandihurst's first vintage flowed in 1992. Recently, Sandihurst has shared its plant, equipment and a winemaker (Andrew Meggitt) with nearby Sherwood Estate (see page 256), but from 2003 the vinification process may once again be based entirely at the Sandihurst winery.

With an output of only 1000 cases in 2002, Sandihurst is a small producer — much smaller, in terms of vineyard area and production volumes, than a few years ago. John Brough is now in his mid-sixties, but is still committed to the wine industry and especially to Pinot Noir: 'It's the only variety grown around here that has definite export potential.'

Top vintages of the Gewürztraminer and Pinot Gris have been impressive, with the substantial mouthfeel and rich, rounded flavours typical of Alsace. The Pinot Noir is typically medium to full-bodied, with crisp, berryish, spicy flavours seasoned with smoky oak. There is also a Premier Pinot Noir, based on a selection of 'the best fruit and the best barrels'.

Address	St Helena Wine Estate, Coutts Island Road, Belfast
Owners	Bernice and Robin Mundy
Key Wines	Canterbury Riesling, Pinot Blanc, Pinot Gris, Reserve Pinot Gris, Chardonnay, Reserve Chardonnay, Pinot Noir, Reserve Pinot Noir; Marlborough Sauvignon Blanc, Chardonnay

St Helena

■ St Helena no longer bestrides the Canterbury wine scene the way it did in the 1980s, when its gold medal Pinot Noirs electrified the fledgling local wine community and put the region firmly on the New Zealand wine map. The typically medium-bodied, attractively scented and supple Pinot Noir is still the company's highest profile wine, but the Chardonnay, Riesling, Pinot Blanc and Pinot Gris are of equal quality.

Canterbury's oldest commercial winery was founded by Robin and Norman Mundy. After nematode worms rendered their potato farm unprofitable, the brothers — and their father, Trevor — early took heed of the results of Lincoln University's pioneering viticultural research and by 1978 St Helena's first vines were planted at Coutts Island, near Belfast, 20 minutes' drive north of Christchurch. In 1994, Norman Mundy withdrew from the venture, leaving Robin and his wife, Bernice, as St Helena's proprietors.

The 20-hectare vineyard, planted in free-draining, high fertility soils, is established principally in Pinot Noir, with smaller areas of Pinot Gris, Riesling and Pinot Blanc. Bounded by branches of the Waimakariri River, the vineyard needs no irrigation because of its high water table. The river flow also encourages air movement, reducing but not eliminating the risk of frost damage to the vines.

St Helena's original goal was to produce only estate-grown Canterbury wines, but the company now buys grapes from growers, and also has an ownership stake in Marlborough vineyards planted principally in Sauvignon Blanc.

With Danny Schuster at the winemaking helm for the early 1981 to 1985 vintages, St Helena scooped a gold medal for its 1982 Pinot Noir, only the second time the variety had been awarded a gold medal in New Zealand. 'We didn't expect a gold for that wine,' recalls Robin Mundy. 'It really set us on our feet for the first few years.' St Helena's 1984 Pinot Noir also won a gold medal. Following Schuster's departure, the wine has been made by a series of winemakers and consultant winemakers: Mark Rattray, Petter Evans and Alan McCorkindale.

In the insulated aluminium winery erected in 1981, in an average year St Helena produces 20,000 cases of wine. The partly barrel-fermented Pinot Blanc is a decent dry white with a subtle bouquet and pleasing depth of savoury, earthy flavour. 'Pinot Blanc is the most underrated grape in the country for a good dry white,' says Mundy. 'It crops almost twice as heavily as Chardonnay, and at five years old can taste quite Chardonnay-like.'

The Riesling offers fresh, slightly sweet, green-apple flavours in a light, delicate, tangy style. The barrel-fermented Chardonnay varies in quality according to the vintage, but the Reserve Canterbury Chardonnay is mouthfilling, with very good depth of flavour, crisp, toasty and mealy.

Robin Mundy planted Canterbury's first commercial vineyard in 1978 and scooped the region's first gold medal with St Helena's legendary 1982 Pinot Noir.

The Pinot Gris and Reserve Pinot Gris, both tank and barrel-fermented, in top years offer rich varietal character, peachy, spicy and smooth. The Marlborough Sauvignon Blanc is crisp, herbaceous and sharply priced.

The early vintages of St Helena Pinot Noir were powerful, dark and richly flavoured, but of late the wine has grown markedly lighter. This is now a good but not outstanding wine, appealingly fragrant, raspberryish, spicy and smooth. A fuller, richer and more complex Reserve Pinot Noir is also made in favourable seasons.

Other producers

■ Bentwood Wines
On the Akaroa Highway at Tai Tapu, Ray and Robyn Watson have 3 hectares of Gewürztraminer, Riesling, Pinot Blanc and Pinot Noir vines. Launched from the 1995 vintage and made by Grant Whelan at the Rossendale (see page 263) winery, the wines include a consistently enjoyable, mouthfilling Pinot Blanc with plenty of lemony, appley, slightly nutty and buttery flavour.

■ Darjon Vineyards
Darjon vineyard and restaurant lies at Swannanoa, north-west of Christchurch, where John and Michelle Baker planted the first vines in 1989. Due to a varying combination of frosts, rain, hail and low autumn temperatures, the 2 hectares of Riesling and Pinot Noir failed to produce a ripe crop in the 1999, 2000 and 2001 vintages. I have tasted a light, strawberryish Pinot Noir and floral, citrusy, slightly honeyed Riesling, but in 2002 Darjon was for sale.

■ French Farm Vineyards
The handsome restaurant and winery at French Farm Bay, on Banks Peninsula, released its first wines from the 1991 vintage. Production ceased in 1994, but has since resumed. The small amount of estate-grown Chardonnay and Pinot Noir is mostly consumed in the restaurant.

■ Gatehouse Wines
Unpretentious, flavoursome wines, priced right, flow from the Gatehouse family's winery at West Melton. The first vines were planted in 1982 and the first wine flowed in 1989. The 4-hectare vineyard is planted mainly in Riesling, Gewürztraminer, Pinot Noir, Merlot and Malbec. For Peter and Carol Gatehouse, Riesling is the speciality — slightly sweet, limey and minerally, with good longevity.

■ Larcomb Vineyard
After planting their first vines at Rolleston, south-west of Christchurch, in 1980, John Thom and Julie Wagner made their first wines in 1984. Owned since 1995 by Michelle and Warren Barnes, the 5-hectare vineyard is planted in Chardonnay, Pinot Gris, Breidecker, Sauvignon Blanc, Riesling and Pinot Noir. The wines, which include a mild, slightly sweet Breidecker and a crisp, light Pinot Noir, are sold exclusively in the cosy vineyard restaurant, at on-site functions or in the cellar door shop.

■ Morworth Estate Vineyard
Chris and Leonie Morkane own a 15-hectare vineyard — planted mainly in Pinot Noir and Riesling — winery and restaurant at Broadfield, on the main road from Christchurch to Lincoln. The Morkanes also have 20 hectares of Sauvignon Blanc and Chardonnay in Marlborough. The wines, produced since 1997, include a medium-bodied, spicy and crisp Canterbury Pinot Noir and a weighty, peachy, full-flavoured Marlborough Chardonnay.

■ Rosebank Estate
Near Belfast, north of Christchurch, Brian and Margaret Shackel run a popular vineyard restaurant. The company does not make its own wines, but purchases grapes and has them processed elsewhere. Some of the early Rosebank Estate wines, launched from the 1993 vintage, were good, but the wines I have tasted in recent years have been plain.

Central Otago

Is it the romantic pull of living in such a lovely, lonely and lofty landscape? The pioneering urge or even mundane economic factors, such as the availability of large blocks of cheap land and the absence, until its discovery at Alexandra in early 2002, of the root-sucking aphid, phylloxera? Or the proof in the glass of those seductively perfumed, fruit-crammed and supple Pinot Noirs?

For these and other reasons, Central Otago was the country's fastest-growing wine region in 2001; more than half the vines had yet to produce their first crop. With 650 hectares planted (some unofficial estimates went much higher), Central Otago ranked as New Zealand's fourth-largest wine-growing region, ahead of Canterbury, the Wairarapa, Auckland and Nelson. On Central Otago's arid, tawny ranges, pastoral sheep farming — especially for fine merino wool — has long been the foundation of the economy, but the region is also acclaimed for its stone-fruit: apricots, nectarines, peaches, cherries and plums. Today, trailing only agriculture and tourism, wine ranks as the region's third-largest income earner. The precise boundaries of Central Otago are unclear, but the local wine-growers define the region as the areas under the jurisdiction of the Central Otago and Queenstown Lakes District Councils. The four distinct viticultural sub-regions — Wanaka, Gibbston, Cromwell Basin and Alexandra — are discussed separately here. Vines are also sprouting near Kurow, in the Waitaki Valley of North Otago, where by 2002 some 37 hectares had been planted.

History

Otago's majestic inland basins and valleys yielded some of the earliest New Zealand wines. A Frenchman, Jean Desire Feraud, planted his first vines near Clyde in 1864 and won a prize for 'Burgundy' at Sydney in 1881. Touring viticulturist Romeo Bragato affirmed in 1895 that Central Otago was 'pre-eminently suitable' for winemaking (see page 14). At a public meeting later held in Dunedin, Bragato stirred up such enthusiasm that a Central Otago Vine and Fruitgrowers' Association was born. The word 'Vine', however, was later dropped from the title, and the eagerly anticipated new wine industry never burgeoned in the interior. From the 1950s onwards, trial blocks of vines planted by individuals and later the DSIR in the Alexandra area (see page 282) proved that classic *vinifera* grape varieties would ripen in Central Otago.

During the 1970s and 1980s a small knot of pioneers finally set Central Otago wine on a commercial footing. Bill Grant, of William Hill Vineyard, planted his first experimental vines at Alexandra in 1973, followed in 1976 by Rolfe Mills at Rippon Vineyard, Wanaka. Ann Pinckney obtained a business grant to plant 200 vines at Dalefield, near Queenstown, in 1976. Alan Brady at Gibbston Valley, and Verdun Burgess and Sue Edwards at Black Ridge, Alexandra, planted their first vines in 1981. In 1985, from grapes air-freighted north to the viticultural research station at Te Kauwhata, Dr Reiner Eschenbruch made a trickle of Central Otago wine. Then in 1987, after 4 tonnes of grapes had been crushed at the tiny Taramea winery, the first commercial wines of the modern era flowed under the Rippon, Taramea and Gibbston Valley labels.

Climate

At 45° south, Central Otago's vines are cultivated in the world's southernmost wine region. At 200 to 450 metres above sea level, Central Otago is also the country's highest wine region and the furthest inland. In the semi-continental climate, the daily and seasonal temperature variations are greater than further north. This is a region of climatic extremes — the country's highest and lowest temperatures were both recorded near Alexandra. The marked diurnal (day/night) temperature swings are believed to enhance the grapes' flavour and colour intensity. Summers are typically hot (with temperatures often soaring to 30–35°C), dry and short; autumns cool and dry, with clear, cold nights; and winters icy, with snow often covering the vines. The 'heat summation' figures for most parts of Central Otago (see below) are hazardously low for commercial wine-growing, and spring and autumn frosts are a constant threat (helicopters, wind machines, water sprinklers and heat pots are used on flatter sites). Site selection is therefore of major importance. In such a relatively cool viticultural region, a warm and sunny, north-facing slope with a low frost risk is a critical asset. Much of Central Otago is semi-arid. Dry autumn weather (especially in the east) is a key viticultural asset, encouraging the winemakers to leave their grapes late on the vines, often into May, to ripen undamaged by autumn rains. Due to the relatively low humidity, there is a low risk of fungal diseases and 'noble rot' is rare.

Soils

From broken schist and clays to heavy silt loams, gravels and light sands, Central Otago's vines are planted in a wide range of soils. Most have stony sub-soils, which promotes good water drainage; irrigation is essential, at least when the vines are young. Schist is the major bedrock, with smaller areas of greywacke. Built up by glacial outwash, mixed by the rivers and wind-blown, the soils' impact on wine styles is only beginning to be understood.

Wine styles

Central Otago grapes often attain high sugar readings while retaining a high level of acidity. The region's finest wines are its perfumed, richly flavoured and supple Pinot Noirs, which often have a suggestion of herbs. Chardonnay, Sauvignon Blanc and Gewürztraminer have shown some potential, but the best white wines are the light, intense Rieslings and crisp, spicy Pinot Gris. The high acid levels of the region's grapes also points to a strong future in bottle-fermented sparklings.

Sub-regions

Far from being a small, homogeneous wine region, Central Otago's vineyards are far-flung. The Mount Maude vineyard at Lake Wanaka lies 100 kilometres north of Black Ridge at Alexandra. Another 75 kilometres of mountains and gorges divide the most westerly plantings at Lake Hayes, near Queenstown, from Alexandra in the south-east. Over two-thirds of the region's vines are clustered in the Cromwell Basin, followed by Gibbston (with about 20 per cent of plantings), Alexandra (7 per cent) and Wanaka (3 per cent.).

Principal grape varieties

	Producing area 2002	% total producing area 2002
Pinot Noir	264 ha	62.9%
Chardonnay	62 ha	14.8%
Pinot Gris	37 ha	8.7%
Riesling	23 ha	5.4%
Sauvignon Blanc	15 ha	3.6%

Vintage chart (1993–2002)

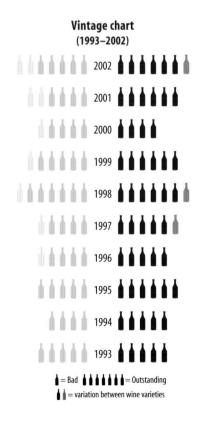

🍾 = Bad 🍾🍾🍾🍾🍾🍾 = Outstanding
🍾🍾 = variation between wine varieties

Previous page: Rippon's much-photographed vineyard on the shore of Lake Wanaka produces mouth-wateringly crisp white wines and a deliciously fruity and supple Pinot Noir.

Summary of climate statistics

Meteorological station	Latitude	Height	GDD	MTWM	Rainfall, Oct–Apr	Air frost days (annual)
Cromwell	45.02'S	213 m	989	17.7°C	276 mm	85
Earnscleugh	45.14'S	152 m	910	16.6°C	243 mm	107

Height — *above sea level* **GDD** — *growing degree days, Oct–Apr, above 10°C* **MTWM** — *mean temperature, warmest month*

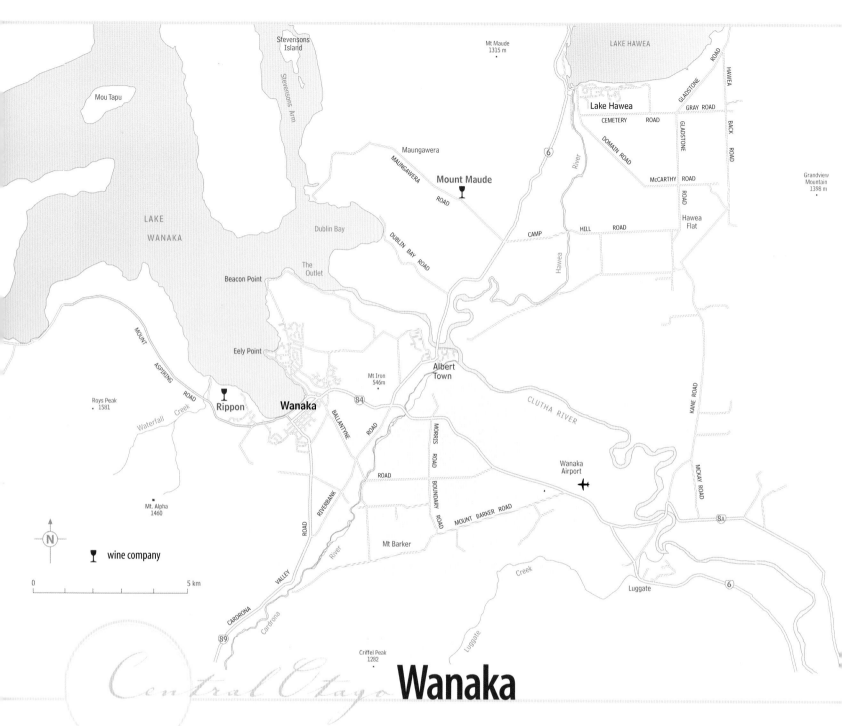

Wanaka

By far the smallest of Central Otago's sub-regions, with 3 per cent of the vineyard area and two wineries, Wanaka nevertheless enjoys a high profile. Its most famous wine, Rippon Vineyard Pinot Noir, is consistently impressive and the alpine lakeside setting is of riveting beauty.

History

When Rolfe Mills established his first vines — Albany Surprise and Seibel hybrids — on the shores of Lake Wanaka in 1976, his only previous link with wine 'was drinking it. I'd been to Portugal and seen land in the Douro Valley that looked like the family land at Wanaka. I knew vines would grow here, but didn't know if they would ripen fruit.' After Mills began to monitor Rippon Vineyard's temperatures and rainfall in 1977, he was able to bury his doubts about the site's ability to ripen grapes. He and his family spent nine months in 1981 learning about wine in Bergerac, south-west France, before the first, minute batch of Wanaka wine flowed in 1984.

Climate

Central Otago's northernmost sub-region, Wanaka lies close to the snowy peaks of the Southern Alps. Due to its relative exposure to the West Coast weather influences, Wanaka is cooler and wetter than the Cromwell Basin, according to most of the region's winemakers. Wanaka in some seasons is very cloudy, and katabatic (down-flowing) winds give it a relatively cool viticultural environment. Most sites, especially those on low-lying land, are too cool to fully ripen grapes and face a high frost risk in spring and autumn. Site selection is therefore of critical importance. At Rippon Vineyard, a sheltered, north-facing slope and reflected radiation from the lake give adequate heat for ripening and a low frost risk.

Soils

At Rippon Vineyard, the vines are cultivated in a glacial moraine, with silty topsoils carried down by erosion over deep schist gravels. Around the lake to the north-east, the vines at Mount Maude grow in stony gravels threaded with seams of clay.

Wine styles

Rippon Vineyard and Mount Maude have both succeeded with richly flavoured Pinot Noirs and intense, freshly acidic Rieslings. In blind tastings, I have often found the Rippon Vineyard Pinot Noir to be green-edged, which probably reflects the cool growing environment.

Mount Maude

■ Sited further north than any other wine producer in Central Otago, Mount Maude lies in the Maungawera Valley, between Lakes Wanaka and Hawea. Its dry, tautly structured Riesling and weighty, deeply flavoured Pinot Noir are both rewarding. Terry Wilson, a former general practitioner and anaesthetist, and his wife, Dawn, a potter, planted their first vines in 1994 as a semi-retirement project, but are 'now working harder than ever'. Their daughter, Sarah Kate, a qualified winemaker who has worked for several Australian wineries, has also been involved in the decision making.

The 3.5-hectare vineyard is draped across a steep, terraced, north-facing slope, looking towards Mount Maude. In gravelly soils with seams of clay, Pinot Noir, Riesling and Chardonnay are the key varieties, with a smaller plot of Gewürztraminer. The first wine flowed in 1999. At 600 cases in 2001, Mount Maude's output is still tiny; some of the grapes are sold to a much bigger winery. The early vintages have been made on a contract basis by Dean Shaw at the Central Otago Wine Company (COWCO) in Cromwell.

The Riesling is lemony and minerally, tight and dry, with crisp, strong flavours. The Gewürztraminer is a bone-dry style with a musky perfume and strong gingery, spicy flavours. The Pinot Noir is full-bodied and ripely flavoured, with oak complexity and very satisfying depth of plummy, spicy flavour.

Address	Mount Maude, Maungawera Valley Road, Wanaka
Owners	Terry and Dawn Wilson
Key Wines	Pinot Noir, Riesling, Chardonnay, Gewürztraminer

Rippon

■ The achingly beautiful view at Wanaka isn't Rippon's only claim to fame. One of Central Otago's oldest vineyards, at 310 metres above sea level it is also one of the highest. When Rippon won a gold medal for its seductively perfumed, richly flavoured and rounded 1991 Pinot Noir, it was the first gold ever awarded to a Central Otago wine.

Rippon Vineyard runs down a gentle schist slope to the shores of Lake Wanaka. The blue-water view to the majestic snow and cloud-capped peaks of the Buchanan Range at the head of the lake is sublime, and has graced the covers of countless wine publications.

The founder, Rolfe Mills, who died in 2000 at the age of 77, was the grandson of Sir Percy Sargood, who once owned Wanaka Station. (Mills named the vineyard after his great-grandmother, Emma Rippon, who married Frederick Sargood.) After a career as the sales director of the family clothing and footwear company, Sargoods, Mills came to Wanaka with no clear plans for the future. After experimenting with vines from 1976 onwards (see opposite page), the first tiny batch of Rippon Vineyard wine flowed in 1984, produced by Dr Rainer Eschenbruch at the Te Kauwhata research station.

A white-haired, gentlemanly figure who celebrated his seventieth birthday by cycling in one day from Wanaka to Dunedin, Rolfe Mills was one of the key pioneers of Central Otago wine. Pinot Noir, he declared, 'has to be the most interesting wine to produce, one of the most satisfying to drink and possibly the most stimulating one on which one may ponder'. Mills took delight in quoting a French proverb: 'Burgundy [Pinot Noir] is for kings, Chardonnay for duchesses and claret [Merlot and Cabernet Sauvignon] for gentlemen.'

From 1986, when Tony Bish became the first full-time qualified winemaker in Central Otago (followed by Rudi Bauer, who made the 1990 to 1992 vintages), Rippon came up with a string of regional breakthroughs. Rippon Pinot Noir 1989 won Central Otago's first medal in 1990; a year later, Rippon Gamay Rosé 1991 won the first trophy. In 1992 came the first gold medal for a Central Otago white wine, Rippon Sauvignon Blanc 1992, followed in 1993 by the first red-wine trophy, for Rippon Pinot Noir 1992. In 1998 the first bottle-fermented sparkling, Emma Rippon 1993, was launched, followed in 1999 by the production of the region's first botrytised sweet white, La Nina Noble Riesling.

Mills' wife, Lois, also heavily involved from the start, is now the executive director of the company. The winemaker from 2002 is Rolfe and Lois' son, Nicholas ('Nick'), who grew up working in the vineyard and winery, and from 1998 until 2002 lived in Burgundy, studying for a degree in winemaking and working for such prestigious producers as Domaine de la Romanee-Conti. The 15-hectare, north-facing vineyard is planted in a glacial moraine, with free-draining schist soils. Pinot Noir covers 40 per cent of the vineyard area, with smaller plots of Riesling, Sauvignon Blanc, Chardonnay, Gewürztraminer, Osteiner and Gamay.

Rippon's annual production is about 7500 cases and growing. The drink-young wines include New Zealand's only Osteiner, a crossing of Riesling and Sylvaner which yields a light, slightly sweet and tangy, lemon and

Address	Rippon Vineyard, Mt Aspiring Road, Rapid No. 246, Lake Wanaka
Owner	Lois Mills and the estate of Rolfe Mills
Key Wines	Pinot Noir, Rosé, Osteiner, Gewürztraminer, Sauvignon Blanc, Riesling, Chardonnay, Hotere White

apple-flavoured wine; a light, crisp, medium-dry blend called Hotere White; and a pink, buoyantly fruity and berryish Rosé, blended from Pinot Noir and Gamay.

The partly barrel-fermented Sauvignon Blanc is grassy and freshly acidic, with some complexity. The Gewürztraminer is crisp and appley, but often lacks real ripeness and richness. The Riesling is more impressive — a steely dry style that with cellaring unfolds strong, flinty, minerally flavours. The Chardonnay is typically a Chablis-like wine with appley, citrusy flavours, fresh and appetisingly crisp.

Rippon Vineyard Pinot Noir is a wine of floral, supple richness. Reflecting its very cool-climate origins, in cold years it can be green-edged, but typically offers sweet, ripe fruit characters and a lovely array of cherry, plum, spice and nut flavours.

Its close proximity to the Southern Alps gives Rippon Vineyard at Lake Wanaka one of Central Otago's coolest climates for viticulture.

Gibbston

A carpet of green stretches along north-facing terraces and fans above the tumbling Kawarau River, between Queenstown and Cromwell. With about 20 per cent of the total vineyard area, Gibbston is Central Otago's second-largest sub-region.

On the river's eastwards journey — draining Lake Wakatipu into Lake Dunstan at Cromwell — at Gibbston the valley opens out for about 10 kilometres, before it narrows at Nevis Bluff into the tortuous Kawarau Gorge. The valley at Gibbston is not wide: from the crest to the foot of the strip of vines is only a kilometre or two. A short drive from Queenstown, the vineyards at Gibbston are a major tourist attraction — Gibbston Valley is New Zealand's most-visited winery.

History

Vines have long been cultivated in the Queenstown area. When viticultural expert Romeo Bragato toured the country in 1895, he tasted his first glass of New Zealand wine at Arrowtown. Made by a Mrs Hutcheson 'after the most primitive fashion, it reflected great credit on the producer and need not be despised by anyone'. Former horticulture student Ann Pinckney established a small vineyard at Dalefield, near Queenstown, in 1976, and in 1980 began planting at Taramea, closer to Arrowtown. 'To prove they would grow', Alan Brady planted the first 350 vines at Gibbston Valley in 1981 and 1982. Five years later, after uprooting fruit trees, Rob and Greg Hay planted the first vines at Chard Farm.

Climate

Gibbston lies closer to the West Coast than the Cromwell Basin or Alexandra sub-regions, so — like Wanaka — is typically cooler and wetter. In the Upper Kawarau Basin (including Queenstown and Arrowtown), on average the annual rainfall is double that of Alexandra. Polar winds from the south-west cool the Queenstown district, but the topographic mix of mountain ranges and hills,

terraces, lakes and rivers creates a variety of mesoclimates, some suitable for viticulture. Gibbston is significantly warmer and drier than Queenstown. The major risk is lack of sufficient warmth over the ripening season — harvest dates can be a month later at Gibbston than at Bannockburn. However, with the river draining cold air down the valley, the frost risk at Gibbston is low. Gibbston's cooler temperatures, compared to the Cromwell Basin, allows ripening to proceed more slowly, which can enhance the grapes' build-up of colour and flavour. However, with the grapes not being picked until late April or early May, in a poor season there is a greater risk of insufficient ripeness, autumn frosts and rains.

Soils

The common silty loams and free-draining gravels can vary markedly in terms of depth and consistency, even within individual sites. At Chard Farm, the vines are grown on an interconnecting series of alluvial fans, with silty loams and some clay bands of moderate fertility overlying shingly sub-soils. The Gibbston Valley estate vineyard is established in very fine silt, stones and broken schist.

Wine styles

Compared to Pinot Noir from the Cromwell Basin, Gibbston Pinot Noir is typically lighter in colour, less opulent, plummy and tannic, but more perfumed and savoury, with raspberry and strawberry flavours. 'They're more feminine wines, nicer to drink early,' says Grant Taylor of Gibbston Valley. Within the valley itself, the winemakers are also starting to identify flavour differences, especially between grapes cultivated at the top and bottom of the slopes.

Address Amisfield Vineyards,
Cnr Lake Hayes Road and
State Highway 6,
Lake Hayes

Owners Rob Hay, John Darby and
Tom Tusher

Key Wines Arcadia NV Brut, Central
Otago Cuvée, Lake Hayes
Pinot Noir, Chardonnay,
Sauvignon Blanc

Amisfield Vineyards

■ Built from local schist and ironwood timbers rescued from West Coast bridges, the Amisfield Cellar has a spectacular view across Lake Hayes, near Queenstown, to Coronet Peak. Amisfield owns substantial vineyards at Lowburn, in the Cromwell Basin, and produces wine under the Lake Hayes and Arcadia brands.

Amisfield is a partnership between Rob Hay, co-owner of Chard Farm; Queenstown businessman John Darby; and Tom Tusher, a former chief executive officer of Levi Strauss International, who has been investing in Central Otago since 1988. The Amisfield Cellar, opened in 2002, has been purpose-built for wine tasting, dining and barrel-aging Pinot Noir. The wines are currently made at Chard Farm, but a specialist Pinot Noir winery will be erected at Lowburn in 2004.

At the Amisfield Vineyard, where planting began in 1999, 40 hectares have been established in Pinot Noir (predominantly), with much smaller areas of Sauvignon Blanc, Pinot Gris and Riesling. The initial plantings were on the easiest land nearest to Lake Dunstan, but more challenging sites at higher altitude are now being developed. Amisfield also buys grapes from growers at Lake Hayes and in the Gibbston Valley.

Winemaker Jeff Sinnott is a Roseworthy College graduate who crafted some brilliant wines at Isabel Estate between 1998 and 2001, and has travelled and worked extensively in Australia, California and France. The early wines have been regional blends, but from 2002 onwards, Amisfield's primary focus will switch to single-vineyard wines.

The table wines are marketed as Lake Hayes and the sparklings as Arcadia. The early releases have included a vibrantly fruity, easy-drinking and smooth Pinot Noir; a partly barrel-fermented, crisp and lively Chardonnay; a soft, strawberryish, moderately yeasty Arcadia NV; and a distinctly classy 1998 Arcadia Central Otago Cuvée, a Pinot Noir-dominant style with intense, citrusy, biscuity, beautifully harmonious flavours.

Address Chard Farm Vineyard,
Chard Road,
Gibbston

Owners Rob Hay and Gerda
Schumann

Key Wines Riesling, Judge and Jury
Chardonnay, Closeburn
Chardonnay, Sauvignon
Blanc, Pinot Gris, River Run
Pinot Noir, Finla Mor Pinot
Noir, Blacksmith's Pinot Noir

Chard Farm

■ Pinot Noir has been the greatest success at Chard Farm. 'When we started planting vines 15 years ago, most of the talk was about Central Otago being suited only to German varieties,' recalls Rob Hay. 'But it's warmer here than people think. We took a punt on Burgundian varieties — and that punt has been successful.'

On a north-facing ledge 70 metres above the Kawarau River, with a riveting view across the gorge to the snow-draped Cardrona Range and Coronet Peak, Chard Farm has one of the country's most strikingly beautiful vineyards. 'We picked the site solely with quality wine in mind,' says Rob, 'not for its tourism potential — which is what many people think.'

Chard Farm lies just off the main highway, 20 kilometres east of Queenstown. The precipitous access route to the vineyard, skirting sheer bluffs with a steep plunge to the river for the unwary, was once the Cromwell–Queenstown road; Chard Farm starts at the cattle-stop. The land was originally worked by Richard Chard in the 1870s as a market garden, supplying food to the miners heading for the goldfields. Later, Chard Farm became a dairy farm and a stone-fruit orchard. Rob Hay and his brother, Greg (who withdrew from the venture in 1996 and is now at Peregrine) uprooted the fruit trees before they planted their first vines in 1987.

Born in Motueka, Rob Hay graduated from Otago University with a BSc, and then embarked on a three-year study

Tourists who survive the death-defying drive to Chard Farm are rewarded by a lineup of fresh, immaculate white wines and a quartet of Pinot Noirs.

and work course in Baden and Wurttemberg: 'I went to Germany to study winemaking in a genuinely cool climate,' he says. After working at Babich and Ruby Bay, in 1986 Hay came to the deep south and was the inaugural winemaker at the Gibbston Valley winery from 1987 to 1991. In moderately fertile silt loams with some clay bands overlying shingly sub-soils, the 11-hectare estate vineyard is planted in Pinot Noir, Chardonnay and Pinot Gris. Chard Farm also owns the 9.5-hectare Redgate Vineyard at Cromwell, established in Pinot Noir, Pinot Gris, Chardonnay and Riesling, and the 10-hectare Amisfield Block Nine Vineyard at Lowburn, planted in Pinot Noir. About 30 per cent of the annual fruit intake is bought from growers, but Chard Farm is moving increasingly to company-owned or leased vineyards.

The 1989 to 1992 wines were produced along the road at Gibbston Valley, but Chard Farm's own large winery was erected for the 1993 vintage. With its current annual production level of 15,000 cases, Chard Farm ranks among Central Otago's largest producers, and Rob Hay is also involved in Amisfield Vineyards (see opposite page).

More successful than most Central Otago wineries with Chardonnay, Chard Farm produces a fresh, crisp, lemony, slightly buttery Closeburn Chardonnay, partly oak-aged; and a fully barrel-fermented, tight, mealy and complex Judge and Jury Chardonnay, citrusy, nutty and long.

At its best, the tank-fermented, lees-aged Pinot Gris offers excellent depth of lemony, appley, spicy flavour. The Riesling is a slightly sweet style with freshly acidic lemon/lime flavours. The Sauvignon Blanc is grassy and nettley, but in warm seasons also shows some riper, tropical-fruit characters.

The Pinot Noirs ascend from the fresh, subtly oaked and smooth River Run, a drink-young style, to the attractively perfumed, strongly flavoured and supple Finla Mor, grown in the Cromwell Basin. Bragato, for many years the flagship Pinot Noir, is currently being replaced by two single-vineyard bottlings, one from Lowburn, the other (Blacksmith's) estate-grown at Chard Farm.

Gibbston Valley

■ The rust-red Gibbston Valley winery and restaurant is New Zealand's most-visited winery, each year attracting 50,000 visitors. Its multiple gold medal and trophy-winning, powerful, firmly structured Reserve Pinot Noir ranks among the region's — and the country's — most distinguished reds.

The founder, Alan Brady (who now owns the nearby Mount Edward winery), purchased the land, then covered in briar, in 1976. After Brady planted 350 grapevines in 1981 and 1982, 'to prove they would grow', the first commercial vintage of Gibbston Valley wine was bottled in 1987.

Today, Gibbston Valley is owned by a small group of investors, with a controlling interest held by American Mike Stone. Formerly an investment banker for Merrill Lynch in San Francisco, Stone first came to New Zealand in 1978 and thought: 'God, what a wonderful place.' After emigrating to New Zealand in 1986, he started investing in Gibbston Valley in 1992 'and just kept upping the shareholding'.

On a north-facing schist ledge at the foot of rocky bluffs, the 2-hectare estate vineyard is close-planted in Pinot Noir and Riesling. At Bendigo, at the head of Lake Dunstan in the Cromwell Basin, 24 hectares have been planted since 1999 in Pinot Noir, Chardonnay, Riesling, Pinot Gris and Pinot Blanc. At Alexandra, Gibbston Valley planted a 6-hectare Pinot Noir vineyard in 1998, and a second, 9.5-hectare vineyard at Gibbston has been established in Pinot Noir and Pinot Gris. A steadily declining proportion of the company's grapes (currently 40 per cent) are bought from contract growers.

For winemaker Grant Taylor, who was raised in North Otago, wine has always been a hobby: 'I used to get into Dad's wine cellar, check what he had the most of, and take a bottle of that.' After graduating from Lincoln University with a Diploma of Agriculture, he was assistant winemaker at Pine Ridge winery in the Napa Valley, and chief winemaker at Domaine Napa, before joining Gibbston Valley in 1993.

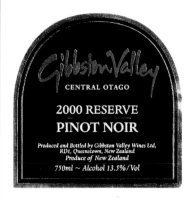

Address	Gibbston Valley Wines, Queenstown–Cromwell Highway, Gibbston
Owners	Mike Stone and shareholders
Key Wines	Pinot Noir, Reserve Pinot Noir, Riesling, Pinot Gris, Greenstone Chardonnay, Reserve Chardonnay

The dimly lit, 50-metre long tunnel at Gibbston Valley provides a stable year-round environment of 12–13°C, ideal for barrel-aging Pinot Noir and Chardonnay — and a romantic setting for tastings.

The 1990 vintage of Gibbston Valley Pinot Noir — along with Rippon Vineyard's — first proved that Central Otago can produce top-flight wine. Looking back, Taylor says the key factor in improving Pinot Noir quality has been lower cropping levels. 'We give our growers incentives to *reduce* their crops to about 6.5 tonnes per hectare. Leaf-plucking has helped with acid reduction and skin colour development, and growing the grapes in warmer sub-regions has given us riper tannins.'

Of Gibbston Valley's current annual output of 16,000 cases, about half is sold at the winery or in Queenstown. The Central Otago Pinot Noir is a middleweight style with subtle, cherryish, spicy flavours, French oak complexity and silky tannins. Its Reserve big brother, matured in all-new French oak barriques, is typically a very substantial wine with notable depth of cherry, plum and spice flavours in a complex, savoury and firm style, built for cellaring.

The Riesling is tangy and garden-fresh, with strong, slightly sweet lemon/lime flavours. The Pinot Gris is also a medium-dry style with peach, lemon and spice flavours and lively acidity. The Sauvignon Blanc is a very cool-climate style, mouth-wateringly crisp and strongly herbaceous.

Crisp, lemony and appley, the Greenstone Chardonnay is a vibrantly fruity, unwooded style, designed for early consumption. Fully French oak-fermented, the Reserve Chardonnay is citrusy and buttery, with very good weight, complexity and depth.

Mount Edward

Address Mount Edward Winery,
34 Coalpit Road,
Gibbston Valley

Owner Alan Brady

Key Wines Pinot Noir, Riesling

■ After 17 years 'growing and managing' the Gibbston Valley winery, Alan Brady shifted a few kilometres along the road to establish Mount Edward, one-tenth the size of the company he previously founded. Mount Edward, says Brady, now in his mid-sixties, has allowed him 'to get back in touch with the reality of wine — working in the vineyard, the sweat and toil of vintage, and the excitement of watching the wine emerge'.

Brady, who came to New Zealand from Ireland as a 23-year-old, is a former print and television journalist. The first to plant vines at Gibbston in 1981, he named Mount Edward after the mountain that looms behind his steeply sloping, 1-hectare vineyard, planted entirely in Riesling. However, Pinot Noir dominates Mount Edward's output, based on grapes from the adjacent, 12-hectare Drystone Vineyard (in which Brady is a shareholder), and a smaller amount from the Hawkdun Rise vineyard at Alexandra.

The keys to making top-flight Pinot Noir, says Brady, are to 'get the right site, manage the canopy and cropping level right, and make sure the fruit is clean and ripe'. Richness and harmony are the crucial qualities he's after, but not at the expense of longevity. Launched from the 1998 vintage, the Pinot Noir is deliciously fragrant and supple, with rich, sweet-fruit characters and velvety tannins. Full of drink-young charm, it also develops with bottle-age.

In his small, concrete, terracotta-coloured winery, Brady also crafts a light, floral, medium-dry Riesling with strong, citrusy, limey flavours, cut with fresh acidity.

MOUNT EDWARD

2000 PINOT NOIR
CENTRAL OTAGO

e75cl   PRODUCE *of* NEW ZEALAND 13.5% Vol

Peregrine

Address Peregrine Wines,
Kawarau Gorge Road,
Gibbston

Owners Greg Hay and Wentworth Estates

Key Wines Pinot Noir, Sauvignon Blanc, Riesling, Pinot Gris, Chardonnay, Gewürztraminer

■ Named after the falcons found in the rugged uplands of Central Otago, Peregrine swiftly achieved prominence when its debut 1998 Sauvignon Blanc won the trophy for champion Sauvignon Blanc at that year's Air New Zealand Wine Awards.

Lying at the eastern end of the Gibbston Valley, at the base of the Crown Range, Peregrine is a partnership between Greg Hay and Wentworth Estates. A marketing graduate from Otago University, Hay founded the Chard Farm winery with his brother, Rob, in 1987, but left in 1996 to work as a viticultural consultant and establish Peregrine, of which he is the managing director.

Wentworth Estates, owned by Adam Peren, Philip Anderson and Paul Glass, has subdivided land in the Gibbston Valley to develop 'lifestyle' vineyards and residences. The individual landowners lease their vineyard to Peregrine, or have it managed by the wine company. This arrangement secures Peregrine the grapes from 30 hectares of vineyards, planted in Pinot Noir (predominantly), Chardonnay and Pinot Gris.

Peregrine also has numerous contract growers throughout Central Otago's sub-regions, with vineyards ranging in size from 2 to 25 hectares.

The company's office, tasting and sales facilities have been based in a 120-year-old woolshed and old musterer's cottage, and the wines have been made on a contract basis at Cromwell. However, Peregrine's own winery will be operational at Wentworth prior to the 2003 vintage. Winemaker Duncan Forsyth, formerly of Chard Farm, joined Peregrine in 2001.

With an output of 9500 cases from the 2001 vintage and 15,000 cases from 2002, Peregrine is one of the region's largest and fastest-growing producers. The medium-dry Riesling is scented and racy, with excellent flavour depth. The Gewürztraminer is lush and mouthfilling, with strong flavours of ginger, spice and lychees and a fractionally sweet finish. Fleshy, with an oily texture and deep, peachy, spicy flavours, the Pinot Gris is one of the region's finest. The Sauvignon Blanc offers gooseberry and capsicum-like flavours, crisp and strong, although the striking intensity of the 1998 has yet to be repeated. Peregrine Pinot Noir is consistently excellent — weighty and warm, with deep plum/cherry flavours, French oak complexity and smooth tannins.

Two Paddocks

■ Everyone wants to drink Sam Neill's wine. After the launch of the debut 1997 vintage of Two Paddocks Pinot Noir, José Hernandez, of Neill's New Zealand distributor, Eurowine, wished he 'had 2500 cases, rather than 250, to sell'.

A popular, down-to-earth member of the Central Otago wine community, Neill is acclaimed for his roles in such films as *The Piano* and the *Jurassic Park* series. His father, a general merchant who imported wines and spirits through his Dunedin-based company, Neill and Co., early sensed Central Otago's wine potential. 'Dad would say: "People should be growing grapes here. It's just like the Rhine, just like Burgundy!"'

After building his Ian Athfield-designed house on a hilltop overlooking the Wakatipu Basin, Neill was inspired in the early 1990s by Rippon Vineyard's 'really astonishing Pinot Noirs. That's what made me think, well, bugger it, if Rolfe [Mills] can do it, I can too.'

In 1993, the first vines sank root in Neill's Two Paddocks vineyard in the Gibbston Back Road. Since then, planting has spread to the Last Chance and Red Bank Paddocks, both at Earnscleugh, near Alexandra.

The wine is made at the Central Otago Wine Company (COWCO) in Cromwell, in which Neill is a shareholder. After the tragic death of winemaker Mike Wolter, Two Paddocks Pinot Noir has been made by Rudi Bauer and, since 1999, Dean Shaw. The initial Pinot Noirs were good but not outstanding, but the 1999, 2000 and 2001 vintages are finely scented, with strong, sweet cherry and plum flavours, savoury, spicy complexities and a firm tannin underlay.

'If there's one thing I've learnt about winemaking,' says Neill, 'it's that it's not something one's ever going to make any money out of. But while I'm still in work elsewhere that doesn't really worry me as long as it pays for itself. The bonus is how much fun and satisfaction we get out of it and it's a tremendous kick.'

Address	Two Paddocks, c/- PO Box 722, Queenstown
Owner	Sam Neill
Key Wine	Neill Pinot Noir

Other producers

■ Hay's Lake Vineyard
Richard Bunton, a Dunedin surgeon, owns vineyards at Lowburn, Lake Hayes (4 hectares of Pinot Noir) and Gibbston (8 hectares of Chardonnay, Pinot Gris, Sauvignon Blanc and Pinot Noir). Launched from the 1998 vintage, the range includes a Sauvignon Blanc with strong fresh-cut grass flavours; a peachy, lemony Chardonnay with firm acid spine; and a plummy, spicy Pinot Noir with good depth.

■ Nevis Bluff Vineyard
Named after a jagged outcrop of rocks at the eastern end of the Gibbston Valley, Nevis Bluff is owned by a consortium of Dunedin investors. On a gentle, north-facing slope with sand and clay soils, the 8-hectare vineyard is planted in Pinot Noir and Pinot Gris. The wines, made at a contract winery in Cromwell, include a lemony, lightly oaked, appetisingly crisp Chardonnay; a peachy, appley, spicy Pinot Gris with excellent depth; and a generous, genial Pinot Noir, packed with plummy, cherryish flavour.

■ RD1
Film director Roger Donaldson's vineyard at Gibbston is next door to Sam Neill's block. The name Two Paddocks originally applied to both vineyards, but is now Neill's; Donaldson's became RD1. Launched from the 1999 vintage and made at a contract winery in Cromwell, the wine is not widely seen.

■ Taramea Wines
In Speargrass Flat Road, near Arrowtown, where in the late 1980s she made some of the first, experimental Central Otago wines, Ann Pinckney now plans to re-enter the wine industry, with a special focus on Gewürztraminer.

■ Valli Vineyards
Valli is the personal label of Grant Taylor, winemaker at Gibbston Valley since 1993, whose great-great-grandfather, Giuseppe Valli, emigrated from an Italian winemaking background to New Zealand in the 1870s. Launched from the 1998 vintage, the early wines have been based on contract-grown grapes, but Taylor has also recently planted his own 3.5-hectare block of Pinot Noir at Gibbston. Both the Colleen's Vineyard Pinot Noir, grown at Gibbston, and Anne's Vineyard Pinot Noir, grown at Lowburn, are sturdy, vibrantly fruity, complex and flavour-packed.

■ Waitiri Creek
At the eastern end of the Gibbston Valley, Waitiri Creek has since 1994 planted 8 hectares of Pinot Noir and Chardonnay, with a 'play' amount of Gewürztraminer. The company is owned by Paula Ramage, a former barrister, her husband, business consultant Alistair Ward, and the Ward family. Launched from 1998, the wines include a toasty, buttery, crisp Chardonnay; a well-spiced, subtly oaked and rounded Gewürztraminer; and a solid, full-flavoured Pinot Noir.

Cromwell Basin

A decade ago, the oldest vines were striplings — barely a year old — yet today the Cromwell Basin is by far Central Otago's most important wine sub-region, with over two-thirds of the region's plantings. The Clutha River flows south from Lakes Hawea and Wanaka into the narrow, man-made strip of Lake Dunstan, created by the Clyde dam. On both shores of Lake Dunstan — from Bannockburn in the south to Lowburn, Mount Pisa and Bendigo — and further up the Clutha River, near Tarras and Luggate, grapevines are mushrooming.

History

Viticultural expert Romeo Bragato found grapevines flourishing outdoors at Cromwell in 1895, 'a convincing fact to me that the summer climatic conditions here are conducive to the early ripening of the fruit'. However, the wine-growing potential of the Cromwell Basin lay dormant for almost a century until John Olssen and Heather McPherson, 'inspired by visiting Gladstone Vineyard in the Wairarapa', planted the first vines at Olssen's of Bannockburn in 1991. A year later, across the road Stuart Elms began planting the Felton Road vineyard and Robin and Margie Dicey, now partners in Mt Difficulty, founded their Full Circle vineyard, also in Felton Road, Bannockburn. Laurie and Anne McAuley pioneered the Lowburn district in 1992, planting the first vines at Packspur Vineyard, followed by Kawarau Estate in 1993.

Climate

East of Gibbston, in the less elevated and hotter Cromwell Basin, lies the old gold-mining town of Bannockburn, where the vineyards overlooking the Kawarau arm of Lake Dunstan grow on some of the warmest sites in Central Otago. With temperatures in February and March usually over 25°C and often exceeding 30°C, harvest dates are up to a full month ahead of Gibbston. Most of the Cromwell Basin has a moderate frost risk, but on many sites turbulent north-westerly winds make shelter belts a necessity. Lowburn is windier and more frost-prone than Bannockburn.

Soils

In Mt Difficulty's four vineyards at Bannockburn the several soil types are free-draining and of medium to low fertility. At Olssen's of Bannockburn, 10–15 centimetres of topsoil covers deep, gravelly yellow earths. In the Felton Road vineyard, where the main soil type is Waenga silt loam, fine colloidal clays retain moisture, reducing the need for irrigation. Pinot Noir is planted on the heavier, more clay-based soils; Chardonnay and Riesling on lighter, stonier, schist-based Lochear soils. At Lowburn, Kawarau Estate's vines are cultivated in free-draining silts. The Quartz Reef vineyard at Bendigo is planted in Waenga and Molyneux soils (stony, sandy soils formed from greywacke and schist).

Wine styles

The top Pinot Noirs from the Cromwell Basin are notably fragrant, robust and concentrated. On the best sites and in warm seasons, there is a danger that the grapes will over-ripen into jamminess, losing their most delicate varietal characters, but overall these are among Central Otago's most powerful, memorable reds. Of the whites, Chardonnay, Sauvignon Blanc and Gewürztraminer all show promise, but Pinot Gris (fresh, crisp and spicy) and Riesling (at its best intensely aromatic and racy) are emerging as the flag-bearers.

Queensberry
MAORI POINT ROAD
TARRAS RD
Lindis River
ARDGOUR ROAD
Clutha
LOOP ROAD
Bendigo
Bendigo Creek
Mt Pisa
LOOP ROAD
Crippletown
PISA RANGE
Kawarau Estate
Pisa Range Estate
Pisa Moorings
PISA
Lake Dunstan
SWANN ROAD
LOWBURN VALLEY ROAD
HEANEY ROAD
Packspur
Roaring Meg
Roaring Meg
Mt Michael 1163
Lowburn
COTTAGE ROAD
Kawarau Gorge
McNAB ROAD
Mount Michael
Kawarau
ROAD
Mt Difficulty 1282
Ripponvale
RIPPONVALE
ORD ROAD
McNULTY ROAD
Cromwell
Quartz Reef
PEARSON ROAD
CARRICK RANGE
River
Olssens
FELTON ROAD
Felton Road
Mt Difficulty
HALL ROAD
Bannockburn
BANNOCKBURN ROAD
CORNISH POINT ROAD
Carrick
Bannockburn Heights (Akarua)
CAIRNMUIR MOUNTAINS
Lake Dunstan
Cromwell Gorge
DUNSTAN RANGE
Dunstan 1699
Leaning Rock 1647

N

0   5 km

🍷 wine company
🍇 notable vineyard
◔ weather station

Felton Road

■ So swiftly did this Bannockburn winery shoot to stardom, its debut 1997 Pinot Noir sold for $US45 in the United States; the rare 1997 Block 3 Pinot Noir commanded $US75. Yet Stuart Elms, a few years after founding one of New Zealand's most brilliantly successful small wine companies, sold up.

A former Dunedin hotelier with a keen interest in fine wine, Elms completed a postgraduate diploma in viticulture and wine science at Lincoln University, and pored over soil maps and climate data before in 1992 he planted his first vines on sheltered, north-facing slopes at the end of Felton Road, Bannockburn.

After Elms (hence the elm tree logo) retired in 2000, control of Felton Road passed to Nigel Greening, an Englishman in his early fifties with a background in producing special effects and films for pavilions, amusement parks and advertising campaigns. The other key figure since the first vintage has been winemaker (and now director and shareholder) Blair Walter, who gained a first class honours degree in horticultural science from Lincoln University and has worked in Australia, Oregon, California and Burgundy. Walter adopts a 'relatively hands-off' winemaking approach, such as indigenous yeast fermentations and minimal or no filtration.

The 14-hectare estate vineyard, The Elms, was divided on the basis of its different soil types (with varying amounts of stones and clay) into 13 blocks and planted in Pinot Noir (the major variety), Chardonnay and Riesling. At the opposite end of Bannockburn, the 8-hectare Cornish Point vineyard (planted by Greening before he bought Felton Road) is a 'Pinot Noir laboratory', with 23 different combinations of Pinot Noir clones and rootstocks. Felton Road also leases two other blocks in Felton Road — The Sluicings and Calvert Vineyard.

In a three-level, gravity-flow winery built into the hillside, much expanded in 2002, Walter currently produces 6000 cases of wine, but expects Felton Road's output to climb to a maximum of 15,000 cases by 2006. The wines are always immaculate and the Pinot Noirs and Rieslings can be of breathtaking quality.

Felton Road was the first winery in the region to produce a great Riesling. 'The exciting thing,' says Walter, 'is that due to the dry climate and lack of disease pressure, we are able to make really clean Rieslings from low-sugar grapes in a low-alcohol style similar to Mosels. These are virtually unique in New Zealand.' Felton Road's Dry Riesling, medium Riesling and gently sweet Riesling Block 1 are all strikingly intense yet delicate wines with a distinctly Germanic scentedness and fragility. The Chardonnay is mouthfilling, in a full-flavoured and crisp, fruit-driven style; the Barrel Fermented Chardonnay is the finest in the region — peachy, biscuity and creamy-smooth, with notable concentration and harmony.

With his powerful, astutely crafted Pinot Noirs, Blair Walter is intent on 'expressing the site. It'll take years for us to clearly understand the personality of the site and the *terroir* factors that give us the taste that let's people say: "Wow — that's Felton Road."'

The Pinot Noir is deeply coloured, fragrant and supple, with a surge of rich, sweet fruit flavours and good weight. The Block 5 Pinot Noir is fleshy and lush, with silky tannins. Grown in soils with a high clay content and matured in 75 per cent new French oak barriques, the famous Block 3 Pinot Noir is one of New Zealand's most majestic reds, with dense, plummy, spicy flavours and commanding mouthfeel.

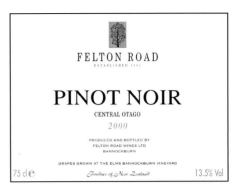

Address Felton Road Wines, Felton Road, Bannockburn

Owner Nigel Greening

Key Wines Pinot Noir, Block 3 Pinot Noir, Block 5 Pinot Noir, Riesling, Dry Riesling, Riesling Block 1, Chardonnay, Barrel Fermented Chardonnay

The Felton Road vineyard and winery at Bannockburn is internationally acclaimed for its perfumed and rich Pinot Noirs, but winemaker Blair Walter takes equal pleasure from his ravishingly scented, intense and racy Rieslings.

Address	Kawarau Estate, Cromwell–Wanaka Highway, Lowburn
Owners	Wendy Hinton and Charles Finny, Nicola Sharp Hinton and Geoff Hinton
Key Wines	Chardonnay, Sauvignon Blanc, Pinot Noir, Reserve Chardonnay, Pinot Noir

Kawarau Estate

■ One of New Zealand's few organic vineyards, Kawarau Estate lies on the western shores of Lake Dunstan, nestled against the foothills of the Pisa Range, just north of Lowburn. Its Reserve Pinot Noir is sturdy, firmly structured and full of cherryish, spicy, gamey flavour.

The company first planted vines at Lake Hayes, near Queenstown, in 1992, but sold that vineyard in 1997. In 1993, planting began on the Pisa Flats, where 11.5 hectares of Pinot Noir, Sauvignon Blanc, Chardonnay and Pinot Gris are now established in free-draining, silty soils. A $35,000 wind machine stands guard against Jack Frost. Awarded full Bio-Gro status in 1996, the vineyard is managed without herbicides, pesticides, insecticides, fungicides or synthetic fertilisers. 'It creates a lot more work in the vineyard,' says part-owner Geoff Hinton, 'especially the hand-weeding with hoes. But it's a marketing opportunity and we don't need to use chemicals.'

Kawarau Estate is owned by Hinton, a computer consultant based in Invercargill, who also manages the vineyard; his wife, Nicola Sharp Hinton, who handles the administration and marketing; and Wellington-based Wendy Hinton and Charles Finny. Launched from the 1995 vintage and entirely estate-grown, the wines are made by Dean Shaw at the Central Otago Wine Company. Production reached 3300 cases in 2001. The Sauvignon Blanc is one of the best in Central Otago, with fresh, penetrating gooseberry and lime flavours, vibrantly fruity and tangy. The Chardonnay is a fruit-driven style, crisp, lemony and appley; the French oak-fermented Reserve Chardonnay is full-flavoured and crisp, with fresh, grapefruit-like flavours and a slightly buttery finish.

Fresh, light and berryish, the lightly wooded Pinot Noir is a drink-young charmer. The Reserve model, matured in French oak barriques (25 per cent new) is a very different beast: dark, powerful and rich, with deep cherry and spice flavours and a gamey, smoky complexity.

Mt Difficulty

■ The Mt Difficulty wine company doesn't own vineyards — it's the other way around. Mt Difficulty was set up by the owners of four separate vineyards, who pooled their grapegrowing and financial resources to establish a new winery with a single wine brand.

Mt Difficulty, the peak dominating the eastern entrance to the Kawarau Gorge, overlooks the vineyards on sloping terraces below Bannockburn. The company is chaired by South African-born Robin Dicey, who studied viticulture and oenology at Stellenbosch University, later set up vineyards in the North Island for Corbans, and now owns the 13-hectare Full Circle Vineyard in Felton Road, planted in Pinot Noir, Chardonnay, Riesling and Pinot Gris. Together with the adjacent, 8-hectare Manson's Farm vineyard, the nearby 7-hectare Verboeket Estate, and 11.8-hectare Molyneux Vineyards (a dramatic site on the upper side of Felton Road, where the vines grow against a backdrop of eroded cliffs and pinnacles) Mt Difficulty has a combined vineyard resource of 40 hectares.

First produced in 1998, the wines have been skilfully made and show good intensity. Winemaker Matthew ('Matt') Dicey — the son of Robin and Margie Dicey — gained a Master of Applied Science (Viticulture and Oenology) degree with first class honours from Lincoln University, and has since worked in South Africa, Oregon and Tuscany. The company built a desert sand-coloured winery in Felton Road prior to the 2001 vintage, which yielded 8500 cases of wine.

The Dry Riesling is racy, with strong, lemony flavours, and the slightly sweet Target Gully Riesling shows good balance and intensity. The Sauvignon Blanc is mouthfilling, with plenty of crisp, limey flavour.

Both tank and barrel-fermented, the Chardonnay is delicious in its youth, with ripe fruit characters to the fore and a seasoning of butterscotch and toasty oak. Showing cool-climate freshness and vivacity, the Pinot Gris is peachy, lemony and spicy, with nutty, yeasty characters adding complexity.

The Pinot Noir is weighty and rich, with berryish, plummy, smoky flavours, warm and lingering.

Address	Mt Difficulty Wines, Felton Road, Bannockburn
Owners	Mt Difficulty Wines
Key Wines	Pinot Noir, Pinot Gris, Riesling Dry, Target Gully Riesling, Chardonnay, Sauvignon Blanc

Olssen's of Bannockburn

■ There's nothing pretentious about Olssen's, which hosts an annual 'scarecrow gathering', 'barrel parties' and a bi-annual 'music in the vines'. But there can be no doubting the quality of its top Pinot Noirs, which have won numerous gold medals, five-star ratings and trophies on both sides of the Tasman.

When John Olssen and his wife, Heather McPherson, planted their first vines in 1991, they pioneered viticulture at Bannockburn and in the Cromwell Basin. A nurse, Heather McPherson later worked in public health management; John Olssen is a forester turned manager and business consultant.

The vineyard (called Olssen's Garden Vineyard) is tucked into a

Address	Olssen's of Bannockburn, 306 Felton Road, Bannockburn
Owners	John Olssen and Heather McPherson
Key Wines	Pinot Noir, Jackson Barry Pinot Noir, Slapjack Creek Reserve Pinot Noir, Barrel Fermented Chardonnay, Riesling, Sauvignon Blanc, Gewürztraminer

sheltered corner at the end of Felton Road, with 8500 shrubs and trees giving the vines extra shelter and warmth during the growing season. Ten hectares have been planted in Pinot Noir and Chardonnay (principally), with smaller blocks of Riesling, Sauvignon Blanc and Gewürztraminer. After the early crops were sold to established wine companies, Olssen's of Bannockburn's first commercial wines flowed in 1997.

At the company's winery in Cromwell, Peter Bartle makes about 4500 cases per year of Olssen's of Bannockburn wine, plus wine for other growers on a contract basis. Bartle learned the ropes of winemaking at Villa Maria and then Forrest Estate, before joining Olssen's in early 2001.

The Barrel Fermented Chardonnay is a fleshy, full-flavoured wine with firm acid spine. The Gewürztraminer is rare but offers excellent depth of lychees and spice flavours and substantial body. The Sauvignon Blanc is fresh, intensely herbaceous and zingy, and the Riesling is floral, with plenty of slightly sweet, lemony flavour. There is also a very refined, light and lovely Desert Gold Late Harvest Riesling.

The Pinot Noir is a graceful, supple wine with excellent depth and complexity. So muscular, ripe and rich is the Slapjack Creek Reserve Pinot Noir, in some years it can be mistaken for a wine from much warmer regions. There is also a Jackson Barry Pinot Noir, with a soft entry and deliciously warm, rich cherry and spice flavours.

Quartz Reef

■ 'We're aiming to conquer Burgundy and Champagne,' says Rudi Bauer with a grin. Based in a no-frills, ex Ministry of Works building in the industrial zone of Cromwell, Quartz Reef won't be causing the French too many sleepless nights yet, but its Pinot Noir, Pinot Gris and sparkling Chauvet are all of eye-catching quality.

Born in Salzburg, Bauer worked in Austria and Germany, gaining diplomas in viticulture and oenology, before joining the Mission in Hawke's Bay for the 1985 to 1989 vintages. A driving force in the production of many top Central Otago and Canterbury Pinot Noirs, he was previously winemaker at Rippon Vineyard and Giesen Wine Estate. Clotilde Chauvet, Bauer's partner since 1996 in Quartz Reef (and his successor at Rippon Vineyard in the early to mid-1990s), has a viticulture and winemaking degree from Montpellier and belongs to a family which owns the small Champagne house of Marc Chauvet.

The vineyard lies at the north-east end of Lake Dunstan at Bendigo Station, which has the largest quartz reef in the country. Fifteen hectares of Pinot Noir, Pinot Gris and Chardonnay have been planted since 1998 in sandy clay soils on a north-facing slope described by Bauer as a 'seriously warm site, at least as warm as Bannockburn'. Another 15 hectares of grapes are purchased from contract growers.

One of Central Otago's top small wineries, Quartz Reef is on a rapid growth path, with its output planned to surge from 5000 cases in 2001 to 18,000 cases in 2008. The Pinot Gris, grown at Gibbston and aged on its yeast lees for several months before bottling, is refined and rich, with lovely weight and depth of citrusy, peachy flavour.

Grown at Mount Pisa Estate, Lowburn, the Pinot Noir is powerful in warm seasons, lighter in cool years, but consistently complex, savoury and supple. Chauvet, a non-vintage, Pinot Noir-dominant sparkling, offers strawberryish, nutty, yeasty flavours with excellent intensity, harmony and vivacity.

Address	Quartz Reef, c/- PO Box 63, Cromwell
Owners	Rudolf Bauer and Clotilde Chauvet
Key Wines	Pinot Noir, Pinot Gris, Chauvet

Other producers

■ Bannockburn Heights
Since 1996, Sir Clifford Skeggs has planted a large, 51-hectare vineyard of Pinot Noir, Chardonnay and Pinot Gris in Cairnmuir Road, Bannockburn. The wines, sold under the Akarua brand and launched from the 1999 vintage, have included an appley, spicy, slightly buttery Pinot Gris; a mouthfilling, fleshy and toasty Chardonnay; a charming, drink-young Pinot Noir, labelled The Gullies; and a supple Pinot Noir with plenty of cherry/plum flavour.

■ Carrick
Three adjoining Bannockburn vineyards on the Cairnmuir Terraces came together to establish the Carrick winery and brand. Steve Green and Barbara Robertson Green own the largest, 12-hectare Cairnmuir Vineyard, planted in 1993 in Pinot Noir (principally), Chardonnay, Pinot Gris and Sauvignon Blanc. Launched from 2000, the wines have included a fresh, flinty Chardonnay and a firm, plummy, spicy Pinot Noir with plenty of character.

■ Mount Michael Vineyard
Named after a peak in the Pisa Range, the Mount Michael vineyard overlooks Cromwell township to the east. Sue and Martin Anderson planted their first vines in 1994 and now have 4 hectares of Pinot Noir and Chardonnay. First made in 1999, the Chardonnay is an elegant wine with crisp, finely balanced peach, citrus fruit and French oak characters, and the Pinot Noir is fragrant and sturdy, with strong berryish, spicy flavours.

■ Packspur Vineyard
The Packspur track crosses the Pisa Range, above Laurie and Anne McAuley's vineyard and winery at Lowburn. First planted in 1992, the vineyard covers 4 hectares of Pinot Noir, Pinot Gris, Riesling and Sauvignon Blanc. The wines, launched from 1998 and made on-site, have included a tight, flinty Riesling and a full-bodied, appetisingly crisp, nettley and nutty Barrel Fermented Sauvignon Blanc.

■ Pisa Range Estate
Warwick and Jenny Hawker's 3-hectare Pinot Noir vineyard is on the Pisa Flats, north of Cromwell. Launched from the 2000 vintage and made by Rudi Bauer (who also buys grapes from Pisa Range for his own Quartz Reef label), Pisa Range Black Poplar Pinot Noir is finely fragrant, charming and supple, with good fruit sweetness and harmony.

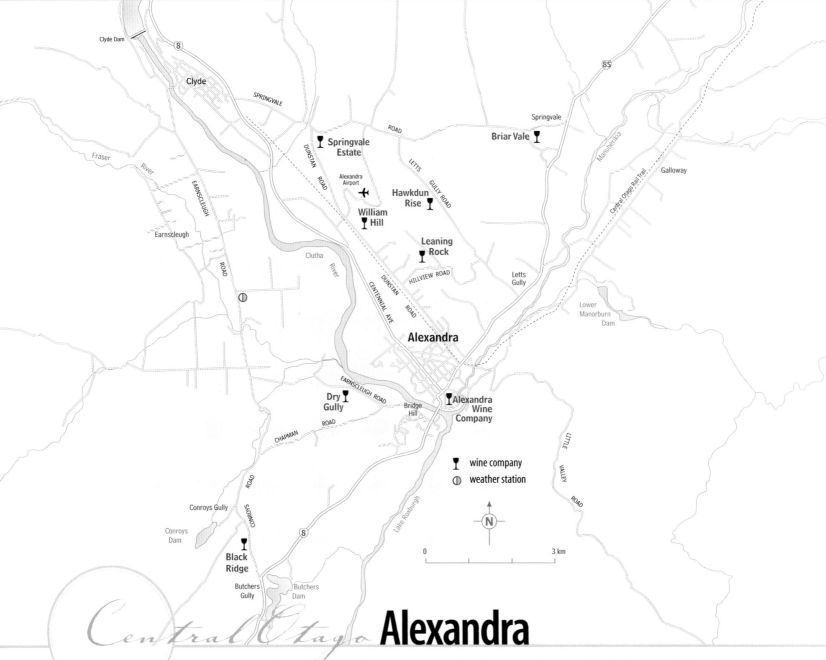

Alexandra

Below the Clyde dam, where the Manuherikia flows from the north-east into the mighty Clutha — which drains most of Central Otago — lies the river town of Alexandra. With about 7 per cent of the region's vines, Alexandra and its surrounding district form Central Otago's third-largest sub-region.

Due to Alexandra's distance from the bustling Queenstown tourism scene, the early pace of viticultural expansion was slow. Now, from the foothills of the Dunstan Mountains, on the outskirts of Alexandra, to Earnscleugh and Clyde in the north-west, and south to Conroy's Gully (and even further south, at Roxburgh), vineyards are mushrooming.

History

On the Dunstan Flats near Clyde, the first wine grapes in Central Otago were planted in October 1864 by a Frenchman, Jean Desire Feraud, and his early partner, M. Bladier. By 1870, 1200 vines were cultivated at Feraud's Monte Christo farm and his wines, bitters and liqueurs commanded high prices on the goldfields. Feraud's Constantia wine captured a First Class of Merit award at the Dunedin Industrial Exhibition, and his Burgundy a Third Class of Merit at Sydney in 1881. Today, Feraud's stone winery is still standing and two of his deep-blue wine bottles can be seen in the Clyde Museum. Romeo Bragato, the touring viticultural expert, found grapevines flourishing outdoors at Clyde in 1895. The present resurgence of activity dates from the late 1950s with Robert Duncan, of Gilligan's Gully, who planted thousands of vine cuttings near Alexandra, but failed to protect his plants from birds, wasps and frost. Trials later conducted on the Earnscleugh orchard of R.V. Kinnaird proved that fully ripe grapes could be harvested by the end of April, notably Müller-Thurgau and Chasselas. Another trial block established in 1972 by the DSIR under frost protection sprinklers at Earnscleugh successfully ripened Pinot Noir and Gewürztraminer. Of the new breed of commercial winemakers, Bill Grant planted the first vines at William Hill Vineyard in 1973, followed in 1981 by Verdun Burgess and Sue Edwards at Black Ridge.

Climate

Alexandra is an area of climatic extremes. As Mark Hesson and Dhana Pillai, of Leaning Rock, put it: 'It's very hot, very cold and mostly dry.' Many parts of the sub-region are too cool over the growing season for commercial viticulture, and frost poses a major threat on the flats. Yet specific sites have proven themselves to be warm enough to ripen wine grapes. The low annual rainfall (even by Central Otago standards) keeps the disease risk to a minimum, and very cool night temperatures leading up to the harvest promote good skin colours in Pinot Noir. According to viticulturist Steve Moffitt, just south of the town there are 'lots of north-facing, sheltered and sunny, 10-hectare blocks ideal for vineyards'.

Soils

Soil types vary in Alexandra, as elsewhere in the region. At Black Ridge, among massive outcrops of schist, the vines struggle in a thin layer of topsoil over a band of clay and a hard, rocky sub-soil. A few kilometres away, in the Dry Gully vineyard, fertile river silts run to a depth of 7–8 metres. At William Hill Vineyard, the soils are dry and sandy. The Leaning Rock vines are planted in very deep, fast-draining alluvial gravels.

Wine styles

Alexandra's white wines are typically aromatic, with firm acid spine. Most of the Pinot Noirs to date have been scented, elegant and supple, in a graceful, slightly lighter style than the top wines from the Cromwell Basin.

Black Ridge

■ Black Ridge is a vineyard blown out of rock. Bulldozers carved the dramatic, rock-strewn landscape to enable pockets of vines to be established, before each post hole was blasted with a stick of gelignite. Where grapes cannot be cultivated, wild thyme still grows on the wildly shaped schist outcrops.

One of the southernmost vineyards in the world, Black Ridge lies on a north-facing slope at Conroy's Gully, near Alexandra. The Old Man Range and Dunstan Mountains provide a panoramic view from the vineyard. Verdun Burgess and his partner, Sue Edwards, planted their first vines in 1981. Born in Invercargill, Burgess came to Alexandra as a builder, but when the Clyde dam was finished, work dried up. Grapegrowing looked to be 'the most economic thing to do with the land', so a year after their first wine flowed in 1988, Burgess moved into wine on a full-time basis.

Tall, rugged, moustachioed, pipe-smoking, extroverted — Burgess is a forceful personality. 'We're cowboys around here,' he grins. 'I love shooting rabbits. They're good fun and they don't shoot back.'

The 8-hectare vineyard is planted in a few centimetres of topsoil overlying a layer of clay, with a hard, almost impenetrable rock sub-soil. For Burgess, this 'rough, rocky terrain has a particular beauty I love'. A visiting wine merchant took one look and labelled it a 'hero's vineyard'.

Burgess believes the schist flavours the wine. 'Riesling has a very tough root system. It can squeeze water out of a stone, and it sucks minerals out of the rock. Black Ridge flavours are especially pronounced in the Riesling.'

The vineyard is sheltered from cold southerly winds. In summer, temperatures are often still hovering around 30°C at 6 o'clock at night.

Pinot Noir and Gewürztraminer are the featured varieties at Black Ridge, followed by Chardonnay, Riesling and Breidecker. Cabernet Sauvignon is planted on the top slope, where, Burgess says, 'it's too hot for anything else'.

In the two-storeyed winery, built out of rocks in the style of a nineteenth-century Central Otago barn, about 3000 cases of wine are produced each year. The winemaker since 2000 has been Kevin Clark, who learned the ropes at Black Ridge during several vintages as assistant winemaker.

Black Ridge Riesling is crisp and green appley, at its best showing a Mosel-like delicacy and lightness. Gewürztraminer yields a big, dryish, appley and spicy wine with clear varietal character. The Chardonnay is a lightly oaked, fruit-driven style with lemony, appley flavours, fresh and crisp. Otago Gold, a slightly sweet blend of Breidecker, Riesling and Gewürztraminer, is floral and fruity, light and mild in a smooth, very easy-drinking style.

The Cabernet Sauvignon (a rare beast in these parts) lacks real ripeness and stuffing but is pleasantly fruity, berryish and smooth. Black Ridge Pinot Noir in the past demonstrated that an excellent red wine could be coaxed from the lowly rated (except for sparkling wine) Bachtobel clone. Since 1997, several other Pinot Noir clones have come on stream, which are expected to add complexity and longevity to the wine. This is typically a fleshy, richly coloured and perfumed red with oodles of cherry, plum and spice flavours, deliciously fresh and vibrant.

Address	Black Ridge, Conroy's Road, Alexandra
Owners	Verdun Burgess and Sue Edwards
Key Wines	Riesling, Gewürztraminer, Chardonnay, Otago Gold, Pinot Noir

At Conroy's Gully, a few kilometres from Alexandra, Black Ridge produces a consistently appealing Pinot Noir and — far less predictably — a trickle of Cabernet Sauvignon.

PINOT NOIR
2001

Address	William Hill Vineyard, Dunstan Road, Alexandra
Owners	The Grant family
Key Wines	Pinot Noir, Chardonnay, Gewürztraminer, Riesling

William Hill

■ Frosts, birds and wasps caused heartaches during the establishment years, but now William Hill Vineyard is in rapid expansion mode, with its perfumed and supple, dangerously drinkable Pinot Noir selling swiftly in the United States.

For several years Bill Grant, the founder, produced only a trickle of Alexandra wine: 'A few thousand bottles a year, sold in a couple of months at my back door. I just wanted to prove it could be done; those who come after me can expand it.'

William Hill Vineyard lies on a sandy terrace above the Clutha River, on the western edge of Alexandra. Grant — whose full name is William Hill Grant — was raised in Dunedin and for many years was a schoolteacher. Stone quarrying and building have been his major activities in Alexandra. While travelling in Europe, however, he became convinced there were climatic parallels between the Rhine and Alexandra.

Grant planted his first two rows of vines in 1973. 'I waited for everyone else to do something, then when I heard Ann Pinckney was going ahead at Taramea [near Queenstown], I thought I'd better get cracking too.' By the early 1980s his vineyard had expanded to a half-hectare. After the first, experimental wines had been 'either drunk or disposed of', William Hill's first 'commercial' wines flowed in 1988.

The 10-hectare vineyard, equipped with overhead sprinklers for frost protection, is planted principally in Pinot Noir, with smaller amounts of Chardonnay, Gewürztraminer and Riesling. Pinot Noir 'ripens well even in a bad season, with good crops, good colour, good everything', says Grant. His son, David, who graduated from Otago University with a Bachelor of Mineral Technology degree, worked as a stonemason and engineer before he took over as managing director of William Hill in the 1995. William Hill is also a shareholder in other young Pinot Noir vineyards at Alexandra. When the extra grapes come on stream, the company's output is expected to quadruple between 2002 and 2006, reaching about 9000 cases. The winemaking duties are shared by David Grant and Gerry Rowland, an Australian winemaker based in California. The early vintages of William Hill were far lighter than the richly flavoured wines of today. 'We've made a concentrated effort in the vineyard,' says David Grant. 'We've reduced shading of the fruit, we're doing more vine-trimming and leaf-plucking, and the winery is much better equipped.'

The Gewürztraminer is perfumed, with slightly sweet, citrusy, well-spiced flavours and well-defined varietal characters. The Riesling is lemony, appley and tangy in a medium-dry style with good freshness and liveliness.

Matured in French and American oak casks, the Chardonnay is peachy, citrusy and crisp, with good fruit/oak balance. Delicious in its youth, the Pinot Noir offers very good depth of cherryish, plummy flavours and a seductively smooth finish.

Other producers

■ Alexandra Wine Company
David and Shona Garry, owners of the 3.5-hectare Davishon vineyard, and Murray and Chris Bell, of the 2-hectare Crag an Oir ('Hills of Gold' in Gaelic) vineyard, produce wines jointly under the Alexandra Wine Company brand. Made on a contract basis at Cromwell, the range includes a freshly acidic, slightly sweet and flavoursome Crag an Oir Riesling; a barrel-fermented, citrusy, peachy, buttery Ferauds Chardonnay; and a floral, vibrantly fruity and supple Davishon Pinot Noir.

■ Briar Vale
A few kilometres north-east of Alexandra, on a very steep, gravelly, north-facing slope, in 1990 John and Judy Currie began planting their 1.8-hectare vineyard in Riesling, Pinot Blanc, Pinot Gris, Chardonnay and Pinot Noir. Of their tiny output, I have tasted a crisp, appley Riesling and a ruby-hued, pleasant but light Pinot Noir.

■ Dry Gully
On the outskirts of Alexandra, Bill and Sibylla Moffitt have 1.5 hectares of Pinot Noir on a silty, free-draining site, previously planted in apricots. Made on a contract basis at Cromwell, the Pinot Noir has shown varying levels of intensity, but is consistently attractive, with sweet fruit characters and easy tannins. The Moffitts' three sons have each planted other vineyards, to add complexity and volume to the label.

■ Hawkdun Rise
Pinot Noir specialists Roy and Judy Faris have a 4-hectare vineyard at Alexandra. Made on their behalf by Alan Brady (who also buys part of their crop to blend into his own Pinot Noir) at the Mount Edward winery at Gibbston, the Hawkdun Rise Pinot Noir is mouthfilling, vibrantly fruity and harmonious, with plenty of raspberryish, plummy, spicy flavour.

■ Leaning Rock Vineyard
Named after a prominent point of the Dunstan Mountains, Leaning Rock's gravelly, 3-hectare vineyard lies on the northern outskirts of Alexandra. Mark Hesson and Dhana Pillai, former geologists, planted their first vines in 1991 and processed their first vintage in 1995. The wines, made on-site since 1997, have included a Chardonnay of variable quality; a flavoursome, minerally and racy Riesling; a vibrantly fruity, berryish and smooth blend of Cabernet Sauvignon and Pinot Noir, labelled Obelisk; and a ripe-tasting, plummy, spicy Pinot Noir with some complexity.

■ Springvale Estate
The owners of three Alexandra vineyards (Tony and Joanne Brun, Peter and Marilyn Morrison, and Stuart and Annette Beattie) produce wine under the Springvale label and also run a charming café, with wine-tasting facilities, between Alexandra and Clyde. The wines, made on a contract basis at Cromwell, include a perfumed, full-flavoured Gewürztraminer; an uncomplicated, lemony, appley Unoaked Chardonnay; a crisp, buttery, flavoursome Oaked Chardonnay; and a Pinot Noir that in top years can be impressively mouthfilling and generous.

Bibliography

Books

Brooks, C., *Marlborough Wines and Vines*, 1992.

Campbell, B., *Cuisine Wine Annual*.

Cooper, M., *Classic Wines of New Zealand*, 1999.

Cooper, M., *Pocket Guide to Wines of New Zealand*, second ed., 2000.

Cooper, M., *The Wines and Vineyards of New Zealand*, fifth ed., 1996.

Cull, D., *Vineyards on the Edge: The Story of Central Otago Wine*, 2001.

de Blij, H., *Wine: A Geographic Appreciation*, 1983.

George, R., *The Wines of New Zealand*, 1996.

Gladstones, J., *Viticulture and Environment*, 1992.

Halliday, J. and Johnson, H., *The Art and Science of Wine*, 1992.

Halliday, J., *Wine Atlas of Australia and New Zealand*, second ed., 1999.

Jackson, D. and Schuster, D., *The Production of Grapes and Wine in Cool Climates*, 1994.

Johnson, H. and Robinson, J., *The World Atlas of Wine*, fifth ed., 2001.

Judd, K., *The Colour of Wine*, 1999.

Kelly, J. and Marshall, B., *Atlas of New Zealand Boundaries*, 1996.

Kirkpatrick, R., *Bateman Contemporary Atlas New Zealand*, 1999.

McLintock, A. (ed.), *A Descriptive Atlas of New Zealand*, 1959.

Molloy, L., *Soils of the New Zealand Landscape*, 1988.

Robinson, J. (ed.), *The Oxford Companion to Wine*, 1994.

Saunders, P., *A Guide to New Zealand Wine* (annual).

Schuster, D., Jackson, D. and Tipples, R., *Canterbury Grapes and Wines 1840–2002*, 2002.

Scott, D., *Pioneers of New Zealand Wine*, (first edition entitled *Winemakers of New Zealand*, 1964), second ed., 2002.

Stewart, K., *Taste of the Earth: Creating New Zealand's Fine Wine*, 2001.

Sturman, A. and Tapper, N., *The Weather and Climate of Australia and New Zealand*, 1996.

Thorpy, F., *Wine in New Zealand*, 1971, revised ed., 1983.

Wards, I., *New Zealand Atlas*, 1976.

Williams, V., *Penguin Good New Zealand Wine Guide* (annual).

Wilson, J., *Terroir: The Role of Geology, Climate and Culture in the Making of French Wines*, 1998.

Theses

Douglas, C., 'Latitudinal Limit of Commercial Viticulture in New Zealand', MSc, University of Otago, 2000.

Mahn, L., 'The Winemakers of the Wairarapa', MA (App. Soc. Sc.), Victoria University of Wellington, 1994.

Norrie, B., 'The Development of Viticulture and Winemaking in Marlborough', MA (Geog.), University of Canterbury, 1990.

Townsend, M., 'Location of Viticulture in New Zealand', MA (Geog.), University of Auckland, 1976.

Workman, M., 'Geographic Organisation of the Wine Industry in New Zealand', MA (Geog.), University of Auckland, 1993.

Articles, Papers, Bulletins and Magazines

Fitzharris, B. and Endlicher, W., 'Climatic Conditions for Wine Grape Growing', *New Zealand Geographer*, 52(1), pp. 1–11, 1996.

'General Survey of Soils of the North Island', *NZ Soil Bureau Bulletin* 5, 1954.

'General Survey of Soils of the South Island', *NZ Soil Bureau Bulletin* 27, 1965.

Grapegrower magazine, published quarterly.

Hessell, J., 'The Climate and Weather of the Auckland Region', *NZ Met. Serv. Misc. Pub.* 115 (20).

Hessell, J., 'The Climate and Weather of the Gisborne Region', *NZ Met. Serv. Misc. Pub.* 115 (8).

Mair, R., Collen, B. and Thompson, C., 'The Climate and Weather of Northland', *NZ Met. Serv. Misc. Pub.*, 1986.

Manson, P., 'Changes are Inevitable in Global Climate Within Decades', *New Zealand Winegrower*, Autumn 2000, p.25.

Maunder, A., 'Climate and Climatic Resources of the Waikato, Coromandel, King Country Region', *NZ Met. Serv. Misc. Pub.* 115 (7).

McGinn, R., 'The Climate of Christchurch', *NZ Met. Serv. Misc. Pub.* 167(2), 1983.

Moran, W., 'Terroir: The Human Factor', Pinot Noir New Zealand 2001 Conference.

Naylor, A. and Trought, M., 'The Terroir of the Wairau Plains, Marlborough', *Proceedings of the Lincoln University Annual Grape and Wine School*, pp. 115–121, 2000.

New Zealand Winegrower magazine, published quarterly.

Pascoe, R., 'The Climate and Weather of Marlborough', *NZ Met. Serv. Misc. Pub.* 115 (12).

Perry, P.J. and Norrie, B.P., 'The Origins and Development of a New World Vignoble: Marlborough, New Zealand, 1970–90', *Journal of Wine Research*, 1991, Vol. 2, No.2, pp. 97–114.

Ryan, A., 'The Climate and Weather of Canterbury', *NZ Met. Serv. Misc. Pub.* 115 (17), 1987.

'Soils and Agriculture of Awatere, Kaikoura and Part of Marlborough Counties', *NZ Soil Bureau Bulletin* 9, 1953.

'Soils and Agriculture of Gisborne Plains', *New Zealand Soil Bureau Bulletin* 20.

'Soils and Agriculture of Waimea County, New Zealand', *New Zealand Soil Bureau Bulletin* 30, 1966.

'Soils of New Zealand', *New Zealand Soil Bureau Bulletin* 26, 1968.

'Soils of the Downs and Plains, Canterbury and North Otago', *New Zealand Soil Bureau Bulletin* 14.

'Soils of New Zealand Part One', *New Zealand Soil Bureau Bulletin* 26 (1).

'Summaries of Climatological Observations to 1980', *New Zealand Met. Serv. Misc. Pub.* 177.

Tessic, D., Hewitt, E., Woolley, D. and Martin, D., 'Terroirs of Hawke's Bay, New Zealand', *Proceedings of the Fifth Cool Climate Viticulture and Oenology Symposium*, 2000.

Thompson, C., 'The Climate and Weather of Hawke's Bay', *NZ Met. Serv. Misc. Pub.* 115 (5).

Thompson, C., 'The Weather and Climate of the Wairarapa Region', *NZ Met. Serv. Misc. Pub.* 115(11).

Tomlinson, A. and Sansom, J., 'Rainfall Normals for New Zealand for the Period 1961–1990', *NIWA Science and Technology Series* No. 3.

Tomlinson, A. and Sansom, J., 'Temperature Normals for New Zealand for the Period 1961–1990', *NIWA Science and Technology Series* No. 4.

Trought, M., 'The New Zealand Terroir: Sources of Variation in Fruit Composition in New Zealand Vineyards', *Proceedings of the Fourth International Cool Climate Viticulture and Oenology Symposium*, 1996.

'Water and Soil Resources of the Wairau', Vols. 1 (1987), 2 (1988) and 3 (1990).

WineNZ magazine, published bi-monthly.

Index

Photographs

All photographs are by John McDermott except for those attributed below:
Auckland Institute and Museum, page 12 (Samuel Marsden and James Busby), page 14 (Henry Stokes Tiffen); Khaleel Corban, page 16; Marti Friedlander, page 20; Mason Chambers, page 13; Matariki Wines, Jeff Worsnop, page 33; Michael Cooper Collection, pages 15, 17, 18 (Robin Morrison), 22 (Robin Morrison), 23, 26; Michael Seresin, page 236; Montana Wines, pages 11, 21, 129; Te Kauwhata Viticultural Research Station, page 14 (Romeo Bragato); Wine Institute, page 24.

Maps

The publishers would like to thank Andrew Shelley of the AA for fast and invaluable help at critical stages, and the School of Geography and Environmental Science at the University of Auckland, particularly Mark Kumler and Roger Gibbs for their early guidance, and Pip Forer for assisting cartographer Jan Kelly in the creation of the maps.

Photographer's Acknowledgements

John McDermott wishes to acknowledge the continued support of Kodak and Leica.

Cover photographs

Front cover, top: Pukawa Vineyard, Lake Taupo
Front cover, bottom: The Tom McDonald Cellar, Church Road, Hawke's Bay
Front inside flap: Vineyard at Hunter's, Blenheim, Marlborough
Back cover: Stony Batter Estate, Waiheke Island
Back inside flap: Grove Mill, Renwick, Marlborough

National Library of New Zealand Cataloguing-in-Publication Data
Cooper, Michael, 1952-
Wine Atlas of New Zealand/by Michael Cooper; photographs by John McDermott.
Includes bibliographical references and index.
ISBN 1-86958-921-1
1. Wine and winemaking — New Zealand. 2. Viticulture — New Zealand.
I. McDermott, John (John Bryan), 1956- II. Title.
641.220993 — dc 21

ISBN 1-86958-921-1

Designed and produced by Hodder Moa Beckett Publishers Limited
Project Manager Linda Cassells
Designer Nick Turzynski
Editor Brian O'Flaherty
Photographs by John McDermott
Cartography by Jan Kelly
Illustrations of grapes by Deborah Hinde
Scanning by Microdot, Auckland
Printed by Toppan Printing Co. Ltd, Hong Kong